More Praise for *Cont*
Someone E

"The rules for succeeding in business have changed. *Control Your Destiny or Someone Else Will* superbly defines those changes and explains how Jack Welch engineered one of the most successful transformations of a corporate culture in American business history. Anyone at any level in business will profit from this account of the renaissance of GE."

—Benjamin M. Rosen, former Chairman of the Board,
Compaq Computer Corporation

"The deal-by-deal commentary of *Control Your Destiny or Someone Else Will* makes fascinating reading for anyone who likes thinking about why corporations like behaving the way they do. . . . There is at least as much to be learned here as from reading Peter Drucker, John Kenneth Galbraith or Michael Porter."

—David Warsh, *Boston Globe*

"*Control Your Destiny or Someone Else Will* is an inspiration. Its possibility-thinking message—that we can face the facts and take responsibility for our own lives—is just what we need in these times of tumultuous change."

—Dr. Robert Schuller, Founding Pastor, Crystal Cathedral Ministries

"It isn't just GE that brings good things to life, it's life that Jack Welch brought to GE. *Control Your Destiny or Someone Else Will* is an utterly fascinating look into a business that the pundits tell us no longer exists: an American company that is healthy, flexible, creative, and run by a brilliant leader. The rough times ahead—the challenges that confront all of us in business—may be less burdensome in light of this extraordinary account of how Jack Welch turned GE around and created an astonishingly strong ecology for growth and viability. *Control Your Destiny or Someone Else Will* is terrific—it's a shot in the arm, and a totally involving read."

—Harvey B. Mackay, author of *Pushing the Envelope:*
All the Way to the Top

"A third of the increased earnings has come from increased productivity. General Electric now has about the same growth in efficiency as its overseas competitors. . . . But getting to that point . . . has been a desperate struggle. . . . That struggle is told in a new book about Welch and General Electric—*Control Your Destiny or Someone Else Will*."

—Houston Chronicle

"A remarkable, accurate, and refreshing story of the dramatic change and redirection of one of the world's most successful companies. Jack Welch's leadership can serve as a valuable tutorial for business managers who are attempting to drive change."

—Lawrence A. Bossidy, retired Chief Executive, AlliedSignal,
and former Vice Chairman, General Electric

"Noel M. Tichy and Stratford Sherman tell a remarkable tale. . . . This book is full of managerial gems such as 'change before you have to,' 'don't manage—lead,' and 'if you don't have a competitive advantage, don't compete.' The authors insist that although Jack Welch is a remarkable leader, anyone can revolutionize a company for the better."

—Industry Week

"Managers discuss cultural change frequently, but seldom achieve it. This has become increasingly clear to me as we struggle to make our company a more dynamic, competitively effective enterprise. *Control Your Destiny or Someone Else Will* explains how General Electric's strong and unyielding leadership got GE focused on a simple, yet powerful vision. This book—and the 'Handbook for Revolutionaries' that accompanies it—is filled with practical tools for change."

—William L. Weiss, retired Chairman of the Board, Ameritech

"What Tichy and Sherman supply is an explanation of the strategy and its execution that alternately made Welch the most feared and respected leader in American business. . . . The book serves as a primer on how American companies need to restructure their focus on global economy and just how daunting that task is in the face of a company's bureaucracy. . . . [It] also serves as description of how a company's bureaucracy can derail the ideas of leaders. . . . Finally, the book explains why the massive restructuring of American business must continue despite employee dislocation, to enable the U.S. to be more competitive in global markets that threaten to undermine our core industries."

—*Pittsburgh Post-Gazette*

"More insight per square inch than any business book I've read in years. Everyone should read it."

—Herbert J. Siegel, former Chairman of the Board, Chris-Craft Industries

"If Jack Welch didn't write the book on corporate restructuring, it's only because Noel M. Tichy and Stratford Sherman beat him to it. *Control Your Destiny or Someone Else Will* is not only the title of their fascinating book but one of the mottoes of the man who put GE through the wringer a full decade ahead of everyone else. . . . The authors cite Mr. Welch's work at GE as a successful model of how business will adjust to changes in the marketplace. . . . Mr. Welch has redefined the process, shifting power from the managers to the people who do the work."

—*Atlanta Journal-Constitution*

"The authors do a substantial job of presenting the research, which included more than 100 hours of interviews with Welch. Recommended for all business libraries."

—Rebecca A. Smith, Harvard Business School Library, in *Library Journal*

"*Control Your Destiny or Someone Else Will* is a harbinger of the future for managing global corporations. CEOs can use it as sort of a template against which to evaluate their own style. For the rest of us, it offers insight into one of America's most powerful corporations."

—*Toronto Star*

"Tichy and Sherman do a remarkable job conveying the mechanics of changing an organization. . . . The mix of ideology, drama, and practical examples make this book a groundbreaker on how to succeed in the global economy. Its themes—empowering workers and then expecting a lot out of them, obliterating bureaucracy, continuous improvement, and more—can be adopted by any business that dares to. *Control Your Destiny or Someone Else Will* makes you want to give it a try."

—*Soundview Speed Reviews*

"This book captures the essence of competitiveness, which is vision, leadership, and a hunger to succeed. It contains essential lessons that need to be learned by all of corporate America."

—P. R. Vagelos, M.D., former Chairman and Chief Executive Officer, Merck

"Tichy and Sherman focus on the process that is making it possible for Welch, through GE managers and employees, to shape a flexible, responsive set of businesses out of what was once an elephantine bureaucracy. They insist that others could and should emulate this process."

—*Training* magazine

"Noel M. Tichy and Stratford Sherman provide an insider's account of Welch and GE. . . . Welch quickly set down some now-famous ground rules on the businesses in which GE would participate. . . . But GE's revolution went far beyond that, the book points out. Welch's leadership energized the company's workers to accept change and challenge. . . . Welch brought GE's workforce to life."

—*Investor's Business Daily*

"*Control Your Destiny or Someone Else Will* forces you to confront organizational and leadership self-evaluation. It is impossible to read this account of Welch's transformation of GE without simultaneously questioning your own organization's structure and operation. This book is filled with thought-provoking ideas."

—Robert B. Palmer, former Chief Executive, Digital Equipment Corporation

"This is a good book for leaders, hopeful leaders-to-be, and the people who will work under their direction."

—*Report on Business* magazine

CONTROL
YOUR DESTINY
OR SOMEONE
ELSE WILL

Noel M. Tichy and Stratford Sherman

HARPER

NEW YORK • LONDON • TORONTO • SYDNEY

HARPER

A hardcover edition of this book was originally published in 1993 by Doubleday, a division of Bantam Doubleday Dell Publishing Group, Inc. It is reprinted in an arrangement with Doubleday.

HarperCollins books may be purchased for educational, business, or sales promotional use. For information, please write to: Special Markets Department, HarperCollins Publishers, 10 East 53rd Street, New York, NY 10022.

First Collins Business Essentials edition published 2005.

Designed by Stratford Publishing Services, Brattleboro, Vermont

Library of Congress Cataloging-in-Publication Data

Tichy, Noel M.
Control your destiny or someone else will / by Noel Tichy and Stratford Sherman.
p. cm.
Originally published: New York: Doubleday, ©1993
Includes index.
ISBN-10: 0-06-075383-8
ISBN-13: 978-0-06-075383-2
1. General Electric Company—History. 2. Electrical industries—United States—Management—Case studies. 3. Welch, Jack (John Francis), 1935– 4. Industrial management—United States—Case studies. I. Sherman, Stratford. II. Title.
HD9697.A3 U575 2001
338.7'62'0973—dc21   2001039371

11 12 13 ❖/RRD-H 10 9 8 7 6

To Noel's mother, Ella Tichy,
and
to Gurumayi

Contents

Authors' Note   *xiii*

Editor's Note   *xvii*

Acknowledgments   *xix*

Act One
THE AWAKENING   1

Introduction by Stratford Sherman (2001)   **3**

1. The GE Revolution   **17**
2. The Business Engine   **27**
3. The Hand He Was Dealt   **44**
4. The New Leader   **61**
5. The Power of Ideas   **80**
6. "Kick-Starting the Revolution"   **93**
7. Nothing Sacred   **108**
8. Facing Reality   **118**
9. The Mirror Test   **132**
10. The Turning Point   **146**

Act Two
THE VISION   157

11. Crotonville   **159**
12. The Politics of Speed   **180**

13. The New Order   190
14. Getting Excited   203
15. Globalization   219

Act Three

REVOLUTION AS A WAY OF LIFE   233

16. Work-Out   235
17. The Twenty-First-Century Organization   256
18. Head, Heart, and Guts   271
19. Jack Welch Speaks His Mind (1992)   285
20. Jack Welch Speaks His Mind (1999)   298
21. Afterword by Noel Tichy (2001)   313
22. Afterword to the 2005 Edition   351

GE TIMELINE   557

GE Timeline   358
Jack Welch's Annual Letters to Share Owners,
    1981–2000   395
Notes   557
Sources   577

HANDBOOK FOR REVOLUTIONARIES   593

Index   675

Authors' Note

Publication of this edition of *Control Your Destiny or Someone Else Will,* twelve years after the book's initial release, brings to mind a proposition from ancient India: Only that which is eternal is real; that which is not eternal is not real. It's the sort of notion that puts one's accomplishments into perspective—by that measure, we've achieved nothing at all. Even by conventional standards, the most we can claim is that we appreciated, explained and popularized ideas worthy of public attention. But we're human. We were shamelessly excited when the initial hardcover edition became a best seller. Since then, it has been satisfying in a more enduring way to witness the book's longevity, seeing it taught in business schools and reaching substantial numbers of new readers each year. For those who have taken the trouble to write, certainly it is gratifying to be read. For authors ardently committed to certain understandings about leadership and responsibility, it has been thrilling to see so many able leaders striving to put them into practice. What may be most satisfying of all, though, is the recognition of something lasting at the core of the story we were honored to tell in 1993.

The essence of Jack Welch's leadership and the inspiration for this book is the principle of *facing reality and adapting.* Simple as it sounds, the challenge of seeing things as they are and responding appropriately has outmatched leaders and heroes throughout recorded history; it has enlivened great stories, both tragic and comic, since the age of Sophocles at least. The situation is no different in business today: As any employee or shareholder knows, corporations can be hotbeds of delusion and denial. When they are, the cost is high.

That the son of a conductor on the Boston & Maine railroad, a man who may stutter when he speaks and cannot always conceal his foibles, could embody this daunting principle to the degree that Welch has, that he could induce General Electric's hundreds of thousands of employees to cleave to it, and then that this man and those thousands together could produce business results so extraordinary that the virtue of the idea uniting them utterly defied contest—this, to our minds, is something great. Not eternal, surely, but enduring. The practical lessons offered in this volume—about leadership, the organization of human effort, and the foundations of success—seem no less relevant and powerful now than they did to us when Welch was still unsung.

As the previous edition of this book went to press in 2001, Welch was preparing to retire after 20 years as the CEO of GE. He was beset in those days by such extreme adulation—honored as the manager of the century, the best executive in the world, etc., etc.—that despite our admiration of the man we felt compelled, in the introduction to the 2001 edition, to gently remind readers of his imperfection. Then the transaction expected to cap Welch's GE career, a mammoth $48 billion acquisition of Honeywell that led Welch, amid some criticism, to delay Jeff Immelt's succession to CEO, was thwarted by the European Commission.

Not long after an exit thus diminished in glory, Welch became embroiled in a notorious divorce proceeding, during the course of which the value of his retirement perks was publicly disclosed to widespread disapproval. Through no fault of Welch's, the stock market crashed, the U.S. economy slid into recession, and the value of GE's stock plunged along with that of other companies. The maraschino cherry atop this confection of woe was the series of multi-billion-dollar accounting scandals at Enron and elsewhere. While these, too, had nothing to do with Welch or GE, they made people anxious. Some investors long delighted by the somewhat opaque financial reports that GE had issued under Welch now viewed them with distrust. And so just as Welch's admirers, at the peak of the millennial frenzy, may have exaggerated his merit, for a little while it became fashionable to denigrate Welch's accomplishments.

The passage of time overwhelms such vicissitudes. Now a consultant, writer and speaker, remarried and living in Boston, Welch is justly respected. General Electric thrives under the leadership of Jeff Immelt, who rivals his predecessor in eagerness to reinvent in response to new circumstances. By the time Immelt is done pushing into new fields, from nanotechnology to security to water purification, GE may scarcely resemble the company Welch left behind, yet prove no less admirable. We regard the accomplishment of a successor among the most accurate measures of any CEO's success. In contrast to IBM, Hewlett Packard, Motorola, and Merck, GE bestowed upon Welch the advantage of selecting from a group of exceptionally qualified internal candidates for CEO. This is no coincidence: It is another facet of Welch's achievement.

This dynamic of learning and leadership development has made General Electric the world's leading producer of first-rate executives, and may be more lastingly important than the wealth GE produced for shareholders during Welch's tenure—an amount that exceeded $430 billion. It is well known that two of Immelt's rivals for GE's top job went on to run 3M and Home Depot, while less prominent GE executives are routinely offered CEO posts at *Fortune* 500 companies and even obscure GE leaders are harassed by headhunters' calls. What is less understood is *how* Welch systematically and reliably brought out the best in GE's leaders.

This, ultimately, may be the relevance and legacy of *Control Your Destiny or Someone Else Will.* The story this book tells is an elaboration of a single imperative: *face reality and adapt.* The recognition, during an era of ferocious competition and technological change, that reality must be faced is what generated throughout GE such exceptional, collective eagerness to learn. And it was the urgent need of this enterprise to adapt to its environment that led GE to invest with such enthusiasm in people who could meet the challenge. The particulars of how GE evolved from these ideas will not apply to every reader, but the essential ideas remain pertinent.

We hope you will use this book to explore your own capacity to contribute, taking advantage of the thinking of and the example of Jack Welch in order to make the most of yourselves and your organizations before eternity overtakes us all.

—*Strat Sherman, December 2004*

E d i t o r ' s   N o t e

Although Noel Tichy appears as a character in this book, to reflect his experiences at GE, this book is the product of a collaboration. Tichy and Stratford Sherman made equal contributions to this book.

Acknowledgments

For better and for worse, this is an inside story.

Our goal was not to investigate GE, but to explain it. Long before we decided to write this book, each of us had thoroughly examined the company and gotten to know Jack Welch, its CEO. We had observed GE from very different vantage points: Noel Tichy led GE's Crotonville School for two years and then served GE for several years as a consultant; since 1986, Stratford Sherman had covered GE as a *Fortune* journalist. Our different perspectives—one from within the company, the other from outside—converged in the conviction that GE's dramatic transformation merits book-length discussion.

The experience of writing *Control Your Destiny* has been a humbling reminder to us that our accomplishments are not ours alone. We are deeply indebted to more people than we can name, and offer heartfelt thanks for their kindness.

We are especially grateful to Jack Welch for permitting us to make public this very intimate view of GE. He unfailingly supported our work, even though it frequently made him uncomfortable. And he was generous with his own time: In addition to uncounted meetings with each of us over the years, Welch submitted to some fifty hours of additional interviews with us both. The CEO seemed to favor marathon sessions, two of which began before dusk and ended after 1 A.M. Such intimacy does not always foster respect, but we concluded our reporting with increased regard for Welch and GE.

Tichy benefited from extraordinary access. Even before the research process began, his file cabinets were stuffed with nonpublic

GE documents. More important, he had participated in confidential meetings with GEers from Welch on down, establishing personal relationships with a much broader range of company employees than any outsider could reach. To prepare this book, Tichy formally interviewed scores of GE employees, from factory workers, management trainees, and middle managers to leaders of multi-billion-dollar businesses. Although some requested that their names not be published, most appear in the list of sources beginning on page 567. The present and former GEers who gave most generously of their time to help get the story right were Toby D'Ambola, Carol Anderson, Marie Andrews, Jim Baughman, Larry Bossidy, Paolo Fresco, Reg Jones, Don Kane, John Opie, Paul Van Orden, Jack Peiffer, Jim Paynter, Phyllis Piano, Carl Schlemmer, John Trani, and Bill Woodburn.

Joyce Hergenhan, with the energetic assistance of Carla Fischer, responded cheerfully and effectively to our endless requests for information. Joyce's insights greatly enriched the text, and her company enlivened hours of difficult work. Rosanne Badowski was a constant beacon of light, reliably guiding us through Fairfield's rocky waters.

We are also indebted to Doubleday editors Harriet Rubin and Janet Coleman for the vision, perspective, and stamina they brought to this effort.

For the 2001 edition, we would like to gratefully acknowledge Adrian Zackheim at HarperInformation, who made it happen, and Beth Comstock at GE, who made it possible. Special thanks to Kathy Frey and Gary Sheffer. Once again, we thank Jack Welch for his patience and generosity.

Noel wishes to thank his research team at the University of Michigan, beginning with Connie Kinnear, who created the original data base and GE Timeline and conducted many interviews. For several years Colin Raymond and John Ahlberg provided first-rate research support. Arathi Krishna made a substantial contribution during the final months. On the administrative side, Esther Sheer, Katrina Samuelson, and Nancy Tanner provided invaluable assistance. Nancy Cardwell made an outstanding contribution to the Afterword.

Faculty and colleagues in the field provided insight, ideas, and constructive criticism throughout the process. Noel is especially indebted to Carole Barnett, Kim Cameron, Mary Anne Devanna, Charles Kadushin, Steve Kerr, Art Kleiner, Andy McGill, Len Schlesinger, Patricia Stacey, and Karl E. Weick.

Noel's deepest gratitude goes to his family, who offered much-needed emotional support.

To all those mentioned above, Strat adds his thanks. He is also grateful to the many others who helped him: Ruth McGeehee, Walter Isaacson, Mary Johnston, and Dick Armstrong, for getting him started; his colleagues at *Fortune,* especially Marshall Loeb, for offering understanding and so much rope; the creators of XyWrite and Magellan software, for the enabling technology; Sarah Bartlett and Peter Canby, for leading the way; Kurt Andersen and Geoff Colvin, for pithy criticism; David Howell and Omar Daboutie, for advice worldly and otherworldly; everyone at the Wilton Center, for keeping him centered; Laura Landro, for persevering; Jane Duce, for gracing his family; Sidney Ganis, for true friendship; and Chandler and Spencer Sherman and Meredith Davis, for filling his heart with love. For all this and more, thank God.

NOEL TICHY AND STRAT SHERMAN
1992 and 2001

Act One

THE
AWAKENING

Introduction
to the 2001 Edition

The cult of Jack Welch is so firmly established that it is enlightening to recall how little admired he was during the early 1990s, when Noel Tichy and I were writing the first edition of this book. By early 2001, as Welch's retirement approaches and chairman-elect Jeffrey Immelt prepares to take charge, GE's zestful chief executive has taken on almost godlike prestige. *Fortune,* which once excluded General Electric from its list of most admired companies, now calls John F. Welch Jr. the manager of the century. The *Financial Times* names GE the most respected company in the world. On *60 Minutes,* Welch is lauded as the best executive in the world and gets credit for personally stimulating the 1990s boom in the U.S. economy. GE is honored as the world's best school for business leaders, as its famously effective managers win CEO jobs at a long list of eminent companies that has expanded to include Home Depot and 3M.

    With a recent market capitalization of $450 billion (it was $13 billion when Welch became CEO in 1981) GE is the most valuable company traded on the New York Stock Exchange, as well as the second most profitable business (after Citigroup) in the S&P 500. If

GE unexpectedly manages to close its acquisition of Honeywell, the combined company would employ more people than GE did two decades ago—and as Welch is delighted to note, GE employees now collectively own the largest block of GE stock. For the guy once dismissed as "Neutron Jack," the ambitious train conductor's son who remembers growing up with his "nose pressed against the glass," this is heady stuff. As Welch told us, "I am one lucky guy."

We were sailing into the wind when *Control Your Destiny or Someone Else Will* was published in 1993. Although by then Welch's reputation was improving, our view of GE's transformation as the best model for business leaders worldwide proved extremely controversial. If we were not actually pelted with tomatoes and rotten eggs, we certainly were viewed with suspicion and fierce disapproval. We were championing a competitive approach that undeniably resulted— at least in the short term—in lost jobs, high worker stress, ruthless abandonment of obsolete businesses, and purposeful overturning of the status quo. Back then, remember, the happy ending of soaring productivity, job creation, energized employees, sustainable profit growth, and widespread prosperity had not yet played out.

Nonetheless, this book found its audience, just as Welch found his. Whether through fate or genius, Welch's thinking consistently has proved relevant to the times. "The New Economy," wrote the *Wall Street Journal* in 2001, "is about more than just technology and the Internet. It is about old-line companies finding whole new ways to communicate and operate more efficiently." GE, founded by Thomas Edison in 1878, became a New Economy archetype, setting standards of excellence in advanced technologies *and* in what Welch calls "social architecture." Gradually, people noticed.

Reconsidering Welch and GE in 2001, we reassert that almost anyone can learn something valuable by studying them. We are not cultists, though. We recognize that neither Welch nor GE is perfect and also that some of their appealing attributes are unique, inimitable. Few leaders can match Welch's charisma, energy, and clarity of purpose. Few companies can match GE's vast economic clout, the wealth of ideas it derives from diverse operations, or the discipline and ability to manage complexity that already distinguished the company back in 1960, when Welch drove his Volkswagen Beetle to Pittsfield, Massachusetts, for his first GE job.

As the personification of the new GE, Welch has received more than his share of attention. In person, he is vibrant, blue-eyed, fit, and sizzling with energy. Vitality is his most striking feature: Welch always seems to be enjoying himself—even when he's annoyed—and his intensity, his seething aliveness, the delight he takes in every breath, make him magnetic. Welch is the first to remind others that GE is not a one-man show. Of course that's true—it's an understatement—yet the peculiar workings of Welch's mind, his gifts as a communicator, and the force of his will have made essential contributions to the company's transformation. Perhaps the most carefully reasoned measure of Welch's value is his pay: For 2000, the most recently reported year, GE awarded its CEO total compensation of $76 million, including exercised stock appreciation rights.

Although this story does appear to end happily, it is not a fairy tale. Welch and GE certainly deserve their share of criticism. Burnout remains an intractable problem for many hard-driving GE employees. Despite substantial progress in creating a more diverse work force, GE still has a top echelon dominated by white American males. Welch, though known for his love of intellectual conflict, sometimes seems isolated by the cocoon of adulation that has thickened around him in recent years. And while GE, once scandal-prone, has established a high standard of integrity, the company still outrages many environmentalists by firmly asserting its rights in controversies such as the debate about how to handle PCB pollution in New York's Hudson River.

Far more significant and relevant to the purpose of this book, however, is GE's controversial role as avatar of brutal global competition. During the 1980s and 1990s, while other top U.S. corporations were getting killed in the marketplace, GE kept winning. Other CEOs complained about drastic marketplace change; Welch responded to it. This is the enduring value of the GE story: It demonstrates a successful method for adapting to new realities. So long as the world continues to turn, this will remain a precious skill.

In the tranquil decades following World War II, business was essentially an intramural sport, the United States' principal economic rivals having been bombed to rubble. This game was played, mostly within national borders, by a limited number of contenders, such as General Motors, Ford, and Chrysler in the automobile market. The companies followed a set of gentlemanly rules. Paternalistically, they insulated employees from direct experience of marketplace combat, offering lifetime job security in return for loyalty and hard work. In this game, nobody lost. Everybody won.

This cozy system exploded in the 1970s, just as Welch was climbing the ladder at GE. Germany and Japan, having built new, state-of-the-art factories, invaded the U.S. market, dazzling consumers and dismaying competitors with high-value offerings such as Sony TVs and BMW cars. Suddenly, competition was no longer a low-stakes game. As globalization dawned, markets began to transform dramatically. Operating in this unfamiliar environment, many U.S. companies, hindered by high costs, closed-minded bureaucracies, and inward-looking cultures, became losers. Jack Welch became CEO of GE absolutely determined to win. Recognizing how much the world had changed, he responded with asset sales, job cuts, and bold initiatives that shocked people inside the company and out.

Ever since, Welch has dedicated himself to what might be called competitive transparency. He worships the marketplace, accepting its judgments as supreme. Therefore, he accepts the cruelties of global competition as a given, not a cause for protest. He consciously tries to eliminate anything that insulates GE's businesses or employees from the markets on which their well-being jointly depends. By thus connecting minds to markets, Welch has sought to align the goals of the company and its people, while energizing the enterprise and making it as responsive as possible to customers—who are, after all, the market's representatives. That is why Welch has so aggressively shared information and seized so many opportunities to communicate. He wants every GE employee to share his direct experience of competition, to *feel* it the way a sports car driver feels the road. Similarly, he wants everyone at GE to internalize and contribute to the company's values and goals.

Always yearning for marketplace advantage, Welch seeks opportunities to redefine the terms of competition. He calls this "changing the game." Early on, he relied on improved productivity: Once GE became the low-cost competitor in an industry such as lighting, it gained the freedom to decide unilaterally whether to gain more market share by lowering its prices, or to leave pricing unchanged and enjoy fatter profit margins instead. From the start of his career, Welch also has used advanced technologies to change the game, whether by producing high-value plastics with unique properties, designing more fuel-efficient jet engines, or lowering GE's purchasing costs through use of Internet auctions. As time went on, Welch came to regard GE's increasingly informal culture as yet another way to change the game. Always an enemy of pretension, Welch views informality—candor, quick decision-making, freedom from bureaucracy, an atmosphere of hopped-up collegiality—as GE's secret weapon. He told us, "If the company weren't informal and the people weren't engaged, none of our best practices would amount to much. No one really understands how valuable an informal company is; it's *critical* to understand that."

The theory is that if everyone understands everything, decision-making becomes laser precise and lightning fast. Even an enterprise with revenues approaching $130 billion, as GE's did in 2000, would respond instantly, delightfully, to the individual customer's every twitch. Technology, particularly the Web-based communications systems that Welch has embraced of late, vastly increases the transparency of business, by giving customers real-time access to information, such as product inventories, that formerly was squirreled away in file drawers or offline computers. Welch revels in the trend toward unfettered competition and ubiquitous access to information, because that is the game GE has learned how to win.

As the 1990s progressed, GE's example inspired other businesses, particularly in the U.S. at first, to drastically reshape themselves for the new competitive era. This is why some observers credit Welch for contributing to the country's economic renaissance. Surely global competition would have emerged without any help from Welch, but perhaps the U.S. would have prospered less without his timely influence.

Since the new competitive game produces clear winners and losers, inevitably a substantial number of people feel disadvantaged by it. Jack Welch and GE didn't invent job stress or worker vulnerability, nor have they solved these problems. What they have done, rather, is to embody the era in which these issues emerged.

Our hope is that a discriminating understanding of the GE story will help people in all walks of life to control their destinies. Underlying the developments described in this book is a coherent approach to business, and life, that anyone can adopt. Don't try to reproduce what GE has done—learn from it. Companies trying to emulate GE often copy specific behaviors and practices, without absorbing the core ideas and understandings on which they're based. Such misguided imitators usually end up with the broken shell of the nut, and little of its meat. Some GE practices, such as the Six Sigma approach to quality, can be dauntingly complex. Others, such as the "GE operating system" that produces so many outstanding leaders, require a sophisticated feel for human behavior. To produce great results, even the simplest of GE's practices demands a level of persevering commitment and a concentrated massing of resources that are hard to maintain without deep understanding of their purpose. So if others find they cannot mimic Welch's successes, perhaps they have not yet imbibed the basic ideas that underlie every one of the CEO's accomplishments.

Welch's philosophy—which he apparently received from his mother, Grace—is not complicated. It boils down to: *Face reality and adapt.* Those who would follow this model may start, as Welch did, with a radical, unblinking acceptance of the world, and themselves, as they are right now. That is the substance of the CEO's familiar exhortation: "Face reality as it is, not as it was or as you wish it were." From this fundamental dictum inevitably follows the idea of response. Anyone who faces reality cannot fail to see the need to adjust, endlessly and often dramatically, to actual circumstances. Thus the second half of Welch's philosophy is the ferocious imperative to change. That's really all there is to it. Anyone who fully commits to facing reality and adapting, and who has the guts, brains, and integrity to relentlessly fulfill that commitment, will benefit from the same infinitely powerful inner engine of transformation that created the man and the company we so admire today.

This new edition of *Control Your Destiny*, written in response to intensifying interest, is updated to accommodate events through year-end 2000. We have revised the financial information throughout, to help readers see the long-term impact of GE's transformation, and expanded the GE Timeline, which relates the company's progress to world events. However, our main focus intentionally remains on the crucial first phase of Welch's tenure as CEO, 1981–1993, during which he carefully laid the groundwork for all that has followed.

We have added four new prisms through which to view the ongoing GE story. This Introduction offers a broad perspective on the Welch era at GE. In a long interview presented in Chapter 20, Welch candidly reviews his decades as CEO and details his thinking about the initiatives that have made GE great. This interview was recorded in late 1999. In Chapter 21, Noel Tichy reviews and updates the whole GE story; he also assesses the Welch legacy, with particular emphasis on leadership development. Finally, we provide all of Welch's annual letters to share owners from 1981 through 2000; these letters have constituted the CEO's most complete and detailed public explanations of his leadership. When read as a collection, they reveal the step-by-step evolution of his thinking.

As Welch explains in Chapter 20, he has relied on a series of initiatives to transform GE. The first was reform of the company's business portfolio, with the now familiar demand that each operation be No. 1 or No. 2 in its market. By 2001, he had moved all the way to "digitization," the effort to use Internet communications to get closer to customers and make internal systems more efficient. The digitization push didn't stop GE from attempting the Honeywell deal, a huge transaction initially valued at $48 billion that provoked fatal resistance from the European Commission. What is fascinating to observe, in retrospect, is the care and patience with which the impatient Welch has nurtured each of GE's initiatives. He planted them one by one, finding ways to nourish each one as it took life and became self-sustaining. He has stuck by every one of these initiatives, repeating the same simple messages again, and again, and again.

Over time, each effort has won converts who, in turn, have contributed their own ideas and whose successes have inspired still others. Thus for all our emphasis on Welch, the true heroes of this story are the GE employees who have brought his ideas to life.

GE's initiatives have altered the state of mind and beliefs of GE people worldwide. Consider the Work-Out program (described in Chapter 16), which began in 1988 as a way to make hierarchy less of a barrier for ideas. Once Work-Out had got ordinary workers speaking openly to managers a couple of levels above their own supervisors, something surprising happened. People began to notice *other* barriers to surmount. They asked why lines of business, or geography, should inhibit communication. Why not invite suppliers and customers into the intimacy of GE's candid discussions? Thus Work-Out eventually, unexpectedly, spawned the explicit value of "boundaryless" behavior, which we also discuss at length in Chapter 18. In essence, boundarylessness is the refusal to accept any limitations to the free exchange of information and ideas. It is the complex set of behaviors that permits GE to make the most of its brainpower. Emphasizing the importance of boundarylessness, GE has reinforced this value by firing people who don't share it, such as supervisors who bully their subordinates. That is typical Welch: He found a very simple—and wholly unsentimental—way to clearly communicate his intention to GE's hundreds of thousands of employees. Steadily, purposefully, GE has been distilling its employee population into a group of people who know how to benefit from candor and shared information. The state of mind of this population is what makes GE, as an organization, so adept at learning.

As this example suggests, the best of Welch's achievements can be hard to imitate directly, because they result from subtle processes. The first subtlety is that the line from idea to result almost never is straight. GE's initiatives tend to *evolve,* in an unpredictably organic process. Welch did not launch Work-Out to create a learning organization. His initial goals were limited: He just wanted the guys who designed locomotives to listen to the factory workers who actually built them. It seemed stupid not to solicit ideas from the low-level employees who knew how their jobs got done. What took Work-Out so very far beyond its modest initial goals was Welch's own delight in learning, his own adaptability. As feedback from the program began to reach him, he adapted, integrating his new understanding into revisions of the program. The heads of GE's business units, who had been selected in part for their ability to learn and adapt, behaved similarly. In theory, every member of GE's hierarchy would behave this way, permitting new ideas to cascade through the whole system. That ideal may remain distant, but after two decades of Welch leadership, GE certainly has become more responsive to feedback, enabling the company's initiatives to evolve with increasing speed.

A second subtlety of the GE process concerns the way GE masses its resources. When Welch commits to a program, he commits absolutely. GE will give up if a path becomes a dead end, but until then the team does everything it can to make an initiative succeed. For example, early on, Welch knew he wanted to change the GE culture and the behavior of its people, so he invested heavily in Crotonville, the company's management school; indeed, he has taught there in person for twenty years. Most CEOs would have stopped at that—at the boundaries of the company's formal training center. Not Welch. He drew on resources regardless of their location.

He kept tinkering with the so-called GE "operating system," the interlocking set of processes for managing the company, until it could comprehensively support his goal of leadership development. As this book explains, Welch's team redesigned GE's existing compensation system, spreading stock options through the ranks to motivate high performance. They created new measurements, such as explicitly ranking people on the values of boundarylessness, and tied those measurements to compensation. They transformed the appraisal process, insisting that managers identify and eliminate the bottom 10% of their subordinates. In the process known as

Session C, Welch personally has reviewed the careers of GE's top 500 people every year, using job assignments as a lever to influence their behavior. The more one looks, the more one finds coordination and integration in GE's approach. As the integrated systems and massed resources produced results, the range of possibilities perceived by GE leadership vastly expanded, and so did the ambition of their initiatives. The GE experience thus demonstrates how total commitment can lead to extraordinary results.

Since the first edition of this book was published in 1993, a great many important events have taken place at GE. Welch has launched major new initiatives in service, Six Sigma, and digitization. A long-standing globalization effort, which started slowly, has gained traction. While other lines of business had ups and downs, the financing unit now known as GE Capital Services has flourished, contributing 40% of net income in 2000. Investor enthusiasm has pushed the company's price/earnings multiple from 19 times earnings in 1993 to a recent 36, compared to 21 for the S&P 500 and roughly 15 for financial companies. Meanwhile, the GE culture has been evolving into an intelligent and self-perpetuating organism that advances and integrates new ideas, enhances its constituents' abilities, and produces results that exceed even the CEO's expectations. As Welch's term of office approached its end, he orchestrated not only his meticulously planned succession but the surprise Honeywell deal, which could become the biggest of GE's countless acquisitions over twenty years or a memorable misstep.

The following are major initiatives and events since 1993:

• **Services:** This initiative began in response to the relatively slow growth of many of the industrial markets GE has served, such as light bulbs and aircraft engines. With a limited upside in product sales, GE needed other sources of revenue. At first, the service initiative was meant to ensure that GE units recognized, and got credit for, the services they already were providing to customers. Then GE instructed its product designers to build in new service opportunities, such as easy software upgrades for the diagnostic-imaging equipment that hospitals buy. By year-end 2000, service offerings (including GE Capital's financial services) produced 70% of GE's total revenues.

• **Six Sigma:** This is another way GE squeezes more value from its operations. *Six Sigma* is a statistical measurement of how much a process varies from perfection. One sigma signifies 690,000 defects per million units. "Six sigma" stands for 3.4 defects per million, or a success rate of 99.99966%. The Six Sigma initiative is a rigorous, data-intensive effort to bring the output of business processes up to that standard of near perfection. GE has invested $2.1 billion in this project over five years. Since more reliable products make customers more efficient, they command higher prices; reducing downtime and scrap in GE's own processes lowers the company's costs. In such ways, Six Sigma has generated returns of $7.1 billion. As Welch explains in his 1999 interview (see Chapter 20), GE is training perhaps 30,000 of its most promising executives as Six Sigma "black belts"; through them, Six Sigma is thus becoming yet another instrument of cultural change.

• **Digitization:** GE was late to recognize the importance of electronic commerce, the emergence of which Welch has described as the biggest business event of the last 100 years. "My age and my experience were against me on this one," he told us. But once he understood the opportunity, GE jumped in. Led by Plastics, Power Systems, and NBC, the company began launching websites. Every business participated in the initiative Welch dubbed "destroyyourbusiness.com," finding opportunities to bring their business processes on-line before high-tech competitors could discover and exploit their vulnerabilities. (The program was later renamed "growyourbusiness.com.") During 2001, GE expects to conduct 30% of its purchases from outside vendors on-line, at substantial savings, while gaining fully 15% of its revenues from on-line sales.

• **Succession:** As Welch explains in Chapter 20, the effort to identify his successor formally began in 1991. Among the most obvious candidates initially were GE's business heads, all but one of whom already were chief executives of operations with multi-billion-dollar revenues. In contrast to the famous process through which GE had selected Welch from a short list of contenders working at headquarters, the candidates this time remained in operating roles, in locations such as Evandale, Ohio, and Waukesha, Wisconsin. Seeking a congenial team, Welch discouraged overt competition among them. Groups of GE directors fanned out to spend a day with each candidate and reported their impressions to Welch. The CEO invited candidates to informal tête-à-tête dinners, asking them for not only their visions but their feelings about other GE executives.

In November 2000, GE named Welch's successor: Jeffrey R. Immelt, then forty-four. As head of GE's burgeoning, $7 billion-per-year Medical Systems unit, which makes diagnostic equipment such as CT scanners, the tall and informal Immelt had aggressively promoted initiatives such as Six Sigma and digitization, while getting superior results from his people. The other two finalists also had great records and soon took CEO posts outside GE: Robert L. Nardelli, of Power Systems, which makes turbines, joined retailer Home Depot, and W. James McNerney Jr., of Aircraft Engines, went to Minnesota Mining and Manufacturing, known as 3M.

• **Honeywell:** This unexpected deal, announced just a month before GE named Immelt chairman-elect, was classic Welch. A spontaneous response to marketplace events, it showcased GE's ability to move quickly and, at least within GE's top ranks, certainly changed the game. GE had had its eye on Honeywell for years. Lawrence A. Bossidy, a former GE vice chairman and longtime Welch associate, had led a GE-style transformation of Honeywell's predecessor, AlliedSignal, an industrial conglomerate with interests in plastics, chemicals, and auto parts. In 1999 AlliedSignal bought Honeywell, another old company in need of revitalization, and assumed its name. Bossidy then retired, replaced as CEO by Michael R. Bonsignore. The new Honeywell's business lines meshed nicely with GE's, but Honeywell was not yet producing outstanding financial results. So when United Technologies—which competes with GE in jet engines—

decided to buy Honeywell, Welch quickly crunched the numbers on a competing bid. The math worked out, and the rest is history.

What stunned people inside GE and out was Welch's agreement to stay on extra months as CEO, at Bonsignore's request. The move is controversial: Serving so long as apprentice to the manager of the century seems awkward for GE's chairman-elect and risks tarnishing Immelt's prestige. On the other hand, the challenge facing Welch's successor would have been hair-raisingly complicated even without the additional task of integrating an underperforming, $25 billion-per-year acquisition. As this book went to press in 2001, opposition from the European Commission put the transaction in jeopardy. Ultimately, the deal collapsed.

It is hard to say whether GE or the outside world has changed more during the two decades since Jack Welch became CEO of General Electric. In 1981, as Welch recalls, U.S. inflation seemed out of control, Japan seemed to be on the verge of dominating the global economy, and the price of oil seemed headed for $100 per barrel. Two decades later, as Welch was preparing to retire, the inflation rate was negligible, the Japanese economy was weak, and oil prices, though rising again, seemed almost unimportant. During the entire period of Welch's leadership, no matter what was happening in the outside world, General Electric found ways to thrive, producing record profits in almost every fiscal quarter. This, finally, is what Welch has wrought at GE: a company that can prosper in *any* environment.

In free-market capitalism, the ultimate duty of a corporate leader is to enrich the share owners. When other leaders were muddled, Welch lucidly focused on his duty, rigorously and consistently aligning his actions toward achievement of this one goal. He did his best to face reality and adapt. He pushed hard, and when he saw opportunities, he grabbed them, without worrying much about whether people might disapprove. Along the way, he tried to remain open-minded, to keep learning all the time. If he has won widespread approval, perhaps it is because his words and actions have integrity. He has done what he said he would do.

Stratford Sherman
March 2001

Chapter One

The GE Revolution

O ne evening late in 1985, Noel Tichy dropped in on a classroom at General Electric's Crotonville management training center in Croton-on-Hudson, New York. Ranged around a rectangular conference table, ten young college graduates, all recently hired as GE junior managers, were ferociously debating two propositions scrawled on a flip chart at the front of the room:

> **Jack Welch is the greatest CEO GE has ever had.**
> **Jack Welch is an asshole.**

Rude stuff. At most major companies, including GE just a few years earlier, such irreverence might have cost these kids their careers. But as Crotonville's new director, Tichy was delighted. In place of a traditional curriculum based on texts and lectures, Crotonville was encouraging the sort of no-holds-barred discussion that characterizes the CEO's most fruitful interactions with senior managers. The goal was to implant and nourish the values Welch cherishes: self-confidence, candor, and an unflinching willingness to face reality, even when it's painful.

By then, John F. Welch Jr. had been GE's chief executive for nearly five years, relentlessly pursuing an agenda of change so radical, so fundamental, and so threatening that it amounts to a revolution. He has taken the established order at GE and thrown it out the window; he presided over the elimination of scores of the company's businesses and over one-third of its jobs—affecting a group as large as the entire population of Salt Lake City. As for the employees who remain, Welch has challenged everything they thought they knew.

This forceful man, sixty-six years old in 2001, is creating a new organization at GE that depends as much on shared values as on hierarchy or coercion. Like most major corporations, GE previously relied on the doctrine of scientific management: the theory that any work process—including its human element—can be broken down to its component parts and then reassembled in an efficient or "scientific" manner. That sort of thinking fostered assembly lines and military-style hierarchies, which produced enormous wealth but generally alienated employees. By contrast, the values-based organization that is emerging at GE derives its efficiency from consensus: Workers who share their employer's goals don't need much supervision.

Blue-eyed and hot-blooded, Welch is a rebel who has matured into a leader. At 5'8", he is not physically imposing, but the intensity and power of his personality can overwhelm. His manner conveys urgency even when he's comparing golf scores or making friendly inquiries about your family. Relentlessly positive, he delights in his own enthusiasm; when displeased, he comes on like a battery of howitzers, flattening all opposition. "We've got a disaster here," he'll warn as he walks into a meeting, before even saying hello. Looking you straight in the eye, he'll tell you exactly what he thinks you've done wrong. But if you can withstand the barrage and talk back, Welch will listen; and if you can solve his problem, soon you will be basking in the warmth of the CEO's cheerful high spirits.

Welch's successes as a leader depend less on his personality than on the quality of his thought. Smart, intellectually disciplined, and creative, Welch has developed a management style that exploits the power of breakthrough ideas. Some of his perceptions are primarily of interest to GE's employees; others have the potential to reshape organizations around the world. In our view, the twentieth century produced two business leaders who will be remembered for their ideas: Alfred Sloan of General Motors and Jack Welch of GE.

The company Welch inherited in 1981 was among the bluest of blue chips. Founded in 1878 by Thomas Edison, the inventor of the light bulb, General Electric was one of America's strongest competitors and one of the world's most admired corporations. Hardly anyone, inside the company or out, thought GE needed fixing. But where others saw strength, Welch saw weakness. GE's executives, disciplined but submissive, knew how to follow the company's rigid rules. But when the outside world started to change, many of GE's procedures and systems became irrelevant. The self-confidence that had characterized the company's managers began to erode. Left to pursue its course for another decade or so, this apparently healthy company might have become another Chrysler. Instead of waiting for trouble, the CEO pushed for radical change long before most people recognized it as necessary.

America's eminent corporations, from GE to General Motors to Eastman Kodak, all faced the same new challenges of lagging productivity and global competition. Welch recognized these changes for what they were: threats to his company's survival. He began by acknowledging GE's vulnerability; then he set out to rebuild its strength. Starting with a forceful attack on the company's status quo, he ultimately transformed the very nature of GE, reshaping not only its businesses but its organization and culture as well. No enterprise of comparable size had ever attempted such a task, yet Welch approached it with relish. The CEO's behavior, sometimes harsh and often misunderstood, was a response to real danger. Like a parent who forces a sick child to swallow bitter medicine, Welch was motivated by a desire to heal.

The remarkable story of GE's revitalization teaches lessons essential for the well-being of managers and laypeople alike. *Control your destiny* is more than a useful business idea. For every individual, corporation, and nation, it is the essence of responsibility and the most basic requirement for success. As the world endlessly changes, so must we. The greatest power we have is the ability to envision our own fate—and to change ourselves.

The process of transformation requires personal commitment and the willingness to persevere. It begins with the recognition that change is necessary. An individual with a problem, whether excess weight or a troubled marriage, won't make much progress without admitting that the problem really needs solving. Similarly, the United States surely won't regain its economic primacy until its citizens stop whining about Japan and face the real causes of declining competitiveness, from low productivity to the ballooning national debt.

In retrospect, GE's biggest problems cannot be blamed on previous CEOs or any other employees: The world simply had changed. Corporations around the globe, small and large alike, were beginning to recognize that the emerging business environment of the 1990s and beyond required dramatic new responses. For anyone who has a job and wants to keep it, this is a challenge that must be faced.

In Welch's view, a strong business must consistently grow both revenues and profits: increasing revenues through a constant stream of new ideas and product innovations and increasing profits through unceasing improvements in productivity. Neither innovation nor productivity alone is enough. A winning company has to master both—in Lyndon Johnson's memorable phrase, to walk and chew gum at the same time.

When he became CEO in 1981, Welch saw major obstacles to both kinds of growth. The threat to revenue growth was the company's highly organized bureaucracy—the pitiless enforcer of scientific management—and the corporate culture that sustained it. Once-useful means of disciplining the organization had started to strangle the business. The company was choking on its nit-picking system of formal reviews and approvals, which delayed decisions, thwarted common sense, and often made GE a laggard at bringing new products to market. For executives, mastery of arduous procedures had become an art form, almost a ballet, as well as an unspoken requirement for advancement. The result: Many of GE's best managers devoted far more energy to internal matters than to their customers' needs. As GEers sometimes expressed it, theirs was a company that operated "with its face to the CEO and its ass to the customer."

The bureaucracy seemed unable to focus on GE's customers, whereas Welch wanted to serve them better. Promoting innovation at GE felt like getting a root canal. The company's elaborate controls ranged from detailed monthly budget approvals to an annual strategic planning review that required six to eight months of preparatory research and analysis. Such procedures ensured that any idea, regardless of its merit, would be treated as worthless until entombed in a lengthy formal report.

The elite bureaucrats who vetted budgets and most operating decisions were GE's strategic planners. The meetings they held to review all proposals—whether for a new way of pricing floodlamps or for a dishwasher based on a breakthrough design—were staged as inquisitions. Naysayers by profession, the planners liked to badger executives with "gotchas," GE lingo for tough questions designed to make people sweat. By the time an idea had run this gauntlet, if it lasted that long, its moment of opportunity often had passed.

Welch was dismayed by the results of that behavior. GE was losing share even in light bulbs, the market that had brought GE to life. In consumer electronics and small appliances, General Electric was no longer the manufacturing or technology leader. Brawny international competitors such as Toshiba and Hitachi were eroding GE's position in some key businesses.

Just as bureaucracy slowed GE's revenue growth, low productivity inhibited the growth of GE's earnings. With intensifying foreboding, Welch had been observing the productivity gains of

GE's rivals in emerging global markets. While Japanese companies were boosting productivity by 8% annually, GE's gains had rarely topped 1.5%.

High productivity is essential, says Welch, because it confers flexibility. Gains in productivity drive costs down: A corporation whose costs are lower than its competitors' has the flexibility either to gain share by lowering prices or to hike profits by raising prices—at will.

The CEO wanted an organization that could systematically foster the creation of new ideas, much as the traditional GE culture had long promoted the manufacture of products. The bureaucracy had to go, and with it the inward-looking mind-set that was alienating GE from its customers. At the same time, he wanted GE to operate at least as efficiently as GE's most productive competitors. To Welch the implication was clear: Strong though it was, GE had no choice but to reinvent itself almost from scratch. Though the phrase isn't his, Welch communicated a message of *change or die,* loudly and often. Said the CEO:

> **Changing the culture starts with an attitude. I hope you won't think I'm being melodramatic if I say that the institution ought to stretch itself, ought to reach, to the point where it almost comes unglued.**

Many GE employees—too many—saw Welch as a tough guy who menaced not only their livelihoods but the company itself. For them, fear gradually hardened into stubborn resistance to the program of change. People who believed they would flourish in the new GE—such as workers at the fast-growing Plastics, Medical Systems, and Financial Services units that Welch had overseen earlier in his career—generally thought he was a terrific CEO. But lots of GEers, especially those in weak businesses such as electrical transformers or consumer electronics, thought their CEO was, well, an asshole.

If Welch's vision shocked GE's workers, his behavior terrified them. While he was talking about "liberating" and "empowering" GE's employees, they were worrying, with reason, about their jobs.

He challenged the time-tested compact that governed GE's relationship with its employees: something approaching lifetime job security in return for loyalty, obedience, and performance. In its place he offered a new principle that struck employees as cruelly Darwinian: "Companies can't give job security," he said. "Only customers can." In other words, *Succeed in the marketplace or you're out of a job.*

To Welch, a man who passionately believes that facing reality is one of life's primary obligations, this principle seemed self-evident. Like most of his management ideas, it flowed naturally from observation of the brutal world of commerce. But as GE kept cutting its work force, many employees found it difficult to share the boss's perspective.

The numbers are staggering: Through one means or another, roughly 300,000 people left GE. When Welch began, GE had nearly 420,000 workers on its payroll. Over the years their ranks increased by 150,000 people, who were the employees of companies that GE acquired. At the same time, GE was selling businesses that employed some 135,000 people; they left General Electric, but most, presumably, kept their jobs. The painful part was the cutting of almost 170,000 positions through layoffs, attrition, and other means. The result: By the end of 1991, just under 285,000 people worked for GE; as of July 1993, there were approximately 230,000 employees. By 2001, the combination of internal growth and acquisitions had reversed the trend. If it closes the Honeywell deal, GE would have more employees than it did in 1981.

To enable fewer people to keep their growing corporation under control, GE designed a new organizational structure that increased managers' "spans of control"—the number of people or businesses reporting directly to each manager—from roughly six to as many as twelve, or even more. The idea was to force employees to delegate more and to eliminate unnecessary work. But GE's managers were unaccustomed to making such decisions, and some drowned in the added responsibility. Working twice as hard and half as well, these people began hating their jobs. Mixed signals added to the confusion and stress: Many GEers reported to hardened bureaucrats who scorned the new ideas.

In 1982 *Newsweek* dubbed Welch "Neutron Jack," suggesting the CEO's willingness to vaporize people while leaving the buildings standing. In fact, Welch detonated buildings too: During just his first four years GE sold 125 businesses, including the languishing line of toasters, irons, and other small appliances that many employees regarded as an essential part of the company's identity.

Before long, the opposition to Welch and all he stood for was of epic scale: roughly 200,000 people—a group larger, in all likelihood, than the entire population of Troy in the age of Homer's *Iliad.* But Welch is no Achilles. Measured against 200,000 opponents, he seems surprisingly ordinary: a middle-aged businessman with thinning hair and a Massachusetts accent, who pronounces "ever" as "evah." What distinguishes him is his self-confidence and drive. He has what one close associate calls "an absolute desire to win." Each success seems to increase his strength—and his desire to win again.

Vitality may be Welch's defining characteristic. He is a breeder reactor for energy; perhaps he uses his inner conflicts as fuel. As a younger man he nervously bit his nails, but today his tension shows in less obvious ways. To explain himself, Welch will hastily sketch chart after chart on a pad of paper, often while eating raw carrots or chewing five sticks of gum at once. His eyes sparkle, and the vivid intelligence shaping his words more than compensates for the mild stutter that has dogged Welch since childhood.

His personality integrates many seeming contradictions. Welch has firm convictions about everything from corporate management to matters of right and wrong, yet he loves to listen and readily changes his mind. He is searingly analytical and intuitive at once. In temperament, he is an enthusiast, not a bully, but whether discussing a business strategy or a recent movie, he always aims to convince. Unabashedly emotional, he can be enormously engaging in person—yet this warm and empathetic fellow has made decisions that caused enormous pain.

Change doesn't scare Welch, it excites him. Throughout his career he has benefited from his willingness to create change—not only in the organizations he has run, but in himself. During his years as CEO, Welch has evolved from a demanding boss to a helpful coach, from a man who seems hard to one who allows his softness to show. That is part of what enabled him, long after he had gotten GE's businesses into shape, to win over GE's alienated employees.

No leader can escape dependence on those he leads. Welch has wielded all the power of a CEO, but command alone could not win him the cooperation of his subordinates; without massive support, no one could succeed in a task as large as the one he undertook. This man's long crusade to remake General Electric has been defined less by such conventional managerial concerns as strategy or finance than by the ineffable difficulty of transmuting resistance into allegiance.

The CEO was never completely alone. General Electric's board solidly supported him from the start. Welch calls their endorsement "absolutely essential," arguing that no one could lead an organization through a transformation of this magnitude without strong backing. Welch also could rely on a cadre of like-minded executives and perhaps a quarter or a third of the company's employees. Even with so much backing, the task he faced was daunting.

Welch seems never to have doubted that his ideas were right. His convictions seem rooted in the bedrock of his personality; indeed, he says he learned many of his best ideas on his mother's knee. Much of the power of his ideas derives from the consistency with which he upholds them, regardless of what others believe. "If you have an idea *du jour,* you're dead," remarks Welch.

Reduced to its essence, his main challenge has been communication. His unconventional ideas already had proved their merit: Most of the businesses he had run were standout performers, and their workers had prospered. The trick was getting GEers to believe that they would end up among the winners. Recalls Welch:

> **For a long time our actions muddied communications. We were taking out lots of people. We were taking out layers of management. We were selling off businesses. We were impacting people's lives.**

Welch has plenty of ideas, but his successes as a communicator are the product of struggle. When he became CEO, many of his most powerful ideas were little more than gut instincts. His stutter is no longer an impediment, but his thinking often is more lucid than his language, and his first attempts to express ideas sometimes fail. A memorable flop was his vain attempt, in 1981, to make GEers feel and act as if they "owned" their businesses—despite the obvious fact that those businesses are owned by GE's share owners. But he persisted, spending years refining his message. Eventually he found ways to articulate his vision for a new GE with simplicity, clarity, and vigor. Explains Welch:

> **Companies need overarching themes to create change. If it's just somebody pushing a gimmick or a program, without an overarching theme, you can't get through the wall.**

This is the story of how GE got through the wall, from one man exhorting his subordinates to a team of hundreds of thousands of people working together. A narrative of the key events of Welch's leadership of GE, from 1981 to the present, the tale is marked by dramatic conflict and by failure as well as success. Above all, though, this is a story about ideas in action. Taken together, the concepts that underlie the GE revolution add up to a comprehensive theory of change that can enable any organization—indeed, any person—to seize control of his or her destiny.

Chapter Two

The Business Engine

The GE revolution is still far from complete. Welch, after all, says he hopes to run "the most competitive enterprise on this earth." But the progress to date is astonishing. This train conductor's son, a chemical engineer who inadvertently blew up a small plant early in his career, already has done more than any other U.S. executive to bust through the limits of corporate performance. Along the way he has created and tested a set of practical management principles that are unrivaled as a guide to running a business in the twenty-first century.

To be sure, GE is unique in many respects. Its size, its strength, its business diversity, and its tradition of disciplined management presented Welch with opportunities and problems that other managers may never face. Even so, most of the ideas driving the GE revolution are so basic, so universal, that they apply not just to business management, but to ordinary human life. Consider this list of Welch's six rules, which *Fortune* published in 1989, and ask yourself whether your behavior meets his standards:

- Control your destiny, or someone else will.

- Face reality as it is, not as it was or as you wish it were.

- Be candid with everyone.

- Don't manage, lead.

- Change before you have to.

- If you don't have a competitive advantage, don't compete.

Simple ideas, perhaps, but only a fool would underestimate the difficulty of acting on them. The idea of facing reality, to consider just one, seems banal—until you try to live by it. Welch believes that "facing reality is crucial in life, not just in business. You have to see the world in the purest, clearest way possible, or you can't make decisions on a rational basis."

Facing reality means dealing with what all of us would prefer to avoid: danger, failure, our own shortcomings. One can argue, as Freud did, that in some cases we must turn away from reality in order to survive. But when such psychological defenses are deployed in attempts to avoid the unavoidable, they become symptoms of illness.

Corporations as well as individuals may suffer from this malady. When an automaker, for instance, can't admit that its products cost more, yet are worth less, than those of its prospering overseas competitors, the company's illness soon becomes apparent. Market share plunges, profits drop, employees fret, and investors flee. Welch saw symptoms of that disease at GE.

Welch has enjoyed one great advantage: His ideas work. The clearest proof is GE's financial performance since 1981. Before Welch took office, GE, like Westinghouse and AT&T, was known as a "GNP company," because its profits consistently grew at about the same rate as the gross national product. But by the end of 1992, GE's earnings had grown at an annual rate of over 10% for the prior decade, amounting to one and a half times the GNP's. That is remarkable momentum for an enterprise of GE's mass. In 1992 GE earned $4.7 billion on revenues of over $62 billion. The company's return on equity, a key measure of corporate performance, topped 20%. Throughout the 1990s, GE's spectacular performance continued. In 2000, revenues totaled $129.8 billion; return on equity was 25%.

Another indicator of the company's strength is market share. Peter Drucker—professor, management guru, and a former consultant to GE—greatly influenced Welch by writing, "If you weren't already in the business, would you enter it today?" Welch pondered that question deeply, and acted on the answers. He insisted that every GE business be No. 1 or No. 2 in its market, vowing to "fix, close, or sell" any that didn't meet his standard. Prior to 1993, Welch sold $14 billion worth of GE-owned businesses, including coal mines, semiconductors, and TV sets, while buying $21 billion worth of new businesses, including Employers Reinsurance Corp. and RCA, the owner of NBC. From 1993 to 1999, GE spent another $79 billion on acquisitions, and during 2000, GE agreed to its Honeywell purchase, initially valued at $48 billion. GE's post-1993 divestitures totaled over $10 billion. Among the units shed was scandal-plagued Kidder Peabody, sold in 1994 amid huge financial problems.

Despite the Kidder fiasco and a few smaller flops, the result of Welch's efforts is a company that boasts a leading share in almost every market it serves: from turbines for electric power plants to engines for 747 jets and B-2 Stealth bombers; from 200-ton locomotives to credit card processing services to special plastics for auto bumpers and computer housings.

The measure of performance that matters most to Welch and to GE's share owners is the value of the company's stock, which trades on the New York exchange. At a recent $50 per share, it was worth over 30 times more than when Welch started, adjusted for stock splits. By comparison, the Standard & Poor's index grew less than 400%. In March 2001, as this book was going to press, GE's $450 billion market value made it the second most valuable enterprise in the United States—a monumental improvement from the company's showing in 1980, when it ranked No. 11.

The need to boost both innovation and productivity is the imperative behind the GE revolution and the main challenge confronting any business that competes in world markets. Under Welch, GE has come a long way: in many of its lines, such as aircraft engines, high-risk lending, or the CT scanners doctors use to diagnose disease, GE's products and services are among the world's most advanced.

The company's annual productivity rate has risen from less than 2% in 1981 to an average of roughly 6% throughout the 1990s. Even during the recession of 1990–1992, GE achieved a 4% to 5% rate. For every percentage point of increased productivity, GE's annual pretax profits rise by over $300 million—year after year.

By the end of 2000, GE's productivity remained at 4%. The e-business initiative was expected to improve that performance in 2001, by enabling GE to do some 30% of its purchasing through on-line auctions, at substantial savings.

More important from the employee's point of view, GE's success is making its remaining jobs more secure. Like most U.S. companies, GE still has spot layoffs from time to time, when businesses such as Aircraft Engines hit downdrafts. But the days of slash-and-burn management are long past. And once-troubled operations such as Power Systems, which makes turbines for electrical power plants, have been expanding and creating new jobs, along with consistent winners such as Medical Systems and GE Capital Services. Total GE employment has rebounded, thanks in large part to the growth of GE Capital.

Drastic changes in the competitive environment are driving demand for new ideas about management. A decade of mergers and acquisitions forced consolidation in industry after industry, from food processing to banking, and as a result, markets are increasingly dominated by huge companies with overwhelming financial and political clout. Smaller players are getting shoved out of the game.

Moreover, globalization has changed the rules of competition, suddenly forcing companies to expand beyond their nations' borders even as they face the incursions of foreign companies at home. Efforts to improve productivity, such as "just-in-time" inventory controls, are pushing corporations into an unprecedented dependence on their suppliers. New technologies and management techniques have shortened product cycles, heightening the expectations of customers and forcing an increasing emphasis on speed.

In a paradox that Welch likes to emphasize, winning now requires all the power and resources of a world-class behemoth *and* the agility of an entrepreneurial start-up. And he insists that the game will only get tougher: "If you thought the 1980s were tough, the 1990s will make the 1980s look like a cakewalk. It will be brutally competitive."

GE's experience can provide the ideas needed to respond to these monumental changes. Almost every major corporation—like GM, IBM, and American Express—faces the same global forces of change. Many once-promising upstarts seem less promising now. Even some companies touted in Tom Peter's *In Search of Excellence,* such as Citicorp and Kodak, have stumbled since the book was published. That leaves GE's revolution, unfinished and imperfect though it is, as the best available exemplar of the way ahead.

For the United States as for GE, failure to adapt to market changes could prove catastrophic. A 1990 study by the nonprofit National Center on Education and the Economy lucidly describes the country's dilemma. To compete in world markets, American business must improve productivity in either of two ways: through lower wages or through more efficient organization. To date the country has chosen lower wages. U.S. salary increases between 1975 and 1988 averaged 6.2% per year. That's 2.1 percentage points lower than Europe's rate, and 5.4 points lower than Japan's. But low wages, like low productivity, end up hurting everyone by lowering the national standard of living. The desirable alternative is the one America has not yet chosen: better organization. Yet according to the report, 95% of U.S. corporations still organize work the way they did at the turn of the century.

The old way, exemplified by Henry Ford's production line, calls for top managers to analyze the work that needs to be done, then devise rules even an idiot can follow. Managers, divorced from the actual work, become bureaucrats, while their frustrated subordinates tighten the bolts. Brilliantly though such methods worked during most of this century, they won't help us much in the next. Even so, it is easy to understand why more companies don't change: The revolutionary process is agonizing.

The new way—GE's way—breaks the intellectual framework that defines the limits of traditional management. The goal is to transcend the concept of management itself. Instead of seeking better ways to control workers, Welch says he aims to liberate them. As he explains, that goal is based on self-interest:

> **The old organization was built on control, but the world has changed. The world is moving at such a pace that control has become a limitation. It slows you down. You've got to balance freedom with some control, but you've got to have more freedom than you ever dreamed of.**

Welch insists that GE managers learn to master paradox. In his view, an apparent conflict between two worthy goals is no excuse for not pursuing them both. He regards the simultaneous pursuit of long- and short-term objectives as a basic responsibility of management. While pushing for organizational change, Welch has failed to boost quarterly earnings only five times since becoming CEO. The last downturn came in the third quarter of 1994.

Welch believes in teamwork, not out of idealism, but because he grew up playing hockey: He knows that teamwork wins games. When his teammates score goals, he feels good. As a manager, he knows that the most valuable innovations often come from the shop floor.

A corporation designed to meet the challenges of the twenty-first century must boost performance by stripping out layers of unnecessary management while encouraging all workers to think more, and thus to produce more. The successful organizations will be those that are "lean and agile," to use one of Welch's favorite terms. In structure they will be fluid, poised to respond rapidly to market changes. In spirit they will be relatively democratic, replacing authoritarian rigidity with openness, candor, and a willingness to reach across functional and hierarchical lines. Welch calls this "boundarylessness," his concept of integrating all the constituencies inside and outside the company.

A primary motivation for GE's transformation is the need for speed. Until employees accept personal responsibility for their work, they need supervision, which Welch regards as a waste of time. So whenever possible, GE tries to eliminate supervisory positions, giving people more power to control their own work. Such responsibility can transform the relationship of workers to their employer: Instead of behaving like children who follow their parents' orders, employees interact with their bosses as adults and peers.

Replacing the old way with the new does not happen at the touch of a button. It requires deep convictions, enormous upheavals, a vision of what lies ahead, and perseverance even when the pain seems unbearable. But the ultimate benefits—for stock owners and employees alike—are enormous. And as GE is proving, it can be done.

The methods needed to create the degree of change at General Electric—quantum change, Welch calls it—are fundamentally different from the managerial techniques taught at most business schools and practiced at most corporations. Understanding the new methods, no less than creating them, requires a new intellectual framework. What follows is a framework devised by Tichy.

The process of corporate transformation is a three-act drama. Unlike those of the theater, these three acts usually overlap, but each depends on the one before.

In Act I, the organization awakens to the need for change. This is a time when tyrannical behavior can serve a useful purpose, since the awakening requires a frontal assault on the status quo. The goal of the attack is not to frighten employees, but to arouse the emotional energy of an entire organization. That energy, which manifests itself first as fear and later as personal commitment to a plan of action, is the only fuel that can sustain a revolution.

GE's Act I was largely complete by late 1985, five years after Welch became CEO. At first, Welch's ideas took the form of demands, such as the requirement that each GE unit be No. 1 or No. 2 in its market. Welch backed this idea—stunning at the time—with powerful actions, including massive layoffs and asset sales. During this period, those efforts seemed destructive, because he was dealing more with problems than with solutions. Act I usually leaves workers and junior managers in confusion and despair, because the process destroys what's familiar and comfortable without providing a new basis for emotional security.

In Act II the organization creates a blueprint for the future. As the old ways are swept away, even people who have resisted change begin to recognize the need for something new. The leader responds by articulating a vision. But a vision can't be acted upon until it is shared, so effective communication becomes critical. Henceforth, a leader can no longer rely mainly on his or her own power: The revolution's continued progress now depends on the support of key lieutenants throughout the organization.

At GE, winning the support of executives—especially the thousands of middle managers far removed from GE's Fairfield, Connecticut, headquarters—has proved Welch's most enduring challenge. GE's middle managers can influence tens of thousands of lower-ranking workers far more directly and powerfully than the distant CEO.

Evidence of middle managers' ability to thwart Welch's ambitions surfaced frequently at Crotonville. Students there, old hands as well as new hires, routinely write comments at the end of a course, which Welch carefully studies. It's the equivalent of market research. The most frequent complaint goes something like this:

All the words sound great—entrepreneurship, ownership, risk taking—but that's not the way it is where *I*
work. At my level, making budget is all that counts.

It was during Act II that Welch found ways to get GEers to
embrace his business vision. Walter Wriston, retired head of Citicorp
and an influential member of GE's board of directors, once told
Welch, "No one can remember more than three things at once." The
young CEO began with an inchoate vision of a transformed GE, but
he spent years distilling his complex ideas into a few precepts simple
enough for every employee to grasp.

One of the most powerful images Welch eventually created is
what he calls "the business engine," which explains how each of
GE's businesses fits into the corporate whole. The idea, which did
not occur to Welch until 1988, is so useful, so clear, it is a wonder
that no one thought of it before. Admits Welch, "It would have been
better if we had designed the engine in 1983." For the first time, one
image showed GE's far-flung employees the workings of the entire
enterprise from the CEO's perspective. It also enabled security analysts and investors to distinguish GE from the conglomerates to
which it was often compared.

To further define the concept of the business engine, GE used
"The Financial Engine" in its 1996 Annual Report to explain how
GE leverages the stability of its core products, services, and media
businesses, plus the financial strength of GE Capital Services, to
provide a cash flow of more than $6 billion that results in consistent
double-digit earnings per share growth.

The business engine shows how different GE is from a
conglomerate, a type of holding company that buys and sells
large numbers of unrelated businesses without doing much to
improve them. Any individual GE business, no matter how well
managed, is subject to the ups and downs of the market it serves.
But GE as a whole, strengthened by its participation in many different markets at once, can consistently make smooth financial
progress.

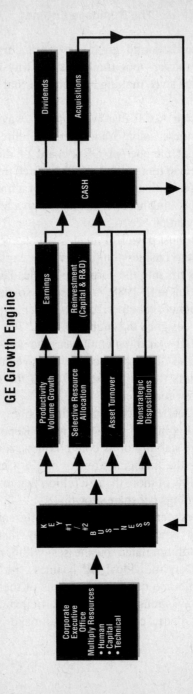

GE Growth Engine

The engine is driven by individual businesses working together like pistons, their performance carefully regulated by the allocation of capital. According to Welch, 40% of GE's employees worked for businesses, such as Lighting, that were growing slowly during the recession of 1991–1992; they produced about 30% of corporate earnings. These less glamorous operations served the engine by generating the cash that was its fuel. By the end of 2000, the business mix changed, with GE Capital Services producing 40% of corporate earnings. The percentage of revenues contributed by consumer products declined sharply. Although the fuel driving the engine has shifted from products to services, the engine itself still churns along, producing the second-highest level of profits among the S&P 500.

Here's how the engine works. During the defense-spending spree of the Reagan years, prosperous Aircraft Engines provided the cash that supported Power Systems' ailing turbine business. By 1993, it was the other way around: Cuts in defense spending squeezed Aircraft Engines, while the revived turbine operation threw off the cash GE needed to develop new engine products. By 2000, both the Aircraft Engine and Power Systems businesses were healthy.

The business engine also uses spare cash to fund dividends that reward share owners, and to pay for acquisitions that, in their turn, make the engine even stronger. Thus each business, while functioning in relative isolation, lends strength to the others and derives strength from them.

By 1988, GE's Act II was complete. With the business engine and other imagery, Welch had communicated his vision to employees.

GE's Act III is still far from over. This act concerns the creation of structures to institutionalize the organization's vision. New practices are created to embody the new ideas; over time, these practices influence the way employees think.

To promote clear thinking and fast decision-making, the CEO often makes operating executives prepare a few simple slides that describe the essence of their business situations. The slides show the answers to basic questions such as these:

- What does your global competitive environment look like?

- In the last three years, what have your competitors done to you?

- In the same period, what have you done to them?

- How might they attack you in the future?

- What are your plans to leapfrog them?

A much more complex technique for pushing cultural change is the ambitious program called Work-Out, which began in 1988. An attempt to extend the benefits of freewheeling debates to the whole company, the program first gathers employees together, regardless of rank, for sessions at which people air their gripes and suggestions. Managers are required to take action on the issues workers raise. Later on, Work-Out organizes employees into carefully targeted teams with the authority to define solutions to business problems.

Other companies have experimented with many of the ideas behind Work-Out, but GE was the first to employ them on such a vast scale. Virtually every GE employee has participated in Work-Out. The program has helped GEers learn how to walk and chew gum. It also has helped to redefine the nature of management at GE: Taking a certain amount of guff from subordinates is now part of an executive's job description.

GE's attempt to reshape itself can be measured in several ways. Its market value, record earnings, and global dominance in every business in which it competes are testimony to the changes that have been made since Welch became CEO in 1981. Perhaps the strongest evidence of GE's success is the strength of its leadership, widely regarded as the best in the world.

Any revolution is based on ideas. In politics, some of the most potent revolutionary ideas, such as Marxist economics, have proved unrealistic. But as GE's financial performance under Welch amply demonstrates, the ideas behind this transformation are entirely practical.

What this company has done, others can do.

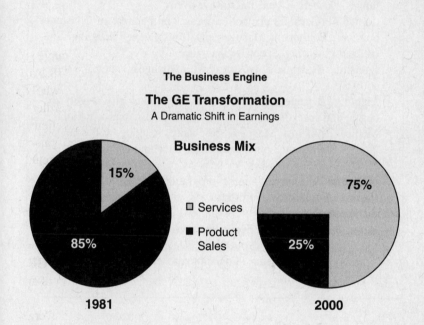

The Business Engine

The GE Transformation
A Dramatic Shift in Earnings

Business Mix

□ Services
■ Product Sales

15%

85%

1981

75%

25%

2000

GE's 2000 Business Portfolio

- Aircraft Engines: Jet engines and parts for commercial and military planes and helicopters, engines for marine propulsion and industrial power, aviation services
- Appliances: Refrigerators, freezers, dishwashers, electric and gas ranges, washers, dryers, microwave ovens
- Capital Services: 28 distinct businesses in the areas of Consumer Services, Equipment Management, Mid-Market Financing, Specialized Financing, Specialty Insurance
- Industrial Systems: Drives, motors, switchgear, control centers, software
- Lighting: Incandescent, fluorescent, halogen, high-intensity discharge and specialty light bulbs, wiring devices, quartz products
- Medical Systems: Magnetic resonance imaging, CT scanners, X-ray systems, ultrasound equipment, nuclear imaging
- NBC: Television network, TV stations, program production, cable-programming services, internet programming, CNBC, MSNBC
- Plastics: Engineered thermoplastics, silicones, resins, laminates, manmade diamonds
- Power Systems: Steam, hydroelectric and gas turbines, generators, pipeline and industrial applications, nuclear fuels and services
- Transportation Systems: Locomotives, electric wheels, transit propulsion systems

Changes in GE's Business Portfolio between 1981 and 1992

MAJOR ACQUISITIONS ($22 BILLION TOTAL)

- Calma (CAD/CAM equipment)
- Intersil (semiconductors)
- Employers Reinsurance Corp.
- Decimus (computer leasing)
- RCA (NBC television, aerospace, electronics)
- Kidder, Peabody (investment banking)
- Polaris (aircraft leasing)
- Genstar (container leasing)
- Thomson/CGR (medical equipment)
- Gelco (portable building leasing)
- Borg-Warner Chemicals (plastics)
- Montgomery Ward Credit (credit cards)
- Roper (appliances)
- Penske Leasing (truck leasing)
- Financial Guaranty Insurance Co.
- Tungsram (light bulbs)
- Burton Group Financial Services
- Travelers Mortgage (mortgage services)
- Thorn Lighting (light bulbs)
- Financial News Network (cable network)
- Chase Manhattan Leasing
- Itel Containers (container leasing)
- Harrods/House of Fraser Credit Cards
- GNA Annuities

MAJOR DIVESTITURES ($14 BILLION TOTAL)

- Central Air Conditioning
- Pathfinder Mines
- Broadcasting Properties (non-RCA TV & radio stations)
- Utah International (mining)
- Housewares (small appliances)
- Family Financial Services
- RCA Records
- Nacolah Life Insurance (RCA's)
- Coronet Carpets (RCA's)
- Consumer Electronics (TV sets)
- Carboloy (industrial cutting tools)
- NBC Radio Networks
- Roper Outdoor Lawn Equipment
- GE Solid State (semi-conductors)
- Calma (CAD/CAM equipment)
- RCA Globcomm (international telex)
- Ladd Petroleum (oil exploration & refining)
- RCA Columbia Home Video
- Auto Auctions (auctions of used cars)
- Aerospace (electronics)

In 1981, only Lighting, Motors, and Power Systems were leaders in their markets. By 1992, all businesses were leaders in their markets.

The Human Story

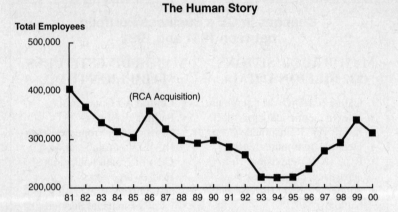

Total Employees

(RCA Acquisition)

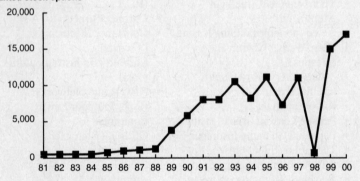

Number of employees
granted stock options

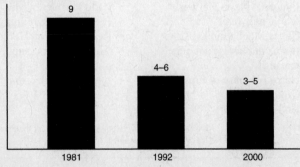

Organizational layers
between CEO and shop floor

9

4–6

3–5

1981   1992   2000

The Performance Story

Revenues
(Billions of U.S. Dollars)

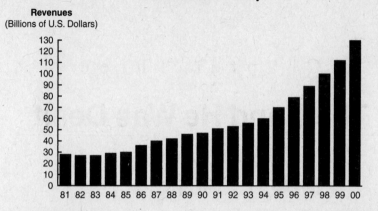

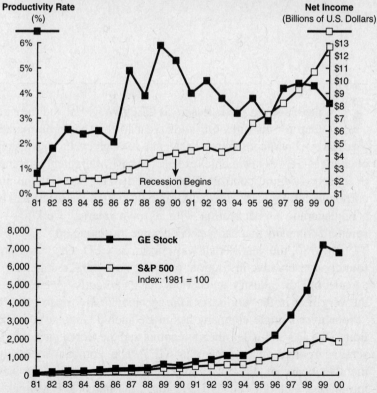

Based on average annual return, assumes reinvestment of dividend.

Chapter Three

The Hand He Was Dealt

Like his seven predecessors as CEO, Welch proved the right man for his time. GE's 115-year history has been marked by consistently robust leadership through cyclic convulsions of change; GE's postwar chief executives have alternately tightened or loosened central controls. Welch inherited an organization and corporate culture marked by admirable discipline but weakened by a bureaucratic preoccupation with its own internal workings—a splendid company that badly needed some loosening up.

In 1980, the year Welch was chosen as CEO, GE was a profoundly conservative institution: proud of its history, recognized as a leader of U.S. industry, and certain that its executives were among the very best in the world. As *Management Today* wrote in 1978: "Probably no single company has made such a singular contribution to the arts and wiles, the viewpoints and the techniques of large scale corporate management as GE." The company's twenty-member board of directors comprised a *Who's Who* of business luminaries, including Lewis T. Preston, chairman of J. P. Morgan &

Co., J. Paul Austin of Coca-Cola, and Ralph Lazarus of Federated Department Stores.

GE's CEO at the time, courtly, British-born Reginald H. Jones, then sixty-three, was a skilled practitioner of scientific management. He was also an accomplished bureaucrat. Long-faced and lean, with a perfect part in his slicked-back brown hair, "Reg" (rhymes with *peg*) Jones was a chain-smoking finance man who had spent his early career on GE's fearsome audit staff. He worked as a line manager for fifteen years before rising to chief financial officer. Once he became CEO, Jones remained aloof from daily operations, exercising power through his mastery of the data in the thick reports he demanded from subordinates. As he later remarked, "I found you never get all the information you'd like."

Unquestionably the most admired CEO of his day—President Jimmy Carter reportedly twice offered him cabinet posts—Jones viewed his eight-year CEO term as distinguished, yet he picked a successor prepared to completely transform much of what he had built.

One can't help wondering what drove GE to choose Welch as CEO. To a degree, members of the GE board may have underestimated Welch's determination to reshape GE, or been unable to imagine the upheavals he had in mind. Says Gertrude G. Michelson, a senior vice president at R. H. Macy & Co. and a GE director: "In a way it has been a revolution, but it did not seem like a revolution as it was happening. It was just Jack's vision of the future."

GE's stewards certainly recognized that change was necessary. Jones's letter to stock owners in the 1980 report describes a "mood of self-renewal" at GE:

> **U.S. business today finds itself challenged by aggressive overseas competitors. National productivity has been declining and, in industry after industry, product leadership is moving to other nations. Companies that refuse to renew themselves, that fail to cast off the old and embrace new technologies, could well find themselves in serious decline in the 1980s. We are determined that this shall not happen to General Electric.**

Jones recognized three challenges grave enough to justify major changes: GE's productivity was growing slowly; it had to speed up the shift from electromechanical to electronic technology; and it needed strong responses to international competition.

He tried to improve GE's productivity mainly by investing in hardware such as factory-automation equipment. That costly approach would eventually pay off, but in 1980 it helped create GE's first negative cash flow in seven years—while productivity continued to sag.

GE's competitive position in technology had slipped dramatically. In 1977, Jones had commissioned a year-long study of the subject, which resulted in a voluminous report that consumed five feet of shelf space. The report convinced Jones that the problem was serious.

Recognizing the growing importance of global markets, Jones stated in the 1980 report that 42% of GE's earnings was earned overseas. Nearly half the foreign earnings came from Utah International, a mining company that sold Australian coal to Japan. (Jones had bought the company as an inflation hedge.) Only three GE units, Aircraft Engines, Gas Turbines, and Plastics, operated on a truly global basis. GE's strength remained in the United States.

At the time, many other U.S. corporations were struggling with the same challenges of productivity, technology, and global competition. But those were not GE's only difficulties. Many of its individual businesses were ailing, among them the troubled unit that built nuclear power plants. After the notorious 1979 accident at the Three Mile Island nuclear plant (built by Babcock & Wilcox), Americans abruptly lost confidence in nuclear plants. Pending orders vaporized, and no new orders replaced them.

Despite Jones's modernization efforts, some GE products were antiquated. In a few areas, notably jet engines and plastics, GE was producing leading-edge products, but most of the company's sales still depended on machine-age technology. In 1970, 85% of the company's earnings came from motors, wiring, appliances, and other businesses dating back to the Edison era. By the time Jones retired, GE depended on those lines for just under half of GE's profits—a great improvement, but not good enough.

Several of these mature operations were in trouble—especially during the second U.S. economic recession in five years—and none was capable of rapid growth. Even with financial services and other high-growth businesses added in, total corporate earnings were increasing at such a sluggish rate that the effects of inflation wiped them out. That wasn't unique to GE: In constant dollars, U.S. nonfinancial corporations' net income had been declining at a 2% annual rate since 1975. At GE, that created a financial squeeze, because the company had to invest huge sums to maintain its position in aircraft engines, nuclear power and, until 1970, computers.

The company's stock was stuck. During 1980 GE's per-share price never topped $16 (adjusted for subsequent stock splits)—13% below its high in 1972, the year Jones took office. The corporation had been steadily paying out nearly half its earnings in dividends to share owners during those years. Even so, anyone who bought GE stock when Jones became CEO, and held it until Welch was named the successor, would have lost about 25% of the investment's value net of inflation, which averaged 8% during the Jones years. During the same period, the value of the Dow Jones industrial average declined some 15%, net of inflation.

Jones probably strengthened GE as much as anyone could without fundamentally challenging the precepts of scientific management. He funded such outstanding businesses as Plastics and Aircraft Engines, adroitly arranged GE's exit from computers, and pushed hard for growth in technology and international markets. But the business environment changed profoundly during Jones's tenure: Scientific management, which had produced enormous benefits at GE and many other companies, had outlived its usefulness and gone into decline. By the late 1970s, traditional management had reached the stage of decadence, spawning wasteful bureaucracy—not just at GE, but throughout corporate America. The only way to accomplish much more than Jones was to abandon the old paradigm and start fresh.

That was easier for Welch. He had spent most of his career at GE Plastics in Pittsfield, Massachusetts, a red-hot start-up venture that had grown to over $1 billion in sales while minimizing contact with the bureaucrats dominant elsewhere in GE. As a young man given to antiauthoritarian views in the 1960s, Welch had freely expressed his resentment of the paper-pushing company men he called "dinks"—a category that included many at GE's headquarters. Unburdened by loyalty to tradition and fiercely intolerant of inefficiency, Welch turned over more rocks than his predecessor. His philosophy of "changing before you have to" led him to attack potential problems before obvious symptoms of trouble appeared.

In temperament and business style, Welch and Jones make a striking contrast: Jones formal and relatively passive, Welch uninhibitedly aggressive. Jones had made most of his decisions in response to information that others provided. To the extent that his courtiers were blind to GE's problems, Jones himself risked blindness. In fairness, he also had spotted some important issues his subordinates didn't, such as GE's weakness in technology. Less obvious, at least to outsiders, are the similarities between the two men. Looking over GE's businesses, they saw the same issues—and reached similar conclusions often enough to enable Jones to trust the younger man.

Welch believed that GE's past successes contained the seeds of present and future difficulties, and he was willing to act on that perception. In an environment of unceasing change, few business ideas remain useful for long; after a while, even successful concepts must be abandoned. But GE's century of business experience was embodied in a rigid corporate culture and an authoritarian organizational structure.

A corporate culture is the sum of the unwritten norms, beliefs, and values that define appropriate behavior. After a while, almost every business develops its own style: Texaco, for instance, is marked by East Coast sobriety and deference to authority, while Pennzoil more frequently exhibits vestiges of cowboy exuberance.

Like human personalities, corporate cultures result from the interaction of temperament and experience. Over time, their dictates slip from consciousness into the realm of habit: People cling to once-useful beliefs and patterns of behavior as if no alternative existed.

In business as in life, sticking to outmoded ways can cause trouble. Tantrums may serve an infant's purposes, but an adult who throws fits invites rejection. Similarly, teaching employees to defer to authority may at first establish needed discipline, yet later suppress creative thought. Discriminating between useful and destructive habits requires a clearheaded objectivity that doesn't come easily, to Welch or anyone else.

The business style that every company develops early in its history is like the genetic code that determines a living creature's characteristics. From generation to generation the mix of genes will change, much as a business will evolve in response to the Darwinian force of competition. Whatever the mix, though, genetic heritage will always exert a powerful influence. In business as in science, our ability to alter underlying structures remains relatively primitive. Any action we take can have unforeseen results that may not become manifest for years.

GE's cultural heritage dates back to the late 1800s, when the "modern" business bureaucracy was just emerging. That is when the German theorist Max Weber extolled the benefits of systematic organizational controls such as clear chains of command and advancement based on merit. Corporations built on the Weberian model have relied ever since on bureaucratic schemes to reduce the inherent uncertainties of business.

The ideal was a system of such clear and enforceable rules that an organization could function with machinelike predictability. People were not expected to have ideas; the ideas were built into the system itself, as in Ford's famous assembly line. Compared with previous methods, this type of organization proved remarkably effective, and businesses around the world adopted it. The larger and more complex the company, the more obvious was the benefit of this so-called scientific management.

GEers fawned on their bosses and did what they were told, even when their orders made no sense. When criticized by superiors, they turned around and "kicked the dog"—company argot for passing on the pain to subordinates. Ambitious GE managers kept their ties knotted and their mouths shut.

The GE organization circa 1980 required business managers to report to two distinct types of authority: a military-style hierarchy of operating executives and a group of independent, headquarters-based staffs that specialized in such functions as finance, strategic planning, and employee relations (GE organization charts appear on pages 563–565). Among the many oddities of this system was that GE's smallest businesses were subject to many more layers of review than larger and more important ones.

GE's organizational structure fostered sprawling staffs of supervisors, rulemakers, and checkers. Over time the bureaucracy established a life of its own, evolving into a self-sustaining organism with a powerful propensity for growth. According to Don Kane, one of GE's key organizational planning experts, the mounting expense of this bureaucracy was a major reason GE became a high-cost producer, vulnerable to foreign competition.

The complex interaction of GE's culture, organization, and bureaucracy created a symphony of not so subtle signals that taught GEers how to behave. But as Jones realized, behavior that had been appropriate in 1878—or even 1978—might prove disastrous in the 1980s.

By then, GEers had come to regard the trappings of status as more important than real operating performance. James Baughman, a bearded sometime musician who headed executive compensation and development and was Tichy's boss at Crotonville, had come to GE from Harvard Business School in midcareer. He remembers noticing that the GE executives who entered his office for the first time would invariably tilt their heads back in an automatic, almost subconscious way. He couldn't figure out why—until someone told him that they were counting the ceiling squares in his office. In an attempt to ensure fair treatment of its workers, GE had assigned all employees to one of twenty-nine civil service–style levels of rank.

At headquarters, people within any given level worked in offices of almost identical size. By counting Jim's ceiling squares, visitors could calculate the square footage of his office, and thus his status in the hierarchy. That told the executives whether to grovel before Jim or boss him around.

GEers regarded this behavior as normal. Unchallenged, such destructive practices spread like cancers. Asked to describe the prevailing attitude, former executive vice president Paul Van Orden, who retired in 1990, recalls an incident that occurred shortly after he was moved to the top job at GE's audiotape operation in the early 1970s:

> There were reports generated that just boggled the mind, but I saw them as the price of belonging in the club. Market share was considered very important in that business, but I had no way of calculating it. When the first call came in from headquarters, I said, "I'll call you back."
>
> I asked my assistant what the share was last month. He said, "15.2%."
>
> I waited a half hour, then I picked up the phone and told them our share was 15.3% this month. I marked that number down on a piece of paper and put it in my drawer. Month after month I would move the number up a tenth or down a tenth, or whatever, and it made everyone happy.

Such antics—and the system that encouraged them—horrified Welch, frustrated him, angered him so much he felt like his hair was on fire. But stopping them would not be easy.

Unlike GE's financial and operating problems, the bizarre patterns of behavior that had become common throughout GE could not be eliminated just by selling assets or making smart decisions. That is why GE's circumstances in 1980 called for a revolution: Just to get the company moving again, Welch had to attack almost everything it stood for.

Welch's situation was hardly unique: Each of GE's CEO transitions had led to considerable change. Management and a willingness to experiment always have been the company's greatest strengths. GE has always expected its leaders to foster change, and it has never been disappointed. During the postwar period, Ralph Cordiner dramatically restructured the organization in order to decentralize control. Next, Fred Borch set off a period of creative ferment and rapid growth. Then Jones established needed financial controls. Welch, having inherited a strong balance sheet from Jones, was free to set off in his own direction.

Almost from its inception, GE was a very large enterprise, producing such basics as wiring and even establishing a streetcar company. The rough-hewn Thomas Edison, who founded the New Jersey laboratory that grew into GE, realized early on that he couldn't sell light bulbs unless people had electricity. He envisioned the whole infrastructure of power stations, wiring grids, and electric appliances that people of our day take for granted.

Edison set out to build much of the system himself. No genius at organization, he incorporated these business units separately, allowing each to become an independent fiefdom. In 1886 he moved three of his principal manufacturing companies to an unused plant in Schenectady, New York. That operation became known as the "Works," a bit of nineteenth-century terminology that survives to this day, describing GE's traditionally autonomous manufacturing centers. To finance all his projects, Edison sought backing from a group of investors that included partners of financier J. P. Morgan.

The money helped, but ultimately cost Edison his job. The investors forced Edison out, replacing him with a former shoe salesman named Charles Coffin. In 1892, just sixteen years after Edison had founded his lab, Coffin reorganized the burgeoning portfolio of businesses under his command into the General Electric Company. The par value of its stock was $35 million—an eye-popping sum at the time and the equivalent of $500 million in 1992.

Coffin, a Quaker, had a flair for corporate organization. In an age when entrepreneurs such as the Rockefellers dominated the business scene, Coffin became known as the father of professional management. Until Alfred Sloan began reshaping General Motors in the 1920s, the management and organizational systems Coffin designed remained the world's most complex.

He created GE's rigid hierarchy, and organized each of the Works around a particular product line. Coffin also instituted extremely conservative financial controls, making GE's AAA credit rating seemingly invulnerable to economic upheaval. He moved beyond electrical products into so many new lines, such as radios and X-ray machines, that GE became the most diversified company in the world.

Far from abandoning light bulbs, Coffin, under Morgan's expert tutelage, did his best to transform that business into a cozy oligopoly. Edison already had won a patent suit that forced other light bulb manufacturers to license GE technology. That gave Coffin the leverage to negotiate cross-licensing agreements with Westinghouse, Sylvania, and many other competitors, even overseas, that effectively eliminated real competition in GE's primary business.

The federal government sued GE several times, charging price fixing and other violations of the Sherman Antitrust Act. By and large, these agreements were judged legal at the time. GE defended itself so effectively that, although the resulting judgments and consent decrees somewhat reduced its clout, the company came of age in protected markets where market shares were fixed and price competition virtually unknown. Until the early 1950s, General Electric's share of the U.S. light bulb market remained around 75% to 80%. Delightful though that experience must have been, it didn't teach GEers the basics of survival.

Gerard Swope, a political liberal who succeeded Coffin in 1922, was no fonder of competition. After serving GE for a decade, he accepted Franklin Roosevelt's appointment as chairman of the Economic Advisory Board of the Department of Commerce. There he designed the so-called "Swope Plan for American Industry," which asserted that "the cause of the Great Depression was the chaos of excessive competition." Some of Swope's ideas helped underpin the New Deal.

When Swope returned to GE, he made the company a leader in enlightened labor practices. He firmly believed that a corporation should help its people avoid uncertainty. Among his innovations were generous employee benefits such as profit-sharing, bonuses, pensions, group insurance, a stock purchase plan, and home mortgage assistance. GE established one of the country's first unemployment pension plans, guaranteeing its laid-off workers $7.50 per week for ten weeks. Swope wanted workers to regard the company as a family. His paternalism paid off, as an implicit promise of lifetime employment attracted talented people to GE. That posture later caused trouble, though, by shaping a work force around a shared aversion to risk.

The pugnacious Charles Wilson became GE's fourth CEO in 1940. He grew up in New York's Hell's Kitchen and boxed as a young man; people called him "Electric Charlie," to distinguish him from Charles "Engine Charlie" Wilson, who was running GM. During Wilson's tenure, much of Swope's good work in labor relations and corporate ethics was undone. Shortly after World War II, when many labor unions were flexing their muscles, GE suffered its most serious strike to date, which alienated both GE's blue-collar workers and its top management.

Then, in 1948, for the first time in its history, GE lost a major antitrust suit. Federal prosecutors charged GE Lighting with illegal patent-licensing practices that helped GE to maintain its market dominance. The company was found guilty. The judge might have broken GE Lighting into pieces, but let the company off with a slap—requiring it to provide its lighting patents to competitors free of charge—and a stern warning.

Subsequently some GE middle managers imagined themselves immune to punishment, expecting their bosses to wink at wrongdoing that helped a business grow. Partly as a result, the company was caught many times in illegal actions—and suffered for them. GE, like other companies, is still vulnerable to wrongdoing by employees, but the winking days are over.

Since Edison's day, the basic organizational scheme at GE had been that of a holding company. A relatively small group of executives at headquarters oversaw the activities of the eleven Works located in distant cities, including Schenectady, New York (turbines);

Louisville, Kentucky (appliances); Cleveland, Ohio (light bulbs); and Erie, Pennsylvania (locomotives). Each of the independently managed Works controlled its own research and development, marketing, and so on, creating expensive redundancies. The local chieftains who ran the Works had become powerful enough to resist repeated efforts by GE's headquarters to expand its authority over them.

Cordiner came closer to breaking this system than any other GE chairman. He did it by overlaying the structures of scientific management atop an older structure with which they were fundamentally incompatible. To exercise more power over the Works, he bolstered an existing bureaucracy of freestanding staffs. He gave the staffs, particularly finance, control over GE's most valuable resources: money and personnel. They enforced his will.

He also ordered a massive reorganization of GE, based on decentralization. Cordiner broke up the company's operations into departments, each small enough, in the CEO's phrase, "for a man to get his arms around." By 1968 the company had 190 departments, ranging in size from $1.7 million in sales to $391 million. These departments reported to forty-six divisions; the divisions reported to ten groups; and the groups reported to the CEO. Accustomed to military hierarchy from service in World War II, most GEers adapted easily to the strict new lines of authority.

But the reorganization caused some problems. It placed separate functional staffs in every department, creating enormous redundancies. It also aroused the ire of executives at the Works, who blocked Cordiner's attempt to consolidate R&D and disperse the Works' central manufacturing operations into smaller units.

Even so, Cordiner pursued his ideas with fervor. In 1951, he assembled a brainy team of GE executives, plus consultants and professors, including Peter Drucker, to recommend ways to improve GE's management. They studied fifty other firms, pored over the personnel records of 2,000 GEers, did time-motion studies of executives at work, and interviewed countless GE managers.

Two years later, they emerged with the Blue Books, a five-volume, 3,463-page management bible. Buried in endless pages of stultifyingly elaborate prescriptions are such powerful concepts as

management by objective—as well as some of the most revolutionary ideas Welch would later espouse. The discussion of decentralization, for instance, sounds a lot like Welch's principle of speed:
"A minimum of supervision, a minimum of time delays in decision
making, a maximum of competitive agility, and thus maximum
service to customers and profits to the company." To indoctrinate
managers in the new principles, Cordiner founded the Crotonville
school in 1956.

The unspoken purpose of the Blue Books was to reduce the
messy human element in corporate decision-making. Cordiner
described human motivation as a "baffling area." He also regarded
people as fungible: "A manager is a manager is a manager," he often
said. Reassigned to a new job, and often a new city, roughly every
three years, GEers gained enough confidence from the Blue Books'
guidance to tackle almost any project with gusto.

When Cordiner's logical theories clashed with human nature,
they sometimes produced loony results. He demanded that every
general manager—the executive responsible for the profit-and-loss
statement of a business unit—produce a 7% return on sales or a
20% return on investment every quarter. That goal proved almost
impossible to achieve, and taught GEers to focus almost exclusively
on short-term objectives. Anxious about expenses in the current
quarter, GE managers often would refuse to invest in essential
equipment such as new machine tools. Only after such decisions
had cost them market share would they belatedly make the necessary purchases. Misguided GEers would even temporarily shut
down factories despite strong demand and fierce competition, just
to keep their expenses from going over budget at year-end.

GE's bureaucracy responded to Cordiner's innovations as if to
a growth hormone. Decentralization added layers of supervisory
management, and the rules in the Blue Books meant nothing without people to enforce them. Cordiner's formal job classifications,
for instance, gave rise to a huge human resources staff that evaluated job descriptions, measured individuals' performance, and
monitored salaries and promotions. Those staffers helped spread
the bureaucratic mind-set throughout the entire company: They

ensured that salaries and bonuses mainly rewarded seniority, not performance. Remembers Walter Wriston, former head of Citibank and a GE board member:

> **It didn't make a hell of a lot of difference if the guy had just screwed up or invented LEXAN [a hugely successful GE plastic]. It was just unreal. You'd take the size of the guy's shirt collar and divide it by the Gregorian calendar and multiply it by the square root of pi, and you'd come out with a number that was totally meaningless.**

Cordiner's term ended on a dismal note. Despite enormous growth in sales, GE's profits, net of inflation, hardly budged. And like Coffin and Wilson before him, he presided over a damaging scandal. A group of managers at the Schenectady Works had entered into an agreement with Westinghouse, Allis-Chalmers, and other competitors to fix prices in turbine generators. Describing Schenectady as "the center of a deep and widespread conspiracy," the government assembled such damning evidence that GE and twenty-eight other corporations had to plead guilty or no contest to the charges. Five GE executives went to jail, and though Cordiner insisted he knew nothing of the conspiracy, it ruined his career.

His successor, in 1964, was Fred Borch, former head of GE Lighting. In contrast to the buttoned-down management of the Cordiner years, Borch's tenure was a time of creative ferment. Borch had a vision of growth, and was willing to make risky investments to produce it. He presided over nine yeasty years of what some people later dubbed "profitless growth." Under Cordiner, GE had been buoyed by the pent-up consumer demand and rapid economic growth that had followed World War II. Trying to match Cordiner's record of 5.3% annual growth in earnings, Borch placed enormous bets on three new, capital-intensive lines: computers, nuclear power, and aircraft engines. He built big businesses, but made little money except in engines, which paid off handsomely. During his nine-year regime, GE's revenues grew to over $10 billion.

Among his most lasting contributions was the first large-scale implementation of strategic planning, one of the most powerful business ideas of the late twentieth century. The concept grew out of a Borch-commissioned study of GE by the consulting firm of McKinsey & Co. Upon completing their investigations, the consultants pronounced themselves "totally amazed" that GE functioned as well as it did, given its bizarre organizational structure. They proposed strategic planning as a technical solution to the problems they saw.

GE's departments were not really businesses, as McKinsey understood the term: Major Appliances alone had twenty departments, some of them created for no purpose other than to be small enough for a manager to "get his arms around." Absurdity ensued. In a company organized around what McKinsey termed "natural business units," all of Major Appliances would have been a single business. The consultants argued that GE was incapable of formulating sensible business plans, since it didn't even know what its businesses were.

McKinsey recommended drastically reorganizing GE into forty-three "natural" businesses. That would have eliminated scores of business units, and with them, scores of the coveted general-manager jobs that were the principal stepping-stones to advancement at GE—what GEers called "the Holy Grail."

Borch dodged conflict by superimposing a new layer of strategic planners on top of GE's existing structure, already creaking under the weight of layers accumulated from previous reorganizations. He defined forty-six strategic business units, or SBUs, which approximated McKinsey's natural business units. Borch then retired, leaving the task of implementing strategic planning to his successor, Reg Jones, who took office in December 1972. The resulting organizational structure was even more complicated than the one that had shocked the consultants at McKinsey. The general manager of one of GE's tiny departments would continue to report about normal operating matters to a totteringly top-heavy hierarchy of divisions and groups: By the end of Jones's term fully nine layers of increasingly isolated executives separated some managers from the CEO. They filtered the information passing up and down the chain of command and often distorted it, as in the game of telephone.

In addition, every general manager now was required to hire a full-time strategic planner and to create a formal strategic plan each year. That hefty document, the product of more man-hours than anyone dared count, went up to one of the forty-six SBUs, which would subject it to intense scrutiny. The SBUs, in turn, would send on the plan to a newly created staff at headquarters.

While it was still a fresh idea, the discipline of strategic planning proved enormously useful. But over time, the planners' success empowered them to build up a bureaucratic infrastructure, which they elaborated until finally it became dysfunctional. Jones says he sees a lesson in this: Outsiders can be invaluable allies in cultural change—but onetime change agents are as likely as anyone else to entrench themselves. The challenge for leaders is to monitor the cycle of transformation and eliminate any process or structure that has outlived its usefulness.

Planners were the most holy of GE's inquisitors, but there were others. To review all capital requests, planners raked executives over the coals jointly with the financial staff, examining all budget results monthly. If, having survived all these examinations, a manager tried to give somebody a raise, employee-relations staffers had to be persuaded that the action did not adversely affect the other 17,356 GE employees at that particular pay level.

Jones fulfilled his mandate to strengthen GE's finances, but the otherwise handsome legacy he bequeathed GE was diminished by the bureaucracy he empowered. The solution to one problem contained the seeds of another.

In late 1977 Jones gave Welch—then forty-two years old and a corporate vice president—his first job at corporate headquarters in Fairfield, Connecticut. *Fortune* described the scene that confronted the young maverick at this bureaucratic bastion:

> There, in a building where the office doors of top executives whoosh open and closed at the touch of a button, Welch encountered a bureaucracy that brings Imperial Russia to mind. . . . Jones's thirst for data led to ridiculous excess. Dennis Dammerman, 43, now GE's chief

financial officer, says that he had to stop computers in one GE business from spitting out seven daily reports. Just one made a stack of paper 12 feet high, containing product-by-product sales information—accurate to the penny—on hundreds of thousands of items.

The bureaucracy routinely emasculated top executives by overwhelming them with useless information and enslaved middle managers with the need to gather it. Old-timers say that as mastery of the facts became impossible, illusion sufficed. Briefing books had grown to such dense impenetrability that top managers simply skipped reading them. Instead, they relied on staffers to feed them "gotchas" with which to intimidate subordinates at meetings.

The cost of all this was enormous, and ultimately incalculable. Scientific management, once a great competitive advantage, had become an obstacle. As Jones himself recognized, the bureaucracy created to strengthen GE had become a weakness.

For all its financial strength and management depth, despite all Jones had achieved, GE was unready for the challenges it would face in the 1980s. No wonder Jones and every other member of GE's board thought the time had come for a change.

And they were to get one.

Chapter Four

The New Leader

The management-succession process that placed venerable General Electric in Welch's hands exemplifies the best and most vital aspects of the old GE culture. Jones spent nine years selecting Welch from a group of candidates so highly qualified that almost all of them ended up heading major corporations. Despite Jones's conservatism—and GE's—the process convincingly demonstrated that Welch's revolutionary leadership was what GE needed, and the company's board of directors gave him an explicit mandate for change.

Always thorough, Jones insisted on a long, laborious, exacting process that would carefully consider every eligible candidate, then rely on reason alone to select the best qualified man. The result ranks among the finest examples of succession planning in corporate history, and highlights Jones's considerable virtues as a manager.

Some of his personal contributions to the effort were strikingly imaginative—starting with his decision to add Welch to the list of contenders. Despite the spectacular profit increases Welch had produced wherever he went, the younger man was, if not exactly a renegade, at least a maverick by the company's straitlaced standards. Compared with the paths most GE executives had followed, Welch's career to date had been highly unconventional. Instead of taking on a wide variety of jobs around GE, for example, he stubbornly remained in Pittsfield—Plastics' headquarters—for seventeen years.

Only thirty-eight when the CEO search began, Welch was GE's youngest group executive, with a reputation for immaturity and abrasiveness. He enforced his high standards by cutting any member of his team who didn't meet them; his intolerance of the bad financial habits most GEers took for granted had turned whole businesses upside down. Many people who didn't know Welch personally assumed he was fearsome. He was known for conviviality after business hours and ferocious determination at all times: Once he spent a whole day skiing despite a dislocated knee. Some of Welch's colleagues called him a "wild man." In a 1973 appraisal form, Welch acknowledged that he needed "improvement in handling socio-political relationships." (He also stated that his goal was to become CEO.) The evaluation noted that Welch had a marked tendency to operate "outside the dots," that is, outside bureaucratic norms.

Jones began the winnowing process by asking Theodore LeVino—the soft-spoken but intense senior vice president who ran GE's Executive Management Staff—to identify the top twelve in-house candidates for the CEO jobs. EMS was an elite group within the employee-relations bureaucracy; one of its main functions was to evaluate and plan the development of the company's most promising managers. Ted LeVino, one of Jones's closest confidants, pushed his staff to a central role in the CEO succession process.

When, after almost a year of careful study, LeVino gave Jones his staff's list of twelve candidates, the name of GE's future CEO was not on it. At the time LeVino didn't consider Welch qualified. That's ironic, since he later became one of Welch's strongest supporters. Indeed, once Welch got the job, LeVino and his EMS colleagues Don

Kane and Ray Stumberger became part of the CEO's inner circle of trusted advisers.

When he first scanned LeVino's list in 1975, Jones remembers, "I asked the EMS staff, 'Where is Welch?' It was clear this was a guy to watch."

The GE culture had many shortcomings, but the company's earnest efforts to make a science of management paid off richly during the CEO search. Jones never had to consider looking outside GE. On the contrary, companies in need of CEOs have routinely raided GE, which has trained more chief executives than any other U.S. corporation. GE alumni are presidents or chairmen of major U.S. corporations from Home Depot to 3M to Owens-Corning to Stanley Works. When *Business Week* ran a story on tough bosses in 1991, three of the five men portrayed on the cover were GE alumni. One was Stanley Gault, a strong competitor to Welch who went on to a career as CEO of Rubbermaid; after retiring at sixty-five, Gault became chief executive of Goodyear, the ailing tire company. A 1999 *Fortune* article highlighted GE's "CEO factory," putting them neck and neck with McKinsey in terms of producing top management talent.

This record is no accident. The harsh demands of GE's bureaucracy forged executives who could meet them, and the people who took shortcuts—though numerous—rarely rose very high. GEers were justly famed for their financial discipline, analytical skill, and devotion to strategic planning. The company's diversity, combined with its practice of shuttling people from one job to another, provided a breadth of business experience few companies can match. And GE's size has enabled even its second- and third-tier managers to run businesses with over $1 billion in sales.

GE's meticulous, nit-picking ways added depth to the CEO selection process. The candidates' thick files were worth reading, containing not only performance data but pungent subjective impressions as well. Employee-relations staffers had routinely interviewed the bosses, colleagues, and subordinates of key GE managers to produce reports called "accomplishment analyses," which included hard data on managers' accomplishments, strengths, and weaknesses.

LeVino's EMS team supplemented those files with round after round of fresh interviews with the candidates and people who knew them. Among those interviewed were retiring executives, who could afford to be honest.

As the field narrowed—first to six men, then to three—Jones tested the contenders with challenging new jobs. He personally conducted several probing interviews with each of the finalists, asking some devilishly ingenious questions. To balance his subjective impressions, he asked EMS to rate the executives on fifteen categories ranging from toughness and intelligence to "ego management" and compassion. As a last step, Jones asked each of the remaining candidates to write a long memo assessing his strengths and weaknesses. Those memos proved fascinating—and influential.

Perhaps inevitably, the search for GE's next CEO turned into an old-fashioned horse race. The candidates, naturally, all wanted to win, and each had his backers cheering from the stands. In retrospect, Welch wonders whether Jones erred in creating such an intense, divisive competition among the aspirants for the top job. Corporate politics played its role in the process, with the EMS staff playing up its favorite candidates. But LeVino and his subordinates remained willing to change their allegiances as new information came flooding in.

Welch won for a number of good reasons. His thoroughly researched business decisions consistently paid off. The financial results he produced were superb, enabling him to outdistance his competitors. None of them matched his experience running high-technology operations. But his most important characteristic, the one that won Welch the job he coveted, was his ability to change.

By 1980, when Jones finally picked Welch, he had decided that GE needed a changemaker. During the years that Jones and LeVino were watching Welch closely, they saw the young man mature. Unflattering stories about Welch still circulated in Fairfield, but most of them concerned events long past. Welch's demonstrated ability to adapt to altered circumstances was a powerful point in his favor. Don Kane, then a senior member of the EMS staff, explains why:

> The company had a tremendous need to change, so you needed a different kind of person—a change agent—to come in. But if that change agent had not been able to change himself, how could you trust him to change the company?

When we show videotapes of Welch to executives from other companies, they often say, "Is there any hope for us? Because we don't have a Jack Welch."

The response is always the same: "Bull."

Every company has its Jack Welch, most likely several of them. If no forceful changemaker has made his or her way into the higher echelons of management, that can only be because corporate politics have blocked the way. Look harder, and you'll find the person your business needs to meet the challenges of the twenty-first century.

Pulling off a transformation on this scale does require a special sort of personality. Even run-of-the-mill CEOs need brains and energy. Vision, physical stamina, and a sense of urgency are essential, of course. So are respect for other people and the ability to express complex ideas in simple ways. But leading people through agonizing change draws on another, ultimately indefinable quality: the human equivalent of a planet's gravitational pull. Whatever it is, that's not something you can pick up at business school.

We respect Welch as a leader, and like him as a man. Anyone who dismisses him as simply fearsome is missing the point. Sure, he can be witheringly forceful, and he's no fun to be around when he's mad. His willfulness can make him overbearing at times: He will "revisit" a seemingly closed issue again and again until he is satisfied with the result. He is tough, but his is the sort of toughness that brings the Jesuits to mind: He is ruthless in service of deep-rooted beliefs. For better and for worse, Welch is an honest man.

He seems to see himself as a regular guy, only smarter. Informal and unpretentious, he can be a comfortable companion. If he is charismatic—and some think he is—it's because he so obviously enjoys other people.

In 1989 Welch, having divorced, married for the second time. Jane Welch, née Beasley, is a plainspoken and fiercely intelligent former mergers and acquisitions lawyer, whom he met on a blind date arranged by Walter Wriston, the GE board member. Welch's personal life, including his relations with four adult offspring from his first marriage, seems to consume a lot of his attention.

Welch didn't expect to become one of the most successful corporate executives of his age—or a businessman of any kind. While growing up in Salem, Massachusetts, he says, "I never thought about it." Welch grew up middle class—not poor, but poorer than he wished to be. As he puts it, "I always had my nose pressed against the glass." Intensely competitive, he has spent his whole life setting tough standards for himself, and usually meeting them. Yet he insists, "My life has been very easy."

The pattern was set as soon as he was born, says Welch. "I was an only child, so I was loved, nurtured, kissed, and praised much more than most people." By 1935, when he was born, Grace and John Welch, Sr., had been trying to have a child for sixteen years; they never had another. Welch's grandparents on both sides were Irish immigrants, and neither of his parents graduated from high school. John was a train conductor for the Boston & Maine railroad, a committed union man. Welch remembers his father as kind but "passive"—a calm, quiet fellow who faded into the background. John left for work at 5:30 A.M., frequently returned after 7:30 P.M., and had relatively little influence on his son.

By contrast, Welch's mother, who died in 1966, was a monumental figure in Welch's life. Grace Welch assured her son that he could succeed at anything he tried, and he believed her. She was the one who taught him to be independent, self-confident, and resourceful; she gave him many of his best ideas. Welch still speaks of her often, and with unabashed emotion:

> **She was a very important part of my life. As an only child, I hung around with her a lot. She was smart as**

could be. Honest as the day is long. Saw reality—no mincing words. Whenever I got out of line, she'd whack me one. But always positive. Always uplifting. Always constructive. Control your own destiny—she always had that idea.

She felt I could do anything. If I was having trouble in algebra or something, she'd say, "Just go upstairs and study. You can do better than anyone." She wanted me to be independent, so I'd take the train to Boston alone when I was twelve years old. She'd take me to ball games, the Braves, the Red Sox. We'd sit in the bleachers. We also played fast games of cards, blackjack and lots of gin rummy. She loved to beat me. "Gotcha!" she'd say. And I'd try to beat her back. I was just nuts about her.

Scrappy and sure of himself, Welch grew up playing street hockey, and though his innate athletic ability was not exceptional, he became captain of the high school hockey team in a town that takes hockey seriously. He also led the varsity golf team. At the University of Massachusetts, where Welch got his B.S. in chemical engineering, he lived in a jock fraternity and played intramural sports. His delight in locker-room camaraderie continues to this day.

Hockey is a metaphor for the confrontational but free-flowing business style that Welch developed. During a game, players will smash you into the boards; when it's over, they'll cheerfully invite you out for a drink. In hockey, individuals' roles blur, as the play moves uncontrollably all over the ice at high speed. There are no time-outs. Players must adjust to new situations constantly, thinking for themselves while looking out for the team as a whole. By contrast, Welch's predecessors had run GE on a football model: Everyone had a carefully defined role in plays that the coach ordered in advance. They were accustomed to gaining ground a few yards at a time, if at all.

As a young man, Welch says, he was "an incredibly serious, believing Catholic." An altar boy through high school, he met his first wife, Carolyn, while attending Lenten masses as a graduate student. Then, with his mother's death, Catholicism suddenly lost its grip on him.

At the University of Illinois, Welch earned his M.A. and Ph.D. degrees in chemical engineering. The physicality of the subject appealed to the pragmatist in him: "It's not just a paper exercise," he remarks. Welch wrote his Ph.D. thesis on the role of condensation in nuclear steam-supply systems. Welch values the experience for teaching him to "wallow" in an intellectual problem until he finds a solution. He thinks he still does that as a manager:

> **The important part [of writing the thesis] for me was going down all the blind alleys, repeating myself, feeling frustrated, until I got it to where it was simple. I'm a firm believer that simple is the most elegant thing one can be. One of the hardest things for a manager is to reach a threshold of self-confidence where being simple is comfortable.**

John Sr. gave his son a brand new Volkswagen Beetle as a graduation gift. In 1960, already a husband and soon to be a father himself, Welch drove the VW to Pittsfield, Massachusetts, 160 miles from his hometown, where GE Plastics had offered him his first full-time job: an engineering post at one of GE's least important businesses, with an annual salary of $10,500.

Although Plastics was classified, Cordiner-style, as a department, it was really an R&D skunkworks with a couple of promising ideas. Its only going business was in silicones, the malleable, water-resistant sealant used in bathroom caulk and children's Silly Putty, a GE invention.

If serendipity hadn't led Welch to this isolated outpost, GE probably would have crushed Welch's entrepreneurial instincts. But Plastics was too tiny to attract much attention at headquarters, so its managers enjoyed unusual freedom. "We were all by ourselves, and we were all equal," he remembers. Casual and freewheeling, the business influenced Welch, nurtured him, and allowed him to develop the idiosyncratic business style that serves him well to this day.

His first assignment, as a junior engineer, was to help launch PPO (polyphenylene oxide), a polymer GE chemists had invented in 1956, into a commercial product. The stuff was strong and tantalizingly resistant to heat—but it was hard to mold, and it yellowed with age. No one was sure whether it would sell.

After only a year at GE, Welch suddenly quit, planning to take a post at International Minerals & Chemicals in Chicago. GE had given him the standard $1,000 raise for his job classification, and the proud young man thought he deserved more. Reuben Gutoff, the boss of Welch's boss and thenceforth Welch's mentor, sweet-talked Welch into returning. From then on, Welch got bigger raises than most of his peers. A believer in incentive compensation, he later gave similarly outsized bonuses to subordinates who performed well—and no bonus at all to those who didn't.

By 1963 GE was ready to start selling PPO, and placed Welch in charge of the new product—an important responsibility. His first important decision as a manager was to move the PPO group to a manufacturing site in Selkirk, New York. By then GE also was selling a tough, durable plastic called LEXAN, and the young manager didn't want his team to labor in LEXAN's shadow.

Just as the Selkirk plant began producing PPO, chemists back in Pittsfield made an important discovery. A blend of PPO with polystyrene, the plastic used in foam coffee cups, created a material that was somewhat less resistant to heat than pure PPO—but it didn't yellow, and it was much easier to mold into products. Welch faced the choice of continuing to manufacture PPO, or investing in new processes to produce something better. After a brief debate, Welch soon recommended modifying the PPO line. With approval from Gutoff and Charles Reed, Gutoff's boss, Welch converted the line to a new plastic blend called NORYL. Remembers Michael Modan, a group member, "Now we had something we could sell."

Welch's decision-making methods have not changed much since his days at Plastics. He would corral everyone he could find who knew something relevant about the subject at hand—whether chemists, production engineers, or finance types—and thoroughly debrief them. He wanted on-the-spot answers, not formal, written reports. Then he would join his subordinates in fierce, no-holds-barred debates about which decision to make. Welch calls this "constructive conflict." His theory is that if an idea can't survive a spirited argument, the marketplace surely will kill it. Says Stephen Eickert, a product manager at GE Plastics, "He likes to be challenged. He likes to get into a pretty animated discussion."

The challenge of selling NORYL gave Welch's people the chance to distinguish themselves. There was no market for NORYL—no one wanted it—so the Plastics sales force had to create demand from thin air. As a first step, they rejected the conventional wisdom at GE that a high-grade engineering product such as NORYL should be sold to engineers on the basis of technical specifications.

Instead, they relied on "application development." Salespeople would visit the manufacturers they regarded as potential customers, looking not for immediate orders but for components made of metal, glass, or rubber that could be made out of NORYL instead. If a salesman noticed, for instance, that an automaker used glass taillight housings, he would bring a sample back to the office and ask GE engineers to custom-design the same housings in NORYL—at GE's expense. When the NORYL parts proved cheaper or more useful than the original ones, as was often the case, GE usually would make the sale. NORYL went from a standing start to $50 million in sales and $5 million in earnings by 1973.

GE rewarded Welch in 1968 by making him, at thirty-three, the corporation's youngest general manager. His assignment: to oversee both LEXAN and NORYL, important enough by then to be consolidated into a department of their own.

Taking advantage of Plastics' independence and the strong support of Gutoff and Reed, Welch broke Blue Book rules by keeping the two plastic operations separate and encouraging them to compete ferociously with each other. Glen Hiner, who later became senior vice president of GE Plastics, remembers the consternation that the NORYL-versus-LEXAN free-for-all caused customers: "They'd pull out a big folder of business cards with a rubber band around them—and they were *all* from GE Plastics." The rivalry, though messy, forced everyone to fight hard for orders. Welch didn't care which plastic GE sold. He was still trying to get customers used to the idea of replacing traditional materials with GE's plastics, and he figured that every sale broadened the market.

Welch advertised LEXAN and NORYL with the same techniques used for soda pop or ladies' lingerie. Pitching LEXAN to Detroit's design engineers as a replacement for steel in auto bumpers, he aired goofy commercials featuring comedians Bob and Ray on a popular local radio station. The ploy paid off: Ford soon started installing LEXAN-based components on its cars. By the end of the 1960s, the average car made in Detroit contained 2.5 pounds of GE plastic.

He even used TV. A memorable commercial, comparing LEXAN to glass, showed a bull in a china shop breaking everything that wasn't made out of LEXAN. As *Fortune* wrote, "That image—rude havoc revealing a Darwinian truth—is Welch in a nutshell."

The shared experience of Darwinian havoc helped build a strong team spirit among Welch's subordinates. They came to see themselves as winners. One of his main goals as a manager always has been to stimulate positive emotional energy in subordinates: He says he wants "turned-on" people. In the old days, according to Larry Buckley, an EMS staffer, Welch "had the best team he could assemble from the people around him, but they weren't exactly the highest quality people available in GE." Their performance shone nevertheless: Under Welch's leadership, Plastics earnings increased at an average annual rate of 34%, compounded; by the end of 1992 its revenues reached $4.85 billion; and by 2000, revenues topped $7.7 billion.

That kind of growth, almost unknown at GE, provided Welch with what GEers call "air cover": the career-saving support of higher-ranking executives. Gutoff, for one, was delighted to protect Welch: "Jack made *my* career go faster," says he. "Jack always had the understanding that what matters in a bureaucracy is getting results. He was totally dependable." Charlie Reed and the late Herman Weiss, who was then a GE vice chairman, also consistently supported Welch. "They made my life easy," he remembers.

With their backing, Welch ran Plastics "like a family store," he recalls. "We were able to take on the big chemical companies and do very well, because we could outrun them. We had the strength of a big company and the speed of a small company." Welch never trained anyone: He'd give a person an assignment and wide latitude, and then expect results. Stealing a phrase from the flower children of that era, he told the GEers under his command to "do your own thing."

No less an information junkie than Jones, Welch lacked the patience to wait for formal reports. Instead, he just dropped in on people and grilled them. Anyone who couldn't answer a basic question wouldn't last long. Welch kept his office door open and allowed subordinates to challenge him or any other boss who seemed to be making a mistake. Delighting in the rough contest of ideas, Welch favored the feisty, hard-shouldered types who knew their stuff and challenged him often.

Perhaps the most important management idea Welch developed in those days is what Tichy calls "planful opportunism." Instead of directing a business according to a detailed, GE-style strategic plan, Welch believed in setting only a few clear, overarching goals. Then, on an ad hoc basis, his people were free to seize any opportunities they saw to further those goals. Welch operated that way instinctively, but the notion crystallized in his mind in the late 1970s, after he read Johannes von Moltke, a nineteenth-century Prussian general influenced by the renowned military theorist Karl von Clausewitz. Von Moltke argued that detailed plans usually fail, because circumstances inevitably change. A successful strategist, he wrote, always must be willing to adapt; even broad goals must be flexible enough to respond to new events.

A typical example of planful opportunism was Welch's early decision to push into overseas markets. Pursuit of one goal—to keep overseas companies from selling LEXAN-type plastics in the United States—led him to another, far broader one: making a market of the entire world. Unlike NORYL, which was protected by patents, the polymers that made LEXAN were in the public domain, and one European outfit—Bayer of Germany—already was selling LEXAN equivalents.

Figuring, characteristically, that the best way to keep those companies out of his turf was to invade theirs, Welch built a $55 million plant in Bergen op Zoom on the coast of Holland. Explains Eickert, "If you're not a player everywhere, we felt, you're going to get clobbered." After the Dutch plant became profitable, GE Plastics negotiated manufacturing joint ventures in Japan and Australia, and created marketing centers in Germany, England, and France. By 1977, GE Plastics was the world leader in the plastics it produced, getting 26% of its revenues overseas. By the time people began talking about globalization, Welch had been living it for years.

GE Plastics grew so fast that Welch frequently had to petition his corporate masters for extra investment capital. Instead of waiting until demand was straining a factory's capacity, he would request expansion funding long before it was needed, so that shortages would not impede the business's growth. *Change before you have to* was his rule even then.

While managers elsewhere in GE aspired only to grow their business as fast as the U.S. GNP, Plastics set a higher standard. As Welch tells it:

> **I came from businesses with great strength. Everybody should work in a fast-growing business like Plastics or Financial Services, because if they did, their standards would be higher. If a guy's spent all his life in a business that's growing 3% a year, and he gets to 3.5%, he thinks he's got a hell of a business. A lot of managers don't know what a good business looks like.**

Though he openly despised it, Welch learned to dance the bureaucratic minuet. Remembers Modan, "I think Jack's first impression was that the people in the bureaucracy were there just to criticize projects about which they had no competence." To outwit them, Welch made sure his capital requests were impeccably researched, financially conservative, and usually prefaced by a cover page that ticked off the results of his previous investments. Says Gutoff, "It showed he always delivered on his promises. Being able to deliver on your promises was the absolute magical secret."

Welch became expert at outwitting the bureaucracy. "He was the worst offender," remembers Don Kane, the EMS staffer. "He knew the game we were playing in Fairfield, and no one played the game better than Jack Welch." He became a master of chartsmanship—and of packaging. Before long he was custom-binding his strategic reports in handsome folders. Headquarters loved those reports, and smart managers throughout the company began copying their format. Says Buckley, the EMS staffer, "One of the first things Jack eliminated when he became CEO was fancy reports, because he knew how much money he had spent making them."

In 1973, at thirty-seven, Welch took charge of GE's $1.5 billion a year components and materials group, which included GE Medical Systems (GEMS) in addition to all of Plastics. Instead of moving to Fairfield like a normal group executive, he ran the whole group from Pittsfield. Herm Weiss, then vice chairman, gave Welch permission to stay there, a decision that angered Jones.

Although the products of his two main businesses were utterly different—GEMS made X-ray machines—Plastics and Medical Systems came to share the characteristics of high technology and fast growth. Welch provided the air cover for GEMS' costly decision to introduce computer-assisted tomography scanners, known as CT scanners, which use computers to create enhanced X-ray images of internal organs. The potential market was uncertain, partly because the complex machines sold for a hefty $1 million each.

As it turned out, hospitals around the world paid the price gladly, snapping up as many CT scanners as GE could make. Before long, Medical Systems was growing as fast as Plastics. That success made people at GEMS receptive to Welch's unusual management ideas, which were becoming ever more clearly defined:

- Practice planful opportunism.

- Wallow in information until you find the simple solution.

- Test ideas through constructive conflict.

- Treat all subordinates as equals, but reward each one strictly according to merit.

- Avoid compromise when making decisions.

- Replace hierarchical organizations with close-knit teams, using internal competition to train your varsity players.

- Give your people every chance to identify with their business. Their enthusiasm is your most valuable asset.

In 1977 Jones gave Welch a shot at the top job. By then the CEO had cut his list of potential successors to six men. Jones's initial favorite, finance chief Alva Way, disqualified himself by refusing to take an operating post despite the CEO's repeated urgings. No clear leader had emerged since. Welch, though in the running, was viewed as a dark horse.

Partly to test the contenders, Jones reorganized GE into six so-called sectors, each a multibillion-dollar portfolio of businesses. As a test, Jones tried to assign each CEO candidate to a sector containing businesses unlike any he had managed before.

Welch, GE's growth master, drew Consumer Products and Services: a collection of fusty, old-line businesses such as Lighting, Major Appliances, and Consumer Electronics, which made TV sets. The one ace in his hand was Financial Services, a hardy outgrowth of GE's long-standing practice of offering financing for consumer appliance purchases.

This was Welch's first Fairfield job, and he quickly made his presence felt. Lighting was producing plenty of cash, so he largely left it alone. But with the more than able assistance of Lawrence Bossidy—who was running heavy-equipment leasing when the CEO discovered him—Welch reshaped what is now called Capital Services on the pattern of Plastics and GEMS. Bossidy is a tall, big-boned man, the father of nine, whose intelligence and instincts closely match Welch's.

Together, Bossidy and Welch produced red-hot earnings growth by pursuing a simple, flexible goal: They would shove their way into almost any attractive financial business in which they felt they had an edge. Able to draw on GE's vast assets, the unit pushed deeper into capital-intensive lines such as equipment leasing. Before long, it owned more commercial jets, for example, than any other U.S. company, including the airlines.

Just as Plastics shaped Welch's operating style, Financial Services shaped his attitudes about managing a portfolio of businesses. Dave Orselet of the Executive Management Staff describes the Financial Services mind-set:

> **The Credit Corporation [as it was then called] was completely unlike most General Electric businesses. On a Monday morning you could take ten million bucks and invest in a business that you think is going to pay off. On Friday afternoon, if it doesn't look good, you close the window and you go home. You don't lament, you don't brood. You cut your losses early and get out.**

Bossidy believed that GE personnel, trained in rigorous financial analysis, should excel at a variety of high-risk lending activities such as leveraged buyouts. Because such loans are unusually chancy, and lenders willing to provide them scarce, the loans command exceptionally high rates of interest. (Despite some investor concern, the unit's write-offs remained less than 1% as a percentage of average net investment from 1993 to 1998. GE Capital Services made a killing nevertheless: Its earnings have grown at an astounding rate since 1978, from $77 million then to $1.5 billion in 1992, to a staggering $5.1 billion in 2000. With twenty-eight different financial businesses, GE is the most profitable financial services company in the world. Bossidy rose to vice chairman; in 1991 he left to become CEO of AlliedSignal, a producer of auto parts, defense electronics, and chemicals. Bossidy was named CEO of the Year by *Chief Execu-*

tive magazine. In 1999, AlliedSignal bought Honeywell, creating the combined company that GE agreed to buy in 2000. By then, Bossidy had retired, amid widespread praise.)

The brass in Fairfield loved what Welch was doing with Financial Services, but his behavior at Appliances, which produced refrigerators, dishwashers, and ovens, raised eyebrows. When he asked deeply probing questions at Appliances, he often got unsatisfactory answers. "Why are our costs so high?" Welch particularly wanted to know. Ignoring the world beyond America's borders—where Electrolux of Sweden and Matsushita of Japan were gaining formidable strength in appliances—the GE unit had built up a cost structure high enough to invite attack from overseas.

While Welch was performing his bull-in-the-china-shop routine at Major Appliances, and expanding Financial Services, the other contenders in the CEO race took on distinctly different roles. Gault, a trim Air Force vet, got responsibility for the industrial sector, which included motors and locomotives. A terrific salesman, he was less comfortable with technical matters. He studied his portfolio of unfamiliar businesses, and moved cautiously to guide them. Thomas Vanderslice, articulate and undeniably skilled, proved too impulsive to win the support of LeVino's staff. He went on to become president of GTE, then CEO of Apollo Computer, and then CEO of M/A Com, a producer of microwave components. Robert Frederick, a staff man who always fulfilled his assignments, never got the operating experience he needed to distinguish himself. He went on to the No. 2 job at RCA, which GE later acquired.

The two remaining contenders were Edward Hood, Jr., and John Burlingame. Hood, five years older than Welch, ran the sector that produced aircraft engines, and everyone agrees he did an excellent job. Deeply reserved and unwilling to play politics, Hood allowed his performance to speak for itself. Burlingame, eight years older than Hood, was a big, burly fellow who managed the sector devoted to overseas markets. He was smart, trustworthy, and a solid performer, but because of his age, he could hope to be no more than an interim CEO.

Jones subjected the CEO aspirants to the now-famous "airplane interviews." A variant of the process Jones's predecessor, Fred Borch, had used to pick him, these interviews enabled Jones to understand the whole matrix of relationships among his CEO candidates. Each person experienced the interview twice: first as a surprise, then again after plenty of time to reflect and prepare answers. Each time, Jones recalls, he would conjure up the image of an airplane ride: "You and I are riding together in the GE company jet. Suddenly, the plane crashes. Both passengers are killed. Who should be the next chairman of General Electric?"

Several of the astonished candidates wanted to climb out of the wreckage. But Jones wouldn't allow that. Instead, Jones would spend a few moments describing the challenges he saw ahead for GE. Then he would ask, "Which other top executives could rise to confront those hurdles?"

In 1979, five years after he began the search, Jones proposed Burlingame, Hood, and Welch as vice chairmen. One person who attended the board meeting says Jones's idea came as a stunning surprise to his two existing vice chairmen, Jack Parker and Walter Dance, both of whom favored other candidates. The three new vice chairmen all performed creditably for two years. Although highly qualified, Hood and Burlingame didn't have the characteristics Jones felt GE's CEO would need. Hood's experience was narrow compared with Welch's, and Burlingame's age ultimately worked against him. Moreover, Welch was the only changemaker in the group. When EMS rated the three chairmen according to its fifteen categories, Welch won hands down. EMS judged him the most charismatic, the toughest, the most objective, and the smartest of the lot; he got poorer grades on delegating authority and sharing credit.

Jones's final gambit was his request that each of the remaining candidates write a detailed memo assessing his own performance and aptitude for the CEO job. David Orselet, Larry Buckley, and Don Kane of EMS viewed Welch's memo as "the clincher" that ended the race. Burlingame's memo revealed how little his staff job had given him to brag about, while Hood simply refused to brag at all. Ted LeVino described Welch's memo to Jones as "an unabashed sales pitch on personal qualities and philosophy of managing, winding up with a strong bid for the order."

Welch stressed his virtues and found ways to minimize his flaws. Aware that some accused him of being overbearing, for instance, he wrote: "The people with whom I have been associated have worked harder, enjoyed it more, although not always initially, and in the end, gained increased self-respect from accomplishing more than they previously thought possible."

As he had done so many times before, with his requests for capital and his beautifully packaged strategic plans, Welch overcame his disadvantages and won the prize. On December 19, 1980, the board of directors unanimously named Welch CEO-elect. He took office four months later.

That is when the struggle began.

Chapter Five

The Power of Ideas

A t the end of his first year as CEO, Welch addressed an audience of Wall Street security analysts at New York City's Pierre Hotel. After dutifully running through the basic performance statistics for each of GE's major businesses, he launched into his first public explanation of what he was trying to do:

> If I could, this would be the appropriate moment for me to withdraw from my pocket a sealed envelope containing the grand strategy for the General Electric Company over the next decade. But I can't, and I am not going to attempt, for the sake of intellectual neatness, to tie a bow around the many diverse initiatives of General Electric. It just doesn't make sense for neatness' sake to shoehorn these plans into an all-inclusive central strategy.
>
> What will enhance the many decentralized plans and initiatives of this company isn't a central *strategy*, but a

central *idea*—a simple core concept that will guide General Electric in the eighties and govern our diverse plans and strategies.

Welch went on to cite the teachings of von Moltke, explaining planful opportunism. To wind up the speech, Welch delivered a passionate pitch for his big idea: that GE become No. 1 or No. 2 in every market it serves. As he told the analysts, "We believe this central idea, being No. 1 or No. 2, will give us a set of businesses which will be unique in the world business equation at the end of this decade."

The analysts—practical people who made their livings crunching numbers—looked puzzled. This strategy stuff sounded awfully vague, maybe meaningless. They seemed bored.

As things turned out, of course, Welch's simple strategic idea proved powerful. By 1993, almost all of GE's businesses had become market leaders, and its competitive clout was feared around the world. By 2000, GE continued its dominance in the market, and it was recognized as "America's Most Admired Company" by *Fortune,* ahead of Microsoft, Wal-Mart, and Southwest Airlines.

When the question-and-answer period started, an analyst stood up to ask a question. Excited by his presentation, Welch was eager to debate his ideas with all comers. But an early question set the tone for the rest of the meeting: How would the fluctuating price of copper affect GE's earnings next year?

"What the hell difference will *that* make?" snapped the infuriated CEO. "You should be asking me where I want to take the company!"

Welch answered a series of desultory technical questions about GE's operations, and then the meeting broke up. The analysts trooped back to their offices to prepare their reports. Intrigued with the new CEO, they wrote positive comments—but largely ignored his thinking. Wall Street's best and brightest didn't understand the power of ideas.

You can't blame them. People in business generally see themselves as practical folk, hardheaded doers who sensibly restrict their attention to matters of fact. Executives are supposed to be decision makers who analyze information, make tough choices, and then enforce their wills through the judicious exercise of power.

That is what business schools and corporate experience mostly teach. And that is why many managers are ill-prepared to lead their organizations into the twenty-first century.

Most executives are neither stupid nor hostile to ideas. On the contrary, it takes brains to prosper in business. And when a hot new idea comes along—as strategic planning did in the early 1970s, or quality circles in the 1980s—managers will race to grab it and impose it on their subordinates. Often enough, the results are pleasing. But the old managerial habit of imposing ideas on employees transforms concepts into rules, stripping them of their vitality. Workers change their behavior but not their minds.

In the years ahead, corporations will sort themselves out into those that can compete on the playing field of global business, and those that either sell out or fail. Winning will require the kind of skill, speed, and dexterity that can only come from an emotionally energized work force.

Today, most large corporations are thick-skinned and ponderous beasts, responding sluggishly to environmental changes, if at all. Businesses organized on the old scientific model still build their best ideas into systems instead of encouraging employees to think for themselves. You can recognize such companies by the listlessness of their workers, who lack the conviction, spirit, and drive that characterize champions in any field of endeavor.

Managers at the top of these old-fashioned organizations issue instructions, and then wait while their orders shuttle from desk to desk down the chain of command. When underlings misunderstand, or find ways to disobey, nothing gets done. It happens all the time.

We have witnessed the attempts of many major corporations to transform the way they operate, among them AT&T, Citicorp, Chase Manhattan, General Motors, Honeywell, and IBM. The leaders of those outfits clearly understand the need for fundamental change. What they are struggling with is keeping up with the pace of change, while getting their employees to understand why change is necessary.

In 1990 Tichy led a workshop at another company, one still imprisoned by bureaucratic traditions. Its chairman saw the problem, and assured Tichy he knew how to solve it. "We're going to make some radical changes," he said. "We're going to move fast. We're going to reshape senior management."

"How're you going to do that?" Tichy asked.

"Well," he replied, "we're going to bring in some consultants, and have them study us for six months. Then we'll move on out with the new program!"

It doesn't work that way.

Ideas are the essence of the GE revolution. GEers have referred to Welch's No. 1 or No. 2 concept so often that they slur it into a single word, **number-one-or-number-two**. But that is not the company's only big idea. By the end of the 1980s, employees were talking about **integrated diversity**, the principle that GE's varied businesses can maintain their operating independence while working closely together as a team, sharing everything from financial data to people to best practices. The business engine is an application of that idea.

GEers are talking about **boundarylessness** now. This is the value that underlies GE's increasingly supple organizational style. A boundaryless organization should break down the internal barriers of hierarchy, geography, and function, while nudging the company into closer partnership with its customers and suppliers. The ability to face reality and communicate candidly is a prerequisite of boundarylessness.

Above all, GE people talk about **speed, simplicity, and self-confidence**. Since his grad school days, Welch has believed that it takes self-confidence to simplify complex issues. Simple procedures, in turn, are a prerequisite for the fast action that enables GE to win in the marketplace. At bonus time, GEers' ability to manifest speed, simplicity, and self-confidence pays off in dollars and cents.

Ideas such as these serve as GE's signposts of change, but every company has ideas. What's revolutionary—and ultimately far more important than the ideas themselves—is the way GE is weaving its guiding principles into the fabric of its culture. GE's values aren't abstractions: They are becoming the basis of the corporate organization. Exclaims Welch: "We're doing it!"

Executives have substantial power over employees, but they can't tell people what to believe. Creating the pumped-up, turned-on, in-synch work force that Welch envisions requires an honest intellectual exchange between bosses and subordinates—conducted as a dialogue of equals. Welch, who enjoys paradox, calls this "leading while being led." As he declared in a 1987 speech to employees:

> We've learned a bit about what communication is *not*. It's not a speech like this, or a videotape. It's not a plant newspaper. Real communication is an attitude, an environment. It's the most interactive of all processes. It requires countless hours of eyeball-to-eyeball back and forth. It involves more listening than talking. It is a constant, interactive process aimed at [creating] consensus.

Convinced that only the best ideas can survive an open discussion, he doesn't necessarily care whose ideas ultimately win, just as he didn't care whether GE's customers bought LEXAN or NORYL. Welch's focus is on the larger mission: creating a team of like-minded people who believe in what they do and work better as a result.

American to the bone, Welch believes in the ideals of individual freedom and responsibility, and in the principle of human equality. As far back as his days in Plastics, he understood that the power of command could not get him the heartfelt allegiance that he craved. He treats subordinates as his intellectual and social peers, and rewards merit where he sees it.

The persuasive Welch usually can win over anyone he spends time with face-to-face. But as GE promoted him higher and higher, he became responsible for more people than he could possibly meet for one-on-one talks. Years passed before he discovered how to earn the allegiance of strangers. His secret? Acknowledging and respecting the considerable power that even the most junior employee commands—the power of independent thought.

Sure, Welch and every other GE executive constantly make decisions and impose them on subordinates, but they also want workers to think for themselves. Why? Because speed now translates into competitive advantage. GE cannot match the agility of small start-ups, but pitted against sumo-sized contenders such as Hitachi or Siemens, GE can win by being more nimble—just as Plastics rose to become a powerful competitor of Bayer and Du Pont.

The corporation can't afford to tell its employees exactly what to do—that would take too long. But like any CEO, Welch needs assurance that his workers will further the corporation's goals. He needs people who not only understand GE's objectives but sincerely believe in them. Only when managers and subordinates are on the same wavelength does turning people loose—"liberating" them, as he puts it—become a sound business decision.

The CEO often talks about the need to win "the hearts and minds" of workers. Even in a dialogue of ideas, he believes, hearts are every bit as important as minds. Bitter experience has taught him how profoundly emotions can influence human thought and behavior—and entire organizations. When GEers felt fearful, as many did during the early 1980s, they fought Welch to a standstill; when they felt successful, as at Plastics, Medical Systems, and Financial Services, their enthusiasm carried him to new heights.

Most organizations don't know how to deal with emotion, so they try to pretend it doesn't exist. By design, corporations seem emotionally barren. Feelings, one understands, are best expressed at home, where they won't gum up the machinery of scientific management. The emotional sterility of the business environment is a *cordon sanitaire* around the fear, jealousy, resentment, rage, longing, pride, ambition, and God-knows-what-else that seethe in human hearts. But the sense of sterility is largely symbolic.

Work, inevitably, is an emotional experience; healthy people can't just drop their feelings off at home like a set of golf clubs. Yet management theory long neglected this realm, and we are just beginning the search for ways to harness the vast power of workers' emotional energy.

Though Welch is a passionate person, and more than a casual student of human nature, his Darwinist creed led him to behave in ways that seemed coldhearted. Awash in the flood tide of organizational change, many GEers ignored or resisted him. Understandably enough, they were devoting much of their emotional energy to worrying about themselves: Their job security, prospects for advancement, and workday routines all seemed threatened by the changes Welch made. Says he, "I was intellectualizing the issues with a couple of hundred people at the top of the company, but clearly I wasn't reaching hundreds of thousands of other people." The employees he wasn't reaching felt that instead of throwing out lifelines to them, the CEO was shouting at them. The message they heard—*Swim better!*—wasn't much help.

Not until 1988 did Welch finally find a way to open a real dialogue with GE's whole work force. Then began the long process— still very far from complete—of winning the large mass of employees over to his way of thinking. Here is Welch's explanation:

> It's not that I changed. We just expanded the reach of our communication. We refined it, got better at it, and it began to snowball. If you have a simple, consistent message, and you keep on repeating it, eventually that's what happens. Simplicity, consistency, and repetition—that's how you get through. It's a steady continuum that finally reaches a critical mass.
>
> By then we had taken out the fat. Over 100,000 people were gone. For a lean organization, the only route to productivity is to build an energized, involved, participative, turned-on work force, where everyone plays a role, where every idea counts.

Like a rock thrown into a still pond, Welch's message has spread out to expanding circles of GE employees. The CEO first created a Corporate Executive Council of GE's thirty top executives— business leaders and senior staffers—who spend two intense days with the CEO each quarter discussing the biggest issues facing GE. Then he transformed Crotonville into a forum for ideas: Its training sessions, both on campus and off, gave 10,000 GEers a year of extended opportunities to debate Welch's ideas. Work-Out, designed to reach the entire work force, is the most inclusive forum of all.

If Welch's ideas are powerful enough, they will survive this process and take hold throughout the company. If not, perhaps better ideas will prevail instead. Either way, the company wins.

These touchy-feely, egalitarian methods may strike people from other countries as peculiarly, perhaps even laughably, American. Without question they are rooted in American culture. But GE is no longer simply a U.S. business. Operating in over fifty countries, in partnerships with many non-U.S. corporations, GE earns over 30% of its operating profits abroad. The No. 3 U.S. exporter, GE boasts a positive balance of trade of $5.9 billion, but it is also the largest corporate exporter in France. GE's methods can work almost anywhere. Its techniques for openly airing conflicts succeed even in Japan, where reverence of authority is a way of life.

Global competition is one of many forces that are, for better or worse, rapidly diminishing the cultural differences that divide nations from one another. In another decade or two, those differences surely will seem less important than they do today. Back in 1989, Welch described GE's place in world competition:

> It's clear that the U.S. system has the most free enterprise in the world. Britain's comes next; after that, it falls off dramatically. In Japan the relationships between the government, the banks, and the companies are very intertwined. Your bank allows you to have low returns, and your government will support your R&D and finance your exports.
>
> Or take Europe. Ronald Reagan goes to Russia, and he talks about nuclear disarmament. Helmut Kohl comes one week later with all the German businessmen, and they sign contracts to do deals. That's their system.

What the U.S. system has is freedom. It allows people like me to become chairman of GE in one generation. It allows the talented young engineers in our company to move up fast. If we put bureaucracy and rigidness into our system, we play into our competitors' hands in global markets. Because we don't get the benefits of the protected markets, the government support, the presidential relationships. But if we let our people flourish and grow, if we use the best ideas they come up with, then we have the chance to win.

Our urge to liberate and empower the GE work force is not enlightenment—it's a competitive necessity. When you look at the global arena, that's what our competitive advantage is. We have got to unleash it.

Before much longer, the world's biggest corporations will reach rough parity in finance and technology. To gain competitive advantage, they'll need organizations that unleash and harness the emotional energy of workers. The winners of this corporate olympiad will be flexible, constantly focused on learning. Employees will work under intense pressure; the confident ones will respond with grace.

None of this will surprise readers of management books. Peter Drucker, Rosabeth Moss Kanter, Tom Peters, and many others have described the organizations of the future. What they haven't explained is how to create them. The path GE is blazing helps show the way.

Tichy finds it useful to analyze Welch's ideas, and the actions he took to implement them, in terms of what he calls **TPC**. The initials stand for the three main aspects of organizational behavior: the **Technical, Political,** and **Cultural**. By separating the main threads that define the nature of a complex institution such as GE, TPC clarifies the workings of the larger whole. It also reveals the effect of managerial actions by defining which aspect of the corporation they touch.

Envision TPC as a three-stranded rope, in which technical, political, and cultural ideas weave together. To the extent that the three strands are tightly interwoven, the rope is strong. When the rope unravels—as it inevitably does during the revolutionary process—it must be braided anew. Applied to the task of transforming an organization, this image highlights the need to deal with each strand separately in order to strengthen the corporation as a whole.

The first strand is the technical. This concerns not technology but technique: the mundane, practical strategy-setting and decision-making with which executives usually are most comfortable. In general, technical acts are those, such as acquisitions, divestitures, and reorganizations, that a highly placed executive can accomplish by fiat. The tradition of scientific management, at GE and elsewhere, encouraged managers to focus primarily on the technical strand. During his first four years as CEO, Welch focused on it, too.

His most powerful technical idea is the rule of No. 1 or No. 2 market shares. Welch's predecessors already had built a massive enterprise, so the new boss made a virtue of scale, focusing on huge, capital-intensive businesses with high barriers to entry, in which GE's management expertise and deep pockets could provide competitive advantage. With a vision of market mastery in mind, Welch used GE's enormous financial resources to help lift each GE business to a position of market leadership.

His method, also technical, was the rule that GE fix, close, or sell any business that didn't meet that standard. During the 1980s and 1990s, GE bought and sold billion-dollar businesses the way kids trade baseball cards. Using No. 1 or No. 2 as a guide, GE sold cyclical businesses such as Utah International, central air conditioning, and small appliances. He bought either top-ranked businesses or companies that could boost GE's existing units to leadership positions.

Welch believes managers should be "hardheaded but softhearted"—in other words, tough-minded in competition, but considerate in dealing with people. When he and Vice Chairman Burlingame sold the Utah International mining subsidiary for $2.4 billion in 1984, Welch offset the gain by socking away over $1 billion to fund generous severance payments to the tens of thousands of people GE was dismissing. The layoffs themselves were extremely hardheaded, but Welch tried to conduct them humanely.

The second strand of the rope is the political. This concerns the more delicate matter of power relationships among people. Hiring and firing, replacing opponents with allies, forcing independent-minded people to work together—these are political acts. Welch largely exhausted the possibilities of the technical realm before taking dramatic political action. Hoping to win the voluntary support of his subordinates, he tried to avoid unnecessary conflict while consolidating his power.

GE's resisters weren't just hourly workers; they included some of GE's business leaders, ranking just below the sector chiefs who reported to the CEO. Courteous, long-suffering company men, they didn't dare to oppose the CEO directly. But they sat on their hands instead of pushing for change, and as Welch learned, passive resistance can slow you down to a crawl.

Starting in 1985, GE "delayered" and then reshuffled its top management, removing high-level resisters and placing hand-picked executives in GE's most important jobs. The Corporate Executive Council, or CEC, helped Welch consolidate these gains. The members of this group are directly accountable to the CEO.

Serving as a central information exchange, the CEC helps promote the integration aspect of integrated diversity, which is Welch's main political idea. To encourage diversity, Welch granted increased autonomy to business leaders, while cutting the central staffs in half and reversing their role: Instead of dictating to the businesses, staffers henceforth were obliged to assist them. One result: GE has replaced its single, companywide compensation scheme with more plans than it can count, each adapted to local needs.

The third strand of the TPC rope is the cultural. This is the most nebulous area of corporate management, and by far the most challenging. It is about changing the often unspoken values and beliefs that guide any organization's conduct. Executive power can't accomplish much here; subordinates' voluntary cooperation becomes essential. The difficulty of the task is such that even revolutionary leaders usually place cultural change last on their agendas. But no transformation is complete without it. Corporate cultures continue to direct behavior long after the most dramatic technical and political acts have been forgotten.

How do you change a culture? Welch has started the process by orchestrating a corporationwide dialogue of ideas. To the degree that Welch can get employees thinking about big ideas, he can get them used to the revolutionary notion of thinking for themselves on the job. Welch is using every means at his disposal. In the technical realm, for instance, the company urged operating units to come up with compensation procedures to directly reward employee behavior that accords with GE's values. The CEO also used political means, placing committed allies in charge of businesses that were resisting change. And in the cultural realm, he promoted company-wide debates about what GE's values should be. Taken together, such methods should transform new ideas into accepted habits; as that occurs, the culture should change.

Welch's thinking has changed in response to GE's dialogue of ideas. An ardent believer in quantum change, the CEO once insisted that incremental change does not work. Since then, he has changed his mind. Welch always has seen the revolutionary process as endless, simply because the world beyond the corporation never stops changing. But he has come to appreciate the value of small changes, too. Now striving to achieve both quantum leaps and incremental change, Welch has discovered that each feeds the other. (An illustration of this principle appears on page 611.) The big breakthrough opens the way for countless small improvements, and then the accumulation of small gains builds the organization's confidence to attempt another quantum leap.

The revolutionary process is agonizing for employees, and many GEers were deeply shaken by the experience. But Welch upset his employees for a reason: He could not create a new order without tearing down the old. Economist Joseph Schumpeter called that process "creative destruction." It's necessary, but it hurts.

GE's bureaucratic ways had been enormously comforting to employees. When the old ways vanished, anxiety began to eat away at GEers' self-assurance. The old job classifications had ensured predictable raises, regardless of how one performed. The many-layered hierarchy had provided plenty of general manager posts to those who sought advancement. In 1980 some 300 GE managers held jobs with P&L responsibility; by the end of 1992, fewer than 50 did. Suddenly jobs were no longer secure, and the company's requirements were less clear.

Before employees could join Welch's cause, they had to come to terms with their loss—the emotional equivalent of losing a parent. First people must disentangle their feelings of connection to what is gone; psychologists call this "disidentification." Next comes "disenchantment," the realization that disillusionment is an inevitable part of growing up. For example, the idea of lifetime job security was enchanting, but by 1981 it had no more basis in reality than Santa Claus. A mature person can understand the need to give up beliefs that don't make sense.

Adjustments like these take time. While GEers were struggling with their own emotions, many responded to the threat Welch represented by fighting his program of change. Some resisted passively, by ignoring his demands. A few battled the CEO directly. Thus the conflict between the old GE and the new became overt, making the process of transformation doubly difficult for everyone.

During Welch's early years, the three-stranded rope of GE's identity frayed. By 1993 he had twisted the technical and political strands of the organization tightly together. By 2000 he had made great progress on the cultural strand. Indeed, as Welch approaches retirement, GE's informal culture may be his greatest achievement.

Chapter Six

"Kick-Starting the Revolution"

During the first two years after Welch took office in 1981, his main goal was kick-starting the revolution. In those days, relatively few people shared his vision of the new GE—many had no idea what he wanted. Trusting his instincts, the CEO relied on charm, brute force, and personal intervention to get his message across to the troops.

Jim Baughman, the fellow who later became Tichy's Crotonville boss, remembers the earful Welch gave him at the January 1981 annual meeting of GE's top 500 managers, in Bellaire, Florida. Welch had just been anointed as Jones's successor, but would not become CEO until April. Baughman, who'd left Harvard only four months earlier, was still finding his feet as a corporate executive. The two men had never met.

Welch buttonholed Baughman at a cocktail party at the Bellaire Biltmore Hotel and hurtled straight into an explanation of his goals for GE. "I want a revolution," he said forcefully. "And I want it to start at Crotonville."

After just a minute or two of crisp elaboration—plus a cordial invitation to lunch—Welch moved on to assault the composure of another high-ranking GE executive.

Though he didn't always express himself quite so plainly, Welch's message was clear from day one: GE was going to change—and fast.

The CEO, then forty-five, began yelling "Fire!" to anyone who'd listen. In October 1981 he harangued GE's 120 corporate officers. Though he is considerate in his personal contacts with workers, Welch feels no inhibition about slamming his highest-ranking subordinates into the boards. Pacing the stage aggressively, he laid out his agenda for change: No more bureaucratic waste. No more deceptive plans and budgets. No more hiding from difficult decisions.

> **Our issue is facing reality about having a troubled business situation. We [top managers] can take good news and we can take bad news. We're big people and we've been paid well, all of us. Don't sell hats to each other.**
>
> **You own these damn businesses. The idea of [your] coming into Fairfield, and Fairfield yells, and Big Daddy gets you—it's an insane system we've built. No, you are the owners of your businesses. For God's sake, take them and run with them. Get us out of the act.**
>
> **Look at where you are in 1981, where you'll be in 1985, and probably more important, where you'll be in 1990. Can you play in that arena as a No. 1 or No. 2 player?**

Any business that could not become a No. 1 or No. 2 player, he warned, would not remain part of GE.

The implication should have been perfectly clear: Now that Welch had become el supremo, many of the executives in the audience wouldn't last long at GE either.

But from the officers' perspective, Welch's speech was a big yawn. These experienced company men had seen chief executives come and go. They'd heard a zillion of these speeches. Nothing much had ever changed, nor ever would. The new boss would learn that soon enough. As far as they were concerned, GE already was a No. 1 player—*the* No. 1 player, by God! While Welch was warning that the sky was about to fall, the company was posting record financial results. Some GEers couldn't figure out why the CEO was bellyaching—after all, net income was up 9%, to nearly $1.7 billion. Only nine corporations in the Fortune 500 had earned more!

Welch had expected GEers to dislike his message. But he believed they'd see the obvious benefits of joining the revolution. He thought they'd understand. He thought they'd agree. He thought they'd help.

He was wrong. Glen Hiner, the Plastics veteran who was a close Welch comrade for decades, explained why in 1989:

> I think Jack had the vision very early, and he articulated the vision almost immediately. The trouble was, he expected to get everything done quickly. He didn't understand how big GE was. He didn't understand how deep he had to go to effect these changes. Even today, I think he continues to be amazed by the questions he gets asked at Crotonville, the ongoing lack of understanding.

Although a substantial core group of employees responded as Welch had expected, the greater mass did not. When he took office, the average employee had served GE for thirteen years; the old mind-set dominated their behavior. Some actively resisted Welch's ideas. A great many more seemed paralyzed, like deer caught in the headlights of an oncoming car.

The CEO couldn't understand their behavior. It seemed insane—either suicidal or self-deluding. Did these people expect the onrushing future to swerve?

What Welch saw, and many others didn't, was the evanescence of GE's prosperity. The company was coasting on massive backlogs of orders for such products as locomotives, steam turbines, and nuclear power plants, which customers request years before delivery. In

1981, GE's backlogs totaled over $28 billion, and contributed one-third of annual revenues. Customers had placed most of those orders during the 1970s, long before business conditions had changed. The backlogs would continue to produce a rich stream of revenues for several years to come, but they obscured the mounting difficulties GE was experiencing in winning new orders for steam turbines and nuclear power equipment.

Welch was trying to avoid the boiled frog syndrome. If you put a frog in a pan of cool water and then gradually turn up the heat, the frog will just stay put until it dies. But if you drop a frog into boiling water, it will jump right out—and survive. It is human nature to say, "If it ain't broke, don't fix it." Left to themselves, people will ignore warnings of danger, scorning opportunities to change early and with a minimum of pain.

We see it all the time. During the mid-1980s, IBM was lulled by its unprecedented profits from mainframes. So Big Blue missed the shift from big computers to workstations and PCs—and its performance suffered greatly for several years. IBM was able to regain some of its lost stature after a long period of poor results. The convulsions that have wracked IBM and several other of America's great corporations are forceful arguments against delaying needed change.

The boiled-frog phenomenon is not uniquely American. Philips—one of GE's major European competitors in lighting and, until 1987, consumer electronics—spent the 1980s posturing about a coming business restructuring that somehow never came. In 1990 the Dutch company abruptly ousted its CEO and laid off 55,000 workers.

Back in 1981, Welch's challenge was to remake GE before its comforting backlogs ran out. With plans that would require every dime GE could produce, he could not afford to wait. When employees ignored his warnings, conflict became inevitable.

No traditional "GNP company" could prosper in the economy of the 1980s, he thought. The U.S. was suffering a recession when Welch took office, and he expected the gross national product to grow less than 3% yearly on average during the decade. According to his calculations, GE would need to boost its profits one-and-a-half to two times faster than the GNP in order to finance the reshaping of its businesses while adequately rewarding employees and investors. As he told a reporter in 1982, "Managements that hang on to weakness for whatever reason—tradition, sentiment, or their own management weakness—won't be around in 1990."

To many, Welch's goal for growth seemed preposterous. Jones had aimed only for growth that outpaced the GNP, however slightly. But a 1980 memo by Daniel Fink, then GE's vice president for planning, predicted that even Jones's relatively modest target was beyond GE's reach. Fink argued that unless the company could miraculously fatten its profit margins—or quickly boost revenues by a seemingly impossible 25%—GE's earnings increases would not even keep pace with the GNP. In four years, Fink warned, the annual net income shortfall would approach $400 million.

By 1982 slackening demand already had caused GE's total sales to drop 3%, the first revenue decrease since 1960. Of itself that decline, to $26.5 billion, might have seemed a mere hiccup for this giant enterprise, but it worried the CEO. He surveyed GE's portfolio of businesses and pronounced it incapable of meeting his demands.

Any number of measures pointed to GE's weakness in 1981. Only a few of GE's 150-odd business units were No. 1 or No. 2 in their markets, among them Lighting, Power Systems, and Motors. Some of these market leaders were ailing, including Lighting, which was charging too much for commodity products and losing market share. Of GE's major businesses, only Plastics, Gas Turbines, and Aircraft Engines were strong overseas, and only Gas Turbines could claim worldwide market leadership. Two-thirds of GE's sales depended on aging businesses that were growing slowly or not at all. The corporation's stars—Plastics, Medical Systems, and Financial Services—were in emerging areas such as technology and services. But GE's efforts in those areas were still relatively modest, contributing under one-third of total corporate earnings in 1981. Another concern: Many of GE's operating units, particularly fast-growing or high-technology businesses such as Aircraft Engines, routinely consumed more cash than they produced.

The rule of No. 1 or No. 2 became the CEO's overarching strategy for solving all these problems. A business can be profitable without a No. 1 or No. 2 market share, of course, but Welch wanted a stable of champions. The huge revenues and fat profit margins that usually accompany leading shares would give GE the financial flexibility to dominate its markets. Welch's urge for market leadership is such that, as he later admitted, he didn't really want to allow even No. 2 businesses into the GE stable. He explains his views on competition:

> **Some people say I'm afraid to compete. I think one of the jobs of a businessperson is to get away from slugfests and into niches where you can prevail. The fundamental goal is to get rid of weakness, to find a sheltered womb where no one can hurt you. There's no virtue in looking for a fight. If you're in a fight, your job is to win. But if you can't win, you've got to find a way out.**

Thus Welch's vow to fix, close, or sell any business that could not achieve market leadership. This was a long-term strategy: GE would readily invest in weak units if they promised to become strong. Fixing a business, in the GE lexicon, meant solving its operating problems, or increasing market share through acquisition, or both. Selling the losers raised cash for investments to strengthen the company. Closing a business down was a drastic last resort, rarely applied to an operation much larger than a factory. Over the course of years, this approach would reshape GE's portfolio, assembling a group of winners with the muscle to meet GE targets.

In the meantime, though, the CEO was insisting on regular increases in quarterly profits. How to achieve them? GE's sales, in those early days, were sluggish at best. Welch had big plans for boosting productivity, but those efforts would not produce significant results for years; GE's productivity rate still hovered around 2%. Welch saw no alternative but to cut costs.

That meant layoffs—big ones. The linkage was inescapable. Employee compensation was GE's second largest cost, after materials and supplies, amounting to 41% of annual expenses. Here's how Welch explained his reasoning: If inflation is running at a hypothetical 5% rate and productivity at 1%, a general manager starts off four percentage points behind the previous year's performance even before he starts making mistakes. As the CEO imagines the scene:

> So what does the manager do? He immediately grabs the sales manager by the shirt, and says, "Get prices up." He feels he has no choice—he's got to make his budget or there won't be any earnings. But what usually happens when he raises prices? He loses share. He's strangling!
>
> But if he could gain 6% productivity, he'd start out ahead—despite inflation. The general manager can cut prices and gain share, or he can raise prices to increase profits. He is in control of his destiny.

Layoffs alone could not produce the productivity gains GE needed; the company also was investing billions of dollars in efficient new equipment. Nevertheless, by the end of 1982 the process euphemistically called "downsizing" already had squeezed out 35,000 employees, almost 9% of the 1980 total. Not all of those jobs were lost: GE says roughly half of them moved with the ongoing businesses that it sold to other companies.

Without those job eliminations and others that followed, GE might have settled like so many other Rust Belt companies into ponderous insignificance. Simple arithmetic suggests why: In 1982 GE's net income was $1.8 billion. Imagine that GE had not already terminated 35,000 employees. Their average salary and benefits of a little over $25,000 per person would have increased GE's pretax expenses by nearly $900 million.

Of the hundreds of top GE executives who heard Welch's early speeches, only a few score initially brought much conviction and energy to the cause of reshaping GE. Among them were Larry

Bossidy of Financial Services, whom Welch soon installed atop one of two new sectors devoted to high-growth businesses; Paul Van Orden, who had taken over the consumer sector when Welch became vice chairman; Glen Hiner of Plastics; Walter Robb of Medical Systems; Brian Rowe of Aircraft Engines; Frank Doyle, the senior VP in charge of human resources; Ted LeVino of EMS; and John Burlingame and Ed Hood, who stayed on as vice chairmen under Welch.

This group faced widespread, but mostly passive, resistance at first. In a corporate organization such as GE's, open rebellion isn't a viable option; besides, few potential opponents judged the new regime a serious threat. So the resisters simply ignored unwelcome orders, or delayed implementing them, or screwed them up.

Executives demonstrated their alienation most clearly in response to demands for cost cuts, and the layoffs they implied. Ever since Swope's days as CEO, layoffs had been unthinkable at GE, except in such extraordinary circumstances as the period after the end of the Vietnam war, when defense budgets suddenly shrank. Welch had a hard time convincing some business leaders that the cuts were necessary.

He dealt with the issue obliquely. Instead of setting numerical targets for layoffs, as so many companies have done, Welch forced executives to accept ambitious earnings goals that could only be achieved by cutting costs. He insists that he has never told a business leader to cut headcount by a certain percentage. Welch explains why not:

> If you did that, people would argue with you—and that's an easy argument to lose. The idea of having a discussion about whether you should lay off 2,000 people, or 3,000, or 4,000 is nonsense. You should be talking about how to deliver the results that a healthy business should deliver. It makes sense to talk about an earnings number. *That* number will force whatever headcount or other changes the business needs.

GE gave its leaders the freedom—and responsibility—to decide for themselves how to reach the earnings targets. If they could reduce costs by means other than layoffs, such as by cutting inventories, that was fine. As a practical matter, though, the earnings goals frequently made job cuts unavoidable.

Perhaps foolishly, Welch expected his resentful subordinates to handle the downsizing with sensitivity. He wanted managers to think carefully about whom they let go, so that the resulting work force would retain the proper mix of skills. And he believed the victims of layoffs deserved compassionate treatment—not only generous financial settlements, but humane consideration of their feelings.

Most of the layoffs were handled decently, but not all. The CEO kept getting reports of mindless across-the-board cuts that shoved the wrong people out of GE, or of employees laid off just before Christmas. He personally answered letters of complaint from laid-off employees, and directly intervened in cases of injustice that came to his attention. (A sample of this correspondence appears on pages 554–556.) Executives who mismanaged the downsizing felt his wrath.

While striving to create a new organization, Welch could not allow the old one to squirm out from under his thumb. To accomplish anything at all, the CEO had to reach GE's employees directly, then totaling roughly 400,000 people. To consolidate his power, Welch immediately seized the revolutionary's three main levers of control: the police, the media, and the schools.

To a leader forced by resistance to bypass traditional chains of command, these three institutions offer the most effective means of influencing the population at large. History shows that without the support of police, media, and schools, a revolution almost certainly will fail. Consider the 1991 coup d'état in the former U.S.S.R.: The plotters foolishly left the media free to publicize the opposition movement that ultimately triumphed. Welch instinctively understood this principle, and spent his first days in office seizing the crucial levers of power. Corporations have their equivalents of police, media, and schools. At GE, the "schools" were Jim Baughman's bailiwick, Crotonville. The "media" included executives' speeches and publications from employee magazines to the corporate annual report. Aware of the media's importance, Welch writes all his own speeches, prepares his own charts, and ad libs his Crotonville talks.

GE's "police" were the cadres of professional nit-pickers and second-guessers on the strategic planning and finance staffs, who reviewed every operating decision and supervised the allocation of capital. It was Welch's inspiration to turn the GE bureaucracy against itself: Once he got the planning and finance staffers under his thumb, every one of those reviews became an opportunity to influence the behavior of the people who actually ran GE.

Both the media and the schools submitted readily, but the police recognized the new CEO as a threat. He pinioned the high-flying strategic planning staff right away. GE first froze its budget, then eliminated 80% of its jobs. Before long, only a dozen corporate planners remained in Fairfield, as part of the business development staff; operating executives gained responsibility for their own strategic planning. Overall, Welch "downsized" the miscellaneous corporate staffs in headquarters—including finance and EMS—from 2,100 people to 900.

Once tamed, the police became powerful allies. Welch recognized that a chief executive, unlike less senior managers, has limited opportunity to run a business directly. All he or she can do is set strategy, select a team of executives, and supervise the allocation of capital. During the revolution's early days, the last of these powers was most vital. Because so many of GE's operating units were so hungry for capital, the CEO's ability to grant or deny them money proved a source of real power. Some of Welch's subordinates may not have liked his ideas, but they needed that dough.

In the organization Welch had inherited, the police on the corporate staffs played a central role in capital allocation. Every year, each of GE's forty-six strategic business units was required to submit a detailed plan for approval in Fairfield. In addition, every business unit that produced a profit-and-loss statement would undergo a formal budget review at least twice a year. Troubled units, such as Major Appliances in the early 1980s, were scrutinized as often as once a month.

The police caught business chiefs in a tight pincer grip. To win approval of plans, budgets, and capital requests, executives now had to satisfy Welch's demands: consistent increases in quarterly earnings, *and* long-term market leadership as defined by the rule of No. 1 or No. 2. These paired demands forced many GE managers to slash costs drastically while completely rethinking their businesses.

To guide the managers' thinking, GE designed a self-sustaining process—a sort of business engine—that in the short run forced layoffs, and eventually purged GE of almost all its substandard operations. The process began with the CEO's ambitious performance goals. Then it provided financial incentives potent enough to counter managers' deeply ingrained aversion to layoffs: GE set up a central corporate restructuring fund that paid severance costs including retraining, job counseling, and outplacement services, plus lump-sum payments for laid-off workers.

The setup allowed the entire economic benefit of a payroll reduction to go straight to the individual business's bottom line. That, in turn, enabled the business to produce the improved results GE required.

Closing the loop, the company financed the restructuring fund with the proceeds from sales of its assets. The businesses it sold were those, such as Central Air Conditioning and Utah International, that weren't market leaders or otherwise failed to make the cut.

Over the years such divestitures poured billions of dollars into the restructuring fund, providing more than enough money to finance generous severance payments for terminated employees. At the same time, the divestitures demonstrated Welch's determination to enforce his rule of No. 1 or No. 2. That message, in turn, encouraged managers to focus on productivity. Once started, the cycle ran on by itself.

The formal reviews gave Welch and the vice chairmen the opportunity to meddle personally with GE's operations. Instead of delegating police work to his staff, the CEO meets several times a year with each of GE's hundred-plus top managers, reviewing their strategic plans, budgets, operating results, and personnel.

Dave Orselet of EMS, who served as a consultant for the consumer products sector while Welch was running it, observed such visits. Orselet recalls how Welch pushed downsizing:

He has an incredible ability to analyze data, but he also does it by feel. Jack would press and press and press and press, until he felt that they [the managers] were screaming loud enough that the cuts probably had gone about as deep as they should go.

Responds Welch: "The starting point was always lousy financial returns. It would become obvious that cutting costs was the only solution."

Nuclear Power was one of several businesses that Welch watched particularly closely. Ranked No. 2 behind Westinghouse, it seemed on the verge of extinction. The problem was not market share, but profitability: After Three Mile Island the business began accumulating losses. In 1981 its leaders pitched a wildly optimistic strategic plan that assumed GE could win orders for three new nuclear plants every year.

When he saw the plan, Welch was incensed. "You can't believe that!" he cried to the assembled Ph.D.'s from Nuclear. "You just *can't*!"

Belatedly, Nuclear Power's leaders began to rethink the whole business, returning with a revised plan that assumed no new plant sales at all: Henceforth their main business would be providing nuclear fuel and services to existing plants. Eliminating the imaginary plant sales from the budget clobbered projected earnings. To produce an acceptable level of profits, the business now proposed massive cost cuts.

This time, Welch approved. By 1991, Nuclear Power eliminated 4,400 jobs, more than half of the total before Welch became CEO. At the 1982 meeting of GE's general managers, he happily predicted a turnaround in Nuclear that would produce $700 million of earnings over the next decade; its actual profits turned out to be closer to $1 billion.

As Welch acknowledged in the mid-1980s, the experience was extremely painful:

> Our people were the best and the brightest. They'd given thirty years of their lives to nuclear power. When I said, in 1981, that there was not going to be another nuclear plant built in the U.S., they were upset, they were angry, they were writing letters.
>
> Even today, if you ran a survey of Nuclear, and asked *How do you like our strategy?* they'd say they don't like it. Not because of anything wrong with GE's strategy. They just don't like what's happened to their situation. They don't like reality. I feel for them. It's a tough deal. But the world decided nuclear power was not what it wanted.

Welch is an information junkie: When he needs a fix, nothing gets in his way. Scorning organizational charts and established procedures, Welch roamed freely throughout GE, cultivating his own sources of information among relatively low-ranking executives. As a result, he sometimes knew more about a particular business than the person who ran it. That spelled trouble, as Orselet remembers:

> With all his nosing around, Welch might be sitting there with better numbers than you had. In dealing with a fellow like Welch, if you're confident about what you're doing, and willing to stand up for what you believe, you're probably going to be okay. That doesn't mean you won't be in for some criticism from time to time.
>
> The one thing you can never do with Jack is wing it. If he ever catches you winging it, you're in trouble. Real trouble. You have to go in with in-depth information. Stand up for what you believe, but acknowledge what you don't know when you don't know it.

Paul Van Orden, who'd been one of Welch's reliable sources of information earlier in his career, remembers a chance meeting with the CEO in the early 1980s.

Van Orden was running the Consumer sector then, struggling with a portfolio of deeply troubled businesses. The sector's TV sets, clocks, and toasters were market laggards and frequently unprofitable. And at Major Appliances, known as Majors, a potentially deadly combination of high prices and declining quality was cutting into sales of refrigerators, dishwashers, and washers and dryers for clothes. In 1981, the sector's profits dropped 7%.

As the two executives were passing in a hallway at headquarters, Welch hailed Van Orden.

"How're you doing?" Welch asked. "How're things at Majors?"

"They're really struggling, Jack," replied Paul.

"Hey, is there anything I can do to help?" offered Welch.

Van Orden considered the CEO's offer for a moment, then told him, "Yeah. You can stop referring to Majors as a cesspool."

"I'll call them anything I like," snapped Welch.

"Well," Van Orden said amiably, "thanks for all the help."

By the end of 1982, GE was beginning to respond. Despite the recession, myriad operating problems, and declining revenues, the corporation reported a surprisingly healthy 10% rise in profits that year. Buoyed by a rising stock market, the price of GE's shares soared from a 1981 low of $13 (adjusted for subsequent stock splits) to $25 in 1982.

But while the corporation's performance was on the rise, the morale of its work force had begun to decline. The ideas in the CEO's crazy speeches—the ideas so many GEers wanted to ignore—were visibly changing the company. The accumulating carnage of layoffs and asset sales was causing anxiety and pain. The time of trauma had begun.

During those first two years the true nature of Welch's leadership did not become obvious even to GE's employees. Most visible was mounting evidence of drastic cost-cutting and the terrible agony of terminated employees. Beginning in 1982, when journalists started calling Welch "Neutron Jack" and describing him as ruthless, the CEO could not convincingly answer their charges. Profits were up, and so was the stock price—but productivity barely budged. The torment seemed pointless. And so what had begun as passive resistance slowly began to transform itself into active opposition.

Chapter Seven

Nothing Sacred

Welch and his allies had thrown off plenty of sparks during their first two years. But all the yelling and meddling, the agony of layoffs and the soaring rhetoric of new ideas—all this heat somehow failed to kindle an awareness within GE of how profoundly the organization still needed to change. It just made people mad.

Resistance spread from the imperiled hourly ranks all the way to top management. Some business chiefs stolidly thwarted Welch's plans to transform the company. Rather than oppose the CEO directly, they would say *yes* when they meant *no,* doing what they thought best for their businesses instead of pushing Welch's agenda of change. Shell-shocked and fearful, unwilling to change, people throughout the hierarchy stubbornly refused to let go of the old GE.

But by the end of 1984, the old GE no longer existed. Welch had cleared it away. That forced GEers to admit that change was unavoidable. And with that recognition, the GE revolution took hold.

Welch got to that point by devoting 1983 and 1984 to a nonstop deal-making spree that dismantled GE's century-old portfolio of businesses and horrified many old-timers. Making good on the vow to fix, close, or sell any operation that didn't measure up, GE divested 117 business units, from coal mines to Light 'N Easy irons, during Welch's first four years, liquidating one-fifth of GE's 1981 asset base of $21 billion.

The early acquisitions proved as shattering to the old culture as the divestitures. Some of the businesses the company bought seemed so alien to GE's proud legacy that they might have been headquartered on Mars. GE's biggest buy of that period was Employers Reinsurance Corp., acquired from Texas for $1.1 billion. It turned out to be among the most profitable of Welch's career, but some people wondered why the heck GE was selling insurance. Why not invest the $1.1 billion in Motors or Lighting instead? Even the people in Nuclear thought they deserved some of that loot.

The lack of consensus encouraged Welch to use force. He had a lot to accomplish, little time, and less help than he'd hoped for. Hounded by the need to win every game he played, Welch maintained his demand for steady quarterly earnings growth, even as preparations for the more distant future forced heavy investment and the turmoil of large-scale reorganizations.

Welch's critics during that period often charged that much of his activity was destructive. But there was method to the mayhem: This was the creative destruction that precedes renewal. Having faced reality early, and responded, GE prospers today while its more timid peers brace for agonies worse than any GE has faced under Welch.

In the three-act model of the revolutionary process, the first act is about awakening people to the need for change. It calls for decisive, unilateral action, and a willingness to engage in conflict. This is when a leader must eliminate whatever obstacles stand in the way.

"You're either the best at what you do or you don't do it for very long," Welch wrote in the 1983 annual report. By then, wised-up GEers understood that this was no mere expression of philosophy.

The CEO meant to affirm his high hopes for GE, but anxious employees read doom in those words.

Events justified their foreboding. Having slashed the work force by 9% during Welch's first two years, GE cut 10% more—another 37,000 human beings—during 1983 and 1984.

Instead of gathering the allies he needed, the CEO often alienated people. To be sure, he won a good many converts to his cause during those early years. But the aspects of Welch's character that had most disturbed his critics—his combativeness, his ferocity, his willingness to bulldoze opponents—all came more visibly to the fore.

At the same time, Welch's public reputation came under attack. The tens of thousands of GEers whose livelihoods were in jeopardy, or whose jobs had changed under Welch in one of a thousand stressful ways, had reasons to bad-mouth the boss. And some outside observers, especially in the press, were dismayed by the spectacle—familiar today but shocking back then—of a seemingly healthy company closing plants and cutting jobs.

The severest damage accompanied the 1984 publication of a *Fortune* story ranking Welch "the undisputed premier" among America's toughest bosses. Wrote the magazine's Steven Flax:

> **According to former employees, Welch conducts meetings so aggressively that people tremble. He attacks almost physically with his intellect—criticizing, demeaning, ridiculing, humiliating. "Jack comes on like a herd of elephants," says a GE employee. "If you have a contradictory idea you have to be willing to take the guff to put it forward."**

The drastic, seemingly arbitrary changes in GE's business mix attracted other criticism. Michael Porter, the eminent Harvard Business School professor, later set forth the view that Welch had produced little more than a retooled version of a 1970s conglomerate. Tom Peters, author of *In Search of Excellence* and, briefly, a Crotonville professor, dubbed GE's business portfolio "a hodgepodge." (Later in the decade Peters would change his mind and call

Welch, along with the late William McGowan of MCI, one of the two best managers of the 1980s.)

The defining moment of this bleak era came in 1984 with the sale of GE Housewares—the small-appliance business—to Black & Decker. The $300 million deal was modest by GE standards and based on solid logic. Nevertheless, the divestiture provoked such loud, agonized yowling from GEers and the press that you'd have thought Welch had murdered the Pope with his bare hands and then sold the Vatican to the Mob.

His crime? By selling Housewares, his accusers cried, Welch was wrenching the GE meatball from the very heart of the American home. The "meatball," in GE parlance, is the familiar corporate logo showing the letters *G-E* in antique script within a stylized circle. The terms of the sale gave Black & Decker the right to market certain products with GE's name and logo for three years; thereafter, the meatball would disappear from small appliances.

Outsiders may not easily understand the agony this prospect caused within GE. Here is another example of the surprising power of human emotion in the purportedly rational world of commerce.

Housewares had become a lousy business, but nostalgic GEers didn't care. Ever since their company had sold its first toaster in 1905, Housewares had been part of the corporate identity. The beloved GE meatball, affixed to irons, toasters, clocks, juicers, coffee makers, and hair dryers—the sort of artifacts that once defined the modern American home—was emblem of a tradition and pride that harked all the way back to Edison's lab. In the minds of some GE employees, it symbolized what almost amounted to a holy compact binding millions of U.S. consumers to GE.

Over time, that feeling evolved into something more dangerous: the view that Housewares was somehow essential to GE's identity. The business had become sacred, and by selling it, Welch branded himself a heretic—a threat to everything GE stood for. As the *New York Times* wrote, "It was as if GM had suddenly abandoned car making."

Tichy observed the emotions. By then he was consulting for the company and spending time with GE managers at Crotonville.

They shrugged off the $2.4 billion divestiture of Utah International, the mining company GE had bought in 1976. Vice Chairman John Burlingame brilliantly engineered that divestiture. Though ten times the size and importance of Housewares, Utah's commodities business had never insinuated its way into the corporate psyche. But GEers *loved* Housewares, the way they loved hamburgers and baseball. When they talked about the sale, it was in terms of betrayal, and you could see the hurt in their eyes. By attacking such a vivid symbol of the old GE, Welch had, in effect, declared war on his own employees.

Perhaps blinded by his own rationality, Welch initially had viewed the sale of Housewares as an easy, obvious decision. He knew that the most important customers, the ones whose purchases actually were making GE's earnings grow, were not householders buying electric can openers at less than $20 a pop. Already in 1984, three-quarters of the corporation's operating profit came from sales to big, impersonal enterprises such as airlines, power companies, department stores, and manufacturers.

The GE Welch foresaw would be primarily a vendor of items selling for $1 million or more: jet engines, turbines, credit card processing services, high-impact plastics sold in bulk. Indeed, by 1991 the company's remaining consumer products, such as light bulbs and refrigerators, contributed only about 10% of corporate profits.

Besides, Welch had been observing Housewares' financial weakness since his days atop the Consumer sector. In 1984, despite 50% market shares in a number of its lines, Housewares was generating no cash, and teetering frequently into the red. The advantage of the business's No. 1 status was diluted by the unusual structure of the market it served. The small-appliance market is fragmented into scores of freestanding and relatively tiny business niches: coffee makers, hair curlers, and so on. These appliances sell largely on technology and design. Companies that focused on a particular product, as Con-Air's Cuisinart did in food processors, consistently stayed ahead of generalist GE in product development. And few of the individual niches were big enough to justify GE spending big money on catch-up R&D. Like Welch, Robert Wright, the head of

Housewares, couldn't see a compelling reason to keep the business. A balding, tough-minded lawyer, Wright had been a Welch protégé since his early stint as Plastics' chief counsel; he went on to run Financial Services and then became head of NBC television, which GE acquired as part of RCA in 1986.

The sale of Housewares was the first of many assaults on GEers' sentimentality that made enemies among the very people Welch meant to lead. The corporate equivalent of blasphemy became a trademark of his regime. Although the moves were financially sound, they hurt his public reputation.

Nevertheless, the conflicts this fiery Irishman sparked with such relish hastened the process of self-discovery at GE, forcing unexamined issues into the open. For the first time in memory, employees throughout the company seriously began to ponder GE's mission, questioning assumptions and discussing the unspoken.

They began, at last, to think for themselves.

During 1983 and 1984, as he focused on reshaping GE's portfolio, Welch struggled to articulate the vision guiding his actions. While he made rapid progress in the technical realm, he had little impact on GE's politics and culture.

That dichotomy, much as it frustrated him, is typical of the early stages of the revolutionary process. Given power, a leader can easily force technical changes such as buying or selling business units; changing minds is harder. Lenin created collective enterprises throughout the Soviet Union, but power could not make those enterprises thrive.

The CEO kept trying to explain his thinking, but his early efforts often failed to convey his ideas. By far the most widely communicated expression of his grand design in those days was a sketch of three interlocking circles that he scribbled on the back of an envelope in 1982.

As a rebuttal to those who dismissed GE as a conglomerate, Welch's three circles defined broad categories of endeavor that promised better than average growth: Technology, Services, plus "Core," a group composed of the strongest of GE's old-line manufacturing

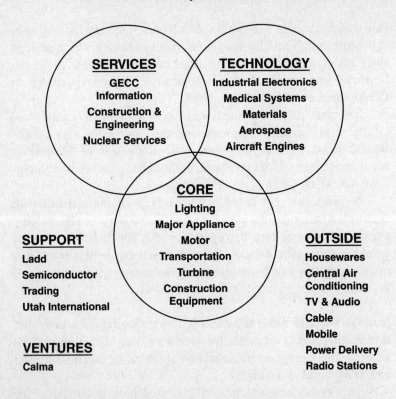

SERVICES
GECC
Information
Construction &
Engineering
Nuclear Services

TECHNOLOGY
Industrial Electronics
Medical Systems
Materials
Aerospace
Aircraft Engines

CORE
Lighting
Major Appliance
Motor
Transportation
Turbine
Construction
Equipment

SUPPORT
Ladd
Semiconductor
Trading
Utah International

OUTSIDE
Housewares
Central Air
Conditioning
TV & Audio
Cable
Mobile
Power Delivery
Radio Stations

VENTURES
Calma

units. Within the circles were the existing GE businesses that Welch intended to keep—fifteen in all. Each of these consolidated business units contained many previously freestanding operations. Together, they add up to most of the existing GE, producing 90% of corporate earnings in 1984.

As Welch explained, only No. 1 or No. 2 businesses were allowed inside the circles. "Anything outside the circles," he said later, "we would fix, sell, or close." What many GEers noticed first were the businesses that fell outside the circles. Of these, Semiconductors and a few other "support" operations were safe for the time being. Everything else—Housewares, TV sets, cellular communications, and more—was subject to the imperative of fix, close, or sell. Few of those businesses remain part of GE today.

The three-circles diagram began to clarify Welch's intentions. Both Lighting and Large Transformers might have sounded like core manufacturing operations, yet only Lighting found its way inside the circle. The reason: Lighting was a financially healthy market leader, while Large Transformers had essentially earned nothing for two decades.

A statement of the four main goals behind the portfolio changes appeared in 1985, as part of a draft of GE's corporate values:

• **Market leadership:** The rule of No. 1 or No. 2.

• **"Well-above-average real returns" on investments:** Welch refused to set inflexible numerical targets. During the mid-1980s, though, one measure to beat was GE's 18% to 19% return on share owner equity.

• **A distinct competitive advantage:** The best way to avoid "slugfests" is to provide value no competitor can match.

• **Leverage from GE's particular strengths:** GE is well equipped to prevail in large-scale, complex pursuits that require technology, massive capital investment, staying power, and management expertise: jet engines, high-risk lending, industrial turbines. In fast-changing industries dominated by nimble entrepreneurs, GE might be at a disadvantage.

You may disagree with these ideas. Tom Peters, for instance, used to think the rule of No. 1 or No. 2 stifled creativity. But these principles reveal that Welch's wheeling and dealing was not arbitrary. Housewares had to go because, despite its No. 1 market position, it failed the test of above-average returns. GE was to abandon TV set manufacturing in 1987—despite the front-page lamentations of damp-eyed newswriters—because it lacked a distinct competitive advantage. On the other hand, the seemingly outlandish Employers Reinsurance deal made sense: By exploiting GE's vast capital and the analytical expertise of its managers, the operation could handily top GE's accustomed returns on investment.

The best of GE's existing businesses already met all four of its requirements. In 1984 the Cincinnati-based Aircraft Engines unit demonstrated the value of holding such a winning hand. For eight years, it had been pitted against United Technologies' Pratt & Whitney in a competition to develop new-technology engines for America's F-16 fighter planes. Reporters dubbed this "the great engine war." GE pushed the envelope of engine and manufacturing technology, and won big: U.S. and international contracts worth $7 billion over eight years.

GE also lost a few hands. Starting in 1981, Welch invested $500 million in a visionary attempt to become the preeminent supplier of factory automation systems to manufacturers. Under Reg Jones, GE had been an early user of such equipment as computer-guided robots in its factories. At plants making products as diverse as dishwashers and locomotives, the emerging automation technologies were producing impressive productivity gains. GE predicted a $30 billion market for automation equipment by 1990.

Welch believed in the vision. "We thought we could sell this directly to the CEOs," he explains. "But the people who ran the plants didn't buy the concept, and they killed us." Before Welch realized that, GE bought Calma and Intersil, relatively small companies that made, respectively, computer-aided-design equipment and semiconductors, to expand GE's automation capabilities.

The business didn't grow as expected. After accumulating losses of $120 million, GE bailed out, selling Calma and Intersil, and folding its remaining automation business into a now-profitable joint venture with Fanuc of Japan.

The lessons? One is that GE can't handle small, freestanding acquisitions. As Welch readily admits, "We don't know how to do it right. So we'll put our assets in what we do well: big, powerful, muscle-using businesses." A second lesson may be that big corporations are too thick-fingered to manage the delicate process of creating start-up businesses from scratch.

A third is that Welch believes in admitting mistakes and cutting his losses: "I don't mind being wrong," he says. "The key is to win a lot more than you lose."

Welch's own behavior slowed the very process of organizational change that he was so urgently trying to accelerate. His efforts to change radically a corporation that most people still regarded as healthy caused deep emotional trauma. And as the CEO was beginning to realize, clearly communicating the reasoning behind his ideas to GE's complacent work force was enormously difficult. At the company's 1983 corporate officers meeting, held in Phoenix, Welch said:

> As people come to Crotonville I ask them: "How many of you feel that communications have improved?" We're getting 15% to 20% responses. Basically, we haven't made a hell of a lot of progress. . . . Without everybody embracing what we want to do, we haven't got a prayer.

Chapter Eight

Facing Reality

Before Carl Schlemmer became the first great hero of the GE revolution, he nearly destroyed his business. Completely misjudging the market for locomotives, he decided in 1979 to invest a budget-busting $300 million in a new model called the Dash 8—just before demand disappeared.

As Schlemmer recalls, the financial projections he used to sell the Dash 8 investment to Welch said that the locomotive market would probably double in size during the 1980s. He was as wrong as a man could be: By 1986 the global market for locomotives would shrink to a quarter of its former size. As a result, a deadly combination of plummeting sales and outsized investment soon threatened to bankrupt Transportation Systems.

What subsequently made Schlemmer's reputation was his readiness to admit how completely he'd screwed up—and then to solve the problems he'd caused. Acknowledging that his predictions were wrong, he simply changed course. He scaled back his expansion plans, focusing instead on improving productivity. By

1987 Schlemmer cut $65 million out of the Erie, Pennsylvania, operation's costs—enough to swing the business from a devastating potential loss to a $34 million profit. Working closely with a union-ized labor force once known for its hostility, Schlemmer and his teammates created a stripped-down, muscular organization capable of breaking even in awful market conditions—and producing out-sized profits in normal times. Overcoming his grave errors of judgment, Schlemmer reinvented the locomotive operation, trans-forming one of the company's most troubled units into a leading exemplar of GE's emerging business style. Lessons drawn from that experience still guide GE managers.

Thanks to methods like those Schlemmer employed, in busi-ness after business GE has been the only U.S.-owned producer to survive the 1970s in good health. General Motors' Electro-Motive Division (known as EMD) was the U.S. leader in locomotives a decade ago; now EMD is ailing and GM is trying to unload it. In lighting, power generation, and medical diagnostic imaging—all fields that used to boast several domestic producers—GE is the only entirely U.S.-owned entity to survive.

The ultimate goal of the GE revolution is for all employees to act for the good of the company without having to wait for orders. That means getting people to face facts and take responsibility—an astoundingly difficult thing to achieve, especially in large organizations.

At GE in the early 1980s, only the leaders in such upstarts as Plastics, Medical Systems, and Financial Services were showing such independence. The older businesses, which still dominated the company, crippled the incentives for individual action with their bureaucratic *yessirs* and *gotchas*. Of the men who headed those tradition-bound manufacturing units, Schlemmer was the only one who proved capable of adapting to a rapidly deteriorating market environment.

A trim, white-haired statesman, equally at ease in a Fairfield boardroom or an auditorium packed with angry blue-collar work-ers, Schlemmer ran GE Transportation Systems from 1974 to 1989.

He wasn't a dirt-under-the-fingernails manager. An engineer named Rick Richardson, his second in command during the 1970s, followed by Jack Dwyer, a marketing man, handled most of the operating details. Schlemmer was known for strategic thinking and salesmanship—the skills that nearly became his undoing, and then salvaged his career.

Schlemmer, Richardson, and Dwyer weren't entirely to blame for Transportation Systems' weakness. The business had long suffered from below-average financial returns. It ranked a distant second behind General Motors' EMD, which commanded well over three-quarters of the U.S. market for locomotives, and perhaps 40% overseas. With a much smaller market share, No. 2–ranked GE couldn't hope to beat its higher-volume competitor on price. And GE's locomotives were clearly second-rate—90% of them failed during their first 150,000 miles, versus a 10% failure rate during the first 250,000 miles for GM's engines.

By the late 1970s the solution seemed obvious to Schlemmer: GE needed a new product superior enough to enable the business to leapfrog GM. With the right locomotive, he believed, GE could quickly boost its market share, for a huge increase in profits. The key technological issues were reliability, fuel efficiency, and pulling power. Schlemmer set his engineers to work incorporating those attributes into a new engine design that became the Dash 8. They introduced what Schlemmer calls "space-age" computer controls to reduce breakdowns and limit energy use, along with modular construction techniques that cut manufacturing cost and improved quality.

In addition to design innovations, Schlemmer's plans called for massive productivity gains and $100 million of investment in factories. That money would buy a highly automated new diesel engine plant in Grove City, Pennsylvania, plus equipment to support a big increase in the capacity of GE's existing locomotive plant, from 500 units per year to 800.

Had the domestic demand for locomotives doubled, as Schlemmer expected, that level of investment might have paid off richly. Instead, his misguided strategy only demonstrated the futility of attempts to predict the future.

While Schlemmer was concocting his plans during the late 1970s, economists both inside and outside GE expected the U.S. economy to grow steadily through the next decade. The railroads, after losing business to truckers for years, seemed poised for recovery, in part because of deregulation. Financially strengthened by a series of mergers, GE's railroad customers were looking forward to significant growth—and that implied surging demand for locomotives. Overseas markets provided half the GE unit's sales; the forecasters spotted no problems looming there.

"There were some very optimistic expectations," remembers Schlemmer. Based on those expectations, he pitched the Dash 8 project to Welch, then a vice chairman, and to the GE board. He thought he saw an opportunity for GE to earn $280 million from locomotives in 1990, over five times more than the unit's peak annual earnings to date. Schlemmer explains: "We figured that if we had the right product and the right facilities, we could capture a major share of that rapidly expanding market. Jack heard us out, and said, 'Do it.'"

Because the improvements were scheduled in phases, Transportation Systems had completed less than one third of its $300 million planned investment before the business jumped off the rails in 1983. Here's how Schlemmer describes the hellish situation he faced:

> The U.S. got into a deep, deep recession beginning in 1981; in my industry the recession lasted until 1988. The locomotive business has always been cyclical but there was never a cycle like this. Out of a total fleet of 27,000 locomotives in this country, the railroads junked or mothballed 6,000.
>
> We got hit by a whole series of things. There was a major restructuring of heavy industries, which hit the railroads hard. Steel, for example, knocked out 30% to 40% of its capacity during the 1980s. Then President Carter imposed a grain embargo on the Russians, which walloped the Santa Fe Railroad. Meanwhile, the recession was forcing the railroads to work on their productivity. That helped them get their fleets down by over 4,000

locomotives—two years' worth of production. Then our Dash 8 proved so powerful and reliable that three of our new locomotives could do as much as four of the old ones in some applications—so we sold fewer units. On top of everything else, prices were falling.

Our export market went down at the same rate as the U.S. market. We had a major contract with Mexico. After we'd delivered about 450 of their 1,000 locomotives they called up and said, "Sorry about this, but we don't have any money, so we won't need any more locomotives. And by the way, we're not going to pay you for the ones you just shipped." We ultimately collected, but it was scary. Then Brazil got into the same kind of trouble. And Africa and most of our Far East customers fell apart completely.

By the early 1980s I couldn't see any light at the end of the tunnel.

The first signs of trouble had appeared in 1981. Earnings were still growing, but at a rate that suddenly began to slow. More ominous, new orders declined. No one worried much, even so. "We made a few minor adjustments," recalls Schlemmer. "We still thought this was a little dip. We expected things to get back to normal soon."

They didn't. In 1982, as Transportation Systems was starting to spend serious money on the Dash 8 program, its U.S. unit sales plunged 50%, to 244 locomotives, and business overseas was just as bad. "We began to have a substantial amount of discussion about what was going to happen to the economy in the 1980s," Schlemmer says. "We had experienced fairly sharp declines before, and the market had always recovered relatively quickly. We were getting concerned, but not alarmed."

By 1983, though, outright panic would have been justified. The world locomotive market contracted from 2,000 units annually to 500. GE was selling roughly 300 of those. Although Transportation Systems had greatly increased its market share, the market was smaller, so the business was selling fewer locomotives than before. Its new Dash 8 was not yet producing revenues. Net income was falling through the floor, down 50% to $37 million.

Schlemmer could no longer evade the truth: Transportation Systems was in mortal jeopardy. As he recalls, "We were in a state of semipanic. We weren't sure we could resurrect the business." In 1983 he gathered his key managers for a brainstorming session at the White Inn in Dunkirk, New York. As he tells the story, they didn't waste much time denying the danger they faced:

> We asked ourselves, "What happens if this market isn't what we said it would be? How should we reprogram the expenditures?"
>
> We all agreed we had to do something dramatic, but we still didn't know what dramatic was. We decided to eliminate all the new capacity that we were planning to add. We already had expended some money on facilities, particularly in Grove City—but from then on we were going to limit ourselves to productivity programs. That decision alone took $100 million of potential expenditure out of our plans.
>
> At that point we expected the market to stabilize around 1,000 or 1,500 locomotives a year. We figured that if we got the productivity gains we wanted, and the market went back to normal, and we offered a superior product, we'd do a hell of a lot better financially because we'd have taken so much cost out of our structure.
>
> If I had realized what was going on, I would never have held that meeting in a place called Dunkirk. When we got back, we essentially pulled the rest of the management team in and said, "Guys, we're on the beaches and the Germans are right over there. We've got to find a way out of this." That was what started the restructuring of the business.

By then, Welch had been CEO for years, but he'd kept his eye on Transportation Systems through the regular ritual of budget and planning reviews. Time after time, Schlemmer showed up with sales projections he'd revised downward since his last visit. The numbers looked dreadful.

Why didn't Welch fire Carl Schlemmer as soon as his plans went awry? According to Jim Paynter, who was then head of Schlemmer's employee-relations staff, the reason was candor. "Welch loved Carl," explains Paynter, "because he was always very forthcoming and he always had a solution. Carl always told Welch, 'Here's the problem and here's what we're doing about it.' The only surprises came from the marketplace." His openness paid off in support from Welch.

The CEO certainly liked Schlemmer's style. As he says:

The leadership of our transportation business did a terrific job. They had a vision, and then that vision fell apart in the recession. The world had changed. They went through hell. But this team said, "Hey, we called it wrong." We didn't have to change anyone—they had the self-confidence to change by themselves.

When Schlemmer began restructuring Transportation Systems in 1983, he still had no idea how catastrophic market conditions would get. At the nadir in 1986, GE ultimately sold just 173 locomotives in the U.S.—down 85% from 1979—and roughly 130 overseas. By then GM had shut down its U.S. locomotive factory, greatly reducing its presence in the business—so GE's puny sales amounted to 80% of the world market.

Always uncertain of what was to come, Schlemmer attacked his cost problem in increments, cutting deeper and deeper as sales continued to plunge. He eliminated a quarter of the unit's 3,000 professional employees; ultimately he slashed their ranks by 60%. He took out some 40% of his 8,000 hourly workers.

Cuts as deep as these required a complete rethinking of the Transportation Systems organization and its working methods. Decisions that would have seemed impossible a few years earlier became the norm. Recalls Schlemmer:

We knew we had to make basic changes in the way we ran this business. As the market continued to get worse, we had to change our perception of how much we could cut and still function and be economically viable. Under circumstances like those, there's no way a business can survive if it can't get its costs in line with the realities of the market.

The Schlemmer team set a pattern that has since become almost routine at GE: They eliminated whole layers of management, consolidated overlapping jobs and business units, and forced employees at every level to take far more responsibility for their own work. If something wasn't absolutely necessary—such as placing advertising in railroad magazines—they eliminated it.

Schlemmer's description of the change is memorable: "We learned to do only what's necessary, not what's nice." They stopped gathering unnecessary financial data, eliminating reports concerning minor product lines, for example. In the plant, equipment operators became responsible for the quality of their own work, reducing the need for inspectors.

The process began at the top of the organization, then worked its way down. Schlemmer called a series of meetings with all department heads, plus employee-relations staffers, including Paynter. They used storyboards—pieces of paper attached to a conference room wall—to map out roughly how the work might flow through a radically smaller organization. To fill in the details, they created multifunctional teams led by their most able executives. As Schlemmer explains:

We told each of these team leaders, "You have responsibility for one function. You can restructure the organization any way you want to. Start at the top, start at the bottom, start at the side—nothing is sacred."

We urged them to substantially reduce the top of the organization, which was sort of a unique idea at GE at that time. There aren't many people up there, but they're very expensive.

We also said, "You may decide to eliminate your own job. If so, don't worry about it, because we will get you another job."

And I told them they'd have access directly to me. I said, "You don't have to worry about the reaction of any other individual in this organization, not even your boss."

When Schlemmer presented the result of these deliberations to Louis Tomasetti, his sector chief, he remembers Tomasetti warning, "You've bitten off more than you can chew." By contrast, says Schlemmer, "Every time we reviewed our plans with Jack, he'd say, 'Why aren't you doing more?'"

Schlemmer needed more than approval from on high to put the new strategy into action. By their very nature, the changes he was proposing required cooperation from workers—particularly the thousands of United Electrical and Electronic Workers members on the factory floor. Were they ready to move from bolt-tightening to independent thinking?

Their assent could not be taken for granted: Transportation Systems had a history of trouble with labor. In 1976, the union staged a violent strike in which people were injured and property was damaged; the courts subsequently fined the union. Paynter, a steelworker's son, joined the Transportation Systems' employee relations staff two years later—right after a management decision to eliminate Sunday overtime, which had enabled union members to earn double their normal hourly wage. The union protested the decision with a slowdown that caused serious delays in locomotive shipments and threatened profits. Recognizing an urgent need to improve union relations, Paynter and several other executives spent months virtually living in Building 10, where final locomotive assembly took place.

Their efforts during the late 1970s made possible Schlemmer's revolutionary changes in the management-labor relationship at Transportation Systems during the 1980s. Indeed, Paynter's work clearly foreshadows GE's Work-Out program, which began a decade later. He told how it all began:

> We wanted to know what was going on in Building 10. Why were we behind schedule? We met with the supervisors. We met with union stewards. We met with the employees—salaried, hourly, everybody. We tried to find somebody who'd tell us the truth.
>
> Then this one welder came and stood in my doorway. He said, "The union would shoot me if they saw me here, but here's the problem we have in this building. . . ." He told us that the flow of subassemblies coming in from other buildings was so erratic that employees often had nothing useful to do. They'd do something useless instead, and get paid for it. He said, "If you'll get the work coming in here, we are very willing to do more—so long as you don't reduce our wages."
>
> So we reorganized the flow of work coming in from the other shops and we changed the way they got paid. It was a win-win situation.

From that modest start, Richardson, Paynter, and a few other Transportation Systems executives developed a new style of employee relations that depended on candid communication. Four times a year Richardson would brief union officers in his conference room in Building 14. Paynter says that the managers held almost nothing back:

> We told them everything that you'd ever want to know—market share, income, what orders we thought we had a chance to win, and what that meant in terms of jobs. Fairfield used to get nervous, because at that time the company was not sharing income data with unions.
>
> We always tried to focus in on two things: serving the customer—the reason we were in the business—and beating the enemy, which was General Motors, not General Electric.

The executives also briefed the hourly employees, in groups of 1,000 at annual meetings held in a local high school auditorium. They got booed the first time, but by the early 1980s their disclosures inspired a measure of trust.

Paynter and his colleagues weren't above using gimmicks. Among the simplest and most successful was an offer to provide free coffee and doughnuts to workers once the plant met its monthly production quota. "It sounds like a small thing," says Paynter, "but it proved how interested employees are in being recognized for a job well done. We dug the business out of the hole it was in, and the doughnut guy got rich."

Another of Paynter's ideas was the "customer awareness trip." He'd gather a group of 150 employees—a mix of hourly workers and supervisors, plus a few managers—charter a plane, and take them on an overnight visit to one of the railroads that bought GE's locomotives.

> The idea was to talk about quality. It gave the people who maintained the locomotives out in Omaha or wherever the chance to talk to our people. The electrical guys could ask, "Why did you wire it that way?" Once they'd talked out an issue like that, the best way to make the product usually became obvious. I can't stress enough how important it is to go to somebody else's turf. That's how you learn.

The first harsh test of the unit's improved labor relations came in 1983, after Schlemmer finally acknowledged the locomotive market's collapse. Instead of merrily handing out free doughnuts, executives suddenly began ordering major layoffs. Remembers Paynter:

> The darkest days were when we started into the layoffs. "Betrayed" is too strong a word, but employees were disappointed that we couldn't find a way to keep more locomotives coming through their shops.

People did complain about the $7 million we were investing in a new, 40,000-square-foot learning and communication center. They'd say, "Why are you spending all that money when we're getting laid off?" Well—that was a fair question.

In the end, though, the credibility we had established paid off. They didn't like what was happening, but they accepted it. They believed that we were doing everything in our power to win all the orders we could.

We demonstrated that if you talked to the people, asked them what to do about something, and then did what they said, your business normally runs better. It's a simple idea that some managers with IQs of 150 can't bring themselves to understand.

A big test came in 1984, when the business snagged the first of two contracts to sell 420 locomotives to China. With permission from Fairfield, Schlemmer agreed to sell those machines barely above cost, as a bridging strategy to keep the factory working until the market recovered. Once the deal closed, he says, Welch wrote him a letter asking how he planned to avoid losing money. Schlemmer called the Erie employees together and explained the need for more cost cuts. "You've got to do something about this," he said—pretty much the same message Welch had just given him.

The workers responded, boosting the operation's profit margin by six percentage points. In one example, workers decided, without management prompting, to redesign the locomotives' cabs, for a 45% cost savings. When a manager inquired why no one had ever mentioned the inefficiencies of the old design, the workers replied, "You never asked." Such efforts by rank-and-file employees enabled the overall business to break even, instead of losing tens of millions of dollars.

Amazingly, Transportation Systems never posted a loss during the 1980s. In 1984, its worst year, the business earned $12 million, then it rapidly improved. Without cost cuts, Schlemmer estimates, the business would have lost $100 million in 1987. Instead, it earned $34 million—about as much as it had been making before the trouble started.

By consistently lowering expenses even faster than his sales volume was dropping, Schlemmer managed the feat of posting earnings increases while revenues declined. He explains his method:

> **I finally developed a philosophy: If Jack has to tell you what to do, you're way late. You have the responsibility to respond, and it seems to me that if your challenge is the size of a grapefruit, your response ought to be the size of a basketball.**

Carl Schlemmer whipped the "indictment of leadership" problem. Everybody makes mistakes but no one likes to admit them. Corporate executives are no exception: Look at any number of famous CEOs who deny that they have anything to do with their companies' problems.

You can't deny reality and control your destiny at the same time. To turn his business around, Schlemmer had to admit that his own decisions were wrong. No one could blame him for what happened to the market, but Schlemmer was the one who had signed off on those optimistic projections. He was the one who pitched the $300 million Dash 8 investment. His willingness to indict himself freed him to take the actions needed to save the business.

He went nose to nose with Welch and said, "I'm responsible for those projections. I know they're wrong. Now I want to stay and clean up the mess."

The Schlemmer story is inspiring. What's disappointing is that we know of no other such story at GE. Executives who make big mistakes often begin to doubt themselves; though Welch has been slow to oust such people, sooner or later many of them leave GE. "Damaged self-confidence is difficult to repair," Welch comments.

That's a problem at any company hoping to revitalize itself. The paint-by-numbers solution is to get rid of the old leaders and bring new people in—but the costs, in human pain and squandered experience, are terribly high. On the other hand, hanging on to executives who can't face facts usually turns out worse: Their mistakes can cost the jobs of thousands of lower-level employees.

Often it is easiest to face reality in a crisis situation such as Schlemmer's. It's harder to come to grips with a gradually deteriorating business situation, as at GE Lighting and Power Systems. A decline that is slow and subtle can be denied. "Hope is one of the worst things that can happen to a manager," says Welch. "Hope can overcome reality."

Managers of very successful businesses can lose touch with reality, too. According to Welch, "One of the hardest things is to get the maximum out of a rising business. The worst sins are committed in boom times, when everybody feels satisfied. That's when managers get fat and arrogant."

Facing reality, in good times and bad, is an *ethical* obligation for managers—indeed, for anyone whose actions affect other people. If that sometimes requires indicting oneself, tough. Business heads are extremely well paid these days, at least in the United States. Their employers have a right to expect responsible behavior in return.

Chapter Nine

The Mirror Test

J ust as one leader can revolutionize a corporation, one crook can damage it. In a business the size of GE, with almost 300,000 employees, even the most scrupulous management can't ensure that no misguided employee will ever commit a crime. Yet the consequences of corporate wrongdoing potentially can be so severe that even a very low crime rate simply isn't good enough. One of the toughest challenges a manager can face is responsibility for the mess left behind when an employee breaks the law.

Such a mess confronted Welch in 1985, when the government charged that GE middle managers had fraudulently doctored time cards in a scheme to overcharge the federal government on defense contracts. Because it occurred on the job, the alleged wrongdoing implicated GE, which pleaded guilty to felony charges and paid a substantial fine.

The time-card scandal surprised and angered many GEers. It also gave Welch an opportunity to clarify his message to employees: He expects them to win with their integrity intact. The CEO urged every GEer to take what he calls the "mirror test," critically examining his or her own actions for integrity.

That test is tougher than it sounds. Even those who honor the law can fail in other ways. Self-respecting executives commonly take home office supplies, or ask their secretaries to type their kids' résumés. Strictly speaking, that's theft. Most people who take the mirror test seriously find something in their own behavior to change.

Let's face it: People are susceptible to ethical lapses. In the real world, competitors may cheat, suppliers or customers may demand bribes, regulators may tacitly or even explicitly allow rules to be broken. Some corporate criminals may be ordinary thieves, but many are weak enough to convince themselves that they're basically honest folk doing what's necessary to get their jobs done. Instead of acknowledging the law as black and white, they convince themselves they're operating within areas of gray.

Too often, they're wrong: Studies show that well over half of all major U.S. companies have experienced corporate crime. One study of Fortune 500 firms showed that from 1975 to 1984, some 62% were involved in one or more incidents of corrupt behavior. Another study, by Clinard and Yeager, surveyed the 477 largest manufacturing and 105 largest service, retail, and wholesale companies. It found that 50% of those businesses were charged with at least one federal offense during the two-year period 1975–1976.

This is not simply a corporate problem: As a society, the United States may be failing to convince people of the value of honesty. In 1990, Donald McCabe, a Rutgers ethics professor, questioned some 6,000 university students about cheating in school. His data show that 76% of those planning business careers admitted cheating at least once, while 19% said they'd cheated at least four times, qualifying them as "regulars." Students anticipating careers in other fields, such as law, medicine, and education, cheated somewhat less—but still often enough to dismay anyone who values integrity.

At GE the challenge of keeping employees honest is tougher than at many companies. As a supplier to the military, and as a global company selling big-ticket items in every corner of the world, it participates in areas where abuse frequently occurs. GE's missteps are highly visible. Because the company does so much government work, the offenses of its employees are disproportionately likely to become public knowledge. Businesses serving private customers are rarely compelled to reveal their ethical lapses, and most keep them quiet. Moreover, GE is unique among leading U.S. defense contractors in selling both military and consumer products under the same brand name. Relatively few Americans think of GM as a defense contractor, even though it owns Hughes Aerospace, which produces guided missiles and has also been subject to employee crime. When something goes wrong at GE—the company that "brings good things to life," according to its TV commercials—it's front-page news.

Compared to its defense-industry peers, GE doesn't look so bad: Between 1985 and 1991, the U.S. Department of Defense took 38,731 legal "compliance actions" against the department's employees and corporate suppliers: indictments, convictions, settlements, suspensions, and debarments. Only twelve of these actions concerned GE; three resulted in convictions.

We trust Welch's integrity and would argue that he has done as much as any CEO to promote high ethical standards. The substantial checks and balances GE has put into place include corporate ethics policies that are clearly articulated and enforced, and a statement that all salaried employees sign annually, stating that they either know of no wrongdoing or have reported it. Nevertheless, charges of malfeasance by GEers still grab headlines. In addition to the time-card scandal, the most serious incidents of the Welch years are these:

- The 1988 "MATSCO" case, in which employees of GE's Management and Technical Services Company, a subsidiary of GE Aerospace, overcharged the government on battlefield computer systems it was installing in military vehicles. Two GEers were sentenced to jail, and the company paid a $10 million fine.

- The so-called Dotan case, named for Israeli Air Force general Rami Dotan. He allegedly colluded with an employee of GE's Aircraft Engines business to divert over $30 million of U.S. government funds into personal accounts. Dotan was convicted in Israel and is serving a prison sentence there; the accused GEer has been fired. GE cooperated with federal investigators and signed a $69 million settlement.

In addition to these serious crimes, which GE acknowledges and regrets, the company has gotten more than its share of public-relations black eyes from matters that may have nothing to do with breaking the law. Not all of the bad press has been deserved.

In 1992, amid great publicity, the U.S. Justice Department was investigating accusations from a former GE employee that GE conspired with De Beers Consolidated Mines of South Africa to fix prices of industrial diamonds illegally. As of mid-1993 no charges had been filed. GE describes the matter as "unsubstantiated allegations by a disgruntled former employee who was removed for performance shortcomings." The company flatly denies his charges.

Some people object to perfectly legal behavior by GE on grounds of morality or politics. GE's role as a defense contractor has prompted a call for a boycott of GE products by a group called INFACT. In 1991 Hollywood gave an Academy Award to a short documentary produced by INFACT. During the Oscar telecast, which reached some 1 billion people worldwide, the producer repeated the boycott call. The film, called *Deadly Deception,* alleged among other things that GE's operation of the government-owned nuclear facility near Hanford, Washington, between 1946 and the mid-1960s, caused health problems to neighbors. GE cites government health studies that have not established such health problems. No charges have been filed concerning any of INFACT's claims.

Some environmentalists object to GE's role in nuclear power, for instance, or its production of plastics. According to the Environmental Protection Agency, GE is a "potentially responsible party" for fifty-one Superfund toxic-waste sites, more than any other listed company. Superfund rankings imply no wrongdoing, but rather the accumulation of waste permitted during times when manufacturers and ordinary citizens were not sensitive to the environment. GE says one reason for its ranking is that the company has more U.S. plants in more different industries than any other company. The other leading Superfund companies are Du Pont, Monsanto, and General Motors.

But Welch argues that there is a world of difference between debatable issues such as these and outright crime. While he is in accord with anyone who regards criminal behavior as abhorrent, he emphatically disagrees with those who criticize GE on moral or political grounds.

Almost from the beginning, the otherwise proud history of General Electric has been marred by instances of employee wrongdoing. An undeniable part of the heritage of many old-line manufacturing companies, including GE's, was a tough-guy willingness to bend and sometimes break the rules in order to win.

At GE, the attitude has its roots in the 1890s, when the company came of age. In those days, when the Harrimans and Rockefellers were forming monopolies, big business openly sought to control markets. Under CEO Charles Coffin and his successors, GE did the same. During the first half of this century, growing up in industries of its own creation—from light bulbs to electrical products—GE became accustomed to pushing the Sherman antitrust rules to their limits.

GE settled its first antitrust case in 1911, agreeing not to conceal its ownership of subsidiaries. In 1924, representatives of GE, Philips, and several other leading electrical companies met in Paris to divvy up market shares around the world; GE's CEO at the time, Gerard Swope, was the fellow who blamed the Great Depression on "excessive competition." Though the cartel, known as Phoebus, was not illegal under the laws of that era, it probably would not pass muster today. During the 1940s, GE was involved in thirteen antitrust cases; once the war ended, Electric Charlie Wilson, then CEO, negotiated a deal in which GE signed consent decrees but avoided the breakup of its lighting business.

There's no evidence that any of GE's CEOs ever committed or authorized wrongdoing. But by 1961, when the Justice Department brought GE's great antitrust scandal to an end, some GEers evidently assumed high-level managers would "wink" at crimes that benefited GE's bottom line. The result was a humiliating price-fixing scandal that finally shocked GE out of its complacency. In its 1961 story about the scandal, entitled "The Incredible Electrical Conspiracy," *Fortune* quoted a GE executive who remarked, "Sure, collusion was illegal, but it wasn't *unethical.*"

That conspiracy was the U.S. electrical industry's dim-witted response to chronic overcapacity. Companies could have addressed the underlying business issues by closing factories, improving products, or consistently competing on price. Instead, executives from many of the major outfits selling such products as industrial circuit breakers—including GE, Westinghouse, and Allis-Chalmers—tried to eliminate the risks of competition. The companies agreed on the U.S. market shares each would maintain for each product; GE's usually was the largest. The conspirators gathered two or three times monthly, often in hotel rooms, to decide which bids each company would be allowed to win. They swapped supposedly confidential pricing information, agreeing in advance on the amount of the winning bid on each particular project.

These meetings—dubbed "choir practices" by the conspirators—fundamentally corrupted the electrical business. Customers relied on the prices submitted in sealed bids to select the best supplier for each contract, and the bidding process was the market's primary means of encouraging competitive pricing. When every supplier but one intentionally submitted bids set too high to win, the ritual became meaningless.

In the end, seven GE executives went to jail and twenty-four received suspended sentences. CEO Ralph Cordiner was never formally accused of participating in the scheme, but his reputation had to be diminished by the scandal.

The Great Electrical Conspiracy taught GEers a harsh but necessary lesson: Never again could employees expect the company to wink at wrongdoing.

Welch sees high ethical standards as a business essential: "In the end," he says, "integrity is all you've got."

His approach to ethical issues suggests the lingering influence of his religious upbringing. Welch says he remained a "passionate" Catholic well into his grad school years; as a mature man he still seems to believe in unambiguous distinctions between right and wrong. Whenever an employee's actions has put GE on the wrong side of the law, he has hastened to cooperate with investigators, admit guilt, and take prompt corrective actions. Those corporate *mea culpas* have served the company well. In the time-card case and others, candor and a determination to ally GE with the forces of law have enabled GE to emerge with a minimum of agony.

The CEO seems to have trouble understanding antisocial acts. Honest himself, he's perplexed when others are not. He has no sympathy for anyone who responds to his ever-escalating demands for performance by resorting to crime. Indeed, he argues that the people who cheat are not doing it for competitive reasons. "Excellence and competitiveness are totally compatible with honesty and integrity," he asserts. "The A student, the four-minute miler, the high-jump record holder—all strong winners—can achieve those results without resorting to cheating. People who cheat are simply weak."

In many countries outside the United States, of course, the integrity issue is complicated by the prevalence of bribery. In accordance with U.S. law, GE policy prohibits the payment of bribes. In Germany, by contrast, corporations can claim tax deductions for the "facilitating" payments they pay abroad. Welch insists GE's strict rules don't make it less competitive:

> **In a global business, you can win without bribes. But you better have technology. That's why we win in businesses like turbines, because we have the best gas turbine. You've got to be the low-priced supplier, but in almost all cases, if you have quality, price, and technology, you win—and nobody can sleazeball you.**

During Welch's tenure, GEers' transgressions have occurred in defense businesses. In the Reagan era, as military spending surged, defense contracts became a central and fast-growing source of profits. To some individuals, the temptation to cheat must have seemed almost irresistible, as trillions of taxpayer dollars changed hands.

The 1985 time-card scandal was the first significant ethical challenge of Welch's twenty-five-year GE career. GE Re-Entry Systems was making a new nose cone for the Air Force's Minuteman missile. Federal prosecutors in Philadelphia charged it with 108 counts of criminal fraud. The indictment alleged that GE managers had altered workers' time cards, creating improper charges totaling $800,000.

Two days after the indictment was filed, Air Force Secretary Verne Orr suspended GE, then the No. 4 U.S. defense contractor, from doing business with the U.S. government. That decision might have caused big trouble for GE: Government work provided nearly one-fifth of its revenues. For mischarges that added up to less than $1 million, the company stood to lose over $5 billion of annual revenues.

The trouble occurred in a tiny corner of GE. In 1985, General Electric was producing a wide variety of military equipment, such as F-101 jet engines and Phalanx seaborne radar. Re-Entry Systems, where the crimes occurred, was a small part of GE Space Systems, based in historic Valley Forge, Pennsylvania; Space Systems produced just 3% of GE's total sales. Re-Entry Systems had won Air Force contracts to design, produce, and test the new Mark 12A nose cone, whose electronic innards steer the atomic warheads of Minuteman missiles as they plunge back into the earth's atmosphere from space. As it happened, GE's work went over budget, producing estimated losses of $3 million. According to the Philadelphia indictment, middle managers at Re-Entry Systems doctored the time cards that hourly workers submitted, misrepresenting production or testing charges as design work. The alleged falsification reduced GE's losses. Since the proceeds from the mischarges went into GE's coffers instead of the employees' pockets, the company became legally liable.

The accused managers never claimed anyone had told them to do it. Nor did they get a cent for themselves. The motivation for the mischarges, presumably, was to limit the deficits caused by the cost overruns in order to avoid career damage. Ultimately, one manager pleaded guilty; others were acquitted in court.

By then, GE had already been punished. Through the severe penalty Secretary Orr imposed, the company suddenly lost the right to sell *any* product—even light bulbs—to any government entity, from the National Weather Service to the Veterans Administration. GE's reputation and a lot of its jobs were on the line.

Two challenges faced GE: the immediate financial, legal, and public relations crises and, just as important, the long-term need to raise employees' awareness somehow of the need for high ethical standards.

The CEO's first goal was to regain control quickly over GE's destiny. A brief investigation convinced him that GE could be in the wrong. When the government attacked, he refused to accept the role of adversary; instead, he allied GE with its accusers, and thereby won the trust of government officials. GE cooperated with federal investigators and accepted responsibility for the acts of its misguided employees. Once Welch ascertained that GE had indeed mischarged the government, the company repaid the $800,000. And the day after one of its employees finally admitted wrongdoing, GE pleaded guilty to felony charges.

Less than three weeks after the indictment, Welch personally called on Orr, presenting a comprehensive proposal for cleaning up the mess and preventing such failures in the future. Welch promised to deliver progress reports to Secretary Orr in person every month. He created a top-level review board within GE to oversee compliance, and appointed GE's ombudsman to investigate reports of misconduct.

In private, Welch warned Orr that cleaning up the defense industry would take years. The CEO subsequently enlisted seventeen other defense company leaders to form a new organization called the Defense Industry Initiative on Business Ethics and Conduct. The group—which later expanded to more than fifty companies—drew up a long-overdue code of ethics for the defense industry. It also required an annual audit of each member's compliance by an independent public accounting firm.

On the level of damage control, Welch's efforts were almost completely successful. The day after his first meeting with Orr, the U.S. government began buying GE products again. Only Space Systems remained ostracized, for a total of five months—a tolerable penalty, and one that Welch has said was well deserved. As he told share owners that year, the suspension had "no significant financial impact."

The most enduring effect of the time-card episode is GE's more rigorous and systematic approach to ethics. Part of the deal it struck with the government was a comprehensive new policy statement that created a clear chain of responsibility for any wrongdoing at GE. Since 1985 the corporation has held its managers accountable for "inadequate leadership and lack of diligence" that enables subordinates to engage in improper activities. Compliance issues have become part of job descriptions and performance evaluations. And nearly every Crotonville course added a section on ethics as a prerequisite to success.

As the CEO recently reminded an audience of GE executives:

> On the question of integrity and company policy, the message is very clear. You are responsible for your organization's behavior. We will not shoot the Indians and let the chiefs go. There's no place in this company for any behavior by anyone that could condone or give the implication of condoning any violation.

Although his public statements remained cautiously moderate, in his internal speeches and discussions with GE managers Welch was outspoken about defense procurement. He described a system grounded for too many years in too close a relationship between the government and defense contractors. He made it clear that GE would not tolerate anything less than "100% ethical behavior."

Welch used every available medium to transmit the message to employees. As he explains, "You can't audit integrity into a system any more than you can inspect quality into a machine. Where you *can* make a difference is by changing the culture, by tireless, forceful leadership that won't tolerate winking, rule-bending, or looking the other way." In memos and speeches, Welch explained the new attitude; for reinforcement, GE created new training procedures, distributed posters, and even made new time cards for some businesses with the words *Mischarging Is Illegal* printed in boldface.

During discussions at Crotonville shortly after the 1985 incident, managers from defense-related businesses frequently groused to Welch, "When are we going to get the government off our backs?"

His stern reply usually went like this: *You have lost your right to not have the government on your back. The system failed, there was dishonesty, and both the government and GE will stay on your back until we clean up this mess.*

The best expression of GE's new cut-the-crap approach to ethics was Welch's mirror test. He'd ask GEers, *Can you look in the mirror every day and feel proud of what you are doing?* Instead of writing down lots of rules, or debating fine points in legalese, he used that one simple question to address the conscience of every individual GE employee directly. It is characteristic of his leadership, which consistently appeals to individual responsibility, that he assumes every person not only has a conscience but cares about its dictates.

To put GE's transgressions into perspective, Welch often compared the corporation to Newark, New Jersey, and St. Paul, Minnesota, cities with populations about the same size as GE's: In a typical year, Newark's 1,000-person police force must cope with roughly 100 murders, 300 rapes, 4,300 assaults, and 12,500 thefts. Statistics from St. Paul tell a story almost as grim. Argued the CEO, "It's utterly naive and ludicrous to believe that we have hired the only 300,000 people in the world who won't steal or cheat or take drugs or do a lot of other things."

In May 1985, a couple of days after GE pleaded guilty to the time-card fraud, Welch addressed a group of 110 senior GE managers. He explained the background of the guilty plea, and then responded to comments from his audience. When someone expressed contempt for the problems at Re-Entry Systems, Welch got angry:

> **Before you point your finger, look in the mirror at yourselves. We've all got to take a much closer look at the way we behave. I'm tired of going to the gym at headquarters and finding that someone has stolen the comb from the locker room. The mirror test is a daily test for every one of us.**

He believes corporate cultures will change in response to clearly articulated ideas—if the ideas are endlessly repeated, and backed by consistent action. The mirror test is a simple and lucid idea, and he hasn't been shy about repeating it. Just as important, Welch has responded to each successive ethical challenge in essentially the same way.

Perhaps the clearest example is the Kidder Peabody insider trading case. In 1986, GE bought the Wall Street investment bank. Six months later, a former Kidder banker named Martin Siegel confessed that he had engaged in criminal insider trading with arbitrageur Ivan Boesky, in return for suitcases stuffed with cash. Siegel's revelations, melodramatic and pitiful by turns, bolstered the government investigations that resulted in the jailing of Ivan Boesky and Michael Milken, then Drexel Burnham Lambert's overlord of junk bonds.

Along the way, Siegel's actions implicated Kidder Peabody; GE, having acquired the Wall Street firm, was stuck with legal responsibility for Kidder's crimes.

Enter Larry Bossidy, then GE's vice chairman. Beefy, brilliant, and blunt-talking, he so closely matched his boss in attitudes and skills that one GE director described him as "Jack Welch, Jr." Bossidy launched an investigation of Kidder's potential vulnerability to civil and criminal charges.

Quickly concluding that the firm "had no choice" but to settle, he helped negotiate agreements with both the SEC and U.S. Attorney Rudolph Giuliani. Kidder did not admit or deny guilt, but agreed to pay fines of more than \$25 million. In addition, GE made management changes at Kidder that ravaged morale at the investment bank, but saved it from destruction. Several years later, the firm was enjoying unprecedented profitability.

As in the time-card case, the crisis quickly passed. The government was satisfied, the press portrayed GE as unwise but honorable—and the company reinforced its unyielding insistence on ethical behavior.

Since GE is an organization of human beings—fallible by nature, and eternally subject to temptation—a certain amount of lawbreaking is almost inevitable. But that does not make any wrongdoing acceptable.

David Calhoun, the corporate vice president in charge of GE's audit staff, regularly reports on wrongdoing by GEers to the audit committee of the board of directors. His data cover all allegations from all sources, and range from trivial personal grievances to potentially significant ethical violations. The number of reports has been rising since 1985, as GE's ethics education programs have taken hold; the company regards them as a healthy demonstration that the reporting system is working. Roughly a quarter of the 1992 reports concerned violations of GE's ethics policy. GE's internal investigations determined that only two of those violations were "both significant and intentional." The government defines "significant" violations with specific criteria such as impact of at least \$25,000. GE policy requires the disclosure of its violations, including all significant ones, to the government.

To the degree that it is rooted in human nature, employee misbehavior lies beyond the reach of any corporate ethics program. The example of General Electric illustrates the difficulties such programs face. Some people simply can't cope with our society's schizophrenic system of rewards and punishments. On the one hand, we tell people they've got to win; on the other we insist they play fair.

GEers are as subject as any to that double bind: Their CEO creates fierce profit pressure, but also insists, "It is better that profits be lost than corners cut or rules bent." No GEer has any reason to believe that the company will "wink" at transgressions. Promptly repaying overcharges, admitting guilt, and siding with the forces of law at every opportunity serve as visible demonstrations that GE's commitment to ethics is real. But the insistence on performance is real, too.

This is what Tichy calls the "no-wink paradox." Some people are just incapable of working it out for themselves—and not only at GE. The paradox explains why some corporate employees break the law, why some Olympic athletes take drugs, why some politicians accept illegal campaign contributions. Losers who feel compelled to win can convince themselves that wrong is right. Dealing with such people remains one of the great challenges of management.

Welch's mirror test shows a path through the morass of corporate ethics that has the virtues of simplicity, honesty, and common sense. But that approach depends on his own strong personal convictions—values and beliefs that other executives may not share. The challenge for all corporations is to find management systems to ensure that employees live up to high standards of integrity.

As Welch concedes, he is still searching. GE continues to experiment with new methods, such as interactive videos, to get the integrity message through to employees. And Welch personally spends a half day per year with each of GE's thirteen businesses reviewing their compliance with GE's ethics policy. On international trips, he conducts compliance reviews with local GE managers in every country he visits. Obviously, he'll never get GE's hundreds of thousands of employees to behave impeccably at all times—but it won't be for lack of trying.

Chapter Ten

The Turning Point

ometime in 1985, GE's progress seemed to stall. When Tichy started consulting there, after a turbulent half decade of Welch's leadership, many GEers seemed exhausted, emotionally drained. Tichy observed what he saw as a spreading malaise that, unchecked, might have destroyed the very spirit of the GE revolution.

The danger stemmed more from such human imponderables as fatigue, anxiety, and hurt feelings than from any tangible difficulty in operations or finance. Welch was demanding much more of employees than dutiful compliance with his ideas: He needed people as zestfully committed as he was.

Many of them still weren't. Far from it. This was the era, remember, when some of the GEers attending Crotonville were calling their CEO an "asshole."

So relentlessly upbeat is Welch that he now denies GE stopped making headway in 1985. "I never felt that," he later told us.

I think you're dead wrong. You came out into Crotonville, a place where ferment is constant, where complaints and concerns and objections are not only encouraged, but expected, and you concluded the company's morale was a disaster. It simply wasn't.

Of course there was some anger and resistance and fatigue in 1985. It was there in 1982 and it will always be there. Massive change in a company of hundreds of thousands of people does not come without it. But we never lost momentum, even in a year when the economy was in the tank.

If your actions get results, you keep getting satisfaction, and so your self-confidence builds. As your self-confidence builds, you try more—and the feedback generally gets better and better. That's been the experience of all my years here.

Welch and Tichy will always disagree on the depth of resistance in 1985. We had different vantage points. At Crotonville and in workshops for managers, Tichy was close to the pain, exhaustion, and frustration that were inevitable in times of radical change. Welch saw the bigger picture: the flow of change since 1981 and GE's long-term momentum. Besides, he is an optimist who characteristically describes the glass as half-full, never half-empty.

There's no denying that the pace of GE's financial gains slowed dramatically around 1985. The U.S. economy turned sluggish that year, slowing sales companywide. As a result, corporate net income increased just 2% that year, versus an average annual gain of nearly 11% since Welch had become CEO. He points out, correctly, that GE's small earnings gain in 1985 outpaced the S & P 500, whose earnings dropped 12% that year.

Productivity also slowed: By 1983 GE had nudged its rate roughly from 2% to 2.5%—but then it plateaued. GE was still far below the 6% productivity rate that Welch regarded as necessary for effective competition against its global competitors.

Some GEers were demoralized by the company's recently acknowledged flop in factory automation—the "$30 billion industry" that never was. Symbolically, automation had become GE's best hope of building an important new business from scratch. Creating a new venture big enough to budge GE, whose revenues topped $29 billion in 1985, now began to seem almost impossible. Even Welch became resigned to adding new lines primarily by acquisition.

But GE wasn't buying much, either—which reinforced the impression that GE's sails were luffing. Welch had been making good on his promise to fix, close, or sell any businesses that didn't fit GE's strategy: By the end of 1985, the company had unloaded operations worth $5.4 billion. So far so good, but GE hadn't reinvested all that money in productive assets. Indeed, despite a few large acquisitions such as Employers Reinsurance the corporate balance sheet still showed $2.5 billion of cash.

The takeover market was white-hot in those days, with acquired companies routinely fetching 50% more than their stock was worth before a bidder approached. GE was reluctant to fork over premiums of that size. So even though GE staffers considered some 6,000 potential acquisition candidates, and then winnowed their list to the best 100 or so, Welch couldn't find many companies he was willing to buy.

Among the manic dealmakers of the mid-1980s, General Electric seemed awkward, even frumpy. It was as if GE insisted on dancing an old-fashioned foxtrot when everybody else was rocking out. In the era of down-and-dirty junk bonds, Welch clung to GE's impeccable AAA debt rating; while hostile takeovers were becoming commonplace, he insisted on friendly deals. And when other CEOs were throwing share owner money around as if it were worthless—practically lighting their cigars with the stuff—Welch fretted about overpaying for assets. Today he seems wise, but at the time, some thought him a wimp.

To any GEer inclined to resist Welch, the bloodletting of the early 1980s—the nonstop layoffs, factory closings, and asset sales—had become a call to arms. At Crotonville, Tichy talked to many GE managers who seriously believed their CEO was ruining the company. The 1984 "toughest bosses" story only bolstered their case; Welch says it marked one of the worst moments in his career.

GE's naysayers regarded the defense industry scandal of 1985 as the final proof that their company was falling apart. In their view, GE's famous control systems hadn't worked, and Welch had betrayed loyal employees by failing to stand up to the government. The result was that their proud corporation had suffered its worst public humiliation since the electrical-conspiracy trials of the early 1960s.

The defense scandal became what management theorists March and Cohen call a "garbage event"—an incident that causes people to focus on their bad feelings. In emotional terms, it seemed to give any depressive on the GE payroll ample reason to conclude that the company was going to hell. So instead of experiencing snowballing enthusiasm, many employees felt miserable about working for GE.

At Crotonville, Tichy noticed a marked increase in signs of unrest. Managers were spending more time complaining, particularly about the CEO. GEers increasingly characterized Welch as "heartless," a man with "brass balls." Frightening, unfounded rumors spread wildly. Tichy often heard that the GE board was demanding Welch's resignation. People told baseless stories about Welch's ruthlessness as a hockey player, alleging that he spent more time in the penalty box than anyone else on his high school team.

Thus Tichy's view that 1985 was a hard year for GE. As if aware that defeat was inevitable, the forces of resistance came out of hiding to make their last, futile efforts to block the GE revolution. Welch's job was never at risk, though: The price of GE's stock had been increasing at a 25% annual rate since Welch took office.

In 1984, Welch commissioned a survey of GE's top several hundred officers, asking them how they viewed the company. When the results came back the following year, they conveyed the mixed feelings and frustration felt by many of these managers. Characteristically, Welch used the negative data to help refine his message, but interpreted the survey as a demonstration that GE was making progress.

GEers needed something powerful enough to cause a complete shift in mood; if GE had been a person, you'd have been tempted to throw a bucket of cold water in its face.

The CEO did the only thing he could: He persevered. And before too much longer, he found a way to bring GE back to life.

Welch wasn't exactly gloomy in 1985—he's not the type—but as the months dragged on and the problems piled up, he struck Tichy as shorter-tempered, more obsessive, noticeably less exuberant than usual. Then, a couple of weeks before Christmas, Tichy found himself walking past his office at headquarters. The shirt-sleeved CEO was visible from the corridor, cracking jokes with his two secretaries at the time, Helga and Sue. Tichy immediately noticed the change of mood: Welch's irrepressible glee was back. Welch turned to greet Tichy as he passed, and Welch's blue eyes sparkled as he grinned.

Tichy didn't know it, but GE had just agreed to buy RCA for $6.3 billion in cash. A big, bold, attention-grabbing deal, this transaction became the biggest nonoil acquisition to date—and the emotional inspiration that GEers desperately needed. Suddenly, their company was back in the game, playing to win.

Welch, of course, had been playing to win all along, but his efforts had been concealed from public view. When Ted Turner briefly threatened a hostile takeover of CBS in the spring of 1985, GE privately offered to protect CBS through a friendly "white knight" deal. Nothing came of that: Turner ended up buying the MGM-UA film company, and CBS eventually fell into the tight grasp of Laurence Tisch, the tough-minded billionaire who also controlled Loews Corp.

But the CEO had discovered broadcasting, which in 1985 was still one of the richest businesses in the world. Largely thanks to NBC, the top-rated TV network and the owner of a money-minting string of television and radio stations, RCA was producing $300 million of cash annually. Much of that came from the hugely popular *Cosby Show.* Hungry for a deal substantial enough to affect GE's financial performance, Welch began breakfasting regularly with Felix Rohatyn of Lazard Frères, one of New York's most respected investment bankers. According to the *New York Times,* Welch kept pressing Rohatyn to set up a meeting with RCA Chairman Thornton Bradshaw.

On November 6, Rohatyn invited Bradshaw and Welch to cocktails at his Park Avenue apartment. According to Welch, they discussed U.S. competitiveness, the Japanese—everything but the GE-RCA deal that was on their minds. "We both thought we knew what we were talking about," he says.

One month later, he called the RCA chairman. Bradshaw invited him to a tête-à-tête in Bradshaw's apartment at the Dorset Hotel, a few blocks from RCA's Rockefeller Center headquarters. There Welch informed his fellow chairman that GE was offering to buy RCA for $61 per share in cash, a substantial premium over RCA's $47 market price. In less than a week, they had a deal.

The press loved the transaction. Front-page stories nationwide certainly didn't portray Welch as frumpy. He had moved quickly many times before—negotiating the Employers Reinsurance deal in a single day, for instance—but this time he got public credit. GE presented the business combination as a patriotic victory, arguing that the GE-RCA merger would "help improve America's competitiveness in world markets"—that is, against the Japanese. Raved a *Washington Post* headline: "MERGER TO CREATE GLOBAL POWERHOUSE."

Time magazine described the deal as a "reunion of technological titans." In 1919, a few years after buying the U.S. rights to Guglielmo Marconi's radio technology, GE created the Radio Corporation of America. RCA did not become an independent company until 1933, when GE sold it under threat of antitrust litigation.

Fifty-two years later, RCA and GE still seemed to belong together. RCA, with 85,000 employees and 1985 revenues of $10.1 billion, increased its new parent's size by one-third, bumping it from No. 10 to No. 6 on the Fortune 500. Though ranked only No. 23 among U.S. military contractors, RCA got some 15% of its sales from defense work. To a remarkable degree, RCA's products complemented GE's: In radar, for example, RCA produced seaborne equipment, whereas GE's was used on land. GE made military satellites; RCA's were civilian. Its TV set business, though weak, bolstered GE's. The broadcasting operation strengthened GE's position in services. And, as Wall Street investment analysts immediately recognized, the NBC network's cash flow was prodigious enough all by itself to justify the entire acquisition financially.

The parts that didn't fit soon would be sold, quickly reducing the cost of buying RCA by $1.4 billion, or one-fifth of the purchase price. Among the RCA businesses GE unloaded were RCA Records, Coronet Carpets, and the Nacolah Life Insurance business.

Financially, the RCA deal was a home run, to use one of Welch's favorite expressions. He says GE's discounted rate of return from RCA has averaged 14% annually. NBC alone produced $1.9 billion of cash during its first six years under GE ownership. After a brief downturn in the early 1990s, NBC has delivered eight consecutive years of double-digit growth in earnings and has grown its family of offerings with the addition of CNBC and MSNBC.

Over the years, RCA has created its share of minor headaches for GE, as well. As the new head of NBC, Bob Wright alienated broadcasters. He couldn't help noticing that the inexplicably complacent network TV industry had been losing viewers for years to cable, videocassettes, and other competition. David Letterman, the irreverent host of NBC's *Late Night* talk show, routinely described his new corporate masters as "knuckleheads." And GE horrified sentimentalists in the U.S. press once again when it swapped the consumer electronics business to Thomson S.A. for the French company's medical-imaging unit in 1987.

The greater difficulty was dealing with RCA's bureaucratic traditions and its many employees. The CEO worked hard to ensure that RCA people got equitable treatment, and its top executives initially did well at GE. In every business where GE and RCA combined their separate operations into a single unit—such as consumer electronics, semiconductors, radar, and communication services—an RCA executive won the leadership job. But GE subsequently sold semiconductors and consumer electronics. By 1993, one member of the Corporate Executive Council hailed from RCA: Eugene Murphy, the head of Aircraft Engines.

Thousands of lower-ranking people from RCA soon left GE. By 1988 GE had fewer people on its payroll than it had the year before it bought RCA. Many of those who left ended up working for other companies, when GE sold the businesses for which they worked. Some of the remainder stayed on as GE employees; many others lost their jobs.

The closing of the RCA deal in 1986 marked the end of Act I of the GE revolution. By 1986 the fusty, bureaucratic company Welch had inherited no longer existed. The weak businesses, the huge staffs, the padded budgets—all were gone. Exercising his power as CEO to the fullest, Welch had cleared away most of the obstacles in GE's path.

As yet, though, he hadn't clearly defined the new GE he hoped to build. Welch's vision still seemed too amorphous to win the gung-ho allegiance of employees. Clarifying the vision, and winning converts, would be the work of Act II.

The RCA deal reenergized Welch and marked a turning point in the GE revolution. But despite the CEO's enthusiasm, GE still had a long way to go. Evidence of how much the corporate culture still needed to change was a video that David Letterman showed on *Late Night*. It captures the pathos of a transformation that led so many thousands of people to fear that they might soon lose their jobs.

Shortly after General Electric announced that it would buy RCA, Letterman visited the old GE building in New York City with a camera crew. The resulting videotape, broadcast to a national audience, is a hilarious send-up of uptight corporate behavior.

Letterman introduced the segment from his desk:

You never know what you're in for when you get a brand-new boss. So when General Electric bought this company, RCA and NBC, I thought I would drop by the

GE building here in midtown Manhattan, meet my new employers, kind of, you know, get things off on the right foot.

Then he cut to the videotape: Wearing a baseball jacket and carrying a large, cellophane-wrapped basket of fruit in both hands, Letterman addressed the camera, in his patented folksy deadpan, as he walked down Lexington Avenue:

Sometime in August, I guess, the takeover will be complete, and we're all now getting a little curious as to what kind of effect it's going to have on NBC as we know it today—the programming and, I guess, specifically, how is it going to influence me? And what I'm really trying to get at here is, am I going to have a job? So this is the General Electric building, and I have a little gift, and we thought: What the heck? Let's just drop in and say hello, just see how it's going. They can't object to that, can they?

At the doorway of GE's former headquarters, Letterman was greeted not by a person but by a disembodied voice from a loudspeaker: "This is not a building to film in," said the unseen security guard. "Clear the front of the GE building, please."

"Yes, sir," said Letterman. "We just wanted to drop off a little fruit basket and say hello to the folks on the board of directors."

A woman stepped through the revolving doors, flanked by a male security guard. "I'm not sure you're able to do this," she warned. "We haven't gotten any authorization."

"You mean we need authorization to drop off a fruit basket?" Letterman asked. He faced the camera. "Oh, this is going to be fun to work with these people, isn't it? To drop off a fruit basket you need paperwork."

After some more chat, Letterman faced the camera again. "I'll just go on in and see what happens." He and the crew jostled their way through the revolving door.

Inside, a scowling security officer in a suit accosted them. "I'm going to ask you to turn the cameras off, please," he said.

Letterman gave the man a big, toothy grin and stuck out his hand. "Okay," he said. Letterman presented the classic mask of corporate passive resistance: a tone of cheerful acquiescence unaccompanied by any effort to comply with requests. The cameras kept rolling. "We just wanted to drop off this basket of fruit—"

The officer started to shake hands, but abruptly pulled his hand away, jabbing his thumb up in the air instead. "Shut off the camera, please," he insisted.

The impasse ended when the security officer blocked the lens with his hand and (as far as the viewers could tell) threw them out of the building.

That night the GE videotape became the highlight of Letterman's show. "Maybe you didn't realize that we got to see a glimpse of the official General Electric handshake," he chortled. Then Letterman presented, in slow motion, the image of the "security gentleman," as he called him, almost shaking the talk show host's hand but then evading contact. Letterman showed the "GE handshake" again and again, while crowing in voiceover.

GE's reaction to the spectacle demonstrated how far the company had progressed since Welch became CEO. Instead of ignoring or condemning it, Welch brought a copy of the videotape to the GE boardroom, where he showed it to the assembled directors. He says they found it hilarious. "It was fun," he remembers. "We'd tease the guard when we went in the building—give him the 'GE handshake.'"

Since the directors had all seen it, Tichy figured it was okay to show the tape at Crotonville. He has used it ever since, to demonstrate the disastrous effects of the bureaucratic mind-set. Thus David Letterman became part of the Crotonville curriculum.

Act Two

THE VISION

Chapter Eleven

Crotonville

W elch's vision for GE hasn't changed much since his days at Plastics, but by the mid-1980s he still hadn't expressed it powerfully or clearly enough to win over GEers. Before the CEO could hope to change the corporate culture, he had to refine his message and implant it in people's minds. Crotonville, which provided advanced training to 10,000 GE executives per year, was the logical place to start.

In 1985, Tichy signed on for a two-year stint as manager of GE's Management Development Institute, overlooking the Hudson River. The new job put him in charge of GE's management education worldwide. His assignment: to accelerate the transformation of Crotonville, so Crotonville could help transform GE. Tichy reported to Jim Baughman; after running Crotonville for five years, and beginning the process of change there, Baughman had been promoted to head of organizational planning, management development, and executive compensation. Baughman challenged Tichy to work with him and the Crotonville team to lead an even more radical transformation.

By the time Tichy accepted the job, he had been consulting for GE long enough to know that he had to establish his credibility fast, particularly since he was an academic who was parachuting in for just two years. GE's performance-driven culture is so powerful that when you start a new job as manager, you want to demonstrate your self-confidence and leadership right away, to establish your credibility with your fellow workers. Tichy felt he had just one turn at bat—and he'd better hit a home run. If he missed, he feared, GEers would lose respect for him, maybe forever. His boss might not give him the "air cover" he'd need to get budgets approved and keep the corporate office off his back. His subordinates might ignore his orders and find ways to make him look bad.

The pressure was exhilarating and scary—and not only for Tichy. Baughman, who knew better than anyone what the job entailed, understood that he was taking a big risk by hiring an outsider to lead an institution as crucial as Crotonville. He later said that Welch and Jack Peiffer, the head of the Executive Management Staff, were worried, too. They all decided to take the risk.

The CEO himself had interviewed Tichy for the job—twice—and his expectations were extremely high. He was relying heavily on the police, the media, and the schools, and counted Crotonville among his principal instruments of change.

Hiring Tichy was one of many expressions of the CEO's intense interest in Crotonville. While cutting costs almost everywhere else, GE was spending $45 million on new buildings and improvements there—a decision that, in the context of so much cost-cutting, outraged some GEers. Welch stuck to his decision despite the protests: He insists that investing in sources of future productivity, such as management training, is entirely consistent with running a lean organization. GE regularly approved the institution's hefty annual budget, even though the return on that investment was impossible to calculate.

The CEO was confident the payoff would come. A devotee of creative ferment, he saw Crotonville as a laboratory to create a new kind of management, and a place to produce new ideas. He wanted "action learning" based on solving real, pending business problems. He wanted participants to learn teamwork skills, while developing companywide networks of contacts to aid them throughout their GE careers.

Above all, he wanted Crotonville to provide a wide-open channel of communication between GE's top management and the more junior employees taking courses. Welch didn't simply want to lecture—he also wanted to listen. "That's how we get the pulse of the organization," he says.

His needs inspired unprecedented candor. To promote the no-holds-barred debating style that Welch sees as the best way to "fertilize ideas," the Crotonville team had to build on what Baughman had done, eliminating any remaining constraints of rank and hierarchy from an institution whose cultural heritage traditionally had reinforced them.

Welch also expected Crotonville to indoctrinate managers in GE's new values, from constructive conflict to integrity to "ownership." So Crotonville had to become deliberately evangelical, its every graduate a missionary capable of spreading the word to the larger organization. As Welch had told Baughman, "I want Crotonville to be part of the glue that holds GE together."

In addition to the pressure from Fairfield and from the heads of GE businesses, Tichy faced a challenge below. Knowing he couldn't accomplish anything substantial by himself, he set out to build a team, but some on his staff were ready to resist. Baughman had assured Tichy that the folks at Crotonville were delighted he'd been hired. No doubt they'd told him that, but it simply wasn't true.

The support staff, administrators, trainers, and other members of the Crotonville organization were a microcosm of the GE work force. Proud of their accomplishments, they saw themselves as contributors to a very successful operation that didn't need fixing. Many viewed Tichy with skepticism, and some saw him as an interloper and a threat. Some of the highest-ranking Crotonville staffers had to struggle hard to follow his leadership despite harboring deeply ambivalent feelings about him.

Even though Baughman had brought in many new staffers while running Crotonville, some people there seemed more focused on Crotonville's glorious history than its future. Crotonville had been the corporate world's first major in-house business school, and it remains the most prestigious. Its success spawned imitators around the globe, from IBM's Sands Point School to Hitachi's Management Development Institute in Japan.

By defining, codifying, and teaching GE's most effective techniques, Crotonville had greatly enhanced the company's reputation as a leader in management science. It popularized any number of breakthrough ideas, including strategic planning and management by objective. The very idea of training executives as general managers, which today seems as basic as brushing your teeth, began there in the 1950s.

At first, Crotonville was an effective instrument of change. By the late 1970s, however, Crotonville's mission was no longer clear. The institution began to lose touch with some of its customers, the GE businesses that were sending participants to courses. Unlike a profit and loss center, Crotonville was not clearly accountable to anyone, and its performance seemed impossible to measure. The staff drifted into the habit of comparing Crotonville to other schools. As a result, the courses—which were mostly taught by leading academics from major universities—gradually became more generic and less relevant to GE.

Tichy's modest legacy to GE is the set of developmental processes he helped introduce at Crotonville. He teaches people how to change large organizations radically. One of his inspirations was political historian James MacGregor Burns, who defined the term "transformational leadership." This is leadership that transcends the mere management of what already exists, to create something fundamentally new. The field itself is new, a study not of heroes, but of the ways ordinary people can bring institutions through the convulsions of dramatic change. A goal is to foster leaders who can address human emotions and values—the "soft" issues, in B-school parlance—as well as the traditional "hard" issues of market share and financial performance.

Over the years, with substantial borrowings from others, Tichy developed an instructional stagecraft designed to transform students or workshop participants into effective agents of change. The key is to put people at risk—intellectually, emotionally, and at times even physically—so they can experience the personal breakthroughs that enable them to change.

The challenge of the new Crotonville team was to clear away the last remnants of the old methods while developing programs that exemplified GE's new ideas. Instead of helping people become leaders, conventional programs usually teach them how to execute orders. The emphasis is on skills training and cognitive development—learning new ways to think about problems. That's fine as far as it goes, but it's superficial.

Change can be terrifying. Anyone who hopes to revolutionize an entire organization had better know how to cope with change on the personal level. You can't teach that with case studies or books; it comes from experience. To provide participants with that experience in a way that's safe, reliable, and cost-efficient, Crotonville drew on a wide variety of disciplines and techniques, from academic social psychology to the "compressed action learning" of Outward Bound training.

Adults learn best in conditions of moderate stress, so conflict and discomfort are essential parts of the process. Outward Bound brilliantly shows the way: They'll take deskbound executives, give them forty-five minutes of training in rock-climbing techniques, and then order them to rappel down a sheer, hundred-foot granite cliff—and climb right back up. To the executives, the assignment seems life-threatening. It isn't—safety measures include alert instructors and stout ropes to halt any slip—but the illusion of great risk spurs performance and transforms learning into a life experience.

Action workshops can achieve similar effects even in conventional corporate surroundings. The trick is putting participants to work on real business issues, with measurable results. The managers who take these programs arrive in teams, each sent by its employer with an assignment to solve an actual, pending problem. For instance one team had to figure out how to patch up the relationship with a major Japanese supplier infuriated by their business's frequently changing product specifications.

The stakes are clearly defined. By the end of a workshop, each team must present its proposals to its boss, for rejection or implementation. If the ideas are good, they can be put to use at once. To add rigor to the process, GE surveys the boss, colleagues, and subordinates of each workshop participant, once before the session begins, and again a couple of months after it ends. The feedback from these assessments also helps participants learn about themselves and develop as leaders.

The teamwork aspect of this training is not just fun and games: Participants feel that if their team's proposals stink, the career of every member might be hurt. So people learn to work together— some for the first time in their lives. And when the participants return to normal work, they remain part of the team they formed in class. Working together as a group, the team members are far likelier to change their organization than any individual would be.

Properly run, such workshops can serve usefully as miniature corporate think tanks. By generating plans and ideas that actually get used, the learning center vastly increases its ability to influence organizational change directly.

That's the ultimate goal. Though Tichy has spent most of his career in academe, he sees himself not as a professor, but as a professional agent of change. He formed his world view during the activist 1960s, when everybody wanted to change the world. He earned a Ph.D. in social psychology at Columbia, writing a thesis on different types of change agents. Among them were community organizer Saul Alinsky, consultants with McKinsey & Co., activists working with Ralph Nader, members of the Black Panther party, and radical anarchists. The result was a typology of change agents, based on their values, how they conceptualized organization, and their methods—which ranged from linear programming to investigative studies to setting bombs.

* * *

Right after Tichy arrived at Crotonville in September 1985, he met with his new team to discuss goals. The marching orders he'd gotten from Baughman were to continue the process of dramatic change at Crotonville, by introducing new methods, new courses, and new goals. The job was to make Crotonville a leading influence over the change process at GE. If that made the participants in our programs nervous, fine. If it meant exposing Welch or any other corporate officer to face-to-face criticism, so much the better: Crotonville should be a learning opportunity for them, too.

The staff members at the meeting were all terribly polite, but some of them obviously thought Tichy was nuts. Some thought he could be stopped, or at least ignored. In the decorously passive-aggressive manner common to corporate types everywhere in the world, they began saying *yes* to him when they really meant *no*. They were making the best of something that didn't suit them at all.

Tichy's first turn at bat came with the Corporate Entry Leadership Conference, or CELC, held soon after he arrived. This brand-new, three-day course was Welch's idea, a way to reach, in groups of 100, all of the 2,000 engineers and other professionals GE hired straight out of college each year. The sessions would orient the new recruits to global competition and GE's changing values, while helping them figure out how they fit into the company.

Designing a suitable course was challenging. As a consultant to GE, Tichy had interviewed middle managers by the score, so he knew the company was in turmoil in 1985. Many employees were scared, or angry, or both. Resistance to Welch and all he stood for seemed to be reaching an emotional peak. Although the opposition was not organized or even very visible, it included business heads as well as thousands of middle managers and hourly workers. At the same time support for Welch was growing rapidly. The result, increasingly, was polarization.

Baughman encouraged Tichy to redesign the course himself. "Give it your best shot," he said. "That's why we hired you."

The goal was to give new hires an honest orientation to GE. The team couldn't expect anyone to commit to GE's emerging values unless they understood the ideas and reasoning behind them. And let's face it: If they didn't like the values, you couldn't expect them to stay at GE. That's why the team required that each CELC participant interview four seasoned GE managers before arriving at Crotonville, as described in Chapter 1.

When the first group of 100 recruits arrived on campus one Sunday afternoon in October, they brought the results of their 400 interviews. You can imagine how the most disaffected of GE's old-timers responded to those questions: That's where the kids got the "Jack Welch is an asshole" statement. But the interviews captured the whole range of feeling among GE managers, from hostility to ignorance to interest to enthusiasm.

The group had plenty to talk about. And since openness, candor, and constructive conflict were prominent among GE's emerging values, the group had a *way* to talk about it—uncensored debate.

After an introductory session and dinner, the participants broke up into small discussion groups, with more experienced GE managers as facilitators.

By 11 P.M. they had boiled down the concerns of GE's middle managers to three big questions:

- How can GE motivate its work force without offering job security?

- How can GE help reindustrialize America when it is moving jobs offshore?

- Does Jack Welch really have a strategy or is he just reshuffling the portfolio?

The next morning, at eight o'clock sharp, the whole group gathered in the intimate, 110-seat Crotonville amphitheater that GEers call "the Pit." The time had come to get answers to the young managers' three questions—but not from Tichy. Facing the participants was Larry Bossidy, then the second most powerful person at GE.

The prospect of this morning's dialogue had horrified the traditionalists on Crotonville's staff. Rather than exposing the vice chairman to such uncertainty, they'd urged Tichy to send Bossidy a complete list of questions ahead of time. Otherwise, they warned, the session would only alienate him—and the rest of GE's top management—from Crotonville and this reckless new training approach.

Remembering their qualms, and feeling some of his own, Tichy asked the vice chairman at the last minute whether he wanted a briefing before going into the Pit.

Bossidy is not as polished as Welch, but he's one of the smartest people around. "Nah," he said. "I'll just go in and interact."

The mood in the Pit was electric. The young people piling into the room were visibly pumped up from their Sunday debates, more than ready to take on the No. 2 man at GE. As for Tichy, he felt this would make or break his GE career. A few of his Crotonville colleagues in the Pit seemed to be gleefully awaiting his comeuppance.

Soon after Bossidy came on stage, a young professional bluntly raised the job-security question. The room hushed. Everyone had known this moment was coming—but still, the kid had just delivered the corporate equivalent of a sock in the jaw. How would the big guy react?

Bossidy took the blow with grace:

You're right to raise this. It's an extremely tough issue, and very relevant. We think the only honest way to handle this is to tell people that there is no job security in GE—other than what the customer can provide. Therefore, if you're making turbines that cost 40% more than Korean or Japanese turbines, and they make a better turbine with more quality, then you will face downturns. That's the reality of the marketplace. . . .

This is very painful, and I think you need to empathize with the middle managers who have worked for GE for twenty-five years and face terrible downsizing.

> We must deal with this with compassion, and with fairness—but we must deal with it.

Asked about the effects of moving U.S. jobs to other countries, Bossidy responded with candor: "Maybe we're paying the price for being sloppy and poorly managed for so many years after World War II. But what alternative do we have now? All we can do is try to make our businesses stronger."

After a spirited discussion of GE's values, from integrity to constructive conflict, here's how Bossidy wrapped up the meeting:

> I passionately believe in these shared values. But I'm not naive enough to think that everyone in GE believes in them. Some people don't know about them; some managers think the values are a crock. But I believe in them, and my challenge to each of you is that you need to decide. Get clear on what your values are and whether they fit with GE. If they don't fit, make the decision to get out. If they do fit, terrific—but make that decision based on a clear understanding of what GE is, what we are attempting to accomplish, and what you want to do.

By the time Tichy took Bossidy back to the car, Tichy was feeling terrific. The vice chairman evidently had relished the give-and-take, and so had the new managers. Even so, it was great to hear Bossidy say he was glad that difficult questions were raised.

Tichy wasn't the only one who gained confidence that day: As they met with other GE officers during the remainder of the course, the new recruits demonstrated a healthy willingness to challenge any idea, regardless of who presented it. One corporate officer tried to dodge a criticism about job security by saying, "We don't have that problem in my particular business, so I really can't answer you."

A newcomer shot back, "Now wait a minute—that's a cop-out. As an officer of the General Electric Company, don't you have to take some responsibility for what's going on?"

Roger Schipke, then head of Major Appliances, addressed the group late Monday afternoon:

> **This has been one of the toughest days of my career. I did not realize how bad it was in GE. That's not a reflection on you; the data you've collected from the middle of the organization is profound and troublesome. I leave here very troubled, but committed to want to do something about it.**

Listening to Schipke, Tichy knew they'd hit a home run.

Crotonville couldn't have accomplished much without solid support not only from Baughman, but from Welch. Every time the team needed backup he gave it, and he demonstrated his commitment to Crotonville in the most visible way: Once every few weeks a GE helicopter would thunder down from the sky. As soon as it landed, the CEO would burst out, ready for another Crotonville debate.

Welch loved being in the Pit, bashing big ideas back and forth with GEers. After all, he hadn't promoted constructive conflict for theoretical reasons—it was his natural way of communicating. In face-to-face discussions he's hard to resist, and he knows it. Welch relishes every opportunity he can get to win others to his point of view, and the Crotonville Pit allowed him to do it to 100 people at a time.

Candor is his secret weapon. It wins him trust, and affection, too. Whatever is on his mind, the CEO usually says. According to a joke that circulated around Plastics when he worked there, the worst way to hurt Welch is to tell him a secret and then lock him in a closet before he can tell anyone else. Welch protects himself, as much as he can, by strictly barring journalists, security analysts, and even consultants from the Pit. (Tichy wasn't allowed in until he became Crotonville's manager.) But inside that safe room, with fellow initiates of the GE fraternity, Welch will say almost anything.

In 1986, after the RCA deal had closed, a manager from RCA's Coronet Carpets unit raised his hand at Crotonville. Coronet was a tiny business by GE standards, and everyone knew it didn't fit into the three-circles strategy. Obviously worried, the executive asked Welch what would become of Coronet.

The CEO didn't hesitate. "I'd better tell you this," he said. "You know that we've been thinking about selling your business? Well, we arranged a deal this morning."

A similar thing happened during another session. A manager from the Robotics group in Orlando—a component of GE's unsuccessful factory-automation business—asked about its future.

Welch replied, "If I were you, I'd get my résumé ready. I know you don't want to hear that. But we're not making it in that business. To be fair to you, you've got to face that." At the cocktail party after the session, he made a point of spending a few minutes with the man from Robotics, making sure the fellow was okay. That's what Welch means by the phrase "tough-minded but soft-hearted."

The CEO spends so much time talking that some people don't realize how carefully he listens. At Crotonville, he installed a systematic new approach to gathering feedback, requiring every participant to fill in a one-page appraisal sheet that asks three questions:

- What did you find about the presentation that was constructive and clarifying?

- What did you find confusing or troublesome?

- What do you regard as your most important takeaway from this session?

In practice, those comment sheets are report cards on his stewardship of GE. Welch reads them by the hundred, with the eagerness of a brand manager absorbing test market data.

Not all the comments are pats on the back:

- "Somewhere between the corporate office and the department workers, the information flow ceases. I believe there would be less fear of the changes to come if the reasons for change were presented."

- "It sounds like GE is becoming a conglomerate."

- "Welch's shots at middle management bothered me. I'm middle management and I work very hard to stay current and guide my business into tomorrow. Maybe we should come at this problem with middle management from a positive side rather than the negative."

- "Perhaps the upper management is not up to the challenge. I have my résumé ready in case my group gets killed."

Welch hears the same complaints over and over and comes back for more. Even years later, when griping was less common, the complaint most frequently aired comes from managers who say they share Welch's values but their bosses don't.

The problem frustrates Welch, too. Once, in 1986, while he and Tichy were driving from Crotonville's helipad to the Pit, the CEO grimaced as they discussed the comments he'd been reading. "This is unbelievable!" he exclaimed. "I'm getting the same questions I've gotten for five years! Doesn't anyone understand anything? I'm just not getting through to them."

"What's the alternative?" Tichy asked. "They obviously haven't gotten the message yet. Don't you have to keep saying it over and over again?"

"You're right," he said. "I've got no alternative." He pulled himself back into his usual upbeat mood, and strode into the Pit for another energetic session. The perseverance to repeat the same message day after day, year after year, with no end in sight, may be Welch's greatest strength.

The CEO's personal participation greatly adds to Crotonville vibrancy, but the programs must create excitement without him— indeed, roughly half take place on GE business sites far from the campus. Tichy's team redesigned every one of Crotonville's programs and assembled many new ones. Typical of the new workshops was a five-day Team Experienced Manager Course that took place in Gotemba, Japan, in March 1987.

Bossidy, an instinctive populist, used to keep asking what Crotonville was doing for the tens of thousands of GE middle managers who weren't invited to the prestigious courses held on Crotonville's campus. Workshops like this one, held at the base of Mount Fuji, were an answer to his question.

The Gotemba course gathered about thirty midlevel managers, five each from the local operations of six different GE businesses. As in most Crotonville workshops, the goal was to develop leaders as change agents while solving real business problems. Each five-person team came with an assignment, such as these:

- Plastics needed to coordinate its research and development activities in Japan more closely with those in GE's U.S. labs.

- Power Systems, facing declining turbine sales in the U.S., needed a strategy for attracting new customers in Asia.

The session opened with a half-day, stage-setting presentation on transformational leadership. This was more than a lecture: For instance, after explaining TPC—the analysis of business issues in technical, political, and cultural terms—the participants would examine their own work projects in those terms.

These middle managers were too far down in the organization to see how they fit in to the larger picture, so in the afternoon Don Kane, GE's organizational-planning expert, explained how the corporation itself was being transformed.

After dinner that evening and every other, the teams separated to work on their own assignments.

On day two Harvard professor Mike Yoshino talked about global strategy. His function was to give the participants some necessary conceptual tools.

The group spent that afternoon outdoors, working Outward Bound–style on building team skills.

On day three, Hiro Takeuchi, a marketing professor from Hitotsubashi University in Tokyo, taught global marketing for half a day.

In the afternoon the group conducted "visioning" exercises. To explain how forcefully a clear vision can influence events, the leaders showed Martin Luther King's "I Have a Dream" speech. They discussed the essential components of King's vision, then abstracted them into terse points written on flip charts. Then the managers had to craft a vision for their projects by each writing a magazine-style article, set two years in the future, describing the project and its effect. Afterward, their colleagues interviewed them and wrote down the main themes on flip charts. Each team member's themes filled one page.

Although the overlap was substantial, the visioning exercise didn't create a consensus. To achieve that, each of the teams gathered to define its goals formally. The debates, often highly emotional, lasted until midnight. But by the time the managers went to bed, each team had its own clear vision.

The next morning, the teams met separately to translate their visions into specific plans. The Power Systems group had set a goal of opening three new Asian markets, for example. Now the question was, how? How much would it cost? How would they get the money?

After lunch on day four, they staged a dress rehearsal of the presentations to business leaders that were scheduled for the next day. Members of all the other teams listened to each presentation, then offered critiques—hardball criticism as well as ideas for improvements.

The business leaders arrived in time for dinner. While the teams of middle managers feverishly polished their presentations, the leaders explained the rules to their bosses: After listening to his team's presentation, and discussing it with the team, the executives were required to announce what action they'd take on each recommendation. Any business leader who failed to take the process seriously risked alienating the managers who'd been working eighteen hours a day to put these proposals together. And once the business leader made the public announcement, he'd have to live with his decision. So tomorrow would test the bosses as well as the students.

On the final day, the teams made their presentations, and then everyone gathered to hear each of the six business leaders declare whether or not he would implement his team's ideas. Another home run for the Crotonville team. At Gotemba, the bosses accepted almost all of the proposals.

Again and again Welch has said, "There are no textbook answers to the problems we face. We have to write our own textbooks every day." His commitment to that approach was most evident in the drafting of the GE values statement, a Crotonville preoccupation for years.

The work was well underway by 1982. Tichy joined Jim Baughman, Don Kane, and Jack Peiffer in the creation of a document intended to define the new GE culture: a simple sounding list of the corporation's core beliefs. The group met endlessly and created countless drafts, consulting often with Welch and Vice Chairmen Larry Bossidy and Ed Hood.

At some companies, a group like that might just have typed up a list of its values—or, more likely, the CEO's—and considered the job done. That's not the GE way. Welch wanted the final statement to be something all GEers could "own." He insisted the group keep exposing its draft values to debate at Crotonville, until thousands of managers had considered them and given their responses.

The process was exhausting, but it gave Tichy a visceral understanding of why top managers must constantly engage workers in dialogue. The feedback is very useful, but that's not the most important thing. By listening to people, you encourage them to think; and by encouraging them to think, you can win their involvement and commitment. The years spent interminably discussing and revising the GE values statement at Crotonville resulted in more than a piece of paper listing ideals. Those who criticized Welch for his inability to nail down a final values statement missed the point: A statement of values never should be considered done. This process forced a large percentage of GE's most influential managers to consider what the company's values should be. Continuous reexamination and discussion is what makes values come alive.

In 1985 the group wrote a discussion document that was, admittedly, an expression of its members' own beliefs. This five-page manifesto (similar to the one Larry Bossidy referred to in the Pit) contained simple statements without much explanation. Each was controversial enough, new enough, or bold enough to spark an emotional reaction. Here are a few samples:

- Only satisfied customers can provide job security.

- Change is continual, thus nothing is sacred. Change is accepted as the rule rather than the exception.

- Leaders share knowledge rather than withholding it as an element of power. Everyone benefits when they know what the leader knows—nothing is "secret."

- Paradox is a way of life. You must function collectively as one company and individually as many businesses at the same time. For us, leadership means leading while being led, producing more output with less input.

- We encourage the sharing of these values because we believe they are both fair and effective, but we realize they are not for everyone. . . . Individuals whose values do not coincide with these expressed preferences will more likely flourish better outside the General Electric Company.

When GEers read the document, their reactions were almost always the same. They'd get to that final paragraph and their jaws would drop. "You've got to be kidding," they'd say, often with anger. That final statement—the "flourish off," as it came to be known—affronted some. They said it felt like being asked to take a loyalty oath. Remembers Welch, "The feedback shocked us."

A typical comment:

The paper should end on a positive note. The tone of the last paragraph appears to contradict much of the discussion under openness and constructive conflict. The same intent could be accomplished by a positive statement such as "We believe that these values are both fair and

effective. We are firmly committed to instilling them throughout the General Electric Company."

Every idea in the statement found both allies and opponents. Some said the document was too long; others, that it was too short. It was pabulum, or too tough. It sounded like "shape up or ship out"; or like "motherhood and apple pie." Some wondered: "Why even bother to write it down?" Others, often younger managers, were glad to see some stakes firmly planted in the ground. "At last!" they'd say.

To many GEers, the values document was profoundly challenging. As one executive wrote on a comment sheet:

> In my view, no one is comfortable with the notion of change. Some would argue that there are things in this world that are sacred: family, identity, one's self-determination, and it would seem that constant change can cause confusion. Do we value change or even the process of questioning and looking for change?

At first, few participants in these debates believed GE really cared about their comments. Those doubts were reinforced when Welch included parts of the values statement in the 1985 annual report. Suddenly the ideas seemed set in stone: "Jack Welch's commandments," one manager called them.

Instead of giving up, Crotonville continued to hold debates on values. Welch's personal presence at Crotonville, his obvious willingness to listen, convinced participants that the discussions were worthwhile. A new draft of the values document came out in 1987; anyone who compared it with older versions could see how the statements had changed.

Welch described the long process in a speech at the Harvard Business School:

> We went to the organization. We took two or three years to develop this thing on values . . . reality, candor, integrity, etc. We worked out every word. It was brutal. We

> talked to five thousand people at Crotonville. Now
> we have the words. . . . We're measuring our people
> against these values and now we're in the process of
> transforming.

Tichy never wanted to be a manager; that's one reason why he accepted the Crotonville job only for a two-year term. Nevertheless, by taking on the assignment he accepted the responsibilities of a transformational leader, with none of the cop-outs and escape hatches usually available to academics and consultants. The experience of helping reshape Crotonville, though admittedly small in scale, helped him better understand the larger revolution Welch was leading at GE.

Like Welch, Baughman, and so many others, Tichy faced stiff resistance. His way of dealing with it doesn't deserve the highest marks. To begin with, he shot himself in the foot by letting everyone know he'd be gone in two years: That encouraged resisters to try to wait him out. For true bureaucrats and company men, there exists a corporate equivalent of geologic time—and from that perspective, Tichy's Crotonville stint would be over in the blink of an eye. So they stalled.

During the early months at Crotonville Tichy struggled in particular with one person who reported directly to him. This person seemed unimaginative, and incapable of providing leadership for new initiatives. Tichy observed and worked with him for several months to make sure his judgment was sound, and gathered the views of others. Then he made a very tough decision. He went to Jim Baughman and made the case for removing that manager. Baughman considered the evidence and supported the decision. Then came the hard part: Tichy had to talk the decision through with the manager, take care of his outplacement counseling and financial needs, and help him find another, better job. The process took months, but ended well for all concerned.

By giving Tichy permission to replace that manager, Baughman signaled GE's commitment to the work Tichy was doing.

Everyone on the Crotonville team understood that ignoring him wouldn't enable them to avoid change. Unfortunately, such demonstrations of power seem to be an essential part of the transformation process.

But you can't replace everyone. In the end, leaders have to work with the people they've got. To define Crotonville's goals and shared values, Tichy held a series of off-site meetings with Crotonville's top five managers, trying hard to promote open debate. They would argue and compromise until they at least approached consensus.

It was at one of those meetings that Tichy finally confronted his biggest mistake as a leader. His colleagues were complaining about him with unprecedented bitterness. They seemed uniformly upset—allies and resisters alike. Tichy was pushing too hard, they said, *much* too hard. He was bulldozing people even when they agreed with him, alienating his own supporters. The clear message: *Back off, Noel!*

It became obvious that they were right. Much of the behavior Tichy had been interpreting as resistance actually was exhaustion. Crotonville was changing or adding so many courses so fast that its administrators simply felt overloaded. Every now and then someone would blow a fuse. Instead of understanding, Tichy would brand any sluggish response as resistance, and push doubly hard for whatever he wanted. Well, it didn't work. Belatedly Tichy realized that he was the person who needed to change.

Baughman and Welch took big risks and every time the Crotonville team needed backup, they gave it without hesitation. Ultimately, Welch deserves the credit for Crotonville's success. The operation has become a vital, central part of his ongoing effort to reshape the GE culture; indeed, its effectiveness in that role is what inspired Work-Out. After Tichy left, Chief Learning Officer Steven Kerr led Crotonville far beyond its modest beginnings, until it became recognized as the world's premier school for developing leaders. In 2001, the prestigious investment bank Goldman Sachs Group recruited Kerr as its chief learning officer.

The achievement of Crotonville is that it gave thousands of GE managers the benefit of hands-on learning. The combination of powerful stagecraft and an environment that deliberately encouraged risk-taking provided 10,000 people per year with experiences profound enough to change them. Today, those people are changing GE.

Chapter Twelve

The Politics of Speed

Only after five years of pushing technical change and consolidating his power did Welch dare to address the political problems he faced within GE. Then, in December 1985, GE eliminated the sectors—the layer of executive vice presidents who intervened between the CEO and the heads of the company's thirteen main businesses. That delayering enabled Welch to seize direct political control of GE at last.

Inevitably, a shakeout soon followed. Eight months after eliminating the sectors, and one month after closing the RCA purchase, GE parted company with the heads of three businesses. These events helped trigger a broader reshuffling of top management: By the end of 1986, GE had placed new leaders in roughly two-thirds of its main businesses. For the first time since Welch took office, the CEO had the luxury of deciding which person belonged in which job.

The sector chiefs had stood in Welch's way even though they largely shared his values. That's because the very existence of sectors slowed communication and reduced the integration of GE's businesses, allowing bureaucratic ways to continue. When you try to move information through layer after layer in an organization, it's like playing the children's game of telephone: The data get corrupted.

GE's new structure eliminated the twilight zone that had separated the office of the CEO from the operating units. So long as the sectors had insulated GE's business heads from one another, they could comfortably maintain values and goals that differed from the CEO's. But once in direct contact with the CEO, they could only agree or clash.

What's remarkable is that the CEO had waited so long, both to get rid of the sectors and to pick his own executive team. The RCA deal, by introducing more new executives to GE's top ranks than the company needed, had made some sort of rationalization inevitable. And it had seemed odd that a company that could eliminate so many tens of thousands of jobs should be reluctant to act against a few top managers.

Welch admits that he hesitated to move against the sectors:

> **I delayed fixing the structure for two reasons: First, I felt I hadn't been in the job long enough, and I didn't want to disrupt the place. And second, I liked the people. They were my friends—I'd put some of them into those jobs.**
>
> **The problem with the sectors was the structure, not the people. They were some of our best people, but they were stuck in impossible jobs.**

The sectors, in turn, prevented the CEO from directly observing the underlying businesses closely enough to be sure of his own judgments about their leaders. Says Welch: "The biggest challenge is to be fair. No one trains you to be a judge." But once the sectors were removed, the need for new leadership in certain businesses became glaringly obvious.

Welch saw no need for the sectors. Jones had created them, in 1977, partly to protect the CEO from a deluge of undigested information from the newly formed strategic business units. Sectors also provided a handy testing ground for Jones's potential successors; Welch himself had run the Consumer Products and Services sector.

The organizational structure Welch inherited was complicated. At the bottom were departments, which produced and marketed particular products such as refrigerators or circuit breakers. These departments were collected into divisions, the divisions were collected into groups, the groups reported to the sectors, and the sectors reported to the CEO. Within that operating structure, GE had superimposed the forty-odd strategic business units, which regrouped those same departments a different way for planning purposes.

Welch viewed all this complication as unnecessary. He already had shifted responsibility for strategic planning back to GE's operating managers. With years to go before his own retirement, he certainly had no interest in running another CEO horse race. And he gathered far less information than Jones, enabling him to oversee more businesses.

From the CEO's point of view, the sector organization wasted time and got in the way. As Welch explains:

> The people running the sectors had no power. Their role was transmitting information, so they acted as filters. They were in-betweeners, with no way of actually knowing anything firsthand. They would waste three days getting ready to come to talk to us. Then we would talk to them for one day. And none of us would know any facts! We would ask a question and we wouldn't get the answer. When I'd ask a question, they had to go check with somebody who knew—someone who was running a business.
>
> People think of delayering as a cost reduction, but it's really a way of enhancing management. We did a study that showed we saved $40 million by removing the sectors, but that's just a fraction of the real value. That doesn't account for the improved quality of our leadership, or how fast we can get to market now. Delayering speeds communications. It returns control and accountability to the businesses, which is where it belongs.

We got two other great benefits from the sector delayering. First, by taking out the biggest layer of top management, we set a role model for the whole company
about becoming lean and agile.

Second, we identified the business leaders who didn't
share the values we were talking about—candor, facing
reality, lean-and-agile. We exposed the passive resisters,
the ones who were right for another time but didn't have
the energy to energize others for the global challenges
ahead.

The first act of the GE revolution had come to an end. "Sometime
in 1985," remembers Dave Orselet of the Executive Management
Staff, "Jack began to feel that all the years he'd spent relentlessly
driving, pushing, screaming, and kicking were beginning to pay
off. I don't mean he was satisfied, because he never is. But he could
see that this monstrous ship he was steering was finally beginning
to turn."

Like it or not, employees were becoming accustomed to
change. Gone were the comforting orderliness and certainty that
once had defined their professional lives. Now hazard and risk, like
a low-lying fog, obscured the path ahead. Once-complacent GEers
were energized—but also frightened and confused. They could no
longer deny their need for leadership.

For Welch, this was the great opportunity that defined the second act of the revolutionary process. To seize it, he had to help his
organization define a new guiding purpose, a new set of rules—a
new vision. This is not something a leader can impose by fiat. And
Welch had nearly reached the limit of his ability to influence the
organization through unilateral, mostly technical, actions. The time
had come to deal with the political strand of the rope. Before the
CEO could lead GE much farther, he had to win GEers' allegiance.
Together, somehow, the leader and the led had to define a vision
that everyone could share.

The sectors had borne such a heavy load in the architecture of
GE's organization that eliminating them forced a radical redesign

of the whole corporate structure. To use Jim Baughman's imagery, GE had been organized vertically like a many-tiered wedding cake; henceforth it would look like a cartwheel lying on its side, with a hub in the middle and spokes radiating out.

The hub was the so-called "office of the CEO": Welch and Vice Chairmen Larry Bossidy and Ed Hood, plus Executive Vice President Paul Van Orden. The spokes were GE's thirteen main business units, which would now report directly to Welch or one of the vice chairmen.

The main effect of this new order was to empower the autonomous business leaders, the class of managers that included Roger Schipke of Appliances, Gen Hiner of Plastics, and Brian Rowe of Aircraft Engines. For instance, GE greatly increased their authority over capital allocation, one of the most important functions of management. In the old days, no executive below sector level could approve a major capital investment without going to the CEO. Now business chiefs have the same authority to approve investment as the CEO. When they need to spend more than they can approve themselves, they present their cases directly to GE's board.

The hub-and-spoke structure obliterated much of GE's lingering bureaucratic uniformity. Suddenly it seemed natural to custom-tailor compensation schemes and other policies to the needs of each of GE's wildly dissimilar businesses. Before long, variation became the rule. The effect, as Baughman notes, was to create organizational structures driven by the needs of the market rather than the bureaucracy.

Welch didn't want to entrust GE's operations to people who thought only of pleasing their bosses and meeting their budgets. Marketplace performance and leadership were the qualities he valued most. As he told a group of managers at Crotonville in 1987:

> **The world of the 1990s and beyond will not belong to "managers" or those who can make the numbers dance. The world will belong to passionate, driven leaders— people who not only have enormous amounts of energy but who can energize those whom they lead.**

Unhappy with the sector structure from the first, Welch had urged Don Kane of the Executive Management Staff to study GE's organization. In typically methodical GE style, Kane analyzed the effect of the company's management structure on the entire business, from Fairfield to the factory floor. He recommended eliminating the sectors on the basis of the data he collected, and in the context of a whole program of delicately interrelated structural changes. The basic theme of his argument applies to almost any company: Eliminating layers increases an organization's responsiveness to leadership.

Welch had been cautiously and very publicly testing the notion of eliminating sectors for years. When he took office, the company had six sectors. Carefully, delicately—probably too delicately—the CEO cut the number of sectors to four without attacking the structure itself. One sector vanished in 1984 with the sale of Utah International, the mining outfit; another, Services and Materials, was abolished when its chief, Larry Bossidy, became a vice chairman.

Kane was impressed by the experience of businesses that once had reported to sectors but now dealt directly with the CEO. Among them, Kane observed:

- Far fewer time-consuming requests for information

- Less time spent in the formal review process

- Much faster decisions

- Quicker, clearer communication

He proposed what he called a "next step in the evolution of our GE management system," defining a new collegial style of interaction to replace the old hierarchical ways. Kane cautioned that CEO edicts would only impede the process of change, and Welch eagerly accepted the point. He was already trying to build consensus through Crotonville debates and other means, but progress was slow. As he remembers, "We knew we wanted GE to move faster. We knew we needed people who represented the shared values. And we wanted to communicate faster and better with people."

Gradually, Welch recognized the structure of the GE organization as one of the major obstacles remaining in his way. When he became CEO, the most powerful resistance had emanated from some of the planners and business heads. By the end of 1982, GE had virtually abolished the central strategic-planning staff. The logical next step was clearing the sectors out of the way, to permit direct interactions with the business heads.

Under the old system, the CEO met with his sector chiefs every month. Spending all their time in the netherworld between the CEO and GE's businesses, these men were out of touch by definition. When they were unable to answer questions about the operations under their command, Welch expressed his frustration to them in a manner that made those meetings uncomfortable. Then, in time-honored GE fashion, the sector heads would turn around and "kick the dog," sharing their discomfort with the business leaders who reported to them. And then those executives would kick their direct reports, and so on down through the hierarchy.

Distanced from operations, the sector chiefs had no alternative but to focus on numbers and budgets. Every month, before their meeting with the CEO, the sector chiefs scheduled full-day performance reviews with each of their main businesses. Despite Welch's efforts to stem the collection of useless data, the sectors had routinely scrutinized business results in excruciating—and unnecessary—detail. The required reports compared a business's projections against its actual sales, with data segmented by market and by channel of distribution—the equivalent of an internal planning audit every month. Preparing reports for just one business's monthly sector review could occupy twenty people full-time for a week.

Line executives didn't go to these meetings expecting to learn anything. Their goal was to emerge from the ritual unscathed. After studying the sector structure, Don Kane concluded that it fostered a tendency to minimize personal risks, to volunteer nothing, and to restrict channels of communication. In such an atmosphere, Kane wrote, a CEO had few tools to influence the organization.

A high-ranking GE executive described another pernicious effect of sectors on the business heads:

> I think we would have accomplished more if [our sector chief] had just run the business himself. It's like a lot of things in life: You get used to the role you have. You begin to rely on the sector chief's involvement. You want to have him involved in your decisions. So frequently you would elevate the tough decisions to that level, one step farther away from your business. You'd gotten used to the mothering.

When he finally announced the decision to "delayer the sectors," Welch presented it as a necessary refinement of GE's organizational structure. He had no need to fire the sector chiefs, nor even to criticize them. One of the sector chiefs retired; the other three stayed on in big jobs. Paul Van Orden of the Consumer Products sector joined the office of the CEO as executive vice president. John Urquhart of International became head of the Power Systems business. Louis Tomasetti of Industrial Products took charge of Aerospace.

As executive coups go, this one was remarkably genteel.

Welch didn't understand until later the enormous cost of having tolerated the resisters hidden beneath the sectors. The business leaders who opposed the GE revolution were all fiercely loyal to the company. Their ultimate goals were identical to Welch's; they just disagreed about how to get there.

The resisters didn't need to take on the CEO directly: Their passive-aggressive behavior did at least as much damage as open opposition could have. They presented new ideas without enthusiasm, damned them with faint praise, and embodied the old way while feigning allegiance to the new. Some business leaders pretended to push the new program while behaving in ways that blocked it.

Feelings of vulnerability provoked many resisters. All three of the business leaders who lost their jobs in 1986 had been running once-prominent businesses that suffered marketplace reversals and deteriorating financial results. But unlike Carl Schlemmer, whose Locomotives unit faced even graver difficulties, these managers never fully faced reality. Well-intentioned but reluctant to change, they were right for another time, but unready for the intensely competitive late 1980s. Despite the CEO's efforts to help them transform their businesses, they had left many of their operating problems unsolved.

Taking away the sectors shone a spotlight on the attitudes as well as the performance of the business heads. It wasn't always flattering.

Some couldn't stomach constructive conflict. The *Wall Street Journal* called it Welch's "hazing-as-shouting-match approach, that requires managers to argue strenuously with [Welch] even if they agree." One of the three top executives GE replaced in 1986 later complained to the *Journal:* "You can't even say hello to Jack without it being confrontational. If you don't want to step up to Jack toe-to-toe, belly-to-belly, and argue your point, he doesn't have any use for you."

Others had trouble—to use Welch's phrase—"facing where we're going to be." One major GE business, which produced heavy machinery, was coasting on profits from its five-year backlog. It lost its technological lead to Japanese competitors, yet continued to price its products up to 40% higher than theirs. The unit's huge backlogs acted as a narcotic: During the early 1980s, as its orders began to drop, the business enjoyed the highest net income of its history.

By 1982 the CEO had seen that a major downturn was inevitable in that business. Bypassing the sector chief, Welch says he and Bossidy spent years "jawboning" the business's leader. They asked for cuts in investment and staff, with the goal of lowering both costs and prices. The executive appeared to agree intellectually, and did seek local tax breaks. But he ignored suggestions about downsizing and fundamentally repositioning his business. He made excuses for the "temporary slowdown" his unit was experiencing, and talked about the comeback ahead.

His backlog had begun to run out by 1985. As a "bridging strategy" to slow the loss of market share to more efficient competitors, the unit began to bid on projects at prices at or below their cost. The worst of these deals produced millions of dollars in losses, but the business announced the order with great fanfare, as if it were a major financial coup. The local city government and the unions saw nothing to celebrate: If GE was doing so well, they wondered, why the hell did the company need so many concessions? Larry Bossidy, to whom this particular business reported, saw nothing to celebrate either.

Before long, GE removed the business's leader, who had presided over the loss of several points of market share, leaving his successor no choice but to downsize the operation by thousands of jobs. Had GE moved sooner, many of those jobs might have been saved.

Once the restructuring was complete, Welch had allies, or at least like-minded people, in all of GE's biggest jobs. Bob Wright, who made a name for himself at Plastics, Housewares, and Financial Services, became head of NBC. John Opie, a star as general manager of GE's $1 billion-a-year construction equipment unit, moved up to a bigger job running Lighting. David Genever-Watling gave up a corporate vice presidency assisting Bossidy to head Motors. In all, the CEO picked new people for sixteen of GE's biggest jobs.

Eliminating the sectors and putting the new team in place drastically reduced the political friction that had been slowing GE. No high-level resisters remained. For the first time since Welch took office, the people who controlled the company—not just the CEO, but the executives who actually ran businesses—largely agreed about what they were doing, and why. It's amazing how much easier it is to run a company that way.

Chapter Thirteen

The New Order

I t sounds simple: Zap the sectors, pop the right people into the right jobs, and presto, your company runs like a charm. The reality isn't so simple. Don Kane, the thirty-year EMS veteran whose thinking helped guide GE's mid-1980s reorganizations, points to some of the subtleties:

> We were changing the entire fabric of the business—the management system by which the enterprise is orchestrated—not just some boxes and lines on the organization chart. Not only did the process change radically, but nearly everyone changed jobs concurrently. I'm not simply referring to those who switched to brand-new positions, but also the myriad folks whose titles and offices were unchanged, but whose roles were very significantly changed.

The purpose of any organization is control. GE's old wedding cake structure achieved control by brute force. At every level of the organization, managers spent professional lifetimes issuing and enforcing orders: from the CEO to the sectors, from the sectors to the business chiefs, from them to the heads of smaller and smaller operating units—and all the way down to the hourly workers who weld pipes or answer phones and don't get to boss anyone around until they get home.

When you think about it, this sort of hierarchy isn't much more complicated than "me Tarzan, you Jane"; simplicity is one of its main virtues. At GE, as at most American companies, the formal structure created an unambiguous chain of command that reliably kept the enterprise under control.

But as a side effect, it also shaped the attitudes and behavior of employees, often in destructive ways. People learned to do what they were told and not much more. They avoided conflict with their supervisors. They evaded responsibility, forcing their bosses to sign off on decisions they could have made themselves. Emotionally, the structure fostered a schoolyard sullenness, with bosses acting as disciplinarians and subordinates as kids. Open communication was almost unthinkable.

Once Welch decided that the old hierarchy was slowing the company down and limiting its competitiveness, he could not avoid fundamental organizational change. And no matter what new method of organization he chose, the CEO knew he'd be toppling dominoes by the thousands. That made the task of designing a better system dauntingly complex.

Getting rid of the sectors was not enough; the CEO needed something to replace them. Though troublesome, the sectors had helped bind GE together, encouraging a measure of unity among the corporation's otherwise independent operating units: Everyone was saluting the same flag (or, in this case, meatball). But what would unite GE's collection of largely autonomous businesses from then on? And what would induce GEers to start thinking for themselves?

The new hub-and-spoke structure didn't resolve those issues. Though it shortened the lines of authority, it was every bit as hierarchical as the old sector organization. Indeed, by making the business chiefs directly answerable to the CEO, the new order increased Welch's ability to dominate the corporation.

Far from uniting GE, the new organization seemed by its very design—a hub with thirteen spokes but no encompassing wheel or rim—to abet the centrifugal forces that have always threatened to pull GE apart. Relations among GE's business chiefs traditionally were cordial, but distant. They rarely saw one another. And these men were competitors, struggling against one another to win more capital, to win the CEO's favor—and perhaps one day to win his job. Now, without the sectors to impose a crude communality upon them, the heads of businesses such as Aircraft Engines might have even less reason to care about, say, a problem in Appliances.

Welch's solution, in 1986, was to create the Corporate Executive Council, or CEC. A group of GE's thirty highest-ranking business chiefs and senior staffers, it meets quarterly to discuss the most important issues facing GE, whatever those might happen to be at the time. The embodiment of Welch's ideas about leadership, this executive council has little overt authority and no clear role in decision making, yet has come to function effectively as GE's political center.

Two of the CEC's members are women. Joyce Hergenhan, vice president for public relations, works directly with Welch and is respected in her field. Hellene Runtagh, president of the $650-million-a-year Information Services unit, joined GE straight out of college in 1970 and worked her way to the top of one of GE's thirteen main businesses. She is one of six women who run GE operations with combined annual earnings of $220 million.

The CEC provides a structural context for the more collegial style of management Welch is trying to promote. It is also a device for indoctrinating GE's leaders in the corporation's shared values. The council's formal mandate is to share information, swap ideas, and help guide GE toward its goals. In practice, the CEC is a high-level think tank, where the company's best informed (and presumably most talented) people work together on issues of common concern. If the definition sounds fuzzy, that's partly intentional: A main purpose of the CEC is to build trust and kinship among executives who might otherwise be slitting each other's throats.

GE's executives are free to lead their own businesses, each according to its own culture and rules; but CEC members are always expected to subordinate their interests to those of GE as a whole. When Welch talks about his "team," it's more than a smiley-face metaphor: He expects these people to work together. Tichy once asked the CEO how he could possibly expect teamwork from CEC members. After all, GE's compensation schemes are designed to reward good financial results in any given business, without regard for behavior toward the rest of GE.

Without hesitation Welch shot back, "Yes, we reward them for performance. But they won't last long if they're not team players."

The CEC's gatherings take place at Crotonville, in a cozy little amphitheater called the Cave. Coats and ties are taboo, as are formal reports. When he isn't addressing the group, Welch sits amid the other executives, to reinforce his view of the CEC as an assembly of peers.

Fascinated by the architecture of social relationships, he thinks deeply about the design of the CEC's gatherings. Much as Walt Disney insisted on orchestrating every aspect of the Disneyland experience, Welch thinks it's essential to create a seamless environment to help the CEC fulfill its potential. He never stops tinkering, and no detail is too small to attract his notice, from the suitability of the council's agendas to the length of its coffee breaks. One early change was the addition of dinner speeches by outsiders he admires, such as Donald Soderquist, vice chairman of Wal-Mart, Wayne Calloway, CEO of PepsiCo, and management consultant Peter Drucker.

In the Cave, as in Crotonville's larger Pit, openness and candor are the rule. Says Welch:

We strive for the antithesis of blind obedience. We want people to have the self-confidence to express opposing views, get all the facts on the table, and respect differing

> opinions. It is our preferred mode of learning; it's how we
> form balanced judgments. We value the participation,
> involvement, and conviction this approach breeds.
>
> It works partly because people feel comfortable in a
> "pit." Everyone's close together. The people asking ques-
> tions are looking down at the speaker. Somehow that
> opens up the questioning.

The wide-open debating style that Welch calls constructive
conflict illuminates more than ideas: It reveals the participants
themselves. If someone lacks confidence or interpersonal skills, it
shows. There's no place to hide, and snow jobs don't work. Unlike
budget reviews, CEC meetings are not meant to be combative, but
nervous executives and newcomers sometimes have found them so,
particularly during the CEC's early years. As one described his first
days on the council: "Boy, those are tough meetings. Really uncomfortable at times. Not a lot of fun. If you come there with a bullshit
synergy idea, Welch will nail you."

Welch insists the atmosphere isn't so tough:

> If you were a first-timer there, you might feel a little
> intimidated. But there's a lot more sensitivity. If someone
> comes the first time and doesn't have a good presenta-
> tion, everyone there feels it, senses it. But he gets a call
> after the meeting, not at the meeting.

During the earliest CEC meetings, some executives were
reluctant even to speak. As Kane remembers, "It was too much a
dialogue between Jack and other individuals." But over time, as
members got used to the process, the level of trust increased. "We
tee up a subject and then they take each other on," says Welch. "We
end up with a consensus." His relative youth encourages easy communication: With the CEO succession so many years away, CEC
members have little incentive as yet to play politics.

A typical session begins with a scene-setting talk from the
CEO: an overview of GE's current status and prospects, and a sounding of the big themes Welch wants to cover. Each member presents

a very brief oral report—rarely longer than ten minutes—on his or her business situation. From then on, loosely guided by a prepared agenda, the meeting is given over to wide-ranging discussions marked by profanity, jokes, and frequent interruptions.

The main agenda items usually concern either problem solving or the sharing of good ideas. Or sometimes both: In the late 1980s, for instance, Welch and a few CEC members became worried about signs of volatility in the U.S. inflation rate. In an enterprise the size of GE, the difference between setting prices that do or do not reflect the actual inflation rate can amount to a substantial swing in operating profit. Professional economists can't help much: Dependent on price data gathered on a quarterly basis, they are chronically behind the times. What to do?

Deciding that early information about price rises could be a valuable competitive advantage, CEC members agreed to start faxing data to one another about changes in the prices their businesses were paying for supplies. Precisely because those businesses are so diverse, that information provided a reasonably accurate, up-to-the-minute gauge of inflation, which individual managers used to adjust their prices. The CEC's informal fax network lasted six months. Then, once it became clear that inflation was no longer a serious threat, the faxes abruptly stopped—there was no need to institutionalize the practice. But the informal fax network has been revived several times since to pool information on other breaking issues.

One of the CEC's functions is to serve as GE's main nerve center, ensuring that good ideas—what GEers call "best practices"—get communicated throughout the company at lightning speed. If Plastics has come up with a great way to cut its insurance costs, or if Aircraft Engines has developed an effective employee-involvement program, the CEC is where they spread the word.

Welch wants a company characterized by "integrated diversity." GE's varied portfolio of businesses makes the diversity part easy. Finding ways to link all those operations, to integrate them into a whole with a distinct identity of its own, is infinitely harder. Without the CEC, GE probably could not have done it.

Sociologist Amitai Etzioni described three methods of organizational control: coercive, utilitarian, and normative.

Coercive control, the least effective type, is what you get when you point a gun at someone and tell him or her to do what you want. The method is alienating, and works only as long as you keep aiming the gun.

Utilitarian control—paying people to do what you want—works much better; it's the method on which most organizations still rely. The weakness of the utilitarian system is that your money buys labor but not goodwill.

Far more powerful is normative control, which relies on a system of shared values to direct behavior. Normative control is what induces people to devote themselves to a cause: An example is the religious missionary who might voluntarily work for years in a hostile environment for poverty wages.

No business can expect to be inspiring enough to rely exclusively on normative methods of control. Corporations exist to make money, after all, and smart employees will always want to share in the loot. Incentive compensation is here to stay.

Nevertheless, we are convinced that the most effective competitors in the twenty-first century will be the organizations that learn how to use shared values to harness the emotional energy of employees. As speed, quality, and productivity become ever more important, corporations need people who can instinctively act the right way, without instructions, and who feel inspired to share their best ideas with their employers.

That calls for emotional commitment. You can't get it by pointing a gun. You can't buy it, no matter how much you pay. You've got to earn it, by standing for values that other people want to believe in, and by consistently acting on those values, day in and day out.

GE's CEO is no sap: He pushes values because that's the way to get results. Delegating more of the control function to individuals—in effect, to their superegos—reduces the need for reports, reviews, and other external mechanisms. A boundaryless organization can achieve the same level of control as a hierarchical one—but at less cost, with less friction, and faster. As Welch told a group of senior GE managers:

> **You have to break down the walls that bind us and slow us down. You have to walk the talk. Never compromise. Go back and look at everybody you've got. Be sure they have the values.**

Welch remains very much the boss, controlling the CEC's membership and agenda, not to mention the salary and career prospects of every participant. But as the CEC has gradually transformed GE's most senior managers into emissaries of the corporate values, he has allowed their collective authority to increase—and spent less of his own energy giving orders.

Managing doesn't interest Welch much. Leadership is what he values, because that's what enhances his control over the organization. He devotes his considerable talents to orchestrating CEC meetings that inspire high levels of emotional energy in participants. To the degree that the meetings are exciting, challenging, fun, and useful, CEC members will emerge pumped up and ready to inspire the people in their businesses to new levels of achievement.

There may be no more efficient way to influence a large organization. Although the public attention that has been focused on Welch might suggest the contrary, his unique personality traits are not what make the system work. Any sizable company employs plenty of people capable of running meetings and interacting with other people with just as much brio. The trouble is that few companies have yet recognized the value of their executives' interpersonal skills, and so have not made them a primary basis for promotion.

GE cherishes those skills, and creates many opportunities for its employees to hone them. Each of GE's operating businesses now has its own version of the CEC, enabling every business leader to play the Welch role. Lower-ranking executives get other opportunities, such as serving as facilitators at Work-Out sessions.

The ability to relate effectively to other people in such settings has become a major factor in performance reviews. GE has begun to breed a new generation of leaders distinguished by the ability to elicit cooperation from others. When, years from now, they rise in large numbers to the company's top jobs, their example may redefine the art of management.

This much is certain: Although the CEC lacks much formal power, it has become a potent instrument of change at GE.

By design, the CEC is a workshop in GE's core values. As at Crotonville, ideas and stagecraft combine to create dramatic effects. Consider the impact of just a modicum of candor:

At CEC meetings, every member gets the details of every other member's quarterly financial results—and discusses them. If one business leader has a problem, the others will propose solutions. This is a startling change from normal corporate practice, in which open discourse about peers' operations is considered a grave breach of etiquette.

Sharing information of all kinds is an important aspect of boundarylessness. As the CEO argues, "Managers traditionally haven't shared information. Information was power, so they held it back. They saw their job as control. I see that as unproductive, a waste of energy." Giving everyone the same data at once speeds decision making and makes for better decisions. The information itself has changed the way CEC members think. Instead of focusing only on their parochial concerns, the line executives now observe the whole of GE from the same lofty perspective as Welch. They can't help but make better judgments.

Welch argues that shared information also helps create consensus:

> If you put a group of bright people together, and you give them the same facts, they'll come up with the same answers. This may not be true in religion and philosophy and a lot of other things, but in business you're dealing with a fairly quantitative process. It's concrete. It's simple. This is not rocket scientist work. If we all have the same information, we'll all come to roughly the same conclusions.

Finally, sharing information creates peer pressure that goads people to ever higher standards of performance. In the old days, GE executives were masters of obfuscation, using splendidly packaged reports and 35-mm slides to avoid the tough issues and snow their masters in Fairfield. But when you're stuck in a room where everyone knows everything, with no props at your disposal, you have to face reality. If your performance stinks, if you're avoiding a major strategic challenge, you won't be able to hide it. The result is openness, candor, and an incentive to produce real results.

The teamwork that the CEC fosters among GE's top executives has been tested by disasters. Among the most memorable was Appliances' $500 million compressor fiasco.

Back in 1981, Appliances had a problem. Borrowing an idea previously used in small air conditioners, GE engineers had designed an advanced rotary compressor to cool its refrigerators. Compared to GE's existing compressors, it would require one-third the parts, half the manufacturing cost, and far less energy to operate. On the other hand, the technology required parts manufactured to tolerances of as little as one one-hundredth the width of a human hair, creating considerable production risks. And the cost included a $120 million investment in a new automated factory. After much agonizing with executives from Appliances, Welch approved the plan to make the new compressors instead of buying them. In retrospect, it was the wrong decision.

According to a middle manager at Appliances, one problem was that frustrated managers there kept bucking decisions up to their bosses: "They were feeling kicked, and pushed, and shoved, and not appreciated. So they just said, 'What do you want me to do, boss?'—and it ended up going all the way to Jack." Says Welch, "With all the layers of approval we had then, no one had ownership of the decision. Ownership is essential."

When the new refrigerators appeared in 1986, people bought so many that GE's market share rose two percentage points. Employees at Appliances were proud of their technical achievements, too: The rotary compressors represented breakthrough engineering. And their new automated factory worked splendidly, turning out one compressor every six seconds.

Then, in July 1987, a rotary-compressor refrigerator broke down in Philadelphia. Soon, others failed, in Puerto Rico and elsewhere. Since these appliances were all covered by GE's five-year warranty, the failures soon came to the attention of GE engineers. Their preliminary investigation suggested that certain critical parts might be far less durable than expected—and very difficult to repair. The conclusion: Many of the new compressors might fail. Eventually, GE decided to replace them all, with conventional compressors purchased from other manufacturers.

In 1988, Roger Schipke, then head of Appliances, had to present this mess to Welch and the whole CEC. A few months earlier, he and GE's other business leaders had submitted operating plans that together would have increased GE's 1988 net income by some $500 million. Although Schipke didn't know it at that time, the pre-tax cost of dealing with the bum compressors would amount to considerably more than half of GE's projected earnings rise.

Here's how the situation would have played out in the old days, according to Welch:

> Let's say we have a disaster in one business where they were minus $30 million. The chief financial officer would call the heads of the other businesses and ask them to make up the $30 million.
>
> The heads of the businesses would say, "Why?"
>
> The financial officer would say, "Because this unit over here blew up."
>
> Then the head of the business would say, "Well, those guys are jerks. They don't know how to run the business anyway. Why are they causing me trouble? I hate them!"
>
> Everybody starts blaming the person who has the problem, and the organization gets very destructive.

But when the refrigerator compressors went bad, CEC members knew they would have to help make up the shortfall. So Schipke's problem automatically became their problem, too. Moreover, Welch has rigged the incentives to force teamwork. CEC members know he is always judging them on that basis, obliging even the most heartless CEC member to come to the aid of a suffering colleague.

So Bob Wright volunteered at one early meeting, "Ad sales are going well at NBC. Our earnings might be up an extra $30 million this year."

Offered Brian Rowe of Aircraft Engines, "Look, I think we may be able to help you by getting a dozen compressor engineers to take a look at that compressor problem." Implicitly, everyone knew that Rowe would pay their costs.

There was no need for Welch to get directly involved. He didn't have to prompt Wright, Rowe, or anyone else to offer help. The CEC members knew what to do.

After replacing more than 1 million defective compressors, Appliances survived, with its market share in refrigerators intact. Schipke kept his job (years later, he left GE to become CEO of Ryland Corp., a builder of single-family homes).

And GE's 1988 net income rose $471 million to $3.4 billion, not far off from plan.

The process has taken years, but by the early 1990s the CEC had become the power center of GE, influencing the company's direction more than any other institution. Though it lacks an explicitly managerial role, the council provides checks and balances to the CEO's authority that certainly exceed any that existed before at GE.

The real power of the CEC is subtle, stemming from its ability to educate. Welch explains:

> The enormous benefit we get from our meetings is that we end up being smarter than anybody else. It's not that we have a higher IQ. But after two days with the CEC, having to talk about everything from TV networks to the Indonesian economy just to understand our own businesses, we can walk out and talk to anybody at a cocktail party, and be the smartest guys in town. And we may not

be as smart as most of the other people there—it's just that we're exposed to so much more information.

During the 1980s there was a trend to break up any multibusiness company. Get rid of the diversity. Focus on a single thing. I think that if we didn't have the CEC, we probably would be unfocused. Diversity was part of the hand we were dealt. In the CEC we've found a mechanism to turn that diversity into our strength.

Chapter Fourteen

Getting Excited

W hen a business becomes productive," says Welch, "it gains control of its destiny." He continues:

In restructuring, you go through trauma, you bottom out—and then you start to see results. Once you get back to being productive, the jobs come back, you succeed in the marketplace, your profit margins rise. You were hurting for a while, but now you feel great.

Lighting is a classic example: It was a high-margin business that was drifting downward. It needed help. In 1986 we put a new man in there, John Opie, and he put in a new team, and they looked at everything, from manufacturing to packaging to distribution to incentive compensation. Three years later, Lighting had the highest productivity rate in GE, around 9%.

That was the breakthrough that showed everyone in GE how productive we can be. By accomplishing so much with one of our slowest growing businesses, Opie and his team broke the dam for the whole company. We put them up on pedestals, we talked about them at every company meeting.

High productivity was supposed to be limited to the exciting, high-growth businesses with new product lines. When the 114-year-old Lighting business got 8% and then 9% productivity, the myth was shattered. No one in the company had an excuse for not becoming productive. Everybody had to go to Cleveland to find out how they did it. And before you knew it, other businesses were getting 5% and 6% productivity rates.

We proved that productivity is not a matter of cut and burn. It has nothing to do with whips and chains. It's a never-ending process that's based on empowerment. It's what happens when you get people excited about finding solutions to their problems.

By 1986 the second act of the GE revolution was well under way. The era of large-scale cost-cutting, of mass layoffs and factory closings, had largely passed. The company had been awakened to the need for change, and Welch was beginning to shape his vision into words employees could understand. Throughout GE the emphasis shifted to the wellsprings of profitability: revenue growth and productivity. Revenue growth, perhaps the clearest demonstration of customer satisfaction, is essential to maximizing profits over the long term. Productivity is the best measure of efficient operation, as well as a potentially rich source of earnings.

Despite all the cutting and burning of the early 1980s, many GE businesses still performed poorly by both measures. Partly because the need to trim RCA's bloated 85,000-person organization had slowed GE's progress, the corporate productivity rate hovered stubbornly around 2%, the prevailing level in 1981. More disturbing, several key businesses, Lighting included, weren't growing their revenues at all.

GE remained a long way from Welch's goal of becoming "the most competitive enterprise on this earth." As the corporation's lingering weaknesses proved, cost-cutting and CEO edicts—what Welch calls "whips and chains"—were not, by themselves, the solution to GE's problems. What the company needed to progress further was positive leadership, based on vision and backed by real-world results.

Lighting, GE's oldest and traditionally most powerful business, was struggling in 1986, when Opie became its leader. Opie's predecessors had eliminated ten factories and 3,000 jobs, but the Cleveland-based operation's costs still were out of line, and some of its light bulb products were technologically out of date. Though still very profitable, GE Lighting was flabby and unready for battle. Yet it faced unprecedented attack from overseas, as Philips of Holland, Siemens of Germany, and myriad Far Eastern importers raided GE's traditional customer base with low prices and new products.

Though GE Lighting remained No. 1 in North America, its awesome market share was eroding from its accustomed postwar level of roughly 50%. The trouble began in 1983, when Philips bought Westinghouse, traditionally GE's main competitor in light bulbs. In that one stroke, the ambitious European outfit displaced GE as the world's leader in lighting. Philips lifted its North American market share from 5% to 21%—and then used that new clout to introduce fiercer competition to a marketplace that had been shaped by the easy give-and-take of oligopoly during the first half of the century. In 1986 Lighting's sales and profits dropped for the second year in a row. GE's market share continued to slide while Philips's increased. Unless GE Lighting radically altered the way it operated, further decline seemed inevitable.

Lighting needed a revolution of its own, and Opie, then forty-eight, was the right person to lead it. He's like a Boy Scout: clean-cut, clear-headed, well intentioned, and utterly self-controlled. Though his emotional range is much narrower than Welch's, and his need for control commensurately greater, Opie has proved he can be an inspiring leader.

His great advantage is the self-confidence that comes with success. An engineer by training, Opie spent part of his early GE career at Plastics, where he witnessed the effectiveness of Welch's methods firsthand. A member of the Welch team from the first, Opie rose fast to division VP in Plastics. Later, as head of the business that makes circuit breakers and other electrical controls, he launched a large-scale transformation effort. Then he got the Lighting job.

Once Opie moved to Cleveland, his confidence showed: Certain he knew how to put together a better business, he didn't hesitate to disassemble it first. When his employees screamed and howled, Opie remained firm, holding the organization together by sheer force of will until Lighting's improved performance in the marketplace finally gave people the reassurance they needed to carry on. According to Bill Woodburn, who then ran Lighting's business development and planning department, "John does not have trouble sticking to his guns. He doesn't have opinions, he has convictions."

Looking back on his tenure at Lighting, Opie defines two distinct periods:

During the first two years, he gained control and pushed change—restructuring management along functional lines, pushing for the productivity gains needed to lower prices, and trying to convince anxious workers that he wasn't going to sell or destroy their business.

Then in 1988 and 1989, as financial results improved, he worked on reshaping Lighting's corporate culture—building a team, indoctrinating managers in new ideas, pushing authority down the hierarchy, and establishing the tenet that productivity and product improvement are never-ending processes.

The essence of Opie's accomplishment, the quality of leadership that has made him a standout on Welch's team, is his ability to make believers of Lighting's disgruntled employees. He defined a vision of what they could accomplish becoming first the low-cost light bulb producer, and then the leading global producer. Then he helped them make that vision a reality.

* * *

GE's overwhelming strength in lighting ultimately became its greatest weakness. From the day in 1879 when Thomas Edison invented the light bulb until a few years before Opie arrived, GE Lighting's stature as the leading lamp producer in North America, where one-third of all light bulbs are sold, remained unchallenged. Comfortable at home, Lighting haughtily ignored the rest of the world until the middle of this century.

For most of that period, GE remained the world's most profitable bulb producer. But by ignoring opportunities for growth abroad, GE ultimately weakened itself and gave Philips its leadership opportunity.

North America used to be GE's safe fortress. Starting with Charles Coffin, GE's early CEOs were men who plainly preferred to avoid competition whenever they could. Taking advantage of GE's patents—which amounted to ownership of essential light bulb technologies—the company used cross-licensing agreements to form partnerships with competitors both at home and abroad that enabled GE to remain unchallenged in the U.S. market.

GE negotiated cross-licensing agreements with its major U.S. opponents, Sylvania and Westinghouse. In return for an exchange of technology, the smaller companies agreed to follow GE's lead. GE signed similar cross-licensing agreements with almost all the world's major light bulb producers. The effect of these agreements was to keep all signatory companies within the borders of their home markets.

Before long, GE controlled 75% or more of North American lighting sales, with Sylvania, Westinghouse, and a few small outfits squabbling over the rest. In his unpublished history, *Problems and Performance of the Role of Chief Executive in GE,* Jim Baughman explains that Lighting's strategy was to protect the domestic market rather than to grow worldwide.

To ensure that its influence persisted even after its patents expired, GE bought equity stakes in light bulb manufacturers around the world. By 1935, according to *Anatomy of a Merger* by Robert Jones and Oliver Marriott, GE owned 10% of Philips, 40%

of Tokyo Electric, 29% of Germany's Osram, 44% of France's Compagnie des Lampes, 34% of Britain's General Electric Company, 100% of China's Edison Electric, and more. In the ensuing decades, GE gradually sold off those stakes—a pity, since they'd probably be worth billions of dollars today.

The Justice Department tried several times to break up the cross-licensing agreements on the basis of antitrust law. But prior to two cases brought in the early 1940s, U.S. courts ruled in GE's favor. In a 1926 case, for example, the court reasoned that the agreements were legal so long as the profits derived from them were "reasonably within the rewards" to which a patent holder would be entitled. The 1940s cases ended with consent decrees that terminated the restrictive cross-licensing agreements and prohibited such agreements in the future. However, GE, Sylvania, and Westinghouse still benefited from the huge market shares that were the legacy of the prewar era, and all continued to prosper.

After World War II, GE's share of the North American market gradually drifted down to roughly 50% and then stabilized at that still handsome level. Meanwhile, the overseas markets Lighting was ignoring had developed characteristics as distinct as those of Galápagos fauna: European electrical power flowed at 230 volts, versus 100 volts in Japan and 120 in the United States; in Southern Europe, consumers picked light bulbs from bins, like onions.

In North America, sheltered from all-out competition, Lighting developed a distinctly complacent corporate culture, relaxed about costs and remarkably willing to pamper employees. In 1913 GE spent $1 million—an extraordinary sum at the time—building the world's first industrial park on a ninety-two-acre site outside Cleveland. In addition to a light bulb factory and a research center, the park offered a swimming pool, bowling alley, gym, tennis and handball courts, rifle range, and fields for baseball, football, and field hockey. The facility kept doctors and dentists on staff, and the park maintained its own bank for employees' convenience. GE even encouraged its people to linger at night, organizing activities from tap dancing and language courses to bridge tournaments and an instrumental band. Few could work there without developing a strong feeling of loyalty.

Bill Woodburn says that Lighting's culture of comfort endured:

The culture was clublike—fraternal to the point that relationships counted more than performance. If you were a part of the right group, you were pretty much protected. Your future was secure.

Protected by its rich stream of profits, Cleveland became the most autonomous of the Works. As a 1987 article in a GE employee magazine recalled, "Lighting's independence drove Headquarters crazy, and GE managers sent to change things were swallowed by the culture and went native, like, some said, the Jesuits in China." In this insular environment, Lighting's leaders saw little reason to change their ways. Nor did Welch push for change when he ran the sector that included Lighting. "The business was very profitable then," he recalls. "Short-term performance can hide many flaws."

But GE Lighting needed to change. Despite enormous unit volumes, it was on the way to becoming the high-cost producer of light bulbs. By 1982, the tentative incursions of overseas competitors had become an invasion, with companies from Hungary, Poland, Japan, Taiwan, Korea, and elsewhere pushing deeper into the North American lighting market. The quality of their bulbs had improved, the market was enticingly vast, and American consumers had amply demonstrated their willingness to buy imported products, from automobiles to TVs to cheese. The newcomers arrived with an unbeatable business proposition: good-quality bulbs priced well below GE's.

This price advantage was based in part on labor costs that GE couldn't match. While GE's workers in Cleveland earned $14.00 per hour, their counterparts abroad made much less: $7.00 in Japan, for instance, and $1.00 in Korea.

Once Philips bought Westinghouse, it fought hard for North American market share, and often won. The Dutch firm slashed prices, invested heavily in consumer advertising, and offered distributors cash or free goods as incentives to handle its products instead of GE's. Philips, which earned most of its light bulb profits elsewhere, suffered little from its expensive price war in the United States.

The cozy environment that had nurtured GE Lighting no longer existed.

Opie's well-meaning predecessors struggled mightily to cope with these unexpected threats. When Lighting's sales finally began to drop in 1985, they maintained profitability by raising prices. GE's opponents didn't match the increase. That left GE stranded with retail prices up to 40% higher than competing brands. The downward spiral began.

Realizing that their costs were too high, Lighting's leaders seized on automation to reduce them. The business spent millions installing three new Pro80 production machines, designed and built by GE itself. Each of these machines could manufacture 6,000 incandescent lamps per hour—roughly twice as many as existing equipment could produce. Within two years, Lighting's team avowed, the Pro80s would lower unit production costs 17%.

Realizing the need to trim costs further, they cut Lighting's R&D budget. That decision cost GE its leadership in new products, an important spur to sales growth. With higher prices and increasingly outdated technology, GE Lighting now had little to offer customers but a familiar brand name. That was no longer enough.

Lighting's weakness was revealed in 1986. Its sales declined again; this time earnings fell, too. The Pro80 machines went into operation, but they were plagued with design problems and operating bugs: It cost GE nine cents *more* to make a bulb with a Pro80 than with the older equipment. Lighting's productivity, which had dropped to zero in 1985, hovered around 3% in 1986.

Lighting decided to raise consumer light bulb prices yet again. Now some of its products were priced up to 50% higher than competitors', and Lighting's market share deteriorated faster than ever.

Then Opie got his turn.

Athletic and intense, relentlessly methodical and focused in pursuit of his goals, Opie is a manager in the Welch mold—analytical, decisive, candid, sometimes abrasive.

Here's how he assessed the situation:

I knew it was going to be a tough job. The business was much worse than it looked. It was on the skids and the numbers were only beginning to show it. The return on investment had dropped from 30% down to 20%, and was headed lower—but right then that 20% return on investment still looked very good. So I knew the reaction of the organization was going to be, "Why are you doing this to me when we're still doing pretty well?"

Though new to Lighting, he quickly defined his vision for the business. Abandoning his predecessors' insular approach, he articulated business goals in the context of a world market for lighting products. As Welch might have done, he boiled his thinking down to a few big ideas, which he called "drives":

- A drive to achieve the industry's lowest costs

- A drive to increase sales by creating new markets, much as GE Plastics had done

- A drive to lead the world in customer service, with sophisticated fulfillment and distribution systems

- A drive to regain leadership in product quality

Opie's push for productivity had the weight of inevitability. Achieving cost leadership had to come first, he knew. Progress toward the other goals would require substantial investment, and since Welch wasn't in the habit of funding losers, the only way to raise the necessary funds was by boosting sales. Later on, new products and new markets would help, but in the short term, the only way to increase sales was to cut prices. And that, in turn, forced cost-cutting, to avoid a sickening slide into unprofitability.

In effect, Opie was designing a scale model of the GE business engine. By lowering prices, he would goose Lighting's sales. Productivity gains would clear the way for higher profits. And the combination would create the cash flow the business needed to invest in its future.

He began by stamping out fires. He canceled all outstanding orders for new Pro80s, and set out to recoup the costs of the machines Lighting already owned. As he later explained, Opie discovered that what had appeared to be technical problems with the equipment were actually cultural problems with the people running it:

> We put foremen and manufacturing engineers on the machines instead of design people. Their orders were to stop running the machines for innovation and new ideas; run them for productivity and lower cost per unit instead. In 1987, they got the cost per unit down about 30%.

At first, almost everything Opie did aroused ferocious resistance. He abandoned the investment-intensive business of designing and manufacturing Lighting's own production equipment. In the past, Lighting made better machinery than outside vendors could supply, and the designs of its factory equipment became trade secrets that Lighting people guarded with fanatical care. But the Pro80 fiasco inspired Opie to probe for facts, and he concluded that GE's machinery was no longer the best available. By implication, the proprietary methods that GEers still treated with mystical reverence actually weren't worth much. Shutting down the production machinery operation saved millions of dollars, but caused an uproar.

Much of the opposition to Opie was rooted in misunderstanding. Employees viewed him as Welch's hatchet man, a characterization that even Opie accepts as fair. But many misjudged his intentions: Remembering the Housewares sale, they wrongly presumed he was preparing to sell Lighting, another treasured emblem of GE's heritage. Some old hands thought Opie lacked the necessary experience to change Lighting's established practices; they viewed him as ill-informed and clumsy, likelier to destroy the business than to fix it. Having observed Welch's exposure to similar criticism, Opie decided the only way to change people's minds was with results. Their complaints did not deter him.

In Opie's opinion, the resisters simply didn't realize how essential it was to lower GE's costs below competitors'. As he explains:

It's one thing to establish objectives. It's another to get people to believe they just *have* to reach them to be successful. Our prices were eroding, and they weren't accustomed to that. We weren't the cost leaders and yet everybody thought we were. So it took a couple of years for people to realize that we didn't have cost leadership, and that we weren't going to win if we didn't get it.

Instead of waiting for employees to catch on, Opie raced ahead with an ambitious, top-to-bottom restructuring of the whole organization. Like Welch, he's comfortable with complexity, playing the managerial equivalent of three-dimensional chess. His team devised a new structure that would not only cut costs, but also simplify and speed decision making and bring the business closer to its customers.

First, he merged Lighting's three P&L centers into one. Stephen Rabinowitz, who was Lighting's technology vice president, explains the principle:

We have a plant that makes wire, a plant that wraps the wire into coils, and a plant that assembles the coils into lamps. If I organize those as three separate businesses and optimize each one, I may not optimize the total.

But if I organize those three plants as a single unit, they can seek the optimum balance of opportunities. It may make sense to make a costlier wire—if it helps us produce a cheaper lamp.

Within the one large operation, Opie created a lean matrix structure of the sort popularized by Procter & Gamble. This flexible type of organization groups employees according to functions, such as manufacturing, human resources, and finance. Each functional group, such as the component manufacturing operation at Lighting, gains responsibility for serving an entire business. Linking the functions together are product managers, each of whom is responsible for a particular product, such as incandescent lamps. To get things done, people from different functions work together in teams; and to force those people into a customer service mentality, product managers are the team leaders. What's confusing about the matrix organization is that most people report to two bosses: a product manager and a functional chief.

The efficiency of the new matrix organization more than compensated for the disruptions it caused. The structure enabled Lighting to reduce seven layers of management to four. In all, the reorganization eliminated 700 white-collar positions. Sales per salaried employee increased 35% in two years, versus 25% for the hourly work force.

Almost everywhere the Lighting team looked, it found opportunities to cut costs and increase effectiveness simultaneously. When Opie arrived, Lighting's distribution depended on a system of thirty-four regional warehouses. At a cost of $35 million, Lighting closed them all, replacing them with nine modern facilities. Similarly, the team shuttered Lighting's twenty-six customer service centers, and invested $25 million in a single, state-of-the-art operation in Richmond, Virginia. "When you're at the other end of a telephone," Opie argues, "nobody cares where you're located as long as you provide the service."

Large measures like these generated more than half of the savings the team achieved. But Lighting's leaders paid as much attention to incremental changes as to quantum leaps. Much of the remaining productivity gain came from small-scale programs designed to get employees involved and reward them for success. Rabinowitz explains:

> Big programs are great if you win. But none of us wins all the time, and when we don't, it's painful. We began with a mix of two-thirds big programs—ones that required investments of many millions of dollars, big project teams, and years to pay off. We very deliberately shifted to two-thirds small programs—each costing a million dollars or less, accomplished by one or two people, and completed in a couple of years at most.

That permitted us to build up a momentum of success. Instead of having ten big programs, you'd have 200 small ones. Ten of them could miss and you wouldn't even notice. But the ones that work give you a very quick infusion of benefits. That helps you fund still more projects—and more important, it builds your confidence.

The Lighting team linked those productivity programs directly to employee compensation. Salaried workers became eligible for bonuses based on their individual performance, and/or the performance of the business as a whole. And every Lighting employee could claim a share of the benefit from suggestions he or she made to increase productivity. A program called Impact, for instance, passed on 10% of the savings from small-scale changes that cost an average of just $14,000 each to implement. A collection of seemingly inconsequential ideas—such as cutting a site's garbage pickups from twice weekly to once—quickly reduced Lighting's costs by millions of dollars per year and helped turn more employees into productivity devotees.

Not all the programs were trivial. Lighting saved big money by selectively purchasing more materials from outside vendors, some overseas. It substantially lowered manufacturing costs by reducing the number of components in its products. Standardizing product packaging created another big savings.

The final element of the productivity drive was Opie's call for "continual change productivity"—in other words, revolution as a way of life. Says Rabinowitz:

The good things that I do today, I fall in love with. So if you come tomorrow and say, "There's a better way," I'll resist you.

I'll say, "Hey, I just thought of that. They gave me a management award. They told me it was good."

So now I've become an obstacle. Somehow you've got to get me to say, "You're right, that's a great idea."

You've got to constantly keep adjusting the organization, so you don't allow those habits and assumptions to become entrenched.

The new methods worked. Within a couple of years Lighting was producing solid results as sales, profits, and market share all rose. Most impressive were the productivity gains: by 1987 Lighting's rate reached nearly 9%.

In a paradox familiar to students of revolution, Lighting's employees resented the changes that had made their business so successful. No one denied the financial success of Opie's strategy; but they had trouble accepting its cost. Between 1986 and 1990 Lighting trimmed more than 6,000 full-time jobs.

When the big cuts began in 1988, employees reacted with disbelief. GE Lighting was generating a handsome amount of cash flow. It was twice as profitable as Philips. No other Lighting business could match its return on sales. Bill Woodburn describes how people felt: "This wasn't an obvious problem like Chrysler in the early 1980s. Why ruin families and destroy lives when we are that profitable, and we are exceeding the industry average by multiples of three and four?"

Now that they'd achieved some success, many employees figured they deserved to relax. Opie remembers:

Questions continued to come up about when we would be through reducing cost. And I kept saying, "Never." Because if we stand still, the competition will go right on by us. Just to maintain our position, we have to keep pushing.

Few employees understood how much more their business still needed to improve. Everyone likes to pause after an early victory. Lighting's managers tried to explain, but the resisters felt too stressed out to listen. The cutbacks had reduced their staffs and resources, while the pressure to perform increased.

Nevertheless, as Lighting's results continued to improve, more employees became believers. Welch's very public enthusiasm about their achievements, the accumulating effects of all the productivity programs, and noticeably fatter paychecks all contributed to improved morale. After years of pushing and shoving, the Lighting team was finding more people who were willing to cooperate. Then came the biggest lift of all, and the biggest challenge: a pair of acquisitions that made GE Lighting a global player for the first time in its history.

In 1989 GE ranked No. 2 in the $9 billion world market for light bulbs, its global share trailing Philips's by only a few percentage points. Yet GE did hardly any business outside North America. In a competition with global players, matching and even beating their prices is not enough. You need access to their markets, for two reasons: first, to maximize your revenue opportunities; second, to weaken your competitors by attacking them in their home markets, just as Philips had hit GE.

After years of transatlantic meetings that led nowhere, Lighting's leaders finally snagged their first big overseas prize in 1989: a majority stake in Tungsram. This Hungarian lighting company suddenly went on the block as communism began to collapse in Eastern Europe. Bill Woodburn, then head of Lighting in Europe, and Paolo Fresco negotiated the deal. Although inefficient, Tungsram produced good-quality bulbs and had 7% of the European market—a nice addition to GE's scrawny 2%, and enough to push GE Lighting back to No. 1 status worldwide. Soon after, the same negotiating team enabled Lighting to buy the light bulb business of Britain's Thorn, which had 9% of the European market. Having accumulated an 18% share in Europe, GE has become a credible opponent to Philips on its own turf. In addition, Lighting has established many smaller ventures in India and elsewhere in Asia.

Going global is a long-term game, and GE Lighting is still learning how to play. With more employees outside the United States than any other GE unit, Lighting faces enormous challenges as it tries to integrate its far-flung operations. Opie admits that Lighting's European operations "are not exactly world-class income generators." Tungsram, in particular, presents a tremendous challenge for GE's revolutionary management ideas. Hungary's inflation rate has soared since GE bought Tungsram, nearly offsetting the benefit of a one-third reduction of the work force. Besides, this business had been run on socialist lines. Individual performance reviews were unknown. Management pushed for production volume, but didn't even track consolidated profits. In 1989, Tungsram's 18,000 workers produced sales of $300 million, while in the United States, 19,000 Lighting employees—a group only slightly larger—produced sales of more than $2 billion. Improving Tungsram's performance—despite the barrier of an unusually obscure language and in a country plagued by all the lingering ills of a Communist regime—surely will take years. By mid-1993, Tungsram's work force had been reduced to about 10,000 people.

Even with these continuing struggles, Lighting has become a demonstrably healthy business. Profits are rising at a respectable rate; sales reached $2.7 billion in 1992, have grown at a 7% annual rate under Opie, versus some 13% for GE as a whole. Lighting's culture is changing, and morale, at least in the United States, is back to normal. But the competitive environment doesn't allow for complacency, and globalization still presents a challenge substantial enough to preoccupy Lighting for years.

Chapter Fifteen

Globalization

W hile in France to attend the French Open tennis tournament in June 1987, Welch met with Alain Gomez, chairman of Thomson S.A., the largest French electronics company. During a half-hour conversation, the like-minded CEOs conceived a transaction based on a major evolution in Welch's strategic thinking. Although smaller in financial terms than the RCA purchase, this deal evidenced a much more important strategic change.

GE agreed to swap its $3-billion-a-year Consumer Electronics business, America's leading maker of TV sets and VCRs, for the Thomson-CGR medical-imaging unit, which was selling about $750 million of X-ray and other diagnostic machines annually in Europe. In addition, since the businesses were of unequal size, Thomson agreed to pay GE $800 million in cash.

This was one of the best deals of Welch's career—"a masterstroke," according to Paolo Fresco, the debonair, silver-haired Italian who rose from GE's senior vice president for international operations to a vice chairman in 1992. He later became chairman of Fiat, the Italian car maker. The TV set business, which GE sold at book value, was in trouble: Despite a 25% U.S. share, it ranked only No. 4 in terms of the world market, and was subject to frequent fits of unprofitability. "There's no room for third-tier players," Welch argues. "In TVs we were at the end of the whip: We'd have a good year, then all of a sudden TV would cost us $40 million."

Thomson-CGR was losing money, but it had over 10% of the European market for medical-imaging equipment—an entrée that the leaders of GE's Medical Systems business believed they needed to ensure long-term prosperity. Siemens and Toshiba had begun chipping away at GE's leading share of U.S. medical-imaging equipment sales.

While roughly half of all CT scanners, X-ray machines, and other such diagnostic equipment were sold outside the United States, GE Medical Systems—known as GEMS—made less than 15% of its sales overseas. The Milwaukee-based business's only major international outpost was a 75%-owned manufacturing joint venture with Yokogawa Electric Works, its former distributor in Japan. The venture company, Yokogawa Medical Systems, or YMS, combines GEMS' technology with Japanese miniaturization to make mid-priced CT scanners. Even with YMS, remembers John Trani, the head of GEMS, "We had a significant imbalance. It was clear that we had to become global."

So the Thomson deal solved two problems at once, greatly fortifying GEMS while eliminating a business that had never measured up to Welch's standards. And it increased GE's cash hoard to nearly $2.7 billion.

To GE's astonishment and dismay, the Thomson deal also provoked furious howls from the U.S. press. The financial and strategic aspects of the transaction attracted scant attention. But the passing of the venerable GE and RCA electronics businesses into foreign hands outraged many newswriters and editorialists. The earlier sale of GE Housewares to Black & Decker also had aroused protest, but at least the buyer was a U.S. company. This was a case of wounded national pride.

The *New York Times* ran a front-page story under the headline "G.E., A PIONEER IN RADIO AND TV, IS ABANDONING PRODUCTION OF SETS":

> The General Electric Company, bowing to unrelenting Japanese competition, said yesterday that it was selling its $3-billion-a-year consumer electronics business to Thomson S.A., France's government-owned electronics giant.
>
> The announcement that G.E. would abandon production of radios, which it had pioneered with the Radio Corporation of America in the 1920s, and television, where it had been one of the industry pioneers in the 30s, sent a shock through the nation's dwindling consumer electronics industry. Only the Zenith Corporation will remain as a major United States manufacturer of television sets and other video equipment.

The *Los Angeles Times* showed less restraint. It asked querulously, "Has GE's controversial Chairman John F. Welch Jr. sold an American birthright for the proverbial mess of pottage?" In a companion piece, the paper quoted an unnamed consultant who complained: "Here is a fabulously wealthy company with so much cash. So why isn't he pouring it into businesses this country can still compete in instead of throwing in the towel to the Japanese?"

The journalists seemed to believe that GE was radically out of sync with American public opinion; Welch thought the press was out of touch with reality. He believes the best way to project jobs is by beating the competition. That was the point of the rule of No. 1 or No. 2.

During the mid-1980s, GE abandoned the domestic context of this most basic strategic tenet. Previously, it had measured the competitive strength of its businesses by their position in the U.S. market. In 1987, Welch announced that "number one or number two, for us, refers to *world* market position." The predations of corporations that drew their strength from international reach had convinced the CEO that leadership in the domestic market no longer ensured success. "Somebody rewrote the script," as he later put it.

> **In the environment of the 1990s, globalization must be taken for granted. There will only be one standard for corporate success: international market share. Success within a particular country will not even guarantee corporate survival. The winning corporations—those which can dictate their destiny—will win by finding markets all over the world.**

Fortress America had become a trap. For nearly a century, GE's main opponent had been Westinghouse; now Matsushita, Philips, Siemens, Toshiba, and perhaps a dozen more emerging global giants were challenging GE's preeminence in markets from light bulbs to CT scanners to industrial turbines. As a GE employee magazine wrote, the huge size of the domestic market, the government protection of certain industries, and the lack of meaningful foreign competition had "delayed the onset of the need as well as the development of the skills needed to hunt in the global wild." What Opie said of Lighting became true for many GE businesses: "We felt that North America was a sitting duck."

Hordes of overseas companies were using mergers and acquisitions to bulk up. In 1986 Sweden's Electrolux bought White Consolidated of Cleveland, a leading U.S. major-appliance company whose products sell under the Frigidaire, Kelvinator, and Westinghouse brands. GE Power Systems faced tougher competition after two of its European competitors joined to form ASEA Brown Boveri, and then bought Combustion Engineering, a major American producer of boilers for power plants. The list goes on and on.

Meanwhile, new technology and increased trade were causing structural change. Computers, fax machines, and improved telephone service were reducing the difficulties of doing business on an international scale. The growth of intercountry and intercontinental trade was stitching together an increasingly integrated world economy. Companies that took advantage of these changes benefited from the savings of purchasing components and labor in low-cost countries, as well as increased sales volumes from entering additional markets. Over time, these global enterprises created their own international networks for distribution, communication, and so on, an infrastructure that further strengthened them vis-à-vis GE.

Once again, Welch was hearing the fearsome call of *change or die.* He responded none too soon—yet long before most Americans saw the need for a global perspective. Inevitably, Welch faced resistance, not only from GEers this time, but also from plenty of his fellow citizens.

In 1987, the year of the Thomson deal, GE was still almost completely preoccupied with its domestic market. Just 23% of its revenues came from outside the United States—one-third less than in 1981, when the Australian mining outfit Utah International had been a big contributor.

Most of the individual businesses suffered from the same made-in-America mind-set that had victimized GE Lighting. To be sure, Lighting's use of patent-licensing agreements to protect its home market during the early twentieth century was unusual; but nearly all of GE's operations had prospered without much consideration of the world beyond their country's borders. Few had experienced much direct competition from sophisticated corporations of global reach. Only three of GE's thirteen businesses—Plastics, Aircraft Engines, and Turbines—functioned on a global basis.

Until the mid-1980s, GE was under no great pressure to build its strength overseas. For most of its early history, the company's main strategy had been to protect and dominate the domestic market. As a result, what it called "foreign business" had averaged less than 8% of GE's net sales from 1892 to 1952. Jones clearly perceived the global opportunity and greatly increased the amount of business GE did overseas. He also chose a successor who had been doing business on a global basis since the 1960s.

As CEO, Welch did not immediately impose globalization on the rest of GE. Until as late as 1984 or 1985, the corporate revolution and GE's domestic problems preoccupied him, so he gave second priority to international efforts. Besides, he was convinced that the only way to make the strategy work was for each business to take responsibility for its own globalization, creating and implementing a plan appropriate to its particular needs. Having witnessed the failure of many corporate-wide policies, he believed that any cookie-cutter approach would be doomed.

One such failure was International General Electric, which GE disbanded not long after Welch took office. For sixty-three years this headquarters-based group had operated overseas businesses structured as mini-GEs. Fresco believes that many people misunderstood the decision to shut it down: "The organization decided that everything which was international was not interesting to the chairman," he says.

Giving autonomy to the individual businesses further slowed the process. In 1983, the CEO introduced the concept of "ownership"—the idea that managers should run their businesses as if they owned them. The idea was to replace bureaucratic, buck-passing habits with a willingness to accept responsibility. To give ownership a chance to work, Welch had to grant the operating businesses a large measure of freedom. And during his first years in office, before he established the CEC, most of GE's autonomous business heads had scant interest in globalization. Recalls Fresco:

**I think the real obstacle was the parochial mentality
of many businesses. They were thinking domestic. And
Jack had to abide by that.**

Moreover, Welch had a few reservations of his own, especially about Europe. Socialistic labor policies in Germany, France, Italy, and elsewhere drastically limited companies' freedom to improve productivity by laying off employees or changing their work rules. Such strictures are anathema to him. Even as Europe warmed to free-market capitalism and began to liberalize its regulations, Welch's concerns lingered.

The main incentive to delay, though, was the inherent difficulty of globalization. Achieving it, particularly at U.S. companies, requires a revolution. And the United States, for all its progress, ranks among the least cosmopolitan of the world's major economic powers, with a citizenry still largely ignorant of foreign languages and susceptible to isolationist urges.

Paolo Fresco urged his boss to act soon. The twelve nations in the European Community, known as the EC or Common Market, had agreed to eliminate most intra-European tariffs and other obstacles to trade with one another by the end of 1992. That would create the world's largest single market, with 337 million consumers. (By making Eastern Europe available, the collapse of the Iron Curtain has since greatly expanded the EC's potential size.) The agreement also promised to make European trade far more profitable, since EC nations had promised to cut back on wasteful regulations.

The opportunity seemed enormous, but no business could benefit from it without access to the European market. While the EC planned to lower internal trade barriers, it would maintain or even raise the barriers around its perimeter. That made 1992 a deadline for non-European companies: To join the club, outsiders had to transform themselves into Europeans—fast. For most of GE's businesses, that meant merging or joint-venturing with local firms, or buying them outright. But that was no longer easy, since everyone else in the world suddenly got the same idea.

Welch might not agree, but Tichy believes the urgency of the need to globalize struck Welch during a twelve-day world tour in May 1985. Accompanied by Fresco, he met with CEOs in Japan, Korea, and Europe. Many, such as Thomson's Gomez, were representatives of a younger generation of leaders whose attitudes matched Welch's surprisingly often. During a meeting in Europe, Olivetti chairman Carlo Benedetti told Welch, "Give me the best CEOs in the United States, and I'll line up the six best CEOs in Europe, and they'll eat your lunch globally."

Welch wasn't exactly intimidated, but he returned with a deepened conviction that the world had changed and the time to globalize was now. Here's Fresco's analysis:

He was exposed to a number of changes which had occurred in Europe. But more important, I think, he was touching hands with a new generation of business

leaders in Europe who thought the same way as he was thinking.

Adds Fresco, "A couple of years later would have been too late."

In 1986, the CEO began pushing hard for globalization. In CEC meetings, the corporation's vulnerability became a frequent topic of discussion, as Welch pitched the idea that GE had to become global to survive. To him, the idea seemed the obvious response to competitive reality; but certain businesses, such as Appliances, initially resisted. Sincerely believing their markets were not global, they figured that remaining best-of-class in the United States was good enough. Building a consensus took time.

The real resistance came from much farther down in the hierarchy. As Welch admits, "The lower you are in the organization, the less clear it is that globalization is a great idea." Fresco describes the plight of a typical Medical Systems employee after the merger with Thomson-CGR:

> **Globalization is to certain people a threat without rewards. You look at the engineer for X-ray in Milwaukee and there is no upside on this one for him. He runs the risk of losing his job, he runs the risk of losing authority—he might find his boss is a guy that does not even know how to speak his language.**

Moreover, for any organization accustomed to domestic success, the introduction of global standards of performance can be deeply threatening. It's a classic example of what Welch calls "raising the bar": demanding a higher level of performance than was ever expected before.

In addition to the complex issues of language and culture, going global requires massive transformations in the way a company does business and measures success. As in domestic competition, only a few top-ranked players can expect to prevail in a global marketplace. Winners must achieve best-of-class status in four areas:

• **Products and services:** Offering the world's best design and technology at the world's best prices.

• **Organization:** Integrating worldwide purchasing, manufacturing, distribution, and marketing networks. Balancing economies of scale with responsiveness to the particular needs of local markets. Institutionalizing learning and communication processes to enable the organization to adopt new techniques quickly.

• **Human resources:** Developing a cadre of cosmopolitan executives marked by what GE calls "global brains": the ability to understand and respect the national and ethnic biases of others, and to feel comfortable anywhere in the world.

• **Alliances:** Finding ways to cooperate with other companies—sometimes even competitors—who can help you quickly surmount trade barriers and other obstacles.

Facing challenges such as these—and having paused to win the agreement of CEC members—the CEO couldn't wait for everyone else in GE to catch on to the need for globalization. The 1992 deadline loomed.

The remaining opportunities to expand overseas were few, and often hotly contested. Welch pushed every business leader to identify potential partners and propose deals, in the Orient as well as in Europe. As he likes to say, business is simple. In each of GE's major lines, only a few companies—rarely more than five—rank as serious global contenders. And within any given country, the important producers of a particular product, whether appliances or gas turbines, are easy to identify. So in a very short time, GE's business leaders defined their main globalization opportunities and set their number-crunchers to work pricing potential deals. They soon knew exactly what they wanted and how much they were willing to pay.

The Thomson-CGR deal is a perfect example of planful opportunism in action. As the Prussian strategist von Moltke had advised, Welch established a clear general goal—globalizing every

GE business—while remaining flexible and open to serendipity about how to reach it. When the opportunity appeared, GE was ready to move fast. Welch explains:

> We didn't need to go back to headquarters for a strategic analysis and a bunch of reports. Conceptually, it took us [Welch and Gomez] about thirty minutes to decide that the deal made sense, and then a meeting of maybe two hours with the Thomson people to work out the basic terms. We signed a letter of intent in five days.

The easiest part was the decision to sell Consumer Electronics, known within GE as Consumers. Welch had never liked selling TV sets, a low-margin commodity business in which GE remained a global also-ran even after the RCA acquisition. GE sold VCRs (putting its meatball on machines made in Japan), but had seen margins erode in that line, too. Welch bitched and moaned about Consumer Electronics' frequent losses but was powerless to prevent them.

The situation demonstrates why the CEO decided that GE must be No. 1 or No. 2 on a global basis. Even though Indianapolis-based Consumer Electronics was the U.S. market leader, it couldn't control its destiny. The world's biggest producer, Matsushita, boasted the industry's lowest costs and unit volumes much larger than GE's. Taking advantage of its edge, Matsushita kept pushing prices down. That left GE with the nightmarish choice of having to give up either market share or profitability.

GE probably could have lifted itself to a No. 1 or No. 2 market position through acquisitions. But since even the top manufacturers were losing money on TV sets, Welch saw no sense in increasing GE's commitment. He preferred to put GE's money into profitable businesses such as medical equipment, in which the company had the advantages of technological and financial strength. Selling Consumer Electronics was the obvious solution. The trick was finding a buyer.

Medical Systems, meanwhile, was facing many of the same problems as many old-line GE businesses. Despite its high-tech image, the GE unit had been making X-ray machines since 1920. For years after it introduced CT scanners in the mid-1970s, GEMS kept the rich U.S. market largely to itself, and prospered. In 1981 GE negotiated the Yokogawa joint venture. YMS could produce some scanners for considerably less than GE's Milwaukee plant, while providing an entrée into the Japanese market.

GEMS faced its first real challenge in the mid-1980s, when hospitals and other health-care providers introduced new measures to control costs. The rules cut the market for CT scanners in half almost overnight. At the same time, Siemens and Toshiba introduced good-quality scanners at competitive prices. One GEMS marketing manager remembers encountering Toshiba at a trade show:

> **I came back and made a report that said in five years Toshiba would be a major competitor. To the product representative I said, "If the Japanese are half as good in medical as they are in automobiles, we're in big trouble."**

When Trani arrived at GEMS in 1986, the business was losing ground globally. Impressed by the productivity of the joint-venture plant in Japan, GE boosted its ownership share of YMS from 51% to 75%. He realized that GEMS also needed to expand in Europe, where its presence was very small. Remembers Trani:

> **We started to ask, "Where is the market?" We told Jack that our position in Europe was not terrific, especially in X-ray. Outside the United States, we had just a 3% share of X-ray. We knew there were certain medium-sized players who might be viable, and Thomson-CGR was one of them. So when the opportunity presented itself, we were ready.**

Welch and Fresco spent several months trying to buy Thomson-CGR. But Gomez didn't want to sell—until he came up with the idea of swapping it for Consumer Electronics. The deal left both parties with stronger businesses. Thomson moved from the back of the pack to No. 2 among the world's TV-set producers, while GEMS moved from No. 2 in diagnostic imaging equipment to No. 1.

Corporations rarely achieve globalization in a single, dramatic stroke like the one that transformed GEMS. In 1993, GE was still struggling, business by business, to grow stronger overseas while improving the organization of what it had already got. It was no longer simply a domestic company, but not yet completely a global one either. GE lost a good part of its non-U.S. sales when it sold Utah International; since then, non-U.S. revenues have more than doubled, to $16 billion.

As the pieces fell into place, the importance of the soft issues became more obvious. Ninety percent of GE managers were U.S. citizens. Some were extremely sophisticated; others were middle-American engineering types. As Welch acknowledged, building a cadre of managers with "global brains" ranked among his most substantial challenges.

Inducing GE's most talented executives to move overseas wasn't always easy. While international stints were a requirement for advancement at Plastics and, increasingly, Medical Systems, executives at some other businesses saw them as a waste of time. If the real action was happening in the United States, that's where managers wanted to be. To fight that tendency, Welch encouraged CEC members to give more big jobs to GEers who had completed overseas stints, in order to create success stories of "people who went overseas and came back and did well."

Crotonville courses also played a role in creating a new breed of global managers at GE. Crotonville routinely sent GE executives on learning assignments overseas, and built teams of managers from around the world.

As with Work-Out or any other ambitious project of cultural change, globalizing GE probably took a decade or more. There's still a very long way to go, but as overseas revenues grew and more GEers became accustomed to the new way of thinking, the rate of progress accelerated.

By the year 2000, Welch was able to report, "Globalization has transformed a heavily U.S.-based company to one whose revenues are now 40% non-U.S. Even more importantly, it has changed us into a company that searches the world, not just to sell or to source, but to find intellectual capital: the world's best talent and greatest ideas."

Act Three

REVOLUTION AS A WAY OF LIFE

Chapter Sixteen

Work-Out

One warm September afternoon in 1988, Welch emerged again from the Crotonville Pit in a state of intense frustration. For the zillionth time, a bunch of middle managers had bombarded him with complaints about the way things worked at their local GE outposts. Stripped of particulars, the grievance was always the same: The speaker believed in GE's shared values, but his or her boss didn't.

The CEO kept hearing comments like these over and over:

The goal of downsizing and delayering is correct. The execution stinks. The concept is to drop a lot of less-important work. But this just didn't happen. We still have to know all the details, we still have to follow all the old policies and systems. We have no time, and more demands than ever.

Or:

If this is the best business in the world, why do I go home feeling so miserable?

Nearly eight years after Welch had become CEO, he knew that far too many GE managers still weren't "walking the talk." By almost any other measure the GE revolution had made enormous progress: The corporate productivity rate, for instance, finally had broken into the 4% to 5% range, roughly twice its previous level. Welch was basically satisfied with GE's portfolio of businesses, and the worst of the layoffs had ended long ago. Progress was visible almost anywhere you looked, resistance had become rare—and yet they still lingered, these unimaginative, frightened, bureaucratic bosses-from-hell, the ones who demanded that fewer people do everything that once had been done by many more. These were the managers or supervisors who snored through the videos of Welch's speeches, then pushed their subordinates to work weekends and nights under intolerable pressure, with no end in sight, often to accomplish tasks that seemed irrelevant, senseless, or worse. When anyone complained, they blamed Fairfield.

Welch had to find a way to get past those people, to directly touch the great mass of GE employees. The boundaryless organization he envisioned couldn't work without the active participation of the whole work force—but he couldn't expect people to participate in something they didn't understand. How to reach them?

On that particular day in 1988, the GE revolution reached its turning point. Welch suddenly experienced an epiphany that enabled him to embody his whole understanding of business in a single, very practical idea. It was a big idea, the sort of transforming thought that comes along only once or twice in a lifetime.

Walking with Jim Baughman to the helicopter that would fly them from Crotonville back to Fairfield, the CEO was angry enough to pound nails with his fist. He'd been hearing the same complaints from GEers for years; unless something changed, Welch feared, he'd still be listening to the same broken record when he reached retirement age. Remembers Welch:

I got in the helicopter, and I said to Jim, "I must have had to say 'I don't know' about twenty times today, or 'That's not my job, that's your job,' or 'I'm sorry, I don't know why you do that stupid thing, and why you don't fix this.' It wasn't much of a learning experience."

And so finally I said, "Jim, we've got to change this. We've got to get these issues dealt with. We've got to put the person who knows the answer to these frustrations in the front of the room. We've got to force leaders who aren't walking the talk to face up to their people."

That was the start of Work-Out. The idea was nothing more than trying to re-create Crotonville in a thousand different places.

Baughman designed Work-Out to Welch's specifications: an ambitious, ten-year program that Harvard Business School professor and GE consultant Len Schlesinger has called "one of the biggest planned efforts to alter people's behavior since Mao's Cultural Revolution."

Welch's desire to make believers of GE's middle managers was based on pragmatism as well as passion. By 1988, as he often said, GE had done about all the slashing and burning it could do. Although in certain areas GE still lagged behind such productivity champions as Toyota, Honda, and Canon, it had largely matched or exceeded the achievements of its direct competitors. At that level of accomplishment, just maintaining GE's productivity rate required enormous effort.

And Welch still believed GE had to improve. As he later wrote, "Without productivity growth, it is possible to lose in twenty-four months businesses that took a half-century, or a century, to build. Productivity growth is essential to industrial survival."

By 1988 GE's top-level executives understood Welch's ideas, and embraced them. The Corporate Executive Council had become an effective mechanism for pushing shared values; CEC members were accustomed to mining good ideas in one part of GE, and moving them quickly to the rest of the company. The CEC, in turn, had spawned similar councils at all of GE's thirteen major businesses, engaging another layer of executives in the new style of management.

But as the complaints at Crotonville indicated, managers farther down in the organization were far less likely to share the new GE values. Middle- and lower-level managers still did not see any urgent need to change. Despite delayering, GE still had a substantial hierarchy; a few levels down in most GE businesses, junior managers were still filling out unneeded reports, taking superfluous measurements, and coping with draconian goals.

Although Welch's ideas were clear, his communication methods still weren't effective enough to change people's minds. In one way or another, the police, media, and schools all failed him. The police (financial controls) could deal only with such technical matters as budgets and plans; the schools (Crotonville) lacked the capacity to affect enough people. As for the media, Welch said:

> I learned pretty early on that videotapes and speech reprints alone are of little value. Because people don't use them. They're not alive or dynamic. The idea is to convene a group, use the videotape [of a Welch speech] as a catalyst, and then have a discussion. Well, what managers would do is just show the tape. There would be no communication with the people. Nobody talked to them.
>
> Worse than that, with their body language some would communicate their own reaction to the tape—that it was bullshit.

Welch identified the problem in a tersely worded memorandum he wrote to CEC members a few months before his fateful helicopter ride with Baughman. The memo started off with a statement of the problem: "Disconnect between CEO and middle management on what CEO says and what middle managers feel." Among the possible causes he suggested was this: "Business leaders like the hierarchical system. . . . They don't want to buy in." In other words, resistance.

The memo lists and rejects two possible solutions: changing the corporate message, or eliminating it. In both cases Welch's response begins with a telegraphic "Don't want to." Finally, on page five, Welch arrives at the solution he recommends:

1. Buy into Corporate message. If cannot: Come and talk to any of us [Welch or the vice chairmen] about what bothers you and what you would like to change/ modify. We can/will react to what is troublesome.

2. After buying in, sit with all direct reports and dialogue about Corporate message. Invite us to participate, as you see fit, in sharing the Corporate message with your direct reports.

3. Ask your direct reports what they can buy into—and what they can't. Dialogue to achieve consensus on Corporate message. Use examples and illustrations pertinent to your business.

4. Have each of them meet with their direct reports—and you participate. Then bring it to the next level until every manager in the Company has met with his/her leader— and if they are troubled, see you.

5. Devote some time—at each staff meeting, at each level— to discussing progress in support of the Corporate message. One-time announcement/discussion will not achieve intended result.

THE OBJECTIVE IS TO HAVE EVERY PERSON IN THIS COMPANY BE EXPOSED TO AND HAVE A DIALOGUE ON THIS CORPORATE OPERATING OBJECTIVE AND ITS SUPPORTING MESSAGES BY JULY 1, 1988.

The idea excited Welch, but his July deadline came and went without much action. A few CEC members took his memo to heart, but most dawdled or simply forgot about it. The hoped-for transformation never happened.

The CEO was fed up, both with the issue and his inability to resolve it. "One of the things we can't do as top management is solve local problems," he admits. That's why Welch had been preaching liberation and empowerment and responsibility for years: He wanted local people to find their own solutions.

To illustrate what he was up against, Welch tells the story of a typical question-and-answer session that took place at GE Plastics' factory in Holland:

> This engineer says to me, "The plant is nothing like it used to be. It's nowhere near as much fun as it was ten years ago. What the hell are you going to do about it?"
>
> I looked at him and said, "Let me tell you what I'm going to do. I'm leaving for Paris in about thirty minutes and I won't be back within a year, maybe two years. So, personally, I'm going to do very little about it.
>
> "Why don't you get fifty people who were here ten years ago, and why don't you, for the next two and half days, go and write down, in the left-hand column, why it was fun before? And in the right-hand column, put down why it isn't fun now. And then why don't you fifty people change it and move everything back to the left side, so you're having fun again. Because you're the only people who can do it."

As Welch will cheerfully concede, the intellectual underpinnings of Work-Out, from worker involvement to continuous improvement, are concepts familiar to the point of being shop-worn. The uniqueness of the program is its vast scale, evidence of GE's commitment: By mid-1993, more than 200,000 GEers—85% of the work force—had experienced Work-Out. As of early 2001, nearly every employee has been through Work-Out, and elements of the program are incorporated into new employee orientations. Within just a few years, Work-Out had touched almost every single person at GE. By contrast, Crotonville programs annually can reach just 10,000 people, an elite 4% of the corporate population. In 1999, GE began an additional round of company-wide Work-Out programs designed to rid the company of new bureaucracy.

A mechanism to change minds, Work-Out is designed to deliver the Crotonville experience to the great mass of GE employees. Crotonville can powerfully affect those who go there, but it can't touch those who hear about it second-, third-, or fourth-hand, because the experience depends on personal participation. You've got to be there. In the Pit, employees directly confront the CEO. In workshops, they learn by doing. People get emotionally involved. They grow.

Trying to replicate that rich experience for 300,000 people was like trying to design a mass-market Rolls Royce, but GE found a way. Work-Out began with four major goals:

• **Building trust:** GEers at all levels had to discover that they could speak out as candidly as CEC members do, without jeopardizing their careers. Only then would GE get the benefit of its employees' best ideas. Welch regarded this goal as so important that he allowed the program to proceed for years without proof that it was working.

• **Empowering employees:** The people closest to any given task usually know more about it than their so-called superiors. To tap workers' knowledge and emotional energy, the CEO wanted to grant them much more power. In return, he expected them to take on more responsibility. "There's both permission and obligation," he says.

• **Elimination of unnecessary work:** The quest for higher productivity was only one reason for pushing this goal. Another was the need to provide some relief for GE's overstressed workers. And Welch hoped to show employees some direct, tangible benefits from Work-Out, to generate enthusiasm for the program.

• **A new paradigm for GE:** Ultimately, the CEO wanted Work-Out to define and nurture a new boundaryless organization. The process was analogous to the way Crotonville participants defined GE's shared values, but the scale was much larger. In effect, Welch wanted the whole organization to participate in defining itself.

Once Baughman designed Work-Out, he formed a small GE team at Crotonville to implement it. He retained two dozen outside consultants, all world-class experts on organizational change. Each was assigned to work with the top management team of a GE business to implement the generic design and tailor it to specific needs. Baughman and his Crotonville team, responsible to Welch, led the company-wide effort. Their role was to integrate the Work-Out activities of the GE units and their consultants, and to facilitate the sharing of best practices throughout GE. Tichy was one of the outside consultants Baughman retained. He assigned Tichy to Medical Systems because the consultant was already involved in a program there called the New Way Workshop.

Work-Out began in October 1988. The first stage was a series of local gatherings patterned after New England town meetings. In groups of 30 to 100, the hourly and salaried employees of a particular business would spend three days at an off-site conference center discussing their common problems. No coats. No ties. The setting and behavior were so different from business as usual that Work-Out consultant Steve Kerr called these meetings "unnatural acts in unnatural places."

To ensure that people could speak candidly without fearing retribution, bosses were locked out during discussion times. And Welch made it clear to managers that he would treat any obstruction of Work-Out as "a career-limiting move." Facilitators, all outside consultants at first, ran the workshops.

Meeting in small groups, the employees would define problems and develop concrete proposals. On the final day, the bosses would return. According to Work-Out's rules, they had to make instant, on-the-spot decisions about each proposal, right in front of everyone. Some 80% of proposals got immediate yes-or-no decisions; the remainder that needed study had to get decisions within a month. As Welch had hoped, the process quickly exposed those GE managers who didn't "walk the talk."

At first, people spent much of their time griping. In his 1991 story on Work-Out, *Fortune*'s Thomas A. Stewart quoted an electrician from Aircraft Engines' Lynn, Massachusetts, plant, who explained, "When you've been told to shut up for twenty years, and someone tells you to speak up—you're going to let them have it."

But in the course of complaining, GEers also would identify lots of problems that could be fixed without too much effort. As Opie and Rabinowitz had demonstrated in their productivity drive at Lighting, picking such "low-hanging fruit," as GEers call it, is a way to build momentum and trust in a hurry. A middle manager at Appliances tells how the Work-Out process worked at one plant there:

> We were getting screws from one supplier that was not so good. The bits would break off the screw heads, and scratch the product, and cut people's hands—we had one guy get eighteen stitches. Tempers flared, but management never went and fixed it. They said, "Okay, we'll go get you some screws from the good supplier." But then the bad screws would always reappear.
>
> So a shop steward named Jimmy stood up at Work-Out and told the story. This guy was a maverick, a rock thrower, a naysayer. He wanted to test us, to see whether we really wanted to change.
>
> He knew what he was talking about. And he explained the solution, which had to do with how deep the bit could be inserted into the screw head, and also the point contour on the screw.
>
> We listened, and then said, "Okay, what do you suggest?"
>
> And he replied, "We need to go tell the supplier what the problems are."
>
> Well, I was nervous about it, but I decided to charter a plane to fly Jimmy and a couple other guys to the plant in Virginia where they made the bad screws. They left that very night.
>
> Jimmy got the problem fixed, and it sent a powerful signal to everyone here. He became a leader instead of a maverick, simply because we gave them the forum and

allowed him to have some ownership. Now we don't even have supervision in his part of the plant. He carries a two-way radio, and if he needs help he asks for it.

As the GE revolution progressed, the pace of change continued to accelerate. Act I lasted until 1985; just three years later Act II began. By 1988 Welch had clearly defined his vision. Through trial and error, he had reduced it to a few simple ideas: integrated diversity, boundarylessness, global leadership, the business engine. In technical and political terms, GE already was largely transformed; the time had come to change its corporate culture.

Preeminent among Welch's ideas is boundarylessness. Here's how the CEO described it in an annual report:

Our dream for the 1990s is a boundaryless Company, a Company where we knock down the walls that separate us from each other on the inside, and from our key constituencies on the outside. The boundaryless Company we envision will remove the barriers among engineering, manufacturing, marketing, sales, and customer service; it will recognize no distinctions between "domestic" and "foreign" operations—we'll be as comfortable doing business in Budapest and Seoul as we are in Louisville and Schenectady. A boundaryless organization will ignore or erase group labels such as "management," "salaried," or "hourly," which get in the way of people working together. A boundaryless Company will level its external walls as well, reaching out to key suppliers to make them part of a single process in which they and we join hands and intellects in a common purpose—satisfying customers.

This is an admittedly grand vision, requiring unprecedented cultural change, and we are nowhere near achieving it. But we have an idea of how to get there—an idea that is rapidly becoming reality across the Company. It's called Work-Out.

Only through boundarylessness, Welch argued, could the corporation reach its productivity goals. But even for a much-changed GE, boundarylessness remained a challenging proposition. It implied much more than just eliminating bureaucracy: "Ultimately," Welch said, "we're talking about redefining the relationship between boss and subordinate." He envisioned the replacement of hierarchy with cross-functional teams, the transformation of managers into leaders, and a radical empowerment of all the workers who were still getting bossed around. As he explained:

> My view of the 1990s is based on the liberation of the workplace. If you want to get the benefit of everything employees have, you've got to free them, make everybody a participant. Everybody has to know everything, so they can make the right decisions by themselves.
>
> In the old culture, managers got their power from secret knowledge: profit margins, market share, all that. But once you share that information with everyone, it often turns out that the emperor has no clothes.
>
> In the new culture, the role of the leader is to express a vision, get buy-in, and implement it. That calls for open, caring relations with every employee, and face-to-face communication. People who can't convincingly articulate a vision won't be successful. But those who can will become even more open—because success breeds self-confidence.

Work-Outs took place all over GE, hundreds of them. As Stewart wrote: "Like kernels of corn in a hot pan, they began popping one at a time—in GE Plastics' silicones unit in Waterford, New York; at NBC; in the lighting business—then in a great, noisy rush."

By 1989 the pent-up demand for change was enormous. Work-Out's carefully designed stagecraft made employees feel safe, freeing them to voice their complaints. Managers added to the momentum by sharing once-secret data. In those early Work-Out sessions they picked a lot of low-hanging fruit.

The key was an insistence on emerging from every session with a list of "actionable items"—things people were committed to start working on right away. At the Schenectady turbine plant, for instance, hourly employees bitched about the milling machines they used. They won authorization to write the specifications for $20 million worth of replacement machines, which they tested and approved themselves.

The result: cycle time—the time needed to mill steel—dropped 80%, lowering inventory cost while increasing responsiveness to customers. Wrote Welch, "It is embarrassing to reflect that for probably eighty or ninety years, we've been dictating equipment needs and managing people who knew how to do things much better and faster than we did."

While Work-Out was getting started, a related movement called Best Practices got under way. One of GE's great weaknesses always was its susceptibility to the "not invented here" syndrome. The corporation had been so accustomed to producing good ideas for so long—ever since Edison, really—that GEers rarely bothered to find out what other folks were thinking. Figuring that no company could corner the market for good ideas, Welch forced the organization to look outside.

His systematic approach was characteristic of GE management tradition. While Welch railed against bureaucracy, he never lost his reverence for the thoroughness and diligence with which GEers think through business issues. During the summer of 1988, Welch assigned Michael Frazier of GE's Business Development staff to develop a list of companies worth emulating, and then to study their achievements. Frazier and his team selected nine companies to study, including Ford, Hewlett Packard, Chapperell Steel, and two of Japan's best-known multinationals, both of which participated on condition their names be kept confidential. The team's ten members fanned out around the world, and spent a full year collecting on-site data at these companies. Although they absorbed lots of minutia, they retained an Olympian perspective: They were seeking answers to the question, "What is the secret of your success?"

Their report argued that the accomplishments of the world's productivity champs depended on common traits:

- They managed processes rather than people. Instead of tracking how *much* they produced, they focused on *how* they produced.

- They used process mapping and benchmarking to spot opportunities for improvement. Process mapping is a matter of writing down every single step, no matter how tiny, in a particular task. Benchmarking means comparing oneself to an objective standard, such as a competitor's performance.

- They emphasized continuous improvement, and lauded incremental gains.

- They relied on customer satisfaction as the main gauge of performance. That overcame the tendency to focus on internal goals at customers' expense.

- They stimulated productivity by introducing a constant stream of high-quality new products designed for efficient manufacturing.

- They treated their suppliers as partners.

No less valuable to GE than these overarching ideas were the mind-blowing stories of these companies' achievements. A typical one came from the laundry products business of one of the Japanese participants, a leading producer of washing machines in Japan. According to GE's case study, this company had realized by 1984 that demographic changes would soon fragment its market into niches. That implied a need to switch from producing a few washing machine models in high volumes to making a broad selection of models, which would sell at lower volumes. The challenge was to accomplish that without creating profit-threatening assembly line snafus.

The company created a flexible production system designed to respond directly to the ebb and flow of sales. In five years it tripled the number of new washer models it introduced. The washer factory became accustomed to eleven model changes per day, versus two and a half daily in 1985. Spending only $2 million to $3 million per year to make all these changes, the business doubled both its manufacturing capacity and the dollar amount of sales per employee. At the same time, quality dramatically improved.

After hearing the Frazier team's presentation, Welch became an instant convert. He ordered up a major new Crotonville course on Best Practices, and assigned to Work-Out teams the task of spreading Best Practices throughout GE. He frequently quoted a favorite Baughman line: "Best Practices has legitimized plagiarism."

In phase two of Work-Out, which gathered steam through 1990, GE shifted to unnatural acts in *natural* settings. Now the sessions began to involve groups of people who would ordinarily work together, such as the cross-functional teams of finance, manufacturing, purchasing, and marketing experts collectively responsible for a particular product. Their sessions would begin with a clearly defined problem and a mandate to solve it. With that shift, Work-Out began to become a regular part of the GE way of life. And self-sufficiency became a key goal: GE trained its own people as facilitators, to replace the outsiders.

Work-Out now depended heavily on tools acquired from the Best Practices study, process mapping in particular. In business after business, GEers would gain control over processes by identifying every step in them. Some process maps were so complex that they covered whole walls and resembled diagrams of the wiring in computer chips. The maps noted even such seemingly minor matters as the signatures required to approve purchases or shipments. Since a document tends to sit on a desk for a day before it's signed, cutting out a few unnecessary approvals can significantly speed up a process. (When process mapping failed to help, it usually was because the attention to detail got out of hand.)

To forge a shared commitment to speed and customer satisfaction, GE invited customers and suppliers such as 3M and Sears to join in these sessions. These gatherings were very effective at building trust, but not always pleasant: At a similar session, Tichy remembers feeling deeply embarrassed to hear the complaints aired by three companies that worked with GE Aerospace—a Union Carbide division, a major shipbuilder, and a large construction consulting firm. Point by point, executives from the other companies demonstrated how arrogant behavior by GEers was costing them business. It was clear that this part of the company still had its "ass to the customer and its face to the CEO."

An early example of GEers vaulting over the high bar was the Quick Response program at Louisville-based Appliances. Process mapping there showed that while a fifth of the parts in any given appliance model were unique, only 5% were expensive enough to affect inventory costs substantially. GE found that it could speed manufacturing and cut costs by keeping ample stocks of the cheap components, while working out just-in-time programs with suppliers to deliver quickly the others as needed. The biggest gains of all came from controlling the sequence in which parts were delivered from a plant's loading dock to its assembly line.

Measures such as these enabled Appliances to reduce its inventory by $200 million—and to increase the business's return on investment by 8.5 percentage points. Appliances cut the eighty-day cycle time from receipt of an order to delivery of a finished product by over 75%. As he had done earlier with Lighting's winning team, Welch put the Appliances group up on a pedestal, touting it as a leading in-house example of Best Practices.

Louisville became a regular stop for executives from all over the company. But this was more than a corporate tourist attraction: To create a corps of Quick Response experts, each GE business sent a few managers for a full year of action learning in Louisville. By the time these people returned to their own units, they had mastered the intricacies of Quick Response and could serve as effective advocates of the method.

More recently, Aircraft Engines used Work-Out to help it figure out how to meet a heroically ambitious 1992 income target. A big winner during the defense-spending spree of the Reagan years, the unit had produced stellar results through the 1980s and thereby avoided the need to do too much hard thinking about productivity. But demand for military engines is slowing down. "Where's the enemy?" Welch asks with a shrug. In 1992, Aircraft Engines' sales declined slightly from 1991 levels of about $7.9 billion and were expected to decline further in 1993. Yet the CEO challenged the business to reduce its inventories by $1 billion, to help reach a net income goal of $750 million—as much as it had made in its very best year.

To achieve that, logically, Engines must match its revenue cuts with cost cuts. For months, Aircraft Engines' managers searched for ways to achieve the massive productivity gains they needed to meet their earnings target. During Work-Out, they decided that the business could increase its efficiency enough to halve the time between customers' orders and the delivery of finished engines. That would boost cash flow and enable Aircraft Engines to cut its inventories by up to 40%, reaching Welch's goal.

Is the CEO crazy to set goals so high? He doesn't think so:

What right do I have to do that? It always works. And it's rational. This is not a business that's going to recover any time soon, so it's reasonable to squeeze. And there were lots of inefficiencies built in during the boom times.

One of the hardest things is to get the maximum out of a rising business. You're satisfied, so you don't try as hard. Why did America become noncompetitive in the 1970s? Because it was living off the fat of the 1960s. When are the most sins created in business? In boom times, when managements get arrogant.

In a growing business, it's hard to know whether you've picked the right goal. You pick one based on the peak returns of other global businesses—but maybe that's too low.

During a slump you have to find out what you can do. Our Aircraft Engines business is going to get to four inventory turns a year—then five, seven, who knows? We've been trying to get them for three years, but they've

**been stuck at 2.5, 2.7, 2.8 turns. Now they're going to do
it, because it will reduce the number of employees they
would otherwise have to let go.**

GE spent nearly a decade getting in shape; then, in just a
couple of years, Work-Out enabled GE to bust through the wall.
Tichy was a facilitator at the Aircraft Engines Work-Out in 1992.
Observing the managers debating ways to cut their inventories,
Tichy noticed that no one was arguing that the cuts were unnecessary. The same phenomenon had been apparent all over the company during the early 1990s: GEers weren't resisting much
anymore. They understood the imperatives of global competition,
and they were determined to win. So instead of bitching when the
bar is raised, they focus on how to surmount it.

Phase three of Work-Out began in 1992. Called the Change Acceleration Program, or CAP, it was a systematic attempt to use Work-
Out to breed a new type of GE manager. Welch wants all GE's
leaders to be professional change agents rather than mere managers. The idea behind CAP is to disseminate to top management
all GE's accumulated knowledge and wisdom about the change
process itself: how to initiate change, how to accelerate it, and how
to make it stick.

Work-Out is a forum for teaching the skills that Welch expects
to prove most valuable in the years ahead. Here is where GEers
explore the implications of boundarylessness, where competence
becomes more important than position, where nobody can hide
behind a title or a desk. If the CAP training works, outside facilitators won't be needed. Program graduates will fan out throughout
GE to spread the revolutionary message. "In seven years," says
Welch, "people who are comfortable as coaches and facilitators will
be the norm at GE. And the other people won't get promoted. We
can't afford to promote people who don't have the right values."

The epiphany that Welch experienced in the helicopter with Baughman was emblematic of his own transformation as a leader. The

cranked-up ferocity of the CEO's interactions with subordinates was giving way to a more wholesome attitude—an urge to respect and empower people that began to seem convincing and genuine. Having started out as the man with the bullhorn, in effect yelling at subordinates who couldn't keep pace, he evolved into a coach, willing to pause (for a nanosecond or two) to help others along.

To some observers, the change was astonishing. As a GE manager said:

> You know, I've watched the rebirth of Welch, or the renaissance of Welch, or whatever has happened to him. I don't know all the elements that went into his being born again, and I don't even care what they are. But I'm sure glad it's happened. He's a different man than he was in 1981.

When we suggested to Welch that he seemed to have remade himself by around 1988, he challenged us with every bit of his old aggressiveness:

> I haven't changed a thing! I try to adapt to the environment I'm in. In the seventies, when I was helping grow new businesses—at Plastics, at Medical—I was a wild-eyed growth guy. And then I got into the bureaucracy and I had to clean it out, so I was different in 1981. And now I'm in another environment. But that's not being "born again."
>
> The ideas were always the same. We've been talking about reality, agility, ownership, and candor since the beginning. We just got it simpler and more carefully articulated over time: Work-Out, eight years later, is a more meaningful way of communicating the idea of ownership—but it's the same idea.
>
> You don't get anywhere if you keep changing your ideas. The only way to change people's minds is with consistency. Once you get the ideas, you keep refining and improving them; the more simply your idea is defined, the

better it is. You communicate, you communicate, and then you communicate some more. Consistency, simplicity, and repetition is what it's all about.

I think it's been a steady continuum that finally reached a critical mass. We were always consistent in how we talked. We went from videotapes to more meetings, to talking to groups, to round tables, and then to Work-Out. We never changed, we just got better at it. And after a while it started to snowball.

Unquestionably Welch's thinking has remained consistent from the first. But the man himself does seem to have changed. Some smart people share that point of view. Said Gertrude G. Michelson, who was a senior vice president of R. H. Macy and a GE director, "He's changed from competitive to cooperative, in the broadest sense—he understands that's the real top leadership role." Adds Larry Bossidy:

I do think there was a change, vividly, from yelling and screaming for performance, to a much more motivational kind of approach. He became a lot more understanding, much more tolerant: *Hey, if you get the job done even though your style is different from mine, that's fine.* He wasn't that way in the beginning.

The nice thing about Jack is that he keeps growing. The Jack Welch who took over GE is not the Jack Welch you see today.

We view Work-Out as evidence of a major change in Welch's thinking. The CEO used to argue against incremental change, on the theory that only quantum leaps made enough of a difference. Work-Out represented Welch's personal commitment to the Japanese idea of *kaizen,* or "continuous improvement." This is really a cultural attitude guiding people to seek ways to get better constantly; small improvements are as important to the process as big ones. By 1988, *kaizen*-style methods had produced impressive results at Lighting and Transportation Systems, and he became a convert.

Another major shift, made possible by GE's progress during the previous eight years, was "from hardware to software," in his phrase. Once the organization's survival was no longer at risk, Welch had the luxury of working on the soft issues of corporate culture and employee behavior, freeing Welch to devote more energy to boosting self-confidence. That, in turn, required different behavior from the CEO: You can't boost people's self-confidence by yelling at them.

Welch had always been interested in the soft side of management; now he was beginning to appreciate its power.

Work-Out has not been perfectly successful. Cynical GEers have described it as "Work-In." We know many stressed-out GEers who still regard liberation as little more than a distant dream.

As occurred earlier with strategic planning, the change-makers GE brought in to spread new ideas are becoming part of the corporation's establishment. There's always the danger that former revolutionaries, having achieved their goals, will entrench themselves and remain on the scene long after they are needed. It would be dismaying if the members of GE's brilliant Work-Out team made that mistake.

By now, so much low-hanging fruit has already been picked that it's reasonable to wonder how much longer GE can sustain the momentum of the last few years. But as the Work-Out process becomes more muscular and people gain trust, more opportunities for improvement come into view. The supply of low-hanging fruit may be inexhaustible. A Work-Out session led GEMS, for instance, to patch a major supplier into its internal electronic-mail network. The two companies also decided to build new-product prototypes jointly. As they work more closely together, they keep stumbling over additional opportunities to improve designs, lower costs, and speed processes. As in human relationships, intimacy can become its own reward.

Work-Out's success is hard to measure. As Welch explains, that's intentional:

> **It's best to present big ideas without time frames or rigidly defined goals, because there is resistance to every**

idea that's different from the current norm. If you allow the naysayers to measure and quantify your idea, they can come back and blow it away before it has a chance to work.

For the first year of Work-Out, some people would have loved to measure it. Then they'd have been able to say, "I held twenty-one meetings and 591 people attended, so now it's over."

How will we know if Work-Out is successful? We'll know because over time we'll become more productive. Our attitudes will be better, people will be happier, better ideas will flow.

Work-Out has made believers of GE's top 1,000 or 2,000 executives. We've been inside scores of the world's best and biggest companies, and we can't think of another where intellectual freedom and like-mindedness coexist to an equal degree.

As a formal mechanism for sustaining a revolutionary process—and for transferring real power to employees—Work-Out is unsurpassed so far. But for those tempted to try the program themselves, we offer this caution: GE's already successful transformation is what enabled Work-Out to succeed. Without that foundation, without all the pain and difficulty of Welch's early years, we doubt Work-Out's techniques would have much effect. As Welch says, "You better be lean before you play these games."

Chapter Seventeen

The Twenty-First-Century Organization

Welch defines an effective corporate executive as "someone who can change the tires while the car's still rolling." John Trani, fifty-five in 2001, fits the description. His challenge has been to create a boundaryless organization in a high-tech, rapidly globalizing business—while engaged in an all-out slugfest with first-rate competitors. Trani has made Milwaukee-based GEMS the equivalent of an R&D lab for organization, testing new ways of applying the lessons of the GE revolution, from the abstract idea of boundarylessness to the pragmatic focus on processes learned in Work-Out. His experiments haven't all worked, but the process he went through is interesting to observe.

In GE-speak, keeping the car rolling means producing terrific financial results. Under Trani's leadership, GEMS' income has grown at double-digit rates for the last six years, while sales tripled. But the numbers tell only part of the story. One legacy of his years may be the global organization that has been evolving at GEMS since Trani took over in 1986. The latest of their organizational innovations began in mid-1991, when GEMS launched an effort to create a process-based management system. New systems usually prove difficult to implement, and this one will likely go through many permutations before reaching its final form. But if GEMS succeeds, it may represent an important advance in the quest for the twenty-first-century organization.

GEMS' transformation occurred in three phases. In the first, which Tichy calls the "hardware" phase, the business focused on technical issues such as cost structure and acquisitions. The second, "software" phase emphasized the transmission of new values and a global mind-set.

Medical Systems has been operating in uncharted territory because of globalization. GEMS had to go global to seize opportunities in markets abroad, and to defend itself from aggressive competitors from overseas; thus the Yokogawa venture in Japan and the Thomson-CGR deal in France. GEMS' non-U.S. sales rocketed from less than 15% of the total in 1985 to well over 40% three years later.

Warp-speed overseas expansion compounded the already considerable difficulties of managing Medical Systems. As local interests ceased to be paramount, many employees felt anxious— regardless of whether they were located in Milwaukee, Tokyo, or Paris. In addition to the normal conflicts between GEMS' various product lines (ultrasound versus CT scan, say), and between management functions (such as marketing versus manufacturing), managers began to have differences based on geography.

Trani, a brainy, warmhearted, self-styled "win-aholic" from a blue-collar neighborhood in Brooklyn, established himself as a grow-or-die manager before taking charge of GEMS. He is one of the most intense, focused, and determined business leaders around. He has a forceful personality, a booming voice, and a propensity for laughter. Uncompromising about holding people to their commitments, he also has great personal warmth, and goes out of his way to offer emotional support when his managers need it.

Since Tichy left Crotonville in 1987, he has worked for Trani as a consultant; Trani's willingness to experiment with social architecture made GEMS an interesting place to work. Trani devotes tremendous amounts of time and energy to trying to understand the business he runs. That involves much more than mastering the numbers: He's also fascinated with organizational design and the many levers that influence organizational behavior and performance.

The son of a longshoreman, Trani joined GE in 1978 at thirty-two, after stints in engineering, financial management, and strategic planning at other companies. During those early years he also attended night school, earning three master's degrees, in industrial management, operations research, and business. In every GE business he has led, sales, earnings, and market share have grown, and new-product development has accelerated. Placed atop GE's Audio unit—which Welch had placed outside his three circles—Trani achieved No. 1 market share in radios and No. 2 share in tape recorders. He also pushed Audio into the emerging business of selling telephones, a very profitable, $130-million-a-year operation by 1987, when Thomson bought the business from GE. Trani's next posting was at Mobile Communication, a troubled unit that made commercial radio-communication equipment. He quickly turned it around; Ericsson of Sweden eventually bought the business from GE for a handsome price.

Appreciating Trani's skills and the results he produced, Welch put him in charge of GEMS. With sales of over $1 billion in 1986, Medical Systems already was the world's biggest maker of diagnostic-imaging equipment. Its product line ranged from ultrasound and X-ray equipment at the low end, through several types of CT scanners, to the high end of magnetic resonance machines.

Under Walt Robb, Trani's able predecessor, GEMS had developed its technology leadership. Until the mid-1980s, the ability to produce the clearest possible images of internal organs was what customers wanted most, and GEMS' images were the best. Although the machines cost as much as $1 million apiece, they enabled doctors to save money—and lives. The images facilitated early diagnosis of medical problems, often on an outpatient basis;

diagnostic imaging provided a very attractive alternative to cutting people open with scalpels and visually inspecting their innards. GEMS led the U.S. market with shares as high as 50% for certain products. It consistently ranked among GE's fastest-growing businesses, along with Plastics and Financial Services.

Even so, Trani's arrival followed a startling wake-up call for GEMS. By 1986 technology was no longer Medical Systems' most critical need. Its cost structure had been premised on continual growth—but the market had changed, and the growth of the business had nearly stopped. In order to grow, GEMS had to globalize, and in order to globalize, it had to reshape its organization. To use Larry Bossidy's word, the operation was showing early signs of becoming "disheveled." People in GEMS' various functions and product lines were accustomed to focusing on their own little boxes, paying scant attention to the business as a whole. To many of them, globalization seemed more threat than opportunity.

GEMS already had a foothold in Japan, through Yokogawa Medical Systems, and was increasing its ownership share in the venture from 51% to 75%. When GE swapped its TV set operation for Thomson-CGR, GEMS suddenly became General Electric's most complex global enterprise.

That forced a radical change in Medical Systems' identity. Nothing in the lives of GEMS' employees had prepared them for the changes they now faced. Globalization would require unprecedented levels of teamwork among people who didn't know each other, felt they had little in common, and in some cases distrusted each other. Some executives in Milwaukee were barely on speaking terms with their colleagues in Europe and Japan. Before moving Trani to Medical Systems, Welch had installed a new head of GEMS' European operation, instructing him to "ignore the Milwaukee bunch" and do whatever was necessary to build business in Europe. The European chief did just that; he was not the most popular man in Milwaukee.

The Thomson-CGR deal introduced thousands of unhappy Frenchmen to an organization that already had many anxious Americans and Japanese. The French felt betrayed by their former masters at Thomson, and fearful of GE. The joint venture with Yokogawa also caused rancor. The Japanese company aroused scorn from some of the technologists in Milwaukee. For their part, the Japanese at YMS criticized GEMS for its quality and cost problems. And they resented any interference from GE, even though GE owned a majority of their company. The Japanese believed their destiny was to fight Toshiba within Japan, and only secondarily to help the American owners.

The conflicts annoyed Welch. Tichy remembers hearing a Milwaukee manufacturing manager confront him: "Sell machines made by Yokogawa Medical Systems? Why should we give them the business over our own people?"

Replied Welch, who had overseen Medical Systems earlier in his career, "Them is us. We *own* YMS. Now figure out what to do."

Like so many of the markets GE served, the diagnostic-imaging business began to change dramatically during the mid-1980s. Pressured by the U.S. government and their own patients, health care providers became cost-conscious buyers. And CT scanners, once the pinnacle of rarified technology, had become a product that several competent manufacturers could supply. Siemens and Toshiba saw an opportunity to penetrate the U.S. market with lower-priced machines.

In 1985 profits fell, and GEMS had to lay off hundreds of employees. That compounded the difficulty of building a global enterprise. Deeply concerned, Welch commissioned a Boston Consulting Group study of Medical Systems' costs; it concluded that GEMS's cost structure was higher than Siemens'.

Once Trani arrived, change came in cascades. The hardware phase began with a program called Focus 80 to wring out the excess cost and make the business leaner and faster. As you'd expect, Trani delayered, consolidated manufacturing sites, laid people off, reduced inventories, redesigned products, and so on. He created countless task forces to involve as many people as possible in these efforts, delegating to them the power to decide what to cut.

The Trani team also had to shepherd GEMS through a painful cultural transition—from a single-minded focus on leading-edge technology to simultaneous concentration on technology *and* marketing, manufacturing, and cost. In organizational terms, the goal was to retain the best qualities of GEMS' independent, free-spirited frontiersmen and teach them the disciplines necessary to achieve sustainable cost-competitiveness. He insisted that productivity and R&D investment were directly related: The higher the productivity, the more GEMS could spend on research. Medical Systems' productivity rose from less than 2% in 1985 to over 7% in 1992, while R&D investment quadrupled.

Inevitably, Trani aroused resistance. Says he:

> **What we have to avoid is breaking people's spirits. I would argue that the most sensitive approach is to err on the side of action. Decide what you're going to do, and then do it quickly. There is nothing worse than change by a thousand cuts. As for organizations—they are much more malleable than people think, and their fragility is, sometimes, only in people's minds.**

Globalization added exponentially to the difficulty of running a business that was already entangled in the intricacies of running five high-tech product lines. Trani regrouped GEMS into three geographic "poles"—based in Milwaukee, Paris, and Tokyo—each with worldwide responsibility for a particular group of imaging products.

That new organization scrambled existing power structures throughout the business. For starters, Trani insisted that "no kings were allowed," meaning that he would not permit Milwaukee to dominate. The poles would share responsibility for developing and manufacturing products to be sold worldwide, but each pole would independently market those products within its geographic sphere of influence. In addition, each pole would take primary responsibility for certain products. The United States got top-of-the-line CT scanners, ultrasound systems, and nuclear-imaging equipment. The

Japanese took charge of mid-priced CT scanners and ultrasound machines. The French got most X-ray systems.

Suddenly, getting ordinary jobs done required crossing more boundaries than ever before—not just the familiar boundaries defined by function or product line, but time differences of up to fourteen hours, language barriers that sometimes forced GEMS to hire simultaneous translators for meetings, and the deep-rooted prejudices of three of the world's most arrogant national cultures.

The Americans, French, and Japanese each see themselves as superior, an attitude that injects conflict into any endeavor involving all three. This isn't unique to GEMS; we have seen it at many global companies. As employees were quick to notice, each culture had its downside. In workshops, they complained that the Americans too often acted like cowboys, impulsive and careless. They said the French, enraptured with Cartesian logic, sometimes carried on annoyingly pointless arguments for hours. And the Japanese, unwilling to offend, could smile and nod in apparent agreement with an idea—and then resist it with all their might.

Everything became more complicated. Even a global electronic-mail system, which has become an essential means of binding this business together, was difficult to launch. Creating a single, integrated network was technologically challenging. Many Japanese and some of the French weren't fluent in English. Another obstacle was that many of them didn't know how to type. The pieces came together only gradually.

By the time Tichy arrived in 1987, GEMS' software phase had begun. Trani asked him to help manage the transition to a global organization, so Tichy formed an international team that also included Ram Charan, originally from India, Michael Brimm, a professor from INSEAD in France, and Hiro Takeuchi from Tokyo. The mandate was to create a program using Crotonville-style compressed action learning to indoctrinate GEMS managers in new ways of working—while they were developing solutions to pressing business needs.

The essential skills the team wanted to teach included the ability to communicate effectively with others despite the barriers of language and geographic distance, and the capacity to motivate and work comfortably with teams. Inventiveness and flexibility were important, too: There's no paint-by-numbers approach to globalization.

Under what was called the Global Leadership Program, seven small teams, each with executives from the United States, Europe, and Japan, were assigned major projects that took nine months to complete. Sample assignments: devising a system to quickly transfer new technologies across the business; globalizing new-product planning; and creating a strategy to compete with Siemens, the world's No. 2 producer of diagnostic-imaging equipment, in its home market of Germany.

Trani regarded the program's goals of long-term executive development and short-term problem-solving as equally important. In the early years, the Global Leadership Program also served to build the human network that helped tie GEMS together, while Trani's team experimented with more formal mechanisms.

The first event of the Global Leadership Program took place in June 1988, not long after Trani's three-pole reorganization. The team yanked fifty-five high-ranking GEMS managers out of their normal lives, and flew them to Faro, Portugal, for an introductory workshop. There, colleagues from America, Japan, and France met for the first time.

Early on, they debated whether GEMS really needed worldwide teamwork to win. The topic was plenty controversial, but the emotional energy of the discussion was deflated by the simultaneous translation, which slowed the pace of conversation. Even so, the participants managed to display all their native prejudices and resentments.

The ice broke—or at least cracked—during the Outward Bound-style activities of the second day. The leaders set up two challenges designed to force people to communicate despite the barriers of language. In the first, multinational teams of people had to grope their way across wobbling rope bridges while wearing blind-folds; that forced them to communicate by touch and tone of voice. Each safe crossing inspired another small increment of confidence.

Then the group faced a sheer, fourteen-foot wall, with orders to surmount it using nothing but their bodies. That called for trust, thoughtful teamwork, and lots of sweaty exertion. By the end of the day, exhausted participants were beginning to like each other more than they liked the people running the program—the sort of healthy, us-against-them camaraderie that Marine boot camp inspires.

Then, between lengthy classroom teaching sessions, the hard work began. After dividing the group into seven teams, the leaders handed out the assignments. Each team also got a senior GEMS manager as its coach. One of the rules was that the coaches all work outside their areas of expertise: The head of the technology staff, for instance, coached the team working on a marketing project. That helped the coaches leave the hard business issues to the teams, which were qualified to handle them, while helping out with subtler human problems.

These so-called soft concerns often proved hard to deal with: How, for example, were people accustomed to hierarchy supposed to act in a team that had no designated leader? The idea perplexed many participants.

At the end of the five-day Faro event the leaders assigned the groups one last physical challenge. In just a few hours, each team had to design, build, and race a raft in a nearby inlet of the Atlantic Ocean. Each raft had to carry an entire seven-member team plus the coach. Using the barrels, wood, and rope we provided, the teams lashed together rough crafts and tried to paddle them around some buoys several hundred yards offshore.

Besides being a lot of fun, this event tested the teams' ability to handle conflict and cultural differences. Under intense time pres-sure, and without a shipwright's skills or the aid of simultaneous translators, they had to reach consensus on a raft design, then build and race the craft. The contest produced clear winners and losers. One team got around all the race buoys, while another team's raft capsized almost immediately in the shallows. That provided a vivid demonstration of the benefits of teamwork—and the penalty for lacking it.

At the end, every workshop member got feedback from the group on his or her behavior. The leaders wrote these comments down on flip charts, a practice that proved especially useful with the French and Japanese, whose comprehension of written English often far exceeds their understanding of conversation. The process forced the shy, silent types out of the shadows.

The teams' work on their projects continued long after the Faro workshop ended. Knowing they would have to report real results to a real boss, participants had to teach themselves how to communicate with their teammates across two oceans via fax, electronic mail, two-way video systems, and in-person meetings. People who'd never left the United States became accustomed to flying to Tokyo one week, and Paris the next. As team members quickly discovered, globalization is a pain in the ass. The discomforts range from lost sleep to the resentment of the stay-at-home managers stuck with the work that globetrotters leave behind.

The only reason to put up with so much complication and disruption is that globalization so clearly seems to be the winning strategy. Market forces are compelling businesses to transfer technology and expertise throughout their organizations regardless of geography. And the economies of scale that come with globalization are impressive; if you can't figure out how to exploit them, your competitors will.

Halfway through the first year of the Global Leadership Program, the seven teams reconvened at the Hotel Seiyo in Tokyo's Ginza District. This meeting, soon dubbed the "Ginza event," proved awkward and painful for all participants. Everyone was suffering from the stress of coping with so much novelty and extra work. They couldn't reach a consensus about what was important; one divisive question was whether to focus on soft issues such as values, or hard business matters. The meeting lasted three days and resolved nothing. Participants returned home feeling serious reservations about the whole process. But GEers are disciplined folks, so everyone kept pursuing the assignments even so.

The Global Leadership Program's final event occurred in March 1989 in Chicago. At this meeting, the seven teams presented their functional plans; after spending a half-day evaluating each project, Trani and the leaders from the three geographic poles announced which proposals they would adopt. By the end of the day Trani had allocated millions of dollars.

When the participants reported what they'd learned, several key themes emerged:

- When the Americans dominate team discussions, as they are prone to do, people of other nationalities quickly lose interest and nothing gets done. It helps to speak slowly and write things down—and sometimes to restrain the impulse to speak.

- The French love of argument can make emotionally neutral remarks seem combative and hurtful.

- The Japanese too often keep their good ideas to themselves.

- Almost everyone was astounded at the amount of time and effort necessary to accomplish meaningful work across global boundaries. The consensus was that true globalization would require years of effort.

- The program's most obvious payoff was the grid of interlacing global networks formed by participants. Forcing people to get to know one another during the workshops, and then obliging them to work together, encouraged people to form lasting personal bonds. Those networks of personal relationships provide the best way to steer work projects through the maze of a global organization.

One of the participants summarized it well when he wrote:

If there's anything we've learned, it's to give equal time to both the project and the globalization experience. If you walk away from this with an excellent project completion, but don't know how a Frenchman lives, don't

know why a Japanese businessman gets promoted, haven't tasted sushi, haven't ridden in the British subway, etc., you've blown it.

To be global, you must know how the other poles think, what their customers want, and basically, what makes them tick.

This isn't as complex as it sounds. Just talk to them as colleagues, not aliens.

In the distant future, no doubt, the skills required for international communication will become more widespread. For now, though, it makes no sense to waste resources teaching language and other complex skills to the adults who are already established in business organizations. Welch, one of the best global managers around, speaks no language but English. Trani, though widely traveled, is not the sort of guy who visits temples while in Japan. You don't need to know how to bow correctly, or enjoy eating brains, to succeed as a global manager.

If you're good at what you do, and know how to get along with people, you're 90% of the way there.

By 1991 GEMS' software phase ended. The Global Leadership Program had produced some 250 graduates, a group of change agents large enough to influence the entire organization. Trani felt GEMS was ready for the next big step: an evolution of the organizational structure designed to address the complexities of global business.

As he tells the story, Trani began to see a process-based organization as the way to get beyond GEMS' limitations:

We decided to try to get five times better in both quality and speed by 1995. Before we even got to the question of how to get there, we had to figure out how to measure our progress. We got a group together and started talking about it, and everybody had a different measurement.

Well, everyone was siting around the table, thirty people. And it was impossible to get them to agree.

> **It became clear that this wasn't going to work. It wasn't really until after that meeting, when I thought about the complexity of it, that I realized processes were the way to go.**

Trani believes that the way to cope with complexity is with a stripped-down, extremely flexible organization that trusts employees to find their own paths through the maze. In simpler, more leisurely times, leaders could achieve greatness by telling people exactly what to do; today the most advanced organizations are forced to rely on individuals who can make decisions by themselves.

The formal networks laid out in organization charts rarely work as well as the informal ones that people create ad hoc. Anyone who has served in the military knows that the best way to get supplies is not through the cumbersome official requisition process, but through back channels, as Milo Minderbinder did so memorably in the book *Catch-22*. Individuals' ability to outsmart the organization becomes more crucial as corporate structures become more complex. At GEMS, one person may simultaneously be working on several project teams, reporting to several different people in widely scattered parts of the business, and working closely with multiple sets of colleagues, some of whom may be located thousands of miles away. A few months later, the same person may be working on entirely different projects and dealing with a new cast of characters. Organizations simply aren't smart enough to cope with so much complexity; only people are.

Trani moved to the third phase of the organization's development: the creation of a new social architecture. His team designed an organization built on six basic processes:

• **Advanced Technology:** The equivalent of research and development, this is the process of developing the basic technologies on which future products will rely.

• **Offerings Development:** The design of products and services based on those technologies.

• **Go-to-Market:** The identification of market needs—including the particular demands of individual national markets—and the fine-tuning of product designs to meet them.

• **Order-to-Remittance:** This sprawling process encompasses everything that gets done from the placing of a customer's order to the delivery of the equipment, including sales, purchasing of supplies, manufacturing, distribution, on-site installation and testing, and billing and collection. Here's where GEMS can leverage its global position and integrate its operations to achieve important economies of scale.

• **Service Delivery:** Providing repairs and upgrades to the installed base of GEMS machines—a business that produces a very substantial portion of GEMS' profits.

• **Support:** This includes all the staff functions, from finance to human resources to government relations.

If it occurs to you that these processes should all work together, Trani would heartily agree, In particular the first two processes, concerning product development and production, need extremely careful synchronization. One of Trani's goals is to force employees into an awareness that, no matter how it is divided, GEMS remains a single organization with the shared goal of serving customers. That idea got lost in the tangle of functional, product, and national rivalries.

The most important links between processes will be informal. Trani is counting on help from the Group Operating Council, the GEMS equivalent of GE's corporate Executive Council. Trani also expects the growing ranks of global executives under his command to develop their own person-to-person lines of communication across the various process-based organizations.

Trani didn't try to define the links himself. Instead, he assigned teams of GEMS executives the task of inventing systems to suit their needs. The result will be a plan that they can "own." With their commitment bolstering Trani's—and their detailed knowledge of the businesses refining his more general ideas—the new vision should be easier to implement.

In 1991, Trani named an eight-person team for each process, consisting of a chief, two senior executives from each of the three geographical poles, and one staffer. Even though the Milwaukee-based "Americas" pole accounts for more than half of GEMS' sales, Trani gave it no more representation than the other poles; he was determined to foster teamwork. He gave the teams enough authority to commandeer whatever people and resources they would need, and instructed them to return in a year with detailed plans.

Creating the new process-based organization proved more complicated than Trani expected. Trani is candid about the difficulty of creating a global organization:

> **An organization is a learning laboratory. The more we get into this, the more we realize we have to scale back and simplify. It was just too complex to try to do the whole thing at once. We're discovering that to get global is even more difficult than what you might think.**

If the process structure succeeds, Medical Systems will better balance three competing goals: maximizing economies of scale, to lower costs; maximizing responsiveness to local markets, to increase sales; and maximizing the whole organization's ability to learn from the experiences of each of its parts, to push both productivity and revenue growth. No business as large and complex as GEMS— its 1992 revenues reached just over $7.9 billion—has ever done that. Being the first would give GEMS a boost likely to keep it ahead of the competition for years.

Since the first edition of this book, much has changed at Medical Systems. It became the final proving ground for the new CEO, Jeff Immelt, who took over from John Trani as CEO of Medical Systems in 1997. Trani left GE to become CEO of Stanley Works. GEMS is still the most global business in GE.

Chapter Eighteen

Head, Heart, and Guts

M anagement is fine as far as it goes, but leadership is the way to win. GE has created an organization designed to demand leadership from every one of its members. As an employee at Appliances wryly notes, "We hired the arms and backs and legs of people for years, and we never knew the brains came free."

Delayering and drastic staff cuts eliminated the bureaucratic infrastructure that used to prop people up. That has forced GEers to understand better their businesses, instead of delegating the responsibility to strategic planners or subordinates. And GE executives can't avoid tough decisions about what's important enough to spend time on: They once directly supervised an average of seven people each; now they typically oversee fifteen to twenty and sometimes more.

The only way to cope with so much responsibility is to lead—management would take too much time. GEers have no choice but to find their own resources, design their own organizations, and invent their own ways of getting jobs done. Leaders' success depends on the ability to assemble and motivate teams of people who can accomplish tasks by themselves. Measured in terms of human stress, the cost of GE's leadership system is still extremely high—but it remains unmatched as a method to deliver new ideas to the marketplace fast.

The real substance of the GE revolution is the new relationship it created between employer and employee. The traditional corporate hierarchy, premised on the mutual mistrust of workers and bosses, was too plodding and cumbersome to suit Welch. In its place, the CEO envisioned an enterprise that relied more on ideas and shared values to win the commitment of employees. "The glue is an affinity among people who want to grapple with the outside world and win," he says. Based on emotional energy rather than coercion, the new organization had to be flexible enough to allow many workers to manage themselves, and nimble enough to beat competitors still bound by bureaucratic controls. Today, that vision is becoming a reality.

The notion of an organization based on shared values evolved from the CEO's perception that control had become a competitive liability. His thoughts on the subject bear repeating:

> **The old organization was built on control, but the world has changed. The world is moving at such a pace that control has become a limitation. It slows you down. You've got to balance freedom with some control, but you've got to have more freedom than you ever dreamt of. To measure value, we're trying to look at what you contribute instead of what you control.**

Looking back over the Welch years at GE, it is clear that he always intended to create a values-based organization. Those who dismissed him as "Neutron Jack" in the early years completely missed the point. The urge to unlock the latent power of ideas explains almost everything Welch has done since he became GE's chief executive in 1981. From the first, his goal has been to get GE's employees to see the world as it really is, and then to act on that understanding. That's what he means by "facing reality." The idea sounds simple, but the turbulent history of the GE revolution demonstrates the difficulty of putting it into practice. It also shows that the payoff can be enormous.

When Welch started out, the values that counted at GE admittedly were mostly his own, as the CEO acted on strong personal convictions about matters ranging from personal ethics to fine points of corporate management. In 1993, the values that count at GE are shared by thousands of employees. With roughly 230,000 people on its payroll, the company surely harbors some dissidents, but anyone who spends much time at GE can feel the energy that results when allegiance once compelled by force is given freely.

Increased unanimity may be the greatest achievement of the eleven years Welch has spent refining and repeating the same handful of big ideas. Much as he cherishes diversity, in people as well as businesses, he knows that teams of people need common goals to win. The emerging consensus about GE's goals is the ultimate result of everything the CEO has done, from the painful early decisions to sell off weak businesses and lay off unneeded employees, to the soft-and-fuzzy concerns of the late 1980s and early 1990s: the Crotonville debates about values, Work-Out, and the ongoing effort to create a boundaryless organization.

The outside world finally began to understand GE's long obsession with values when the company released its 1991 annual report. In his chairman's letter, Welch repackaged one of his oldest ideas in a way that suddenly riveted the attention of business people around the world. He defined four types of executives:

> **The first is one who delivers on commitments—financial or otherwise—and shares the values of our Company. His or her future is an easy call. Onward and upward.**
>
> **The second type of leader is one who does not meet commitments and does not share our values. Not as pleasant a call, but equally easy.**
>
> **The third is one who misses commitments but shares the values. He or she usually gets a second chance, preferably in a different environment.**

Then there's the fourth type—the most difficult for many of us to deal with. That leader delivers on commitments, makes all the numbers, but doesn't share the values we must have. This is the individual who typically forces performance out of people rather than inspires it: the autocrat, the big shot, the tyrant. Too often all of us have looked the other way—tolerated these "type 4" managers because "they always deliver"—at least in the short term.

And perhaps this type was more acceptable in easier times, but in an environment where we must have every good idea from every man and woman in the organization, we cannot afford management styles that suppress and intimidate. Whether we can convince and help these managers to change—recognizing how difficult that can be—or part company with them if they cannot, will be the ultimate test of our commitment to the transformation of this Company and will determine the future of the mutual respect and trust we are building. . . . We know now that without leaders who "walk the talk," all of our plans, promises, and dreams for the future are just that—talk.

Such talk draws credibility from the consistent record of action. Since 1989, GE has rated its top 200 or so managers on shared values such as candor, speed, and self-confidence—and relied on those ratings in decisions about pay raises and bonuses. The CEO claims that when GE executives fall short of the company's standards these days, the problem in the vast majority of cases is not financial performance but a failure to live up to the shared values. "If *you* wouldn't want to work for somebody, why would anyone else?" he asks.

Welch has applied this test to his own executive team. The CEO recently said that for the first time since he took office, he is satisfied with every member of the CEC. The council's lineup has continued to change as other companies lured away such prized executives as Larry Bossidy and former Plastics chief Glen Hiner, who became chief executive of Owens-Corning Fiberglas. But Welch also quietly removed a few people who didn't belong.

The manifesto about the four types of managers may become one of Welch's most broadly influential ideas, but those who would apply it won't succeed by taking shortcuts. Though other companies have long been accustomed to picking up hot management ideas from GE, from strategic planning to management by objective, such borrowings more often consist of the husks of ideas than their substance. When stripped of context and commitment, concepts lose meaning; divorced from the revolutionary gestalt, the idea of rating executives on values doesn't mean a thing.

At GE, the integration of shared values into the management process represents the culmination of a long, arduous, and highly disciplined effort. The focus on soft values was always accompanied by the demand for financial performance. Transforming the GE of 1981 into today's revved-up business engine required all the layoffs, asset sales, and reorganizations that made the early 1980s so agonizing at GE.

Those hardheaded decisions, in turn, forced a redefinition of the psychological contract between the company and its employees. As Welch explained in an interview Tichy conducted with Ram Charan for the *Harvard Business Review:*

> Like many other large companies in the United States, Europe, and Japan, GE has had an implicit psychological contract based on perceived lifetime employment. This produced a paternal, feudal, fuzzy kind of loyalty. You put in your time, worked hard, and the company took care of you for life.
>
> That kind of loyalty tends to focus people inward. But given today's environment, people's emotional energy must be focused outward on a competitive world where no business is a safe haven for employment unless it is winning in the marketplace. The psychological contract has to change.

> **The new psychological contract, if there is such a thing, is that jobs at GE are the best in the world for people who are willing to compete. We have the best training and development resources and an environment committed to providing opportunities for personal and professional growth.**

The new compact gives employees more freedom than ever before, and potentially, greater rewards for performance. But their jobs remain at risk every day. Over time, the idea of exposing every member of the organization to the common risk has become one of GE's most fundamental values and an essential part of the corporate culture.

This is not for the weak or the squeamish. As a GE deal-maker puts it: "The company gives me all the resources and independence I need. If I perform well, I can make more money here than any-place else. If I don't, I'm out. That's the way it works at GE, and I knew it when I came. We all know it." About 45% of the corporation's current employees arrived after Welch became CEO: They knew what they were getting into when they signed on. The old-times who can't stand the risk have mostly bailed out.

GE's toughness and its emphasis on shared values are not contradictory. Both spring from the same source: the insistence that the company control its own destiny. They are different manifestations of a single idea, that the competitive realities of the late twentieth century and beyond require a new relationship between employer and employee. In the years ahead, even a well-tuned business engine won't be enough. The winning corporations will be those that can create *human* engines, powered by turned-on, committed, responsible employees. Companies with old-fashioned, control-based organizations will disappear in the dust.

By revolutionizing the way GE was organized, Welch inadvertently robbed many GEers of the sense of how to get ahead. Shared values helped employees adjust.

The decentralized GE organization Welch inherited in 1981 was based on some 150 business units. Each was devoted to a single product or product line and equipped with all the necessary support functions, from finance to manufacturing. Each had its own profit-and-loss statement. Though not always meaningful as a token of managerial independence, P&L responsibility became the "Holy Grail" to ambitious GE managers, who generally started their careers in functional posts. Since general managers got all the big jobs, promotion, not increased pay, became the most prized reward for performance.

The CEO likened GE's proliferating business units to "popcorn stands," and railed at their inefficiency. The old organization called for redundant functional staffs and encouraged battles over turf that thwarted teamwork. He toppled the whole edifice, consolidating related businesses and minimizing the number of P&Ls. Appliances, for instance, went from a collection of six P&Ls to just one. By 1992, GE had fewer than fifty jobs with P&L responsibility—roughly one per 5,500 employees. Businesses also consolidated their staffs, increasing the responsibility of functional jobs but reducing their number, too.

Given the scarcity of senior management positions, the tradition of frequent promotions had to go. As the image of climbing the ladder became an anachronism, it hasn't always been easy to convince people that the available management jobs were good ones. Functional posts, long scorned as mere stepping-stones, are about the only ones left. To replace the "Holy Grail," GE now emphasizes challenge, increased responsibility, opportunities to learn—and handsome financial rewards, such as stock options and bonuses. In 1981, only 500 GEers received stock options; by 1992, the number had soared to nearly 8,000.

Having changed the way it operates, GE began looking for a new kind of manager, with different skills than the old general-manager jobs required. Most GE units have turned to product-management matrix organizations of the sort used in Lighting and Medical Systems. Such organizations are cost-efficient, customer-focused, and wonderfully adaptable, but complex: Staffers from different functions work together in teams led by product managers. The ability to collaborate and to find one's own way through the maze become essential. Also vital is the ability to cope with constant change: People usually work on several teams at once, and as they complete their tasks, they get new assignments and teammates. Globalization adds additional layers of complexity, as managers join teams of people scattered around the world, intensifying the need for independence and interpersonal skills.

The company's expectations have changed in other ways. GEers once feared getting "entrenched" in any job or business: a much-cited study by Don Kane of the Executive Management Staff showed that the company's 248 top managers had changed jobs every 2.2 years, on average, during their careers. But Welch, who values commitment and experience, wants people to stick around—often for four years or more in a single job.

Forced to give up their expectations, many GE managers initially felt screwed. During Tichy's time at Crotonville, he joined Don Kane and Eugene Andrews, also of EMS, in a task force assigned to chart a new career path for GE managers. As their 1987 report noted, they found "malaise, confusion, and disorientation increasingly evident across our professional and managerial population insofar as their own careers are concerned."

The new organization couldn't work unless GEers came to see their own roles in it as meaningful and rewarding. Incentive compensation alone can't buy the depth of employee commitment Welch is after. That's why values became a central element of Welch's reorganization plans.

The CEO's vision of a boundaryless organization is as much an expression of values as a description of corporate structure. Boundarylessness is such an all-encompassing idea that many people have trouble understanding it. Welch uses the term to express the quintessence of everything GE stands for: A boundaryless manager should embody speed, simplicity, and self-confidence; serve customers with devotion; act with integrity; serve as an active agent of unceasing change; and more, much more.

At the most basic level, boundarylessness is a matter of cooperation across all the artificial barriers that can separate people with common interest. To explain his thinking, Welch uses the image of a house, which presents barriers in three dimensions:

• The **horizontal** barriers are the walls—such as function, product line, or geographic location—that divide groups of peers into isolated compartments. Why shouldn't Marketing talk to Design, or Tokyo to Milwaukee?

• The **vertical** barriers are the layers—the floors and ceilings—that come with hierarchy. Even a boundaryless organization needs a few layers; at GE an average of four or five now separate business leaders from factory workers. But when differences in rank obstruct open communication, hierarchy becomes self-defeating.

• The **external** barriers are the outside walls of the company itself. Beyond them are found many groups with whom close relationships are essential, such as customers, suppliers, and venture partners.

The idea of boundarylessness is particularly useful at GE, which specializes in complicated businesses that involve processes too complex for individuals or even small groups to manage alone. Indeed, the company's ability to handle complexity ranks among its chief competitive advantages in many lines, from Aircraft Engines to Locomotives to Financial Services. Succeeding at such businesses requires teamwork on a grand scale, making cooperation an essential characteristic of organizational success. Given the right kind of people and clearly understood goals, intricate webs of informal networks among employees can accomplish much more than any rigid, traditional organization, producing tangible competitive advantages.

Not everyone is suited for this style of work. Welch makes the cut on the basis of what he calls "head, heart, and guts." By **"head,"** he means intelligence and technical expertise. **"Guts"** is just another word for self-confidence, one of the qualities he values most in people. As for the elusive quality of **"heart,"** it is a mixture of human understanding, consideration, willingness to share—and the ability to keep one's ego in check. Not many executives embody all three attributes. People with "head" aren't hard to find, but the business world attracts fewer capable people with "heart" than it needs. As for "guts"—many of those who appear to have it actually don't; genuinely self-confident people are surprisingly rare.

Accustomed to producing many more talented managers than it needs, GE almost never recruited outsiders for senior positions until Welch became CEO. In order to change the culture, the company occasionally hires brainy outsiders. They serve two purposes: introducing new perspectives, and providing an objective standard against which to benchmark GE's homegrown managers. Many of these transplanted executives start out in GE's corporate Business Development staff, which evaluates potential mergers and acquisitions. Graduates include Michael Carpenter, a Boston Consulting Group alumnus who handled the RCA deal and now runs GE's Kidder Peabody investment bank; Chuck Peiper, also from B.C.G., who heads Lighting's European businesses; and Nigel Andrew from Booz Allen, who runs Plastic's multi-billion-dollar-a-year North and South American operation.

GE's main focus, though, is on developing in-house talent. Welch is convinced that people with "head" are easy to find, and those who don't have "guts" can acquire it by surmounting failure and experiencing success. As for "heart"—Welch has always insisted that sensitivity can be developed, too. We wonder if he is still so sure. Without question, GE can help shape a more humane new generation of leaders, with a recruiting program that values heart, and the sort of relationship-based leadership training that the company offers in its Work-Out Change Acceleration Program and elsewhere. But inspiring teamwork is a lot harder than bossing people around; some GEers once regarded as terrific managers turn out to be type fours. The only way to deal with inveterate bullies may be to part company with them.

Long before Welch came to power, GE's human resources system was among the most disciplined and sophisticated in the world.

By combining the best of the old GE procedures with the new emphasis on values, Welch fostered an effective apparatus for corporate transformation.

The CEO's personal commitment is what made those methods work. We have never encountered a chief executive who devotes as much time to people issues as Welch does. Take a look at his calendar: At least twice every month, he spends a half day or more talking with rank-and-file employees, either at Crotonville or local Work-Out programs. Every January, he devotes several days to reviewing and adjusting the incentive compensation for each of GE's top 400 executives. And he spends a full month every year on the rigorous management-appraisal and succession-planning reviews called "Session C."

The CEO's Session C is the pinnacle of a painstaking system for appraising executives and helping them improve their skills and plan their careers. GE's 3,500 or so most senior managers have traditionally been regarded as corporate property, although nearly all of them work in operating businesses. Out of this group, the CEO figuratively "owns" the top several hundred. During the yearly Session C reviews, the CEO spends a day visiting each of GE's thirteen business leaders and their staffs, discussing the qualifications, achievements, and developmental needs of every single member of that top echelon of managers. These are substantive discussions based on hard information. Rated on their ability to develop subordinates, business leaders take that responsibility seriously.

GE's elite, six-person Executive Management Staff amasses information to bolster those judgments. As you might expect, a GE personnel file is no random collection of scribbled notes. It includes comparisons of the GE manager's work goals to actual results, and the appraisals prepared for compensation reviews and for annual succession and development evaluations.

Perhaps the most fascinating such report is the Accomplishment Analysis, a ten-to-fifteen-page document that two-person teams of HR professionals spend a full week preparing. Each contains a detailed, thoughtfully argued appraisal of a manager's strengths and weaknesses, covering anything that seems relevant, from financial performance to psychological quirks to physical fitness. The reports suggest ways to develop further: recommending an overseas posting, or a graduate course—or things as basic as showing up at meetings on time, or treating underlings with respect.

Accomplishment Analysis was designed in the 1970s as a tool to evaluate executives. Under Welch it has become a device to help them grow, part of the extensive feedback and coaching process GE uses to develop its executives.

An HR team begins the process by conducting a very lengthy interview with the target executive: These sessions often last five or six hours. Next they interview the subject's bosses, former bosses, colleagues, subordinates—sometimes even customers and suppliers. The development process begins when the subject of the report reads it and discusses it with the HR staffers. These meetings are often textbook examples of constructive conflict at work. Trained to be truth-tellers, HR people are very polite but don't pull their punches; their candor forces managers to confront themselves. The feedback can cause considerable pain, but GE's HR professionals are trained to help people through the emotionally turbulent process of self-discovery: shock, anger, rejection, and acceptance. Repeated exposure to this challenging process has helped GE's managers earn their reputation for excellence.

Accomplishment Analysis is one piece in the complex system that culminates in Session C. Others include:

• **Recruiting:** Welch has urged business leaders to visit campuses personally, instead of delegating the job. New recruits learn about GE's values during their initial interviews.

• **Compensation:** To increase flexibility, most GE businesses have reduced the twenty-nine pay levels that existed in 1981 to a few broad bands. Incentive pay such as bonuses now comprises an average of 25% of total compensation for GE's 3,500 most senior employees; in addition, most of them also get stock options. For the top 450, incentive pay amounts to 35 to 40% of compensation. Type-one employees—those who produce good financial results and share the values—do best.

• **Appraisals:** GE asks employees to rate themselves—and their peers, subordinates, and bosses—by any number of criteria, including the shared values. The person being rated always sees the data and discusses it with a capable person.

• **Training:** Crotonville exists only to further the development of GE leaders. Since 1986 every single program the school offers has included explicit discussion of GE's shared values, and most programs are designed to further them.

• **Reward and Punishment:** A system of values is meaningless unless enforced. GEers who can't live up to the shared values are less likely to rise—and major shortfalls are punished with dismissal. People who embody the values can advance very fast: Most of GE's thirteen business leaders are in their forties.

By 1989 the CEO had begun systematically using shared values to run the company. Welch recalls the howls of protest that greeted his suggestion that GE numerically rate executives on their adherence to GE's shared values:

> We must have discussed this for two hours in the CEC. People kept saying "You can't put a number on how open somebody is." Or, "How can you put a number on how directly people face reality?"
>
> I said, "You're going to have to. Come up with the best numbers you can, and then we'll argue about them."
>
> And that became one of the tools for our Session C review. Are they power oriented? Fair? Are they open, are they self-confident? Do they believe in boundaryless-ness or are they protecting their turf? Are they mean-spirited? We're forcing an evaluation of all our people against these values.

The particular values that GEers share aren't for everyone. Reflections of a distinct corporate identity, they shouldn't be imposed willy-nilly on anyone else. But the broader idea of using shared values as the guiding principle of corporate organization may be Jack Welch's greatest contribution to the art of management.

Chapter Nineteen

Jack Welch
Speaks His Mind
(1992)

As GE's managerial focus has shifted from cost-cutting to the murky realm of human values, you may wonder whether the man once dubbed America's toughest boss has gone soft after twelve years on the job.

Not bloody likely.

"Our standards are tougher than ever," says Welch. "They have to be. The Value Decade has already begun, with global price competition like you've never seen. It's going to be brutal. When I said the 1980s was going to be a white-knuckle decade and the 1990s would be even tougher, I may have understated how hard it's going to get."

He is pushing soft values because he sees them as the only way to maintain the pace of GE's productivity drive. To prevail in the coming years, he argues, GE must keep improving its productivity. But most of the company's fat is long gone. Since 1981 GE has more than doubled its revenues, to more than $62 billion, while greatly reducing total employment. The only way such a lean, disciplined organization can continue to better its performance may be by inspiring the remaining workers to produce more.

Welch has been pushing soft values all along, but GE became receptive to them only recently. It took the CEO years to get his ideas across, first to GE's top-management elite, then to wider circles of executives. At the same time, he was relentlessly pushing hard values, such as global market leadership. Through a gradual, cumulative process, those efforts profoundly altered GE—and then, rather suddenly, the organization ripened, ready for a different kind of change. So now, for the first time, Welch has the opportunity to put his soft ideas into practice on a mass scale.

The revolutionary process, once begun, can never end; each achievement reveals a new challenge. With its portfolio of efficient businesses and willing work force, GE is well into Act III of its transformation. But the dream of a boundaryless organization is not fully realized, and the urgent need for cultural change is undiminished. So long as the world keeps spinning, change will remain a constant, and self-renewal the mark of success.

In mid-1992, we went to GE's headquarters for one final interview. We met in a small, by now familiar conference room with a round table and an expansive view of Fairfield's wooded hills. As Welch struggled for nine hours to summarize his years at GE and his sense of what lies ahead, his energy and stamina were striking— indeed, almost dismaying. The CEO, fifty-seven, had just returned from a fifteen-day, seven-country world tour that had taken him from Saudi Arabia to Indonesia, India, and much of Europe. After a workday crowded with meetings he met us in mid-afternoon—and the conversation continued till 1 A.M., interrupted only for the few minutes we spent serving ourselves a cold buffet dinner.

Here's the gist of what he said:

My main takeaway from all that running around the world is that the capacity-demand equation in most industries is out of whack, and could remain that way for several more years. That's why the Value Decade is upon us.

Everywhere you go, people are saying, "Don't tell me about your technology, tell me your price." To get a lower price, customers are willing to sacrifice the extras they used to demand. The fact is, many governments are broke, and people are hurting, so there's an enormous drive to get value, value, value.

During the global expansion of the 1980s, companies responded to rising demand by building new factories and facilities in computers, airplanes, medical equipment—almost every industry you can think of. Then, when the world economy stopped growing, everybody ended up with too much capacity.

Globalization compounds the problem: It doesn't matter where you are anymore, because distribution systems now give everybody access to everything. Capacity can come from anywhere on the planet, and there's too much in just about every industry in every developed country. No matter where you go, it's the same story.

This worldwide capacity overhang, coming at a time when everybody feels poor, is forcing ferocious price competition. As it intensifies, the margin pressure on all corporations is going to be enormous.

Only the most productive companies are going to win. If you can't sell a top-quality product at the world's lowest price, you're going to be out of the game. In that environment, 6% annual improvement in productivity may not be good enough anymore; you may need 8%, or 9%. And while that bar keeps getting raised higher, higher, higher, we're all going to be experiencing slow revenue growth. It's brutal!

We're focusing our efforts on value-driven products because in business after business, wherever you look, value is what people are buying. With a few exceptions such as pharmaceuticals, the demand for the newest, most expensive, fanciest products is not booming. Look at the sales of European luxury cars—or supercomputers, for that matter. That's not what people want anymore.

In Aircraft Engines, our customers aren't asking about the latest advances, the last 2% of fuel burn. They want to know, *How much will it cost? Can we provide financing? Can they walk away from the lease?* Boeing and ourselves just lost a $1 billion-plus bid at United Airlines to Airbus. Simply put, we couldn't afford to sell them the planes.

Technology is still absolutely critical, but in industry after industry it will be value-driven. Who can make the most energy-efficient light bulb or refrigerator? Whose medical-imaging system is the most cost-effective? The medical diagnostic-imaging business is a perfect example of what's happening everywhere. The market is shifting away from the "technology leader" in the high-end niche to the guy with the basic, proven, low-priced systems that produce acceptable images. Governments have decided they don't want to pay more for health care, so if you're trying to pitch some new hot technology, the customer's going to say, "See you later."

Environmental soundness is another form of value. For instance, we recently won an order from Swissair for jet engines because ours produced the lowest emissions. Multinational companies have to maintain world-class environmental standards wherever they go—even where local laws are lax—in their plants as well as their products. In the end, there's going to be a global standard for the environment, and anyone who cuts corners today will wind up with enormous liabilities down the road. If we're going to be global citizens, we can't have one set of standards in some countries and different standards in others.

Some of the biggest dangers I see ahead come from governments. You can do everything right as a manager and then government deficits, or interest rates, or whatever, can cause a currency to change value by 30% or 40% and knock your business completely out of whack. About 65% of GE's manufacturing base is still located in the U.S. I have to worry about whether government policies here will allow us to deliver the productivity we need to win on a global basis.

But it's not just the United States: Wherever you travel these days, you encounter increasing fear of government. Constituents want more. And to get more, they seem willing to accept enormous increases in government power. I worry about a return to overregulation and protectionism. I don't want to see governments meddling in industrial policy—bureaucrats picking winners and losers. Governments set out to create Silicon Valley and wind up building the Motor Vehicle Department.

In terms of jobs, government may become the world's main growth industry. When the European Community was formed, it created thousands of jobs for bureaucrats. Now they are telling the French which cheese is good and which isn't. It's frightening!

I think the U.S. is in a great position, competitively. We're looking better compared to Germany and Japan than we did five or ten years ago, and many of our companies are in a position to win. We've restructured our industries. Our businesses have better leaders than ever before. Our people have learned the value of their jobs, and the principle that job security comes from winning. Some of the most passionate pleas for worker productivity I've ever read have been made by tough union leaders. They lecture our managers on the subject at Crotonville. That change in attitude is one of the most positive developments I've seen.

The U.S. did have a gap in product quality before, but during the 1980s we made great strides in closing it. Our cars are better, and so are our computers and semiconductors. We thought they'd all be Japanese by now, but they're not. And if you look at the J. D. Power surveys of customer satisfaction—U.S. versus foreign auto companies—we're pretty close. A few years ago, not many would have believed that could happen.

The United States faces some serious issues—but our country isn't being torn apart to the extent of Czechoslovakia, say. What we have to do now is educate our people. Companies have to get involved in the school systems, with dollars and volunteers. Within GE, we've got to upgrade workers' skills, through intense and continuous training. Companies can't promise lifetime employment, but by constant training and education we may be able to guarantee lifetime employability. We've got to invest totally in our people.

For U.S. companies, at least, globalization is getting increasingly difficult. The expansion into Europe was comparatively easy from a cultural standpoint. As Japan developed, the cultural differences were larger, and U.S. business has had more difficulties there. Looking ahead, the cultural challenges will be larger still in the rest of Asia—from China to Indonesia to Thailand to India—where more than half the world lives. U.S. companies will have to adapt to those cultures if they are to succeed in the twenty-first century.

Trying to define what will happen three to five years out, in specific quantitative terms, is a futile exercise. The world is moving too fast for that. What should a company do instead? First of all, define its vision and its destiny in broad but clear terms. Second, maximize its own productivity. Finally, be organizationally and culturally flexible enough to meet massive change.

The way to control your destiny in a global environment of change and uncertainty is simple: Be the highest value supplier in your marketplace.

When I try to summarize what I've learned since 1981, one of the big lessons is that change has no constituency. People like the status quo. They like the way it was. When you start changing things, the good old days look better and better.

You've got to be prepared for massive resistance.

Incremental change doesn't work very well in the type of transformation GE has gone through. If your change isn't big enough, revolutionary enough, the bureaucracy can beat you. Look at Winston Churchill and Franklin Roosevelt: They said, *This is what it's going to be.* And then they did it. Big, bold changes, forcefully articulated. When you get leaders who confuse popularity with leadership, who just nibble away at things, nothing changes. I think that's true in countries and in companies.

Another big lesson: You've got to be hard to be soft. You have to demonstrate the ability to make the hard, tough decisions—closing plants, divesting, delayering—if you want to have any credibility when you try to promote soft values. We reduced employment and cut the bureaucracy and picked up some unpleasant nicknames, but when we spoke of soft values—things like candor, fairness, facing reality—people listened.

If you've got a fat organization, soft values won't get you very far. Pushing speed and simplicity, or a program like Work-Out, is just plain not doable in a big bureaucracy. Before you can get into stuff like that, you've first got to do the hard structural work. Take out the layers. Pull up the weeds. Scrape off the rust.

Every organization needs values, but a lean organization needs them even more. When you strip away the support systems of staffs and layers, people need to change their habits and expectations, or else the stress will just overwhelm them. We're all working harder and faster. But unless we're also having more fun, the transformation doesn't work. Values are what enable people to guide themselves through that kind of change.

To create change, I believe in the Crotonville/Work-Out concept: Direct, personal, two-way communication is what seems to make the difference. Exposing people—without the protection of title or position—to ideas from everywhere. Judging ideas on their merits. You've got to be out in front of crowds, repeating yourself over and over again, never changing your message no matter how much it bores you.

You need an overarching message, something big but simple and understandable. Whatever it is—*we're going to be No. 1 or No. 2, or fix/close/sell, or boundarylessness*—every idea you present must be something you could get across easily at a cocktail party with strangers. If only aficionados of your industry can understand what you're saying, you've blown it.

Another takeaway for me: Simplicity applies to measurements, too. Too often we measure everything and understand nothing. The three most important things you need to measure in a business are customer satisfaction, employee satisfaction, and cash flow. If you're growing customer satisfaction, your global market share is sure to grow, too. Employee satisfaction gets you productivity, quality, pride, and creativity. And cash flow is the pulse—the key vital sign of a company.

One thing I've learned is the value of stretching the organization, by setting the bar higher than people think they can go. The standard of performance we use is: *Be as good as the best in the world.* Invariably people find the way to get there, or most of the way. They dream and reach and search. The trick is not to punish those who fall short. If they improve, you reward them—even if they haven't reached the goal. But unless you set the bar high enough, you'll never find out what people can do.

I've made my share of mistakes—plenty of them—but my biggest mistake by far was not moving faster. Pulling off a Band-Aid one hair at a time hurts a lot more than a sudden yank. Of course you want to avoid breaking things or stretching the organization too far—but generally, human nature holds you back. You want to be liked, to be thought of as reasonable. So you don't move as fast as you should. Besides hurting more, it costs you competitiveness.

Everything should have been done in half the time. When you're running an institution like this, you're always scared at first. You're afraid you'll break it. People don't think about leaders this way, but it's true. Everyone who's running something goes home at night and wrestles with the same fear:: *Am I going to be the one who blows this place up?* In retrospect, I was too cautious and too timid. I wanted too many constituencies on board.

Timidity causes mistakes. We didn't buy a food company in the early 1980s because I didn't have the courage of my conviction. We thought about it, we discussed it at Crotonville, and it was the right idea. I was afraid GE wasn't ready for a move like that. Another thing we should have done is eliminate the sectors right away. Then we could have given the sector heads—who were our best people—big jobs running businesses. We should have invented Work-Out five years earlier. I wish we'd understood boundaryless-ness better, sooner. I wish we'd understood all along how much leverage you can get from the flow of ideas among all the business units.

Now that we've got that leverage, I wonder how we ever lived without it. The enormous advantage we have today is that we can run GE as a laboratory for ideas. We've found mechanisms to share best practices in a way that's trusting and open. When our people go to a Xerox, say, or their people come here, the exchange is good—but in these "fly-bys" the takeaways are largely conceptual, and we both have difficulty getting too far below the surface. But when every GE business sends two people to Louisville for a year to study the Quick Response, program in our own appliance business, the ideas take on intensity and depth. The people who go to Louisville aren't tourists. When they go back to their businesses to talk about Quick Response, they're zealots, because they're owners of that idea. They've been on the team that made it work.

All those opportunities were out there, but we didn't see them until we got rid of the staffs, the layers, and the hierarchies. Then they became obvious. If I'd moved more quickly in the beginning, we'd have noticed those opportunities sooner, and we'd be farther ahead than we are today.

The only way I see to get more productivity is by getting people involved and excited about their jobs. You can't afford to have any-one walk through a gate of a factory, or into an office, who's not giving 120%. I don't mean running and sweating, but working smarter. It's a matter of understanding the customer's needs instead of just making something and putting it into a box. It's a matter of seeing the importance of your role in the total process.

The point of Work-Out is to give people better jobs. When people see that their ideas count, their dignity is raised. Instead of feeling numb, like robots, they feel important. They *are* important.

I would argue that a satisfied work force is a productive work force. Back when jobs were plentiful and there was no foreign com-petition, people were satisfied just to hang around. Now people come to work with a different agenda: They want to win against the competition, because they know that the competition is the enemy and that customers are their only source of job security. They don't like weak managers, because they know that the weak managers of the 1970s and 1980s cost millions of people their jobs.

With Work-Out and boundarylessness, we're trying to differentiate GE competitively by raising as much intellectual and creative capital from our work force as we possibly can. That's a lot tougher than raising financial capital, which a strong company can find in any market in the world.

Trust is enormously powerful in a corporation. People won't do their best unless they believe they'll be treated fairly—that there's no cronyism and everybody has a real shot.

The only way I know to create that kind of trust is by laying out your values and then walking the talk. You've got to do what you say you'll do, consistently, over time.

It doesn't mean everybody has to agree. I have a great relationship with Bill Bywater, president of the International Union of Electronic Workers. I would trust him with my wallet, but he knows I'll fight him to the death in certain areas, and vice versa.

He wants to have a neutrality agreement in GE's nonunion plants. He wants to recruit more members for the union.

I'll say, "No way! We can give people everything you can, and more."

He knows where I stand. I know where he stands. We don't always agree—but we trust each other.

That's what boundarylessness is: An open, trusting sharing of ideas. A willingness to listen, debate, and then take the best ideas and get on with it.

If this company is to achieve its goals, we've all got to become boundaryless. Boundaries are crazy. The union is just another boundary, and you have to reach across, the same way you want to reach across the boundaries separating you from your customers and your suppliers and your colleagues overseas.

We're not that far along with boundarylessness yet. It's a big, big idea, but I don't think it has enough fur on it yet. We've got to keep repeating it, reinforcing it, rewarding it, living it, letting everybody know all the time that when they're doing things right, it's because their behavior is boundaryless. It's going to take a couple of more years to get people to the point where the idea of boundarylessness just becomes natural.

Who knows exactly when I'll retire? You go when it's the right time to go. You pray to God you don't stay too long.

I keep asking myself, *Are you regenerating? Are you dealing with new things? When you find yourself in a new environment, do you come up with a fundamentally new approach?* That's the test. When you flunk, you leave.

Three or four times a year, I hop on a plane and visit something like seven countries in fifteen days. People say to me, *Are you nutty?* No, I'm not nutty. I'm trying to regenerate.

The CEO succession here is still a long way off, but I think about it every day. Obviously, anybody who gets this job must have a vision for the company and be capable of rallying people behind it. He or she has got to be very comfortable in a global environment, dealing with world leaders. Be comfortable dealing with people at all levels of the company. Have a boundaryless attitude toward every constituency—race, gender, everything. Have the very highest standards of integrity. Believe in the gut that people are the key to everything, and that change is not something you fear—it's something you relish. Anyone who is too inwardly focused, who doesn't relish customers, who isn't open to change, isn't going to make it.

Finally, whoever gets the job will have to have what I call an "edge"—an insatiable passion for winning and growing. In the end, I think it will be a combination of that edge and those values that will determine who gets this job.

Well after midnight, Welch finally began to show signs of fatigue. The forest beyond the conference room window had disappeared into blackness. The round table at which we sat was littered with financial charts, dirty dinner plates, candy wrappers, and scribbled-on pads of paper. Time to leave.

Looking at Welch across that table, searching for a final question, we reflected on some lingering concerns about the GE revolution. Can any company maintain such momentum indefinitely? Won't employees eventually burn out?

Over the years, GE's financial and stock market performance seemed to legitimize Welch's controversial decisions. But what if the numbers betray him? Although GE is outperforming most industrial corporations of comparable size, its growth has slowed during the recession of the early 1990s. Meanwhile, the fast-growing Financial Services business is producing ever larger percentages of corporate earnings. In 1993, over 30% of GE's earnings are expected to come from financial services, versus less than 9% in 1981. The trend could become awkward: Since the 1987 stock market crash and the savings-and-loan crisis, wary investors have generally traded the stocks of financial services companies at a steep discount to the S & P 500. What if Wall Street cools on GE?

Ultimately, the question is whether Welch's sometimes fuzzy-sounding ideas about empowering employees can produce the concrete results—in terms of cash flow, and customer and employee satisfaction—that GE will need to prevail in the Value Decade ahead. In 1992 *Time* magazine wrote up the former Neutron Jack in an article titled, "Is Mr. Nice Guy Back?" That sounds like progress—but does Mr. Nice Guy have what it takes to win?

So we asked our last question: What's your response to those who dismiss your talk about values and empowerment as bunk?

For an instant, Welch seemed dumbfounded by the idea that anyone could seriously entertain such a thought. Then, reaching his hands toward us, he made one final effort to explain:

I think any company that's trying to play in the 1990s has got to find a way to engage the mind of every single employee. Whether we make our way successfully down this road is something only time will tell—but I'm as sure as I've ever been about anything that this is the right road.

If you're not thinking all the time about making every person more valuable, you don't have a chance. What's the alternative? Wasted minds? Uninvolved people? A labor force that's angry or bored? That doesn't make sense!

If you've got a better way, show me. I'd love to know what it is.

Chapter Twenty

Jack Welch
Speaks His Mind
(1999)

With hindsight, you can make everything we've done look like a pretty picture. But it's not. Everything we've done, every initiative, was just a way of trying to move the ball forward. A lot of what we did early on was groping around. We didn't know then how to get an initiative like Work-Out or Six Sigma or e-business through the organization. What we've learned is that if you focus on just a few initiatives and stick with them, they grow and they get a life of their own and they build. They grow like crazy! You start an initiative. You don't know where it's going to go. You stay with it, and always keep the intellectual kettle boiling. Good people get involved, and they add their intellect; it goes off in new directions, and the results are amazing. Launch and learn! That's what we know now; we didn't understand all that in the beginning.

Look at almost every best practice we have here. If we still had all the underbrush of bureaucracy and reports, if the company wasn't informal and the people weren't engaged, none of our best practices would amount to much. If you go back to the very first annual report in 1981, the stated objective was to develop a high-spirited, high-energy company where people felt "ownership" of GE. That word *ownership* turned out to be troublesome for us. People didn't understand what we meant. The idea was to engage everyone. We want our people to act like owners.

Everyone forgets that early in my career, when I left Plastics to run a GE division, I ran that business from a Hilton hotel in Pittsfield, Mass. I didn't want the new Plastics guy in Pittsfield to feel I was running him, so I moved the division headquarters to the hotel to get out of his way. There were seven of us there—a lawyer, a business development guy, a finance guy, among others—and we ran Medical, Semiconductors, and some other things. We would take off in the morning and fly to Milwaukee or wherever to work with a particular business, and we'd come back at night and stay up late drinking and reviewing the day's events. We'd do all those crazy things. But what we experienced was *ownership*—we thought we owned our businesses. And we acted like owners. We're all creatures of our experiences; ownership had been my model all along. We ran that division in a totally informal way—we didn't know any better! And so every time I came to these GE businesses that were formal, where people didn't feel ownership, I was stunned.

In the beginning, we were groping for ways to get GE's people to understand a new way of thinking. First of all, as we said in the 1981 report, the idea was to get a good portfolio of businesses. None of these ideas work if you don't have good hardware. In every one of GE's businesses, there's a moment in time where the business cycle isn't right for them. You've got to have staying power to weather the cycles. But if they're good operations, and you give them time, they're going to win. That was the idea behind *No. 1 and No. 2* and *fix/close/sell*. And that is a big deal! Power Systems used to be a drag, but now Power Systems is helping to carry GE. Aircraft Engine had a period of being a drag; now it's having a great run.

At first we didn't have the mechanisms to engage everybody, but we were looking for them. Building Crotonville was part of our attempt to explain this tremendous transition our people were going through. GE in 1981 was a company that held onto everything, that was filled with layers, that was very formal. It was a good company, right for the times—but I didn't think that the way we were then was going to be right for the *next* 20 years. And my predecessor, Reg Jones, obviously didn't think so, either. So, the question we had to answer was, *Why are we making all these changes to a good company?* I responded to that by going to Crotonville again and again to explain the rationale for change. Today, lots of leaders do that sort of thing, but in the early 1980s, it wasn't common for a CEO to sit in front of classes.

Despite that, people were still confused. At the same time as we were building Crotonville—putting in a new residence hall, remodeling the place—GE was shedding layers and selling businesses. People were outraged! It seemed totally in conflict to be investing in this campus while people were losing their jobs. For a while I didn't know how to get the organization to understand why this approach made sense.

Fortunately, I wasn't alone. A good third of the people in the company had worked with me in Plastics, Medical, and the other businesses that I had run. They understood what we were doing. There's a myth that I was taking on the whole company. Well, no one could do that. I had a whole battery of supporters from the very beginning.

We have been working on the same basic ideas since we started. What has changed over time is that we've found mechanisms to bring these ideas into reality. The turning point came when we started Work-Out in 1988. Work-Out, clearly, was hugely important—but no one understands it. Work-Out was a process that took three to five years, and tens of thousands of meetings. It wasn't a tinker. It was a true *commitment,* repeating the same things over and over and over for years. Today, our people can go to a meeting, decide what they're going to do, and then just do it. But before Work-Out, you had to get endless approvals. In one 90-day period, GE did 64 acquisitions. Try to imagine doing 64 acquisitions in 90 days if you had to get approvals from all the staffs we used to have, with all their reviews—you couldn't do it! Work-Out is what cleared out the underbrush that was getting in our way.

Initially, Work-Out was aimed at getting our people to be candid. The people closest to the work knew more about it than their supervisors did, so we wanted to hear their ideas. We wanted people at the bottom of the hierarchy to talk to people at the top. We created a process that enabled the person on the floor to share ideas with the person about two layers above his boss. We did that over and over and over again, all over GE. And that's all it was, at first. We didn't start it thinking, *Let's get rid of the prejudice against anything that's not-invented-here.* Our plan wasn't, *Let's go out and touch every company in the world.* But over time, as we kept on repeating it, one Work-Out after another, the effort grew and expanded, and we kept on learning—until one day we found ourselves talking about boundaryless behavior. *Boundaryless* wasn't in our vocabulary when we started. *Boundaryless* is a very powerful word, because it expanded our horizons—it got us thinking about crossing more boundaries than we'd initially had in mind. *Boundaryless* is what got us going outside the company and talking to customers and suppliers. It was a natural evolution from Work-Out.

Cultural change wasn't our original intention with Work-Out. The intention was to get everyone in the game, to create for everyone the informal atmosphere that we liked so much at Crotonville. At Crotonville people could ask tough questions, because they weren't identified. They could take incredible swings at me. The problem was, when they went back to their office, they wouldn't dare say to their boss what they had been saying to me. That's what motivated Work-Out. It was about getting everybody to vent their feelings.

Maybe *groping* is the wrong word to describe the process we've undergone. What I'm trying to say is: You begin an initiative with an objective. Let's look at globalization, for example. The objective, at first, is to get GE products sold around the world. That's what you're thinking about. Then, as the initiative develops, you begin staffing overseas offices with locals. Then you start making stuff in the local country. Then you see the opportunity to start making components there to import back to the U.S. And then, all of a sudden, you start thinking about *intellect*. So now we're building a $50 million R&D center in India. In Prague we've got a lab doing great metallurgy work. There is a guy who has built a massive collection center in Bangalore—he's calling all around the world collecting payments for us. Our average cost per aircraft engine engineer ought to be going up; instead, it's coming down because we're moving them to low-cost sites like Mexico. We're doing all sorts of things now because we finally noticed that we've been getting great intellect from all around the world. When we launched the globalization initiative, it wasn't about sourcing intellect. But as we stuck with it year after year, the initiative *evolved* from sourcing to selling product to sourcing intellect.

Or take the services initiative. We went from adding a service component to our products, to thinking about service itself as the product, to our new understanding that the key to success in services is the introduction of a whole lot of technology. That is the future. We started the service initiative just to make sure we weren't giving away service for free; now it's most of our revenues. We did it by getting better people to start thinking about service. We did it by focusing on maximizing the service opportunities for our products. And then—it expands. You start thinking about other people's products, ways to use our technology to service other people's products. And then the thinking goes to technology itself: Every time you start a new product design, you're thinking about the service opportunity ten years out. You build something in, like software capabilities in a CT scanner, so a customer can upgrade it later. You add lots of software to your product, lots of monitoring, lots of information technology.

I was very slow to buy into Six Sigma. I thought the quality movement was bull. Larry Bossidy is the one who got me into Six Sigma, after he had been running AlliedSignal for a while. Larry hated quality more than I did. And then one day he said, "Jack, this works. I'm getting all kinds of results."

I said, "You like quality?" I couldn't believe it! Larry and I used to laugh at those quality circles.

Larry said, "No, I'm telling you the truth."

Then he came and gave a speech at the CEC, pitching Six Sigma. Our guys almost fainted! But we all said, "Gee, if he likes Six Sigma this much, there must be something there, because we like Larry."

Six Sigma got us focused on spans. *Span* refers to the measure of variation. Before, when we measured something, like the time we take to deliver a product to a customer, we'd look at the average time, or the mean. We'd work hard, and we'd make big improvements by those measures, but the customer wouldn't feel it. We know, because the customer told us.

Here's the problem: Say we make four deliveries to you. The first one takes 20 days; the next, 16 days; then 40 days for the third one; and 2 days for the last one. Our average time for those four deliveries is around 20 days. So then we go out and make a lot of changes to our business process, and the next four deliveries come in at 16 days, 4 days, 21 days, and 19 days. Now our average delivery time is down to 15 days—that's a 25% improvement, which looks pretty good to us. But the customer isn't seeing any benefit!

What Six Sigma taught us is the importance of variation: The customer doesn't want the delivery 40 days early, and he doesn't want it 40 days late. What he wants is the smallest standard deviation in the delivery time, so that he doesn't have to waste a lot of money and effort adjusting his business process to ours. Now, all our guys are thinking about spans—how many days early or how many days late are we, compared to a customer's demand? I can show you businesses that have tightened spans from 35 days, to 4 days, or to 2 days. Believe me, the customer feels that!

Besides the improvement in customer satisfaction from Six Sigma, we've gained a lot of pricing power. Let's go back to the CT scanner. We introduced a product called Light Speed, which was designed from the bottom up to meet Six Sigma standards. Plug it in, it runs. The Light Speed CT sells for $1 million versus $800,000 or so for the previous unit. Six Sigma enabled us to change the game.

Eventually, maybe in another couple of years, Six Sigma will become the way we just naturally work. Each of our big businesses is now graduating 120 to 130 Six Sigma black belts a year. To get a black belt, you have to complete three Six Sigma projects. We're on the way to having somewhere around 15,000 to 30,000 black belts, which means that these people will make a critical mass within GE's leadership. Black belts are getting all the leadership jobs now—if you're not a black belt, you're not among the top candidates. That's a good example of how we take an initiative and embed it into the culture so that it becomes a way of life.

Looking back, Six Sigma prepared us beautifully for e-commerce. If you had tried to operate an e-business before Six Sigma, you'd be disappointing customers every day with partial shipments and all sorts of other problems. E-commerce is about customer satisfaction and fulfillment.

E-business is the biggest game in town, probably the biggest idea that has come along in 100 years, and let's be honest, we could have missed it. My age and my experience were against me on this one. I thought it was nonsense at first. It was Jane, my wife, who finally got me into e-commerce. I saw her doing all kinds of stuff online: Jane basically lives at E*Trade. Or we'd be going somewhere on vacation and she'd show me the virtual tour. I was just blown away by all the things she could do. Then, during the Christmas season of 1998 I saw everyone in the office ordering gifts.

So I got started. I was afraid of typing at first, so I got the Mavis Beacon learn-to-type software, and worked on it at home on weekends and nights—now I can type pretty well. I began using e-mail, and I started going to the chat rooms to see what they were saying about GE. I still check those chat rooms almost every day, just to see what people are saying. I'm totally hooked.

The next breakthrough was getting myself a mentor. I was in the U.K., at a GE business review. The young man who was running it told me he was being mentored in e-business by one of the junior people in his office, who knew all about the Web. I didn't get it at first—usually, in a mentoring program, it's the boss mentoring the young person. But what a great idea! The next week, when I came back from Europe, I sent out an e-mail to 500 people, telling them they all have to get a mentor—a young one!—to teach them about the Internet. That tipped our whole organization upside-down, because suddenly the youngest people are teaching the most senior ones. This is what I appreciate about our culture: First, everybody did it, they all got young mentors. Second, they all *liked* it, because it related to the e-business initiative we're all working on, and everyone wanted to get better at it.

We used to think these websites were magic—that you needed Nobel prizewinners to start one. Then we had a group of 11 information-management trainees from Penn State working for us; in 16 days they put together a site to auction off commodities in transportation. The cost to create that site was peanuts; it saved us $4 million in the first six months. That experience broke the mystique of the Web for us. We lost our fear. We also began to appreciate the beauty of e-business. It's so transparent! Everything is visible to the customer—your inventories, your shipping, your behavior. There's nowhere to hide.

Our approach to e-business is the same as for any new initiative: Launch and learn. We made some silly decisions, at first, such as partnering with more experienced companies that tried to get in between us and our customers. We saw our mistake pretty quickly: We cut those guys off and now we don't let third parties anywhere near our customers.

E-commerce is a game we can win. We already have the brand, the capital, the infrastructure, and the distribution know-how; and we have learned how to pour tons of technology into a project to make it work for our customers. What GE can do, that none of these startups can do, is to transfer our best practices to the customer, so that he can run his own business more effectively.

We're going to help him win every day. So in diagnostic imaging, we can connect all of our machines in hospitals everywhere to gather data. Nobody else has information like this. So first thing in the morning, we can send out an e-mail to Dr. So-and-So. It says, "Good morning. You ranked in the 71st percentile in the world in the last 36 hours on MRI scans. Click here, and we'll bring you the CD-ROM upgrade to improve your performance." You can do the same thing in utilities: "Your utility's output ran at 71% efficiency against a national average yesterday of 81%. Here's what you can do. Click here, we'll be out to fix it."

The more proprietary information you have, the more valuable your game is, and the more ruthlessly you can cut out these intermediaries who want to get in between you and your customer. We've got the information or the know-how to do something like this in almost every one of our businesses. In our credit business, it's our risk models. In Fleet, which leases vehicles, it's our physical distribution ability. In some cases we build our own sites; in other cases we trade our knowledge for substantial equity positions in sites owned by others. We have been buying data mining companies, because our whole game is intellect. The initiative is all laid out. And to show you how these things all tie together, Crotonville reinforces the initiative: Every Crotonville class is going out focused on e-business. They've lived it!

You always wish you had started these initiatives earlier—every one of them. We'd be so much farther along. But on the other hand, you're always afraid that if you move off an existing initiative too quickly, you'll kill it. So you always have to come up with a new plan, new programs, new reward systems to keep an initiative hot. In order to be sure we did not abandon Six Sigma when we started e-commerce, we gave special stock options, in equal amounts, to all the e-business leaders *and* to the Six Sigma people. You want the initiative to take on a life of its own, to get assimilated. Work-Out, for example, is still there: In 1999 we had a 90-day across-the-company blitz. It was about the same old stuff—getting rid of meetings and reports—and it did us a lot of good. Globalization is still there. It's a way of life.

To make an initiative successful, you've got to commit yourself to it totally, and *stay* committed. The last thing you want is to turn these programs into the "flavor of the month." You need to be relentlessly persistent. That's why, after a meeting on one of these things, I will send out my notes to all the participants, to make sure we're all on the same page. Clearly, it has slowed us down to make sure that each one of these initiatives stuck. We'd stay with an initiative two or three years before bringing the next one in, doing them deliberately one after the other, in sequence. Between Six Sigma and e-commerce, for instance, three years passed. In an ideal world, we would have started each of them three or four years earlier. On the other hand, though, the programs worked.

We put great people on our initiatives. The effort blossoms with great people, with their intellect, their ideas. Then we take the successes, and make those people the role models who talk about it to others. That way, we keep building and building, and we end up a long way from where we started.

All that is one way of describing how our operating system works. Session C and the CEC and the annual leadership meeting in Boca Raton are all integral parts of it, too—we could have spent all our time discussing them instead. Put it all together and you see that this GE operating system is our competitive advantage. It's our mechanism for cultural change. Over time, it alters the way we think.

This operating system is our social architecture. It's built around dialogue, which came from Work-Out, which led to boundaryless behavior, which led to maximizing individual and collective intellect. It is reinforced by trust, which leads to responsibility, which gets us to values. Responsibility gets you a job at GE: By making the numbers, you get to play the game. You get *promoted* through the values. So, everyone in the game has made the numbers; we try to identify anyone who doesn't live the values, and get them out of here. We still make mistakes; we still have some bullies. But in our game, making numbers has nothing to do with how far you go in the company. Getting promoted is all about values: boundaryless behavior, being open to ideas from anywhere, energizing others, high integrity, all that stuff. It's about being somebody who can excite and maximize individual and collective intellect through boundaryless behavior, open to ideas from anywhere. That's our culture.

Everyone wants to know about our succession process. It was very straightforward. It was never about selecting one person—it was about building a *team*. How do you get to the right group of people who, together, have the complementary skills needed to take GE to the next level and beyond?

The process started around 1991. Every six months we'd go to the board with a list of the most likely candidates. We started talking to the board more seriously about succession in 1994. The obvious candidates were the business leaders—ten people plus a broader field. In 1996 the board started going out to meet them. They'd go out in groups of five, without me, to visit the business leader for a day. They'd meet his staff, go to a ball game together, have dinner. When they got back, they'd summarize their impressions for me. That was very useful.

Then I would have dinner with the candidates. Very informal. Different from the process I went through. We'd have a glass of wine, and talk about who in the organization they like, who they don't like. How do they feel about their peers? What do they want to do in life? What are their objectives? I asked them the same questions people ask me: What do you think the leader of the next century looks like? What's your vision of the game? We'd talk about everything from baseball to family. We talked about life. These were very comfortable meetings.

Meanwhile, none of these people were stuck in a holding pattern, waiting to be selected. For one thing, they weren't all gathered at headquarters, competing against each other. They were all out in the field, in great jobs—CEOs running $7 billion-, $8 billion-, $10 billion-a-year companies. And when we all got together for CEC, there was no backbiting, because that's not our game. So throughout the whole process we tried hard to maintain the atmosphere of business as usual.

What I was thinking about the whole time, and what the board was thinking about, was chemistry: How do we end up with a group that works well together? We want a collegial team here, because no one person can run this company.

The only reason for me to retire is so that things can change. The new team will have to find their own way, their own form, their own structure, their own initiatives, and they may do it with different businesses, perhaps. That's all up to them. The only thing that would disappoint me is if GE were broken up. No one around here has been thinking about that, but that's the one limit I'd want to see on GE's strategy going forward. If we did that, we'd lose the value of our integration and intellectual capacity. Having so many businesses and so many geographies is what stimulates us and gives us so many fresh ideas. It would break my heart to see this company broken up, to watch others picking its bones apart. I don't think that's possible.

I just want this team to win the next game, whatever it is. GE clearly is going to have to get faster, more customer-centered. In the e-business world everything is faster and more transparent. There's nowhere to hide. These people can do it. The CEC is the most capable group of people you will ever see in one room. They're all smart as hell, they all have ideas, they're all hitters. And when you think about it, the only thing a big company can really do is take swings. So we go to bat all the time.

Winning in the century ahead is going to require a passionate, total commitment to making sure your customers win. That will be your mind-set. You will spend every day finding ways to make the customers more productive, more effective. You will be totally outward-looking, because your whole organization will have become transparent. The employees are going to know every key piece of information. Databases are going to be everywhere. Everyone's going to know everything. Managers will have to be energizers— cosmic, exciting people, raising the barn, rewarding people with great job offers. Half your people might be in offices. A lot of them will be working at home. There will be a total change in hierarchical relationships: The only thing that keeps companies in hierarchical mode now is information, and the authority one gets from holding on to information. But everyone's going to know everything! All these changes clearly will be in place by the end of the decade. It will start in the U.S., but the rest of the world is coming so fast, it's unbelievable.

Energizing leaders aren't the whole story—you need exciting atmospheres. The atmosphere you create is what you'll use to compete for the best people. You've got to be growing, offering exciting new opportunities, and you've got to give people good lives. Many people enjoy the intellectual stimulation of a multibusiness culture, they like working with vast resources, so there will always be a role for GE.

We are competing for talent with companies that have started with a clean sheet of paper, and have created exciting, informal atmospheres. It's much harder for older companies to do that. That's why we need mechanisms that provide training and contribute to fresh understanding. That's what our initiatives are all about. During the 1980s and 1990s, our training efforts, and our focus on values and leadership—those were nice, they were very helpful. But as you look forward to the century ahead, those things become *critical*. You absolutely need them. No one really understands how valuable an informal company is; it's *critical* to understand that. So, we've got a jump on the game. But I'll tell you, we probably did it the hard way. We started with no idea what we were doing. Today, there are models out there that show you how to get it done pretty easily. Our model isn't the only one. The thing to remember is that it takes a total commitment of leadership.

When all the paraphernalia is stripped away, the leader must articulate a vision. People in my job don't know how to design the engine, or how to fix the car. That's not what we do. *Our job is developing people to build the company.* That's it. Allocating resources and developing people.

I'm one lucky bastard. I probably wanted to be CEO by the time I was 20. I always had my nose pressed against the glass. Now, it would be insane to want anything more. Sure, I'd have like to have been a better athlete, a great golfer or a great hockey player.

But even *thinking* that is almost sinful from where I sit. I never have my nose against the glass anymore. I'm happy for everyone's success. When people were getting rich in dot-coms, my feeling was, God bless them! I hope they get tons! I never have to be envious of anybody or anything. On the other hand, it is clear that having my nose against the glass did bring a lot of energy into my life. It was always easy to keep trying to win. It was always easy to want to do better.

I still want to do better. Why stop? So we're boiling the ocean, trying to create perfection. Run for your life. Launch and learn. Build it in days, pulse it in minutes. Yeah.

Afterword to the 2001 Edition

J umpin' Jack Flash" was a headline in the 1980s referring to Jack Welch's quick-action style. He was still true to form less than six months before his carefully planned April 1, 2001, retirement date. He pulled an early April Fools' Day. He agreed to buy Honeywell for $48 billion and as part of the deal promised Wall Street he would stay till January 2002 to see that the integration got off to the right start. This was not Welch figuring out a way to hang on; it was the kid who could not pass the candy store without going in.

The failure of the proposed Honeywell acquisition did not fundamentally alter his legacy. It was consistent with his modus operandi for twenty years, and the succession process went as he had planned it. Welch's decision to delay retirement in order to complete the acquisition would have been a mixed blessing under any circumstances. When the deal subsequently collapsed it cast a pall on what might have been a triumphal exit for GE's longtime leader.

During his twenty years as CEO of GE, Jack Welch set many new standards for business leadership and built GE into what he calls the "world's most competitive enterprise." But only now at the end of his career can it be evaluated in perspective. What emerges as his single greatest legacy is the depth of leadership he left behind at GE.

As Welch prepared to leave office, many people in the business world were amazed by his masterful handling of the succession process. Two years before his retirement, as the endgame opened, he had seven fully qualified internal candidates. During the winnowing and final selection, he managed to keep all the players fully engaged and contributing to the company. And he is handing over to his successor, Jeffrey Immelt, a company that is well positioned for the e-commerce era, has forward momentum, and is cleaned up and ready for the new leader to make his mark.

Welch delivered the most skillfully orchestrated CEO succession in business history, but the succession was just the culmination of a twenty-year leadership development effort. Almost as soon as Welch came into office, he began to build leadership and developing leaders into the fabric of life at GE. The smooth succession was just a marker of his success in creating a company with an abundance of highly developed leadership talent and a process for continuously developing leaders. As one analyst has summed it up in a remarkably mixed metaphor, "Not only did Jack create bench strength, but he built a DNA that is institutionally bulletproof for a long time."

In this book we have chronicled the steps Welch took to create the continuous GE revolution. It is one that simultaneously built the world's best cadre of business leaders and the world's most valuable enterprise. GE is the only company from the original Dow Jones Industrial Average over 100 years ago that is still on the list, and it is the No. 1 company, to boot. It is also the premier "transition" company moving from the twentieth to twenty-first century. In fact, its success in marrying "old economy" power with new dotcom speed has made the GE formula the recipe that "new economy" CEOs are increasingly seeking to duplicate.

Obviously, Welch wasn't around for the early years of GE's more than 100-year run, but he did remodel and revitalize it during a critical period. While many of its old industrial peers were slipping off the radar screen, Welch was rebuilding GE not only to survive, but to be the world leader at the beginning of the twenty-first century. In 1980, GE ranked 14 in total market value, and Westinghouse, Burroughs, and Digital Equipment were still blue chips. In early 2001 GE is worth $460 billion, and its closest rivals, Microsoft, Intel, and Cisco, are companies that were infants, if they existed at all, when Welch took office.

Welch has been lauded as the most admired and important CEO of the twentieth century. This is a status I believe he earned and deserves, yet, having worked for him and known him for more than twenty years, I think that those who romanticize and lionize Welch misconstrue who he really is as a leader. He is a flawed human being, like all of us. He is unreasonable at times, dead wrong in some of his decisions, and at times out to lunch in his demands. At the same time he is a very warm and caring human being. Every year, he takes the time to write personal notes to literally thousands of people, both inside and outside GE. He is really all about emotion. The good side of that is that he is amazingly insightful when it comes to reading people and situations. He can empathize with people, and then figure out what's needed to energize and excite them. The dark side of this emotional drive is a demonic intensity to win. Thus you can find him acting like a careful, listening learner even as he impatiently and impetuously pursues an agenda that he has declared to be urgent. The mixture is what makes him who he is.

It is through this lens of human strengths and frailties that Welch and the GE transformation must be viewed. The Welch-led GE legacy is built on ordinary people doing some pretty extraordinary things. It is a company that continues to shape much of the global business community. It is both revered and resented. I have never met a business leader who is neutral on GE or Jack Welch. But whether they idolize or condemn, most are off the mark, because they don't really understand GE, Welch, or the other GE leaders he has nurtured.

The Welch Track Record

There is no question that Jack Welch will go down in history as the most significant and influential business leader of the twentieth century. Both his ideas and his performance are remarkable, and the record of his accomplishments in the past twenty years is astounding. Under his leadership,

- GE has created billions of dollars in value for its share owners. A $1,000 investment made when Welch took over GE is now worth more than $45,000. Its market capitalization in the fall of 2000 had increased fifty-five-fold to $550 billion from $10 billion. It has paid out more than $27 billion in dividends.

- GE has transformed itself from a plodding producer of appliances and industrial equipment into a high-tech provider of industrial and financial services. GE still makes hardware, but that's just the ante that opens the game. GE creates value and stays ahead of its competitors by providing services that help customers operate the hardware more effectively and efficiently.

- GE has revamped its business model and built a growth engine that has propelled double-digit revenue and profit growth for the past fifteen years. For the previous eight decades, GE had been a reliable "GNP company" whose results year after year matched the performance of the overall economy. Under Welch's leadership, GE divested itself of $23.8 billion of businesses that did not live up to his dictate that they be No. 1 or No. 2 in their markets and acquired $127.5 billion (+$40 billion if the Honeywell deal closes) of businesses that did. Matching the economy is no longer considered success at GE. In the past twenty years, the company has outperformed the economy by 27%.

- GE has dismantled its bureaucracy, even though it was widely acclaimed as a managerial paragon. The stifling layers of bureaucrats have been replaced with a radically new corporate architecture that facilitates the sharing of ideas, values, and information. The old GE bureaucracy controlled far-flung operations through rules and strictures. The new GE coordinates and aligns its global businesses by providing a shared base of knowledge and a framework of core values for making decisions.

- GE has transformed its internal culture from fierce competition to corporate-wide cooperation. The result is that the time and energy that used to go into political maneuvering and turf battles now go toward activities that create real value—pleasing customers, generating growth, and improving efficiency.

- GE has implemented a world-class Six Sigma quality program that has transformed all areas of GE operations and focused them on recognizing and eliminating the causes of defects. GE did not invent Six Sigma, but it has implemented the approach with such vigor that it has delivered $7.1 billion in returns based on an investment of $2.1 billion in only five years.

- GE has wholeheartedly embraced e-business. When it seemed that Internet start-ups would take over the world, GE showed that in fact fast and flexible, rather than new and small, are the qualities that make companies winners in the "knowledge economy." Under Welch's insistent prodding, GE managers have figured out how to use Internet technology to make the big, old company fast and flexible as well. "Every year we got better, faster, hungrier, and more customer-focused—until the day this elixir, this tonic, this e-business came along and changed the DNA of GE forever by energizing and revitalizing every corner of this Company," enthused Welch in his 1999 letter to share owners.

These are just some of the reasons most people name Jack Welch as the business leader they most admire and *Fortune* proclaimed him the "manager of the century." Welch set out in 1981 to build "the world's most competitive enterprise." The result of his vision is an amazing tale of leader-driven transformation. Welch took over the reins of a company that was deemed by just about everyone to be highly successful and—before most people sensed any trouble on the horizon at all—managed to shake up its culture and rebuild its business model so that when other old-line industrial companies suddenly found themselves in fast-paced global markets where they were unable to compete, GE was ready with a powerful new engine for producing growth and profits.

Welch kept the revolutionary process going, creating an organization that thrives on change. In his 1998 letter to share owners, he describes a company that "is both challenged by the unexpected and confident in, as well as capable of, dealing with whatever comes along." Coaching, cheering, prodding, and directing, he has led the men and women of GE to achieve the remarkable feats listed above. He describes them in much more detail and sets them in the context of GE's continuing success in his annual letters to share owners, which are included in their entirety in this book. These letters represent Welch's teaching notes. They clearly lay out the GE agenda every year. Reading them provides a clear track of how Welch led GE.

Welch the Teacher

Jack Welch's legacy is captured best in the many successful leaders, both inside and outside of GE, whom he has taught. All his life, Welch has been a coach and teacher and cheerleader. A scrappy only child of an Irish working-class family in Salem, Massachusetts, Jack was the ringleader of the kids in the neighborhood and captained his hockey team in high school. When he went to GE after getting a Ph.D. in chemical engineering from the University of Illinois, he started the Plastics business from a hotel room in Pittsfield, Massachusetts. He then built it into one of the company's fastest growing business units by collecting a maverick group of players and fashioning them into a winning team. It would be an understatement to say that winning is extremely important to Welch, but he learned early in life that in group activities, consistent success comes only through teamwork and leadership, so he is a relentless team builder and leadership coach.

If you audit Welch's calendar for the past ten years, you will see that he spends more than 50% of his time on matters directly related to human resources and leadership development. Every several weeks for his twenty-year tenure as CEO, he went to GE's Crotonville Leadership Development Center to teach. He personally reviewed the performance evaluations and career plans, in detail, of the top 500 executives and, in less detail, the next 1,000. He spent twelve- to fourteen-hour days in each of the major GE businesses, going through a grueling succession planning process called Session C. Here are a few examples from former GE executives as well as a young entrepreneur who was a friend of Welch's son in Pittsfield.

Essentially, Jack Welch's secret to success is that he is a world-class learner and teacher. He is curious about the world. He is insatiably hungry for new ideas, information, and insights. And once he has learned something, he can't keep it bottled up. He has to spread it around. He is also a risk-taker. Because he often acts impulsively and is willing to try things that are less than sure bets, he has probably made more mistakes than most people. But what he has that most people don't have is an exceptional ability to recognize his mistakes, learn from them, and translate them into lessons that he then uses for himself and passes on to others. Whether a screw-up is caused by risk-taking, misjudgment, or just plain stupidity, Welch is a master at confronting reality, figuring out what went wrong, even if the fault is his, and then moving on, wiser for the experience. In fact, because he learns so well from mistakes, part of his strength as a leader/teacher is his track record of mistakes—on investments, acquisitions, partnerships, products, people, structure.

As recounted in this book, in 1981 GE bought Calma, a computer-aided-design firm. Welch's plan was that GE would become a leader in the factory-automation business. Instead, Calma turned into a money pit and was losing $50 million a year by the time GE sold it in 1988. But from the experience, Welch learned about nurturing the value that acquired companies bring to the table and not letting bureaucracy smother innovation. This was the start of a much deeper understanding of how to make acquisitions successful, which GE has done with literally hundreds of acquisitions since the mid-1980s, adding up to over $175,226 billion through the 1990s.

The refrigerator compressor fiasco was another expensive mistake that yielded a valuable lesson. In the mid-1980s GE decided to put a new compressor derived from air conditioners in its refrigerators. It was a top-level decision made in the interest of economics. Unfortunately, none of the people who were in the room when the decision was made, including Welch, knew anything about compressors. The subsequent refrigerator repairs and replacements cost GE about $1 billion. The lesson for Welch: Fear of breaking things had made him too slow to clear out layers of bureaucracy. He had removed some layers, but the panicked reactions of the threatened bureaucrats had kept him from going far enough. In a leaner organization, the people making the decisions would be closer to the action. After that, the reorganization moved much more quickly.

A fundamental shift that Welch made in response to feedback was to change from being what I call a social Darwinist to becoming a coach. In the early years, as he began to remove layers, Welch believed in survival of the fittest. The fittest would figure out how to do their jobs in the leaner environment. In fact, many of them did, but the price was rapid burnout. When spans of control in Medical Systems went from seven to twenty direct reports, I can remember working with midlevel engineering managers who could not figure out how to get their work done. The ways they set work goals and managed day to day were leading to constant seven-day weeks and massive overload.

After a few years, Welch saw that social Darwinism would destroy the company. GE had good, smart, dedicated people, and they needed help. Welch dropped the sink-or-swim Darwinism and became a coach. Throughout the company, he gave speeches, held meetings, and set up programs to help people figure out how to operate more efficiently in a leaner organization. By 1988, the Work-Out program was engaging everyone in the company in workshops to drive out bureaucracy, liberate time, and figure out new ways of working. Since then Change Acceleration, Best Practice sharing, and Six Sigma training have all become Welch-led coaching enablers for GE.

What makes the management precepts and practices that Welch developed at GE astounding is that they are just as valid, and even essential, for tiny Internet start-ups as for industrial behemoths. What Welch did, as he puts it, was figure out how to "get a small-company spirit into the big-company body." In Welch's case, the challenge was teaching the elephant to dance. GE was already big; what he needed to do was to make it creative, energetic, and responsive to the music that the customers are playing. In the new economy, CEOs have a different challenge. Their companies are often energetic, creative dancers, but they are scrawny. What they have to do is to bulk up the dancer so it won't get knocked off the stage by the elephants. But, regardless of the starting point, success in the new knowledge economy demands that companies be big, fast, and smart.

In the non-Welch world, those qualities compete with one another. Big versus fast. Fast versus smart. Welch's gift was to rewrite the rules. GE became fast *because* it was big and smart *because* it was fast. He figured out how to turn liabilities into assets and in doing so delivered such spectacular results that he redefined the game.

Scott McNealy, the founder of Sun Microsystems, is on the GE board and is just one of Jack Welch's Silicon Valley disciples. Microsoft's Bill Gates and Steve Ballmer and Cisco's John Chambers have publicly said that they have looked to Welch for guidance. Joe Liemandt has fashioned much of Trilogy Software around Welch teachings. Keith Krach is scaling Ariba using Welch and GE concepts. Nigel Andrews left GE Capital to help Internet Capital Group take its portfolio of 70 start-ups and try to build the GE of twenty-first-century Internet companies. The point is, Welch is the teacher for all varieties of businesses. His principles are universal because they are about creating a winning organization of leaders at all levels.

Welch's Succession Process

GE stands unique among companies in the world for having incredible bench strength. In the recent past, blue chip companies such as AT&T, IBM, Hewlett Packard, Kodak, and Merck have had to go outside to find new CEOs. One of the most significant failures of any institution is to have not developed the next generation of leadership. Not only did GE find its successor, but in the last few years there were seven or eight fully qualified successors and a team that included several vice chairmen that could have ended up as CEO. This didn't happen by accident.

Most companies go into crisis mode, or at least lose focus, as the CEO approaches retirement age, but GE just got stronger and more effective in the final years of Jack Welch's tenure. The reason is that for twenty years, Welch made developing leaders throughout GE a top priority. As a result, when the time came to choose a successor, there was a full pipeline of leadership talent. The abundance, in turn, allowed Welch to keep the competition centered on ever-improving results rather than on executive-floor politics. GE seems to have actually gained energy and focus from the succession process.

To understand Jack Welch, and the GE that he led, you have to understand that teaching and developing leaders were the means through which Welch managed and led the company. All companies do a certain amount of training and human development, because they need qualified people to fill jobs, but in Welch's GE, creating leaders was a core competence. Welch believed that GE would win or lose according to its ability to develop the leadership skills of its people. He built GE into a teaching organization, one in which teaching and learning are woven into the very fabric of the company.

From the day he became CEO in 1980, Welch focused on developing leaders. In the early years, the headlines were riveted on his reshaping of the GE business model. Previously, anything related to electricity had been deemed suitable for its "general electric" portfolio. When Welch arrived and began closing plants and selling underperforming units to fulfill his "No. 1, No. 2, fix, close, or sell" edict, this grabbed the public attention. But the reshuffling of the GE business portfolio was just a piece of Welch's agenda. At a young forty-five, he knew that barring health issues or a colossal screw-up, he probably would have twenty years in office. Nonetheless, he took the approach that everyone should be groomed as if they were going to become the CEO. By developing everyone in the company to be leaders, he not only provided the selection committee with a plethora of choices twenty years later, but also built the bench strength to make GE a winner while he was in office and keep it a winner when he was gone.

Welch as Leader/Teacher: His Teachable Point of View

All of his life, Welch has been a voracious learner and an enthusiastic coach. He knows more than most people because he will listen to anyone he thinks may have ideas or information that he can use. And he has had more influence than just about any twentieth-century business leader, because he will share his knowledge and judgment with just about anyone who will listen. He is a true leader/teacher.

As a kid, when he was captain of his hockey team, he would coach others, trying to make sure that everyone's level of play improved. Later, in his early days at GE, he built Plastics into one of the company's fastest growing units. In those days his teaching was informal, day-to-day coaching, instant feedback, and constant dialogue and debate with his team.

As Welch's leadership pond expanded, so did his learning about how to teach. Scale forced him to learn a couple of important lessons. First, the larger the number of people, the more critical it was to have a point of view that was clear and concise so that people could comprehend it. Second, scale required ultimately building a GE teaching infrastructure for reaching all employees.

Having a teachable point of view, as Eli Cohen and I explain in *The Leadership Engine* (HarperBusiness, 1997), is one of the keys to being a winning leader. A teachable point of view is what you have when you have figured out how to take the implicit information inside your head and make it explicit to others. It means not only that you have a point of view but that you know how to articulate it and communicate it. Everyone has points of view. We all have a wealth of knowledge and experience from which we create assumptions about the world and how it operates. We use them every day to orient ourselves in new situations and make decisions about how to proceed. In order to pass that knowledge on to others, leaders must be able to articulate their points of view in ways that people can understand. Successful leaders need a teachable point of view that includes (a) the key business ideas for the company; (b) the values that shape and drive behavior; (c) an understanding about how to energize people emotionally so that they live the ideas and values; and (d) a determination to exercise edge, which means making tough and courageous decisions.

Jack Welch's ability to develop teachable points of view is perhaps his greatest strength. The reason for this is embedded in the way his mind works. Welch is a brilliant strategist because he's an excellent learner. He is competitive, but he never lets his ego blind him. He is avid for what he called "the straight scoop." He wants to know what is really happening in the world without any filters or shadings of wishful thinking. So he's always watching and listening. He latches onto and uses every piece of information that comes across his path. And he trolls for ideas the way a seiner goes after fish.

In addition to having a voracious appetite for facing reality, Welch is always drawing lessons and extracting concepts from his constant stream of data and ideas. For Welch, the process of learning isn't complete until he has both applied the lessons himself and managed to convince other people of their validity. In other words, teaching is an essential part of Welch's learning process. Developing teachable points of view is how Welch makes sense of the world for himself. It isn't always easy, but he works at it. He works at improving the articulation of his ideas. He was talking about tearing down walls, delayering GE, and sharing information for years before he finally came up with the term "boundarylessness." He also is constantly working at improving his underlying points of view to make them more applicable as circumstances change.

In the early 1980s, for example, his simple business idea was "No. 1, No. 2, fix, close, or sell." By the mid-1980s, however, GE needed a more dynamic business model, so he developed the Business Engine, which we describe in Chapter 2. In the mid-1990s he further modified his business ideas for GE, stating, "A shift to services is a much better mix for deflationary times." He continued,

> **This is a global services company making competitive products, not a global product company with an offshoot of services. You have got to get your heads changed on this. Customers will always need high-quality hardware, but what they must have more than ever are productivity solutions that help them win in their markets. Our challenge in the years to come will be to continuously find new ways to help them fight their competitive battles, by providing more sophisticated added-value services.**

Welch is not wishy-washy or ever out of focus. Once he has an idea, he is extraordinarily thorough in making sure that everything about the company and everything that he does support the fulfillment of that idea. But he is not fixed or rigid, either. He makes a plan, and he sticks to it with incredible fidelity, but only until a better plan comes along. And he is always checking the world around him and sifting his incoming information in search of a better plan. Thus, the late 1990s saw the emergence of Six Sigma and then e-business as central GE business ideas.

When e-business finally took off in 1999, Welch framed it as the most important shift in business in the last seventy-five years. In his 1999 letter to share owners, he explained why even though GE had been late getting on the bandwagon, it had an advantage in e-business: "Start-ups have energized the business landscape, supported by a strong venture capital environment and healthy IPO market; however, much of their resources must go to establish brand, develop real content, and achieve fulfillment capability. We already have that! We already have the hard stuff—over 100 years of a well-recognized brand, leading-edge technology in both product and financial services, and a Six Sigma–based fulfillment capability." While other old economy CEOs lamented that they were too big and slow to get into the game, Welch was teaching his point of view about why GE would win.

Welch was equally clear in identifying, articulating, and teaching the values that GE people would need to drive his business ideas. By the year 2000, Welch had crafted the following list of values that would drive GE to success:

GE LEADERS . . . Always with unyielding integrity . . .

- Are passionately focused on driving customer success.
- Live Six Sigma Quality . . . ensure that the customer is always its first beneficiary . . . and use it to accelerate growth.
- Insist on excellence and are intolerant of bureaucracy.
- Act in a boundaryless fashion . . . [and] always search for and apply the best ideas regardless of their source.
- Prize global intellectual capital and the people that provide it . . . [and] build diverse teams to maximize it.
- See change for the growth opportunities it brings . . . i.e. e-business.
- Create a clear, simple, customer-centered vision . . . and continually renew and refresh its execution.
- Create an environment of "stretch" excitement, informality, and trust . . . reward improvement . . . and celebrate results.
- Demonstrate . . . always with infectious enthusiasm for the customer . . . the 4-Es of GE leadership: the personal ENERGY to welcome and deal

> with the speed of change . . . the ability to create
> an atmosphere that ENERGIZES others . . . the
> EDGE to make difficult decisions . . . and the
> ability to consistently EXECUTE . . .

Welch firmly believes that one of the critical roles of a leader is to generate positive emotional energy. To sustain success, organizations must constantly change. To do that, the people within them must have the enthusiasm and the self-confidence to take risks. Welch instilled these qualities in GE's more than 300,000 employees by constantly encouraging them and engaging them in dialogue and debate. The GE values and business ideas were his rallying points. "This place wants to become a bureaucracy every day," he told them. "Kick it, break it."

He backed up this point of view about fighting the system by creating a culture that encouraged informality. When people can sit around, share ideas openly, and engage in constructive conflict, they make much better decisions and make them more quickly than they can in hierarchies that require them to make formal presentations, follow rules, and cover their asses. He used to challenge his people to stay only if they were energized, telling them, "If GE doesn't give you what you want, then get the hell out, because with your brains and with your résumé, you can get a job anywhere."

When it comes to his teachable point of view regarding edge—the courage to make the yes or no decisions on business issues and people—Welch is unequivocal. This is the core of what he believes strong leadership is all about. A leader must have the guts to face reality and then make yes or no decisions, not just study the situation, set up committees, and hire consultants to avoid making a decision. A leader must act decisively.

One example of his coaching on edge is a talk he gave his top 500 executives at their annual Boca Raton meeting in the mid-1990s, when he was squeezing the organization for cost savings. He warned them about the danger of falling into weak, bureaucratic behavior. His specific target was wishy-washy, across-the-board cost-cutting when tough, differentiated cutting and simultaneous additions would be more effective:

> Any manager who says share the pain, 10 percent across the board, if we find you, you are in real trouble. Your whole reason for being is to differentiate. Pour the coals to some and squeeze the others. Your kid could come in in a rocking chair and say, "Ten percent out from every-one." Leaders differentiate. It's your whole reason for being, to invest in some and squeeze others . . . so invest in quality, globalization, and information technology while slashing the hell out of overhead.

Welch's strongest coaching about edge was in terms of people, and he spent the last half of the 1990s pushing for better differentiation among the people at GE. He wanted only A players, people who both delivered business results and embodied the GE values. C players were defined as those who did not perform and did not embody the values listed above. The values were measured by 360 surveys and taught in all programs at Crotonville as well as discussed in almost all of Welch's meetings. Welch taught his team that they could not be A players if they had any C players on their teams; they had to have the guts to remove them. He even had a module that he taught to younger managers at Crotonville so they would learn to evaluate and differentiate talent early in people's careers; this way, if they had to remove employees from GE, they could do it when the employees were more mobile and able to get on with their careers in other companies. Coaching younger managers to develop edge was a passion for Welch.

Like all great coaches and teachers, he repeatedly stresses the fundamentals. His teachings on business, values, emotional energy, and edge are simple. He is able to continuously excite himself and others with these fundamental building blocks. The teachable point of view that Welch articulated over and over again provided the framework for everything that he did at GE.

The GE Teaching Infrastructure

As we discuss earlier, Welch built a huge teaching infrastructure at GE, and used the "schools" as a means of leading and injecting new ideas into the company. GE is the largest business academy in the world, providing leadership development for all 340,000 of its workers worldwide. The major elements of the GE teaching infrastructure are Crotonville, Work-Out, Change Acceleration, Six Sigma, and e-learning.

Crotonville: GE's Leadership Development Center
The fifty-acre campus overlooking the Hudson River in Ossining, New York, has a world-class teaching and living environment. It enrolls more than 5,000 GE leaders a year, ranging from entry level to senior executives.

From the beginning, Welch intuitively understood that Crotonville was a lever for change. It was a place where he could have input into the heart and mind of his organization as well as get honest feedback and insight into what was going on in the company. While I was head of Crotonville in 1985, he formally changed the center from a traditional management development business school to GE's staging ground for revolution. The mission was to

> **enhance GE's competitiveness in a global environment, providing GE professionals with a broad array of functional and business leadership development and organization effectiveness experiences, and serving as an instrument for cultural change.**

When Welch became CEO, he moved quickly with Jim Baughman, head of Crotonville in the early 1980s, to implement a program for new managers. At the time, first-time managers at GE were mostly bench engineers who were promoted to manage other engineers. The new managers program gave them a developmental experience on how to manage people, implement the new culture, run teams, and do appraisals and hiring. He invested in a new residence facility so it would be a first-class site—a move that met much resistance, since he was simultaneously downsizing the company and selling off assets. But he saw Crotonville as leading GE into the twenty-first century. The investment signaled the importance that the new CEO placed on developing leaders.

Welch was well into using Crotonville as a staging ground for revolution when I became head of the center in the mid-1980s. One of my jobs was to serve on a small task force charged with creating a new model of leadership development at GE. In giving us our mandate, Welch told us that what he wanted to think about was the creation of future CEO candidates. "How I got to be CEO is irrelevant," he said. "We are a very different company, and let's look at what it will take for the future."

Although the actual task force was small, Welch had hundreds of GE leaders participate in the project. He, vice chairman Larry Bossidy, and other key executives were also deeply involved. The leadership development framework that resulted mapped a path from the entry door to the CEO's office. It started with new college hires and the Corporate Entry Leadership Conference. This three-day workshop taught 100 college hires at a time the GE strategy for winning and the GE values and had them examine their own values. More than 2,000 people a year went through the program as a way to imprint the new GE on the leaders joining the company. By the end of the 1990s, GE had moved this program out to its businesses and integrated elements of it into its corporate development programs for college hires, such as the finance program, human resource program, and various engineering programs.

The plan then laid out different levels and types of teaching for new managers, experienced managers, and business heads. It was designed to provide people at each step of the way the tools to move them to the next step. It focused on the developmental challenges at each level in terms of business acumen and skills, as well as how the core values for GE get shaped at different stages of leadership development. These values included such things as embracing change, dealing with paradox, and behaving in a boundaryless manner. It also offered opportunities for addressing these developmental needs through all of the levers available at GE, including primary position assignments, enrichment experiences, coaching opportunities, and development programs. Today, GE has the largest formal leadership development platform of any business institution in the world. It rivals the U.S. military, with its service academies, war colleges, and special forces training, on top of myriad job-specific programs.

The adjacent figure provides a summary of the core experiences that were developed in the mid-1980s, most of which continue into the new millennium. A huge shift at Crotonville was to minimize the use of case studies, readings, and lectures. They were replaced by an action-learning model that included teams of GE professionals working on real problems as part of the development experience. The new nimble GE would need people who could think on their feet, make decisions quickly, and energize their teammates to make things happen. The note-takers and rule-followers of the old GE would be worse than useless; they would be a drag on everyone else. So we revamped all the programs at Crotonville, regardless of their content, to encourage critical thinking, creativity, and decision-making. The assignments included such things as having teams work as consultants to deal with thorny problems plaguing specific GE units or head off in search of joint ventures in Southeast Asia. In all cases, leaders from the units were brought in as both clients and evaluators.

As a result of these changes, going to Crotonville was less a comfortable business school academic experience than a "top gun" or Navy Seals training experience. Participants were stretched, pushed out of their comfort zones into new areas of learning, tested, and renewed. The atmosphere was designed to be unsettling and emotionally charged. Working on real GE problems, presenting results to real GE leaders with honest feedback and evaluation, created productive anxiety and the pressure to lead and succeed.

We also changed the measure of program success from how participants said they felt about the learning experience to how the experience affected their organization and their leadership behavior over time.

CEO

Development Stage V:
Officers Workshops

Developmental Stage V Corporate officers, with participation from the CEO, wrestle with major corporate issues, and develop action plans for implementation in their individual businesses and on a company-wide basis.

Development Stage IV:
Executive Programs

Developmental Stage IV Emerging leaders on a path toward senior management attend the selective executive program sequence: Management Development Course, Business Management Course and Executive Development course. These month-long, intense programs encourage a bias for action, and competitiveness and a habit of decision-making that favors "yesses" and "noes" rather than "maybes."

Development Stage III:
Advanced Functional Courses

Developmental Stage III As professionals move toward the top of their function they attend senior level programs in marketing, finance, information systems and human resources aimed at both increasing the depth of their skill in a given field as well as lifting up their heads to see cross-functional implications and possibilities.

Development Stage II:
New Manager Development Program

Developmental Stage II All newly appointed GE managers attend the New Manager Development Program where the focus is on critical skills, knowledge and values as well as the overriding goal of developing the desire and capability to lead people in an increasingly competitive world.

Development Stage I:
Corporate Entry Leadership Conference I & II

Developmental Stage I New professional hires attend Corporate Entry Leadership Conference I within six months of joining GE. The conference centers on company and individual values. Participants get a chance to meet their peers, form contacts and meet several general managers and a vice chairman. When professionals are in their third year at GE they attend Corporate Entry Leadership Conference II, where the accent shifts to competitive forces and the individuals' role in helping a business win.

Work-Out: How to Energize More Than 300,000 Employees
The paradox of Crotonville is that it frustrated Welch. Its success in developing the few thousand people a year who passed through its programs made him regret all the more that the vast majority of GE employees weren't exposed to the Crotonville experience. So, in 1988, Welch created Work-Out, his next huge leadership investment. The idea was to bring the spirit of Crotonville to everyone at GE. Today, Work-Out is one of the primary developmental mechanisms deeply embedded in the GE culture.

Work-Out started as a fairly free-form workshop. Leaders at all levels were required to hold "town hall" meetings so that the people working for them could speak up and identify the situations, processes, and procedures that were slowing them down and hassling them. The bosses were required to respond and make changes happen. The idea was that the employees knew best where the problems were and giving them a voice would help GE run more effectively in a lean, fast-moving business environment. I ran my first workshop at GE Medical Systems in the latter part of 1988, when John Trani had us work with 100 middle managers in trying to improve the organization. By 1989, Welch had mandated Work-Out for the whole company. Every business had a small consulting team helping facilitate it, and literally thousands of meetings have taken place since that time.

The first official rounds of Work-Out were pretty much over by 1991, but the Work-Out culture has permeated GE. In a 1999 interview, Welch talked about Work-Out:

> Work-Out was clearly a huge deal. . . . When I talk to people, I tell them it was three to five years, it was tens of thousands of meetings. It wasn't a tinker; it was a true, true commitment over and over and over again. Now people get in a meeting and decide what they're going to do, and they do it. But you had to get approval for that in the past. It's led to incredibly new capabilities in GE. We did forty-six acquisitions in the last ninety days. Now think of doing forty-six acquisitions in ninety days if you

had staffs' reviews and all that old bureaucratic stuff. So
Work-Out really got rid of the bureaucracy.

In the fall of 1999, as part of his preretirement housecleaning,
Welch mandated a new ninety-day round of Work-Out. He said the
purpose was to fight the reemergence of bureaucracy. It's about
"throwing out the crap that keeps creeping in—tons of meetings, getting rid of reports that aren't needed, getting rid of crap," Welch said.

Change Acceleration Program

After several years of having outside consultants facilitate the Work-
Out sessions, Welch decided that running Work-Out, teaching people
process mapping, and driving change needed to be a core competency of every single GE leader. That's when the Change Acceleration Program (CAP) began. CAP basically was the next generation
after Work-Out, building the competency of leaders to make change
management a part of everyday life. CAP has been used as a developmental experience for the top 5,000 leaders at GE and continues to
this day. It is now also used with suppliers and customers.

In CAP, a leader and his or her team come together with other
teams and go through a three-workshop sequence. Over the three-
to four-month period, they work on a real business project and also
get training in boundarylessness, team building, and process mapping. Because CAP requires them to solve real problems as they
develop their skills and capabilities, it is another example of how
Welch built teaching and leadership development into the GE infrastructure for running the business.

Six Sigma

The largest developmental infrastructure in the business world today
is Six Sigma training at GE. The best guesstimate is that GE spends
close to a billion dollars a year on this investment. Six Sigma is a statistical measurement of how much a process varies from perfection.
One sigma signifies 690,000 defects per million opportunities. Six
sigma represent 3.4 defects per million opportunities.

Six Sigma has been around since the 1980s, when Mikel Harry
led a team at Motorola to develop techniques to improve the quality

and production efficiencies. In the 1990s Harry helped Larry Bossidy, Welch's old friend and then CEO of AlliedSignal, implement Six Sigma. Bossidy introduced Welch to it.

Six Sigma appeals to the engineer in Welch because it involves rigorous data gathering and statistical analysis to pinpoint the sources of errors and ways to eliminate them. Sometimes the tiniest piece of a process or product can account for an inordinate number of errors. In these cases, a simple fix can save millions of dollars. Projects are carefully chosen with customer input and tracked to see if they deliver measurable results. It also suits Welch's leader-as-teacher style of management, because it is deployed by developing people in the company to be "black belt" teachers. These high-potential leaders in the company then teach others and lead the projects.

In these ways, Six Sigma is fundamentally different from other 1980s approaches to quality, which Welch hated. He saw practices like continuous improvement, quality circles, and kaizen as soft and fuzzy, resulting in little good to the bottom line. In an interview with us in 1999 he told us about his personal transformation:

> I was very slow to get there. I mean I thought [the quality movement] was bull . . . Larry Bossidy's the one that got me into Six Sigma because Larry hated quality [programs] more than I hated it. And then he came up one day and said, "Jack, this works, I'm getting all kinds of results." I said, "You like quality?" Because we hated it, we'd sit there and laugh at those jerks with their slow, you know, almost bureaucratic continuous improvement TQM process and all that crap. He said, "No, I'm telling you the truth!" Then he came and gave a speech at the CEC [Corporate Executive Council] on Six Sigma.

When Bossidy gave the speech, Welch was in the hospital, having open-heart surgery. Welch had been convinced about Six Sigma, but knew that without the buy-in of the CEC, it would never work. After that, GE was totally on board.

Six Sigma has produced enormous financial returns for GE. At the end of 2000, Welch shared the following data with analysts:

Year	Investment in Six Sigma	Return
1996	$200 million	$170 million
1997	$380 million	$700 million
1998	$450 million	$1.2 billion
1999	$500 million	$2 billion
2000	$600 million	$3 billion

In addition, Six Sigma has also become a major influence on the culture and behavior of GE people everywhere. A key part of the Six Sigma process is to make sure that there is a common language and methodology. It is very disciplined, but it is built on a model of action learning, and a model of leaders developing leaders. Today at GE, more than 10,000 full-time, black belt leader/teachers are teaching every employee in the company—all 340,000 employees—how to implement Six Sigma.

The projects, which number more than 20,000 at any one time, are having phenomenal results, ranging from Six Sigma Design for Quality, which resulted in a radically new magnetic resonance machine in medical imaging, to monitoring of Six Sigma quality in tier 2 suppliers in power systems. This means that Power Systems has trained not only its major tier 1 direct suppliers in Six Sigma, but also the companies that supply them. Combining Six Sigma with e-business has produced Internet monitoring of Six Sigma quality in suppliers.

Six Sigma is working so powerfully in GE in part because of the company's previous cultural initiatives, Work-Out, CAP, and boundarylessness. The effectiveness and discipline of Six Sigma are magnified because it is being applied by self-confident people. Thus, the platforms of boundarylessness and leadership are still giving GE returns on its earlier investment. Part of the premium price/earnings ratio for GE includes very high expectations and credit for returns that Six Sigma's already getting. In addition to the black belts who have been trained, there are hundreds of master black belts also teaching, and well over 100,000 professionals in GE have been through first-level green belt training.

E-Learning

Finally, the other leadership development infrastructure that GE is developing is e-learning. As Welch has rapidly embraced e-business, he has also embraced e-learning. It is still at a very early stage, but already the Internet is being used with customers, suppliers, and employees for interactive Web-based training and development. As GE digitizes, e-learning will grow exponentially.

Consistent and Cumulative Long-Term Initiatives

Most large companies tend to fall prey to the "flavor of the month" syndrome. Top management latches on to so many fads—quality circles, "in search of excellence" programs, reengineering, learning organizations—that most companies have a population of very cynical leaders and employees. But this is not the case at GE. Virtually no one thinks, or dares to think, that any of the initiatives are fads. This is because Welch never lets up. Whenever he embraces a plan, you can be sure that it will be carried out, because he will stick with it for years, until all stakeholders, senior business leaders, employees at all levels, and even Wall Street and the journalists get it and how it fits in his teachable point of view. In 1999 when Jack Welch was talking to Strat Sherman and me, he explained how the initiatives build on each other and are embedded in the GE culture: "These initiatives get a life of their own . . . our cultural things, our boundaryless behavior from Work-Out help immensely. Six Sigma will eventually become the same way—the way we just naturally work. . . . Most jobs aren't being filled if you're not a black belt. Black belts are getting all the leadership jobs."

Because he sees leadership development as a core competency, Welch in effect put it into the DNA of every GE process and operating mechanism. Strategy sessions, operations planning processes, and succession planning were all designed to achieve the simultaneous goals of teaching and building teams.

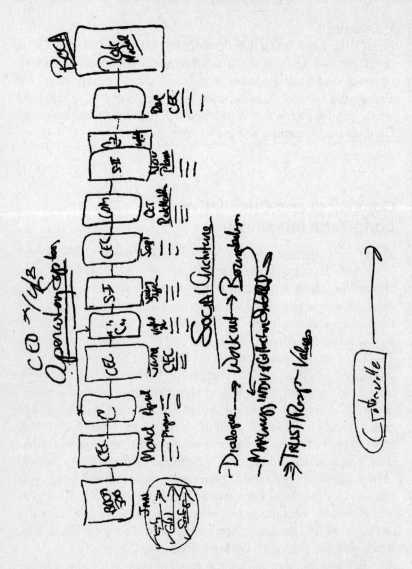

Here is a hand drawing that Welch did in the fall of 1999 for a group of securities analysts who were invited to a session that he ran at Crotonville. This was the first time outsiders were invited to Crotonville. It was a rather amazing teach-in. Welch revealed where the most profound leadership development actually happens in GE. It is not at Crotonville or in the formal developmental processes. Rather, it is in the way the company is run day in and day out.

Welch runs GE with an informal, boundaryless, but hard-hitting, confrontational process. It is a style that runs throughout all levels of the company and is epitomized in the operating mechanisms and practices of the seniormost ranks. Welch included a more detailed overview of the operating mechanisms in the 2000 GE Annual Report.

The year starts with a meeting in Boca Raton, Florida, where the top 500 executives spend several days going over the key initiatives and agenda for the coming year. For the last couple years, the focus was on e-business and Six Sigma. This meeting, where best practices are shared and people are highlighted as well, sets the stage for the year. The leaders of each of the GE units spend the final day of the meeting wrestling with how they will implement the new initiatives in their own business.

Each year, Welch's letter to share owners is really his personal write-up of the Boca Raton meeting—a brief summary of results for the previous year, and then a teaching message for the organization to set the stage for the coming year. It is the reason we have included in this book all of Welch's annual letters to share owners through 2000. They are the best examples of his teachable point of view. They are his teaching notes.

The start of spring brings Session C, that is, succession planning in which the top 500 positions are examined in great detail as well as several thousand contenders and candidates for those jobs. The session requires that thousands of people conduct similar reviews deep down in the organization. Welch then spends twelve- to sixteen-hour days in the businesses going through the Session C process. It is important that he physically go to their setting so he can talk to people, see people, get a feel for them.

Many companies make the mistake of having the business leaders come to the headquarters rather than having senior leaders go out on site. With Welch, both the hard and the soft issues are reviewed. A typical agenda for Session C includes a review of all

First Quarter

**Operating Managers
Meeting ("Boca")**
600 Leaders
INITIATIVE LAUNCH
• Case for New Initiative
• Outside Company
  Initiative Experience
• One Year Stretch Targets
• Role Model Presentations
• Re-Launch of
  Current Initiatives

JANUARY

• Intense Energizing
  of Initiatives Across
  Businesses

FEBRUARY

**Corporate Executive Council:
(CEC at Crotonville)**
*35 Business and Senior
Corporate Leaders*
• Early Learning?
• Customer Reaction?
• Initiative Resources Sufficient?
• Business Management
  Course (BMC)
  Recommendations

MARCH

**Anonymous Online
CEO Survey:**
11,000 Employees
• Do You "Feel"
  Initiative Yet?
• Do Customers Feel It?
• Sufficient Resources
  to Execute?
• Messages Clear
  and Credible?

APRIL

Globalization
Six Sigma Quality
Product Services
e-Business

GE Values

DECEMBER

Corporate Executive Council:
(CEC at Crotonville)
*35 Business and Senior
Corporate Leaders*
• Agenda for Boca
• Individual Business
  Initiative Highlights
• Business Management
  (BMC) Course Recom-
  mendations

NOVEMBER

**Operating Plans
Presented:**
All Business Leaders
• Initiatives Stretch Targets
• Individual Business
  Operating Plans
• Economic Outlook

OCTOBER

**Corporate Officers
Meeting: (Crotonville)**
150 Officers
• Next-Year Operating
  Plan Focus
• Role Models Present
  Initiative Successes
• Executive Development
  Course (EDC)
  Recommendations
• All Business Dialogue:
  What Have We
  Learned?

SEPTEMBER

**Corporate Executive
Council: (CEC at Crotonvi
*35 Business and Senior
Corporate Leaders*
• Business Management
  Course (BMC)
  Recommendations
• Clear Role Models
  Identified
• Outside Company Best
  Practices Presented
• Initiative Best Practice
  (All Businesses)
• Customer Impact of
  Initiatives

Fourth Quarter

The GE Operating System

The Operating System is GE's learning culture in action—in essence, it is the operating software of the Company.

It is a year-round series of intense learning sessions in which business CEOs, role models and initiative champions from GE as well as outside companies, meet and share the intellectual capital of the world: its best ideas.

The central focus is always on raising the bar of Company performance by sharing, and putting into action, the best ideas and practices drawn from our big Company-wide initiatives.

The Operating System is driven by the soft values of the Company—trust, informality, simplicity, boundaryless behavior and the love of change. It allows GE businesses to operate at performance levels and speeds that would be unachievable were they on their own.

What may appear in the diagram to be a typical series of stand-alone business meetings is in reality an endless process of enrichment. Learning at each meeting builds on that of the previous, expanding the scope and increasing the momentum of the initiatives.

Globalization has been enriched through more than a dozen cycles, Six Sigma is in its fifth cycle, Services is in its sixth, and e-Business its third. The GE Operating System translates idea to action across three dozen businesses so rapidly that all the initiatives have become operational across the Company within one month of launch, and have always produced positive financial results within their first cycle.

Second Quarter

Leadership Performance Reviews at Business Locations:
All Business Staffs
- Initiative Leadership Review
- Level of Commitment / Quality of Talent on Initiatives
- Differentiation (20% / 70% / 10%)
- Promote / Reward / Remove

MAY

Corporate Executive Council: (CEC at Crotonville)
35 Business and Senior Corporate Leaders
- Initiative Best Practices
- Review of Initiative Leadership
- Customer Impact
- Business Management Course (BMC) Recommendations

JUNE

JULY

Session I: 3 Year Strategy
- Economic / Competitive Environment
- General Earnings Outlook
- Initiatives Update / Strategy
- Initiative Resource Requirements

AUGUST

- Informal Idea Exchanges at Corporate and Businesses

Third Quarter

key people's performance and leadership behaviors and action plans that will benefit them and take the business where it needs to go strategically. Often there is a specific initiative that Welch wants to talk about. Some years its focus is the sales force; other years, it may be black belts. The day's agenda is fluid in that certain items may take longer, depending on how much the leaders want to talk. Session C is followed up in the summer with a video conference session to see what's going on, and another follow-up in the fall.

In the summer there's an S1 strategy review meeting, where the business heads come in to corporate headquarters and spend a half-day or day around Welch's conference table, reviewing the business, discussing it, and debating. The S2 process in the fall essentially wraps up the year and puts together the plan for the next year and the budget. The officers meeting, also in the fall, is very critical, in that it sets the stage for the Boca Raton meeting. It begins to wrap up the year and set the stage for the next year.

All of the operating mechanisms are open, interactive sessions in which real decisions get made and there are no formal pitches. Rather, teams work together problem-solving with Welch and his key executives. He takes opportunities to coach during these sessions, call time-outs, see where people are learning, and summarize.

The Succession Endgame for Welch

At the end of 1999, Strat Sherman and I interviewed Welch about the endgame of the process for selecting and installing the next CEO. Welch's first comment was, "The process is very straightforward. It's all about building a team. How do you get to the team that looks like it has the right complementary skills to take the position from here to there?" He tried to make it sound simple, but it was anything but that.

Welch orchestrated an incredibly thorough succession process that involved wide-ranging interviews and data-gathering by both himself and independent teams of board members. It went far beyond simply running a horse race to determine a successor. It included cleaning house to get rid of some key leaders he felt might get in the way of the new CEO, managing the competition to minimize its potentially destructive effects on the organization, and priming Wall Street so GE's stock wouldn't tank upon his departure.

Board Involvement

Welch involved the board in ways that have never been seen in large corporate America. In 1996, Welch began sending board members out to the field to spend time with the candidates without him around. Five board members would spend a day with a candidate in a mix of business and social settings. For example, Welch said, "The board goes to dinner with them, goes to a ball game with them, spends time with their staff." Then the board members would "write up notes for me." This active involvement of the board gave Welch another point of view, and also created the kind of free-flowing dialogue that stimulates Welch most.

Sending the board members into the field gave them a much deeper understanding of the candidates than most directors ever get before they vote a person in as CEO. In other organizations, the board may have a series of one-on-one meetings at corporate headquarters or over dinner, but they don't get the opportunity to see the candidate at work or to meet his or her staff and talk off-line. Candidates were in charge of setting the schedule for the visit, which was another test: How did they use the board's time? How well did they allow the board members to see the full operation of the organization? Did the board members get the opportunity to meet the candidate's team members in a setting where the latter could give candid assessments of candidate?

Welch's Database

Welch was thoroughly turned off by the succession process he went through in the late 1970s. He thought that the head-to-head competition among candidates at corporate headquarters and the stress interviews, such as the "airplane interview" that we describe in Chapter 4, disrupted corporate operations and weren't really necessary.

Instead of conducting intense stress interviews, Welch engaged the candidates in long discussions that included topics that weren't explicitly business related. Says Welch, "We'd talk about things such as who do they like, who don't they like, how do they feel about peers, how do they feel about other things, and what do they want to do in life. What are their objectives?"

Welch often did this in informal settings. "We'd have a one-on-one dinner. We'd talk about everything from baseball to life to family . . . about what's your vision for the company. What do you think the leader of the next century looks like, what's your vision of the game. I don't ask anybody to pick themselves and that stuff. . . . We had a martini or two and sat around and talked."

The one-on-ones and the board involvement gave Welch the data he needed to develop his complementary team. At the end of 1999, he said, "All of this informal data collection, very systematically done since 1996, is in parallel to all the regular Session C [succession] process that goes on, the regular evaluation of the performance of these business leaders, and the day-to-day running of GE. The process is on top of a very disciplined leadership assessment and development process."

Conflict Management—Avoiding the Pitfalls of Competition
One of the boldest and perhaps most brilliant elements of the GE succession was that it did not re-create the process that Welch went through, whereby three vice chairmen ran in a horse race at corporate headquarters. When Welch reflected on this, he noted the dysfunctional nature of having vice chairmen at the corporate level competing for the CEO job. They had time and resources to engage in politics. This cost the company in terms of relationships and in terms of the business.

Welch came up with an alternative, which was to leave the final three contenders—Bob Nardelli, Jeff Immelt, and Jim McNerney—out in the field running their businesses. Everyone knew there was a competition, but in order for them to win, they had to run their businesses well. Plus, they physically were in three different parts of the United States. Nardelli was leading Power Systems in Schenectady, New York; McNerney was heading Aircraft Engines in Evendale, Ohio; and Immelt was running Medical Systems in Waukesha, Wis-

consin. This, and the fact that there was no business interdepend-
ence, minimized daily interactions among the three. However, they
all attended CEC meetings, where Welch valued teamwork and collaboration, so any demonstrations of competitiveness there were not
acceptable. Finally, each of them knew that the only way to stay in
the game was to keep his own business producing top-tier results.

Early in 2000, Welch added an important wrinkle. He
appointed chief operating officers, number two executives, in each
of these three businesses. He did this to give himself and his successor an insurance policy: (a) The person who became CEO would be
leaving that business, so he would have an individual ready to step
in, and (b) the two who lost out in the CEO race were very likely to
take CEO jobs outside of GE, which they have done. McNerney is
now CEO of 3M and Nardelli is now CEO of Home Depot.

Cleaning House

One thing that many CEOs don't do for their successors is make
sure they are handing over a strong company with a team that will
help and support the new boss.

In the past decade, as he evaluated CEO candidates, Welch
systematically looked at the whole leadership corps at GE. Among
other things, he identified the people he feels will add value going
into the future and those who would be better off taking CEO
assignments outside of GE.

One very successful GE leader who was seen a decade ago as
one of the potential contenders was John Trani, CEO of GE Medical Systems. When Welch decided that Trani was not going to be
among the finalists for the CEO job, he honestly let him know that.
Trani, being the hard-charger CEO type, decided mutually with
Welch that he would look for an opportunity where he could run his
own show outside of GE, and amicably moved on to become CEO
of Stanley Works. They continue to be good colleagues.

Another transition, which was a bit more acrimonious, was the
exciting of Gary Wendt, the very successful former CEO of GE
Capital Services. For over a decade, Wendt had driven GE Capital
to achieve phenomenal average annual growth rates of 20% a year.

Over time, the relationship between Wendt and Welch, however, became quite contentious. It wasn't helped by the fact that Wendt went through a very controversial and publicly played-out divorce toward the end of his tenure. Welch felt that it was particularly important that Wendt leave before another person became CEO. He reasoned that Wendt was a strong leader heading a unit that was producing nearly 40% of GE's net income. If he stayed in place, the new CEO would have a hard time dealing with the most powerful unit. Therefore, as effective and good as Wendt was in driving GE's bottom line, Welch made the tough call. Wendt left and, after a hiatus of several months, became CEO of Conseco, Inc.

Wall Street Expectations

Another thing that Welch did for his successor—and GE share owners, including himself—was to stage a campaign explicitly to assure investors, business partners, and the media that GE would continue to produce strong results even after he left. He didn't quite succeed in convincing the Honeywell board that he was inessential—their demand that he continue to serve as CEO until 2002 was part of the agreement to sell Honeywell to GE for stock. He did a masterful teaching job, nonetheless.

In press conferences, annual letters to share owners, interviews, anytime he got the opportunity, Welch explained over and over how the whole GE organization was built to succeed. One of the most significant events was the series of analysts' meetings a Crotonville in the fall of 1999, when Welch diagrammed how GE produces leaders and how they systematically raise the bar and take the company to higher and higher levels. He described the leadership development, operating mechanisms, and social architecture of the company.

The response was amazing. In the week after the meetings, GE's stock rose and some of the analysts began to call GE "bullet-proof." Within hours, concepts that Welch had introduced to the analysts, such as "social architecture," the importance of an open, interactive environment, and the need to embed sound values and attitudes into the "DNA" of a company, became buzzwords on Wall Street.

Throughout the succession period, Welch's teachable point of view was clear: Leaders need to help prepare the ground for their successors in many ways. They need to leave a company financially sound, but that is not enough. The company must be in very top form, primed for success. This again demonstrates Welch as the social architect, who planned every element of the succession that he could think of, all with an eye toward the future.

The Hand That Jeff Immelt Has Been Dealt by Welch

The GE that Jack Welch is handing over to Jeff Immelt is the world's most valuable and competitive enterprise. However, it will retain those titles only as long as it continues to grow and to adapt to new demands and new markets. Caretakers are never long-term winners; only transformational leaders are. Success in the present and the future will continue to require the revolutionary cycles of creative destruction and reinvention.

Welch is handing over a smoothly running machine, but if Immelt simply tinkers with it and doesn't make fundamental changes, it will not run smoothly for long. In the next few years, the key areas that the new leadership will have to address include a number of hard business issues and some soft people issues. Our view of these challenges is as follows.

Hard Business Issues

THE IMPACT OF HONEYWELL: Had the deal gone through, the integration of Honeywell into GE surely would have been one of Immelt's major challenges, necessitating layoffs and divestitures. Instead, the European Commission blocked the deal; the time, money, and emotional energy invested in the transaction became writeoffs. Immelt's energies were consumed instead by unexpected factors. After the terrorist attacks of 9/11 the U.S. economy tipped into recession. A rash of high-profile corporate scandals, none involving GE, suddenly resulted in pressure on all publicly-traded companies to provide more transparent financial reporting and comply with tighter regulation, to overcome an upwelling of mistrust on the part of the public, regulators, and investors. Immelt seized the opportunity to become a role model for reform, reporting stock options at GE as expenses, increasing the company's financial transparency, revamping the Board, and strengthening the corporate commitment to global corporate citizenship.

GE PORTFOLIO OF BUSINESSES: The mix of GE business is never perfect. There are always some winners and some losers. The Welch No. 1, No. 2 mantra should continue to be the focus in the future. But that means that there inevitably must be some moves to reconfigure the portfolio for the first half of the twenty-first century. What will stay, what will go, and what will be acquired are big issues for the new leadership.

E-BUSINESS: The digitization of GE is off to a fast start, but it's far from over. It has moved fast because of the informal, flexible leadership platform that Welch built. It will require a quantum leap forward to make GE the global leader in this area across its diverse set of businesses. The diversity, however, also gives GE a unique strength, namely, a way to do quick-cycle learning in multiple-industry environments and rapidly share best practices across GE.

SIX SIGMA: This is a hand that Welch played very nicely for the new leadership. The momentum is incredible, and the recent phase of Six Sigma, with its customer focus and the design for Six Sigma in GE's products and services, is beginning to pay off. It amounts to a rich annuity for GE. It is because this Six Sigma effort is so good that the leadership must be vigilant to prevent any complacency slipping into GE's leadership. Leaders must keep the pedal to the metal, or the investment will erode to become a bureaucratic ritual with little long-term payoff in new products and services and the ultimate success of GE customers.

NEXT GREAT PLATFORM FOR CHANGE AT GE: Welch handed Immelt two great platforms—e-business and Six Sigma—for turbocharging GE. These efforts are well into their life cycle and clearly must be played out. The challenge is to come up with the next one. What is the platform from which GE will leap to its next level of enhanced performance? The clock is ticking on this one, because without a new injection of innovation, inertia will become apparent in just a few years.

The Soft Human Issues

DIVERSITY: On September 3, 2000, *the New York Times,* captured the diversity challenge by publishing a picture gallery of the top GE leaders on the front page of the Sunday business section. The point was clear: Among the thirty-one faces, there were no women and only one African American. Welch got away with low grades in building diversity into the top team at GE. It was not that he was unsympathetic and did not make strong efforts in this area, but in the end his drive for the kind of competitive leaders he was used to having around him did a pretty good job of subtly screening out women and minorities or making it difficult to recruit them. The new leadership cannot win in this millennium with only white American males in all the key leadership spots.

OPERATING MECHANISMS: The strategy process, the CEC sessions, the Session C succession planning, the budgeting process, and the officer meetings were very bureaucratic when Welch took over. He made them his informal vehicles for intellectual debate, learning, and teaching. They need to be recrafted for tomorrow's GE and the style of the new leadership team. This requires that Immelt play a role that he has not had an opportunity to demonstrate his competence in, namely, that of large-scale social architect.

E SQUARED, OR EMOTIONAL ENERGY: Welch had the capacity to energize more than 300,000 employees through his skillful use of Crotonville, Work-Out, Six Sigma, and the operating mechanisms, along with his constant use of informal communication networks and the channels he developed over his forty-one years at GE. How fast Immelt and his team can develop their own modus operandi for energizing GE's huge work force is critical. There is a short window, possibly no longer than nine months, for this to happen, and it must happen in the face of the layoffs and divestitures resulting from the possible Honeywell acquisition and the inevitable comparisons that will be made between Immelt and Welch.

Success is about change. If it is to succeed in the future, GE must change and continue to change. Welch has turned the company over to a leadership team he developed and one he believes are change masters. They are, says Welch, "challenged by the unexpected and confident in, as well as capable of, dealing with whatever comes along."

Noel M. Tichy
March 2001

Afterword to the 2005 Edition

W hen the previous edition of this book went to press, Jack Welch had just announced a proposed $48 billion acquisition of Honeywell Inc. That announcement, coming just weeks before Welch's scheduled retirement as CEO of General Electric on April 1, 2001, prompted me to open the Afterword to the 2001 edition with the remark that the man whose quick-action style had once earned him the headline "Jumpin' Jack Flash" had pulled an early April Fools' Day joke.

In the ensuing months, the European Commission turned the joke back on Welch and GE. They blocked the acquisition. Some observers contended that this setback seriously tarnished Welch's record. At the time, even when I believed that the deal would take place, I said that the proposed Honeywell acquisition would not fundamentally alter his legacy; when the acquisition failed to occur, that continued to be true.

Welch's legacy is all about leadership and the pipeline that continues to build leaders at GE. All you have to do is look at how GE, under the leadership of Jeff Immelt, has fared in the three years since Welch's departure. Immelt's success thus far is not only navigating GE through rough times, but also positioning GE for future success and maintaining its status as the world's most valuable corporation. These examples are ample proof of the Welch leadership factor at work.

When the Honeywell acquisition was proposed, Welch had promised Wall Street that he would stay on until early 2002 to see the acquisition through. But when the deal fell through, he pushed his departure up to September 2001. On September 7, 2001, Immelt became the next CEO of GE.

Four days later on September 11th, Welch was on NBC's *Today* Show starting to promote his book *Jack: Straight from the Gut,* when the program was interrupted by news of the attack on the World Trade Center. He sat there in shock along with the whole world. Meanwhile, Immelt was on the West Coast watching the events unfold and experiencing the awful feeling of knowing friends and colleagues had died in the attack. "In addition to the human tragedy," he later remarked, "I saw planes with our engines hit buildings we insured, covered by a network I owned. To be honest, I was a little bit afraid for GE and our country." With his plane grounded on the West Coast, Immelt sprang into action, mobilizing GE's response which included marshalling emergency generating equipment and lighting for rescue workers.

The world dramatically changed at that moment. Since then, corporate America has been rocked by scandals ranging from Enron, to Arthur Anderson, to Tyco, to Imclone, to HealthSouth, among others. Add in a recession and wars in Afghanistan and Iraq. Immelt has had to operate in a totally new environment that Welch might have imagined only in his wildest fantasies. But the company Immelt has led has continued to build success upon success. This success is, to a large extent, thanks to Jack Welch.

But, Jeff Immelt has made many changes at GE in its portfolio of business as well as in its day-to-day operations. He is his own man who makes his own decisions. But he has been able to make these changes and succeed so well because Jack Welch left him with a company that is fast, flexible and not afraid of, even embraces, change. Thanks to Welch, hundreds of thousands of people at GE know how to deliver on change. Six Sigma, globalization, digitization and other initiatives do not tell Immelt where to take GE, but they have been the enabling platforms.

Meanwhile, Welch's stature as a business leader has continued to grow. In the first edition of *Control Your Destiny or Someone Else Will,* we predicted that Welch, more than any other CEO, would be the business leader of the twentieth century. We compared him at the time to Alfred Sloan and made the case that Welch's approach to running a large corporation and his development of leaders would set the benchmark for corporations for years to come. Since then *Fortune* has agreed, naming him the manager of the century. And in 2004, *BusinessWeek* recognized him as one of the great innovators of the last 75 years in part because he developed "the deepest bench of executive talent in U.S. business."

Welch's Leadership Pipeline and Teaching Machine

The most important job of a leader is to develop other leaders and to build a pipeline that produces leaders for the future. Jeff Immelt as CEO of GE stands as living proof of Welch's success at this. Immelt is a product of the leadership development system that Jack built. GE's pipeline not only insured that GE had a great successor for Welch, it purposely overproduced leaders. Those that did not get the gold medal at GE have gone on to lead major corporations. Jim McNerney and Bob Nardelli, the runners up to Immelt, are running 3M and HomeDepot respectively. Other GE leaders are running over 35 major corporations including Intuit, Albertsons, Honeywell and Polaris.

The GE leadership pipeline is one of the key legacies that Welch left for Immelt. There is a worldwide system and process for sourcing talent from all over the globe and then placing these talented future leaders into the GE talent system. These employees then receive careful appraisal, developmental feedback, and career planning from early on in their careers. Immelt has not altered this system, and it is what has enabled him to rapidly drive change at GE.

In fact, Jeff Immelt is spending as much time and attention on the GE leadership pipeline as Welch did. He is out in the field spending as many as 20 days in the spring leading "Session C" initiatives, GE's term for succession planning sessions. He spends all day and into the evening at each business site, involved in vigorous dialogues with the business' leadership team. They discuss their talent base, current performance, developmental needs, action plans, career moves and future potential. Immelt has created the Welch "Session C" process on steroids. It is what enables Jeff to lead 315,000 people through key leaders who he understands and takes personal responsibility for developing.

Welch views all human interaction as an opportunity to learn and teach. He thus created the operating system and the GE annual calendar of leadership events to be informal and interactive. He led through learning and teaching events. As a result, the famed Crotonville (now the John F. Welch Leadership Center) programs are a key asset of GE's pipeline. Crotonville's action learning programs continue to be a CEO lever for change and development. Jeff Immelt has used Crotonville to assess global strategy, to explore global citizenship for GE and as a vehicle for changing the GE shared values. In his 2003 annual report Jeff shares how this happened and the results.

> "About a year ago, one of our executive development classes suggested that we reformulate our values to capture the spirit of GE as a growth company. Values can't just be words on a page. To be effective, they must shape action. We looked to make them simpler, more inclusive and inspirational.
>
> "With this in mind, we reshaped GE values around four core actions: *Imagine, Solve, Build* and *Lead. Imagine* at GE is the freedom to dream and the power to make it real. This requires the values of passion and curiosity. *Solve* reflects GE's unique ability to tackle the world's

toughest problems and expresses our values of resourcefulness and accountability. Build requires a performance culture that creates customer and shareowner values, and the word captures our values of teamwork and commitment. *Lead* reflects our spirit of optimism that embraces change, and our values of openness and energy; it's what it will take to win." (GE 2003 Annual Report, Letter)

All of the other learning and teaching mechanisms that Welch implemented—Six Sigma, the Change Acceleration Program (CAP), and Work-Out—are alive and well under the Immelt umbrella. Jeff has utilized these mechanisms and built upon the foundation Welch left behind by adding new programs. He has created a program—Experienced Commercial Leadership Program— where very high potential MBAs take part in a fast path talent development program. It is illustrative of how the platforms Welch created at GE can quickly support new leadership development efforts.

Even though Jeff Immelt is only three years into his what will probably be a 20-year tenure as CEO of GE, he is already refilling the leadership pipeline and developing his successor. The real test of Welch's legacy will be the talent that Jeff Immelt develops, and if he will continue to produce as many leaders.

Conclusion

In retirement, Welch continues to be a world-class leader/teacher. His latest big project is to develop leaders in the New York City School System. He is working pro bono with Mayor Bloomberg and Schools Chancellor Joel Klein to launch a Crotonville type leadership development infrastructure for New York City principals. I have had the privilege to work with Jack on this and he is as inspiring now as when I ran Crotonville for him in the 1980s. In New York, he was instrumental in recruiting Robert Knowling, a talented executive and former CEO of several high technology firms. Knowling agreed to take several years out of the business world to be CEO of the New York City Leadership Academy. Welch and I have worked closely with Knowling to support the world's most ambitious leadership development effort in schools, and we have derived the designs of these workshops from Crotonville's Work-Out and Change Acceleration Program designs built with Welch at GE. So far, all 1200 NYC principals have been through multiple workshops and leadership experiences run by the Leadership Academy.

Jack's contribution to this program has been multifaceted. He has been a key partner with Knowling and with the Leadership Academy's board in raising over $60 million. He is a coach and mentor to Knowling, meeting several times a month one on one, and he regularly comes to workshops and teaches the principals. Welch's energy and enthusiasm are as high as any time during the more than 25 years I have known him. He continues to build on his legacy. He continues to teach and to learn. And he continues to be Jack Welch.

Noel Tichy
December 2004

GE TIMELINE

GE Timeline

	WORLD EVENTS	COMPANY CORE IDEAS
1879	**1882** Pearl Street Station lighted one square mile of New York City.	**THOMAS ALVA EDISON 1879–1889** Edison's vision was of a company that would light a nation, producing all the components of electrical power stations and electric lamps to accomplish this feat. He believed that politics should not constrain business, that businesses should receive the rewards derived from patents, and that management and not unions should make business decisions.
1885	**1886** American Federation of Labor (AFL) founded.	
1890	**1891** The manufacture of incandescent lamps in Europe begun by Philips Holland Company. **1893** Financial "Panic."	**CHARLES A. COFFIN, PRESIDENT 1892–1895; CHAIRMAN 1913–1922** Coffin broadened Edison's vision to include any and all applications of electricity in GE's domain. He set in place GE's domestic policies of business governed by the principles of market control through patents and alliances with competitors to enforce licensing agreements. The liquidity of the company was of primary concern to Coffin after a cash shortage threatened GE's existence during the economic recession known as "The Panic of 1893."
1895	**1895** Roentgen announced the discovery of x-rays.	
1900	**1903** Wright Brothers flight.	
1905	**1907** Niagara Falls illuminated by arc searchlights with 1.15 billion candlepower.	

COMPANY EVENTS	PRODUCT INTROS	FINANCIAL RESULTS (in millions)
ORGANIZATION Began as a loose federation of independent manufacturers, but the need for control brought Edison to establish the Schenectady Works where all manufacturing was consolidated. **1879** Edison Electric Light Company founded.	**1880** First incandescant light bulbs sold commercially.	
1886 Manufacturing facilities moved to Schenectady "Works."		
LABOR RELATIONS Edison sought to reduce the influence of the growing labor union movement on his company by moving all facilities out of New York City to Schenectady, N.Y. **1891** Edison received patent on thin-filament, high-vacuum incandescent bulb. **1892** Merger with Thomson-Houston formed the General Electric Company.		**1892** Revenues $11.7 Net Income $2.9 Employees 4,000
1896 Working agreement with Westinghouse to share patents. **1898** The assets of the Fort Wayne Electric Corp. were purchased, becoming the Fort Wayne Electric Works of GE.	**1895** GE built the world's largest electric locomotives (90 tons) and transformers (800 kw).	
ORGANIZATION Coffin created a hierarchical, vertical organizational structure for GE. Reporting to him directly were the functional vice presidents of Sales, Accounting, Manufacturing & Engineering, Law & Patents, and Treasury. Sales forces were deployed along product lines. The managers of GE "Works" facilities reported to the vice president of Manufacturing & Engineering. R&D was located at each "Works," with Research & Engineering Labs at Schenectady. Functional disputes were settled by CEO. **1900** Steinmetz established the General Electric Research Laboratory, first industrial research laboratory in the U.S. **1900** Registration of the GE trademark (the monogram). **1901** Formation of National Electric Light Assoc., with 40% GE backing centered in Cleveland, Ohio.	**1902** James J. Wood, consulting engineer at the Fort Wayne Works, received patents for stationary and revolving electric fans. **1903** First large Curtis Steam Turbine introduced.	**1900** Revenues $28.8 Net Income $6.9 Employees 12,000
1905 GE controlled 97% of U.S. lamp business and organized Electric Bond & Share to aid small utilities. **1907** The Stanley Electric Manufacturing Co. of Pittsfield, Mass., became the Pittsfield Works of GE.	**1905** GE's first electric toaster, the model X2, placed on the market. **1905** Commercial electric refrigerators with compressor motors and controls manufactured by GE were sold by Federal Automated Refrigeration Co.	

	WORLD EVENTS	COMPANY CORE IDEAS
1910	**1914** World War I began.	
	1914 The Panama Canal opened with controls by GE's Switchboard Engineering Department and using GE's towing locomotives.	
1915	**1917** Bolshevik Revolution in USSR.	
	1918 World War I ended.	
1920	**1923** Transcontinental airmail service began using GE radio transmitters and receivers.	**OWEN D. YOUNG, CHAIRMAN 1922–1939, 1942–1945; GERARD SWOPE, PRESIDENT 1922–1939, 1942–1945** Under Swope and Young, there was a broad diversification of the number of products manufactured by GE for the electrification of the American home. The growing demand for these products also resulted in increasing sales of the generating and distribution equipment needed to provide electricity. Swope and Young also initiated an extensive enlargement of GE's advertising, marketing, distribution, and service organizations. Swope's plan calling for industry associations to establish and enforce codes of fair competition influenced FDR's New Deal. Swope also espoused the idea that the company was the steward of the balanced best interests of shareholders, workers, and customers, called Corporatism. Swope expanded GE's domestic market control policies by entering into nonaggression pacts and by investing in foreign competitive manufacturers.
1925	**1927** The first home television reception took place at the residence of GE scientist E. F. W. Alexanderson.	
	1927 Lindbergh's transatlantic Solo Flight	
	1929 Stock Market Crash	

COMPANY EVENTS	PRODUCT INTROS	FINANCIAL RESULTS (in millions)
1911 Dept. of Justice required GE to purchase remaining interest in NELA and it became the National Quality Lamp Works of GE; NELA Park became GE's lighting center.	**1910** George Hughes, founder of Hotpoint, manufactured his first electric range.	**1910** Revenues $71.5 Net Income $10.9 Employees 36,200
1912 The General Electric Pension Plan began.	**1912** GE began the molding of plastic parts using phenolic resins.	
1913 GE applied for a patent on an inert gas-filled lamp, improving lamp efficiency.		
1913 E. W. Rice, Jr. became the second president of GE; Charles A. Coffin was elected Chairman of the Board.		
1919 International General Electric Company formed.	**1917** Limited production of the first household refrigerator began at GE's Fort Wayne Works.	
1919 Under the encouragement of the U.S. government, GE organized the Radio Corporation of America (RCA).		
REORGANIZATION Swope and Young believed that each of GE's six "Works" should produce all product lines to encourage competition in all areas of development, engineering, and manufacturing. Under Swope, R&D began reporting directly to the CEO. The CEO was involved throughout GE in all financial issues.	**1920** William D. Coolidge developed an x-ray tube and transformer assembly weighing only 20 pounds and suitable for dental and portable x-ray use.	**1920** Revenues $318.5 Net Income $35.4 Employees 82,000
1922 General Electric radio station WGY, Schenectady, began regularly scheduled broadcasting using its 1500-watt transmitter.		
1924 Phoebus Contract with foreign lighting manufacturers entered into.		
1925 Formation of Plastics Department.	**1927** The GE Electric Refrigeration Department was established and began production of the "Monitor Top" hermetically sealed refrigerator.	
1928 GE's station WGY initiated broadcasting of TV programs twice weekly.		

WORLD EVENTS	COMPANY CORE IDEAS

1930

1930–1940 The Great Depression.

1933 Roosevelt began the New Deal.

1935

1935 The first major league night baseball game played under GE Novalux lamps.

1937 Howard Hughes set a transcontinental air record employing the GE supercharger.

PHILIP D. REED, CHAIRMAN 1939–1942, 1945–1958; CHARLES E WILSON, PRESIDENT 1939–1942, 1945–1950 Under Wilson and Reed, GE greatly expanded its defense-related business and moved into several new markets under the slogan "Progress is Our Most Important Product."

1940

1940 GE's television station WRGB became the first to relay television broadcasts from NYC, marking the formation of the first TV network.

1941 U.S. entered World War II.

COMPANY EVENTS	PRODUCT INTROS	FINANCIAL RESULTS (in millions)
LABOR RELATIONS Corporatism had a large impact on labor relations. It espoused the importance of communication and personal contact between management and labor. Compensation was based on piecework, profit bonuses, and pension plans to keep employees happy and away from union influence.	**1931** The one-millionth GE electric refrigerator, a product introduced only four years earlier, was presented to the Henry Ford Museum.	**1930** Revenues $376.2 Net Income $60.5 Employees 78,400
1930 The General Electric X-ray Corporation name given to GE affiliate the Victor X-Ray Corporation.	**1932** The three-way lamp was developed for multi-level illumination.	
1931 The Swope Plan proposed.	**1932** The first GE dishwashers were marketed.	
1932 Swope became Chairman, Economic Advisory Board of the Dept. of Commerce.	**1934** The first fluorescent lamp was constructed at NELA Park.	
1932 GE Contracts Corporation began to finance purchases of refrigerators (ancestor of GE Financial Services).		
1932 The GE Air Conditioning Department was established to develop electric devices for home heating, humidifying, and temperature control.		
1932 RCA became an independent company when the U.S. government decreed that it should be separated from GE. The memory of GE lingered on in the notes of the famous NBC chimes—GEC—which stand for the General Electric Company.		
1939 The GE Radio and Television Department was formed; the first lines of TV and FM receivers were announced.		
LABOR RELATIONS Policy of "Management Knows Best." Influenced work force directly to avoid union conflict. Expanded number of facilities from thirty-five to sixty to disperse union influence.	**1942** GE built and tested first U.S. jet engine.	**1940** Revenues $411.9 Net Income $56.2 Employees 76,300
1942 To meet wartime needs, GE plants manufactured 400 plastic parts for aircraft, demonstrating important engineering plastics applications.		
1942 Wilson resigned to become a member of the War Production Board; Swope came out of retirement to serve as GE President. Reed resigned to help administer the Lend-Lease Program and later became Chief of the U.S. Mission for Economic Affairs in London; Young returned as GE Chairman of the Board.		

WORLD EVENTS	COMPANY CORE IDEAS

1945

1945 World War II ended.
1949 NATO founded.

1950

1950 U.S. entered the Korean War.

1951 Start of the European Economic Community (EEC).

1953 The Korean War ended.

RALPH J. CORDINER, PRESIDENT 1950–1958; CEO, CHAIRMAN 1958–1963 Cordiner sent GE on a path to take advantage of the new markets and technologies that opened after WWII. Following his slogan of "Go for it," GE saw a twentyfold increase in the number of market segments it competed in during Cordiner's tenure. GE's organizational structure changed to a market and product focus under Cordiner's decentralization. Management Science became the main tenet of Cordiner's career philosophy; Crotonville was established to teach how to manage.

COMPANY EVENTS	PRODUCT INTROS	FINANCIAL RESULTS (in millions)
1945 International GE had 5,000 employees selling and manufacturing products abroad. **1946** GE began study of power generation by nuclear energy. **1946** Nine-week labor strike against GE. **1947** GE found guilty in carboloy suit.	**1947** The first completely automatic clothes washer was introduced. **1947** The Erie Plant produced the first two-door refrigerator-freezer combination.	
ORGANIZATION Cordiner's decentralization of GE changed its fifteen centralized components to more than forty-six Executive Office and one hundred Operating Departments, including those in such new markets as aircraft engines, computers, nuclear energy, and aerospace. Each operating department had P & L responsibilities and managers were appraised primarily on profit goals. Teaching managers how to manage any business with standardized procedures was the purpose of the Crotonville Management Institute. Great expansion of Corporate staff occurred in the areas of management consulting, research, employee and public relations, and all functional coordination. **1950** Ralph Cordiner became GE President. **1951** Cordiner cut the dividend rate for GE stock for only the eighth time in GE's history; it has not been reduced since. **1951** Construction began on Appliance Park, Louisville, Ky. **1952** Cordiner's decentralization reorganization began with the company's fifteen centralized components converted into more than one hundred operating departments. **1953** GE's foreign sales 10% of its total sales.	**1953** Dr. Daniel W. Fox combined heated bisphenol A and diphenyl carbonate and discovered a tough, unbreakable, impact resistant, transparent, polycarbonate thermoplastic. This discovery led to the development of LEXAN® thermoplastic. **1954** First industrial installations of numerical controls for machine tools. **1954** GE designed J79, world's first jet engine to move aircraft twice the speed of sound.	**1950** Revenues $2,233.8 Net Income $179.7 Employees 206,000

WORLD EVENTS	COMPANY CORE IDEAS

1957 USSR launched Sputnik I.

1961 Alan Shepard first U.S. astronaut in space.

FRED J. BORCH, PRESIDENT 1963–1968; CHAIRMAN, CEO 1968–1972 Borch called the GE Growth Council which identified nine growth sectors in the U.S. economy and GE decided to "Beat the GNP" by entering them all. During his tenure, Borch essentially added another GE to the one whose direction he assumed. GE's sales and earnings doubled between 1963 and 1972. Borch commissioned the McKinsey Study, which called for greater corporate strategic planning to manage the increasingly decentralized structure and to prioritize investment decisions.

COMPANY EVENTS	PRODUCT INTROS	FINANCIAL RESULTS (in millions)
LABOR RELATIONS GE's number of production facilities grew greatly due to the need to specialize production in each facility for its own product line. The training given managers at Crotonville served to create a growing division between management and labor. **1956** Management Development Institute opened in Croton-on-Hudson, N.Y. **1959** GE's International Business was organized as one of the Company's major Groups.	**1955** GE announced creation of industrial-grade diamonds. **1955** America's first commercial nuclear power is distributed over the Niagara Mohawk Power Company system; a GE turbine-generator and the Seawolf submarine nuclear reactor prototype were used to produce electric power from a plant in West Milton, N.Y. **1956** PPO discovered by Alan S. Hay. It represented a fundamentally new way to make polymers and became GE's biggest scientific breakthrough in polymers. **1957** The U.S. government's first nuclear reactor license for the five megawatt Vallecitos atomic power plant near Pleasanton, Calif., was granted. **1957** GE Housewares Division introduced the first commercially marketed spray steam and dry iron.	**1955** Revenues $3,463.7 Net Income $208.9 Employees 250,300
1960 Federal grand jury indictments were handed down against seventeen GE executives for participation in a conspiracy to set prices in turbines and electrical machinery. **1963** Fred Borch succeeded Cordiner as President of GE. **1964** GE Plastics globalization began with a joint venture with Algemene Kunstzijde Unie NV in the Netherlands to market the PPO polymer in Europe.	**1960** GE entered the plastics market with the commercial introduction of LEXAN® resin. **1961** The GE Space Division developed NIMBUS, an earth-oriented meteorological satellite, the first of a series of seven that supplied scientific data on atmospheric and environmental conditions.	**1960** Revenues $4,197.5 Net Income $200.1 Employees 250,600

WORLD EVENTS	COMPANY CORE IDEAS

1965 American troops entered combat in Vietnam.

1969 Neil Armstrong stepped on the moon with boots of GE silicone rubber and a helmet visor of LEXAN polycarbonate.

1970 Invention of the Computed Tomography (CT) technology in England.

1973 Last U.S. ground troops left Vietnam.

1973–1974 Energy Crisis.

REGINALD H. JONES, CHAIRMAN, CEO 1972–1981 Jones, a man whose background was in finance and who believed in running GE with a rein of strong financial control, increased the role of corporate review of business strategy and investment prioritization. Jones believed in the importance of R&D in providing growth and instituted Sector Executives as the positions within GE charged with looking for long-term opportunities for growth. Jones felt that it was important to build a constructive dialogue between business and government. To this end, he accepted positions as the Chairman of The Business Council and Co-Chairman of The Business Roundtable.

COMPANY EVENTS	PRODUCT INTROS	FINANCIAL RESULTS (in millions)
ORGANIZATION During Borch's tenure, the number of departments within GE grew to more than 350. These were divided into forty-three strategic business units (SBUs) considered to be truly viable businesses. Planning staffs in each of these SBUs were added to GE's already large layers of management. Strategic business plans were reviewed annually by a new corporate planning staff and a newly established Corporate Executive Office of the CEO and three Vice Chairmen.	**1966** NORYL production began in Selkirk, N.Y.	**1965** Revenues $6,213.6 Net Income $355.1 Employees 333,000
1968 At age 33, Jack Welch was named general manager of the entire Plastics Department; he had been promoted through four management levels in only eight years.	**1968** In the first commercial order for GE engines, GE CF6 engines with 40,000-pound thrust were chosen to power the McDonnell Douglas DC-10 trijet wide-bodied airliner.	
1968 The McKinsey study led to the establishment of GE's SBU organization and the instituting of strategic planning for GE's component business.	**1969** GE Appliance Division announced the first side-by-side refrigerator-freezer with an automatic dispenser for ice cubes and chilled water through the door.	
1969 GE sales were at an all-time high while profitability was at an all-time low.		
ORGANIZATION Jones ended the dual organization structure of Departments and SBUs, having only the SBUs be planning units within GE and allowing each of the now forty-nine SBUs to organize internally along product (department) lines or functionally. A new corporate management layer consisting of six Sector Executives was created as the position to which SBU managers reported and were reviewed. The recommendations of the Sector Executives for each business were reviewed by the Corporate Executive Office.		**1970** Revenues $8,762.7 Net Income $328.5 Employees 396,600
1970 GE bought land in Bergen op Zoom, the Netherlands, for a production facility for LEXAN and NORYL in Europe.		
1970 International sales accounted for 16% of GE's total sales.		
1971 New $30 million Medical Systems complex built in Waukesha, Wis.		
1974 The General Electric Company officially transferred its corporate headquarters from New York City to a new facility in Fairfield, Conn.		

WORLD EVENTS	COMPANY CORE IDEAS

1975

1979 Three-Mile Island nuclear facility accident.
1979–1980 U.S. Energy Crisis.
Hostage Crisis ended January 1979.

COMPANY EVENTS	PRODUCT INTROS	FINANCIAL RESULTS (in millions)
1976 GE Medical systems first CT prototype installed at Univ. of California San Francisco School of Medicine. **1978** GE's international system employed over 100,000 people outside the U.S.; it included 129 affiliated companies manufacturing products in 23 countries and using more than 350 distributors serving markets in 150 countries.	**1975** The Aerospace Electronic Systems Department built the GEOS-3 Radar Altimeter; GEOS, the Geodynamics Experimental Ocean Satellite, studies, measures, and maps the oceans from orbit. **1976** A computed tomography (CT) scanner developed by the Medical Systems Division took detailed cross-section x-ray pictures of the human body in less than five seconds, four to sixty times faster than other total-body scanners in use. **1977** GE Medical Systems introduced the CT8800, the world's most successful CT scanner. **1978** The largest nuclear plant in the world is completed in Japan, jointly built by GE and three of its licensees in Japan. **1978** The largest rated turbine-generator in the world, Palo Verde I, was shipped to the Arizona Nuclear Power Project; the unit was capable of producing 1,559,100 kva.	**1975** Revenues $14,105.0 Net Income $688.0 Employees 380,000

WORLD EVENTS	COMPANY CORE IDEAS

1980

1980–1982 U.S. Recession with highest rate of unemployment since the Depression.

JOHN F. WELCH, JR. 1981 A chemical engineer by training, Welch rose through the ranks while building the GE Plastics business. Upon becoming CEO, he realized that, with key markets growing more slowly, technology moving faster, and world competition intensifying, only businesses on top of their markets would survive in the 1990s and beyond. He articulated a strategy whereby businesses that were not #1 or #2 in markets in which GE wanted to participate would have to be fixed, closed, or sold.

THE #1 OR #2 STRATEGY AND FIX/CLOSE/SELL With key world markets growing more slowly, technology moving faster, and world competition intensifying, only businesses on top of their markets would survive in the 1990s and beyond. With this in mind, Jack Welch divided the GE businesses which met the requirements of being #1 or #2 globally into three strategic circles: Core Manufacturing, Technology-intensive, and Services. Any businesses outside these circles would have to be made more competitive or be closed or sold.

1981

COMPANY EVENTS	PRODUCT INTROS	FINANCIAL RESULTS (in millions)
PRODUCTIVITY Factory automation investments were designed to make GE businesses more cost competitive with their global competition. Programs designed at eliminating waste, downtime, excess inventory, and distribution problems were instituted in plants. The result was an increase in productivity from 2% for the period from 1981 to 1986 to greater than 4% in 1987 and 1988. Each 1% of productivity improvement equaled nearly $300 million in pre-tax profit contribution. **1980** GE Medical Systems (GEMS) acquired portions of Thorn-EMI medical equipment sales and service operation and entered the Ultrasound modality. GE Corporate R&D in Schenectady, N.Y. began Magnetic Resonance (MR) development project for medical diagnostics.		**1980** Revenues $24,959.0 Net Income $1,514.0 Employees 402,000
DOWNSIZING/DELAYERING LEAN AND AGILE Between 1981 and 1988, approximately 100,000 positions at GE were eliminated through restructuring, attrition, and dispositions. Jobs aimed at producing information, "nice to know" but not "necessary to know," were cut. Many layers of management were removed. With less bureaucracy, less second-guessing and reviewing of decisions, GE businesses could be faster-acting and more competitive.	**1981** Introduced CT 9800 scanner for medical diagnostic imaging. Introduced Quick-Fix system for do-it-yourself appliance repair. The USS *Ohio,* first of the TRIDENT class ballistic missile submarines was commissioned, powered by nuclear reactors designed at GE's Knolls Atomic Power Laboratory and GE Power Systems.	**1981** Revenues $27,240.0 Net Income $1,652.0 Employees 404,000

1982

JACK WELCH'S ORIGINAL KEY ISSUES As he sought to define his vision of GE's new culture, Jack Welch spoke of key attitudes and policies which were to be reshaped and reworked over the decade of the 1980s. No longer would there be formal, inwardly focused *budgets*. Managers were to take *ownership* of their businesses, working with a spirit of *entrepreneurship* and *stewardship* and in an environment in which *reality* and *candor* and *open communications* were the mode of operations. Managers were to demand *excellence* from themselves and others. GE's businesses were to be *lean* so that they could be *agile* and fast moving with *quality* in everything produced. Lastly, *investment* as each business required would be made to make each business its very best.

QUANTUM CHANGE As Jack Welch gained experience with trying to change GE, he came to believe that quantum, or bold, large, structural change was required. Incremental change was easily circumvented by established bureaucracy and gave outside competitors time to thwart the strategy. As Welch said, "Understand today fast. Shape tomorrow in your mind, and then leap to tomorrow."

COMPANY EVENTS	PRODUCT INTROS	FINANCIAL RESULTS (in millions)

DIVESTITURES GE businesses which were not #1 or #2 in their markets or which did not provide GE with any unique comparative advantage were divestiture candidates. Among those sold were: Utah International, Consumer Electronics, Housewares and Central Air Conditioning. In total, $8.5 billion in cash was generated.

1982 Opened the GE Answer Center, award winning 24-hour toll-free customer service answering center.

Dedicated $130-million expansion of R&D Center in Schenectady, N.Y.

Invested $130 million into automating locomotive business in Erie, Pa.

Sold central air conditioning business.

Joint venture with Yokogawa Electrical Works of Japan established Yokogawa Medical Systems (YMS); GE had 51% ownership.

OWNERSHIP/ENTREPRENEURSHIP/STEWARDSHIP/ EXCELLENCE The goal of ownership within GE was to delegate more decisions and drive the ability to act down several layers. Entrepreneurship meant the creation of an atmosphere in which ideas from all levels could surface. Stewardship was an obligation to take the assets of the business and make them grow. All this required excellence, managers demanding and reaching for the very best from within themselves and from each coworker.

1982 Introduced GE Medical Systems' first Magnetic Resonance (MR) machine.

GE Plastics introduced XENOY thermoplastics for use in automotive exterior body parts.

GE Lighting introduced the Miser Maxi Light, a 55-watt bulb that delivered as much light as brightest setting of the 150-watt three-way-bulb and has 4-6 times the life of ordinary light bulbs.

1982 Revenues $26,500.0
Net Income $1,817.0
Employees 367,000

WORLD EVENTS	COMPANY CORE IDEAS

1983

1983 The Reagan Era.

COMPANY EVENTS	PRODUCT INTROS	FINANCIAL RESULTS (in millions)
EXTERNAL FOCUS The only results that counted were those in comparison to external competition: Do sales show increasing market share? Do margin figures show that GE had a cost advantage versus its competition? The numbers that now counted at GE were outward-looking and competitively focused.	**1983** Introduced Signa magnetic resonance (MR) technology for medical diagnostic imaging.	**1983** Revenues $26,797.0 Net Income $2,024.0 Employees 340,000
1983 GE sold Family Financial Services, a second-mortgage subsidiary, for $600 million.	XENOY used in bumper of Ford Sierra manufactured in Europe.	
Opened new dishwasher plant in Louisville, Ky., as first phase of $1 billion investment in Major Appliances.		
Refocused nuclear energy business on fuels and service.		
Received major locomotive order from the People's Republic of China.		
Expanded mortgage insurance business by acquiring AMIC Corporation.		
Common stock split two-for-one.		
GE-sponsored Horizons Pavilion opened at Epcot Center in Orlando, Fla.		
GEM Polymers (Japan) established as joint venture between GE Plastics and Mitsui Toatsu Chemical and Mitsui Petrochemical Industries to build $50 million thermoplastic resins plant in Japan to serve automotive, electrical, and electronics industries.		
GE Plastics also began a joint venture with Nagase to build a polyphenol oxide resin plant in Japan.		
Philips purchased Westinghouse Lighting, giving this global competitor a 21% share of the U.S. market.		
REALITY & CANDOR/OPEN COMMUNICATIONS Reality & Candor in GE: seeing the world as it is rather than as one might wish it to be. With this outlook, a change in the marketplace became an opportunity for action and not something to be feared or ignored. Reaching these opportunities required teamwork with two-way, open communication.		

1984

1985

INTEGRATED DIVERSITY GE was not a conglomerate of thirteen unconnected businesses. GE made long-term commitments to winning on a global basis in each of the businesses. In GE, financial, technological, and human resources were moved across and among businesses, best practices were shared, and the success of the entire company was the responsibility of each of its parts. Diversity at GE also meant being both a "big" and "small" company at the same time. To its competition, GE was "big": a well-resourced, highly talented, technology-leading, fast-moving, self-confident, and very formidable competitor. To its customers, GE was to be "small": serving each on a "first-name basis" with real customer satisfaction and retention. GE wanted to be "small" to its employees: making each one's voice and ideas heard and acted upon. Lastly, GE wanted to be "small" in its dealings with the community: taking its place as a responsible part of the environment and a solver of social problems.

THE BUSINESS ENGINE Building on the #1 or #2 strategy, Jack Welch used The Business Engine analogy to show how GE would continue to grow in the future. The office of the CEO allocates GE's human, capital, and technical resources among the businesses for productivity or volume growth, selective resource allocation, asset turnover, or non-strategic disposition opportunities. The outcomes of these opportunities produce earnings and, with earnings, cash for dividends, acquisitions or to provide the resources for the next round of strategic allocations. Each GE business has a critical role in the Engine and should be rewarded for earnings growth and/or cash flow.

COMPANY EVENTS	PRODUCT INTROS	FINANCIAL RESULTS (in millions)
1984 GE sold Utah International, its natural resource subsidiary, for $2.4 billion.	**1984** GE made first flight-test of the CF6-80C2 commercial aircraft engine.	**1984** Revenues $27,947.0 Net Income $2,280.0 Employees 330,000
GE sold its housewares business to Black & Decker for $300 million.		
GE acquired Employers Reinsurance Corp. from Texaco for $1.1 billion; grouped with GECC to form General Electric Financial Services, Inc.		
Began $250 million investment to modernize GE Lighting.		
Received 75% of U.S. Air Force contract for new fighter engines in the Great Engine War.		
GE Medical Systems began joint venture with Samsung in South Korea, forming SMS.		
INVESTMENT/QUALITY To accomplish #1 or #2 businesses today and ten years into the future, money would be allocated to that future, by investing in acquisitions, joint ventures, Property Equipment, and R&D to ensure the long term. The goal of this investment was to have the best products and services for each market served—the quality of offerings needed to stay on top.		
ACQUISITIONS GE acquisition strategy was to add businesses which would either enhance the market position of its #1 businesses or purchase businesses which were already #1 or #2 in their markets. In the 1980s, some businesses acquired by GE were: CGR, Borg-Warner Chemicals, Roper, RCA, ERC, Kidder, Peabody, GELCO, and Montgomery Ward Credit Corp.	**1985** NORYL GTX resin introduced in automotive class "A" surface body panels in U.S. GE shipped the first Dash 8 computer-controlled locomotives.	**1985** Revenues $32,624.0 Net Income $2,277.0 Employees 299,000
ALLIANCES GE has entered into joint ventures with foreign firms to achieve technical or marketing advantages. Every GE business has taken steps to join into such alliances. Potential strategic partnerships are limited in number; speed in achieving them is very important.		
1985 GE Plastics opened facility to produce NORYL resin in Brazil to serve Latin American and African markets.		
GE acquired Decimus Computer Leasing.		
SECTOR REMOVAL In order to improve speed and communication, Welch removed the Sector Executive positions in 1985. Each of the businesses now reported directly to one of the members of the CEO. As a result, more decision-making power was placed in the hands of the business leaders.		

WORLD EVENTS	COMPANY CORE IDEAS

1986 Chernobyl nuclear facility accident.

THE HUMAN ENGINE From the human side of the corporation, growth can only be achieved when emotional energy is released at all levels of the organization, when creativity and feelings of ownership and self-worth exist at every level. The key characteristics of The Human Engine are self-confidence, simplicity, and speed. Self-confident people are able to be simple, not clutter the organization with bureaucracy, and hence create speed.

SHARED VALUES For change to succeed, all players at GE must accept and sign on to common values. The values determined to make GE the best company to work for were openness, ability to face reality, self-confidence, fast action, candor, honest communication, and integrity. At GE such values were not just platitudes, but they were actual measurement issues in personnel review.

COMPANY EVENTS	PRODUCT INTROS	FINANCIAL RESULTS (in millions)

GLOBALIZATION Globalization, becoming a true producer and seller in each of the major markets of the world, became a requirement for GE in the 1980s if it was to maintain its #1 or #2 competitor position in each of its businesses.

1986 GE acquired RCA, including the National Broadcasting Company (NBC), for $6.4 billion in cash.

The Statue of Liberty relighted for 100th anniversary by GE.

GE acquired 80% of Kidder, Peabody & Company.

GE formed factory automation joint venture with FANUC Ltd. of Japan.

GE increased ownership of Yokogawa Medical Systems (YMS) joint venture in Japan from 51% to 75%.

GE Lighting prices for light bulbs began dropping 2-3% per year, instead of rising 2-3% per year as they had in the past.

THE CORPORATE EXECUTIVE COUNCIL (CEC) Two days each quarter, the Corporate Executive Officers, the thirteen heads of GE businesses and the senior corporate staff meet in what is more like a business laboratory. All see and discuss the numbers, the goals, and the problems at the same time and work until consensus is reached. The CEC creates a sense of trust, personal familiarity, and mutual obligation at the top of the company. At each meeting, new programs are discussed so that best practices can be transferred from one business to the next. At the end of each CEC meeting, each leader has the same playbook and knows the plays for each individual business and for GE as a whole.

HUB & SPOKE STRUCTURE GE's hub was its Corporate Executive Office. Here, resource allocations would be made among all GE businesses. The spokes in GE, the businesses, were to be highly differentiated. For example, each had its goal for the GE Engine, its own structural variation, and its own reward and compensation system.

WELCH'S VARSITY TEAM In August 1986, due to the acquisition of RCA, Jack Welch moved many of the business heads to different businesses. Now, he had at the helm people who had bought into his management philosophies and strategies.

1986 GE's Unducted Fan (UDF) engine successfully completed its first flight. The UDF offered expected fuel savings of 40% to 70% over conventional turbofans.

The 1986 Ford Taurus and Mercury Sable represented a landmark of GE Plastics; each contained some seventy pounds of GE resins.

1986
Revenues $42,013.0
Net Income $2,492.0
Employees 373,000

WORLD EVENTS	COMPANY CORE IDEAS

1987

1987 October 19th stock market crash.

LEADERSHIP CHARACTERISTICS Good business leaders create and own a vision, articulate the vision, and relentlessly drive it to completion. They are open, use all channels of communication, and are accessible to all. They are truthful with co-workers. Their job is to create and add value, not control or focus on personal power. A leader's task is to make others more effective.

1988

THE BOUNDARYLESS ORGANIZATION This is a call to break down all barriers to communication and action. All employees should go wherever necessary to get needed information or to give input on decisions they can impact. The goal is to increase the level of mutual respect for the parts played by people in each function, each level, each business across all of GE. Furthermore, communication channels should extend to outside stakeholders in GE to suppliers, customers, share owners, and communities.

COMMUNICATION Communication is *not* achieved through pronouncements on videotapes or in newspapers. Communication comes from give-and-take constant personal interaction aimed at achieving consensus. Everyone must know, understand, and buy into goals or achieving those ends cannot come with speed and decisiveness.

COMPANY EVENTS	PRODUCT INTROS	FINANCIAL RESULTS (in millions)

REVIEW PROCESS In addition to being evaluated on business results, GE managers are also judged on the leadership principles included in the GE values statement: openness, ability to face reality, self-confidence, speed of decision making, honesty of communication, candor, and integrity.

1987 GE swapped the GE/RCA consumer electronics business to Thomson, S.A. of France for CGR, a medical diagnostic imaging business, and $800 million in cash.

GEFS expanded worldwide financial services business by acquisition of Navistar Financial Corporation Canada, Gelco Corporation, and D&K Financial Corp.

GE selected by NASA to produce major portions of its planned space station.

Common stock split two-for-one.

GE acquired WTVJ in Miami; merged with NBC.

1987 Revenues $48,158.0
Net Income $2,915.0
Employees 322,000

REWARD SYSTEMS Each GE business can design its own management compensation and bonus plans to best meet its markets and goals. Furthermore, $30 million has been set aside for management awards to individuals each year.

1988 GE bought Borg-Warner Chemicals, the worldwide leader in ABS resins with sales of $1.25 billion in 1987, for $2.3 billion.

GE expanded its appliance business by buying Roper Corporation for $507 million, outbidding Whirlpool.

GEFS acquired Montgomery Ward Credit Corporation.

GE sold semiconductor business to Harris Corporation.

Formed a joint venture in motors with Robert Bosch of West Germany.

Signed an alliance in lighting with Toshiba of Japan to manufacture fluorescent lamps in the U.S. with 50% of production to be shipped to Japan.

Employers Reinsurance Corporation purchased Baltica-Nordisk Reassurance of Denmark.

GE rated first in quality by U.S. consumers in Gallup Poll.

50% of GE Medical Systems business came from outside the U.S.

1988 Revenues $50,089.0
Net Income $3,386.0
Employees 298,000

WORLD EVENTS	COMPANY CORE IDEAS

1989 Berlin Wall tumbled.

NEW PSYCHOLOGICAL CONTRACT In the modern, highly competitive world, no business is a safe haven for employment unless it is winning in the marketplace. GE is striving to be the best place in the world to work for people willing to compete and take risks. It is not the place for those seeking an implicit lifetime employment contract.

1990 Iraq invaded Kuwait.

WORK-OUT (The Process)
SELF-CONFIDENCE (The Driver)
SPEED Speed is the indispensable ingredient of success in this decade. It is accomplished by implementing the Work-Out processes which create employee self-confidence in pursuit of a boundaryless corporation. With fewer boundaries speed is picked up—or the competitive advantage.

COMPANY EVENTS	PRODUCT INTROS	FINANCIAL RESULTS (in millions)

REAL-TIME PLANNING This idea deals with the removal of any bureaucracy that slows down the decision-making process—reviews, filling out of forms, or preparation of lengthy reports. GE must know clearly what the strategic needs of each business are and be ready whenever an opportunity arises to move fast to grasp the moment.

WORK-OUT Work-Out is a company-wide drive to improve the work process by identifying and eliminating unproductive tasks—unnecessary reports, reviews, forecasts, budgets—so as to energize employees. Removing these tasks will allow more stimulating and creative work environments to emerge. Employees at all levels are asked to give their input on better ways to do their jobs and service customers.

1989 GE authorized $10 billion share repurchase.

Broadcasting record set by NBC with sixty-eight consecutive weeks as top-rated U.S. TV network.

Formed mobile communications joint venture with Ericsson of Sweden.

Opened Living Environments concept house for showcasing the use of plastics in the building construction markets.

Awarded contract from Tokyo Electric Power Company for world's largest combined-cycle power cycle.

"Work-Out" began.

1989 Introduced new line of RCA major appliances.

Announced new arc-discharge lighting for automobiles.

GTX fenders introduced on Cadillac DeVille and Buick Reatta.

CNBC cable-TV network launched by NBC.

1989 Revenues $54,574.0
Net Income $3,939.0
Employees 292,000

BEST PRACTICES One effort of boundary-busting has been the wringing of not-invented-here—NIH—from GE's culture. GE teams are now searching within their own entity, within other GE businesses, and in corporations around the world, for better ways of doing things. One example: a truly innovative method of compressing product cycle time was found in New Zealand, tested in a GE company in Canada, transferred to the largest appliance complex in Kentucky, and is now studied by other GE teams.

1990 GE acquired majority interest in Tungsram Company Ltd. for $150 million.

GE presented with Harvard University's Dively Award for Corporate Public Initiative.

GEFS acquired certain leasing operations of MNC Financial Inc. for $341 million; service operations of the Burton Group, U.K., for $316 million; Travelers Mortgage Services Inc. for $210 million; ELLCO Leasing Corporation for $160 million.

GE sold Ladd Petroleum Corporation to Amax Oil and Gas Inc. for $515 million.

GE Appliances launched Quick Response, reducing cycle time by 70%.

1990 Unveiled the new fuel efficient, super thrust GE90 aircraft engine.

Introduced the F-technology gas turbine, the world's most powerful and efficient.

Introduced Heavy VALOX resin, which can have the feel and aesthetic qualities of glass, ceramic, porcelain, metal, and ivory.

British Airways became launch customer for GE90.

1990 Revenues $58,414.0
Net Income $4,303.0
Employees 298,000

WORLD EVENTS	COMPANY CORE IDEAS
1991	
1991 The Gulf War—Operation Desert Storm.	**BOUNDARYLESSNESS (The Vision)**
1991 Disintegration of U.S.S.R.	**SPEED (The Result)**
	ONLY LEADERS WHO "WALK THE TALK" The ultimate test of the commitment to company transformation will be how it deals with those leaders who deliver on commitments but do not share GE's values. These autocrats and tyrants force performance out of people rather than inspire it. GE has to convince these managers to change or depart. Because without leaders who "walk the talk," all corporate plans, promises, and dreams for the future are just that—talk.
1992	
1992 Civil wars in the former Yugoslavia, Somalia, and Cambodia.	Manage to three core measures: customer satisfaction, employee satisfaction, and cash flow.

COMPANY EVENTS	PRODUCT INTROS	FINANCIAL RESULTS (in millions)

COMMUNITY BOUNDARYLESS In the spirit of boundarylessness, employees volunteer in the communities that the company's hundreds of plants and installations call home. Efforts range from mentoring in schools, working on homeless shelters, to environmental clean-ups. Some GE efforts involve the 35,000-member Elfun Society. Volunteerism has become a winning experience for GE's communities, employees, and company.

TRUST Leaders in the 1990s must trust and be trusted. Successful leaders are those who have the self-confidence to trust and empower others. Empowered, highly involved work forces trust their leaders. Trust is gained over time by walking the talk, creating an environment where trust can flourish— Work-Out, Open Communication, Facing Reality, Candor, Compassion, Integrity.

1991 GE established joint ventures with: MABE, Mexico; Godrej & Boyce Mfg. Co. Ltd., India; GE Hangwei Medical Systems Co., the People's Republic of China; India Petrochemicals Corporation Ltd., India.

GE Industrial and Power Systems cut cycle time in parts of the power generation business by over 80%.

GE Plastics honored with Business Enterprise Trust for community service.

GE ranks #1 on Forbes "Most Powerful" companies list.

NBC acquired FNN.

GE Lighting acquired light source from Thorn EMI.

1991 Introduced "Energy Choice" energy efficient fluorescent lamp.

Introduced CT HiSpeed Advantage system, which permits one-second scan with only a one-second delay between scans.

NBC launches around-the-clock News Channel.

1991 Revenues $60,236.0
Net Income $4,435.0*
Employees 284,000
(*Does not include $1.8 billion non-cash accounting charge.)

QUICK MARKET INTELLIGENCE (QMI) QMI is a process that gives every salesperson direct access, every Friday, to the key managers and the CEO of the business to lay out customer problems and needs. The product of the meeting is not deep or strategic in nature, but action—a response to the customer right away.

QUICK RESPONSE (QR) QR is a cycle-time reduction technique. It erases most of the barriers between the functions of GE businesses and the customers—it took GE Appliances from an eighteen-week order-to-delivery cycle to a 3½-week cycle, on the way to three days.

CO-LOCATION This is the ultimate boundaryless behavior. Teams from all functions are put together in one room to bring new products to life.

1992 GE Aerospace merger with Martin Marietta announced.

GE Lighting completes APAR Ltd. joint venture in India.

GE Capital acquires Avis Lease in Europe.

ED&C's Eurolec joint venture acquires Lemag of Spain.

GE Lighting announces joint venture with Hitachi in Japan.

1992 GE Capital launches GE Rewards credit card.

GE Motors introduces high-efficiency ECM™ programmable motor.

GE Appliances introduces Profile™ line.

1992 Revenues $62,202
Net Income $4,725
Employees 268,000

WORLD EVENTS	COMPANY CORE IDEAS

1993 Economic contractions around the globe.

1994 Mandela released from prison.
Internet gains national media exposure.

1995 Federal Building bombed in Oklahoma City.

Republicans regained the House.

Delayering continues to remove sectors, groups, business units; Work-Out continues.

1996 Clinton reelected President.

Bosnian war continues.

Six Sigma.

1997 Woolworth closes its doors.

Clinton sex scandal begins.

Princess Diana dies.

Continuous learning already resulting in tremendous bottom-line improvement. New stretch goals announced for company-wide Six Sigma implementation by 2000. Six Sigma dedicated to moving quality to near perfection. Core ideas solidified as Service, Globalization, and Six Sigma.

COMPANY EVENTS	PRODUCT INTROS	FINANCIAL RESULTS (in millions)
QUICK MARKET INTELLIGENCE, QUICK RESPONSE, AND CO-LOCATION CONTINUE. **1993** GE Aerospace merger with Martin Marietta completed. GE Capital acquires Weyerhauser's GNA Corp. GE announces $70 million investment for home laundry upgrade at Appliance Park. GE Capital buys forty-five aircraft from Irish Guiness Peat Aviation.	**1993** GE Transportation Systems unveils new AMD-103 passenger locomotive for Amtrak.	**1993** First quarter Revenues $12,900 First quarter Net Income $1,160 First quarter Employees 230,000 (reflects the transfer of GE Aerospace to Martin Marietta)
1994 Liquidation of Kidder, Peabody.		**1994** Revenues $60,000 Net Income $4,700 Employees 221,000
1995 Six Sigma launch with 200 projects. *Tonight Show with Jay Leno* recaptured number one slot in late night programming. NBC is leading broadcaster with five of the top ten shows.	**1995** GE Lighting introduces Heliax compact fluorescents. GE Power Systems develops "H" technology which converts 60% of a fuel's energy into electricity combined cycle operation. GE Aircraft Engines introduces GE powered Boeing 777 twin-jet.	**1995** Revenues $70,000 Net Income $6,600 Employees 222,000
1996 GE invited to opening Wall Street's first trading session as the only surviving company from the original Dow Jones Industrial Average. Six Sigma: 40% of every manager's bonus tied to quality. 1000 projects underway. Continued emphasis on capitalizing on service opportunities with over 120,000 pieces of GE equipment worldwide.	**1996** GE.com launched. MSNBC premieres. GE Capital introduces Socrates Quick Quote™ system. GE Plastics develops LEXAN® pellets for use in CDs, DVDs and CD-ROMs.	**1996** Revenues $79,000 Net Income $7,280 Employees 239,000
	1997 GE Appliances develop Smart Water™ Water Filtration Device. GE Medical launches LOGIQ® 700 ultrasound.	**1997** Revenues $990,840 Net Income $8,200 Employees 276,000

	WORLD EVENTS	COMPANY CORE IDEAS
1998	**1998** U.S. budget surplus $70B. Asian financial crisis expands.	ABC Players: Focus efforts on transforming B players into A players and moving C players out of the organization.
1999	**1999** WTO meets in Seattle amid protests. U.S. enjoys longest expansion in history. Y2K bug plagues computer systems.	E-Business fully recognized as driving force in GE rejuvenation, used throughout GE to enable billions in transactions and serving customers ever more closely.
2000	**2000** NASDAQ records largest one year drop in history. George W. Bush is elected 43rd President.	

COMPANY EVENTS	PRODUCT INTROS	FINANCIAL RESULTS (in millions)
1998 Bayer AG to develop polycarbonate and coatings technology to improve the impact resistance and safety of automotive windows.	**1998** Medical Systems launches Lightspeed QXI CT, first product introduced with Six Sigma. GE Capital Employers Reinsurance launches Hercules Comprehensive Coverage.	**1998** Revenues $100,470 Net Income $9,300 Employees 293,000
	1999 GE Medical Systems introduces functional anatomical mapping. GE Appliances launches Advantium Oven with Speed-clock technology.	**1999** Revenues $111,630 Net Income $10,700, more than $2,000 in E-commerce transactions Employees 340,000
		2000 Revenues $129,900 Net Income $12,700 Employees 313,000

GE Strategy and Performance

... as reported to Share Owners 1981 to 2000

To Our Share Owners

Your Company's underlying strength and resiliency were reflected in its 1981 performance and year-end financial position.

Sales of $27.24 billion were up 9% over 1980. Earnings of $1.65 billion—$7.26 a share—were also 9% ahead of 1980. Total assets exceeded $20 billion for the first time: our debt-to-capital ratio was 19.4%; cash and marketables increased 12%, to almost $2.5 billion.

These 1981 earnings were produced in the face of weak economic conditions in the United States and most foreign markets; they also came on top of record levels of expenditures for research and development ($1.7 billion) and Company investments in plant and equipment ($2 billion). A number of electronics and computer software companies were acquired, strengthening General Electric in two areas targeted for high growth.

In April of last year, Reginald H. Jones retired after eight years as GE Chairman and Chief Executive Officer. Mr. Jones left us a healthy Company, one with a strong balance sheet and a record of sustained earnings growth. His other legacy, to us and to the business community, was the recognition that public policy and social responsibility are not mere adjuncts to business management, but are central to it. We miss him, but are confident we can build upon the strong foundation of financial and social stewardship he left to us.

Rather than focus on the economic environment for 1982, which we see as a continuation of many of the difficulties faced around the world during 1981, we'd like this Annual Report to cover our financial performance, and to communicate the **positioning** we did last year that is designed to serve us well in the future.

First, and most critical, was **people positioning**—making the best possible fits between our managers and the business challenges. Second were **portfolio priorities**—channeling funds into high-growth opportunities in both our new and old businesses. Third were **program investments**—

enhancing the technical strengths that must underlie our drive for worldwide market leadership. And fourth was **attitudinal positioning**—Company climate-setting designed to bring out the best in GE people.

People positioning occurred in the major Company reorganization on September 1, 1981. The people and the structures were selected both to capitalize on growth opportunities and to deal with problem businesses. These are different but equally important management challenges, and we are committed to reward successful execution in both environments. This focus on the selection and reward of people will be uppermost in your Corporate Executive Office priorities.

Portfolio repositioning takes two forms: strengthening our core businesses and developing new, fast-growth businesses. We are revitalizing our cash-generating core businesses by pointing their products and services toward changing market directions and dimensions.

With our core businesses serving as solid, income-producing platforms, our major focus is on developing strong positions in the more vital sectors of the world economy: engineered materials, information services, financial services, construction services, medical systems and natural resources. The challenge to the managers and their entire organizations in these high-growth businesses is "how big and how fast?"

Program investments increasingly have gone toward enhancing our computer software and electronics technology. This will enable us to serve, for example, the emerging megamarket of factory automation—the so-called "factory of the future." We have made the long-term commitments to achieve decisive leadership in this market by applying state-of-the-art technologies in areas where GE experience is second to none.

As for attitudinal positioning, there are three basic concepts we are emphasizing as part of the GE culture.

The first is **reality**. A sure grasp of marketplace realities and a clear understanding of corporate social responsibilities are essential in today's environment. Social expectations rightfully remain high, yet business faces intensified world competition and more rapid shifts in market structures. In this environment, a company must be a lean, low-cost producer of quality goods and services in order to survive, let alone prosper.

Corporate social responsibility in the '80s begins with a healthy company, derived from satisfying customers with quality products and services. Worldwide competitiveness leads to jobs and job security and the ability to support effectively social, educational and cultural endeavors—support that is impossible without a healthy corporate balance sheet.

A second basic concept is **excellence**. This means reaffirming and enhancing the Company's tradition for quality goods and quality services in an increasingly skeptical and quality-conscious age. And it means excellence in people—calling for the best in all of us—in some cases being even better than we thought possible.

The third concept we describe as **ownership**—the call for GE employees to assume full responsibility for the decisions they make on behalf of you and the Company. It means moving more decision-making power to operations—to managers who know their markets best.

We intend to make reality, excellence and ownership the basis for a pervasive operational atmosphere in which people will dare to try new things, where their own creativity and drive will determine how far and how fast they move. Whether in revitalized core businesses, or in the newer growth businesses, the result will be an organization more high-spirited, more adaptable and more agile than companies a fraction of our size.

This decentralized entrepreneurial energy will be aligned and augmented by the very considerable central strengths of General Electric—not just **financial** (a very strong balance sheet), but also **technical** (a research laboratory that is a model of excellence worldwide), and **human** (a manpower development system acknowledged to be among the very best)—all bonded further by the unifying power of the GE monogram—our trademark and most enduring asset.

John F. Welch, Jr.
Chairman and
Chief Executive Officer

John F. Burlingame
Vice Chairman and
Executive Officer

Edward E. Hood, Jr.
Vice Chairman and
Executive Officer

FEBRUARY 26, 1982

To Our Share Owners

Despite deep and prolonged worldwide recession, General Electric is financially stronger today than a year ago, with both earnings and balance sheet significantly improved.

GE earnings of $1.817 billion—$8.00 per share—were 10% ahead of 1981, on slightly lower sales of $26.50 billion.

The Company's return on equity was 18.8%. Return on sales rose to 6.9%. Debt-to-capital ratio at year end was reduced to 16.5%.

In this letter, the Corporate Executive Office would like to highlight some of the actions we are taking to position GE for the future—steps toward our goal of making our businesses Number One or Number Two in their markets, of making General Electric the most competitive enterprise in the world.

Major moves can be seen in four areas:

First, the shifting mix of GE businesses toward high-technology products and high-growth services—supported by heavy R&D investment and an accelerated rate of acquisitions and dispositions.

Second, record investments in productivity, combined with cutting overhead costs, to meet higher margin expectations.

Third, our efforts in the public-policy arena aimed at creating an atmosphere of free and fair trade—a critical element for a healthy, growing U.S. economy.

And fourth, creating a climate throughout the Company that not only attracts the most talented people, but also permits their talents to grow. A climate where the organization can move as quickly as a good idea can carry it.

Looking at 1983, we believe GE is well-positioned to take advantage of any improvement in the economy. Our major concern about the economy lies with interest rates. Uncertainty over fiscal and monetary policy in the face of increasing deficits could lead to higher interest rates and stall recovery in its early stages.

GE's shifting mix: Our strong position for 1983 and beyond derives from GE's unique strengths—its people and its technical and financial resources—which are being focused increasingly on high-technology products and high-growth services markets to meet the world's changing needs. Increasing in relative importance to GE sales and earnings are such high-technology businesses as medical systems, aerospace, plastics and other proprietary materials; and such service businesses as General Electric Credit Corporation, General Electric Information Services Company, and construction, engineering and nuclear services.

The last decade has seen a dramatic shift in our business mix—from the old to the new, from relatively mature businesses to those in their high-growth stages. At the start of the 1970s, three-fourths of our earnings came from traditional electrical manufacturing businesses. By year-end 1982, our dependence on these for earnings had been reduced to under 40%. Their contribution is still substantial and, in absolute terms, the earnings from these businesses grew since 1970 from $200 million to $600 million.

But GE's greatest earnings growth has come from such non-traditional businesses as services, providing 21% of Company earnings in 1982, compared with 14% in 1970; materials, 28% of earnings last year, compared with 8% in 1970; and aircraft engines, 9% of earnings last year, versus virtually no contribution in 1970.

Our emphasis on fast-growing high-technology and services markets has led GE to make both acquisitions and dispositions at an accelerated rate. Over the past two years, we have completed 118 transactions involving acquisitions, joint ventures and formations of new companies, including the acquisition of Intersil and Calma to support our efforts to become the world leader in factory automation. There were also dispositions of 71 businesses that didn't fit our strategy. These transactions involved $1.5 billion: roughly $1 billion for acquisitions and $500 million received for dispositions.

The most significant transaction—announced in late January 1983—is the proposed sale, for about $2.4 billion, of most of GE's holdings in Utah International Inc. to The Broken Hill Proprietary Company Ltd. (BHP), an Australian industrial and natural resources company. This transaction provides a unique strategic opportunity for both companies. For GE, it will enable us to focus our unique strengths on fast-growing high-technology and services markets. For BHP, it will broaden both product and geographic base, and it will increase Australian ownership of one of that nation's important natural resources.

Last year's heavy expenditures for research and development support our increasing shift to high technology. While the total was about equal to 1981's record levels, the long-range "futures" part of our R&D was up more than 20%. This work is carried out mainly at the corporate Research and Development Center in Schenectady, N.Y., where we just completed a $130 million expansion, including construction of an advanced electronics laboratory. In 1982, we also completed our microelectronics research, development and production unit at Research Triangle Park, N.C., and our industrial electronics facility in Charlottesville, Va.

Productivity investments: While our shift to high technology has been significant, we have also been upgrading our core businesses. During 1982 there were strong cost-improvement efforts and major plant and equipment expenditures to increase productivity and assure the competitiveness of these important traditional GE businesses.

We have reduced our costs to lower break-even points—an important factor in producing 1982's earnings growth. But most of the benefits from reduced costs will come in future years, both quantitatively as volume picks up and, above all, qualitatively as we become a leaner, more competitive company with early responses to market changes.

Although 21% below 1981, plant and equipment investments of $1.6 billion in 1982 included continuing record levels of expenditures for productivity improvements. The most significant were factory-automation investments to strengthen the future cost and quality competitiveness of such important core businesses as locomotives, turbines, motors, lighting and major appliances.

Free and fair trade: Inextricably tied to our efforts to make GE the most competitive enterprise in the world is the necessity to make America more competitive. Regaining world-class competitiveness, in our view, is one of the most pressing challenges for the U.S. today.

While we continue to expand our international position in a wide range of products and services, and in innovations like the newly formed General Electric Trading Company, we also need U.S. public policies consistent with worldwide competitiveness—notably free and fair trade. Rising pressures for protectionism both here and abroad threaten this nation's ability to compete in world markets, one of the main engines of economic growth, prosperity and jobs.

Helping to create public understanding and support for policies that will allow America to be more competitive in world markets—thereby creating more jobs at home—is an important responsibility for our Company.

Our people: In the end, though, General Electric's own competitive strength rests with our people. How competitive we are depends upon the climate we create for them—their eagerness to dream, their willingness to dare.

Whether it's bringing new technologies and services to the marketplace or revitalizing our strong core businesses, we want GE to be a place where the bias is toward action—a high-spirited,

world-class enterprise that uses the resources of a large company but moves with the agility of the youngest and smallest.

Of all the values we seek to foster, personal excellence is the most important to the success of our Company. We have great expectations for what can take place when people are challenged—challenged to take what they have that is good, and make it better. Then make the better best.

John F. Welch, Jr.
Chairman and
Chief Executive Officer

John F. Burlingame
Vice Chairman and
Executive Officer

Edward E. Hood, Jr.
Vice Chairman and
Executive Officer

FEBRUARY 18, 1983

To Our Share Owners

This year, we've expanded our letter to highlight:

- General Electric's long-term strategy.
- 1983 results and some significant new business activities.
- Company culture.

Strategy evolution: Over the past three years, in this discussion of our strategy, we've talked about accelerated technological and market change in an era of slower worldwide growth and greatly intensified competition. In such a world, winners and losers are clearly more definable. You're either the very best at what you do, or you don't do it for very long. That's why General Electric formulated a strategy to become the most competitive enterprise in the world by being number one or number two in market share in every business we are in.

Today, this strategy has evolved to where we are focusing on being number one or two in 15 critical businesses in three distinct areas: high technology, services and our leadership core businesses.

Six core businesses (major appliance, lighting, turbine, transportation, motor, contractor equipment) from the heart of our Company. Each is very big, very profitable and has strong market leadership. Our challenge is, through reinvestment in productivity and quality, to be sure that same statement can be made a decade from now. Over the five years, 1981–85, we expect to spend nearly $2.5 billion to renew, restructure and reconceptualize these attractive, enduring businesses. Since 1980, unit volume breakeven levels have been reduced by an average of 17%, with the leverage from expanding margins expected to provide strong earnings growth.

In GE's large, high-tech businesses (medical systems, materials, industrial electronics, aerospace, aircraft engine), our strategy is to make certain these businesses stay on the leading edge through a combination of synergistic acquisitions and substantial investments in research and development. R&D in these five businesses increased 27% in 1983, some seven times the inflation rate.

In our key services businesses (financial services, information services, construction and engineering, nuclear services), our strategy is to grow these opportunities by adding outstanding people, who often can create new ventures all by themselves, and by making contiguous acquisitions. In 1983, we made acquisitions and other investments in services of approximately $650 million.

The three elements are interrelated. Our core businesses need the most advanced process technology and strong service offerings to improve their leading positions. Similarly, in high technology, where customers are seeking not just products, but solutions to problems, the linkage with services is key to higher earnings growth. And, to be competitive, our services businesses must use the latest technologies.

With our strategy focused on these three critical pieces of our Company, there emerges this snapshot of General Electric: In 1980, the core represented 40% of Company earnings; by the end of 1983, even though it grew significantly, the core represented 32% of Company earnings. GE's high-technology piece grew from 25%

to 29%. And services grew from 18% to 31%.

In 1983, we supported our overall strategy with record expenditures for research and development—consisting of GE and customer funds totaling $2.1 billion, an *increase* of about $400 million, or 23%, over 1982. In addition, expenditures for plant and equipment increased 7%, to $1.7 billion.

This spending for the future came on top of significant earnings growth. Following a strong 1982, with earnings up 10% despite a recession, GE continued to achieve strong gains as the recovery began in 1983. Earnings of $2.024 billion—$4.45 per share—were 11% ahead of 1982. Sales of $26.8 billion were up 1%. Our operating margin rose to 9.5% of sales, compared with 9.1% in 1982, as productivity investments in our core businesses produced the intended leverage.

In the consumer-led first stage of the recovery, substantial earnings growth was seen in GE consumer businesses, such as major appliance, and in those businesses which serve consumer industries, such as our high-tech materials operations. Also posting sharp gains were medical systems and General Electric Credit Corporation (GECC), reflecting growth in high technology and services; and our aerospace and aircraft engine businesses, which benefited from increased defense spending.

Our biggest disappointment in 1983 came in Latin America, where extraordinary economic difficulties resulted in an earnings decline of about $90 million and an aggregate operating loss for our affiliates in Mexico, Venezuela and Brazil.

New business development, consistent with our strategy, was stepped up in 1983. Discussed in the sector summaries following this letter, this included:

- The introduction of MR (magnetic resonance)—a non-invasive medical diagnostic system that can produce detailed images of the body's organs and tissues.
- Supportive of our services strategy, 1983 saw acquisitions and expansions by GECC in major equipment remarketing, municipal bond insurance, mortgage insurance, and investment banking and real estate syndication activities.
- The commitment of resources to strengthen GE's historical relationship with the People's Republic of China. This was evidenced not only by an order for 220 diesel-electric locomotives, but also by market development in aircraft engines and such major infrastructure

arenas as power generation and transmission.
- Expansion of our presence in cogeneration, involving a number of GE businesses from turbines to construction and engineering services. A highlight was our joint venture with Houston's Big Three Industries to build, operate and own one of the country's largest cogeneration projects.
- In support of our high-tech industrial electronics strategy, we are using our experience—no other company has a greater variety of manufacturing plants than GE—to focus on factory automation. In this market, estimated to reach $30 billion by 1990, we increased our capability in total systems, gained share in programmable controls, shipped the first production units of our state-of-the-art numerical control system, strengthened our software offerings and opened the Company's first robotics manufacturing plant.
- General Electric Trading Company, formed in 1982, is now among the country's largest, taking on more obligations to serve more markets for GE products through, among other tools, the sophisticated use of barter and countertrade.
- In early 1984, the U.S. Air Force and Navy selected GE's Aircraft Engine Group to supply its F110

engine for future F-16 and F-14 fighters—awards potentially worth $8–11 billion over the remaining production life of the aircraft.

We accelerated our drive in 1983 to divest those businesses throughout the Company that, while good businesses in themselves, don't fit our strategy.

We expect to complete, in the spring, the sale of our natural resources subsidiary, Utah International, to The Broken Hill Proprietary Company Ltd. of Australia, and the sale of our housewares business to Black & Decker. Last month, we completed the sale of Family Financial Services, a second-mortgage subsidiary of GECC, to the Philadelphia Saving Fund Society. We received about $600 million for Family Financial Services and will receive $2.4 billion for Utah (less the value of certain properties we may retain) and $300 million for housewares.

These dispositions reflect our strategy to focus GE's unique technological, financial and managerial strengths in our 15 key businesses where we believe we can add the most value. The evolution of this strategy has led us to complete 118 additional dispositions totaling more than $1.1 billion over the 1981–83 period.

Apart from dispositions, your Company's cash position was further increased in 1983 by a 10% improvement in the productivity of our working capital assets—freeing up about $620 million of cash during the year.

With our increased cash reserves from the sale of Utah and other dispositions, plus improved working capital turnover, the question has been raised: What will we do with the money? The short answer is: It's not going to burn a hole in our pocket.

The cash has given us the flexibility to fund what we've wanted to do internally—new business activities, quality and productivity investments, record amounts of research and development, and new plant and equipment. It has also allowed us to spend more than a half-billion dollars, in 1983 alone, on 62 acquisitions, joint ventures and other equity investments.

Still, some have wondered why we haven't made the **big acquisition**. Frankly, the temptation— and in some ways the easiest route—is to pay too much too fast. In 1983, we undertook a major study of large acquisitions, reviewing in depth more than 100 candidates. We analyzed the premium we'd be paying versus the synergy to be gained. To this we compared the opportunities available internally and in smaller acquisitions, where the synergies overwhelm the market premium. We believe a large acquisition may, in fact, take place; but, at the time of this writing, we've been unable to find the one that would clearly provide real value to GE share owners beyond the transitory excitement it might create in the marketplace.

Looking at 1984: We are expecting 1984 to be a very strong year. GE is well-positioned to take advantage of growth in a number of high-technology and services markets and in consumer spending. Capital spending, which grew only slightly in 1983, is expected to join the recovery, with GE in a position to benefit as a major participant in the industrial equipment and factory automation markets. Internationally, while we don't anticipate a significant upturn in Latin America, we also don't expect our affiliates there to experience the negative year-to-year change some had in 1983. On the trade front, we'd like to think a turnaround is likely, but the past two years have cautioned us against *anticipating* a more trade-competitive dollar.

Beyond 1984, the macro issues are:

(1) Will America continue to reinvest in productivity-enhancing technology so as to enjoy what we have called a "quality recovery"—one with sustainable, long-term gains in productivity and real income? By 1985, with many U.S. manufacturers nearing capacity, it will be critical to *expand* industrial capacity with the most productive, internationally competitive factories conceivable.

(2) Will the United States, in its own long-term interests, pursue non-protectionist trade policies which create international financial equilibrium and preserve the free and fair trading system?

In our view, the ability of the United States to deal favorably with these issues depends ultimately on lower real interest rates. While there is disagreement over the extent to which the current high real interest rates are due to the U.S. budget deficits, there is a strong presumption that interest rates would be lower if the outlook for containing looming deficits were improved.

Company culture: Successfully implementing a strategy to become the world's most competitive enterprise demands a special company culture—one that's strongly cohesive, fostering a high level of understanding of what General Electric is trying to do and be. We are advancing a culture that has a sense of urgency, that demands the very best and that emphasizes how crucial an individual's contribution can be to the success of our enterprise.

The challenge for us, as indeed for many companies as we face this recovery, is to emerge more competitive at the end of the cycle than we were at the beginning. The competitive values—easy to hone in a recession—must become a way of life, sustainable over decades.

At GE, we're driving to be **lean and agile**, to move faster, to pare away bureaucracy. We're subjecting every activity, every function, to the most rigorous review, distinguishing between those things which we absolutely need to do and know versus those which would be merely nice to do and know.

But while we challenge and shrink the non-essentials in our Company, our main goal is to expand—expand the climate for *excellence,* to get more and more people to do what even they thought they couldn't do.

Excellence means rewarding those who win—*and* rewarding those who try: the fuel for

entrepreneurship in a large company. Nurturing entrepreneurship at GE means expunging the punitive aspects of failure from the good try and, instead, focusing on rewards for those willing to dream, to reach, to dare.

Across your Company, a strategy has been formulated, with a clear focus on our three elements and where they're going. The resources are in place to get them there. And most important, an atmosphere, a cultural feeling, has been created where concepts like agility, excellence and entrepreneurship—the real stuff of world competitiveness—are coming to life.

John F. Welch, Jr.
Chairman and
Chief Executive Officer

John F. Burlingame
Vice Chairman and
Executive Officer

Edward E. Hood, Jr.
Vice Chairman and
Executive Officer

FEBRUARY 17, 1984

To Our Share Owners

As we sat down to write this letter, we looked back on what we said a year ago. The numbers have changed, in large part because 1984 was another good year for General Electric, but the direction of your Company—its programs, its dreams, its ambitions—hasn't changed. And rather than write a new letter, with a new theme, we chose to take the same letter and update the results and the outlook.

Strategy evolution: Over the past four years, in this discussion of our strategy, we've talked about accelerated technological and market change in an era of slower worldwide growth and greatly intensified competition. In such an environment, a company—and its businesses—must change faster than the world around it. Winners and losers are clearly more definable; you are either the very best at what you do, or you don't do it for very long. That's why General Electric formulated a strategy to become the most competitive enterprise in the world by being number one or number two in market share in every business we are in.

This strategy has evolved to where we are focusing on being number one or two in 15 critical businesses which we've grouped into three circles: high technology, services and our leadership core businesses. Outside the circles are three businesses (semiconductor, Ladd Petroleum and the General Electric Trading Company) that provide support to the businesses within the circles. Outside, as well, are other businesses: Some have performed marginally; some are in low-growth markets; others are simply a poor strategic fit with the Company. For these other businesses, we have a fix, sell or close strategy.

Each of GE's six core businesses (lighting, major appliance, motor, turbine, transportation, construction equipment) is large, is profitable and has strong market leadership. Our challenge is, through reinvestment in productivity and quality, to be sure this same statement can be made a decade from now. Over the four-year period, 1981–1984, we spent about $2 billion to rebuild, modernize and reconceptualize these attractive, enduring businesses. The payoff from this investment is apparent. Over the past two years, these businesses, as a group, had a 39% earnings increase.

In GE's large, high-tech businesses (medical systems, aircraft engine, aerospace, materials, industrial electronics), our strategy is to make certain these businesses stay on the leading edge through a combination of synergistic acquisitions and substantial investments in research and development. R&D expense in these five businesses increased 42% in the past two years, some five times the two-year inflation rate.

In our services businesses (financial services, construction and engineering, nuclear services, information services), our strategy is to grow these opportunities by adding outstanding people, who often can create new ventures all by themselves, and by making contiguous acquisitions. In 1984, we made acquisitions and other investments in services of approximately $1.3 billion.

The three elements are interrelated. Our core businesses need the most advanced process technology and strong service offerings to improve their leading positions. Similarly, in high technology, where customers are seeking not just products, but solutions to problems, the linkage with services is key to higher earnings growth. And, to be competitive, our services businesses must use the latest technologies.

With our strategy focused on these three critical pieces of our Company, there emerges this snapshot of General Electric: In 1980, the core represented 40% of Company earnings; by the end of 1984, even though it grew significantly, the core represented 34% of Company earnings. GE's high-technology piece grew from 25% to 31%. And services grew from 21% to 24%.

In 1984, we supported our strategy with record expenditures for plant and equipment totaling $2.5 billion, an increase of 45%. In addition, expenditures for research and development were a record $2.3 billion, an increase of about $200 million. The GE-funded portion of this R&D was up 13% over 1983.

This spending for the future came on top of significant earnings growth. Following 1983's earnings increase of 11%, GE continued to achieve strong gains in 1984. Earnings of $2.280 billion—$5.03 per share—were 13% ahead of 1983.

Sales of $27.95 billion were up 4%. When the sales figure is adjusted to reflect the 1984 disposition of our housewares business and most of our natural resources business, sales were up 10%. Our operating margin rose to a record 10.2% of sales, compared with 9.5% in 1983, as productivity investments in our core businesses produced the intended leverage.

Some of our 18 key businesses did better than we anticipated in 1984, some did about what we expected, and some didn't quite measure up to our expectations. Major appliance, lighting, aircraft engine, aerospace, financial services, materials and semi-conductor performed well beyond our expectations. Turbine, motor, construction equipment, medical systems, nuclear, information services, Ladd Petroleum and the trading company were about on plan.

We also suffered three disappointments. In transportation, the market didn't grow as rapidly as we had expected as customer productivity and lower demand reduced the need for domestic locomotive purchases—a market miss. In industrial electronics, the increased acceptance of our electronic product offerings and record sales were not translated into earnings—a management execution miss. And finally, in con-struction and engineering services, the weakened economies in the Middle East and Latin America resulted in dramatically lower earnings in 1984—a market and management miss on the international scene.

New business development, consistent with our strategy, was stepped up in 1984. Among the highlights were:

- The $1.1 billion acquisition by our financial services business of Employers Reinsurance Corpora-tion, which is already proving itself an excellent fit with our financial services strategy.
- Two innovative partnerships— with Ungermann Bass in networking and Coherent, Inc. in lasers—that complement and advance our strategy in industrial electronics.
- A new ceramics business, still in its infancy, but with a chance of playing a big role in an estimated billion-dollar electronics packag-ing market in the 1990s.
- The graphics processor venture—a highly leveraged means of substituting silicon for software in image generation that could provide a key advantage to our aerospace and computer-aided design businesses.
- A new affiliate, General Electric (USA) China Company Ltd., designed to serve as the focal

point for all GE business activities with the People's Republic of China. These activities have increased markedly and now involve the aircraft engine, plastics, motor, drive systems, transportation and power generation businesses. The 1984 highlight was the shipment, on schedule, of 220 locomotives ordered in late 1983.

• The commitment of more than $600 million to expand plastics production facilities around the world. In the wake of strong sales and high market enthusiasm for 1982's introduction of Ultem®, 1984 saw the introduction of Lomod® resin, our first entry into the market for thermoplastic elastomers. 1984 also saw the opening of a $25 million Plastics Technology Center in Pittsfield, Mass., designed to increase our customers' role in applications development and test processes.

• New orders for commercial aircraft engines, in combination with strong military orders, that will raise the backlog in the aircraft engine business to $8 billion by the end of 1985.

We continued our drive in 1984 to divest those businesses throughout the Company that, while good businesses in themselves, don't fit our strategy.

We completed the sale of our natural resources subsidiary, Utah International Inc., to The Broken Hill Proprietary Company Ltd. of Australia; the sale of our housewares business to Black & Decker; and the sale of Family Financial Services, a second-mortgage subsidiary of General Electric Credit Corporation (GECC), to the Philadelphia Saving Fund Society. In total, these three transactions were valued at $3.3 billion.

These dispositions reflect our strategy to focus GE's unique technological, financial and managerial strengths in our 18 key businesses where we believe we can add the most value. The evolution of this strategy has led us to complete 152 additional dispositions totaling more than $1.6 billion over the 1981–1984 period.

The cash from dispositions has given us the flexibility to fund what we've wanted to do internally— new business activities, quality and productivity investments, record amounts of research and development, and new plant and equipment. It has also allowed us to spend more than $1.4 billion, in 1984 alone, on 52 acquisitions, joint ventures and other equity investments, including Employers Reinsurance.

Looking at 1985: With the 2½% to 3½% real GNP growth we see for

1985, we expect our earnings growth to come mainly from nine Company businesses: lighting and construction equipment, from margin expansion; materials, from increased market penetration; aerospace, aircraft engine, and nuclear fuel and services, from increased backlogs; industrial electronics and construction and engineering, from volume increases being translated into profitable growth; and financial services, from continued asset growth.

On the international trade front, we'd like to think a turnaround is likely, but the past three years have cautioned us against anticipating a more trade-competitive dollar. Instead, we accept the reality that we're going to have to do more ourselves: We're going to have to cut costs; do more offshore sourcing and make more offshore investment; enter creative alliances and joint ventures; and step up our marketing efforts to be more competitive in international markets.

Beyond 1985, the macro issues are:

(1) Will the government face up to the federal budget deficit? While there is disagreement over the extent to which the current high real interest rates are due to the U.S. budget deficits, there is a strong presumption that interest rates would be lower—and the dollar would be more trade-competitive—if the outlook for reducing deficits were improved.

(2) Will America continue to reinvest in productivity-enhancing technology so as to enjoy what we have called a "quality recovery"—one with sustainable, long-term gains in productivity and real income? Increased foreign competition makes it critical for U.S. companies to have the most productive, internationally competitive factories conceivable.

Competitiveness, jobs and taxes: Over the past several years, the Congress has enacted a series of incentives to direct badly needed investment capital into America's aging factories and to improve the worldwide competitiveness of American corporations. These incentives permit your Company and others to defer or reduce their federal income tax payments when they invest in new plant and equipment.

In the past four years alone, these incentives helped GE invest a total of $18 billion in our own factories and—through GECC's leasing activities—in new equipment for other companies. This investment created or preserved more than 250,000 jobs, many of them in small and medium-sized businesses. In the nation as a whole, the rate of growth of spending on new plant and equipment in this economic recovery has been more than double that of previous cycles—an indication these capital formation incentives are working.

Now these incentives are in jeopardy—and there is uninformed criticism of companies, such as GE, that are said to have "avoided" the payment of federal income taxes. We don't welcome this misrepresentation. We are proud of the capital investments which have made us and the companies we have helped finance more competitive. The jobs created or sustained by these investments have made a contribution to the nation's economic recovery.

During the congressional debate on tax reform, we will describe America's critical capital investment need and emphasize the major role capital-formation incentives have played in increasing the worldwide competitiveness of U.S. corporations.

Company culture: As we said a year ago, successfully implementing a strategy to become the world's most competitive enterprise demands a special company culture—one that's strongly cohesive, fostering a high level of understanding of what General Electric is trying to do and be. We are advancing a culture that has a

sense of urgency, that demands the very best and that emphasizes how crucial an individual's contribution can be to the success of our enterprise.

The challenge for us, as indeed for many companies as this recovery continues, is to emerge more competitive at the end of the cycle than we were at the beginning. The competitive values—easy to hone in a recession—must become a way of life, sustainable over decades.

At GE, we're driving to be lean and agile, to move faster, to pare away bureaucracy. We're subjecting every activity, every function, to the most rigorous review, distinguishing between those things which we absolutely need to do and know versus those which would be merely nice to do and know.

But while we challenge and shrink the nonessentials in our Company, our main goal is to expand—expand the climate for excellence, to create an atmosphere where more and more people do what even they thought they couldn't do.

Excellence means rewarding those who win, and rewarding those who try—the fuel for entrepreneurship in a large company. Nurturing entrepreneurship at GE means expunging the punitive aspects of failure from the good try and, instead, focusing on rewards for those willing to dream, to reach, to dare.

Nowhere in our Company has this spirit, this culture, been more vivid than in some of our most beleaguered businesses. We learned something about our culture in 1984, and we learned it from our "other" businesses—the ones outside our 18 key businesses.

These businesses have been under an intense internal spotlight. And as their futures are continually scrutinized, we have marveled at the truly heroic efforts of the GE people in them—at their ability to communicate with each other and their communities, at their ability to gain understanding and support for the reality of their competitive position.

These men and women have shown us how to create a spirit of can-do and agility in difficult atmospheres where the reality of the marketplace causes the competitive juices to flow at a rate difficult to achieve in some of our larger,

more successful businesses. Our challenge is to create this same heightened sense of urgency and candor throughout General Electric.

Across your Company, a strategy has been formulated, with a clear focus on our key businesses and where they're going. The resources are in place to get them there. And most important, an atmosphere, a culture, is being created where concepts like agility, excellence and entrepreneurship—the real stuff of world competitiveness—are coming to life.

John F. Welch, Jr.
Chairman and
Chief Executive Officer

Lawrence A. Bossidy
Vice Chairman and
Executive Officer

Edward E. Hood, Jr.
Vice Chairman and
Executive Officer

FEBRUARY 15, 1985

To Our Share Owners

During the past five years, we've shared with you our assessment of the increasingly more competitive 1980s—and our strategy for winning in this era of greatly intensified worldwide competition. In an environment of accelerated technological and market change and slower worldwide growth, a company— and its businesses—must change faster than the world around it. That's why General Electric embarked five years ago on a long-term strategy to become the most competitive enterprise in the world—not only in the 1980s, but in the 1990s and beyond.

Central to our strategy is being number one or two in market share in 15 critical businesses which we've grouped into three circles: core manufacturing, technology and services.

In core manufacturing, we have six large businesses—lighting, major appliance, motor, turbine, transportation, construction equipment—that have a commanding or leading market position. In the past five years, we've invested more than $2 billion in these businesses to help ensure they'll be as strong in the 1990s as they are in the 1980s. The payoff from this investment is encouraging. Over the past five years—despite the cost of the heavy investment, one of the worst postwar recessions, and increased foreign competition (aided by a strong dollar) that battered much of America's manufacturing sector— the earnings of these businesses as a group have increased at an average annual rate of 7%. Equally important, they are well-positioned for the future.

In GE's large technology businesses—medical systems, aircraft engine, aerospace, materials, factory automation—our strategy is to make certain these businesses continue to improve their competitiveness through a combination of synergistic acquisitions and substantial investments in research and development. R&D expense in these businesses was $7.8 billion in the past five years; plant and equipment investment,

$3.6 billion. During the 1981–85 period, earnings in these businesses as a group grew at an average annual rate of 19%.

In our services businesses—financial services, construction and engineering, nuclear services, information services—businesses where ideas overwhelm invest-ment—our strategy is to grow by adding entrepreneurial people, individuals who by themselves can create new ventures, and by making related acquisitions. Employers Reinsurance Corporation, for example, was acquired in 1984 for $1.1 billion and made a positive contribution to earnings in its very first year—even after allowing for all acquisition costs. Our four services businesses—led by financial services—have grown earnings during the past five years at an average annual rate of 16%.

Outside the circles are three businesses—semiconductor, Ladd Petroleum, the General Electric Trading Company—that provide support to the businesses within the circles.

Also outside the circles are GE's ventures—such as our ceramics business and Calma, our interactive graphics affiliate. These ventures represent businesses that have a chance to play a big role in what we estimate to be large markets in the 1990s. At GE today, they're run by entrepreneurs with their own boards—but with all the technolog-ical and financial resources that come with being part of a larger company.

Outside these circles, as well, are other businesses: Some have performed very well in small or low-growth markets; some have performed marginally; others are simply a poor strategic fit with the Company. In general, the managerial performance in these businesses was outstanding in 1985—and just as important to the Company's short-term results as the performance of our more strategic businesses.

In 1980, GE's earnings were about equally divided between core manufacturing—on one hand—and technology and services—on the other. Today, while core manufacturing has grown in absolute terms, about 70% of 1985 earnings came from technology and services.

As part of the ongoing implemen-tation of our strategy, we signed in late 1985 a definitive merger agree-ment whereby GE will pay approx-imately $6.3 billion in cash, or $66.50 a share for common stock, to merge with RCA. After this merger, GE will generate about 80% of its earnings from tech-nology and services—and still have a very strong, competitive and growing manufacturing segment.

RCA's services and technology businesses—the NBC network, the broadcast stations, the aerospace and defense businesses, communications and the RCA Service Company—will complement our own businesses and help improve our global competitiveness.

General Electric already competes successfully in world markets, and we consistently rank among the nation's largest exporters. Our 1985 total exports were $4.0 billion, and our net exports were $2.6 billion positive in a U.S. economy that had almost a $150 billion merchandise trade deficit.

Because of the strong dollar, and our commitment to maintain worldwide share, much of our export sales in recent years had low or no profit margins. But we were able to compete because our strong domestic businesses could support our exports during the period of dollar imbalance. The merger with RCA—with its strong domestic businesses—will greatly improve our already significant global competitiveness by increasing the staying power of an American company, with American workers.

The merger was approved by RCA's share owners on February 13, 1986. During the next few months, it will be subject to review or approval by the Federal Commu-

nications Commission, the Justice Department and other governmental authorities. We anticipate the merger will be completed in the second half of 1986.

Our positioning for the future was accompanied by significant growth during the past five years:

- Earnings have grown 10% a year compounded.
- Our stock, through appreciation and yield, has grown 25% a year compounded.
- We've outperformed, from the standpoint of both earnings growth and stock appreciation, any group of peers—including the S&P 400, the "Blue Chip" (triple A-rated) companies, and the electrical equipment industry.

Looking more specifically at 1985, some of our businesses had an excellent year, but a number of our key markets were flat or down, reflecting the general sluggishness in the U.S. economy. Overall, net earnings were $2.336 billion, an increase of 2% from $2.280 billion in 1984. Earnings per share were $5.13 for 1985 compared with $5.03 for 1984. Sales for 1985 were $28.29 billion, about 1% more than 1984's $27.95 billion. Contributing to the modest improvement in earnings were better operating margins which, at 10.4% of sales, exceeded last year's record 10.2% rate.

In 1985, we also made significant additional progress toward our long-term goal of disposing of businesses that don't fit GE's future and of strengthening the productive capabilities of those that do. Total value of transactions involving sales of assets during 1985 amounted to about $700 million, bringing the five-year total to $5.6 billion. The money from these asset sales has been essential to our restructuring efforts— enabling us to invest in our key businesses and to help make such acquisitions as Employers Reinsurance and RCA.

Also looking to the future, research and development expenditures from Company and customer funds totaled $2.6 billion in 1985, up from 1984's $2.3 billion. R&D expenditures equaled 9% of 1985 sales compared with 8.2% in 1984. Expenditures for plant and equipment were about $2 billion. The five-year investment in GE's future growth—in plant and equipment and in research and development—totaled more than $20 billion.

Some key businesses did better than we anticipated in 1985, some did about what we expected, and some didn't quite measure up to our expectations. Aircraft engine, aerospace, financial services, factory automation, nuclear services, construction equipment, transportation and the trading company performed better than our expectations. Major appliance, lighting, motor, medical systems, materials, information services, Ladd Petroleum, semiconductor, and construction and engineering were about on plan. Turbine, because of the severely depressed worldwide market for electrical generating equipment, suffered a significant erosion in earnings. Outside the circles, very strong performances from Canadian General Electric and power delivery were, unfortunately, overwhelmed by the disappointment in consumer electronics, which had a negative swing of more than $50 million in earnings.

Our factory automation business became profitable during 1985—an achievement of special significance for us. We began this venture five years ago; went through one of the worst postwar recessions; and, as with most new ventures, made several mistakes and invested more money than we had planned. But our staying power, and confidence in the reindustrialization of America, has been rewarded. Today, we have a growing, profitable business in less time than it took us to do so in either plastics or commercial aircraft engine— two other GE technology ventures that are now billion-dollar-plus businesses.

GE business highlights for 1985 are discussed on pages 8–24. They include technology and marketing achievements for our plastics, medical systems, major appliance, lighting, aircraft engine, aerospace and locomotive businesses and the continued strong growth of several businesses, led by financial services. Another highlight—one that crosses several businesses—was the selection of GE in a Gallup poll of U.S. consumers as the first company that comes to mind when they consider worldwide companies associated with high quality.

Our biggest disappointment in 1985 was not operational. It was the indictment and guilty plea in a case involving improper timecard charges on a defense contract back in 1980. This incident was very difficult and painful for the men and women of General Electric, but we learned much from it. We implemented significantly more stringent financial and management controls in our defense-related businesses—including a new corporate policy, a Compliance Review Board and an ombudsman. We are firmly committed to reducing the possibility of future transgressions and to finding—and reporting to the government— transgressions that may have occurred in the past.

In lifting the government's suspension of the Company as a government contractor, then-Air Force Secretary Verne Orr acknowledged the depth of our commitment by stating: "General Electric has been very forthright in uncovering, investigating and reporting to appropriate governmental agencies potential past violations of government procurement regulations. This cooperative self-policing effort provides a means for effectively discovering and resolving problems promptly and constructively."

Another disappointment during the past year was our inability to make the case for the crucial linkages among incentives for productive capital investment, worldwide competitiveness and America's standard of living. Since the 1981 federal tax plan went into effect, with its provisions for investment tax credit and accelerated cost recovery, General Electric and its financial services subsidiary have invested $22 billion in our own plants and in the factories, utilities, airlines and railroads of America, creating or preserving at least 250,000 jobs. While we paid $5.6 billion in taxes other than federal income taxes during the past five years, the $22 billion investment deferred much of our federal income tax liability—a fact that has been misunderstood by some advocates of tax reform.

Although that pro-investment 1981 tax plan helped GE and other companies to modernize and automate their factories and to become more competitive in world markets, current tax reform proposals would reduce or eliminate the incentives that facilitated such investment and would seriously impair the ability of American companies to compete with foreign firms that are strongly supported by their countries' fiscal and trade policies. While we accept the reality that a system in which profitable corporations do not appear to pay taxes is politically unacceptable, we will continue to speak out on the critical need for incentives for productive capital investment.

The economic outlook for 1986 is mixed. Although a few positives have emerged, some negatives stubbornly persist. Interest rates are lower than a year ago, but inflation-adjusted "real rates" are still very high by most yardsticks. The trade-weighted dollar did start to fall in 1985, but still ended the year almost 50% above its 1980 level. Even at today's exchange rates, Japanese wage costs are only about 60% of the U.S. manufacturing average, and Korean worker compensation is about 10% of the U.S. average. Other restraining forces are the still-unsettled state of

U.S. tax reform and the seemingly intractable federal deficit problem.

Against this backdrop, our economists are looking for a modest rebound in the U.S. economy, and operating plans of GE's businesses for 1986 reflect— prudently, we believe—a relatively low-growth scenario with modest earnings growth. Should the economy be more in line with the consensus forecast of close to 4% real GNP growth, we are well-positioned for good earnings growth.

The removal of an entire layer of upper management structure in late 1985 gives significantly more responsibility to the leaders of GE's various businesses, freeing them to compete more effectively in world markets. We were able to make this major organizational change because of the growing recognition by GE people that, while we profit from the cultural diversity of our many businesses, we are governed by common policies and united by shared values. Our shared values include a recognition that:

- Excellence can be measured only in terms of customer satisfaction.
- Change must be accepted as the rule rather than the exception.
- Open, candid, interactive, continuous communication up, down

and across the Company is the key to gaining trust and commitment.

- Effective leadership involves the acceptance and management of paradox. For example, we must function collectively as one Company and individually as many businesses at the same time. Similarly, we must meet our short-term commitments while investing for long-term success.
- Our resource allocation process must be dynamic. Sometimes a business benefits as a net importer of dollars, ideas and talent while at other times the same business will be called upon to be a net exporter for the benefit of the Company as a whole.

As we look to the next five years, our combination of different business cultures and shared values gives GE the ability—and flexibility—to win in world markets. It provides the bond that stimulates our people, the most important asset of any organization, to pursue a common goal—achieving excellence in everything we do.

John F. Welch, Jr.
Chairman and
Chief Executive Officer

Lawrence A. Bossidy
Vice Chairman and
Executive Officer

Edward E. Hood, Jr.
Vice Chairman and
Executive Officer

FEBRUARY 14, 1986

To Our Share Owners

By almost any measure, 1986 was a strong year for your Company—record sales, record earnings, several successful acquisitions and excellent positioning for the future. But to put 1986 in full perspective, one has to go back to 1981 when we first enunciated the strategy that has guided GE through the 1980s.

In 1981, we said that the world was going to get much more competitive, characterized by slower growth with more companies after a smaller pie. That analysis became the cornerstone of what we set out to do. It led to the strategy of being number one or number two in our large key businesses, which we have grouped into technology, services and core manufacturing.

Within that framework, we sold or exited businesses and product lines that weren't central to our strategy, and became much more cost-effective in what we own by consolidating facilities, where needed, and by investing $11.6 billion in our businesses to develop new products and improve productivity.

At the same time, we reduced our work force by more than 100,000 but the strength of our balance sheet allowed us to do so in ways that were fair and compassionate to those involved. Lengthy notification periods, equitable severance packages, retraining and placement centers were used whenever business realities caused us to close a plant or exit a business.

We have also accelerated the use of alliances and joint ventures; 12 of them were either started or expanded in 1986 alone. We view alliances as a means to expand product lines, to open new markets, to become more competitive with existing products in existing markets, and to reduce the investment and time it takes to bring good ideas to our customers.

Our acquisitions—the most visible being Employers Reinsurance Corporation, RCA and Kidder, Peabody—plus internal growth during the past six years have helped shift the overall GE mix toward faster-growing services and technology businesses. In 1986, 70% of our key business net earnings were in technology and services compared to 50% in 1981. Significantly, this shift was accomplished while earnings grew 30% in core manufacturing over these years.

Our positioning for the future has also produced significant growth for investors. For example:

- Earnings have risen 9% a year compounded since 1981, 32% faster than the GNP over the period.
- Our stock, through appreciation and yield, has grown 29% a year compounded. And we have moved from number 10 in market value among all U.S. corporations to number three.
- We absorbed restructuring costs for plant consolidation and employee assistance without taking any one-time restructuring charges of a size that could have broken our string of steady earnings increases.

The acquisition of RCA in 1986 was a significant step in the continuation of our strategy. RCA has been a member of the GE

family since June, and GE and RCA managers, working together, have accomplished much:

- We have added to GE an important new business in NBC, an enterprise with $3 billion in annual revenues and a leadership position in the broadcasting industry.
- In several business areas where GE already participated— aerospace and defense, communications and services, consumer electronics, and semiconductor—integration plans have been defined, management teams put in place and actions initiated that will obtain the greatest advantage from our combined strengths.
- RCA's record company, carpet business and insurance firm, none of which fit GE's long-term strategy, and notes from RCA's 1984 sale of CIT were sold for a total of more than $1.3 billion.
- Corporate staffs have been combined and streamlined, making sure that qualified people in both organizations were retained.

RCA added 14 cents per share to GE's earnings in 1986, even after allowing for all acquisition costs. And we expect the RCA contribution to increase in 1987.

Looking at GE's three groups of key acquisitions at the end of 1986, we believe we have accomplished much of what we set out to do in 1981—developing one of the most competitive and winning sets of businesses in the world by the end of the decade.

GE's five technology businesses— Aircraft Engine, Aerospace, Plastics, Medical Systems and Factory Automation— all have the ability to reach beyond today's boundaries and to anticipate tomorrow's needs. During the 1981–86 period, earnings in these businesses grew at an average annual rate of 26%. For the future, the combination of GE and RCA in Aerospace creates a formidable competitor in the industry. Our other technology businesses are all using alliances to add significantly to their already strong worldwide positions. Some of these alliances are Aircraft Engine's long-term alliance with SNECMA of France and newer alliances involving Plastics with PPG Industries and others, Medical Systems with Yokogawa of Japan, and Factory Automation with FANUC of Japan.

The mix of our services businesses has changed markedly since 1981, and they have grown from providing 20% of key business earnings at the start of the period to 29% in 1986. NBC brings to GE its role as a premier provider of TV programming and its current position as the top network. GE Financial Services has been strengthened by the addition of Kidder, Peabody to an already strong lineup including General Electric Credit Corporation (GECC) and Employers Reinsurance Corporation, which we acquired in 1984. In just six months, Kidder, Peabody added 4 cents per share to GE's earnings, after accounting for acquisition costs, and is an excellent fit with GECC in several areas, such as providing distribution capability for GECC's growing nationwide origination capability. Communications and Services combines several RCA and GE operations to form a business with almost $2 billion in annual revenues.

Our six core manufacturing businesses—Major Appliance, Lighting, Power Systems, Construction Equipment, Transportation Systems and Motor—have maintained commanding or leading market positions by striving to become the low-cost, high-quality global competitors. Since 1981, earnings of these businesses as a group have increased at an average annual rate of 8%, while investments of more than $2.6 billion have been made to help ensure continued strength into the next decade.

Among our support businesses, Consumer Electronics combines RCA and GE operations to provide a leadership position in a very visible, but difficult, market. A talented business team in the GE/RCA Consumer Electronics business has the Company's full support as it undertakes a concerted effort to succeed in a volatile worldwide environment. Our other support businesses—Semiconductor, Ladd Petroleum, Corporate Trading Operations and International—also help GE businesses to win in world markets. In the international arena, Canadian General Electric, for example, has posted strong gains in an important national market and continues to develop unique products to serve global markets.

Looking specifically at 1986 performance, some of our businesses had excellent years, but a number of our key markets were characterized by severe global competition and sluggish growth. Overall, net earnings were $2.492 billion, an increase of 9% from $2.277 billion in 1985. Earnings per share were $5.46 for 1986 compared to $5.00 for 1985. Sales for 1986, which reflect RCA for the last seven months, were $35.21 billion, about 24% more than 1985's $28.29 billion.

Our strong performance has been accompanied by continuing investment in the future of our businesses. Research and development expenditures in 1986, excluding RCA, were $2.9 billion, up 14% from 1985. Expenditures for plant and equipment were about $2 billion.

Several key businesses had excellent years. Aerospace, Aircraft Engine, Financial Services, Major Appliance, Medical Systems, NBC and Plastics, for example, all achieved double-digit growth in earnings. On the other hand, extremely difficult markets in Power Systems, Motor, Construction Equipment and Transportation Systems have caused these businesses to consolidate operations and to redesign products to become even more cost-competitive in anticipation of a time when demand rises. In Power Systems, a sharp downturn in shipments in what historically had been one of GE's most profitable businesses resulted in a negative earnings swing of more than $150 million in 1986, but the growth of other GE businesses allowed the Company to have a record year.

In 1986, GE continued its commitment to ensuring ethical behavior by all employees in business dealings with the government.

New policies and procedures instituted in 1985—including establishment of a Compliance Review Board and an ombudsman—were emphasized with Companywide communication and training. We continue our policy of voluntary disclosure of problems to appropriate governmental authorities, and the government continues to cooperate in our efforts to ensure compliance in the complex area of government contracting.

GE also participated in an industry initiative that produced a set of six principles of business ethics and conduct for the defense industry. These principles were incorporated into the final report given to the President by the blue-ribbon commission headed by David Packard, former deputy secretary of defense, which was charged with suggesting reforms for the nation's defense procurement system. To date, 37 companies representing about half of all defense procurement dollars spent have pledged to implement these principles. We are optimistic that the work of the Packard Commission will result in a more cost-effective, less adversarial system of meeting the nation's defense needs.

Our outlook for the economy during the next couple of years is for modest growth in the GNP.

Our businesses are positioned to do well in such an environment. We expect eight of them—Aerospace, Aircraft Engine, Factory Automation, Financial Services, Major Appliance, Medical Systems, NBC and Plastics—to grow faster than the GNP over the next five years. And we anticipate they will account for about 80% of our earnings by 1991—up from 73% in 1986. We expect the remainder of our key businesses, those in more difficult markets, to grow at about the GNP rate.

The competitiveness of many of our businesses—and indeed much of American industry—is linked inextricably to their ability to trade freely in world markets.

Protectionist trade legislation will again be debated in 1987. It is our view that open, free trade is one of the main engines of economic growth, prosperity and jobs. While we strongly support the government's efforts to improve exports through a more competitive dollar and other export initiatives, we oppose measures that endanger the international trading system and ultimately drive up the cost of domestic manufacturing.

As we look to the future, we see a growing confidence within GE. Confidence in the prospects of the key businesses that will carry us forward and confidence in the men and women who run these businesses.

Leadership at GE means creating a vision for, and within, each business. It means articulating that vision so clearly that an entire organization can rally around it and, more important still, achieve its goals.

This kind of leadership—vision plus achievement—is not reserved for only those businesses doing well. In some cases, the people in our most beleaguered businesses understand the realities of their markets even better than those in businesses that, for the present, are growing rapidly.

Leadership is also not restricted to any one level of the Company. It's an engineer in our Aerospace business seizing an opportunity for new business, gathering a team and pursuing the order—potentially more than a $1 billion order—until it is won. It's a production worker who shuts down a Major Appliance production line upon spotting a potential quality problem. It's a Power Systems manager who makes the difficult, but necessary, decision to close a marginal operation and who then uses the financial strength of the Company to soften the landings for those affected.

While we derive strength from the diversity of GE's businesses, we are also proud that the men and women who lead them share a strong set of values:

- They accept that change is a constant and that success is measured by how well we shape tomorrow.
- They recognize that customers' needs, not internal bureaucracy, are the real drivers of our activities.
- They practice open, candid, interactive, continuous communication up, down and sideways in our organizations—and externally to all our publics—convinced that this is the only way to gain trust and commitment.
- They understand that moral, legal and ethical behavior at all levels is a fundamental prerequisite for working at GE.

In summary, GE is a unique set of different businesses run by a unique group of people with different talents—united by the Company's shared values and strengthened by its human, technical and financial resources. Whether it is Financial Services' ability to adapt to its market environment, or Medical Systems' technology leadership, or Aircraft

Engine's and Plastics' use of
creative alliances, GE's key
businesses are all leaders in the
markets in which they participate.
We believe your Company has a
future unmatched anywhere in the
world. And the people of GE are
committed to seizing that future.

John F. Welch, Jr.
Chairman and
Chief Executive Officer

Lawrence A. Bossidy
Vice Chairman and
Executive Officer

Edward E. Hood, Jr.
Vice Chairman and
Executive Officer

FEBRUARY 13, 1987

To Our Share Owners

The events of 1987 reaffirmed our belief in the strategy your Company has followed throughout the 1980s. GNP growth remained modest; global competition continued to intensify; large transnational alliances became a key ingredient to success throughout the world; and the inextricable relationship of the world's economies and financial markets was clearly demonstrated.

Against this backdrop GE's 14 key businesses all performed well and, more importantly, demonstrated that GE is well-positioned for strong earnings growth in any reasonably good economic scenario.

At the beginning of the decade, we said the world economy would be characterized by slower growth with stronger global competitors going after a smaller pie. That analysis became the cornerstone of what we set out to do. It led to a strategy of being number one or number two in market share in large key businesses that we grouped into technology, services and core manufacturing.

Within that framework, we sold or exited businesses and product lines that were not central to our strategy, and became much more cost-effective in those that were by consolidating facilities and by investing $16.7 billion to develop new products and improve productivity. Our financial strength allowed us to do this in ways that were fair and compassionate to the employees involved. Long notification periods, equitable severance packages, retraining and placement centers were used when business realities caused us to close plants.

As we sold or exited businesses not central to our strategy, we acquired others that would either improve the competitiveness of an existing key GE business or would stand strongly alone in a promising market in which we want to participate.

In our view, a key criterion of strength is being number one or number two in market position; and number one or number two, for us, refers to *world* market position. In 1987, we continued to establish strong global positions for our businesses through acquisitions, cross-sourcing partnerships, asset exchanges and other arrangements with Asian and European companies whose strengths and assets complement our own.

Of GE's strategic moves in 1987, the one that best demonstrates our global business leadership direction is the business exchange we made with Thomson, S.A. of France. In this transaction, we acquired CGR, a European-based medical diagnostic imaging business, and cash from Thomson; in return, Thomson received GE's consumer electronics business.

This move greatly strengthened our global Medical Systems business and allowed us to divest a business that was not strategically important to us. Thomson, which views consumer electronics as central to its strategy, strengthened its ability to compete globally in this industry. In this win-win transaction, both companies became stronger in businesses they feel are key to their future.

Adding CGR's strength in Europe and Latin America, particularly in x-ray products, will complement GE's already strong engineering, marketing and manfacturing operations in the United States and in Japan, where we hold a 75% stake in Yokogawa Medical Systems.

In the exchange with Thomson, we built upon decades of globalization initiatives by several other GE businesses that have long realized that a strong market presence in the major areas of world commerce will be a decisive advantage in the intensely competitive and highly concentrated markets of the 1990s.

Many of our fastest-growing businesses have had their growth fueled by innovative, transnational alliances where each partner's unique assets are shared in return for greater world-market access.

GE Aircraft Engines, for example, has used its 16-year-old partnership with SNECMA of France to help forge a pre-eminent position in world markets, winning the leading share of the world's large commercial engine orders in 1987. GE Plastics, with nearly half its sales outside the United States, has grown 16% annually over the last five years by developing applications in one part of the world, and then multiplying their value through global technology, manufacturing and marketing organizations. Our Factory Automation business, which struggled for years by itself to fulfill a dream of world leadership, now sees that dream becoming a reality via GE Fanuc Automation Corporation, a 50-50 joint venture with FANUC Limited of Japan that includes subsidiaries in Europe, Japan and the United States.

Actions like these are under way in virtually every GE business. Each business understands clearly that an important road to growth is through globalization and through sharing individual strengths such as market access, technology and capital availability. In this "share-to-gain" approach, our businesses are expanding product lines, opening new markets, becoming more competitive in existing markets, and reducing the investment and time it takes to bring products to customers and potential customers.

During the past seven years, consistent application of GE's strategy has produced consistent growth for our investors:

- Earnings have risen 10% a year compounded since 1980, about 40% faster than the GNP over th same period and triple the rate of growth of the S&P 400 companies.
- Our stock, through appreciation and yield, has grown 19% a year compounded, even with last fall's market correction, versus 11% for the S&P 400.
- We have shifted our earnings mix to where we now obtain about 75% of our key business earnings from faster growing technology and services businesses compared with about 50% in 1980,

even though earnings in our core manufacturing businesses have grown at an average of 6% a year over the same period.

By any measure, 1987 was a very strong year for your Company. All of GE's key businesses met their business plans. And, for the third year in a row, virtually all of our key businesses increased their market share.

Overall, net earnings were $2.915 billion, an increase of 17% from $2.492 billion in 1986. Earnings per share were $3.20 for 1987 compared with $2.73 for 1986, reflecting the April 1987 stock split. In 1987, the Company had two accounting changes which resulted in one-time net earnings gains of about $720 million. These gains were more than offset by business restructuring of about $750 million after taxes. Thus, our 1987 earnings growth of 17% was independent of these unusual items, but the restructuring will enhance GE's competitiveness in 1988 and beyond.

Sales for 1987, the first full year in which the RCA businesses are included, were $39.31 billion, up 12% from 1986's $35.21 billion.

We again ended the year in excellent financial condition. Cash, marketable securities and funds held for business development aggregated about $2.8 billion at

December 31, 1987, compared with $2.3 billion a year earlier. GE's short- and long-term debt, which carries the highest credit ratings, improved to a ratio of 25.1% of total capital, down from 28.7% at the end of 1986. Return on share owners' equity improved significantly, to 18.5% from 17.3% for 1986. Measurements of capital efficiency such as return on investment and working capital turnover also were improved.

Our commitment to research and development remained strong. R&D expenditures were $3 billion. In February 1987, GE donated the RCA David Sarnoff Research Center in Princeton, N.J., to SRI International and made a five-year, $250 million commitment to fund research there. This move preserved Sarnoff labs as one of the nation's foremost research centers, a position that might have been jeopardized had we tried to combine it with GE's existing research operations.

Expenditures for plant and equipment during 1987 were $1.8 billion, with significant capacity and productivity investments in Aircraft Engines, Plastics, Lighting and Appliances.

The major contributors to 1987's earnings growth were Aircraft Engines, Financial Services, Medical Systems, NBC and Plastics.

Adding to our internally generated growth is our record with acquisitions. Several large recent acquisitions—for example, Employers Reinsurance, NBC and RCA—have provided net additions to our earnings in their first year of GE ownership and have added significantly since then.

Kidder, Peabody, 80% of which was acquired by GE in 1986, had some difficulties in 1987, including admission by a former employee to securities violations that occurred prior to GE's acquisition; a subsequent settlement with the SEC; and the effects of stock and bond market volatility. Kidder, Peabody was a strong contributor to GE's 1986 earnings, but the 1987 difficulties put Kidder's contribution to GE at about breakeven for the first 18 months of ownership. Kidder is taking the decisive steps needed to weather turbulent times, and it remains an important part of our Financial Services business.

We have had a good track record with major acquisitions; and, although we have the resources for another, we have no set timetable to do one. Our past acquisitions were successful because they were a fit with our long-term strategy. We will continue to be selective, knowing that when the right opportunity presents itself, we have the financial strength and management depth to act quickly.

Our outlook for GE businesses in 1988 is optimistic. While the worldwide collapse in stock markets in the last quarter of 1987 was of concern, we believe that the directions our management team has been emphasizing—agility, quicker response to markets, globalization—will serve GE well during this period of change and uncertainty. Your Company is positioned for strong earnings growth in any reasonably good economy. We made a 1986 prediction of two-year double-digit earnings growth, given approximately 2-3% GNP growth. We have achieved that growth in 1987 and, given about the same economic scenario, we're confident we can do it again in 1988.

Your Company has a vitality, a sense of confidence, a bias for action that even the most optimistic of us could not envision just a few years ago. The sharing, open, adaptive culture we have worked so hard to grow is well-suited to the ever more complex world we face.

None of this has been brought about by more management, but rather by **less management**. Layers have been peeled away, and with them the reviews and the filters have also gone. Approval authority has been delegated downward. Thus, the bureaucratic paraphernalia that often slows and impedes communications and discourages the innovator and the risk-taker has been swept aside; in its place a faster-moving, more action-oriented and personally more satisfying environment has taken shape. We have removed, in addition, the saddle of a corporate bureaucracy from the backs of our businesses and have encouraged them to run in directions, and at speeds, they choose—and run they have.

With the reduction of "management" and the dismantling of bureaucracy, leaders have moved quickly to the front, creating a vision for each business and articulating that vision so clearly and compellingly and consistently that an entire organization can rally around it and turn it into reality. Leadership of that caliber is abundant in this Company and we see it shining from deeper and deeper in the structure of each of our businesses.

Communication, above all other factors, is driving this progress. We will never be satisfied with our performance, but we are proud of the gains we are achieving. Communication, for us, is more than newsletters and speeches and videotapes. It means sharing all the facts, with all the people, all the time. It is, we find, a simple concept but one requiring patience and persistence to imbed in the culture.

Our businesses are on the move—driven by people who talk, listen and share with one another, forging commitments that include everyone. For those businesses individually, and for the Company as a whole, 1987 was a terrific year. We continue to believe your Company has a future unmatched anywhere in the world. And the people of GE remain committed to seizing that future.

John F. Welch, Jr.
Chairman and
Chief Executive Officer

Lawrence A. Bossidy
Vice Chairman and
Executive Officer

Edward E. Hood, Jr.
Vice Chairman and
Executive Officer

FEBRUARY 12, 1988

To Our Share Owners

Nineteen eighty-eight was another exciting and successful year for GE. Earnings per share grew 17%. Earnings were $3.386 billion on revenues of $50.089 billion. The fourth quarter was the first in which GE's reported net earnings broke the one-billion-dollar mark. Return on equity was 19.4%, up almost a point. Operating margins grew, as did total cost productivity, which is now gaining at three times the national average and accelerating.

The year was punctuated by several key acquisitions, alliances and joint ventures that strengthened the Company's position around the globe. The results of these and other globalization efforts were apparent as revenues from international operations approached $11 billion, producing an operating profit of $2 billion—up more than 50% from the level of just two years ago and accounting for more than one-third of GE's total operating profit in 1988. The strong demand for our products around the world helped GE make a $3.1 billion positive contribution to the U.S. balance of trade in 1988, 50% greater than in 1987.

By virtually every measurement, it was a great year. But, as is usually the case in most years, a few thorns can be found among the roses—two, to be exact.

The first was a problem we've experienced with a new type of rotary compressor in certain models of our large refrigerators. There is no safety issue involved, and we are in the midst of an active campaign to replace every one of these compressors with minimum inconvenience to our customers. Our aim is to come out of this situation with our reputation for customer support and satisfaction not only intact but—if anything— enhanced. While the cost to the Company will be substantial, we have set up reserves to cover the estimated cost of the fix—and we still had a record performance in 1988.

The second disappointment of 1988 is one you, as share owners, are quite familiar with: the price of our stock. Those who have held GE shares from the early 1980s have been rewarded handsomely. Appreciation and yield provided a return averaging 20% per year, compounded from 1981 to 1988, even with the October 1987 correction, compared with a return of 15% for the S&P 500. But that's yesterday's performance. In 1988, the stock appreciation didn't keep pace with the Company's performance.

We're not sure why this is the case, but it occurs to us that perhaps the pace and variety of our activity appear unfocused to those who view it from the outside. The general media and the financial press have, for the most part, been more than favorable in their appraisal of our performance, but as we've picked up the tempo, especially in 1988, we began hearing: GE is "too difficult to understand" and "portfolio managing." We even heard ourselves described by the "C" word—conglomerate—with its usual pejorative corollary: "Who knows what they'll buy or sell next?"

You get the idea.

Perhaps a strategy that appears to us crystal clear and consistent—because we live by it—seems less so to some of our key constituencies in the media and financial community.

This is more likely a failure of our communication efforts rather than one of understanding, so we have decided to use a good part of this letter to explain again, without adornment, the operative premises and world view that have guided, without exception, every major move we've made since 1981.

There is no denying we are a diverse company. We are not a computer, or oil, or auto, or steel monolith. Those who track us in the financial analyst community or financial press have much more homework than do those who watch and report on our peers. We have businesses ranging from plastics to network broadcasting to the manufacture of jet engines to reinsurance. But the strategy, the management philosophy that drives the Company, is the essence of simplicity.

We have two basic premises.
The first is that we will run only businesses that are number one or number two in their global markets—or, in the case of services, that have a substantial position—and are of scale and potential appropriate to a $50 billion enterprise. Currently, there are 14 of these businesses, highly diverse in their pursuits but closely knit by common values, shared technology and substantial resources; and they draw upon a pool of management talent we believe is unequaled in the world.

The second premise is that in addition to the strength, resources and reach of a big company, which we have already built, we are committed to developing the sensitivity, the leanness, the simplicity and the agility of a small company. We want the best of both.

These premises shape and explain everything we do.

In acquisition philosophy, for example, being number one or number two dictates that we will only acquire companies that are a direct and enhancing graft onto one of our 14 key businesses or that are large, freestanding and in a position of leadership in their marketplaces. The RCA acquisition, while old news, illustrates this principle very well. NBC was a part of RCA and the nation's number one network. We kept it and added it to our other leadership businesses.

The RCA Aerospace group, on the other hand, was a natural fit with our own GE Aerospace business, so we merged them, strengthening our overall aerospace position. Several discrete RCA businesses that were not strategic to us, such as the carpet company, were neither graftable to our 14 key businesses nor large and freestanding, so we disposed of them almost immediately.

But, for some reason, our trade of the merged GE/RCA television manufacturing business to Thomson of France in exchange for its medical diagnostic business and cash provoked some puzzling responses. Suddenly, the manufacture of televisions became something quintessentially American, like baseball. Some felt we had betrayed our heritage in our compulsion to "do deals." We heard phrases like: "Un-American," "giving up on manufacturing," "exporting jobs."

The facts were these: The combined GE/RCA television business lost $125 million in the 1980s, was a cash drain and was number three or four in the global market with no way in sight of getting to number one or two. Thomson's TV business, while profitable, was in a similar market-share situation— stuck in the middle of the pack. Our trade with Thomson produced the following results. Thomson, including its new employees from GE, broke out of the pack, doubled its volume and moved into a number one or two position in the industry. GE, by acquiring Thomson's medical business, with its $1 billion in sales, and grafting it onto the already strong GE Medical Systems business, became number one in a game central to our strategy. Exporting jobs? Some 21,000 of the 31,000 jobs in the TV business had been overseas for a decade or more. Hurting employees? The employees in that business, formerly endangered by being part of an also-ran in a global market, now have the reach and volume that gives them a real shot at winning.

We think it is one of the most important, logical and universally beneficial moves made anywhere in the 1980s—a win for the employees of the GE/RCA television business, a good deal for Thomson and a key victory for a high-technology GE manufacturing business—Medical Systems—that is now the global technology and market leader.

The divestitures we've made in the 1980s have produced $9 billion in cash, which has been used for acquisitions to strengthen our 14 key businesses. In 1988, we purchased Borg-Warner's chemicals businesses to expand GE Plastics' global market basket. In addition, we bought the Roper Corporation to strengthen the position of GE Appliances in the domestic range market. GE Financial Services (GEFS) acquired the credit card business of Montgomery Ward, a move that effectively doubled our private-label credit card assets and enhanced our number one position in that market segment. GEFS'

1988 integration of the 1987 Gelco acquisition created a leading position in automotive fleet leasing as well as in the cargo shipping container business.

In all, we've invested some $16 billion in the 1980s on acquisitions. We would argue that some $15 billion of these funds has been very successfully invested. Only two niche electronics acquisitions—amounting to about $400 million—didn't pan out and were sold. Another $600 million invested in Kidder, Peabody has thus far had—for a variety of reasons—difficulty in reaching its potential. Even so, Kidder increased its 1988 earnings 20% to $46 million—admittedly a small part of the total GEFS net of $788 million; nevertheless, we see Kidder as a business with important synergies across GEFS that should become more significant in the 1990s.

This track record gives us confidence in the acquisition process as one of the means to strengthen our global leadership positions.

In addition to acquisitions, we continue to invest in alliances and joint ventures with other companies all over the globe to enhance our 14 key businesses. In 1988 alone, we concluded alliances between GE Lighting and Toshiba of Japan and between GE Motors and Bosch of

West Germany, and we expanded an alliance between GE Electrical Distribution and Control and Fuji.

Finally, in early 1989, we signed a series of historic agreements with GEC of the United Kingdom that will open the door to increased European participation by four of our 14 businesses—Medical Systems, Appliances, Industrial and Power Systems, and Electrical Distribution and Control. This move appears complicated on the surface because there are four businesses involved, but it is driven, once again, by the simple strategy dictating that we advance our 14 businesses, on a global basis, whenever we can, consistent with a consistent strategy.

In addition to acquiring, divesting and forming alliances to support these key businesses, we continue to supply them with resources to propel their internal growth—investing close to $16 billion since 1981. In 1988, we made a multiyear, $1.8 billion commitment to build a Spanish plastics complex that will supply the European market, we committed another billion dollars to further fuel the strong growth of GE Financial Services, and we spent a total of more than $1.8 billion on new plant and equipment. Another $3.6 billion—

about $1.2 billion funded by the Company—was spent on research and development, almost exclusively in support of these 14 key businesses.

To those who perceive us as institutionally fickle, we would point to two of our key 14 businesses—Transportation Systems, which is mainly locomotives, and Industrial and Power Systems. Both went through purgatory in the 1980s, in the bottom of market troughs of several years' duration that saw few orders in locomotives and none in large steam turbines.

Instead of closing or selling these businesses, we reduced their costs consistent with the market, invested to make them more competitive ($300 million in locomotives alone) and stuck with them through the lean years—not out of sentimentality or inertia but because they are large, world-leading businesses with big potential and because doing so fits our strategy. And in 1988, we saw a significant market revival under way in locomotives and the approaching dawn of a revival in areas of the turbine business.

That, then, is the first part of our strategy: Creating a company consisting only of world-class global businesses that can compete and win in the 1990s and beyond.

The focus of our R&D, investment, acquisitions and alliances—everything we do—is ensuring the growth and vitality of those businesses.

The second part of the strategy, as we mentioned, is making this $50 billion enterprise as lean, as agile and as light on its feet as a small company—a big company with the heart and hunger of a small one.

We've been grappling with how to achieve this unbeatable amalgam for the entire decade, and, while we haven't yet achieved it, our progress is accelerating. Once again, the actions we have taken are totally consistent with our oft-stated theory of the case.

We believed layers of management were "big-company" encumbrances—so we reduced ours from nine to as few as four, from us in the Corporate Executive Office to the factory floor of any given business. In the mid-1980s, we made a calculated gamble and removed the entire second and third echelons of management in the Company—layers we called sectors and groups. The 14 key businesses now report not, as often in the past, to senior vice presidents who report to executive vice presidents—all with staff entourages—but directly to us three. This arrangement is

dependent for its success on the quality of leadership at the business level. We gambled that we had that quality, and we won. The new arrangement has proved breath-takingly clean, simple and effective. Ideas, initiatives and decisions move, often at the speed of sound—voices—where once they were muffled and garbled by a gauntlet of approvals and the oppressive ministrations of staff reviews.

Secondly, we found ourselves in the early 1980s with corporate and business staffs that were viewed—and viewed themselves—as monitors, checkers, kibitzers and approvers. We changed that view and that mission to the point where staff now sees itself as facilitator, advisor and partner of operations—with a growing sense of satisfaction and cooperation on both sides. Territoriality has given way to a growing sense of unity and common purpose.

The third step toward a small-company management system began in 1988 when we formulated and began planning a project we call "work-out." This will be an intense and continuing program, conducted within the businesses and with support from the Company's management institute, to "liberate" the employees of our Company from the cramping artifacts that pile up in the dusty attics of century-old companies: the reports, meetings, rituals, approvals, controls and forests of paper that often seem necessary until they are removed.

As we succeed over the next three years in ridding our Company of the tentacles of ritual and bureaucracy, we are now better able to attack the final, and perhaps the most difficult, challenge of all. And that is the empowering of our 300,000 people, the releasing of their creativity and ambition, the direct coupling of their jobs with some positive effect on the quality of a product or service. We want each man and woman in this Company to see a connection between what he or she does all day—and winning in the marketplace. Their roles, responsibilities and rewards must become clear to them and to everyone. Small companies thrive and grow on that sense of contribution and reward. We want it as well, and everything we do to evolve our management system will be consistent with getting it.

Liberation and empowerment, as we use the concept, stems from what we believe is a very solidly grounded view of winning and losing around the world. We, as a globally competing company, have some serious disadvantages as we line up against our foreign competi-tors. Some of those competitors enjoy protection from foreign inroads into their markets; others are financially supported by their governments. Some are beneficiaries of nationally focused R&D in key technologies. Others are part of regimented, paternalistic cultures that serve them well.

We complain, on occasion, about all of this, but it is we who have the ultimate advantage, one that few of us, if pressed, would ever wish to trade. It is the fact that we are, despite our mix of global cultures and enterprises, an American company; and, as such, our system, while providing no guarantees, also has the fewest barriers to innovation, boldness and risk-taking—the stuff that will propel the real winners in the 1990s.

And that's the "why" behind our program of liberation and empowerment—more fulfilling work for all and greater competitiveness for our Company. The worst thing we could do is to stifle with bureaucracy our employ-ees—the Americans and Germans, the French and Japanese, and the scores of other nationalities that are now part of the global GE. If we did, we would then have none of the advantages of our competitors—and many of the encumbrances that burden them all. We won't let that happen.

If we can become that big-company/small-company hybrid while pursuing our global strategies and encouraging even more boldness in the leadership of our businesses, we will be within striking distance of the goal we set out in pursuit of eight years ago: We will be a more contemporary, more accessible, more responsive company, in touch with our customers, firmly in control of our own destiny, driven by more-fulfilled people in control of theirs.

We are on the brink of the most exciting and opportunity-rich decade in world business history. We approach it with a strategy that has been both consistent and very successful during the 1980s. If this summary of the strategy we have once again presented in this letter is clear, you will have no difficulty understanding everything we do in the 1990s.

And we intend to do a lot.

John F. Welch, Jr.
Chairman of the Board and
Chief Executive Officer

Lawrence A. Bossidy
Vice Chairman of the Board and
Executive Officer

Edward E. Hood, Jr.
Vice Chairman of the Board and
Executive Officer

FEBRUARY 10, 1989

To Our Share Owners

Nineteen eighty-nine was another excellent year for General Electric—a record year in a decade of accelerating performance. We begin the 1990s with a profoundly transformed Company, and while we are culturally opposed to dwelling on the past, it is important to outline the degree of change we have experienced because in many ways it suggests the direction in which we are headed in the new decade and beyond.

GE entered the 1980s with a strong balance sheet that gave us the financial strength and flexibility to effect dramatic change decisively yet compassionately. Much of that change was aimed at creating a business mix and a system of managing it that would allow us to grow much more rapidly than the world economies in which we operate.

We begin the 1990s with a Company vastly different from the one that existed in the early 1980s:

- In 1980, two-thirds of GE's revenues came from slow-growth core manufacturing and nonstrategic businesses like natural resources. Today, two-thirds of our revenues come from high-growth technology and services.
- In 1980, of our strategic businesses, only two were truly global—GE Plastics and GE Aircraft Engines. We begin the 1990s with a significant global presence in virtually all of our businesses. Our operating profits from outside the United States have grown 30% per year since 1987 and, at $2.8 billion in 1989, amounted to 40% of the Company total. Our exports helped us increase our positive contribution to the U.S. balance of trade to $4.8 billion in 1989, up from $3.1 billion in 1988 and $2.1 billion in 1987.
- We began the 1980s with a bureaucracy of as many as nine management layers in some businesses. Today, all our businesses have significantly reduced layers, some to as few as four, and now we *move* a lot faster—not yet with the speed of the best small companies but with that goal

always in our sights and closer every day.

- Our productivity growth in the early 1980s was representative of the United States—in the range of 1–2% a year. We enter the 1990s approaching the 6% level.
- Earnings grew for 40 consecutive quarters in the 1980s. As the decade progressed, this growth climbed from high single digits to consistent double digits, and we finished the decade with a strong 1989—earnings of $3.9 billion, up 16% from 1988, and 2.6 times the 1980 level. Operating margins are at historic highs; revenues, at $54.6 billion, are double the 1980 level.
- The stock market looked favorably on these moves and changes and the performance they produced. In 1980, we had a total market value of $12 billion, which ranked us 11th among American companies. We left the decade ranked second, with a year-end market value of $58 billion, and that $46 billion increase during the 1980s was the largest of any company in the United States.

In sum, it was a great decade for GE. We are proud of what we did well and smarter for some of the things we didn't do so well. Not every new acquisition worked, although $16 billion out of the $17 billion we spent on acquisitions

will add to 1990s earnings. Not every new product was right—as the refrigerator compressor failure demonstrated. And we discovered in mid-decade that we needed to upgrade substantially our systems for complying with government procurement laws.

And finally, as bold and transformational as we think we have been—as we acquired, sold, restructured and reorganized—it is clear in hindsight that we could have been faster, bolder and less incremental. We will be all of these in the years ahead.

But before we take that look ahead, we would like to share a few thoughts about the type of enterprise your Company has become.

People sometimes grapple with what to call GE. An electrical equipment manufacturer? Sure. But that description ignores two-thirds of our earnings.

Are we a conglomerate? No, not that there's anything wrong with being a conglomerate. We simply aren't one. We're not a collection of stand-alone enterprises, and this label misses the very essence of what makes this Company work so well.

We know what we are: an **integrated, diversified company**. And we'd like to explain what that means and, more important, why we think it positions us uniquely to take on the challenges of the 1990s.

We entered the 1980s with a widely diverse set of businesses and major product lines—as many as 350—that we subjected to a strategic test. Diversity, we felt, could only be a real strength if each business was number one or number two in its particular market. For those that were not, we had a very specific prescription—they were to be fixed, sold or closed.

In line with this simple strategy, we sold businesses that made up 25% of our 1980 sales, including natural resources, consumer electronics, housewares and scores of others that could not become number one or number two. During the same period, we invested $17 billion in acquisitions—NBC as a free-standing business; the Aerospace business of RCA added to GE Aerospace; Borg-Warner Chemicals added to GE Plastics; Employers Reinsurance, Montgomery Ward Credit and Kidder, Peabody as well as many others added to GE Financial Services; the French medical equipment company, CGR, added to GE Medical Systems; and, most recently, Tungsram of Hungary added to GE Lighting—just to name a few. We committed the research and development and plant and equipment investment necessary to keep our current businesses in leading positions, and we undertook the initiatives to ensure that these businesses became global in their scope and reach.

We enter the 1990s with 13 businesses, each number one or number two in the global markets in which they compete, each with strong distribution networks, each in industries requiring enormous capital, technology and human resources for entry.

But diversity, even when based on strong individual businesses, each making significant contributions, is not in itself enough. To truly maximize the strength of our businesses, we had to achieve what we call **"integrated diversity."** To get that, we had to dismantle the multiple layers of management that so smoothly ran the Company in a more predictable era but that had, over time, served to garble communication and hobble action. We removed sectors, groups, span-breakers and much of the other superstructure that we had once used to manage our diversity. The role of staff was turned 180°, from checker, inquisitor and authority figure to facilitator, helper and supporter of "the field"—our 13 businesses. Today, all 13 report directly to the three of us. Important communications are oral. The passion of our business leaders is not diluted by filters, briefers and rewriters. We have put in place a management system that integrates our diversity more simply, allows us to allocate resources more effectively than we ever believed possible and lets us move faster.

Obviously, the 1990s will be as full of unknowns and surprises as the 1980s were, but in our view, some things are dead certain: The pace of change will be faster. Globalization will be more pervasive. Competition will intensify. The need for continuous employee education at all levels will be even greater. Protecting the environment will become a total commitment of every employee at GE.

In the 1980s, we built a management system ideally suited to deal with these 1990s issues— a system that brings the leaders of our 13 businesses together quarterly over a two-day period, not for a parade of sterile, polished business reviews but to grapple together with common problems and share insights and initiatives that are valuable to all.

While our seemingly diverse businesses range from a television network to financial services, from plastics to jet engines, there is a unique common thread—**shared management practices**—that binds them together and creates what we call integrated diversity. All must deal with the urgency of globalization, the need for cultural

change, the protection of the environment and the sudden opportunities in Eastern Europe, where, for example, the experience of a business like GE Lighting, which moved quickly into Hungary, is shared and leveraged across all the businesses.

When one leaves these dynamic sessions, it is impossible to be complacent, impossible to be comfortable with the status quo. The need for faster, more aggressive, more global action comes alive and is obvious to all.

The same dynamics occur every day at our Management Development Institute at Crotonville, N.Y., where 5,000 employees a year, from every business in the Company, share the very best they have observed in areas like customer service, environmental protection and compressing the product development cycle. All these issues and countless others are wrestled with by men and women eager to find a better way of doing things—from anywhere—and translate it into a more productive way back home.

The effect of this constant sharing of common management issues is a reinforcement in the minds of all of the need for speed, continuous experimentation and action.

We've seen, as we shed our bureaucracy and created this integrated diverse enterprise, the enormous benefits of sharing best practices, of helping each other, of asking questions and, above all, of listening. In the 1980s, these practices tended to concentrate in the upper levels of the Company. We are now committed to a decade-long campaign to drive them throughout the enterprise.

Our dream for the 1990s is a boundary-less Company, a Company where we knock down the walls that separate us from each other on the inside and from our key constituencies on the outside.

The boundary-less Company we envision will remove the barriers among engineering, manufacturing, marketing, sales and customer service; it will recognize no distinctions between "domestic" and "foreign" operations—we'll be as comfortable doing business in Budapest and Seoul as we are in Louisville and Schenectady. A boundary-less organization will ignore or erase group labels such as "management," "salaried" or "hourly," which get in the way of people working together.

A boundary-less Company will level its external walls as well, reaching out to key suppliers to make them part of a single process in which they and we join hands and intellects in a common purpose—satisfying customers.

This is an admittedly grand vision, requiring unprecedented cultural change, and we are nowhere near achieving it. But we have an idea of how to get there— an idea that is rapidly becoming reality across the Company. It's called Work-Out.

Work-Out is a fluid and adaptable concept, not a "program." It generally starts as a series of regularly scheduled "town meetings" that bring together large cross sections of a business— people from manufacturing, engineering, customer service, hourly, salaried, high and lower levels—people who in their normal routines work within the boxes on their organization charts and have few dealings with one another.

The initial purpose of these meetings is simple—to remove the more egregious manifestations of bureaucracy: multiple approvals, unnecessary paperwork, excessive reports, routines, rituals. Ideas and opinions are often, at first, voiced hesitantly by people who never before had a forum—other than the water cooler—to express them. We have found that after a short time those ideas begin to come in a torrent—especially when people see *action* taken on the ones already advanced.

With the desk largely cleared of bureaucratic impediments and distractions, the Work-Out sessions then begin to focus on the more challenging tasks: examining the myriad processes that make up every business, identifying the crucial ones, discarding the rest, and then finding a faster, simpler, better way of doing things. Next, the teams raise the bar of excellence by testing their improved processes against the very best from around the Company and from the best companies around the world.

We have progressed well into the first stage of Work-Out in most of our businesses, and some are beginning the transition into the second—or best-practices—phase; but we are under no illusions that this is anything less than a decade-long crusade. We have hardly scratched the surface of the enormous mine of productivity and innovation that we *know* exists in the intelligence and imagination of our 300,000 employees, but we are excited beyond measure by what we are discovering. The natural cynicism that accompanies the announcement of new corporate campaigns and slogans has largely been dissipated as progress and momentum have begun to grow. Work-Out is working.

The hardware of this Company—its businesses and its management structure—is now largely the way we want it. Work-Out is our decade-long vehicle for the software. Restructuring is a road,

not a destination. A company can boost productivity by restructuring, removing bureaucracy and downsizing, but it cannot sustain high productivity growth without cultural change, without totally involving the individual who is closest to the work and therefore knows it better than those who "manage" it. The individual is the fountainhead of creativity and innovation, and we are struggling to get all our people to accept the countercultural truth that often the best way to manage people is just to get out of their way. Only by releasing the energy and fire of our employees can we achieve the decisive, continuous productivity advantages that will give us the freedom to compete and win in any business anywhere on the globe.

We end this decade with enormous confidence in the future of GE. Last November, we announced our intent to repurchase $10 billion worth of our stock over the next five years. This decision was made possible by our earnings and our debt capacity and by the significant cash flows generated by our business restructurings and productivity growth during the 1980s.

The repurchase in no way impinges on investment in the Company. R&D investment is the highest in our history, as are capital expenditures. The businesses, even during the repurchase period, will be given the resources to make modest-size complementary acquisitions, and should a very large acquisition opportunity surface, we have the flexibility to suspend the repurchase program and move decisively.

Our Company will be making exciting business moves in the 1990s—ventures, new product lines, acquisitions, alliances—but the most important campaign will be the daily one we wage to inspire and enlist our employees in the cause of shared excellence and winning.

In the 1980s, we changed the Company. We also challenged the bureaucracy and generally got the better of it. In the 1990s, our task will be to challenge each other and, in doing so, to get the very best out of ourselves. The cool efficiency that many have always associated with business leadership must give way to personal skills and traits like empowering, listening, passion, energy and the capacity to transmit that energy to others. Being "on top of things," controlling them, must give way to sharing, trusting. Most of the bureaucracy that infects business institutions—the reviews, layers, routines and reports—stems largely from a lack of trust. We have seen, with the demolition of the control superstructure we once imposed on our business, and we

are *beginning* to see even more clearly as Work-Out starts to blossom, that controlling people doesn't motivate them. It stifles them. We've found that people perform better, even heroically, when they see that what they do every day makes a difference.

When they see that—when they are allowed to make real contributions to win—they quickly develop increased **self-confidence**. That self-confidence in turn promotes **simplicity**—of action, of design, of process, of communication—because there is no longer a psychic need to wrap oneself in the complexity, trappings and jargon that, in a bureaucracy, signify sophistication and status. And that simplicity will radically increase the **speed** of our businesses and their ability to react to a world whose pace of change will become astonishing in the 1990s. Speed, simplicity and self-confidence will be the operative characteristics of the winning companies of the 1990s and beyond.

We want GE to become a company where people come to work every day in a rush to try something they woke up thinking about the night before. We want them to go home from work wanting to talk about what they did that day, rather than trying to forget about it. We want factories where the whistle blows and everyone wonders where the time went, and someone suddenly wonders aloud why we need a whistle. We want a company where people find a better way, every day, of doing things; and where by shaping their own work experience, they make their lives better and your Company best.

Far-fetched? Fuzzy? Soft? Naive? Not a bit. This is the type of liberated, involved, excited, boundary-less culture that is present in successful start-up enterprises. It is unheard of in an institution our size; but we want it, and we are determined we will have it.

John F. Welch, Jr.
Chairman of the Board and
Chief Executive Officer

Lawrence A. Bossidy
Vice Chairman of the Board and
Executive Officer

Edward E. Hood, Jr.
Vice Chairman of the Board and
Executive Officer

FEBRUARY 16, 1990

To Our Share Owners

General Electric had another strong year in 1990.

- Revenues climbed 7% to $58.4 billion; earnings per share were $4.85, up 11% for the fourth consecutive year of double-digit growth; and net earnings grew to $4.303 billion, up 9%. The performance of our long-cycle businesses such as Industrial and Power Systems, Aircraft Engines and Medical Systems, in addition to Financial Services, more than overcame the softness in short-cycle businesses such as NBC and Plastics.
- Strong productivity growth continued, reaching 5.4% in 1990, the fourth consecutive year we have grown our productivity in the 4–6% range—an improvement central to our competitiveness in the world marketplace.
- Our positive contribution to the U.S. balance of trade in 1990— approximately $4.5 billion, up 15% from the year before—is a clear measure of this global competitiveness.

- Operating margin, another gauge of increasing strength, hit an all-time high of 11.6%.
- Working capital turnover, a measure of efficiency and process speed, improved for the fifth consecutive year to 4.7 turns, and we are targeting 5 turns in 1991. These recent improvements in working capital turnover have freed up a total of $2.3 billion in cash.
- All of these improvements combined to produce a record return on equity of 20.2%.
- Revenues from international operations grew to $15.4 billion, up 18% from 1989.
- Our total R&D expenditures increased 9% in 1990 to a record amount, $4.3 billion, and a record percentage of sales, 9.9%, demonstrating our confidence in the Company's technological future.
- Our stock buyback continued in 1990 with the repurchase of 37.9 million shares at a cost of $2.4 billion.
- And finally, GE's balance sheet remains strong with a debt-to-

capital ratio of 23.6% and a Triple-A rating.

Those are the numbers, and we are pleased with them. For the remainder of our letter, we would like to share with you the progress we continue to make in turning our 1980s vision into reality and the promise we see in the vision we outlined last year for our Company in the 1990s.

Our vision of the 1980s has been described to you for a decade. We believed that only businesses that were number-one or number-two in their markets could win in the increasingly competitive global arena. Those that could not were to be fixed, closed or sold. Consistent with this view, we divested $10 billion worth of those that could not meet the number-one or number-two criterion and made $19 billion of acquisitions to strengthen the world-class businesses that could.

These moves during the 1980s, and our focused investment, have shaped the 13 businesses we have today, each at, or very close to, the top in its global markets.

In 1990, the process continued. GE Lighting, Mr. Edison's 112-year-old business, was, up until 14 months ago, almost totally a U.S. business, with less than 2% market share in Europe. When the Iron Curtain lifted, and the EC created

pan-European markets, we moved. First we acquired a majority interest in the Hungarian lighting company Tungsram, and then, in early 1991, a majority of the THORN Light Source business in the United Kingdom. We now have the number-one lamp business in the world, with close to a 20% market share in Western Europe.

Also consistent with our number-one or number-two strategy was our sale in 1990, for $515 million, of a nonstrategic business, Ladd Petroleum.

While restructuring our Company in the 1980s, we spent much of our time talking about the accelerating pace of change: in world politics, in technology, in product introduction and in the increasing demands of customers. We don't have to do that anymore. Change is in the air. Newspapers and networks hammer it home daily. GE people today understand the pace of change, **the need for speed**, the absolute necessity of moving more quickly in everything we do, from inventory turnover, to product development cycles, to a faster response to customer needs. They understand that slow-and-steady is a ticket to the boneyard in the 1990s. What they need, and what we must provide, are the power, the freedom and the tools that will allow them to achieve that speed in everything we do.

From that pursuit of speed—from the understanding that it is the indispensable ingredient of success in this decade—came our vision for the 1990s: **a boundaryless Company**.

What that boundaryless vision means, and where we are headed with it, is something we'd like to share with you.

"Boundaryless" is an uncommon word—perhaps even an awkward one—but it has become a word we use constantly, one that describes a whole set of behaviors we believe are necessary to achieve speed.

In a boundaryless company, suppliers aren't "outsiders." They are drawn closer and become trusted partners in the total business process. Customers are seen for what they are—the lifeblood of a company. Customers' vision of their needs and the company's view become identical, and every effort of every man and woman in the company is focused on satisfying those needs.

In a boundaryless company, internal functions begin to blur. Engineering doesn't design a product and then "hand it off" to manufacturing. They form a team, along with marketing and sales, finance and the rest. Customer service? It's not somebody's job. It's everybody's job. Environmental protection in the plants? It's not the concern of some manager or department. Everyone's an environmentalist.

Perhaps the biggest stride we've made recently in boundary-busting has been our progress in wringing out not-invented-here—NIH—from our culture. Increasingly, GE people are now searching, around the world, for better ways of doing things.

For example, two years ago one of our people spotted a truly innovative method of compressing product cycle times in an appliance company in New Zealand and tested it successfully in our Canadian appliance affiliate.

The methodology has now been transferred to our largest appliance complex in Louisville, Kentucky, where it is revolutionizing processes, reducing the time it takes to produce products, increasing our responsiveness to customers and reducing inventory levels by hundreds of millions of dollars a year.

Teams from all of our manufacturing businesses are now living in Louisville and learning these techniques in real time. The objective: to take this New Zealand-to-Montreal-to-Louisville experience to every business in GE and, by doing so, to raise the bar of excellence yet another notch around this Company.

It is this elimination of boundaries between businesses and the transferring of ideas from one place in the Company to another that is at the heart of what we call **integrated diversity**. It is this concept that we believe sets us apart from both single-product companies and from conglomerates.

Integrated diversity, for us, means the drawing together of our 13 different businesses by sharing ideas, by finding multiple applications for technological advancements and by moving people across businesses to provide fresh perspectives and to develop broad-based experience. Integrated diversity gives us a Company that is considerably greater than the sum of its parts.

Integrating diversity only works when the elements of the diversity—in our case our 13 global businesses—are strong in their own right. A critical mass of competitive advantage cannot be achieved by leaning small businesses on large ones or weaklings on winners. That is why our work of the 1980s— creating strong, stand-alone businesses—was the indispensable forerunner of integrating them in the 1990s.

But the walls that separate our businesses from one another are not the only ones we are removing.

Even the barriers between GE work life and community life have come down. The GE management

society, whose chapters for 63 years met and talked shop and discussed investment funds, has turned its face outward to the needs of the community, and the results are something of which we are more than proud. Hundreds of GE volunteers from the society are serving as mentors and tutors in inner city and rural school systems; and, as a result of their efforts, thousands of under-privileged but promising young men and women will attend college who otherwise would not have had the opportunity. Just a few months ago, Harvard University presented its prestigious Dively Award for Corporate Public Initiative to GE because of the efforts of these volunteers.

So we have knocked down a few boundaries inside the Company and around it, but the walls within a big, century-old Company don't come down like Jericho's when management makes some organizational changes—or gives a speech. There are too many persistent habits propping them up. Parochialism, turf battles, status, "functionalitis," and, most important, the biggest sin of a bureaucracy, the focus on itself and its inner workings, are always in the background. This is no reflection on people but simply a product of the way large organizations have evolved.

We've been pulling the dandelions of bureaucracy for a

decade, but they don't come up easily and they'll be back next week if you don't keep after them. Yes, we've taken out a lot of structure—staff, span-breakers, planners, checkers, approvers—and yet we have by no means removed it all. Those who have ever cleaned out an attic and returned a year later are often shocked to see what they left as "essential"—the pairs of old pants that would never be worn for the painting that would never be done, the boxes of moldy *National Geographics* that would never again be read.

We feel the same way every time we revisit our management system—our processes—and see the barriers that insulate us from each other and from our only reason for existence as an institution—serving customers and winning in the marketplace.

For decades, business has been rewarding people with not only money and promotions—which is appropriate—but with titles as well, the most common of which is "manager" of this or that. Managers, logically enough, see their mandate as managing: controlling, measuring and getting on top of things. Often, by doing so, they unconsciously carve out fiefdoms and then feel compelled to defend them. By the end of this decade, we will have one-third fewer management positions than

we have today—not necessarily fewer people, but fewer titles with their perceived mandates to "manage" rather than facilitate and contribute.

But the root cause of many of bureaucracy's ills—the turf battles, the parochialism and the rest—is deeper and more subtle. It is people's insecurity. Insecurity makes people resist change because they see it only as a threat, never an opportunity. It's that insecurity, that resistance to change, that must be dealt with.

The antidote to insecurity is **self-confidence**. Some people get it at their mother's knee, others through scholastic, athletic or other achievement. Some tiptoe through life without it. If we are to create this boundaryless Company, we have to create an atmosphere where self-confidence can grow in each of the 298,000 of us.

So how do we grow self-confidence, not just at the top, or in the middle, but everywhere in the Company?

We designed a process to give people a voice, a say, to get them talking to one another and trusting one another, a process we believe will eventually lead to widespread self-confidence across the Company.

"Work-Out" is the name of the process. As we've described it to you before, Work-Out began around the Company with assemblies patterned after the New England town meeting—the ultimate boundaryless event. They are attended by a disparate group of people—hourly, salaried, managers, union leaders—people who often had no occasion to speak to one another during the workday.

The sessions quickly became a shooting gallery, with the more egregious manifestations of bureaucracy as targets—10 signatures on a minor requisition, nonsensical paperwork, wasteful work practices, artificial dress codes, pomposity. Most of these were abolished or reformed on the spot, not put "in channels."

For the first time in their work lives, people began seeing action match rhetoric—their trust in the process grew—and the ideas began to come in waves. People who had never been asked for anything other than their time and their hands now saw their minds, their views sought after. And in listening to their ideas, it became even more clear to everyone that the people who are closest to the work really do know it better.

Work-Out is two years old now and it's moving steadily up the learning curve. Today, suppliers and customers are part of many of the sessions, exploring new ways of working together. Sessions are becoming more complex as cross-functional teams map the most complicated business processes and compare them with the very best we can find from companies around the world. Work-Out, incidentally, has proved indispensable to the implementation of the revolutionary cycle-time reduction effort in our appliance business.

Work-Out is building trust, teamwork and self-confidence around this Company.

Now, as we write this, we are conscious that across the Company there are still too many people for whom much of this bears little resemblance to the reality of their lives—people who are still trapped in the web of bureaucracy or work in a place where measurement and reward systems still run counter to the very concept of boundarylessness.

There are others as well who say, "You can talk all you want about Work-Out and boundaryless, but the boss still calls the shots." And they are right. Yes, after all the dialogue and input and debate, priorities must be set, resources allocated and final decisions made by the leadership at every level. The difference—a very big difference—is that the input and ideas upon which those decisions are based will come from many, not a few.

Leaders in the 1990s must delegate more, facilitate more and listen more. They must trust and be trusted. Leadership will always have responsibility for the final call, but it will have an equal responsibility to make the decision rational to those who provided the input. The successful leaders of the 1990s will be those whose decisions, however difficult, will be understood, accepted and rallied around by a highly involved work force.

Work-Out is allowing self-confidence to flourish around our Company. As that self-confidence grows, the boundaries are beginning to fall; and as they fall, GE is picking up speed, and with that speed a competitive advantage.

Some people are uncomfortable with this soft stuff and press us to quantify it, to measure its progress. It would be easy to quote numbers of Work-Out sessions, best-practice teams, suggestions implemented, money spent on training, and the like; but we've resisted because the last thing this effort needs is its own bureaucracy and measurement systems. But we can tell you it is working. We see it working in people's faces and we hear it in the confidence in their voices. And we are beginning to see its results

in some of those numbers we gave you at the beginning of our letter: working capital turnover, operating margins and, above all, productivity growth.

These are numbers that couldn't be improved as significantly as they have been by the actions of the top one hundred, or one thousand, or even five thousand people in a company our size. They can only be moved by the contributions of tens of thousands of people who are coming to work every day looking for a better way.

We enter a year fraught with global uncertainty, but we do so confidently, with 13 globally positioned businesses and an increasingly clear vision of what we can become—a boundaryless Company with a boundless future.

John F. Welch, Jr.
Chairman of the Board
and Chief Executive Officer

Lawrence A. Bossidy
Vice Chairman of the Board
and Executive Officer

Edward E. Hood, Jr.
Vice Chairman of the Board
and Executive Officer

FEBRUARY 15, 1991

To Our Share Owners

1991 was a tough, terrific year for GE.

For the past few years, those of you who invest in our Company, and share our interest in and affection for it, have patiently read letters from us that dealt only minimally with traditional business data and focused instead on soft concepts and values. We wrote of our belief in simplicity as a critical component of business plans and communications. We defined self-confidence in our people as the catalyst that would release the ideas and energy we craved. We spoke endlessly about what we believe to be the ultimate virtue of a company—speed. We used a big, clumsy word like "boundary-lessness" to describe a mindset that breaks bureaucratic barriers and draws teams closer. And, finally, we described, in largely promissory terms, a concept called Work-Out—our vehicle for pursuing a total transformation of a century-old Company culture, in pursuit of a future of virtually unlimited productivity.

This emphasis on the **software** of our Company followed the **hardware** changes—the restructuring we had undertaken during the early 1980s—that produced excellent results—a 22% average annual return on share owner investment during the decade. But those were good times, and we, like our contemporaries, were helped substantially by the prosperity that characterized much of the 1980s.

But in 1991, all our rhetoric, our 1980s restructuring and our cultural changes were put to their first **real** test when much of the global economy settled into a full year of steady decline.

So how did we do?

- Our revenues grew 3% to over $60.2 billion.
- Our earnings grew 3% to $4.435 billion, and our earnings per share grew 5%.
- We adopted a new accounting rule for retiree health and life insurance benefits, which reduced earnings by $1.8 billion but used no cash.

- We repurchased a billion dollars worth of our stock while keeping a solid Triple-A debt rating.
- Total cost productivity grew 4%, more than twice the rate it did during the comparable recession of 1981–82. Return on equity was close to 20%.
- GE Financial Services had another terrific year, with a 17% increase in earnings. Seventeen of its 22 businesses grew earnings—11 of them with strong double-digit growth.
- Industrial and Power Systems, Lighting, Medical Systems and Information Services compiled powerful double-digit sales increases, much of it offshore. GE exports increased 21% to $8.6 billion, making a strong positive contribution to the U.S. balance of trade.
- And our share owners were rewarded with a 38% total return in '91, including an 8% increase in the dividend.

There were other significant achievements. Most of our businesses overcame much of the negative effect of weak markets with strong productivity, but we did have a few misses as well.

NBC saw a decline in ratings, and that, in combination with a soft advertising market, made for a significant decline in earnings.

Motors and Plastics, because of weak markets and poor productivity, also had a very difficult year. And, finally, two of GE Financial Services' 22 businesses—Commercial Real Estate and Corporate Finance (leveraged buyouts)—were not immune to the endemic problems in those investment areas. Real estate produced only a small profit and LBOs incurred a modest loss.

But enough of the numbers from '91. It's over.

1991 did, however, once again remind us how absolutely critical productivity growth is in the brutally Darwinian global market-places in which virtually all of our businesses compete. We are aware, for instance, that if we had the same productivity growth in '90 and '91 that we had in '80 and '81, our '91 earnings would have been more like $3 billion rather than $4.435 billion. We also are acutely aware that, without productivity growth, it is possible to lose in 24 months businesses that took a half-century, or a century, to build. Productivity growth is essential to industrial survival.

But to increase productivity, you first have to clear away all the impediments that keep you from its achievement—primarily the management layers, functional boundaries and all the other trappings of bureaucracy.

We've been trumpeting the removal of bureaucracy and layers at GE for several years now— and we did take out "Sectors," "Groups" and other superstructure— but much more remains; and, unfortunately, it is still possible to find documents around GE businesses that look like something out of the National Archives, with five, 10 or even more signatures necessary before action can be taken. In some businesses, you might still encounter many layers of management in a small area— boiler operators reporting to the supervisor of boilers, who reports to the utility manager, who reports to the manager of plant services, who reports to the plant manager, and so on.

Layers insulate. They slow things down. They garble. Leaders in highly layered organizations are like people who wear several sweaters outside on a freezing winter day. They remain warm and comfortable but are blissfully ignorant of the realities of their environment. They couldn't be further from what's going on.

Layers are symptoms of a century-old tradition at GE of rewarding people with titles. Giving someone a "manager" title could be likened to issuing a building permit—the functional walls and management floors begin construction, the procedural cement is poured, the no-trespassing signs are posted. Today, more and more, we're cutting back on useless titles, and we're rewarding people based on what they contribute—the quality of their ideas and their ability to implement them—rather than on what they control.

We've made our most significant progress breaking down the horizontal barriers that interrupt the flow within and among businesses. We wrote last year of a remarkable method of compressing product cycle times that we discovered in an appliance company in New Zealand, tested in our Canadian affiliate and then brought to our huge appliance operation in Louisville. That effort, which we call Quick Response, has been an astonishing success in which every function in the business—finance, distribution, consumer service, marketing and manufacturing— worked together to reduce average inventory by $200 million, to speed up the order-to-delivery cycle time from 18 weeks to five weeks and to move that team closer toward a shared vision—building appliances virtually to order—a three-day cycle. And as this effort was unfolding, GE teams from all of our other manufacturing businesses moved to Louisville for up to a year, became deeply involved in the project and now are home using this experience to accelerate their own processes.

Barriers are coming down all around the Company. In Medical Systems, our ultrasound technology is advancing rapidly because of an influx of sonar experts from Aerospace, and scores of military aircraft engineers have moved from Aircraft Engines to help Power Systems cope with the explosive worldwide demand for our advanced gas turbines.

Finally, last year saw the transfer of leadership in four of our 13 big businesses, with the new leaders coming from other GE businesses, bringing with them fresh, recently tested ideas and proven team-building skills.

Whether the flow is people from Aerospace to Medical or technology from Aircraft Engines to Power Systems or key management transfers, the objective is the same—mining the enormous value that exists all over the Company. GE's diversity creates a huge laboratory of innovation and ideas that reside in each of the businesses, and mining them is both our challenge and an awesome opportunity. Boundaryless behavior is what integrates us and turns this opportunity into reality, creating the real value of a multibusiness company—the big competitive advantage we call Integrated Diversity.

Boundary-busting does something else for us. It makes us **faster**.

There is something about speed that transcends its obvious business benefits of greater cash flow, greater profitability, higher share due to greater customer responsiveness and more capacity from cycle time reductions.

Speed exhilarates and energizes. Whether it be fast cars, fast boats, downhill skiing or a business process, speed injects fun and excitement into an otherwise routine activity. This is particularly true in business, where speed tends to propel ideas and drive processes right through functional barriers, sweeping bureaucrats and their impediments aside in the rush to get to the marketplace. Speed helps force a company "outside of itself" and prevents the inward focus that institutions tend to develop as they get bigger. In some businesses, the bureaucracy can warp priorities to the point that a pat on the back from the "boss" and a stick in the eye from a customer amounts to a pretty good day for an employee.

We say "some" businesses—but not all. In 1991, we shared best practices with a number of great companies. We learned something everywhere, but nowhere did we learn as much as at Wal-Mart. Sam Walton and his strong team are something very special. Many of our management teams spent time there observing the speed, the bias for action, the utter customer fixation that drives Wal-Mart; and despite our progress, we came back feeling a bit plodding and ponderous, a little envious, but, ultimately, fiercely determined that we're going to do whatever it takes to get that fast.

And Work-Out is still the process that will help get us there.

Work-Out began three years ago with baby steps: a series of New England-style town meetings with people of every conceivable rank and function chipping away at the bureaucratic barnacles and nonsense that develop on all institutions as they age and grow—wasteful paperwork, duplication, unnecessary approvals and the like. After the initial stages and modest progress, we began to move cautiously into team analyses of how specific functions and processes within businesses could be done better and, above all, faster. Customers were eventually invited into the process as were suppliers.

For a couple of years, we resisted the traditional GE predilection to quantify and measure Work-Out, and, in truth, there was little beyond the anecdotal and atmospheric to report. For a year or so, individual Work-Out

environments seemed to just sit there, as one observer noted, like popcorn kernels in a warm pan. The cynics no doubt believed the warmth came only from the hot air of Company rhetoric. **But all that time, trust was building, confidence was growing and teams were coming together.** Then, suddenly, things began to pop, here and there, with big ideas, process breakthroughs; and today they roar almost everywhere, with both radical transformations in the way we do business and with tangible business results. The Quick Response breakthrough at our Appliances operation would still be years away—perhaps unreachable—without the cooperative team approach Work-Out creates.

In Lynn, Mass., a century-old GE location that traditionally has been a sore spot in labor-management relations, Work-Out has begun to transform the climate into a much more productive atmosphere of mutual respect and cooperation. "We versus them" is increasingly coming to mean GE versus the competition. In 1987, at the Lynn plant, a combustor—a key part of a jet engine—took 30 weeks to make. Through Work-Out, that process was down to eight weeks in early '91; now it's four weeks, and the teams that run it are talking **10 days**. Hardware product cycles are now down an average of 20% across the business, with 50% clearly in sight.

And in our Schenectady turbine plant, another site with a century-old tradition of mistrust between labor and management, Work-Out has grown a team effort that is improving productivity beyond anything we ever envisioned. Just to name one area, in the critical steam turbine bucket machinery center, teams of hourly employees now run, without supervision, $20 million worth of new milling machines that they specified, tested and approved for purchase. The cycle time for the operation has dropped 80%. It is embarrassing to reflect that for probably 80 or 90 years, we've been dictating equipment needs and managing people who knew how to do things much better and faster than we did.

All around this Company in large plants like Schenectady, Lynn and Louisville and in scores of smaller sites like Florence and Salisbury in the Carolinas, Decatur, Ala., and in many other places, compulsive managing and mutual mistrust are giving way to real teamwork. GE has become faster and more energized than any of us ever thought possible.

If one vignette typifies how Work-Out has transformed how we work together in this Company, it is

this: Late in '91 at a best-practices session at our management school at Crotonville, N.Y., two of the key lecturers on the subject of productivity were two of the toughest union officers we face across any table. One of these leaders told the group he used to have three clearly defined enemies in his life—the IRS, Russians and GE management—but with the way things had changed, only the IRS retains that status. Both GE management and the Russians are doing a lot better.

The transformation that is sweeping our Company is not complicated in theory or even original. Much of the intellectual underpinning of Work-Out consists of ideas like worker involvement, trust and empowerment—shopworn and even platitudinous concepts. The difference is that our whole organization is, in fact, living them . . . every day! Most of our 284,000-member Company are, in fact, using soft concepts today as competitive weapons and are winning with them, rather than just inscribing them on coffee mugs and T-shirts.

Yes, there are pockets where things haven't changed, and no, not everyone has been empowered, but the momentum is unmistakable, and we are determined to make it irreversible.

This is a long road we are on, and a difficult one. Trust and respect take years to build, and no time at all to destroy. In the first half of the 1980s, we restructured this Company and changed its physical make-up. That was the easy part. In the last several years, our challenge has been to **change ourselves**—an infinitely more difficult task that, frankly, not all of us in leadership positions are capable of.

Over the past several years, we've wrestled at all levels of this Company with the question of what we are and what we want to be. Out of these discussions, and through our experiences, we've agreed upon a set of values we believe we will need to take this Company forward, rapidly, through the 1990s and beyond.

In our view, leaders, whether on the shop floor or at the tops of our businesses, can be characterized in at least four ways.

The first is one who delivers on commitments—financial or otherwise—and shares the values of our Company. His or her future is an easy call. Onward and upward.

The second type of leader is one who does not meet commitments and does not share our values. Not as pleasant a call, but equally easy.

The third is one who misses commitments but shares the values. He or she usually gets a second chance, preferably in a different environment.

Then there's the fourth type—the most difficult for many of us to deal with. That leader delivers on

---

GE Values . . . GE Leaders throughout the Company:

- Create a clear, simple, reality-based, customer-focused vision and are able to communicate it straight-forwardly to all constituencies.
- Understand accountability and com-mitment and are decisive . . . set and meet aggressive targets . . . always with unyielding integrity.
- Have a passion for excel-lence . . . hate bureaucracy and all the nonsense that comes with it.
- Have the self-confidence to em-power others and behave in a boundaryless fashion . . . believe in and are committed to Work-Out as a means of empowerment . . . are open to ideas from anywhere.

- Have, or have the capacity to develop, global brains and global sensitivity and are comfortable building diverse global teams.
- Stimulate and relish change . . . are not frightened or or paralyzed by it. See change as opportunity, not just a threat.
- Have enormous energy and the ability to energize and invigorate others. Understand speed as a com-petitive advantage and see the total organizational benefits that can be derived from a focus on speed.

commitments, makes all the numbers, but doesn't share the values we must have. This is the individual who typically forces performance out of people rather than inspires it: the autocrat, the big shot, the tyrant. Too often all of us have looked the other way— tolerated these "Type 4" managers because "they always deliver"—at least in the short term.

And perhaps this type was more acceptable in easier times, but in an environment where we must have every good idea from every man and woman in the organization, we cannot afford management styles that suppress and intimidate. Whether we can convince and help these managers to change—recognizing how difficult that can be—or part company with them if they cannot will be the ultimate test of our commitment to the transformation of this Company and will determine the future of the mutual trust and respect we are building. In 1991, we continued to improve our personnel management to achieve much better balance between values and "numbers." That balance will change further in '92 and beyond, because we know that without leaders who "walk the talk," all of our plans, promises and dreams for the future are just that—talk.

In the first week of 1992, 450 men and women who lead our Company convened from around the world to share best practices and review our course for the coming year. It was a very special event, with a unique and spontaneous atmosphere—one we had never quite felt before. It is striking that coming off one of the most brutal economic years most of us can remember, the mood at that meeting was one of exhilaration and bound-less confidence. The commitment to speed and boundarylessness was at a new high.

We put our values, our people and our Company to the test in '91. By our measure, at least, we passed with flying colors. We grew during a bad recession, and as we see recovery on the horizon, it is diffi-cult not to be very, very optimistic about our future.

Thanks for your support.

John F. Welch, Jr.
Chairman of the Board
and Chief Executive Officer

Edward E. Hood, Jr.
Vice Chairman of the Board
and Executive Officer

FEBRUARY 14, 1992

To Our Share Owners

1992 was another strong year for GE in a difficult global economic environment. There is nothing like hard times to try out soft concepts; nothing like reality to test rhetoric.

We have produced our fair share—maybe more—of rhetoric over the recent past, discussing soft values with you in this report and struggling among ourselves at all levels of GE to distill just what the characteristics of a winning company are, what makes work exciting and fulfilling rather than just tedious drudgery, and what kind of leadership traits will galvanize and inspire an organization.

In 1992, these soft values continued to produce hard numbers, and much of our rhetoric rolled into action.

- Consolidated revenues were $62.202 billion, up 3%.
- Earnings were $4.725 billion in 1992, up $290 million or 7%.
- Earnings per share were $5.51, up 8%.
- Total cost productivity, despite the recession, was 4½%, three times the level achieved during the last recession of the early 1980s. This level of productivity maintains the two-to-threefold improvement we've been seeing since we started a cultural thrust called Work-Out several years ago.
- The quickening of the pace of the Company, a staple of our rhetoric in past years, has turned into the reality of faster inventory turns across the businesses, producing $5.3 billion in cash flow from operations—an all-time record for GE.
- Industrial and Power Systems, Plastics and Medical Systems turned in double-digit earnings growth; and the 22 entrepreneurial businesses of GE Capital Services continued their powerful growth in leasing, credit card services, property management, reinsurance, and scores of value-added, "non-banking" activities, producing 18% growth in net earnings. Kidder, Peabody had its second consecutive year of record earnings.

- Our exports of $8.8 billion enabled us to make a nearly $6 billion positive contribution to the U.S. balance of trade.
- The reality of the global marketplace as our true arena was reinforced by a major shift of senior management and resources toward India, Southeast Asia, China and Mexico—the mega-markets of the 21st century and the opportunities of today. We continue to move the center of gravity of GE in the direction of these high-growth markets.
- In November, we agreed to combine our Aerospace business with that of Martin Marietta, creating the world's number-one aerospace electronics company, a new competitor with double the assets and a fraction of the overhead of its two components. When this combination is approved in 1993, GE will have a one-billion-dollar investment in the new company.

These events and numbers were looked on favorably by the market and—along with two dividend increases during the year—rewarded GE share owners with a return of 15%.

Over the years we've analyzed our own Company, with as much objectivity as we can muster, and we've studied and visited hundreds of companies around the globe—either in acquisition efforts or just to learn from them. In doing so, we find that while we like some of the attributes of big companies— particularly their scale and market-place reach—it is small companies that create excitement while big companies, too often, just impress.

What do we like about small companies?

Most small companies are un-cluttered, simple, informal. They thrive on passion and ridicule bureaucracy. Small companies grow on good ideas—regardless of their source. They need every-one, involve everyone, and reward or remove people based on their contribution to winning. Small companies dream big dreams and set the bar high—increments and fractions don't interest them.

We love the way small companies communicate: with simple, straight-forward, passionate argument rather than jargon-filled memos, "putting it in channels," "running it up the flag-pole" and, worst of all, the polite deference to the small ideas that too often come from big offices in big companies.

Everyone in a small company knows the customers—their likes, dislikes and needs—because the customer's thumbs up-or-down means the difference between a small company becoming a bigger company tomorrow—or no company at all.

It comes down to something very simple: small companies have to face into the reality of the market every day, and when they move, they have to move with speed. Their survival is on the line.

We come back again and again to that small company advantage: **speed**. Speed, which brings with it an urgency, an exhilaration and a focus on what really matters, is a vaccine against bureaucracy and lethargy. It is the simple ingredient that drives small companies, and it is the lack of speed that gets big companies in trouble.

But "big" does have its advantages. Big allows us, for example, to spend billions on developing the new GE90 jet engine, or the next-generation gas turbine, or Positron Emission Tomography (PET) diagnostic imaging machines—products that sometimes take years of investment before they begin producing returns.

Size gives us staying power through market cycles in big, promising businesses. It permitted us to invest heavily in Power Systems during several down years in the 1980s, which allowed the business to emerge healthy and ready to capitalize on the global boom now in progress. Size will allow continued heavy investment in new products as GE Aircraft Engines goes through an early 1990s down-cycle, and will permit that business to maintain global leadership throughout that cycle and into the 21st century.

Size gives us the resources to invest over a half-billion dollars a year on education: cultivating, at every level in the organization, the human capital we must have to win.

Offshore, "big" permits us to form partnerships with the best of the large companies, and large countries, and to invest for the long term in nations such as India, Mexico and the emerging industrial powers of South Asia—while still putting billions of dollars into the research and development of products that will be in demand in tomorrow's markets.

But size is no longer the trump card it once was in today's brutally competitive world marketplace— a marketplace that is unimpressed with logos and sales numbers but demands, instead, value and performance.

What we are trying relentlessly to do is get that small-company **soul**—and small-company **speed**— inside our big-company body.

But how do you get that speed in a $60 billion company with 230,000 employees competing all over the earth? Before you begin to accelerate an organization, you have to take the brakes off. The brakes in our case are the boundaries, the barriers, the fiefdoms, the remnants of a bureaucracy that slow us down.

That's what that cumbersome word "boundaryless" is all about and why we focus on it so much in this letter and in every hour of our work day. **"Boundarylessness" is a behavior definer**, a way of getting people outside of their organizational boxes and offices and working together, faster. It also gets us closer to our customers, our suppliers—closer to all of the constituencies upon which we depend.

This behavior definer led us to a process called Work-Out that we've been using for four years now to capture good ideas and run with them—whether their originator is a crane operator on the line or some company on the other side of the earth. Work-Out has been the vehicle that has allowed us to act on a series of innovative ways of removing barriers—always with an eye to becoming faster—becoming better.

These boundaryless initiatives are changing the way our businesses operate. For example:

Quick Response. This is a cycle-time reduction technique we adapted from our Canadian affiliate, which found it in an appliance company in New Zealand, which got it from who-knows-where. Quick Response erases most of the barriers between the functions of our businesses—manufacturing, finance, etc.—and the customers, and has taken GE Appliances from an 18-week order-to-delivery cycle to a 3½-week cycle at the present—on the way to three days. Quick Response has reduced average inventory in GE Appliances 50%, or almost $400 million, and will allow it to break through the 10-turn barrier in 1993—almost double the rate of 1989.

Co-location. Co-location is the ultimate boundaryless behavior and is as unsophisticated as can be: We tear all the walls down and put teams from all functions together in one room to bring new products to life. One room, one coffee-pot, one team, one shared mission.

The standard lament of manufacturing—"What idiot designed this thing?"—is no longer heard because the product is now designed with manufacturing, with marketing, with suppliers, and often with the customers themselves.

GE Medical Systems is using this boundaryless technique to design and manufacture its new ultrasound products. The Profile appliance line was developed this way, as was the GE90 jet engine. Before long it will be the way GE develops **everything** it makes, and every service it sells.

We are finding that once people leave their cherished offices, work as a team and share the excitement and rewards that belong to winning teams, they never want to go back.

Quick Market Intelligence. Too many people in big companies come through the gate each morning to serve the internal bureaucracy. Customers—if they are thought of at all—are some vague abstraction. QMI changes all that. It is a process that gives every salesperson direct access, every Friday, to the key managers and the CEO of the business, to lay out customer problems and needs. The product of the meeting is not deep or strategic in nature, but action— a response to the customer right away. The QMI routine turns the face of everyone in the organization toward that marketplace and, by doing so, makes the bureaucracy stand out for what it really is: silly, irrelevant and even malevolent in its interference in the process of serving customers.

Quick Market Intelligence is our term for the magnificent boundary-busting technique pioneered by Wal-Mart that allows the entire Company to understand, to sense, to touch the changing desires of the customer and to act on them in almost real time. The rhythm of the Wal-Mart intelligence-action cycle encourages experimentation, because whatever doesn't work is never in place for more than a week.

QMI has rooted quickly in long-cycle and short-cycle businesses as diverse as Medical Systems, Lighting, Plastics and Power Systems, and it is dramatically increasing the speed of those businesses. That QMI rhythm— that weekly pulsing of customer needs—will become the rhythm of GE in the years to come and one of the key drivers of our top-line growth. The secret of Wal-Mart is that it keeps its small-company speed and behavior as it grows bigger. QMI is a chance for us to get bigger—by acting smaller.

Rewards. In small companies the punishments and rewards of the marketplace come quickly. If the product doesn't win, the team doesn't eat. If the product wins big, the rewards are substantial—often the stuff of legend.

Stock options are the most powerful tool we have in the Company to approximate small-company incentive systems. In the early 1980s, only 400 of our senior executives held them. We've also broken that barrier, and today, more than 13,000 of our top performers, from foremen to secretaries to newly hired engineers and salespeople, hold stock options. These options are a key part of the linkage we are trying to forge between what a person does on the job every day and winning in the marketplace—and between that winning and the rewards that come with it—rewards felt in the soul as well as the wallet.

Boundaries are crashing down everywhere around this Company. Every day people from finance, manufacturing and sales are taking off their functional uniforms and teaming up to meet common challenges. The face of the customers, and the customers' needs, have become as real, as vivid and as urgent to everyone in the organization as they are to the salespeople who meet with them.

Nowhere can we quantify the results of boundaryless behavior better than in **productivity** and **globalization**.

The removal of functional barriers within our businesses—and between our businesses and their suppliers and customers—has produced productivity figures over the last five years double or triple those of the early 1980s.

In globalization, the overcoming of geographic and cultural barriers has given us, over the past five years, a double-digit average annual growth rate in revenues outside the United States.

Of course, we haven't rid ourselves of all our turf battles and barriers; and, sure, some boundaries remain. And there is one boundary that we continue to maintain, strengthen and make clear to everyone—the boundary that says that no matter how hard we compete—here and around the world—not one foot must ever step outside the line of absolute integrity.

But all the other boundaries are fair game, and **the biggest has already fallen**: the one between us and the world full of good ideas we didn't happen to come up with. Parochialism—"Not Invented Here"—is dead at GE—it has been for a while. We don't claim to be the global fountainhead of management thought, but we may be the world's thirstiest pursuer of big ideas—from whatever their source—and we're not shy about adopting and adapting them. Whether it's QMI from Wal-Mart, or co-location from garage shops, or the "Quick Response" technique from New Zealand, or some blinding insight from some formerly quiet machine operator at a Work-Out session—if it looks like it might make us faster—we try it. And if it works, we spread it across every business in this Company—**fast**.

As we look, eagerly, toward '93 and beyond, we ask every person in every business to ask the tough questions leaders must ask themselves every day:

- Am I facing reality? Am I seeing the situation the way it really is—or the way I wish, or hope, it were? Am I painting flattering self-portraits, or looking honestly in that cold mirror? And when I have grasped the reality, then comes the big, defining question: Am I **acting** on it fast enough?
- Do I see a competitor beating us with lower prices and mutter nervously that "he's nuts" or "he's dumping"—when the real answer is: "he's got lower costs, and I better get my costs down now, or I'm gone"?
- Do I see other competitors racing one new product after another into the marketplace and take comfort in deducing they're "spending too much on product development"? Or do I focus on what they are really doing—increasing the speed of their product development cycle, and beating me to the marketplace?
- Do I wait in hope of some dozing manager suddenly springing into action when he hasn't moved in 10 years? Do I "wish" that the autocrat who sits on people all morning and puts barriers between them all afternoon will change his spots? Or is the reality that I lack the courage to make

the tough personnel calls that I know I have to make if we're going to win?
- Do I shrug in resignation at slow growth, and wait for new government bureaucrats to replace old government bureaucrats and "fix the economy"? Or is the reality that slow growth is largely a mindset that is unknown in start-up businesses and must be unacceptable in big ones?
- Above all, do I recognize the pace of change, which is making obsolete and wrong today what was contemporary and right yesterday? Do I welcome change for the opportunity it always brings—or am I frightened and paralyzed by it?

When most of us look at our careers, if we are honest with ourselves about decisions we've made, changes we've brought about, we have to acknowledge that there was much wishing and hoping and temporizing that has slowed us in coming to grips with reality. But beyond that, our biggest regrets—sometimes our most bitter ones—are often that once we defined reality, and brought it into focus—we didn't act fast enough, boldly enough.

That's what the best companies do best, and our challenge at GE for '93 and beyond is clear—to ignite this big Company with passion, hunger, appetite for change, customer focus, and, above all, the speed to see **reality** more clearly and to act on it **faster**.

Translating the need for speed, for reality, into the language and practices that change people's behavior, that encourage them to renew themselves, to walk through that door every day as if it were Monday morning on a new job—that's what leadership in this Company is all about. No matter how many ideas we try, it all comes back to people—their ideas, their motivation, their passion to win.

Our unending drive to build a boundaryless, high-spirited Company is moving us faster every day in the direction of what we want passionately to become—the world's most competitive global enterprise.

Thanks for your support.

John F. Welch, Jr.
Chairman of the Board and
Chief Executive Officer

Paolo Fresco
Vice Chairman of the Board
and Executive Officer

FEBRUARY 12, 1993

To Our Share Owners

1993 was a very good year for your Company, a year when our soft initiatives turned increasingly into hard results. Despite economic weakness in several of our global markets, we posted our best business results in a Company history that stretches back more than a century.

- Consolidated revenues were up 6% to $60.6 billion.
- Earnings, before a mandated accounting change for employee benefits, were up 10% to nearly $5.2 billion, and, more importantly, the 12 businesses remaining after our Aerospace divestiture grew earnings 16% before restructuring provisions.
- Ten of our 12 businesses had double-digit earnings growth. Only Aircraft Engines, suffering from the effects of a weak commercial engine market and declining defense expenditures, had lower earnings; but even this business had a good year in a difficult market, gaining market share and still producing about $800 million in operating profit.
- The earnings increases were led by GE Capital Services, NBC, Plastics and Power Generation. Kidder, Peabody had its third straight year of record earnings, and two highly visible strategic European acquisitions—Tungsram, the Hungarian lighting business, and GE Medical Systems-Europe—had major turnarounds, generating nearly $100 million more in net income than in 1992.
- Operating margin from ongoing operations grew a full point to 12.5%, a historic high, but just another step toward our stretch target of 15%. All of our businesses other than Aircraft Engines had increases of more than one point.
- Inventory turns, a key measure of speed, rose almost a full point to 6 turns on the way to our stretch target of 10 turns.
- Free cash flow, after dividends and capital expenditures, was

$2.3 billion, the second consecutive year of cash flow over $2 billion.

- Productivity was 3.8% and, excluding Aircraft Engines, was more than 5% for the other businesses combined.

The market responded to these results and rewarded our share owners with a 26% return on their investment in 1993.

The reason for this level of performance and, more importantly, for this accelerating momentum is not some complex business strategy, some unique technology breakthrough, or some new market trend. It's much simpler than that.

We run this Company on a simple premise: the only way to win, in the brutally competitive global environment in which we operate, is to get **more output** from **less input** in all 12 of our businesses and, by doing so, become the lowest-cost producer of high-quality goods and services in the world.

We believe the only way to gain more output from less input—to grow and win—is to **engage every mind within our businesses**—exciting, energizing, involving and rewarding everyone. That is the foundation and philosophy upon which our Company is now operating. While we have a long

way to go before philosophy becomes total reality, our progress has come faster than the most optimistic among us expected.

We are betting everything on our people—empowering them, giving them the resources and getting out of their way—and the numbers tell us that this focus has not only pointed us in the right direction but is providing us with a momentum that is accelerating.

With this objective of involving everyone, we use three operating principles to define the atmosphere and behavior at GE:

- **Boundaryless** . . . in all our behavior;
- **Speed** . . . in everything we do;
- **Stretch** . . . in every target we set.

Boundaryless behavior is the soul of today's GE. We've described it to you in past years. Simply put, people seem compelled to build layers and walls between themselves and others, and that human tendency tends to be magnified in large, old institutions like ours. These walls cramp people, inhibit creativity, waste time, restrict vision, smother dreams and, above all, slow things down.

The challenge is to chip away at and eventually break down these walls and barriers, both among ourselves and between ourselves and the outside world. The progress we've made so far has released a flood of ideas that is improving every operation in our Company. We've adapted new product introduction techniques from Chrysler and Canon, effective sourcing techniques from GM and Toyota, and approaches to quality from Motorola and Ford. We've moved more effectively into the immense potential markets of China with advice and best practices from pioneers like IBM, Johnson & Johnson, Xerox and others.

The removal of those walls means we involve suppliers as participants in our design and manufacturing processes rather than treat them as vendors, left to cool their heels in waiting rooms. It means having major launch customers like British Airways, Tokyo Electric Power or CSX in the room and involved in the design of a new jet engine, a revolutionary gas turbine or a new AC locomotive, or a panel of doctors helping us develop a new ultrasound system.

Internally, boundaryless behavior means piercing the walls of 100-year-old fiefdoms and empires called finance, engineering, manufacturing, marketing, and gathering teams from all those functions in one room, with one shared coffee pot, one shared vision and one consuming passion—to design the world's best jet engine, or ultrasound machine, or refrigerator.

Boundaryless behavior shows up in the actions of a woman from our Appliances business in Hong Kong helping NBC with contacts needed to develop a satellite television service in Asia. On a larger scale, it means labor and management joining hands in the unprofitable Appliance Park complex in Louisville in a joint effort to "Save the Park," with a combination of labor practice changes and GE investment—not two people making a "deal," but 10,721 making a commitment.

And finally, boundaryless behavior means exploiting one of the unmatchable advantages a multibusiness GE has over almost every other company in the world. Boundaryless behavior combines 12 huge global businesses—each number one or number two in its markets—into a vast laboratory whose principal product is new ideas, coupled with a common commitment to spread them throughout the Company.

Some have argued that single-product businesses have a focus that gives them an advantage over multibusiness companies like our own—and perhaps they would have, but only if we neglect our own overriding advantage: the ability to share the ideas that are the result of wide and rich input from a multitude of global sources.

GE businesses share technology, design, compensation and personnel evaluation systems, manufacturing practices, and customer and country knowledge. Gas Turbines shares manufacturing technology with Aircraft Engines; Motors and Transportation Systems work together on new locomotive propulsion systems; Lighting and Medical Systems collaborate to improve x-ray tube processes; and GE Capital provides innovative financing packages that help all our businesses around the globe. These are just a few of the thousands of examples of how our businesses work together. Supporting all this is a management system that fosters and rewards this sharing and teamwork, and, increasingly, a culture that makes it reflexive and natural at every level and corner of our Company.

When we began our pursuit of boundarylessness, we believed that the boundaries just described—the walls, if you will—would be the most difficult to eliminate, while the hierarchical management layers would be the easiest because they could simply be taken out by directive. The big, visible layers at the top of the Company—Sectors, Groups and the like—were easy to get rid of, but deeper within the businesses, the layers—formal and informal—are not only hard to remove, they are often hard to find.

The compulsion to manage, to control, to direct, is a powerful one, reinforced by a century-old tradition at GE of measuring one's self-worth by how many people "work for you" and whether or not the word "manager" appears in your title. The highest compliment you could give GE managers a few years ago was to say they were "on top of things" or had gotten "their arms around them." These techniques, more useful in tackling people than coaching them, are difficult to get rid of.

What we are looking for today at GE are leaders at every level who can energize, excite and coach rather than enervate, depress and control. And never has this atmosphere been more critical. Today, everyone must be engaged if we are to win. The kind of people we need in this Company are those unwilling to "put in their time" in the bowels of the bureaucracy, or grunt along under the heel of some autocrat for years, before they get a chance to make decisions, try something and be rewarded in their souls as well as their wallets.

In some difficult cases this means parting company with some impressive people—Heisman Trophy candidates, to use an American football expression—who won't block for others or play as part of a team. Their debilitating effect on the team can outweigh the benefits of their individual talent. Leaders at GE are now subject to what we call a 360° evaluation, meaning they are rated not just by those above them, but by their peers and their subordinates as well. This has become a powerful tool for detecting and changing those who "smile up and kick down." To be blunt, the two quickest ways to part company with GE are, one, to commit an integrity violation, or two, to be a controlling, turf-defending, oppressive manager who can't change and who saps and squeezes people rather than excites and draws out their energy and creativity. We can't force that creativity and energy from our teams—they have to give it—but we have to have it to win.

To this end, we have also become boundaryless in our rewards and recognition systems. Stock options, once awarded to just a few hundred executives, are now in the hands of more than 15,000 GE employees whose contributions have become visible because of team-like work environments and flatter organizations. Speakers at big Company meetings are selected based on what they know that can be shared, borrowed and expanded on—rather than on their title or rank. Just a few years ago we said that "the people closest to the work know it best," and we said it as if we had produced some deep

insight. Today, it's just a common assumption across the Company.

In a boundaryless atmosphere, a good idea sprouts and blossoms and is nurtured by all, and no one cares where the seed came from. You can feel the explosion of energy and creativity that flows over every process in a business when "not-invented-here" is swept aside, and in its place the behavior that brings reward and recognition is instead the execution or transfer or improvement of a good idea, no matter what its source.

Ideas are now judged at GE on the basis of their quality rather than the altitude of their origin. The status-defining tie on a manager at a GE plant is now about as fashionable as a leisure suit. And because informality is warming every corner of our Company, today's GE has become both a lot more fun to work at—and a lot faster.

Speed is the second element we are after in every one of our operations. A fast organization has the advantage of relishing change because of the constant opportunity it presents. The faster the pace of change, the bigger the advantage.

With the drag and nonsense of boundaries, management layers, bureaucracy, and formality cleared, the organization automatically accelerates. Where we once relied on "moonshot" development programs that took years to reach the market, new GE products are now coming out with drumbeat rapidity. There is now a new product announcement at Appliances every 90 days—unthinkable years ago. The GE90, the world's most powerful commercial jet engine, was designed and built in one-half the normal time, by a boundaryless team. Another team developed a breakthrough ultrasound innovation in less than a year-and-a-half. We designed and built a new AC locomotive in 18 months. We're developing an absolute cascade of new energy-efficient lighting products, plastics for the construction industry, and revolutionary turbines that extend the limits of thermodynamics and materials.

While speed has had its most striking impact on our New Product Introduction process—the driver of tomorrow's top-line growth—its most immediate quantitative impact has been on our asset management. Focusing on the speed of our Order-to-Remittance cycle—from time of order to when we get paid—has increased our inventory turns 27% in two years, throwing off almost $2 billion in cash in the process. Every single-digit improvement in inventory turns produces $1 billion in cash to reinvest for tomorrow.

Speed "redefines capacity," reducing plant and equipment investment. In the past three years, our faster pace has freed up nearly five million square feet of manufacturing space across the Company. To a business like Plastics, that has meant a savings of nearly one-half billion dollars that would have been required for new capacity—like getting a new plant, free.

Speed is allowing us to shift the center of gravity of the Company rapidly toward the high-growth areas of the world, particularly in Asia. Forty percent of our sales now come from outside the United States, up from 30% just five years ago. GE's non-U.S. sales have grown at a compounded rate of almost 10% over the past five years. Lighting, one of our oldest businesses, which less than five years ago had 21% of its sales outside the U.S., today sells 38% in the non-U.S. global market.

And finally, speed, in the form of a technique called Quick Market Intelligence, originally learned from Wal-Mart and evolved and adapted in our businesses, has GE leadership at all levels of the Company, in every business, living in the field with customers. The center of gravity in all our businesses is not only shifting from the U.S. to the world; it's shifting, everywhere, from the office to the field.

The speed generated by a boundaryless organization makes possible, and leads naturally to, our third operating principle—which we call stretch, or reach.

Stretch is a concept that would have produced smirks, if not laughter, in the GE of three or four years ago, because it essentially means using dreams to set business targets—with no real idea of how to get there. If you do know how to get there—it's not a stretch target. We certainly didn't have a clue how we were going to get to 10 inventory turns when we set that target. But we're getting there, and as soon as we become sure we can do it—it's time for another stretch. The CEO of Yokogawa, our Japanese partner in the Medical Systems business, calls this concept "bullet-train thinking," i.e., if you want a ten-miles-per-hour increase in train speed, you tinker with horsepower—but if you want to **double its speed**, you have to break out of both conventional thinking and conventional performance expectations.

Stretch allows organizations to set the bar higher than they ever dreamed possible. Whether it be a 100-fold improvement in quality, 10-fold reduction in product development time or margin rates never before dreamed of—the openness, candor and trust of a boundaryless, fast company allows us to hang those dreams out there, in view of everyone, so that we can all reach for them together.

We used to timidly nudge the peanut along, setting goals of moving from, say, 4.73 inventory turns to 4.91, or from 8.53% operating margin to 8.92%; and then indulge in time-consuming, high-level, bureaucratic negotiations to move the number a few hundredths one way or the other. The point is—it didn't matter. Arguing over these petty numbers in conference rooms certainly didn't inspire the people on the shop or office floor who had to deliver them—in most cases, they never even heard of them. We don't do that anymore. In a boundaryless organization with a bias for speed, decimal points are a bore. They inspire or challenge no one, capture no imaginations. We're aiming at 10 inventory turns, at 15% operating margins, and at the introduction of more new products in the next two years than we've developed in the last ten. In a company that now rewards progress toward stretch goals, rather than punishing shortfalls, the setting of these goals, and quantum leaps toward them, are daily events.

Across this Company, stretch targets are making seemingly impossible goals exciting, bringing out the best from our teams; and the pizza delivery people are getting rich as our people celebrate each milestone along the way to those targets. Celebrating success is a critical element in creating it, and we expect our teams to celebrate, celebrate, and celebrate again.

Putting this all together: boundaryless people, excited by speed and inspired by stretch dreams, have an **absolutely infinite capacity to improve everything**. While we are still learning as we go, and are under no illusions that we have all the answers, we really do have more than two hundred thousand people who get up every morning and come to work intent on finding a better way—every day.

The performance, the standards, the targets, the excitement levels at GE have all been moved to a higher plane than those of the Company you invested in just a few years

ago. We are raising the bar of performance and changing the basis of competition in every game we play. That is why we refer to your Company as "the new GE," and why, as our pace accelerates and our reach lengthens, we will, no doubt, be describing another "new GE" for you in the years ahead.

We enter 1994 with 222,000 self-confident people, proud of our past, excited by our future, seeing change as opportunity and, most importantly, convinced that our best days are ahead of us.

John F. Welch, Jr.
Chairman of the Board and
Chief Executive Officer

Paolo Fresco
Vice Chairman of the Board
and Executive Officer

FEBRUARY 11, 1994

To Our Share Owners

GE had a great year in 1994, with the notable exception of the Kidder, Peabody issue. By any other measure, our 221,000 associates turned in their best performance in the Company's history.

- Earnings and earnings per share from ongoing operations were up 22%.
- Nine of our 12 businesses saw double-digit earnings growth; five of them were up more than 20%. Only Aircraft Engines, saddled with a weak commercial market and declining defense spending, saw a modest earnings decline, but the business still managed to produce more than one-half billion dollars in net income.
- GE revenues from outside the United States continued to outpace our domestic growth. In Europe, they totaled more than $9 billion in 1994. More importantly, our businesses are well positioned for another year of significant net income growth as the European economy continues to recover.

In Japan, we expanded our already substantial presence with a major financial services acquisition and the significant growth of our existing partnerships.

Globalization continued with double-digit top-line growth in the key emerging markets of Mexico, India, China and Southeast Asia. While there will, no doubt, be temporary setbacks on their road to full development, these countries represent the key growth markets of the next century, and we are committed to continue investing in them.

- NBC's cable assets continued their growth, with a valuation now exceeding $1.5 billion. Using the reach and resources of GE, the globalization of the network continued, with well over 60 million homes throughout Europe and the Middle East now being reached through NBC Super Channel. In Asia, NBC's new network is currently distributing programs from the United States and Europe, and, later in 1995, locally produced programming will come on stream from our new Hong Kong studio and be available in more than 25 Asian nations.

- A series of initiatives enabled the businesses to generate more than $2 billion in free cash flow for the third straight year. This enabled GE to undertake a second $5 billion stock buyback in five years, while still retaining our triple-A debt rating.

- In April 1994, the share owners approved a two-for-one stock split, the seventh split since the founding of the Company and the third in the past 12 years. In December, a 14% dividend increase was declared, making 1994 the 19th consecutive year of dividend increases.

These strong operating results, and the actions to enhance share owner value that they permit, are the result of the Company's commitment to involving everyone, a philosophy that is the core of our vision for the future.

Since the early 1980s, as the Company downsized in order to become more globally competitive, we often heard the question, "How much more can be squeezed from the lemon?" This zero-sum thinking did not foresee the immense reservoir of creativity and energy that flows from an engaged work force that increasingly em-

braces three fundamental operating behaviors.

We've described these three behaviors in past letters: boundarylessness, speed and stretch. They have evolved from philosophical, "soft," concepts into behaviors that deliver hard results, and they are the reason for both today's success and the enormous potential we see for tomorrow.

A few examples of where these soft concepts have delivered top- and bottom-line results:

Boundaryless behavior, an odd, awkward phrase just a few years ago, is increasingly a way of life at GE. It has led to an obsession for finding a better way—a better idea—be its source a colleague, another GE business, or another company across the street or on the other side of the globe that will share its ideas and practices with us.

- American Standard, a customer of our Motors and Industrial Systems business, has been using a technique called "Demand Flow Technology" to double and triple inventory turn rates and move toward a goal of zero working capital. GE teams have learned from American Standard and are obtaining dramatic results from Power Systems to Plastics to Medical Systems, producing a second consecutive year of double-digit improvement in working capital turnover.

- Yokogawa, our partner in the Medical Systems business, has been using "Bullet Train Thinking" to take 30–50% out of product costs over a two-year period. This technique, which employs "out-of-the-box" thinking and cross-functional teams dedicated to removing obstacles to cost reduction, is now fully operational in our Aircraft Engines business. This effort should lead this business to double-digit profitability growth in 1995, despite less-than-robust market conditions.

- "Quick Market Intelligence," the weekly direct customer feedback technique, was originally learned from Wal-Mart and implemented with great success in our Appliances business to improve asset turnover. "QMI" has now been adopted by a service business—GE Capital's Retailer Financial Services—in this instance to drive the quality of customer service in its credit card operations and help grow earnings more than 25% in 1994, with double-digit growth expectations for 1995.

- Caterpillar has dramatically reduced its service cost structure and new product introduction time through part standardization disciplines. The implementation of these disciplines is becoming key to the rapid new product introduction successes in our Appliances and Power Systems businesses, where product introduction cycle times have been cut by more than half.

- From Toshiba we have learned of its "Half-Movement"—half the parts, half the weight, in half the time—and tomorrow it will become a key element of engineering design philosophy at each of our businesses.

Boundaryless behavior has become the "right" behavior at GE, and aligned with this behavior is a rewards system that recognizes the adapter or implementer of an idea as much as its originator. Creating this open, sharing climate magnifies the enormous and unique advantage of a multibusiness GE, as our wide diversity of service and industrial businesses exchange an endless stream of new ideas and best practices.

Speed. Today's global environment, with its virtually real-time information exchanges, demands that an institution embrace speed. **Faster**, in almost every case, **is better**. From decision-making to deal-making to communications to product introduction, speed, more often than not, ends up being the competitive differentiator.

In new product introduction, a clear gauge with which to quantify speed, there are several important examples:

• The Lighting business introduced hundreds of new products, ranging from the expansion of its Halogen IR line, to a whole new range of compact fluorescents, to the introduction of GE/Motorola brand electronic fluorescent ballasts.

• Power Systems, a long-cycle business that used to be characterized by glacial product development, completed design of, and brought to market, three new gas turbine-generators in 1994.

• CNBC brought America's Talking, 14 hours a day of original programming, from a concept to on-the-air in less than six months.

• Product development in Medical Systems has gone from a two-year cycle to less than one, and now 70% of our computed tomography products are less than one year old.

• In locomotive manufacturing, the change from "DC" technology—the standard diesel locomotive propulsion for 30 years or so—to "AC" is, in many respects, as profound a change as from steam to diesel. This "traditional," century-old, long-cycle business

had an AC model locomotive on the tracks within 18 months, is changing out its entire product line and, in 1995, will be selling very little that it sold as recently as 1993.

Across every business, the focus on shorter cycles—on simply getting faster—has been the driver of our improved asset turnover rate and strong cash flow.

In an organization where boundarylessness, openness, informality and the use of ideas from anywhere—and speed—with its bias for action—are increasingly a way of life, the third operating principle—**stretch**—is a natural outgrowth.

Stretch, in its simplest form, says, "Nothing is impossible," and the setting of stretch targets inspires people and captures their imaginations.

Target setting at GE begins when business leaders at the beginning of the year set their stretch goals for things like income, cash flow and market share—given the contemporary circumstances of competition, the economy and all other external variables. Because this management team has been together for a long time, trust has grown, and trust is an indispensable ingredient that allows a business to set big stretch targets. GE business leaders do not walk around all year regretting the albatross of an impossible number they hung around their own necks. At the end of the year, the business is measured, not on whether it hit the stretch target, but on how well it did against the prior year, given the circumstances. Performance is measured against the world as it turned out to be: how well a business anticipated change and dealt with it, rather than against some "plan" or internal number negotiated a year earlier.

Stretch does not mean "commitments are out." Stretch can only occur in an environment where everyone is totally committed to a rigid set of core values—integrity, trust, quality, boundaryless behavior—and to outperforming every one of our global competitors in every market environment.

Stretch does mean we are not fixated on a meaningless, internally derived, annual budget number that does nothing but make bureaucrats comfortable.

A stretch atmosphere replaces a grim, heads-down determination to be as good as you have to be, and asks, instead, how good can you be?

"How good can we be?" was the question in 1991 when the Company set two big stretch targets: 10 inventory turns and 15% operating margins by the end of 1995. At that time, those two numbers represented big stretches—after all, it had taken over a century—since Edison's time—and we still hadn't reached five turns and had barely achieved an 11% operating margin.

Well, 1995 is upon us, and 10 turns may be just beyond our reach, but by year's end we'll be over nine. In GE today, this is not a "miss," a "broken commitment" or a "black eye"—but a triumph to be celebrated, an achievement that is providing the cash to finance the acquisitions we want and a stock buyback.

As for the 15% operating margin stretch target by 1995, it's possible, and we're all focused on reaching for it.

The point is, whether we hit our targets or not is not the issue. What does matter is that we've broken out of a 110-year pattern with stretch thinking, and we're on to new targets. The point is made even clearer when we read our letters to share owners from just a few years back. We now cringe at numbers we once crowed about, as they pale beside today's. And the most exciting thing is knowing that tomorrow's "stretches" will make today's numbers look anemic in light of where the Company will be at the time of the 1996 or 1997 letter.

As we look to 1995, we have launched a Company-wide

campaign to overlay our three initiatives, and everything else we do, with something we've talked about for years: **Simplification**. We are going to de-complicate everything we do and make at GE. Our communications with each other will be increasingly straightforward, our presentations to each other and to our customers will be simpler. Their richness will come from the dialogue, not the complexity of the charts. Our engineers will use less-convoluted processes, and fewer parts, to produce designs whose elegance will be measured by their simplicity; and that simplicity will improve their quality, their cost and their speed in reaching the marketplace.

The unfortunate part of 1994 was that the many achievements and terrific performance of GE people were often overshadowed by the well-chronicled problems with Kidder, Peabody.

The Kidder story, and its $1.2 billion loss, is not a pleasant one; and it is tempting to simply relegate it to the past—but we can't.

Whether or not it was a good idea to buy Kidder in 1986 is academic—in the end, it simply didn't work out. In 1994, weak trading markets lowered Wall Street earnings by billions of dollars from the levels of 1993, and Kidder was not immune to the weaknesses in these markets. But Kidder had another problem: a phantom trading scheme by a single employee, directed not against customers but against the firm itself, which cost it $210 million in net income. The combination of the two circumstances—a downturn in earnings, and an employee's wrongdoing—made it clear to us that it was time to get out; thus the sale of the brokerage assets of Kidder to PaineWebber, in return for 25% equity in that firm, and the liquidation of the trading operation.

None of this is to say it couldn't have been done better, but the bottom line is that the type of business Kidder had become— a cyclical trading business—was simply not the place for GE to be.

The tragedy of businesses that are not market leaders, that don't have a broadly based competitive edge—be they brokerage houses or manufacturing plants—is exactly the same; and it goes beyond "one-time charges"—dollars and cents. It's the people—the factory or office workers—who can't just "go down the street"—like traders and managers can—for another job. This human toll reminds us, once again, that nothing we do is more important than staying competitive—keeping that winning edge. Nothing.

Increasing our competitiveness is at the heart of all this "soft stuff"—

boundaryless behavior, increasing our speed and stretch, with an overlay of simplification. And the excitement they produce is, obviously, in the hard results they generate, but even more importantly, it is in the knowledge that what we have done has barely scratched the surface. It turns out that there is, in fact, unlimited juice in that lemon. The fact is that none of this is about squeezing anything at all—it is about tapping an ocean of creativity, passion and energy that, as far as we can see, has no bottom and no shores.

Using 100% of the minds and passion of 100% of our people in implementing the best ideas from everywhere in the world is a formula, we believe, for endless excitement, endless growth and endless renewal.

We now have a Company that is faster, more confident and higher-spirited than at any time in its history—a Company of people who believe in themselves, in each other and in their infinite capacity to improve everything.

Clearly, our best days are ahead—starting with 1995.

John F. Welch, Jr.
Chairman of the Board and
Chief Executive Officer

Paolo Fresco
Vice Chairman of the Board
and Executive Officer

FEBRUARY 10, 1995

To Our Share Owners

Your Company had a terrific 1995—a record year by any measure.

- Revenues rose to $70 billion, up 17%.
- Global revenues increased 34% to $27 billion.
- Earnings were $6.6 billion, up 11%.
- Earnings per share of $3.90 were up 13%.
- Seven of our 12 big businesses produced double-digit earnings increases.
- The quarterly dividend was increased 12%—the 20th consecutive year of dividend increases.
- We repurchased $3 billion of our stock, increased our buy-back program from $5 billion to $9 billion, and extended it through 1997.

This performance was recognized by the market, which rewarded GE investors in 1995 with a total return of 45%.

As strong as the year was, we did not achieve two of what we call "stretch" performance targets: operating margins and inventory turns. Over the last three decades, our highest corporate operating margin hovered around 10%, and our inventory turns around five, so in 1991 we set two "stretch" targets for 1995: 15% operating margin and 10 turns. 1995 has come and gone, and despite a heroic effort by our 222,000 employees, we fell short on both measures, achieving a 14.4% operating margin and almost seven turns. But in stretching for these "impossible" targets, we learned to do things faster than we would have going after "doable" goals, and we have enough confidence now to set new stretch targets of at least 16% operating margin and more than 10 turns by 1998.

The hottest trend in business in 1995—and the one that hit closest to home—was the rush toward breaking up multi-business companies and "spinning-off" their components, under the theory that their size and diversity inhibited their competitiveness. The obvious question to General Electric, as the world's largest multi-business company, was "When are you going to do it?" The short answer is that we're not. We've spent more than a decade getting bigger and faster and more competitive, and we intend to continue.

Breaking up is the right answer for some big companies. For us it is the wrong answer. "Why" is the subject of our letter to you this year.

Our dream, and our plan, well over a decade ago, was simple. We set out to shape a global enterprise that preserved the classic big-company advantages—while eliminating the classic big-company drawbacks. What we wanted to build was a hybrid, an enterprise with the reach and resources of a big company—the body of a big company—but the thirst to learn, the compulsion to share and the bias for action—the soul—of a small company.

Here's how we went about it.

Changing the Hardware

No. 1 or No. 2—or Fix, Sell or Close
The foundation for our future was to be involved in only those businesses that were, or could become, either number one or number two in their global markets. The rest were to be fixed, sold or closed. We made this decision based on our observation that when a number-one market-share business entered

a down cycle, and "sneezed," number four or five often caught galloping pneumonia. Consistent with this view, we divested, in the eighties, $10 billion worth of marginal businesses, and made $19 billion of acquisitions, to strengthen the world-leading businesses we wanted to take with us into the nineties.

Delayering While we were restructuring the businesses, we also changed the management hardware at GE. We delayered. We removed "Sectors," "Groups," "Strategic Business Units" and much of the extensive command structure and staff apparatus we used to run the Company.

We cleared out stifling bureaucracy, along with the strategic planning apparatus, corporate staff empires, rituals, endless studies and briefings, and all the classic machinery that makes big-company operations smooth and predictable—but often glacially slow. As the underbrush of bureaucracy was cleared away, we began to see and talk to each other more clearly and more directly.

As the Company moved through the eighties, the businesses grew increasingly powerful. Freed from bureaucratic tentacles, and charged to act independently, they did so, with great success. Corporate management got off their backs, and instead lined up behind them with resources and support.

Changing the Software

Self-Confidence, Simplicity, Speed As the big-company body was developing, we turned from changing its hardware to the infinitely more difficult task of changing its software—toward creating, in GE, the spirit and soul of a small company.

Most successful small companies possess three defining cultural traits: self-confidence, simplicity and speed. We wanted them. We went after them.

Self-Confidence We began with a theory of the case that valued self-confidence as the absolutely indispensable ingredient in a high-performance business culture. Self-confident people are open to good ideas regardless of their source and are willing to share them. Their egos don't require that they originate every idea they use, or "get credit" for every idea they originate. We began to cultivate self-confidence among our leaders by turning them loose, giving them independence and resources, and encouraging them to take big swings. The inevitable surge of

self-confidence that grows in people who win leads to another natural outgrowth: simplicity.

Simplicity Self-confident people don't need to wrap themselves in complexity, "businessese" speech, and all the clutter that passes for sophistication in business—especially big business. Self-confident leaders produce simple plans, speak simply and propose big, clear targets.

The boldness that comes from self-confidence, and the clarity that comes from simplicity, lead to one of the small company's greatest competitive advantages: speed.

Speed Simple messages travel faster, simpler designs reach the market faster, and the elimination of clutter allows faster decision making. All this happened in the upper echelons of GE. We saw the leadership come alive with energy, excitement and the crackle of small-company urgency.

Involving Everyone The challenge then became to involve everyone— to spread our new openness into every corner of our Company; to give every one of our 222,000 employees what the best small companies give people: voice. We were running out of models at this point, and moving into uncharted territory—at least for big companies—and so our next move, and the centerpiece of culture change at GE, was one we had to invent ourselves. We called it Work-Out.

Work-Out Work-Out was based on the simple belief that people closest to the work know, more than anyone, how it could be done better. It was this enormous reservoir of untapped knowledge, and insight, that we wanted to draw upon. Across GE today, holding a Work-Out session is as natural an act as coming to work. People of disparate ranks and functions search for a better way, every day, gathering in a room for an hour, or eight, or three days, grappling with a problem or an opportunity, and dealing with it, usually on the spot—producing real change instead of memos and promises of further study. Everyone today has an opportunity to have a voice at GE, and everyone who uses that voice to help improve things is rewarded.

Management Selection It was at Work-Out sessions that it became clear that some of the rhetoric heard at the corporate level—about involvement and excitement and turning people loose—did not match the reality of life in the businesses. The problem was that some of our leaders were unwilling, or unable, to abandon big-company, big-shot autocracy and embrace the values we were trying to grow. So we defined our management styles, or "types," and how they furthered or blocked our values. And then we acted.

Type I not only delivers on performance commitments, but believes in and furthers GE's small-company values. The trajectory of this group is "onward and upward," and the men and women who comprise it will represent the core of our senior leadership into the next century.

Type II does not meet commitments, nor share our values—nor last long at GE.

Type III believes in the values but sometimes misses commitments. We encourage taking swings, and Type III is typically given another chance.

Type IV. The "calls" on the first two types are easy. Type III takes some judgment; but Type IV is the most difficult. One is always tempted to avoid taking action, because Type IV's deliver short-term results. But Type IV's do so without regard to values and, in fact, often diminish them by grinding people down, squeezing them, stifling them. Some of these learned to change; most couldn't. The decision to begin removing Type

IV's was a watershed—the ultimate test of our ability to "walk the talk," but it had to be done if we wanted GE people to be open, to speak up, to share, and to act boldly outside traditional "lines of authority" and "functional boxes" in this new learning, sharing environment.

Crotonville Throughout this process of change—much of it wrenching and all of it new—our Management Institute at Crotonville, New York, served as a forum for the sharing of the experiences, the aspirations and, often, the frustrations of the tens of thousands of GE leaders who passed through its campus. It was the glue that held things together as the process of change took hold.

With the new culture in place, Crotonville has become a vehicle for learning and sharing the best practices that can be found anywhere around the globe. Leaders return from these intense courses to their businesses prepared to put these new ideas quickly into action. Entire classes are regularly sent to Europe or Asia, to wrestle with specific potential opportunities. After data gathering, and intense Work-Out style discussion, each class returns and presents recommendations directly to the top 35 officers of GE, who act on them—often on the spot. Crotonville com-

bines the thirst for learning of academia with an action environment usually seen only in small, hungry companies.

Boundaryless Behavior

These changes in the culture of our Company—the profound and pervasive effect of Work-Out and the steady reduction of Type IV management—developed a fresh, open, anti-parochial environment, friendly toward the seeking and sharing of new ideas, regardless of their source. It also encouraged looking outside the traditional boundaries that shackle thinking and restrict vision. Ideas around the Company quickly began to stand or fall on their merits—rather than on the altitude of their originators.

An endless search began for best practices—for ways of getting better, faster. Meetings around the Company that used to consist of self-serving "reports" and windy speeches became interactive forums for disseminating new ideas and the sharing of experiences. A whole new behavior has invigorated and freshened this century-old company. We've seen the emergence of true small-company phenomena: dreaming, which is at the heart of those "stretch" goals we mentioned earlier; and constant celebration of the milestones toward those goals—even if we occasionally don't quite get there. We describe our emerging culture by an awkward but descriptive name: "boundaryless." It is the soul of our integrated diversity and at the heart of everything we do well. It is the small-company culture we've been after for all these years.

The sweetest fruit of boundaryless behavior has been the demise of "Not-Invented-Here" and its utter disappearance from our Company. We quickly began to learn from each other: productivity solutions from Lighting; "quick response" asset management from Appliances; transaction effectiveness from GE Capital; the application of "bullet-train" cost-reduction techniques from Aircraft Engines; and global account management from Plastics—just to name a few. At the same time, we embarked on an endless search for ideas from the great companies of the world. Wal-Mart taught us the direct customer feedback technique we call Quick Market Intelligence. We learned New Product Introduction methods from Toshiba, Chrysler and Hewlett-Packard, and advanced manufacturing techniques from American Standard, Toyota and Yokogawa. AlliedSignal, Ford and Xerox shared their insights into launching a quality initiative. Motorola, which created a dramati-cally successful, quality-focused culture over a period of a decade, has been more than generous in sharing its experiences with us.

Stretch

"Stretch," which we mentioned earlier in connection with inventory turns and margin goals, simply means moving beyond being as good as you have to be—"making a budget"—to being as good as you possibly can be: setting "impossible" goals and going after them. Crucial to stretch is the trust that grows in a boundaryless organization, as self-confident people come to know that it is the quality of their effort toward achieving the "impossible" that is the ultimate measure.

Compensation To reinforce the boundaryless and stretch behavior taking root across the Company, we adapted our compensation system. When we began our journey in the eighties, about 400 of the senior people in GE received stock options. Today, 22,000 individuals, at all levels, have options, and thereby have a clear financial incentive for driving total Company performance by doing everything they can to help their colleagues in their own, or another, GE business.

Today, stock option compensation, based on total GE

performance, is far more significant than the salary or bonus growth associated with the performance of any individual unit or business. This aligns the interests of the individual, the Company and the share owner behind powerful one-company results.

A New Kind of Company

What we have described is the creation of a new kind of company—one that has, and uses, all the strengths of a big company while moving with the speed, hunger and urgency of a small company.

While the excitement, speed and growing confidence can be felt all across GE, its accelerating performance can be quantified as well.

In the first five years of the eighties, as we divested, invested, and restructured our array of big, leading businesses, GE returned to its share owners about $850 million a year in dividends.

Through the following five years, ending in 1990, as the effect of Work-Out took hold across the Company and small-company values began to flourish, we returned nearly double that—about $1.4 billion in annual dividends—and repurchased $2.6 billion of stock.

During the past five years, as boundaryless behavior has taken hold, and the best practices we shared have taken effect, we've returned to share owners about $2.3 billion a year in dividends and repurchased an additional $5.5 billion of our stock.

The pace continued to accelerate in 1995 when $5.9 billion impacted share owner value—$2.8 billion of it in dividends, and $3.1 billion supporting the equity by stock repurchase.

The GE Board of Directors has approved an additional $6 billion of stock repurchase through 1997. That, and our performance objectives in the current global economic environment, should permit us to maintain or increase the $6 billion level of share owner support each year, through dividends and the repurchase program.

Moving from about a billion dollars of share owner support in 1985 to $6 billion in 1995 says more than any of the words we've written about the new GE, and its new look to investors.

Once this big, diverse Company is looked at for what it has become—an accelerating earnings and cash engine—its performance is much easier for investors and analysts to judge. Those who follow GE are increasingly aware that there are very few individual hits or misses of sufficient magnitude to alter the trajectory of a Company moving toward the $100 billion revenue level in any reasonable global economic scenario. By focusing on the scale, breadth and growth of our Company, rather than on the "event of the day"— whether it be a hit or miss, from locomotives to TV programs— investors should look beyond the headline—to the bottom line.

Growing Rapidly into the Next Century

As the millennium approaches, this Company will pick up the pace, as it brings to bear its enormous financial, technical and human resources in support of its big businesses as they move to seize five of the biggest growth opportunities in our history: Globalization, New Products, Information Technology, Installed-Base Service and Quality.

Globalization

- Approaching joint venture partners, and even sovereign states, as multi-business teams, sharing country knowledge, and capable of assembling supportive financing packages from GE Capital, our globalization is accelerating. Global revenues over the last 10 years have increased from 20% of the Company's total to 38% today— and, somewhere around the millennium, we expect the majority of GE revenue to come from outside the United States.

New Products

- The sharing of new product introduction techniques, developed both inside and outside GE, is compressing the cycle of learning and executing, and is already producing a torrent of new products, from jet engines to turbines to washing machines to TV shows.

Information Technology

- The enormous leverage of information technology, combined with our culture of learning and sharing, creates a tremendous opportunity, both internally— with better inventory control and shorter order-to-remittance cycles, for example—and externally—with remote diagnostics in medical imaging and just-in-time inventory replenishment for our customers.

Service

- Improving the profitability of our customers through technology upgrades of the enormous installed base of GE equipment— scores of thousands of jet engines, locomotives, turbines and CT scanners, for instance—is an enormous growth opportunity for us and a profit opportunity for our customers.

Quality

- Already equal to or better than our competitors—quality at GE will be taken to world-leading levels, providing us with yet another competitive differentiator. Our openness to learning, our ability to share across the Company and our bias for speed, as well as the generosity of Motorola and others in sharing their techniques with us, will bring GE to a whole new level of quality in a fraction of the time it would have taken to climb the learning curve on our own.

This is a Company focusing on huge growth opportunities as we look to the millennium—a GE that renews itself constantly, exhilarates itself with speed and freshens itself by constant learning.

We are a Company intent on getting bigger, not smaller—a Company whose only answer to the trendy question—"What do you intend to spin off?"—is "cash—and lots of it."

Two significant events occurred within a couple of weeks of each other as 1995 ended and the new year began. The first was the 100th anniversary of the Dow Jones Industrial Average and an invitation from Dow Jones to GE to open the market with them on the year's first trading session. The reason we

were invited to "ring the bell" was because we are the only surviving company of those in the original Dow Average. We celebrated that occasion, but thought "surviving" an anemic adjective, inadequate to the vibrancy of our Company and the promise of its future.

There was a glimpse of that future in the second event, in that two-week time span, when NBC and Microsoft, a company synonymous with the future, announced they were joining in two exciting new information ventures. The juxtaposition of those two events provides a nice snapshot of GE—a Company with a legendary past, humming powerfully in the present, with its greatest days always ahead.

Thank you for supporting us.

John F. Welch, Jr.
Chairman of the Board and
Chief Executive Officer

Paolo Fresco
Vice Chairman of the Board
and Executive Officer

John D. Opie
Vice Chairman of the Board
and Executive Officer

FEBRUARY 9, 1996

To Our Share Owners

In 1996, your Company had its best year ever.

- Revenues rose to a record $79.2 billion, up 13%.
- Global revenues were up 18% to $33 billion, a record.
- Earnings increased 11% to a record $7.280 billion.
- Earnings per share increased 13% to a record $4.40.
- Operating cash flow rose to $9.1 billion, $3 billion above our previous high.

This performance translated into significant rewards for our share owners.

- Total return to share owners in 1996 was 40%, after a 45% return in 1995.
- Record cash flow allowed us to return more than $6 billion to share owners for the second consecutive year: $3.1 billion in dividends; $3.3 billion in the repurchase of GE stock.
- We increased our quarterly dividend 13%, our 21st consecutive annual increase.
- We expanded our share repurchase program from $9 billion to $13 billion, extending it through 1998.
- The Board of Directors recommended, for share owner approval in April, a 2-for-1 stock split.

The Model

The GE financial model is simple but, we believe, unique in world business. On one side is a group of 11 large businesses, virtually all #1 or #2 in their marketplaces, that consistently improve operating margins, earnings and cash flow and support the "triple A" debt rating of the parent Company. GE's "triple A," in turn, supports a huge, diverse, global financial services enterprise, also rated "triple A."

The uniqueness of this model lies in its **consistency.** The operating businesses in the model consistently grow their revenues, operating margins and working capital turns, while the 27 businesses that make up the financial services arm grow earnings at consistent double-digit rates.

Our model is not in itself difficult to construct, nor are we the first to put together a mix of industrial/service/media and financial services businesses. It is the consistent aggregate performance of these large #1 or #2 businesses over a diverse array of global markets that makes this model work.

While consistent growth is the output of this model, the fuel that drives it—the energy behind it—is our culture . . . **how we behave**.

The Values

Our behavior is driven by a fundamental core belief: the desire, and the ability, of an organization to continuously learn from any source, anywhere—and to rapidly convert this learning into action—is its ultimate competitive advantage.

Driven by this belief, and anxious to get at the learning opportunities that abound in, and around, a multi-business global company, we first had to deal with the myriad boundaries that were impeding the generation and transfer of ideas. There were boundaries within the Company, between management layers, functional disciplines and different national cultures. The boundaries between us and the outside were the product of an NIH (Not-Invented-Here) attitude, that limited our ability to learn from suppliers, our customers and other global companies that had "best practices" that could be of enormous use to us.

We went after these barriers with a massive initiative called Work-Out, which we've described for you in detail in past letters. Work-Out flattened those barriers. It eliminated insularity in our businesses. Work-Out also went after NIH—and eradicated it. GE began to systematically roam the world, learning better ways of doing things from the world's best companies.

We supported this behavior with changes in the management appraisal and compensation systems. We introduced a 360° management appraisal that focused leaders on finding and rewarding people who demonstrated an ability to get every mind in the organization into the relentless search for ideas: for finding the better way—every day.

We made major changes in the compensation system to support this learning behavior. Before Work-Out, we operated under a management philosophy that rewarded "originating" ideas and "standout" performance with bonuses and salary. Today, those bonuses, as well as salaries, reward the **finding** and **sharing** of ideas even more than their origination. Stock options—formerly held by a

few hundred, now by 22,000 GE employees—provide a powerful incentive to learn and share and work together.

You can talk—you can preach—all you want about a "learning organization," but, from our experience, reinforcing management appraisal and compensation systems are the critical enablers that must be in place if rhetoric is to become reality.

As those of you who've read these reports in the past know, we never shut up about the great things that lie ahead of a company whose people get up every morning and come to work knowing—convinced—that there is a better way of doing everything they do—and determined to find out who knows that way and how they can learn it.

It is this learning, sharing and action-driven culture, when laid across the diverse businesses of GE, that gives us our true advantage, an advantage single-industry companies can never match—what we call **"horizontal learning"** across more than 250 diverse, global GE business segments.

The Horizontal Growth Opportunities

As this learning, sharing and doing have become rooted in our culture, we see, beyond our strong #1 and #2 individual businesses, the common growth opportunities that cut across them.

Quality, Globalization, Service, Information Technology and Consumer Savings . . . are part of our answer to the sometimes-posed question of how an $80 billion company—a $7.3 billion net income machine—can continue to grow at double-digit rates.

The biggest opportunity for us to use this horizontal learning to accelerate growth is **Quality**.

Quality Just as Work-Out got us to a culture of learning and openness that defined the way we behave, quality improvement, under the disciplined rubric of Six Sigma methodology, will define the way we work.

Six Sigma quality means the virtual elimination of defects from every product, process and transaction this Company engages in every day around the globe. A Six Sigma quality level generates fewer than 3.4 defects per million operations in a manufacturing or service process.

It has been estimated that less than Six Sigma quality, i.e., the three-to-four Sigma levels that are average for most U.S. companies, can cost a company as much as 10–15% of its revenues. For GE, that would mean $8–12 billion.

Six Sigma quality is already becoming part of our culture and

The GE Growth Model

The Financial Engine

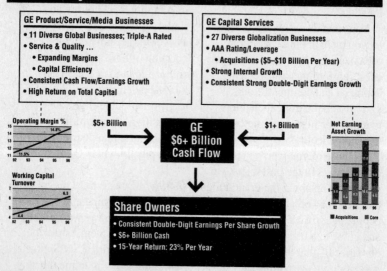

GE Product/Service/Media Businesses

- 11 Diverse Global Businesses; Triple-A Rated
- Service & Quality ...
  - Expanding Margins
  - Capital Efficiency
- Consistent Cash Flow/Earnings Growth
- High Return on Total Capital

GE Capital Services

- 27 Diverse Globalization Businesses
- AAA Rating/Leverage
  - Acquisitions ($5–$10 Billion Per Year)
- Strong Internal Growth
- Consistent Strong Double-Digit Earnings Growth

Operating Margin % 14.8% 11.5% 92 93 94 95 96

Working Capital Turnover 6.3 4.4 92 93 94 95 96

$5+ Billion

GE $6+ Billion Cash Flow

$1+ Billion

Net Earning Asset Growth 92 93 94 95 96 ■ Acquisitions ■ Core

Share Owners

- Consistent Double-Digit Earnings Per Share Growth
- $6+ Billion Cash
- 15-Year Return: 23% Per Year

The Culture ... Finding a Better Way Every Day

GE Leaders ... Always with Unyielding Integrity:

- Have a Passion for Excellence and Hate Bureaucracy
- Are Open to Ideas from Anywhere ... and Committed to Work-Out
- Live Quality ... and Drive Cost and Speed for Competitive Advantage
- Have the Self-Confidence to Involve Everyone and Behave in a Boundaryless Fashion
- Create a Clear, Simple, Reality-Based Vision ... and Communicate It to All Constituencies
- Have Enormous Energy and the Ability to Energize Others
- Stretch ... Set Aggressive Goals ... Reward Progress ... Yet Understand Accountability and Commitment
- See Change as Opportunity ... Not Threat
- Have Global Brains ... and Build Diverse and Global Teams

Horizontal Growth Opportunities

Quality ... $100–$200 Million of Operating Margin in '97 in Second Full Year of Quality Program
Globalization ... $30+ Billion Global Revenues Growing Three Times Domestic
Service ... $8 Billion Equipment Service Businesses Growing Double-Digit in '96 and '97
Information Technology ... $9 Billion Information Technology Businesses Growing Double-Digit
Consumer Savings ... $46 Billion Assets of New "Savings" Business Will Add Several Cents Per Share of '97 Growth

defining how we work. The Six Sigma process is a very specific scientific methodology of measuring, analyzing, improving and controlling every process we engage in, from making jet engine blades, to executing a credit transaction with a customer, to minimizing "dead air" between segments in broadcasting. It involves enormous amounts of training, with thousands of "Green Belts," "Black Belts" and "Master Black Belts" leading projects, teaching, and widening the circle of involvement in the quality initiative throughout GE.

The methodologies of Six Sigma we learned from other companies, but the cultural obsessiveness and all-encompassing passion for it is pure GE. The intensity level involved in our decade-long struggle to achieve a boundaryless culture now seems "laid-back" compared to the near monomania with which we are approaching Six Sigma quality. Forty percent of every manager's bonus is tied to his or her progress on quality results. Quality is the top item on every agenda in every discussion in every business in this Company. For leaders who do not see how critical quality is to our future—like leaders who could not become boundaryless during the 1980s— GE is simply not the place to be.

The momentum of the Six Sigma initiative is unprecedented. From launching this initiative in late 1995, with 200 projects and massive training, we moved to 3,000 projects and even more training in 1996; and we will undertake 6,000 projects, and still more training, in 1997. The $200 million we invested in 1996 has already returned nearly that much in quality-related savings. The additional $300 million we will invest in 1997 will deliver some $400–500 million in savings, producing an additional $100–200 million in incremental margins. This snowball will pick up size and momentum in terms of people trained, projects completed, and customer and employee satisfaction—all driving sales and net income growth. Growth and more growth.

Globalization We now have a $33 billion "global business" that grew 18% in 1996. More than 40% of GE's revenues are now derived from non-U.S. markets—markets where we have grown, and will continue to grow, at three times the U.S. rate.

In Europe, despite the less-than-robust economy, we have grown revenues 42% per year from 1994 to 1996—and almost tripled profits. That growth will continue in strong double digits in 1997. Today there is an $18 billion "European GE."

Asia also is a source of ongoing double-digit growth, and today there is an $8 billion "Asian GE," a big player in the fastest-growing market in the world.

Nowhere is the horizontal learning more important than in globalization. The constant sharing of business experiences and cultural insights, from around the world, is creating a Company whose brains, as well as its businesses, are truly global.

Information Technology GE is a high-growth information company. Along with NBC, CNBC, MSNBC and the network's other ventures, we are well positioned in information services, in satellite leasing, and in a technology management services business created by the acquisition of AmeriData in the United States and CompuNet in Germany. In 1995, our information technology businesses had revenues of $6 billion. We expect to more than double that in 1997, in a market synonymous with seemingly endless double-digit growth.

Information technology is clearly an important business opportunity in itself, but equally important is the role it is playing in the success of every business in the Company. It is making the huge transition from the "function" it was in the 1980s—with its own language, rituals and priesthood—to the indispensable competitive tool, the central nervous system of virtually every operation in the Company. Information technology has drawn us closer to customers via inventory management systems. It enables our engineers to monitor and service products on-line globally. It allows new products to be designed in real time by engineers, 24 hours a day, on two or three continents.

Without the detailed information on process capabilities, our quality initiative would be more art than science, driven more by slogans than by precise methodologies where tolerances are measured in millionths.

And even beyond "changing the game" in virtually every business operation in the Company, information technology is a perfect fit for our culture, as it gets more people "into the game," learning and sharing—and allows them to execute the fruits of that learning—faster.

Consumer Wealth Accumulation and Protection GE is a savings business, focusing on consumer wealth accumulation, with $46 billion in assets. This has been created by the acquisition of insurance and annuity companies such as First Colony, Life of Virginia, GNA, Harcourt General, AMEX-LT Care, Union Fidelity Life and Union Pacific Life.

The scale of this business can be understood in the context of the several cents a share it will add to GE's 1997 earnings growth—this from an activity in which we were not even participating four years ago. It illustrates both the power of our financial services arm as well as the horizontal approach to managing newly acquired companies. Our culture is driving these well-positioned niche players into a closely integrated, stronger whole; they are in the process of becoming a large consumer wealth accumulation business serving the huge demand for the financial, insurance, health care and other needs of the aging baby-boomer population.

Services Expansion Looking across several manufacturing businesses, GE is an $8 billion equipment services business, growing at double-digit rates, with an advantage unique in the world: an installed base of some 9,000 GE commercial jet engines, 10,000 turbines, 13,000 locomotives and 84,000 major pieces of medical diagnostic imaging equipment.

Medical Systems has long been a world leader in remote diagnostics. Thousands of its MRI and CT scan-

ners are on-line 24 hours a day, allowing a doctor in, say, Bombay to get help from Tokyo, Paris or Milwaukee anytime, day or night.

This on-line diagnostic technology has been transferred across all GE equipment businesses and is taking the concept of equipment service into an entirely new dimension.

In Aircraft Engines, all critical operating parameters of GE jet engines can be monitored by our service experts while the engines are in flight. As a result, any out-of-spec performance data can be quickly dealt with when the plane lands, with the engine on the wing, saving airlines millions by increasing the time between off-wing overhauls.

Two joint ventures with Harris Corporation capitalize on related diagnostic and communications technologies—one to help our electric utility customers increase the efficiency of their systems, and the other to radically improve the utilization of rolling stock for the railroad industry. Both of these service initiatives are key to the long-term success of companies in these increasingly deregulated and intensely competitive industries.

Customers will always need high-quality hardware, but what they must have more than ever are productivity solutions that help them win in their markets. Our challenge in the years to come will be to continuously find new ways to help them fight their competitive battles, by providing more sophisticated added-value services.

Services is so great an opportunity for the Company that our vision for the next century is a GE that is "a global service company that also sells high-quality products."

This, then, is General Electric: its financial engine, the culture that drives it, and the opportunity for growth ahead of it as it attacks the largest opportunities in its history across multi-business fronts.

In giving you this picture of a few of these enormous multi-business growth opportunities, we do not for a moment minimize the terrific growth opportunities in front of our individual businesses: a new line of ultrasound products from Medical Systems growing 25% a year in a modest-growth market; a new on-line interactive network—MSNBC; a new high-technology 6000HP locomotive; a new washing machine that has grown share close to three points in a mature market; a new product nearly every day from Lighting; and all the other individual opportunities ahead for these intensely entrepreneurial, world-leading businesses.

Nor do we neglect our traditional tight management of individual business results—accountability is still a part of our culture—but increasingly the important question is not only "How is Plastics or Lighting or Employers Reinsurance or Auto Financial Services doing?" at any given moment, but also "How is GE doing?" in Europe or Asia, in Services, in Information Technology, in Consumer Wealth Accumulation and Protection, and, above all, in Quality.

What better time, with this "learning, sharing, doing" culture in our blood—and with quality growing by the hour in each of our operations around the globe—to have before us not one, but several of the biggest growth opportunities in our history. We are determined to seize them. We are determined to grow.

Thanks for your continuing support.

John F. Welch, Jr.
Chairman of the Board and
Chief Executive Officer

Paolo Fresco
Vice Chairman of the Board
and Executive Officer

John D. Opie
Vice Chairman of the Board
and Executive Officer

FEBRUARY 7, 1997

To Our Share Owners and Employees

In 1997, your Company had a great year—a record year.

- Ongoing revenues rose to $89.3 billion; up 13%.
- Global (non-U.S.) revenues rose to $38.5 billion, now 42% of total revenues.
- Earnings increased to more than $8.2 billion; up 13%.
- Earnings per share increased 14% to a record $2.50.
- Ongoing operating margin rose to a record 15.7%, exceeding 15% for the first time in the history of our Company.
- Operating cash flow rose to a record $9.3 billion. This, in combination with our Triple A debt rating, fueled the investment of $17.2 billion in more than 75 industrial and financial services acquisitions in 1997.
- This record cash flow also allowed us to return $7 billion to share owners: $3.5 billion in dividends and $3.5 billion for the repurchase of GE stock. Dividends were increased by 15%, our 22nd consecutive annual dividend increase.
- In April, our share owners approved a 2-for-1 stock split, the fourth in the last 15 years.

Our share owners—including our active and retired employees, who now own more than $12 billion in GE stock in their savings plans—were rewarded for this performance. The total return on a share of GE stock was 51% in 1997; this followed gains of 40% in 1996 and 45% in 1995.

We delivered these 1997 results by executing on our three major initiatives: globalization, a focus on product services and our drive for Six Sigma quality. Building on these same three initiatives will be critical to our future success.

The uncertainty brought about by the Asian economic difficulties creates both challenges and opportunities. For GE, Asia represents about 9% of our revenues (about half in Japan)—exposure that is by no means insignificant, but certainly manageable—and we are confident that we can minimize any impact on our existing operations.

It has been our repeated experience that business uncertainty is inevitably accompanied by opportunity. The Asian situation should be no exception; it should provide us with a unique opportunity to make the strategic moves that will increase our presence and our participation in what we know will be one of the world's great markets of the 21st Century.

We've been down this path before. In the early 1980s, we experienced a United States mired in recession, hand-wringing from the pundits and dirges being sung over American manufacturing. We didn't buy this dismal scenario; instead, we invested in both a widespread restructuring and in new businesses. We emerged into the recovery a much more competitive and productive company.

Our successful experience with U.S. business uncertainty gave us a very different view of the European malaise of the early 1990s.

To us, Europe looked a lot like the United States in the 1980s, and in need of the same remedies: restructuring, spin-offs, and the like. So, while many were "writing-off" Europe, we invested heavily, buying new companies and expanding our existing presence. Following the restructuring of its industrial and financial structure, as well as a dose of the powerful export medicine of a devalued currency, Europe is now recovering, and "GE Europe" is now a $20.6 billion operation. Our revenues have more than doubled from 1994 to 1997; net income has tripled to more than $1.5 billion; and this growth is accelerating as the European recovery progresses.

Mexico in the mid-1990s was a similar story: dislocation, uncertainty and turbulence. Reacting to the peso crisis of 1995 and its aftermath, GE moved, acquiring 10 companies and investing more than $1 billion in new and existing operations. The result was revenue growth of 60% and a doubling of earnings in the two years following the crisis.

Today, we are determined, and poised, to do the same thing in Asia we have done in the United States, Europe and Mexico: invest in the future.

Globalization

Globalization is one of the engines of GE growth, now and well into the next century. There will be dislocations and speed bumps on the road to prosperity in all the world's critical markets, but one cannot afford to write off any region in difficulty. Bad business management or bad government policies that weaken competitiveness can be remedied by tough restructuring and policy change. The same conditions that made restructuring and reform necessary frequently create a currency weakness that, when coupled with the increased competitiveness brought about by restructuring leads the country out of recession, via internal growth and increased exports. **The path to greatness in Asia is irreversible, and GE will be there**.

Services

Another growth engine, which we have described for you in the past, is Services. By any measure, GE is today a global service company, and in 1998 more than two-thirds of its revenues will come from financial, information and product services. Our second major initiative is focused on high-technology product services. In 1997, we achieved a second consecutive year of double-digit growth in product service revenues and improved ongoing operating margin, while making 20 acquisitions and joint ventures, primarily in the industrial, power, medical and aircraft engine services businesses. Key among these were the $1.5 billion Greenwich/UNC jet engine service acquisition and the recently completed $600 million acquisition of the gas turbine-related businesses of Stewart & Stevenson Services, a global power generation equipment service company.

The opportunity for growth in product services is unlimited. We have the ability, using high-technology services, to make our customers' existing assets (e.g., power plants, locomotives, airplanes, factories, hospital equipment and the like) more productive, and by doing so reduce their capital outlays. This growing capability, much of it information technology-based, will enable us to increase our revenues from product services by more than 30% in 1998—to $13 billion.

Six Sigma

We have described our progress in globalization and services rather quickly so we could cover in depth something we talk to each other about all day: the centerpiece of our dreams and aspirations for this great Company—the drive for Six Sigma quality. "Six Sigma" is a disciplined methodology, led and taught by highly trained GE employees called "Master Black Belts" and "Black Belts," that focuses on moving every process that touches our customers—every product and service—toward near-perfect quality.

Six Sigma project work consists of five basic activities: Defining, Measuring, Analyzing, Improving and then Controlling processes. These projects usually focus on improving our customers' productivity and reducing their capital outlays, while increasing the quality, speed and efficiency of our operations.

We didn't invent Six Sigma—we learned it. Motorola pioneered it and AlliedSignal successfully embraced it. The experiences of these two companies, which they shared with us, made the launch of our initiative much simpler and faster.

GE had another huge advantage that accelerated our quality effort: we had a Company that was open to change, hungry to learn and anxious to move quickly on a good idea.

This learning environment came from a decade-long, soul-transforming cultural initiative called "Work-Out." Work-Out is a continuing effort to achieve what we call "boundaryless behavior"— business behavior that tramples or demolishes all barriers of rank, function, geography and bureaucracy in an endless pursuit of the best idea—in the cause of **engaging and involving every mind in the Company**.

After a decade of Work-Out, most of the old bureaucracy and the boundaries among us have been de-molished. (We are, however, aware that bureaucracy is the Dracula of institutional behavior, and will rise again and again, requiring everyone in the organization to reflexively pound stakes through its

reappearances.) But at GE today— and we are obviously proud of this—finding **the better way**, **the best idea**, from whomever will share it with us, has become our central focus.

Nowhere has this learning environment, this search for the better idea, been more powerfully demonstrated than in our drive for Six Sigma quality. Twenty-eight months ago, we became convinced that Six Sigma quality could play a central role in GE's future; but we believed, as well, that it would take years of consistent com-munication, relentless emphasis and impassioned leadership to move this big Company on this bold new course.

We were wrong!

We are the ones who now find ourselves running to keep up with the excited charge of tens of thousands of GE employees who have seen the transformational magic—the rejuvenation—that this combination of rigid discipline and cheerful fanaticism can achieve in our businesses. Projections of our progress in Six Sigma, no matter how optimistic, have had to be junked every few months as gross underestimates.

Six Sigma has spread like wildfire across the Company, and it is transforming everything we do.

We had our annual Operating Managers Meeting—500 of our senior business leaders from around the globe—during the first week of January 1998, and it turned out to be a wonderful snapshot of the way this learning Company— this new GE—has come to behave; and now, with Six Sigma, how it has come to work.

Today, in the uncountable number of business meetings across GE—both organized and "in-the-hall"—the gates are open to the largest flood of innovative ideas in world business. These ideas are generated, improved upon and shared by 350 business segments— or, as we think of them, 350 **business laboratories**. Today, these ideas center on spreading Six Sigma "best practices" across our business operations.

At this particular Operating Managers Meeting, about 25 speakers, from across the Company and around the world, excitedly described how Six Sigma is transforming the way their businesses work. They shared what they had learned from projects such as streamlining the back room of a credit card operation, or improving turnaround time in a jet engine overhaul shop, or "hit-rate" improvements in commercial finance transactions. Most of the presenters focused on how their process improvements were making their **customers** more competitive and productive:

- Medical Systems described how Six Sigma designs have produced a **10-fold** increase in the life of CT scanner x-ray tubes—increasing the "uptime" of these machines and the profitability and level of patient care given by hospitals and other health care providers.
- Superabrasives—our industrial diamond business—described how Six Sigma **quadrupled** its return on investment and, by improving yields, is giving it a full **decade's** worth of capacity despite growing volume— without spending a nickel on plant and equipment capacity.
- Our railcar leasing business described a 62% reduction in turnaround time at its repair shops: an enormous productivity gain for our railroad and shipper customers and for a business that's now **two to three times faster** than its nearest rival because of Six Sigma improvements. In the next phase, spread across the entire shop network, Black Belts and Green Belts, working with their teams, redesigned the overhaul process, resulting in a **50% further** reduction in cycle time.

- The plastics business, through rigorous Six Sigma process work, added 300 million pounds of new capacity (equivalent to a "free plant"), saved $400 million in investment and will save another $400 million by 2000.

At our meeting, zealot after zealot shared stories of customers made more competitive, of credit card and mortgage application processes streamlined, of inventories reduced, and of whole factories and businesses performing at levels never believed possible.

The sharing process was repeated at another level two weeks later in Paris, as 150 Master Black Belts and Black Belts, from every GE business throughout Europe, came together to share and learn quality technology. This learning is done in the boundaryless, transcultural language of Six Sigma, where "CTQ's" (critical to quality characteristics) or "DPMO's" (defects per million opportunities) or "SPC" (statistical process control) have exactly the same meaning at every GE operation from Tokyo to Delhi and from Budapest to Cleveland and Shanghai.

The meeting stories are anecdotal; big companies can make great presentations and impressive charts. But the cumulative impact on the Company's numbers is not anecdotal, nor a product of charts. It is the product of 276,000 people executing . . . and delivering the results of Six Sigma to our bottom line.

Operating margin, a critical measure of business efficiency and profitability, hovered around the 10% level at GE for decades. With Six Sigma embedding itself deeper into Company operations, GE in 1997 went through the "impossible" 15% level—approaching 16%—and we are optimistic about the upside.

Six Sigma, even at this relatively early stage, delivered more than $300 million to our 1997 operating income. In 1998, returns will more than double this operating profit impact.

Six Sigma is quickly becoming part of the genetic code of our future leadership. Six Sigma training is now an ironclad prerequisite for promotion to any professional or managerial position in the Company—and a requirement for any award of stock options.

Senior executive compensation is now heavily weighted toward Six Sigma commitment and success—success now increasingly defined as "eatable" financial returns, for our customers and for us.

There are now nearly 4,000 full-time, fully trained Black Belts and Master Black Belts: Six Sigma instructors, mentors and project leaders. There are more than 60,000 Green Belt part-time project leaders who have completed at least one Six Sigma project.

Already, Black Belts and Master Black Belts who are finishing Six Sigma assignments have become the most sought-after candidates for senior leadership jobs in the Company, including vice presidents and chief financial officers at some of our businesses. Hundreds have already moved upward through the pipeline. They are true believers, speaking the language of the future, energized by successful projects under their belts, and drawing other committed zealots upward with them.

In the early 1990s, after we had finished defining ourselves as a company of boundaryless people with a thirst for learning and a compulsion to share, it became unthinkable for any of us to tolerate— much less hire or promote—the tyrant, the turf defender, the autocrat, the big shot. They were simply "yesterday."

As we move toward 2000 and beyond, with Six Sigma permeating much of what we do all day, it will be likewise unthinkable to hire into the Company, promote or tolerate those who cannot, or will not, commit to this way of work. It is simply important to our future.

And as we "raise the bar" from three to four to five and then to Six Sigma . . . we must raise, again, the bar of quality as it applies to ourselves. The reality is, we simply cannot afford to field anything but teams of "A" players.

Six Sigma Costs and Benefits

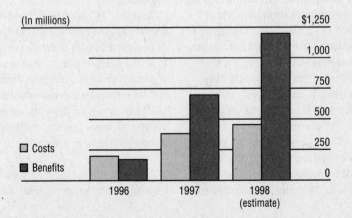

(In millions)

$1,250

1,000

750

500

250

0

□ Costs
■ Benefits

1996   1997   1998
(estimate)

What is an "A"? At the leadership level, an "A" is a man or woman with a vision and the ability to articulate that vision to the team, so vividly and powerfully that it also becomes their vision.

An "A" leader has enormous personal energy and, beyond that, the ability to energize others and draw out their best, usually on a global basis.

An "A" leader has "edge" as well: the instinct and the courage to make the tough calls—decisively, but with fairness and absolute integrity.

As we go forward, there will be nothing but "A's" in every leadership position in this Company. They will be the best in the world, and they will act to field teams consisting of nothing but "A" players. The best leaders—the "A's"—are really coaches. What coach, with any instinct or passion for winning, would field an Olympic swimming or gymnastics team, or a Super Bowl team, that wasn't made up of the absolute best available? In the same vein, what business leader worthy of the name would even consider fielding a team with anything other than the very best, the "A" players?

What characterizes "A" players?

In finance, for example, "A's" will be people whose talents include, but transcend, traditional controllership. The bigger role is one of full-fledged participant in driving the business to win in the marketplace—a role far bigger than the dreary and wasteful budget "drills" and bean-counting that once defined and limited the job.

In engineering, "A's" are those who embrace the methodology of Design for Six Sigma. "A" engineers can't stand the thought of "riding it out" in the lab, but rather relish the rapid pace of technological change and continually re-educate themselves to stay on top of it.

In manufacturing, "A" players will be people who are immersed in Six Sigma technology, who consider inventory an embarrassment, especially with a whiff of deflation in the air—people who understand how to drive asset turns and reduce inventory while at the same time increasing our readiness to serve the customer.

In sales, "A" players will use the enormous customer value that Six Sigma generates to differentiate GE from the competition, to find new accounts, and to refresh and expand the old ones—as contrasted with "C" players whose days are spent visiting "friends" on the "milk-run" circuit of customer calls.

This is now the business of your Company: "A" products and "A" services delivered by "A" players around the globe.

We are feverish on the subject of Six Sigma quality as it relates to products, services and people—maybe a bit unbalanced—because we see it as the ultimate way to make real our dreams of what this great Company could become.

Six Sigma has turned up the voltage in every GE business across the globe, energizing and exciting all of us and moving us closer than ever to what we have always wanted to become: more than a hundred-billion-dollar global enterprise with the agility, customer focus and fire in the belly of a small company.

In our 1994 letter to you, we addressed the perennial question put to management teams, which is "how much more can be squeezed from the lemon?" We claimed, then, that there was in fact unlimited juice in this "lemon," and that none of this had anything to do with "squeezing" at all. We believed there was an ocean of creativity and passion and energy in GE people that had no bottom and

no shores. We believed that then, and we are convinced of it today. And when we said that there was an "infinite capacity to improve everything," we believed that as well—viscerally—but there was no methodology or discipline attached to that belief. There is now. It's Six Sigma quality, along with a culture of learning, sharing and unending excitement.

For GE, these are the best of times, and in our view they will only get better.

Thanks, as always, for your continuing support.

John F. Welch, Jr.
Chairman of the Board and
Chief Executive Officer

Paolo Fresco
Vice Chairman of the Board
and Executive Officer

Eugene F. Murphy
Vice Chairman of the Board
and Executive Officer

John D. Opie
Vice Chairman of the Board
and Executive Officer

FEBRUARY 13, 1998

To Our Share Owners, Employees, and Customers

1998 was another terrific year for your Company—another record year.

- Revenues rose to $100.5 billion, up 11%.
- Earnings increased 13% to $9.3 billion.
- Earnings per share grew 14% to $2.80.
- Operating margin rose to a record 16.7%, up a full point from the record 15.7% of 1997. Working capital turns rose sharply to 9.2, up from 1997's record of 7.4.
- This performance generated $10 billion in free cash flow, which, in combination with a "AAA" debt rating, allowed us to invest $21 billion for 108 acquisitions in support of two of our three Company-wide initiatives: Globalization and Services.
- Record cash flow allowed us to raise dividends by 17% and to further increase share owner value by repurchasing an additional $3.6 billion in GE stock.
- In 1998, GE was named *Fortune* magazine's "Most Admired Company in America" and "The World's Most Respected Company" by a worldwide business audience in the *Financial Times*.

Our share owners—including our active and retired employees, who now own more than $17 billion in GE stock in their savings plans—were rewarded for these actions and this performance—the total return on a share of GE stock was 41% in 1998. GE has averaged a 24% per-year total return to share owners for the past 18 years.

This performance, year after year, is the product of a diverse and powerful portfolio of leading global businesses. This performance has been driven this decade by three big Company-wide growth initiatives: Globalization, Services and Six Sigma quality.

These initiatives, in turn, have been rapidly advanced by a General Electric culture that values the contributions of every individual, thrives on learning, thirsts for the better idea, and has the flexibility and speed to put the better idea into action every day.

We are a learning company, a company that studies its own successes and failures and those of others—a company that has the self-confidence and the resources to take big swings and pursue numerous opportunities based on winning ideas and insights, regardless of their source.

That appetite for learning, and the ability to act quickly on that learning, will provide GE with what we believe is an insurmountable and sustainable competitive advantage as we pursue our three big growth initiatives.

Globalization is the first of those initiatives.

Last year we wrote to you as the difficulties in Asia were causing global uncertainty and unease.

We, like everyone else, had not foreseen these difficulties, but we quickly viewed Asia as similar in many respects to the Europe of the early 1990s—in need of various structural remedies but rich in opportunity. In the case of Europe—and in the case of Mexico in the mid-'90s—we moved decisively and were rewarded with significant and rapid growth. We have grown fourfold in Europe, from a relatively small GE presence in 1990 to $24 billion in revenues in 1998.

We learned from our European successes and saw in Japan the opportunity to do it again—only faster.

We acquired the business infrastructure and sales force of Toho Mutual Life, and—because of the high respect the Japanese have for Thomas Edison—we renamed it GE Edison Life and quickly became a force in the Japanese insurance industry. We also acquired the consumer loan business of Japan's Lake Corporation, with $6.2 billion in assets, and added it to our already rapidly growing consumer finance business there. These acquisitions, along with several other ventures, partnerships and buyouts by our industrial businesses, together with the growth of our ongoing existing businesses in Japan, should allow us to more than double our over $300 million in 1998 Japanese earnings within three years.

Our Japanese initiatives are part of an intense multiyear focus on globalization that produced $43 billion in revenues in 1998 and a growth rate for GE outside the United States that has been double our U.S. growth rate for 10 years.

But market success is only part of globalization. We must globalize every activity in the Company. We've made some progress in sourcing products and components

Growth Through Globalization

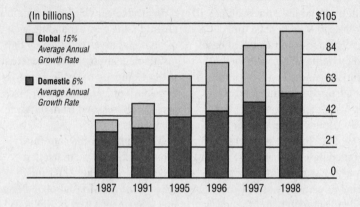

(In billions) $105

☐ **Global** *15%*
  Average Annual
  Growth Rate   84

■ **Domestic** *6%*
  Average Annual
  Growth Rate   63

                                                                                                      42

                                                                                                      21

                                                                                                       0

1987   1991   1995   1996   1997   1998

so critical to survive and win in a price-competitive deflationary world, but our challenge is to go beyond that—to capitalize on the vast intellectual capital available around the globe. In 1999, we will move aggressively to broaden our definition of globalization by increasing the intensity of our effort to search out and attract the unlimited pool of talent that is available in the countries in which we do business—from software designers in India to product engineers in Mexico, Eastern Europe and China.

The GE of the next century must provide high-value global products and services, designed by global talent, for global markets.

Product services is a second continuing growth initiative. This initiative has already changed the headset of the Company from that of a provider of products augmented by ancillary services to a Company that is overwhelmingly a source of customer-focused, high-value, information technology-based productivity solutions—as well as a provider of high-quality products.

With this initiative, as with globalization, we are broadening our definition of services—from the traditional activities of parts replacement, overhauling and reconditioning high-value machines like jet engines, turbines, medical equipment and locomotives, to a larger and bolder vision. We have the engineering, the R&D, the product knowledge, the resources and the management commitment to make the series of hundred-million-dollar investments that will allow us to truly change the performance of our installed base, and by doing so upgrade the competitiveness and profitability of our customers: utilities, hospitals, railroads, factories and airlines.

By adding higher and higher technology to the customers' installed base of machines, we will have the capability of returning them to operation not just "over-hauled" but with better fuel burn rates in engines, higher efficiency in turbines, better resolutions in CT scanners, and the like.

The ability to go beyond "servic-ing" to, in essence, "reengineering the installed base" will dramat-

ically improve our customers' competitive positions.

In product services, as with glob-alization, the new expanding view of both initiatives is driven by the insatiable learning culture inherent in the Company today, learning from each other, across businesses, across cultures, and from other companies.

Six Sigma quality, our third growth initiative, is, in itself, a product of learning. After ob-serving the transformational effects this science, this way of life and work, had on the few companies that pursued it, we plunged into Six Sigma with a Company-consuming vengeance just over three years ago. We have invested more than a billion dollars in the effort, and the

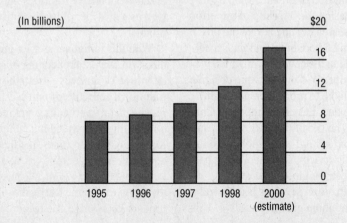

Growth Through Product Services

(In billions)

financial returns have now entered the exponential phase—more than three quarters of a billion dollars in savings beyond our investment in 1998, with a billion and a half in sight for 1999.

The Six Sigma-driven savings are impressive, but it is the radical change in the overall measures of operating efficiency that excite us most. For years—decades—we have been straining to improve operating margin and working capital turns. Our progress was typically measured in basis points for margins and decimal points in working capital turns. Six Sigma came along in 1995 when our margins were in the 13.6% range and turns at 5.8. At the end of 1998, margins hit 16.7% and turns hit 9.2.

These numbers are an indicator of the progress and momentum in our Six Sigma journey.

The ratio of plant and equipment expenditures to depreciation is another measure of asset efficiency. This number in 1998 dropped to 1.2 and will be in the .7-.8 range in the future, as "hidden factory" after "hidden factory"—"free capacity"—is uncovered by Six Sigma process improvements.

All this has taken place in just over three years, after the quarter million of us hurled ourselves into this unknown way of life and work.

Year three of Six Sigma shows how far we have come in training ourselves—with 5,000 full-time "Master Black Belts" and "Black Belts" driving scores of thousands

Six Sigma Progress

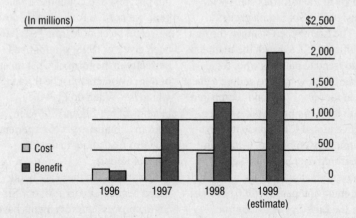

of quality projects around the globe, and with virtually every single professional in the Company a "Green Belt," extensively trained and with a project completed.

As measured by internal performance improvements, and the enhancement of share owner value, Six Sigma has been an unqualified success.

The first major products designed for Six Sigma are just now coming into the marketplace and beginning to touch some of our customers. The new LightSpeed™ CT scanner and the new True-Temp™ electric range, to name two, are drawing unprecedented customer accolades because they were, in essence, designed by the customer, using all of the critical-to-quality performance features (CTQs) the customer wanted in the product and then subjecting these CTQs to the rigorous statistical Design For Six Sigma process.

The LightSpeed scanner, the first multislice CT to reach the market, is a godsend to patients who, for example, now have to endure a chest scan for only 17 seconds compared with the 3 minutes it takes with a conventional CT. A patient with a pulmonary embolism, usually in breathing distress, must lie in a conventional scanner for nearly half a minute compared with 6 seconds for the LightSpeed. A trauma patient, for whom time-to-diagnosis

is a literal life-or-death matter, can have a full-body scan in 26 seconds instead of the 3 minutes a single-slice CT scanner requires. Hospitals, for their part, now get a much higher utilization rate and hence lower per-scan costs. The reception of this product has been remarkable, with $60 million in orders in the first 90 days and with customer acceptance levels and endorsements never before seen.

Every new GE product and service in the future will be "DFSS"—Designed For Six Sigma. These new offerings will truly take us to a new definition of "World Class."

Yes, we've had some early product successes, and those customers who have been touched by them understand what this Six Sigma they've heard so much about really means. But, as we celebrate our progress and count our financial gain, we need to focus on the most powerful piece of learning we have been given in 1998, summarized perfectly in the form of what most of our customers must be thinking, which is: "When do I get the benefits of Six Sigma?" "When does my company get to experience the GE I read about in the GE Annual Report?"

Questions like these are being asked because, up to now, our Six Sigma process improvements have concentrated primarily on our own internal processes and on internal measurements such as "order-to-delivery" or "shop turnaround time."

And in focusing that way—inwardly on our processes—we have tended to use all our energy and Six Sigma science to "move the mean" to, for example, reduce order-to-delivery times from an average of, say, 17 days to 12 days, as reflected in the example below. We've repeated this type of improvement over and over again in thousands of GE processes and have been rewarded for it with less "rework" and greater cash flow. The problem is, as has been said,

"the mean never happens," and the customer who looks at this chart, or charts like it, is still seeing variances in when the deliveries actually occur—a heroic 4-day delivery time on one order, with an awful 20-day delay on another, and no real consistency. The customers in this chart feel nothing. Their life hasn't changed; their profitability hasn't increased one bit. These customers hear the sounds of celebration coming from within GE walls and ask, "What's the big event; what did we miss?" The customer only feels the variance that we have not yet removed.

Example

Customer Dashboard: Customer XYZ
Dashboard Dial: Order to Delivery Time

Order by Order Delivery Times

	Starting Point	After Project	
	29 Days	11 Days	
	10	24	
	7	10	
	19	8	
	6	12	**Mean—Big Change**
	8	8	**17 Days →12 Days**
	16	15	**Variance—Almost**
	19	10	**No Change**
	33	4	
	15	20	
Performance Mean	**17 Days**	**12 Days**	

Customers Feel Variance!

Our challenge, as we move toward 2000, is to turn our Company vision "outside in," to measure the parameters of the customers' needs and processes and work toward zero variability in serving them. *Variation is evil in any customer-touching process*. Improvement to our internal processes is of no interest to the customer.

In 1999, our customers will feel and enjoy the same benefits of Six Sigma that we have been experiencing internally. We will improve variability. We will make this happen. The impetus for this change will come not only from the business leaders but also from the first of the pioneering Six Sigma GE leaders who have now completed their "tours" and have been promoted into leadership positions in the businesses. They are now General Managers, Directors of Finance, Vice Presidents of Sales, Vice President of the Audit Staff, President of GE Mexico, and the like—big jobs.

This next generation of senior GE leadership, and the succeeding waves of Black Belts, share a camaraderie and an esprit forged by their Six Sigma training and the experiences of their tours. They are already predisposed toward hiring only those fluent in Six Sigma language and adept at its methodology. Within a few years, the work

culture and the management style of General Electric will be indelibly, irreversibly, Six Sigma— and it will be focused on the customer's success.

These new leaders are changing the very DNA of GE culture. Work-Out, in the '80s, opened our culture up to ideas from everyone, everywhere, killed NIH (Not Invented Here) thinking, decimated the bureaucracy, and made boundaryless behavior a reflexive and natural part of our culture, thereby creating the learning culture that led to Six Sigma. Now, Six Sigma, in turn, is embedding quality thinking—process thinking—across every level and in every operation in our Company around the globe.

Work-Out in the 1980s defined how we behave. Today, Six Sigma is defining how we work.

The two initiatives—Services and Six Sigma—have one common theme: Only when tomorrow's product and service offerings from GE significantly reduce the plant and equipment expenditures of our customers and increase their productivity will we have fulfilled the GE Services and Six Sigma vision.

These, then, are the three initiatives—Globalization, Services and Six Sigma—fueling powerful growth in your Company and transforming its culture and its soul.

These initiatives are being driven across the businesses and across the globe by a unique brand of 21st century business leader—the GE "A" player, the leader who embodies what we call the four "E's": high *E*nergy; the ability to *E*nergize others; "*E*dge," the ability to make the tough calls; and finally *E*xecute, the consistent ability to turn vision into results.

These "A" players, driving these initiatives, have transformed the very nature of GE—what it does and how well and how quickly it does it.

With our three initiatives, these "A" players will broaden our globalization vision beyond markets and products to the pursuit of the best intellectual capital in the world.

"A" players will see the mission of product services as investing in technology to change our customers' productivity equation and enhance their competitiveness.

And finally, they will turn the face of Six Sigma outward toward the customer and make that customer's profitability the number one priority in any process improvement.

What does a Company with an incredible array of leading global businesses, a learning culture and a depth of "A" player leadership talent have to worry about as we approach the next century? What should keep it awake at night?

Not much, but history points a warning finger toward the arrogance and complacency that have caused others to stumble. It points to the sheer size that has slowed them and limited their agility to change quickly in this era of rapid change.

Already, as we approach the millennium, the pundits are hard at work. Predictions of trends and megatrends are in full production. Their record for accuracy has been spotty, at best. Most recently, less than two years ago, the conventional view of Asia was still one of "onward and upward" without interruption.

Looking back much further, to 20 years ago, when a new GE team moved into leadership, the prognostications were, in many cases, spectacularly inaccurate.

- In 1980, with oil at $35 a barrel, the big questions were when would it hit $100 or if it would be available at all.
- Japan in 1980 seemed to be in inexorable ascendancy, invading and dominating complacent industry after industry. Future American generations were doomed to menial work. The U.S. was losing confidence, experiencing "malaise."
- Twenty years ago, everything was predicated on the expectation of a never-ending

double-digit inflationary environment.

Obviously, these trends did not play out—quite the reverse. Oil is at record lows, Japan is struggling, and the U.S. has moved from "malaise" to exuberance—irrational or not. Inflation has yielded to deflation as the shaping economic force.

So what does this tell us about the future? It tells us that what's as important as predicting trends is a company's ability to cope with any trend.

Sure, early in the next century, Japan will rebound. Oil prices are bound to rise again. Inflation is probably not dead. But spending a lot of time putting too fine a point on the "how" and "when" any of these might happen is less important than growing a culture that is both challenged by the unexpected and confident in, as well as capable of, dealing with whatever comes along.

That's why so much about leading a big company is about assuring that it stays agile, unencumbered by bureaucracy or lulled by complacency—keeping it a company that breathes information, loves change and is excited by the opportunity change presents. It means never allowing a company to take itself too seriously, and reminding it constantly, in the face of any praise or good press, that yesterday's press clippings often wrap today's fish.

Crossing the $100 billion mark in revenue, as we did in 1998, was a milestone, just as the $10 billion mark in earnings will be, but that's all they are—good for a quick pat on the back.

Yes, GE has become a very big company, and with the growth initiatives we have under way, we have every intention of becoming a lot bigger.

But bigger is only better if a company understands and is committed to using the unique advantages of size.

As a big, global, multibusiness company, we have access to an enormous amount of information—and with our learning culture, we have the ability to acquire, share and act rapidly on that information to turn it into marketplace advantage.

Size gives us another big advantage: our reach and resources enable us to go to bat more frequently, to take more swings, to experiment more, and, unlike a small company, we can miss on occasion and get to swing again.

What size cannot be allowed to do to a big company is to let it fall to the temptation of "managing" its size rather than "using" it.

We can never stop swinging! At the same time, we must always be striving to capture the best of a small company—its energy, excitement and speed.

We move into 1999 filled with high expectations and with the confidence that we have the right initiatives, the right culture and the right leadership teams—teams with the agility and speed to seize the big opportunities we know this changing world will present us.

Thanks for your continuing support.

John F. Welch, Jr.
Chairman of the Board and
Chief Executive Officer

Dennis D. Dammerman
Vice Chairman of the Board
and Executive Officer

Eugene F. Murphy
Vice Chairman of the Board
and Executive Officer

John D. Opie
Vice Chairman of the Board
and Executive Officer

FEBRUARY 12, 1999

To Our Share Owners, Customers, and Employees

The final year of the century was our finest, as 340,000 GE people around the globe posted the strongest results in the Company's 122-year history.

- Revenues rose 11% to $112 billion, a record.
- Earnings increased 15% to $10.7 billion, the first time GE has broken the $10 billion mark in earnings from operations.
- Earnings per share were up 15%.
- Free cash flow was a strong $11.8 billion, up 17%.
- Our ongoing operating margin rate grew to 17.8%, a gain of more than a full point from '98 and the third straight year of more than a full point improvement. Working capital turns hit an all-time high of 11.5—an improvement of 2.3 turns. The 80% improvement in this key performance measure over the past three years has added $4 billion to our cash flow.
- GE made 134 acquisitions in 1999, worth almost $17 billion. This marks the Company's third year in a row with over 100 acquisitions, totaling over $51 billion.
- GE was named, for the second consecutive year, *Fortune* magazine's "Most Admired Company in America." Also for the second straight year, we were named "The World's Most Respected Company" by the *Financial Times*. A *Business Week* survey named the GE Board of Directors "Best Board," and *Time* magazine described GE as "The Company of the Century."
- We repurchased $1.9 billion in GE stock in 1999, raised the dividend 17% for the second consecutive year, and proposed a 3-for-1 stock split, the fifth split in 17 years, which will take effect after share owner approval in April 2000.

Our share owners—including our active and retired employees who have $24 billion of GE stock in their savings plans—were rewarded for this performance. The total return on a share of GE stock in 1999 was 54%. This

followed returns of 41% in 1998, 51% in 1997, 40% in 1996 and 45% in 1995.

Understanding GE

In this report, for the first time, the CEOs of the top 20 GE businesses will describe the highlights and, in a few cases, the shortfalls of the year, and their plans for the future. Fourteen of these 20 businesses produced double-digit earnings increases in 1999: five grew more than 40%; four between 25–40%; five between 15–25%; three were about flat; three were down.

We never get it all "right" in any year, and probably never will, but it is the scale and leading market positions of these businesses, and the quality of the teams that run them, that allow us to have one great year after another. 1999 was an outstanding year—our best ever—but the past five have been great as well, as have the past 20. For that matter, it's been a great century. Edison would be pleased.

We believe annual reports are as much about where we can go as where we have been; and our message to you this year should enable you to look forward to the brightest of futures for GE in its third century of operation.

Much has been said of the difficulty of "understanding" GE because of the enormous diversity of its products and services and the breadth of its global operations. But it's actually easy to understand this Company, and to feel confident about its future growth, if you look at its array of world-class businesses and grasp the two fundamental forces that drive GE—its social architecture and its operating system.

The Social Architecture

GE's current social architecture began to form in the early '80s when we became convinced that the only way a company like ours could move quickly and successfully through times of radical change was to use every mind in the Company and to involve everyone in the game—to leave no one, and no good idea, out. To achieve this radical cultural transformation, we developed something we called "Work-Out," which is based on the simple premise that those closest to the work know it best. Over the years there have been literally hundreds of thousands of Work-Out "town meetings," where the views and ideas of every employee, from every function, in every business, were solicited and turned into action—usually on the spot. People saw the value we attached to their intellect and their ideas—and as a result, their ideas began to flow in torrents.

The second facet of the social architecture involved the

cultivation of what we call "bound-aryless" behavior by the removal of every organizational and functional obstacle to the free and unimpeded flow of ideas—inside the Company across every operation, and outside the Company from the best thinking in world business. We measured this boundaryless behavior in our leadership—and rewarded or removed people based on it. We anonymously survey thousands of employees every year to measure our progress and see if our rhetoric matches their reality. When it does not, we take action.

The combination of involving everyone in the game and of responding to this flow of ideas and information turned GE into what we are today—a learning company. By becoming a learning company, we have taken market and geo-graphic diversity, the traditional handicap of multi-business com-panies, and turned them into a deci-sive advantage—unlimited access to the most enormous supply of best ideas, information and in-tellectual capital the business world has to offer.

Our social architecture—our val-ues—is the software that drives what we call the operating system of GE.

The GE Operating System

The operating system of GE was devised to channel and focus this

torrent of ideas and information and put it to use through the medium of Company-wide "initiatives," as well as to track, measure and expand these initiatives as they take hold and flourish.

This operating system is based on an informal but intense, regular schedule of reviews designed to create momentum for the initiative. It progresses with a drumbeat regu-larity throughout our business year—year after year.

A typical initiative—Product Services, say, or Six Sigma Quality—is launched with passion-ate intensity at the meeting of our 600 global leaders in January. A commitment to the initiative is made. Every subsequent event in the Company is developed around implementing and expanding the initiative: resources are allocated; high visibility jobs are created; intense communications start throughout the businesses; and work begins.

Each quarter throughout the year, the leaders of our businesses meet to share what each of them has done to drive the initiative. At these meetings, leaders ranging from the Reinsurance CEO, to the NBC executive, to the head of the Industrial Systems business describe how they are imple-menting the particular initiative in their own operations. The incredible amount of learning that comes from this shared experience expands the initiative and energizes their efforts.

Every Company activity and every Company event during the year add energy and momentum to the initiative. In these same quarterly meetings, for example, every Business Management Course class at our Management Development Institute—50 to 60 of our highest potential leaders— reports back on its three-week experience in the field on the best practices they found from other companies around the world—and they are brutally honest on how we stack up vis-à-vis the best they saw. This candid feedback really picks up the pace.

The same is true for Human Resources reviews. In April and May, the Corporate Executive Office and Human Resources leaders go into the field for full-day personnel reviews at each location, where the people leading and practicing the initiatives present their progress, and a clear assessment is made of the capabilities and the level of intensity of the people involved in the initiative. We want only the best, the brightest and the most committed to be in these leadership roles, and the focus on talent is relentless.

By October, role models— heroes—have emerged in all the businesses, and they are selected to present to the 150 Corporate Officers at their annual meeting. This meeting serves as a platform where each business can measure its progress against that of the best of its peers.

This takes us full circle to January, when the 600 global leaders of our Company meet and focus, once again, on the initiatives. The initiative from the prior January usually occupies the entire first day, and the role models present their stories and share their learning. On Day 2, new ideas around other ongoing initiatives— some several years old—are shared. This year, for example, the first full day was on e-Business. Day 2 covered new thinking in Globalization, Six Sigma and Product Services.

This operating system propels what has become a "learning engine" and embeds these initiatives in the DNA of the Company.

Crucial to the success of this social architecture and operating system is their synchronization with our reward and incentive system. How well people capitalize on these initiatives, how open they are to change, determines the level of their reward. Making the numbers at GE gets you into the game. Living the values and leveraging the operating system is the road to promotions and greater personal rewards.

The remainder of this report will describe how this social architecture and operating system have driven and expanded the four key initiatives that will be the source of GE growth for decades.

Globalization

The oldest current initiative in GE, driven by the GE operating system for about 15 years, is, like Work-Out, becoming so pervasive and ingrained in the Company that it's less an "initiative" now and more a reflex. Globalization began with a GE that derived more than 80% of revenues from the U.S. and has taken us to where we are today, with 41% of revenues from outside the U.S. and moving toward a majority sometime in this decade.

Globalization evolved from a drive to export, to the establishment of global plants for local consumption, and then to global sourcing of products and services. Today, we are moving into its final stages—drawing upon intellectual capital from all over the world— from metallurgists in Prague, to software engineers in Asia, to prod-uct designers in Budapest, Monterrey, Tokyo, Paris and other places around the globe. Our insatiable appetite for more advanced technology is being fed, not by a new wing on our world-class Corporate R&D center in Schenectady, New York, but by a soon-to-open greenfield laboratory in the suburbs of Banga-lore, India.

There has been an enormous amount of comment recently on the subject of globalization. Let us assure you that GE brings only world-class business and work practices and careful, compliant and proactive environmental processes to every one of our global operations. We understand that to be a truly great global company, we must be a great local citizen.

Today, American GE business leaders located outside the United States have become fewer and fewer as local leaders, trained in GE operating methods and steeped in our values but with their own unmatchable customer intimacy and market savvy, are replacing them. Our objective is to be the "global employer of choice," and we are striving to create the exciting career opportunities for local leaders all over the world that will make this objective a reality. This initiative has taken us to within reach of one of our biggest and longest-running dreams—a truly global GE.

Product Services

The precursor to our Product Services initiative was a GE where new product development was primarily "where the action was" for our huge corps of engineers and scientists. The best and brightest of these wanted to work on the highest-thrust jet engine, the fastest medical scan or the leading-edge electrical turbine design. Product services consisted of less-exciting maintenance of our high-value machines—turbines, engines, medical devices and the like.

As recently as 1995, when this initiative was launched, GE derived $8 billion a year in revenues from product services. In 2000, this number will be $17 billion.

The premise for the Product Services initiative was the collective realization that while GE cannot win, and shouldn't play, in the "wrench-turning" game, it could find enormous growth in the high-technology, customer-productivity game—where there are few, if any, who can do the things we can do for that customer.

The human resources focus in the operating system made services the new "place to be" for the best and brightest. Big, exciting, high-technology jobs in services were created. And the GE values system—increasingly tied to customer focus—reinforced the shift.

But the most important key to the long-range success of our services initiative is the understanding that leading-edge technology can only be derived from creating great products. By driving this leading-edge technology back into the installed base of older equipment, we can increase our customers' productivity and, in turn, make them more competitive—with significantly lower investment on their part. We want being a product services customer of GE to be analogous to bringing your car in for a 50,000-mile check and driving out with 100 more horsepower, better gas mileage and lower emissions.

For example, the technology in the world's most advanced, highest-thrust jet engine—the GE90—is now being migrated into yesterday's installed base, refreshing 20-year-old customer engines, improving their thrust, fuel efficiency and time on wing.

"H" gas turbine technology, the world's most advanced, is now improving the efficiency and heat rate of customers' 20- and 30-year-old power plants. Twenty-first century AC locomotive technology is making 1980s' locomotives more reliable; and 1990s' CT machines are producing better scans because of infusions of technology from Six Sigma-designed twenty-first century platforms.

We understand that to be a great services company, we must be a great leading-edge product technology company—they go hand in hand. Using tomorrow's technology to upgrade yesterday's hardware will make our customers more successful and create for GE a rapidly expanding services business for decades to come.

Six Sigma Quality

The Six Sigma initiative is in its fifth year—its fifth trip through the operating system. From a standing start in 1996, with no financial benefit to the Company, it has flourished to the point where it produced more than $2 billion in benefits in 1999, with much more to come this decade.

In the initial stages of Six Sigma, our effort consisted of training more than 100,000 people in its science and methodology and focusing thousands of "projects" on improving efficiency and reducing variance in our internal operations—from industrial factories to financial services back rooms. From there, our operating system steered the initiative into design engineering to prepare future generations of "Design for Six Sigma" products—and drove it rapidly across the customer-interactive processes of the financial services businesses. Medical Systems used it to open up a commanding

technology lead in several diagnostic platforms and has achieved dramatic sales increases and customer satisfaction improvements. Every GE product business and financial service activity is using Six Sigma in its product design and fulfillment processes.

Today, Six Sigma is focused squarely where it must be—on helping our customers win. A growing proportion of Six Sigma projects now under way are done on customer processes, many on customer premises.

The objective is not to deliver flawless products and services that we think the customer wants when we promise them—but rather what customers really want when they want them.

One thing that the truly great companies of the world have in common, regardless of the diversity of their industries, is a total business focus on servicing customers. With Six Sigma as the enabler, we intend to meet that standard.

E-Business

E-business, which entered the operating system at the January Managers Meeting little more than a year ago, is already so big and transformational that it has almost outgrown the bounds of the word "initiative." While we are already generating billions in Web-based revenues, the contribution of e-Business to GE has been so much more. It is changing this Company to its core.

For 20 years, we've been driving to get the soul of a small company into this sometimes muscle-bound, big-company body. We described the contribution of Work-Out, and there was more. We delayered in the '80s, eliminating many of the filters and gatekeepers. We got faster by reducing corporate staff. We launched venture units, in imitation of start-ups. We made close to 30,000 people stock optionees in a Company that used to have under 500. And we ridiculed and removed bureaucrats until they became as rare around GE as whooping cranes.

Every year we got better, faster, hungrier and more customer-focused—until the day this elixir, this tonic, this e-business came along and changed the DNA of GE forever by energizing and revitalizing every corner of this Company.

The first effect of e-business was to further energize and refresh our other three initiatives. For one, it enabled us to put to customer advantage the enormous databases we had compiled on customer processes as part of Six Sigma projects.

What we are rapidly moving toward is the day when "Dr. Jones," in radiology, can go to her home page in the morning and find a comparison of the number, and clarity, of scans her CT machines performed in the last day, or week, to more than 10,000 other machines across the world. She will then be able to click and order software solutions that will bring her performance up to world-class levels. And the performance of her machines might have been improved, online, the previous night, by a GE engineer in Milwaukee, Tokyo, Paris or Bangalore.

The day is almost here when the chief engineer at the local utility may check the heat rate and fuel burn of his turbines—before he has coffee in the morning—to learn how he stacks up with 100 other utilities. Again, with a click to a home page, he can look at what GE services can provide to increase his competitiveness. Here, a number of GE's service packages are offered that will take him quickly to world-class levels.

The efficient harvesting of intellectual capital, which is the state-of-the-art of the globalization initiative, is impossible without the Internet, and GE products are today being designed collaboratively online around the globe 24 hours a day—as our Industrial Systems business does with its "Web City."

But the transformation e-business is bringing about at GE

is more pervasive than even this growing magic.

When you think about this e-Business revolution that is transforming the world, an obvious question comes to mind: Why wasn't the e-revolution launched by big, highly resourced, high-technology companies rather than the small start-ups that led it? The answer may lie, as perhaps is true in GE's case, in the mystery associated with the Internet—the perception that creating and operating Web sites was Nobel Prize work—the realm of the young and wild-eyed. In our case, we once again used a best practice from one of our businesses to overcome this discomfort. We took the top 1,000 managers in the Company and asked them to become "mentees" of 1,000 "with it," very bright e-business mentors—many brand new to GE—and to work with them three to four hours a week, traveling the Web, evaluating competitor sites, and learning to organize their computers, and their minds, for work on the Internet. It was this mentor-mentee interaction—which in some cases resembled that of "Stuart" and his boss in the Ameritrade commercial—that helped overcome the only real hurdle some of us had—fear of the unknown. Having overcome that fear, and experienced the transformational

effects of e-business, we find that digitizing a company and developing e-business models is a lot *easier*—not harder—than we had ever imagined.

Start-ups have energized the business landscape, supported by a strong venture capital environment and healthy IPO market; however, much of their resources must go to establish brand, develop real content and achieve fulfillment capability. We already have that! We already have the hard stuff—over 100 years of a well-recognized brand, leading-edge technology in both product and financial services, and a Six Sigma-based fulfillment capability. The opportunities e-business creates for large companies like GE are unlimited.

But digitizing a company does more than just create unlimited business opportunities; it puts a small company soul into that big company body and gives it the transparency, excitement and buzz of a start-up. It is truly the elixir for GE and others who relish excitement and change.

E-business is the final nail in the coffin for bureaucracy at GE. The utter transparency it brings about is a perfect fit for our boundaryless culture and means everyone in the organization has total access to everything worth knowing.

The speed that is the essence of "e" has accelerated the metabolism of the Company, with people laughing out loud at presentations of business plans for "the third quarter of next year" and other tortoise-like projections of action. Time in GE today is measured in days and weeks.

The accelerating pace of our success in this initiative is leading to a lot of spontaneous celebrating—something big companies, including GE, have always had trouble doing as well as small companies. It generates more fun across a business than anything we've ever seen. The informality, joy of work and endless celebration that comes with "e" life is something on which we are thriving.

E-business was made for GE, and the "E" in GE now has a whole new meaning. We get it—we all get it.

We begin this century with a GE totally focused on the customer, utterly energized and rejuvenated by e-business, and driven by the relentless beat of a unique operating system and social architecture. This Company is poised to move forward to levels of performance, growth and excitement undreamed of in the past.

We thank you all for your support in helping make this future so bright.

John F. Welch, Jr.
Chairman of the Board and
Chief Executive Officer

Dennis D. Dammerman
Vice Chairman of the Board
and Executive Officer

John D. Opie
Vice Chairman of the Board
and Executive Officer

FEBRUARY 11, 2000

To Our Customers, Share Owners, and Employees

2000 was a memorable year for GE: It was a year of record-breaking business performance; a year that saw the proposal to acquire and integrate the businesses of Honeywell; and a year that began the transition to a new leadership team.

- Revenues rose 16% to $129.9 billion—a record.
- Net income rose 19% to a record $12.7 billion, with 15 of GE's top 20 businesses posting double-digit earnings increases.
- Earnings per share increased 19%.
- Cash generated from our operations was a record $15.4 billion—up 31%, or $3.6 billion from 1999.
- Ongoing operating margin—a key metric of business performance—rose to nearly 19%—this from a Company that struggled for 111 years to reach 10%.
- The Company made over 100 acquisitions for the fourth consecutive year and moved quickly to acquire Honeywell, whose businesses are a perfect complementary fit with our Aircraft Engines, Industrial Systems and Plastics businesses. Honeywell share owners approved the merger in January, and GE and Honeywell are working with regulatory agencies to close the transaction as early as possible in 2001.

We expect the acquired Honeywell businesses to give us double-digit earnings-per-share accretion and, within two years, add one to two percentage points to GE's bottom-line growth rate.

- In 2000, GE continued its share repurchase program, raised the dividend 17% and split the stock 3 for 1.
- Our stock price was down 7% but outperformed the S&P 500, which was down 10%. This is not the kind of "outperformance" we've been proud to report in past years—particularly after posting the best operating results in the history of the Company. Still, share owners who have held our stock for five years, including 2000, have been rewarded with

an average 34% total annual return on their investment. Those who have held it for a decade, 29%; two decades, a 23% total annual return.

- Substantial progress was made in 2000 in further diversifying GE's leadership. 26% of the Company's top 3,900 executives are now women and minorities, and over $30 billion of our 2000 revenues were generated by business operations led by female and minority operating managers.
- GE continued to be the world's most honored company—awarded for the fourth straight year *Fortune's* "Most Admired Company in America," as well as, for the third time, "The World's Most Respected Company," by the *Financial Times*.

We write this in a year of transition to a new team, and we would like to use this occasion to reflect on what GE is today: why it works, the values and beliefs it is built upon and how they will serve to take us to the even better days that we know lie ahead for our Company.

First, and most importantly, GE is a growth company, creating, in 2000 alone, the equivalent of an $18 billion, multi-business "company" with earnings of $2 billion. In 2000 the Company not only posted its highest revenues ever, but grew them at one of the highest rates in its history.

Second, through the rigorous pursuit of four big Company-wide initiatives—Globalization, Services, Six Sigma Quality and Digitization—we've changed not only where we work and what we sell, but how we work, think and touch our customers.

Globalization has transformed a heavily U.S.-based Company to one whose revenues are now 40% non-U.S. Even more importantly, it has changed us into a Company that searches the world, not just to sell or to source, but to find intellectual capital: the world's best talent and greatest ideas.

A **Services** focus has changed GE from a Company that in 1980 derived 85% of its revenues from the sale of products to one that today is based 70% on the sale of services. This extends our market potential and our ability to bring value to our customers.

Six Sigma has turned the Company's focus from inside to outside, changed the way we think and train our future leaders and moved us toward becoming a truly customer-focused organization.

As we said in our 1999 letter, **Digitization** is transforming everything we do, energizing every corner of the Company and making us faster, leaner and smarter even as we become bigger. In 2000, these words began to turn into numbers, as we sold over $7 billion of goods and services over the net and conducted over $6 billion in online auctions. Digitization efforts across the Company will generate over $1.5 billion in operating margin improvements in 2001.

The initiatives are playing a critical role in changing GE, but the most significant change in GE has been its transformation into a **Learning Company.** Our true "core competency" today is not manufacturing or services, but the global recruiting and nurturing of the world's best people and the cultivation in them of an insatiable desire to learn, to stretch and to do things better every day. By finding, challenging and rewarding these people, by freeing them from bureaucracy, by giving them all the resources they need—and by simply getting out of their way— we have seen them make us better and better every year.

We have a Company more agile than others a fraction of our size, a high-spirited company where people are free to dream and encouraged to act and to take risks. In a culture where people act this way, every day, "big" will never mean slow.

This is all about people—"soft stuff." But values and behaviors are what produce those performance

numbers, and they are the bedrock upon which we will build our future.

The rest of our letter will describe these abiding values and beliefs because they are at the heart and soul of everything we do, what we stand for, what we stand on and, most important, where we are going.

Integrity

It's the first and most important of our values. Integrity means always abiding by the law, both the letter and the spirit. But it's not just about laws; it is at the core of every relationship we have.

Inside the Company, integrity establishes the trust that is so critical to the human relationships that make our values work. With that trust, employees can take risks and believe us when we say a "miss" doesn't mean career damage. With trust, employees can set stretch performance goals and can believe us when we promise that falling short is not a punishable offense. Integrity and trust are at the heart of the informality we cherish. There are no witnesses needed to conversations, nor the need to "put it in writing." None of that—our word is enough.

In our external dealings, with our unions and governments, we are free to represent our positions vigorously, in a constructive fashion, to agree or disagree on the issues, knowing that our integrity itself is never an issue.

A period of transition is a period of change, and some of our values will be modified to adapt to what the future brings. One will not: our commitment to integrity, which, beyond doing everything right, means always doing the right thing.

Relishing Change

We've long believed that when the rate of change inside an institution becomes slower than the rate of change outside, the end is in sight. The only question is when.

Learning to love change is an unnatural act in any century-old institution, but today we have a Company that does just that: sees change always as a source of excitement, always as opportunity, rather than as threat or crisis. We're no better prophets than anyone else, and we have difficulty predicting the exact course of change. But we don't have to predict it. What we have to do is simply jump all over it! Our moves in Europe, Mexico, Japan and the rest of Asia during the '90s were risky, richly rewarded big swings at fast-breaking change, as was our leap into digitization, and more recently our decision to acquire Honeywell. We strive every day to always have everyone in the organization see change as a thrilling, energizing

phenomenon, relished by all, because it is the oxygen of our growth.

The Customer

Bureaucracies love to focus inward. It's not that they dislike customers; they just don't find them as interesting as themselves. Today we have a Company doing its very best to fix its face on customers by focusing Six Sigma on their needs.

Key to this focus is a concept called "span," which is a measurement of operational reliability for meeting a customer request. It is the time window around the Customer Requested Delivery Date in which delivery will happen. High span shows poor capability to hit a specific date; low span reflects great capability; and zero span is always the objective.

With span, the measurement is based on the day the customer wants the product. When the order is taken, that date becomes known to everyone, from the first person in the process receiving the castings, circuit boards or any other components from the supplier, all the way through to the service reps who stand next to the customer as the product is started up for the first time. Every single delivery to every single customer is measured and in the line of sight of everyone; and everyone in the process knows he or she is affecting the businesswide measurement of span with every action taken.

The object is to squeeze the two sides of the delivery span, days early and days late, ever closer to the center: the exact day the customer desired. Plastics has reduced its span from 50 days to 5; Aircraft Engines from 80 days to 5; Mortgage Insurance took it from 54 days to 1.

GE completed more than 2000 Six Sigma projects "at the customer, for the customer," last year. Here we took GE resources and applied them to our customers' biggest needs, using Six Sigma as a foundation. The focus has been totally inside our customer operations. The wins have been significant: improving locomotive reliability, reducing medical CT scan wait times and improving airline operations. It's not that we know all the answers but we're totally committed to finding them; and committed to externalizing all of our initiatives for the benefit of the customer. Over the long term, we believe this will differentiate GE in the eyes of the customer.

Using Size

One of the biggest mistakes large institutions can make is indulging the compulsion to "manage" their size. They become impressed with how big they are and at the same time nervous about the need to con-trol their size, to get their arms around it. This often leads to more layers, structure and bureaucracy—and eventually stifled and frustrated people.

We see size differently. We understand its inherent limitations—on speed and on clarity of communications, among other things—and we fight every day to create the quickness and spirit of a small company. But we appreciate the one huge advantage size offers: the ability to take big swings, big risks, and to live outside the technology envelope, to live in the future. Size allows us to invest hundreds of millions of dollars in an enormously ambitious program like the GE90, the world's highest-thrust jet engine, and the "H" turbine, the world's highest-efficiency turbine generator. Size allows us to introduce at least one new product in every segment, every year, in medical diagnostics, or to spend hundreds of millions on new plastics capacity, or to continue to invest in a business during a down cycle, or to make over 100 acquisitions a year, year after year.

Our size allows us to do this knowing that we don't have to be perfect, that we can take more risks, knowing that not all will succeed. That's because our size— far from inhibiting innovation, the conventional stereotype—actually allows us to take more and bigger swings. We don't connect with every one, but the point is, our size allows us to miss a few—without missing a beat.

Annihilating Bureaucracy

We cultivate the hatred of bureaucracy in our Company and never for a moment hesitate to use that awful word "hate." Bureaucrats must be ridiculed and removed. They multiply in organizational layers and behind functional walls—which means that every day must be a battle to demolish this structure and keep the organization open, ventilated and free. Even if bureaucracy is largely exterminated, as it has been at GE, people need to be vigilant—even paranoid—because the allure of bureaucracy is part of human nature and hard to resist, and it can return in the blink of an eye. Bureaucracy frustrates people, distorts their priorities, limits their dreams and turns the face of the entire enterprise inward.

In a digitized world, the internal workings of companies will be exposed to the world, and bureaucracies will be seen by all for what they are: slow, self-absorbed, customer insensitive—even silly.

Self-Confidence, Simplicity, and Speed

One leads to the other. Self-confidence is the indïspensable leadership characteristic. It can come from early family life, from sports, from school success, or it can be acquired through opportunities to lead, to take business risks, to be challenged and to win. It is the obligation of every leader to give everyone the business challenges that provide opportunities to develop personal self-confidence. We see, day after day, people's lives—and not just their business lives—utterly transformed by the self-confidence born of meeting big challenges.

Self-confidence in turn allows one to communicate simply and clearly—without the business jargon, busy charts, convoluted memos and incomprehensible presentations that insecure leaders use to mask their self-doubt. Leaders who lack self-confidence use their intelligence to make things more complex. Self-confident people use it to make things simpler.

Simplicity clarifies communications and enhances the chance that everyone in the organization gets the same message. Those clear, simple messages energize people and inspire them to action; thus simplicity leads to speed, one of the key drivers of business success.

Leadership

It's about the four "E's" we've been using for years as a screen to pick our leaders. "Energy": to cope with the frenetic pace of change. "Energize": the ability to excite, to galvanize the organization and inspire it to action. "Edge": the self-confidence to make the tough calls, with "yeses" and "noes"—and very few "maybes." And "Execute": the ancient GE tradition of always delivering, never disappointing.

And it's about the four "types" that represent the way we evaluate and deal with our existing leaders. Type I: shares our values; makes the numbers—sky's the limit! Type II: doesn't share the values; doesn't make the numbers—gone. Type III: shares the values; misses the numbers—typically, another chance, or two.

None of these three are tough calls, but Type IV is the toughest call of all: the manager who doesn't share the values, but delivers the numbers; the "go-to" manager, the hammer, who delivers the bacon but does it on the backs of people, often "kissing up and kicking down" during the process. This type is the toughest to part with because organizations always want to deliver—it's in the blood—and

to let someone go who gets the job done is yet another unnatural act. But we have to remove these Type IVs because they have the power, by themselves, to destroy the open, informal, trust-based culture we need to win today and tomorrow.

We made our leap forward when we began removing our Type IV managers and making it clear to the entire Company why they were asked to leave—not for the usual "personal reasons" or "to pursue other opportunities," but for not sharing our values. Until an organization develops the courage to do this, people will never have full confidence that these soft values are truly real. There are undoubtedly a few Type IVs remaining, and they must be found. They must leave the Company, because their behavior weakens the trust that more than 300,000 people have in its leadership.

Training

We've always had great advanced management training programs at GE. We also have terrific early-career programs in financial management, engineering, manufacturing, the audit staff and others. However, because of our diversity we've never had a truly early-career generic program that would develop leaders for all our functions. All of our big, Company-wide initiatives have led us down serendipitous paths, and Six Sigma has proved no exception. It has, in addition to its other benefits, now become the language of leadership. It is a reasonable guess that the next CEO of this Company, decades down the road, is probably a Six Sigma Black Belt or Master Black Belt somewhere in GE right now, or on the verge of being offered—as all our early-career (3–5 years) top 20% performers will be—a two-to-three-year Black Belt assignment. The generic nature of a Black Belt assignment, in addition to its rigorous process discipline and relentless customer focus, makes Six Sigma the perfect training for growing 21st century GE leadership.

People

Our technology, our great businesses, our reach and our resources aren't enough to make us the global best unless we always have the best people—people who are always stretching to become better. This requires rigorous discipline in evaluating, and total candor in dealing with, everyone in the organization.

In every evaluation and reward system, we break our population down into three categories: the top 20% the high-performance middle 70% and the bottom 10%.

The top 20% must be loved, nurtured and rewarded in the soul and wallet because they are the ones who make magic happen. Losing one of these people must be held up as a leadership sin—a real failing.

The top 20% and middle 70% are not permanent labels. People move between them all the time. However, the bottom 10%, in our experience, tend to remain there. A Company that bets its future on its people must remove that lower 10%, and keep removing it every year—always raising the bar of performance and increasing the quality of its leadership.

Not removing that bottom 10% early in their careers is not only a management failure, but false kindness as well—a form of cruelty—because inevitably a new leader will come into a business and take out that bottom 10% right away, leaving them—sometimes midway through a career—stranded and having to start over somewhere else. Removing marginal performers early in their careers is doing the right thing for them; leaving them in place to settle into a career that will inevitably be terminated is not. GE leaders must not only understand the necessity to encourage, inspire and reward that top 20%, and be sure that the high-performance 70% is always energized to improve and move upward; they must develop the determination to change out, always humanely, that bottom 10%, and do it every year. That is how real meritocracies are created and thrive.

Informality

Informality is not generally seen as a particularly important cultural characteristic in most large institutions, but it is in ours. Informality is more than just being a first-name company; it's not just an absence of managers parading around the factory floor in suits, or of reserved parking spaces or other trappings of rank and status. It's deeper than that. At GE it's an atmosphere in which anyone can deliver a view, an idea, to anyone else, and it will be listened to and valued, regardless of the seniority of any party involved. Leaders today must be equally comfortable making a sales call or sitting in a boardroom—informality is an operating philosophy as well as a cultural characteristic.

One of GE's long-standing management tenets has been the belief that businesses must be, or become, number one or number two in their marketplaces. We managed by that tenet for years, and enjoyed the business success that came, over time, from implementing it. But, once again, insidious bureaucracy crept into the definition of number one or number two and began to lead management teams to define their markets more

and more narrowly to assure that their business would fit the one-or-two share definition.

It took a mid-level Company management training class reporting out to us in the spring of 1995 to point out, without shyness or sugar-coating, that our cherished management idea had been taken to nonsensical levels. They told us we were missing opportunities, and limiting our growth horizons, by shrinking our definition of "the market" in order to satisfy the requirement to be number one or two.

That fresh view shocked us, and we shocked the system. At the July three-year planning review that year, leaders were asked to define their markets in such a way that their businesses would have a 10%-or-less share. Rather than the increasingly limited market opportunity that had come from this number-one or number-two definition that had once served us so well, we now had our eyes widened to the vast opportunity that lay ahead for our product and service offerings. This simple but very big change, this punch in the nose, and our willingness to see it as "the better idea," was a major factor in our acceleration to double-digit revenue growth rates in the latter half of the '90s.

That's the value of the informal culture of GE—a culture that breeds an endless search for ideas that stand or fall on their merits, rather than on the rank of their originator, a culture that brings every mind into the game.

GE, as a **Global Learning Company**, is the result, the culmination, of the values and behaviors we've described. Today, the whole world's intellect and best ideas are ours because we are "boundaryless." More than just being receptive to these ideas, we spend our days seeking them out. Years ago Toyota taught us asset management. Wal*Mart introduced us to Quick Market Intelligence. AlliedSignal and Motorola got us started on our enormous Six Sigma initiative. More recently, Trilogy, Cisco and Oracle helped us begin the digitization of GE.

In today's GE, the rewarded behavior has changed from being the exclusive originator of an idea as a vehicle for standing out among colleagues—to, more importantly, finding a better idea and eagerly sharing it across the business and the entire Company, with the intent and effect of raising the bar of performance for all of GE.

The innovation that keeps every one of our businesses—from Aircraft Engines to Medical Systems—at the leading edge of their industries occurs much more rapidly because of the technology that flows rapidly back and forth

across our Company in countless streams: metallurgy from Aircraft Engines to Power Systems; digitization from Medical Systems to Industrial Systems to Capital Services; span success from Plastics to Mortgage Insurance to every other business.

The GE operating system, which we have illustrated in the pages that follow our letter, is not a bureaucratic series of reviews, budget drills, reports and dog-and-pony shows, but a regular series of sessions devoted to learning and to sharing the best ideas and practices from across the Company and around the world.

Understanding how this learning culture, this insatiable thirst for new ideas fuels and is the central agenda of this operating system, explains how businesses as diverse as Plastics, Aircraft Engines or NBC can grow faster and perform better as part of this system than they would if they were not. It's what makes GE work. It's the fabric of the learning culture. Such an operating mechanism is difficult to bring alive on paper or in a chart, but is vividly clear when one observes the ferment and sharing of ideas that are at the heart of what might look like, from an agenda, just another series of boring business meetings.

It is this passion for learning and sharing that forms the basis for the unrelenting optimism with which we view the future, and for the conviction that our greatest days lie ahead.

The GE of the future will be based on the cherished values that drive us today: mutual trust and the unending, insatiable, boundaryless thirst for the world's best ideas and best people. But the GE of the future will be a faster, bolder GE whose actions will make the Company of today appear slow and tentative by comparison, a GE whose every employee will understand that success can only come from an inextricable link to the success of our customers.

And it will be a GE that will always be, as it is today, grateful for your continuing support.

John F. Welch, Jr.
Chairman of the Board
and Chief Executive Officer

Jeff Immelt
President and Chairman-Elect

Dennis D. Dammerman
Vice Chairman of the Board
and Executive Officer

Robert Wright
Vice Chairman of the Board
and Executive Officer

FEBRUARY 9, 2001

Notes

Chapter One: The GE Revolution

Page 21: "with its face to the CEO and its ass to the customer"

This is one of the core elements in what Tichy calls "Old Way" mechanistic organizations. Other attributes include:

- Large physical locations.
- Many layers from top to bottom.
- Strong functional and staff groups.
- Suppliers regarded as adversaries.
- "Doing it by the book" instead of doing it right for the customer, employee, or business.
- Businesses as islands unto themselves.

From "Creating the Competitive Organization of the 21st Century: The Boundaryless Corporation" by Mary Anne Devanna and Noel Tichy, *Human Resource Management,* Winter 1990, vol. 29, number 4, pp. 455–71.

Page 22: While Japanese companies were boosting productivity by 8% annually, GE's gains had rarely topped 1.5% . . .

GE's measure of productivity is a four-step calculation designed to create a realistic picture of the company's overall performance.

- The first calculation deducts from GE's annual *revenues* the total dollar effect of that year's price increases.
- Step two is the subtraction of inflation's effects from GE's total *costs* for the year.
- In step three, GE divides the revised revenue figure by the revised cost figure, to calculate the ratio of output to input.
- The final step is to calculate the percentage change in that ratio versus that of the previous year. The resulting percentage is the number that defines productivity at GE.

Page 24: "Neutron Jack," suggesting the CEO's willingness to vaporize people . . .

Remarkably, despite all the cuts, GE ranked as the world's twelfth largest employer in *Fortune*'s 1991 Global 500 list.

Chapter Three: The Hand He Was Dealt

Page 52: Coffin . . . had a flair for corporate organization . . .

Charles Coffin set the stage for the GE culture through his eleven interdependent and complementary strategic preferences:

1. Internal growth

   —growth from within preferable to acquisition or merger
   —GE should generate its own capital, technology, and management
   —debt unthinkable

2. Constrained diversity

   GE prior to World War II was a generalist with a specialty—design, manufacture, and sale of goods related to the generation and utilization of electricity.

3. Oligopolistic competition

   —minimizing the number of competitors through control of entry and industry concentration
   —allocation of markets by region, product, and function
   —minimization of price competition
   —nonrelative growth among competitors
   —neutralization of government intervention

4. Domestic saturation
   The goal was to dominate the industry in the domestic market:

   —dominate electrical science and technology
   —maintain fixed ratios of market share and price with competition
   —prevent entry of new competitors
   —do the above legally enough to avoid antitrust prosecution

5. International defense
   Protect its domestic market position through:

   —domestic cross-licenses with Westinghouse and other American electrical manufacturers
   —a set of nonaggression pacts with foreign electrical manufacturers
   —portfolio of foreign securities
   —the International General Electric Company

6. Vertical centricism
   The GE organizational structure resembled a wedding cake.

7. Definite chain of command

8. Functional specialization
Interfunctional problems and opportunities were almost exclusively handled by the president; thus all levels below him were primarily defined in functional terms.

9. Structural uniformity
Each organizational layer had defined authority and responsibility; all operating components at any given level of the company were to be of equal size; ratio type of performance measures; structural uniformity bred a complex and bureaucratic system of procedures, standards, and controls.

10. Liquidity
Pay-as-you-go policy

11. Anticipatory relations
The pursuit of anticipatory and nonadversary relationships with government, labor, and the public.

From James Baughman's unpublished manuscript, *Problems and Performance of the Role of Chief Executive in the General Electric Company, 1892–1974.*

Page 55: In 1951, he [Cordiner] assembled a brainy team of GE executives, plus consultants and professors . . .

The task force Ralph Cordiner put together was led by Harold Smiddy, VP of GE Management Consultation Services Division, a former consultant and partner at Booz, Allen and Hamilton, and president of the Academy of Management. Many of the ideas presented in the Blue Books and by Cordiner bear Smiddy's trademark.

From Ronald G. Greenwood, *Harold F. Smiddy: Manager by Inspiration and Persuasion,* University of Wisconsin.

Chapter Four: The New Leader

Page 61: among the finest examples of succession planning in corporate history . . .

Reg Jones's thoroughness and thoughtfulness in selecting the next CEO is reflected in the carefully planned activities for the last months before he was due to present his evaluation of the vice chairman to the GE board.

Page 67: By contrast, Welch's predecessors had run GE . . .

Welch's predecessors and most of his competitors for the CEO job were caught in the old scientific management mold, reflected in their style and mode of operation. For an in-depth discussion of these concepts, see Peter Drucker, *Concept of the Corporation,* New York: John Day, 1946.

MANAGEMENT ATTRIBUTE/ STYLE	WELCH	ALFRED SLOAN SCIENTIFIC MGMT.
Style of Communication	Speaking	Writing
Behavior	Aggressive	Cautious
	Confrontational	Harmony
Tends to assign responsibility to	Individuals	System
Approach to decentralization	Large units	Small units
	"Business"	Defined as "P & L centers"
Method of integration	Processes	Committees
Relies on	Key data	Reports
	"Employee feedback"	Committees
Belief in planning	Limited	Unlimited
	In tune with market	forecasting
Attitude to uncertainty	Accept	Avoid
Attitude to change	Accept	Control

Page 78: When EMS rated the three vice chairmen according to its fifteen categories . . .

The contenders were rated on a five-point scale ranging from "very weak" to "very strong" on the following items: leadership—even-handed, objective, consistent, charismatic; decisive; savvy; fun; intelligence; balance of delegation/involvement; people judgment; ego—ego management, share the credit; long-term view; toughness.

Page 78: each of the remaining candidates write a detailed memo assessing his own performance . . .

Below is an excerpt from Welch's seven-page letter to Reg Jones, followed by Ted LeVino's assessment:

Obviously, looking at any of these issues, there is great distance today between where you are and all three of us [vice chairmen]. However, I feel I have the intellectual capacity, breadth, discipline, and most of all the leadership to get there. General Electric has been my business life and its importance to me has grown with each succeeding year. Whether I can properly assemble and discharge the multiple responsibility is for others to judge—but obviously I would like the chance . . .

Ted LeVino:

. . . an unabashed sales pitch on personal qualities and philosophy of managing winding up with a strong bid for the order. He had seized this opportunity to state his case with just enough vice chairman accomplishment content to make it appear responsive to the request. It is an extremely well-written amalgam of performance, concepts and achievements, examples, etc. He covers the short-comings you may see in him extremely cleverly.

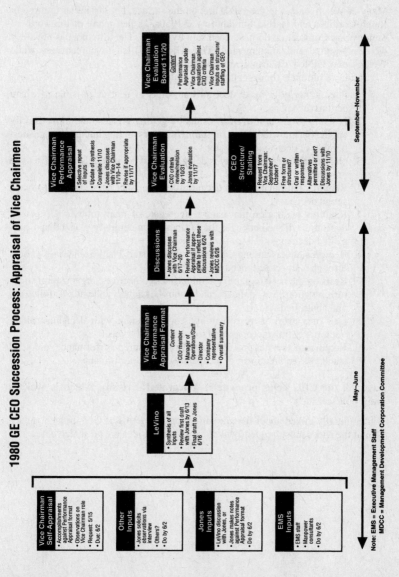

1980 GE CEO Succession Process: Appraisal of Vice Chairman

Note: EMS = Executive Management Staff
MDCC = Management Development Corporation Committee

Chapter Five: The Power of Ideas

Page 83: What's revolutionary—and ultimately far more important than the ideas themselves—is the way GE is weaving its guiding principles into the fabric of its culture.

Many of Welch's ideas in the 1980s are, on the surface, not dissimilar to those of Ralph Cordiner and Harold Smiddy in the 1950s. In fact many of the words of Smiddy and Cordiner could have been said by Welch. The difference is how they were interpreted and implemented. The "Old Way" led to bureaucracy while Welch's new GE led to a lean flexible organization.

Smiddy's rationale for decentralization was:

1. Puts authority to make decisions at points as near as possible to where actions take place.
2. Is likely to get best *overall* results by getting greatest and most directly applicable knowledge and most *timely* understanding into play on greatest number of decisions.
3. Only works if real authority is delegated; and not if details then have to be reported.
4. Requires faith that men in decentralized jobs will have capacity to make sound decisions.
5. Requires realization that natural aggregate of many individually sound decisions will be better for the business than centrally planned and controlled decisions.
6. Requires understanding that main role for "staff" is the rendering of help through a few experienced people.
7. Rests on the need to have general business objectives, organization structure, relationships, policies, and controls known, understood, followed, and controlled.
8. Can only work if responsibility commensurate with decision-making authority is truly accepted and exercised at all levels.
9. Requires personnel practices based on measured performance, enforced standards, and removal for incapacity or poor performance.

Page 90: the CEC helps promote . . . integrated diversity, which is Welch's main political idea.

Welch initially talked about Integrated Diversity in terms of GE's hidden values. Two of the slides most frequently used to explain the idea are presented below:

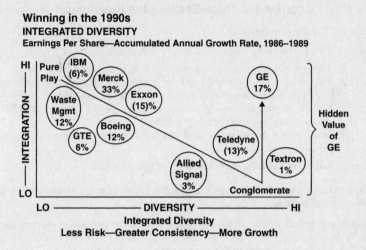

Winning in the 1990s
INTEGRATED DIVERSITY
Earnings Per Share—Accumulated Annual Growth Rate, 1986–1989

Integrated Diversity
Less Risk—Greater Consistency—More Growth

The second diagram is how Jack Welch presented these benefits to the security analysts in 1989. Note the blend of hard and soft issues.

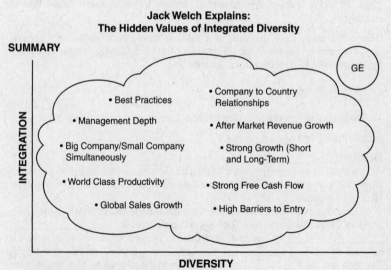

Jack Welch Explains:
The Hidden Values of Integrated Diversity

SUMMARY

The GE Issue:
• **Everyone Understands Diversity**
• **Some Understand Integration**
• **Few Recognize the Hidden Values of Integrated Diversity**

Chapter Six: "Kick-Starting the Revolution"

Page 93: Trusting his instincts . . .

These are four main obstacles to transforming shared values:

1. The lack of clearly articulated and internally consistent shared values.
2. The "do as I say rather than as I do" problem: Failure of role models to live up to shared values creates cynicism in the organization.
3. Pockets of ignorance and/or resistance: Some people remain ignorant of the shared values while others reject them.
4. Overreliance on speeches and one-way communication—the Sunday morning sermon problem.

Values must be built into the everyday fabric of people's lives.

Page 101: As a practical matter, though, the earnings goals frequently made job cuts unavoidable.

During this period of time Welch kept track of who was getting cut in businesses that were downsizing, the chiefs or Indians. When the chiefs weren't getting cut as much as the Indians, Welch would send the business leader a note or call them up to discuss why. The message got clearer and clearer over the years: Start cutting at the top.

Page 101: He personally answered letters of complaint from laid-off employees . . .

Below is a letter from the wife of a laid-off employee, and Welch's personal response, which resulted in the GE business following through on his promise to the spouse to provide relocation assistance.

c.c.: John F. Welch Jr.

August 14, 1985

To: Division Vice-President & General Manager

From: Employee's Spouse

Dear Mr. _____:

    I am giving you an opportunity to read this letter and respond before I share my story publicly. I am in a very traumatic situation that I can't fully comprehend. Here are the details:

    A man interviews with one of the top 100 corporations in America for a sales position. He is offered the job. The man presently lives in _____, _____, a booming metropolis. The job offer will require him to relocate to _____, _____, a small seaside community. The man and his wife decide that the job is worth the relocation. They arrive at this conclusion based on several facts: (1) The position is with a stable, reputable company. (2) The man knows that he will enjoy the job and be successful at it. (3) He foresees opportunity for upward career mobility. (4) The job offers adequate salary and benefits for family support. The man accepts the job. He sells his home in

_____. His wife quits her well-paying job, and they move to _____.

In _____, they rent a place to live and he purchases a company car. Six months pass and they buy a home. The wife becomes pregnant and the couple joyfully await the birth of their first child.

The man works very hard for the company. He frequently works twelve hours a day, arriving home 7:30 P.M. or later. But he enjoys his job. The hard work pays off, and he meets his sales objectives. He has established new dealers, increased business with old ones, and developed large sales with OEMs. After eight months in the field, he reaches 127% of his sales objective. This he accomplished without any hands-on assistance from management. He was an eight-month rookie and he produced! He succeeded in spite of his not knowing how his performance was stacking up by company standards. You see, he was never given a performance evaluation.

Now the man has to sell the home in _____ that he bought two months ago. He and his pregnant wife must prepare to move back to _____, where he will stand a better chance to secure a job to provide for his family.

Why does the man have to move again? He has _just been informed that as of November 1, he will no longer be employed with the company due to "lack of work."_ He asks himself, "How can there be lack of work when I could not get the order department to fill a countless number of orders due to product unavailability?" He wonders, "Why me? What about my family? What about my career? I trusted these people."

This is a true story. The man is _____, _my husband._ The company is the General Electric Company, _____ Division. I realize that you may not know my husband, but I was compelled to write this letter because I can't believe that you are fully aware of the effects of your current policies. My husband is intelligent, sharp, ambitious, and hardworking. Your _____ management will attest to his attributes on the grounds that they hired him. _It seems to me our family is a victim of General Electric's lack of planning and integrity._ How would you explain this situation?

At this point _I feel that the decent and fair thing for GE to do is to purchase our house in _____ and assume responsibility for our moving back to _____._ These requests are quite minimal compared to what we have given you and what we stand to lose because of your actions.

If our experience is indicative of General Electric's regard for the American family, then it's no wonder that the institution of family continues to disintegrate with every height of corporate prosperity.

Sincerely,
Mrs. _____

September 5, 1985

Dear Mrs. _____:
Thanks for your direct and thoughtful letter of August 14.

I wish I could say that no component of General Electric is ever too optimistic in setting its goals, or falls short . . . but clearly you know better. In this case, the _____ industry price collapse was far greater than the manage-

ment of the business anticipated. In fact, the business will lose more than thirty billion dollars in 1985.

"Fair and decent" is precisely what we want to be to each of the individuals
affected by cutbacks in _____, or any of our businesses effecting
reduction in force in the struggle to deal with an increasingly competitive environment.

By the time you receive this letter, I believe the _____ program to
assist your husband in finding a new job and relocating will be known to you. I
hope you both will find it helpful.

Thanks again for your letter. I'm sorry we were so slow in getting our act together.

Sincerely,
Jack Welch

Mrs. _____
_____

_____

bcc: Sector Executive
     Division Vice President

Chapter Seven: Nothing Sacred

Page 108: by the end of 1984, the old GE no longer existed . . .

The "Old Way" GE, with sheltering layers of resistance, can be symbolized by its
organizational structure:

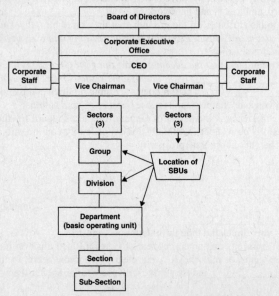

1981 GE Organization Structure

Chapter Eight: Facing Reality

Page 127: Four times a year Richardson would brief union officers . . .

Besides these quarterly meetings, Richardson and Paynter organized **weekly dialogue meetings, monthly operational reviews** with 100 to 120 managers, and **customer awareness trips**—they rented planes and filled them with 150 hourly and salaried employees, to interface with customers.

Page 129: Transportation Systems never posted a loss during the 1980s.

The effects of Schlemmer's team efforts are shown below:

Earnings Profile—With Cost Reductions

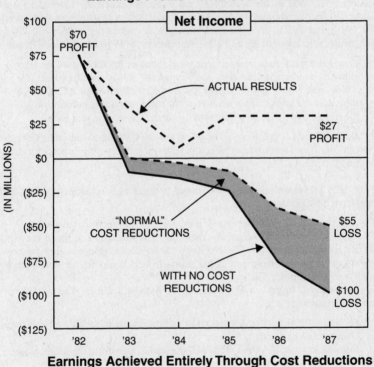

Earnings Achieved Entirely Through Cost Reductions

Chapter Ten: The Turning Point

Page 155: David Letterman became part of the Crotonville curriculum.

Letterman evidently believes he was being courageous by verbally bloodying the GE CEO. Welch spoiled his fun by enjoying the satire. Indeed, several years later Welch tried to return the compliment by personally delivering a fruit basket to Letterman, but the talk-show host didn't seem to get the joke.

Chapter Eleven: Crotonville

Page 159: GE's Management Development Institute, overlooking the Hudson River.

Its forerunner was an organization of top managers called the Electrical Funds Group (ELFUN), who gathered on Association Island in upstate New York during the 1940s and 1950s. Novelist Kurt Vonnegut, Jr., who once worked for GE in Schenectady, lampooned the ELFUN gatherings in his 1958 novel *Player Piano:*

> . . . spent a week each summer in an orgy of morale building—through team athletics, group sings, bonfires and skyrockets, bawdy entertainment, free whisky and cigars; and through plays, put on by professional actors, which pleasantly but unmistakably made clear the nature of good deportment within the system, and the shape of firm resolves for the challenging year ahead.

In Vonnegut's novel every aspect of these retreats—whether you qualify for the "Green" or "Blue" team, whom you bunk with—signifies your prospects for rising within the firm.

Page 163: The emphasis [in conventional programs] is on skills training and cognitive development . . .

We redrafted our ideas about purpose and values for Crotonville into a chart. The top line shows each manager's experience. The left-hand axis shows the focus of any particular program. The challenge facing Crotonville was how to move toward the upper left-hand part of the matrix to help deal with the revolutionary agenda of transforming GE.

That analysis helped us define Crotonville's strategic thrusts. The most important of these were:

> Serving as think tank to develop knowledge about organizational effectiveness, Using action learning, Reinforcing the GE values while helping leaders transform the local culture, Bringing GE's top people to Crotonville.

Page 174: Welch wanted the final [values] statement to be something all GEers could "own."

The values statement changed dramatically over the years. Some highlights:

Depth of Intervention

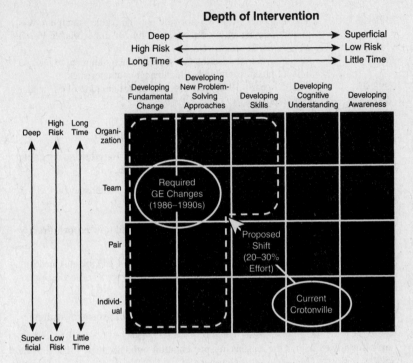

	Jan. 1981	"fast moving, acting like a small organization even though you're a big organization."
	1983	Ten major cultural themes: budgets—comparing to our environment; ownership—more delegation; investment—stay number one; lean and agile; excellence; quality; entrepreneurship; reality and candor; communication; stewardship—obligation to take the assets you have, drive them to newer and better heights through excellence.
	1985	A five-page document on shared values was created.
	Nov. 1985	The EMS staff created a first draft on GE leadership characteristics, built on the values statement.
	1986–87	The values statement was discussed at Crotonville by thousands of participants.
	Spring of 1986	Twenty-five officers attended a Crotonville workshop to discuss leadership and values.
		Image study showed a deteriorating sense of commitment on the part of GE to its employees, to its customers, and to its suppliers.

Mid-1987	The feedback from Crotonville on the value statement was pulled together into a document titled *Toward a Shared Vision and Shared Values for GE*.
1988	Welch further revised the GE shared values statement to include a list of business and individual leader characteristics.
1992	Again, in early 1992 Welch refined his articulation of GE leader characteristics.

Chapter Twelve: The Politics of Speed

Page 184: GE had been organized vertically like a many-tiered wedding cake; henceforth it would look like a cartwheel lying on its side . . .

The GE organizational structure when Welch became vice chairman in 1981 is apparently different from that of 1992 (see page 564).

Page 184: GE's thirteen main business units, which would now report directly to Welch or one of the vice chairmen.

Several months after Vice Chairman Larry Bossidy took the CEO job at AlliedSignal, Welch added two men to the office of the CEO: Paolo Fresco, now vice chairman, and Frank Doyle, now executive vice president.

Page 186: By the end of 1982, GE had virtually abolished the central strategic-planning staff.

Larry Bossidy explained the reasons in a presentation at the Strategic Management Society in Boston, Massachusetts, October 1987:

(a) It is no longer possible to see that far (three to five years) into the future. Five years is an eternity. In fact, it's two careers in Silicon Valley. We manage GE from the perspective that every cliché about events moving faster and becoming more complex is essentially true.

(b) Strategic planning was reluctant or unable to confront the reality of the need to compete internationally. Planners tended to focus on the more coherent and decipherable U.S. market . . . much like the man who searched for his keys near the lamppost, not because that was where he lost them, but because that was where the light was.

(c) Strategic planning inculcated a preoccupation with precision as well as predictability. Sudden change was viewed more often as threat than opportunity.

(d) Strategic planning—at least at its worst—produced operating management that did not participate in the development of strategy, that did not understand it when developed, and often, when understood disagreed with it.

MOREOVER:

A separate planning function can undermine the objective because it permits the manager to sidestep the issue, and it promotes isolation. Don't give the manager a planner. Rather demand a comprehensive strategy review within six months of the manager's assignment. This should force a team-building, participative process, which combines the analytical process with appropriate communications.

BUT:

When we deserted strategic planning, we most emphatically did not abandon strategic thinking or strategic management. . . . Strategic thinking identifies and synthesizes the forces that affect your business while strategic management uses strategic thinking to set business objectives and to communicate this direction to the organization. . . . That's [strategic management] what we're trying to spread at GE today.

Chapter Thirteen: The New Order

Page 194: The wide-open debating style that Welch calls constructive conflict . . .

As Karl Weick points out, constructive conflict depends on face-to-face contact. Previously, GE had used more formal, less rich channels. Karl Weick:

If you want to be informed in equivocal environments, there is no substitute for face-to-face communication. If you are in a more certain environment, then you can get by with formal media.

Page 196: Sociologist Amitai Etzioni described three methods of organizational control: coercive, utilitarian, and normative.

See A. Etzioni. *A Comparative Analysis of Complex Organizations* (New York: Free Press, 1961).

Chapter Fourteen: Getting Excited

Page 207: the company used cross-licensing agreements to form partnerships with competitors . . .

One of these agreements was called "Phoebus." Robert Jones and Oliver Marriott in "A History of G.E.C., A.E.I. and English Electric" in *Anatomy of a Merger* explain:

Phoebus, an allegorical reference to the Sun God, suggesting the necessity of light rather than the morality of the ring. Phoebus was organized through a Swiss limited company, Phoebus S.A. Compagnie Industrielle pour le Developments de l'Eclairage. Its aim was to encourage a complete interchange of patents among members and to fix prices country by country by means of national "Local Meetings."

With one exception, all the world's biggest lamp-makers signed the Phoebus agreement in 1924 and, generally through pressure from Phoebus, a number of smaller producers had fallen into line and signed by 1939. The exception was GE of America, although its subsidiaries in Mexico, Brazil, and China were signators.

What finally cemented GE of America's hold on the world ring was its shareholdings. It owned a major shareholding in every one of the leading lamp-producers in the world in the middle of 1935.

Page 208: building the world's first industrial park . . .

It was founded on April 4, 1913, and called "Nela" Park, drawing its name from the initials of the National Electric Lamp Association, an association of smaller companies that pooled their engineering and research. It was formed in 1894 by Franklin S. Terry of the Sunbeam Company of Chicago and Burton G. Tremaine of the Fostoria Lamp Company in Ohio to compete against such giants as GE and Westinghouse. However, they didn't have the capital they needed to grow, so on May 3, 1901, GE's CEO Charles Coffin purchased 75% of NELA with an option to buy the rest. In 1911, the federal courts ordered GE to consolidate NELA. Terry and Tremaine then pursued their idea of moving the division's headquarters to a bucolic, remote surrounding and convinced Coffin and other top GE managers to lay out $1 million for its purchase and development.

Page 213: Stephen Rabinowitz, who was Lighting's technology vice president . . .

He has since left GE and has been hired by Larry Bossidy at AlliedSignal to run one of the Automative Businesses.

Chapter Fifteen: Globalization

Page 224: International General Electric, which GE disbanded . . .

But in January of 1982 Welch gave a go-ahead to establish the General Electric Trading Company (GETC), which became an independent subsidiary the following July. Its task was to secure GE companies' export orders through countertrade, offset, and bartering.

Chapter Sixteen: Work-Out

Page 242: At first, people spent much of their time griping . . .

To me the evolution of GE's Work-Out efforts follows the phases of a social movement:

Conception Phase: 1987–1989
The launch of town hall meetings and workshops in all businesses.

GE Organization 1981

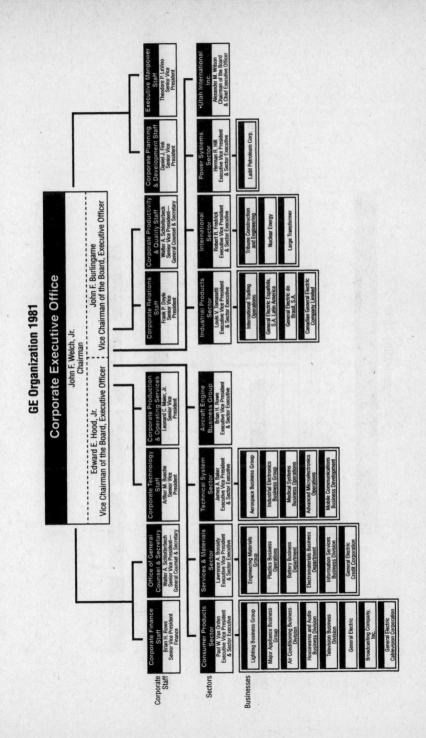

GE Organization 1992

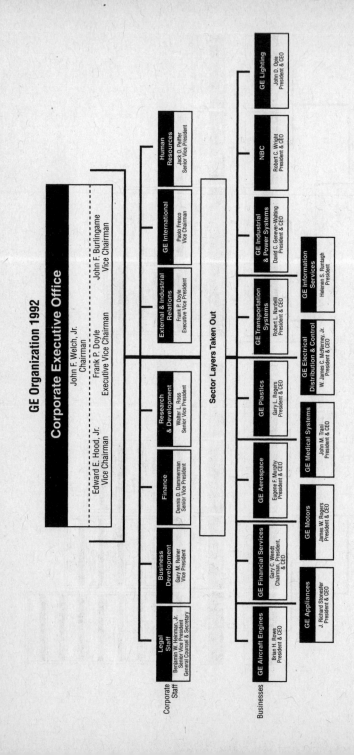

Corporate Executive Office

John F. Welch, Jr.
Chairman

Frank P. Doyle
Executive Vice Chairman

Edward E. Hood, Jr.
Vice Chairman

John F. Burlingame
Vice Chairman

Corporate Staff

Legal Staff
Benjamin W. Heineman, Jr.
Senior Vice President
General Counsel & Secretary

Business Development
Gary M. Reiner
Vice President

Finance
Dennis D. Dammerman
Senior Vice President

Research & Development
Walter L. Robb
Senior Vice President

External & Industrial Relations
Frank P. Doyle
Executive Vice President

GE International
Paolo Fresco
Vice Chairman

Human Resources
Jack O. Peiffer
Senior Vice President

Sector Layers Taken Out

Businesses

GE Aircraft Engines
Brian H. Rowe
President & CEO

GE Appliances
J. Richard Stonesifer
President & CEO

GE Financial Services
Gary C. Wendt
Chairman, President, & CEO

GE Motors
James W. Rogers
President & CEO

GE Aerospace
Eugene F. Murphy
President & CEO

GE Medical Systems
John M. Trani
President & CEO

GE Plastics
Gary L. Rogers
President & CEO

GE Electrical Distribution & Control
W. James C. McNerney, Jr.
President & CEO

GE Transportation Systems
Robert L. Nardelli
President & CEO

GE Information Services
Helene S. Runtagh
President

GE Industrial & Power Systems
David C. Genever-Watling
President & CEO

NBC
Robert C. Wright
President & CEO

GE Lighting
John D. Opie
President & CEO

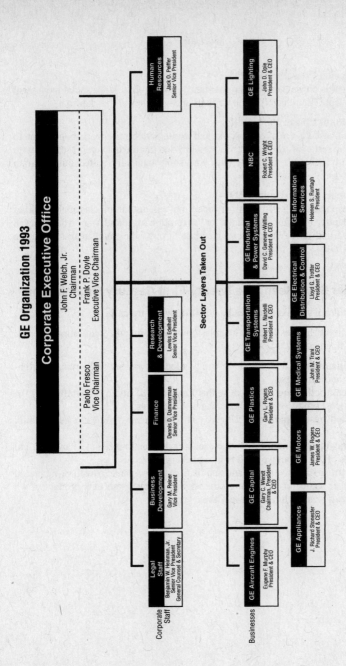

GE Organization 1993

Corporate Executive Office

John F. Welch, Jr.
Chairman

Frank P. Doyle
Executive Vice Chairman

Paolo Fresco
Vice Chairman

Human Resources
Jack O. Peiffer
Senior Vice President

Corporate Staff

Legal Staff	Business Development	Finance	Research & Development
Benjamin W. Heineman, Jr. Senior Vice President General Counsel & Secretary	Gary M. Reiner Vice President	Dennis D. Dammerman Senior Vice President	Lewis L. Edelheit Senior Vice President

Sector Layers Taken Out

Businesses

GE Aircraft Engines	GE Capital	GE Plastics	GE Transportation Systems	GE Industrial & Power Systems	NBC	GE Lighting
Eugene F. Murphy President & CEO	Gary C. Wendt Chairman, President, & CEO	Gary L. Rogers President & CEO	Robert L. Nardelli President & CEO	David C. Genever-Watling President & CEO	Robert C. Wright President & CEO	John D. Opie President & CEO

GE Appliances	GE Motors	GE Medical Systems	GE Electrical Distribution & Control	GE Information Services
J. Richard Stonesifer President & CEO	James W. Rogers President & CEO	John M. Trani President & CEO	Lloyd G. Trotter President & CEO	Helenen S. Runtagh President

Pioneering Phase: 1989–1990
During this phase there was no resistance to Work-Out. It is a social movement that swept GE, reflected in the writings and speeches of the chairman.

Self-Doubt Phase: 1990–1991
In this phase the era of enthusiasm and excitement for the workshops began to wane; in some businesses intense pressures led middle managers themselves to say, "my life isn't any different," and some cynically called this program "Work-In."

Responses to Self-Doubt: 1991–
The responses to "self-doubt" in social movements can be classified as either Maladaptive ("demise by default" or "absorption by default"), or Adaptive. GE adapted and used Work-Out to navigate through the tough recession in the early 1990s.

Chapter Seventeen: The Twenty-First-Century Organization

Page 259: Trani's arrival followed a startling wake-up call . . .

Trani had five strategies to reach his mission of becoming the unquestioned leader in diagnostic imaging:

Globalization: "I don't think we can win locally without really winning globally and vice versa."

Cost competitiveness: "Because that gives us: *(a)* pricing flexibility; *(b)* the low-cost producer wins when the market matures."

Installed base expansion: "Unless you feed the cow, you can't get the milk out."

Technical preeminence: "We have technical preeminence in CG and MR and parts of X-ray, but we need to have it everywhere."

Growth: *(a)* Joint ventures and acquisitions; *(b)* organic growth or increased market share, which among other things means more new products; "we have to turn the line over every three years."

Sources

Personal Interviews

Interviews are by Noel Tichy unless otherwise noted. Multiple interviews are indicated by number in parentheses.

Allen, Jim, Manager, Communication and Community Affairs, GE Appliances.

Andrews, Nigel, Vice President, Corporate Development, GE.

Baughman, James, Manager, Corporate Management Development, GE (5).

Bergstrom, Thomas, attorney for Joseph Calabria, by Arathi Krishna.

Bossidy, Lawrence, Chairman and CEO, AlliedSignal, former Vice-Chairman and Executive Officer, GE (3).

Bowen, Bobby, Director, Finance, GE Lighting Europe (2).

Buckley, Larry, former consultant, GE Corporate Human Resources.

Chadwell, Charles, Vice President and General Manager, GE Aircraft Engines Production Division, by Charles Kadushin and MBA Group.

D'Ambola, Toby, Manager, Human Resources, GE Medical Systems (5).

Dillon, Ronald, Manager, Business Development, GE Plastics, Latin America, by Connie Kinnear.

Donovan, Dennis, Vice President, Human Resources, GE Industrial and Power Systems, by Charles Kadushin and MBA Group.

Doyle, Frank, Executive Vice President, GE (3).

Eickert, Stephen, General Manager, Structured Products, GE Plastics, by Connie Kinnear.

Feit, Josh, Media Director, INFACT, by Arathi Krishna.

Frago, Bill, former Vice President and General Manager, GE Lighting Worldwide Marketing, by Connie Kinnear.

Fresco, Paolo, Vice Chairman and Executive Officer (2).

Hamilton, Jack, former Manager of Human Resources, GE Lighting, by Connie Kinnear.

Hiner, Glen, CEO, Owens-Corning Fiberglas, former Senior Vice President, GE Plastics, by Connie Kinnear.

Jones, Reginald, former Chief Executive Officer, GE.

Kane, Donald E., former Manager, Corporate Organization Planning, GE (10).

Klein, Judy L., General Manager, GE Wiring Devices, by Connie Kinnear.

Kline, Jim, Program Manager, Government Practices, GE Aircraft Engines.

LaMadrid, Lorenzo, former Vice President Marketing and Business Development, GE Aerospace.

Madej, John, Manager, Financial Planning, GE Plastics.

McNerney, James, President and Chief Executive Officer, GE Electrical Distribution and Control.

Michaelson, Gertrude G., Senior Vice President—External Affairs and Director, R. H. Macy and Co., Inc., GE Board of Directors.

Modan, Michael, Manager, Licensing/Technology, GE Plastics Legal, by Connie Kinnear.

Mozgala, Robert P., Vice President and General Manager, GE Plastics Americas Manufacturing Division, by Connie Kinnear.

Murphy, George, Managing Director, GE Lighting Asia-Pacific Operation, by Charles Kadushin and MBA Group.

Najhib, Jalal S., National Executive, GE, Iran, by Charles Kadushin and MBA Group.

Opie, John, Chairman and Chief Executive Officer, GE Lighting (5).

Orselet, David K., Consultant, Corporate Human Resources, GE (2).

Pasmore, Carol, Manager, Organization Effectiveness, GE Lighting, by Connie Kinnear.

Paynter, Jim, Manager, Human Resources, Commercial Engines and Service, GE Aircraft Engines (2).

Peiffer, Jack, Senior Vice President, Corporate Human Resources, GE (4).

Reiner, Gary, Vice President, Corporate Business Development, GE.

Rogers, Gary, President and Chief Executive Officer, GE Plastics.

Saline, Craig, former Manager, Human Resources GE CGR (France).

Schipke, Roger, former Senior Vice President, GE Appliances, currently CEO, the Ryland Group.

Schlemmer, Carl J., former Vice President, GE Transportation Systems (5).

Schuh, Gary, Manager, Sourcing, Tungsram U.S.A. Ltd., by Connie Kinnear.

Shenian, Popkin, former Manager, GE Plastics Ventures Technology, by Connie Kinnear.

Smith, Eva, Executive Secretary, GE Plastics Finance, by Connie Kinnear.

Trani, John, President and Chief Executive Officer, GE Medical Systems (10).

Van Orden, Paul, former Executive Vice President, GE (10).

Welch, John F., Jr.:
  (Note: certain of these interviews were attended by Jack Peiffer, James Baughman, or Joyce Hergenhan.)
  —by Strat Sherman for *Fortune* magazine, 1989: 10 hours
  —by Noel Tichy, 1988–91: 45 hours
  —by Noel Tichy and Strat Sherman, 1991–92: 55 hours
Williams, Walter, former Vice President and General Manager, GE Housewares and Audio Business Division, currently Chairman of Rubbermaid.
Woodburn, Bill, Vice President and General Manager, GE Lighting Worldwide Marketing.
Wright, Robert, President and Chief Executive Officer, NBC (3).
Wriston, Walter, retired Chairman of the Board and former Director, Citicorp and Citibank, GE Board of Directors.

GE Diagnostic and Evaluation Studies
Studies were conducted by Noel M. Tichy and colleagues.

Crotonville Needs Assessment Study 1986–87.
Personal interviews (35); focus groups (25); surveys of managers (220) in Major Appliances, GE Capital, Plastics, Mobile Communications, and Aircraft Engines (with Professor Charles Kadushin).
Globalization Study of GE Medical Systems 1987–91
Tracking and evaluating the impact of the Global Leadership Program (220 personal interviews, 430 surveys) (with Professor Charles Kadushin).
Human Resources Assessment Survey 1986–87
535 surveys completed by managers across all GE businesses (with Professor Chestor Borucki).
Human Resources Strategy Project 1988–90
Interviews with 55 line and human resource managers on the future of GE Organization and People Systems (with Patricia Stacey).
Organization Diagnostic Studies
(a) *GE Lighting* telephone surveys 1984–86 (430).
(b) *NBC Values Assessment* focus groups and interviews of 135 NBC managers and employees.
(c) *Medical Systems Middle Managers* diagnosis and tracking of the Work-Out process (240 interviews/focus groups).

Internal GE Documents

"Advanced Human Resource Management Program," February 6, 1987.
Andersen, Raymond K. "Dashing Down the Line." *Monogram,* May/June 1980.

Barnette, Carole K. and Rich Fortinberry. "The GE Lighting/Tungsram Acquisition: A Case Profile for Acquisitions," August 9, 1990.

"Career Management," 1990.

CEO and the Executive Management Staff. "CEO's Working Paper on GE Shared Values and Leadership," June 11, 1986.

"Change Acceleration Program," 1992.

"Company Organization for the 1970s," February 26, 1970.

"Company Policies."

"Continuous Improvement Project Report."

Corporate Marketing and Consulting. "Lighting: National Customer Service Center." Working Report. August 25, 1988.

"Crotonville Analysis of Participant Feedback."

"Crotonville Needs Analysis Survey," June 1986.

"Customer Focused Process Improvement."

"DoD Compliance Actions: 1985–1991."

"Ethics Education and Communication at General Electric," January 30, 1987.

"The Evolution of GE Lighting—Some Perspective on the Work-Out! Process," Work-Out! Conference Presentation, June 5, 1989.

Examples of Accomplishment Analyses

Executive Management Staff. "A New Framework for Leadership Development at GE," February 5, 1987.

Freeman, Bennett. "Catalyst for Change." *Monogram,* 1986.

GE Annual Reports, 1970–92, 1996, 1998, 1999, 2000.

GE Industry Sales & Services. IS&S Leadership Coaching Workshop: Schenectady, New York, August 26, 1987.

"GE Locomotive Milestone Events."

GE Organization Charts, 1978–92.

GEMS. "Developing Cross-Cultural Teamwork."

GEMS. "Global Leadership Program: Executive Summary" (prepared by Executive Leadership Institute).

GEMS. "Global Leadership Seminar" (handout).

GEMS. "GLP3 Global Leadership Workshop: Workshop 2."

GEMS. "Group Process Mapping: A GEMS Work-Out Tool for Speed, Simplicity, Self-Confidence," 1988.

GEMS. Heritage Reference, 1990.

"General Electric Company Lamp Products Division, Human Resource Index—Results of Survey Administration #1," conducted October/November 1984.

Kane, Donald E. "A GE Case Study: Four Critical Steps to Cultural Change." *Executive Excellence,* November 1984.

Kane, Donald E. "Change and GE," February 1987.

Kane, Donald E. "GE Corporate Management Systems Study," August 5, 1986.

Kane, Donald E. "Multiplying Leadership: A Desirable Next Step in the Evolution of Our GE Management System."

Kane, Donald E. "Resizing the Structure." GE Executive Management Staff.

Kane, Donald E., Noel M. Tichy, and Eugene S. Andrews. "A Leadership Development Framework." GE Executive Management Staff, November 1987. OEN-6.

Lake, Dale G., Noel M. Tichy, and Tom Dunham. "Sourcing: New Frontiers for the Boundaryless Organization," July 1990.

"Launching and Leading the Boundaryless Organization: Work-Out Best Practices." Set of papers by Work-Out consultants, 1990.

Lighting. "GE Lighting History."

Lighting. "Introduction to the Work-Out! Process."

Lighting. "Work-Out! Business Component Meeting," June 1989.

Lighting. "World Lighting Markets—Strategies and Challenges."

Lighting. *GE Lighting News,* June 1989, vol. 15, no. 6.

"The Management Development Institute at Crotonville" (brochure).

McKinsey & Co. "Staff Support Needed for Management of General Electric in the 1970s," December 1969.

Monogram. "220 Locomotives," Spring 1984.

Monogram. "Liberating GE's Energy: An Interview with Jack Welch." Fall 1987, vol. 67, no. 4.

"1985 Management Education Catalog" (course catalog).

"Plant Closings and Product Relocations," January 20, 1987.

Plastics. "The GE Plastics Story."

Plastics. "The History of GE Plastics."

"Preliminary Draft: GE Corporate Management System Study," August 5, 1986.

Saperstein, Marc J. "Criteria for Successfully Implementing Significant Organizational Change." GE Executive Management Staff, January 1986. OEN-2.

Smith, Eva M. "How GE Plastics Became an International Business." GEP, May 1986 (updated November 8, 1988).

"Strategic Alliances as a New Way of Life."

Tichy, Noel M. "Crotonville Strategy." February 19, 1986.

Tichy, Noel M. "Global Mindsets: A Model Building Exercise." GEMS Global Leadership Program.

Tichy, Noel, Toby D'Ambola, and Michael Humenik. "The Phases of Organization Development and Work-Out at GE: A Comparative Look," 1990.

"Toward a Shared Vision and Shared Values for GE." Draft, June 10, 1987, June 19, 1987.

Warshaw, David. "Sharing at Every Level." *Monogram,* Fall 1987, vol. 65, no. 4.

"Work-Out Leaders Guide."

"Work-Out! Improving Product Quality," February 12–14, 1990.

General Electric Blue Books:

Professional Management in GE, 1954
   Book One: History
   Book Two: Organization
   Book Three: The Work of a Professional Manager
   Book Four: The Work of a Functional Individual Contributor, 1959
Some Classic Contributions to Professional Managing, 1956
   Volume I: Selected Papers
   Volume II: Historical Perspectives
Manager Development Workbooks, 1956
Manager Development Guidebooks: Basic Principles and Plan, 1956
   Guidebook I: Managerial Climate
   Guidebook II: Self-Development Planning
   Guidebook III: Manager Manpower Planning
   Guidebook IV: Manager Education
New Perspectives in Management, Dr. Harry Arthur Hope

Burlingame, J. F. to Reginald H. Jones. May 29, 1980.

Executive Management Staff, handwritten Evaluation of Vice President, 1980.

Fink, Daniel, Vice President of Planning. Re: R. H. Jones' Growth Target. 1980.

Hood, Edward E. to Reginald H. Jones. Re: Success in Self-evaluation. June 3, 1980.

Jones, Reginald H. to J. F. Burlingame, E. E. Hood, and J. F. Welch, Jr. Re: Succession Process—Personal Evaluations. May 8, 1980.

Kane, Donald E. Re: Existing GE Beliefs/Shared Values. October 11, 1985.

Kane, Donald E. Re: Projection of GE 1985 Operating Environment.

Kane, Donald E. Re: Corporate Executive Council. April 1988.

LeVino, Thomas P. to Reginald H. Jones. Re: Vice Chairmen Appraisal Process. May 1, 1980.

LeVino, Thomas P. to Reginald H. Jones. Re: Vice Chairmen Performance Assessment Interview Questions. June 9, 1980.

Peiffer, Jack O. to CEO Direct Reports. Re: Evaluating Leadership of Officers, March 7, 1989.

Trani, John to Group Staff. Re: Global Processes. September 3, 1991.

Welch, John F., Jr., to Corporate Executive Council. Re: Values and Middle Management. April 1987.

Welch, John F., Jr., to Corporate Officers. Re: Shared Values. April 7, 1981.

Welch, John F., Jr., to Corporate Officers. January 14, 1992.

Welch, John F., Jr., to Operating Managers. Re: Values. January 14, 1992.

Welch, John F., Jr., to Reginald H. Jones. Re: Success in Self-evaluation. June 2, 1980.

Speeches/Presentations

Baughman, James, November 1990.

Bossidy, Lawrence. "Some Thoughts on Strategic Thinking." Presented at Strategic Management Society. Boston, October 14, 1987.

Company Officers Speaking at Crotonville, February 2, 1987.

Cordiner, Ralph. Management Conference, 1952.

Fresco, Paolo. "Globalization in GE," October 21, 1988.

Hanson, Kirk O. "Managing Ethics." Crotonville Presentation. Stanford Business School and the Hanson Group.

Lighting. "Lighting Productivity Presentation." Boca Raton, 1989.

Schlemmer, Carl:
  "Excellent Opportunities for the 1980s."
  White Inn Presentation, 1983.

Tichy, Noel M.
  "Creating the Self-Renewing Organization." Presentation to the Conference Board, 1986.
  "Strategic Alliances," April 1982.

Trani, John. "1991 Current Business Situation," 1991.

Welch, John F., Jr.:
  "Former Planning Procedures," Question-and-Answer Session with an MBA Class, Harvard Business School, April 27, 1981
  "Audit of Management Systems," 1981
  Closing Remarks at Conference, October 1981
  "Growing Fast in a Slow Growth Economy," December 1981
  Presentation to Financial Community Representatives, December 8, 1981
  Closing Remarks, General Management Conference, 1982
  "The New Competitiveness," June 8, 1983
  "Competitiveness from Within," April 26, 1984
  "Linkages and Leadership," October 17, 1985
  Harvard Business School, October 18, 1985
  Customer Dinner, March 19, 1986

Opening Remarks, Operations Managers Meeting, Boca Raton, January 1987

Introduction to Security Analysts Presentation, January 1987

Report to Share Owners, April 22, 1987

"Globalization," October 1987

Society of Automotive Engineers, October 9, 1987

Crotonville Faculty Day, September 7, 1988

"GE Growth Engine," December 1988

Boca Raton Remarks, 1989

Aerospace Council Meeting, March 1989

Electrical Products Group of New York, May 10, 1989

"A Boundaryless Company in a Decade of Change." GE Annual Meeting of Share Owners, Erie, PA, April 25, 1990

GE OMM, Boca Raton, January 7 & 8, 1991

February 1991

Harvard Business School, November 1991

Speech to Operating Managers, January 1992

Press Coverage

Alexander, Charles P. "Let's Make a Deal." *Time,* December 23, 1985.

Associated Press. "GE to Sell Unit to Black and Decker." *New York Times,* December 17, 1983.

Banks, Howard. "General Electric Going with the Winners." *Forbes,* March 26, 1984.

Barker, Robert. "Commanding General: GE's Management Merits a Premium—But How Much?" *Barron's,* October 15, 1984.

Barmash, Isadore. "At GE, a Change of Course." *New York Times,* October 8, 1984.

Bremner, Brian. "Tough Times, Tough Bosses." *Business Week,* November 25, 1991.

Business Week. "General Electric: The Financial Wizards Switch Back to Technology." March 16, 1981.

Carrington, Tim. "U.S. Suspends GE from Defense Work, Asks It, Pratt & Whitney for Repayments." *Wall Street Journal,* March 29, 1985.

Cincinnati Inquirer. "GE Fined $10 Million: Two Employees Jailed." July 27, 1990.

Clayton, Mark. "GE Goes Light Years Beyond the Light Bulb." *Christian Science Monitor,* March 23, 1987.

Condo, Adam. "GE's Suspension Called Unfair." *Cincinnati Post,* June 5, 1992.

Davis, L. J. "Did RCA Have to Be Sold?" *New York Times Magazine,* September 20, 1987.

Davis, L. J. "They Call Him Neutron." *Business Month,* March 1988.

Dentzer, Susan. "GE's New High-Tech Boss." *Newsweek,* April 6, 1981.

Dickson, Martin. "Why GE Encourages Lese Majeste." *Financial Times,* October 5, 1990.

Dobrzynski, Judith H., and Russell Mitchell. "General Electric's Jack Welch—How Good a Manager Is He?" *Business Week,* December 14, 1987.

Dumaine, Brian. "How Managers Can Succeed Through Speed." *Fortune,* February 13, 1989.

Egan, Jack. "What Makes Giant GE Keep on Growing." *U.S. News and World Report,* November 23, 1987.

Emshwiller, John R. "Reginald Jones Plans April 1 Retirement from GE—John Welch Will Succeed Him." *Wall Street Journal,* December 22, 1980.

Engelmayer, Paul A. "Black and Decker Agrees to Acquire a GE Operation." *Wall Street Journal,* December 19, 1983.

Feder, Barnaby J. "Companies Find Rewards in Hiring G.E. Executives." *New York Times,* March 9, 1992.

Finn, Edwin A., Jr. "What Will General Electric Eat Next?" *Forbes,* March 23, 1987.

Flanigan, James. "Trading a TV Tradition for Profit Margins." *Los Angeles Times,* July 23, 1987.

Flax, Steven. "The Toughest Bosses in America." *Fortune,* August 6, 1984.

Forbes. "Batter-up." September 18, 1978.

Forbes. "Forbes International 500." July 20, 1992.

Guyon, Janet. "Combative Chief." *Wall Street Journal,* August 4, 1988.

Harris, Diane. "Can GE Shake the GNP Image?" *Financial World,* May 15, 1982.

Harris, Marilyn A., with Zachary Schiller, Russell Mitchell, and Christopher Power. "Can Jack Welch Reinvent GE?" *Business Week,* June 30, 1986.

Holusha, John. "G.E. Inquiry into Diamonds Charge." *New York Times,* April 23, 1992.

Industry Week. "Factories of the Future: A Front-Runner Keeps Pushing." March 21, 1988.

Insight. "After Stagnation's Darkness GE Begins to See the Light." April 6, 1987.

Investor's Daily. "GE to Pay $10 Mil. Fine in Settlement of Lawsuit." July 27, 1990.

Jones, Jack. "Slouching Toward the New Millennium." *Los Angeles Times Magazine.* December 24, 1989.

Kanabayashi, Masayoshi. "Scandal Widens at GE Medical Venture in Japan." *Wall Street Journal,* March 7, 1991.

Kanabayashi, Masayoshi, and Jacob M. Schlesinger. "GE Joint Venture in Japan, Contending with Tough Rivals, Is Hit by Scandal." *Wall Street Journal,* February 22, 1991.

Landro, Laura. "Electric Switch." *Wall Street Journal,* July 12, 1982.

Landro, Laura. "GE's Wizards Turning from the Bottom Line to Share of the Market." *Wall Street Journal,* July 12, 1982.

Landro, Laura, and Douglas A. Sease. "General Electric to Sell Consumer Electronics Lines to Thomson SA for Its Medical Gear Business, Cash." *Wall Street Journal,* July 23, 1987.

Lorenz, Christopher. "GE of the U.S.: Life Under Jack Welch—Opportunistic and Tough." *Financial Times,* May 16, 1988.

Lorenz, Christopher. "GE of the U.S.: Why Strategy Has Been Put in the Hands of Line Managers." *Financial Times,* May 18, 1988.

Lueck, Thomas J. "Why Jack Welch Is Changing G.E." *New York Times,* May 5, 1985.

Main, Jeremy. "Managing Now for the 1990s." *Fortune,* September 26, 1986.

Mann, Judy. "Shedding Light on Takeover of NBC." *Washington Post,* December 19, 1986.

McClenahen, John S. "GE's Welch Gambles on Growth." *Industry Week,* April 20, 1987.

Meehan, John. "GE Aims for Nimble Bigness." *International Herald Tribune,* May 5, 1989.

Mitchell, Russell: "Black and Decker in the Kitchen." *New York Times,* January 18, 1984.

Mitchell, Russell, with Judith H. Dobrzynski. "Jack Welch: How Good a Manager?" *Business Week,* December 14, 1987.

Mohl, Bruce A. "General Electric's Man of Action." *Boston Globe,* February 1, 1981.

Morrison, Ann M. "Trying to Bring GE to Life." *Fortune,* January 25, 1982.

Naj, Amal Kumar. "GE Yields to Tiny Rival in Battle over Servicing Medical Machines." *Wall Street Journal,* March 18, 1991.

Naj, Amal Kumar, and Andy Pasztor. "GE Unit Isn't Likely to Feel Impact of Ban." *Wall Street Journal,* June 3, 1992.

Naj, Amal Kumar, and Pauline Yoshi Hashi. "U.S. Broadens Fraud Action Against G.E." *Wall Street Journal,* March 17, 1992.

New England Business. "GE's John F. Welch—General of Excellence or 'Neutron Jack'?" March 1987.

New York Times. "A Change of Course." October 8, 1984.

New York Times. "Mr. Wright? The New Man at NBC." January 19, 1987.

Norman, James R. "Big Changes Are Galvanizing GE." *Business Week,* December 18, 1989.

Norman, James R. "Why GE's Powerhouse Isn't Electrifying Wall Street." *Business Week,* October 31, 1988.

Ottawa Citizen. "Cancer Machine's Malfunction May Cause up to 27 Deaths." February 23, 1991.

Park, Jacob. "Overseas Sales Take Off at Last." *Fortune,* July 16, 1990.

Peters, Tom. "Here's to Another 'Best of Decade' List." *Rocky Mountain News,* December 19, 1989.

Petre, Peter. "GE's Gamble on American Made TVs." *Fortune,* July 6, 1987.

Petre, Peter. "How GE Bobbled the Factory of the Future." *Fortune,* November 11, 1985.

Petre, Peter. "The Man Who Brought GE to Life." *Fortune,* January 5, 1987.

Petre, Peter. "What Welch Has Wrought at GE." *Fortune,* July 7, 1986.

Potts, Mark. "GE Chief Seeks a Strong, Lean Machine." *Washington Post,* May 29, 1988.

Potts, Mark. "GE Sells Consumer Electronics Unit." *Washington Post,* July 23, 1987.

Potts, Mark. "GE's Management Mission." *Washington Post,* May 22, 1988.

Potts, Mark. "GE's Welch Powering Firm into Global Competition." *Washington Post,* September 23, 1984.

Potts, Mark. "A New Vision for Leadership from GE's Visionary." *Washington Post,* March 8, 1992.

Potts, Mark. "Seeking a Better Idea." *Washington Post,* October 7, 1990.

Pound, Edward T. "Charge That GE Conspired to Fix Prices Is Studied." *Wall Street Journal,* April 22, 1992.

Pound, Edward T. "GE Is Expected to Admit Guilt in Dotan Case." *Wall Street Journal,* July 10, 1992.

Pound, Edward T. "Papers Show G.E. Employed Big Guns in Industrial Diamond Market Struggle." *Wall Street Journal,* May 4, 1992.

Pound, Edward T., and Amal Kumar Naj. "GE Launches Internal Probe into Charges." *Wall Street Journal,* April 23, 1992.

Richter, Paul. "GE Selling TV, Electronics Business to French Firm." *Los Angeles Times,* July 23, 1987.

Russell, Mitchell. "GE's Jack Welch—How Good a Manager Is He?" *Business Week,* December 14, 1987.

Sanger, David E. "G.E., a Pioneer in Radio and TV, Is Abandoning Production of Sets." *New York Times,* July 23, 1987.

Sanger, David E. "Pioneers That Grew Up Together into Giants." *New York Times,* December 12, 1985.

Sanger, David E. "Workers at GE Subsidiary Accused by Japan of Bribery." *New York Times,* February 21, 1992.

Schwadel, Francine. "Black and Decker's New Ideas Include Men's Hair Dryers." *Wall Street Journal,* September 14, 1984.

Sherman, Stratford P. "Eight Big Masters of Innovation." *Fortune,* October 15, 1984.

Sherman, Stratford P. "GE's Costly Lesson on Wall Street." *Fortune,* May 9, 1988.

Sherman, Stratford P. "Inside the Mind of Jack Welch." *Fortune,* March 27, 1989.

Sherman, Stratford P. "Today's Leaders Look to Tomorrow: John F. Welch, Jr." *Fortune,* March 26, 1989.

Sherman, Stratford P. "Trashing $150 Billion Business." *Fortune,* August 28, 1989.

Smith, Jim. "GE Admits Guilt, Is Fined 800G Scan." *Philadelphia Daily News,* May 14, 1985.

Smith, Richard Austin. "The Incredible Electrical Conspiracy." *Fortune,* April 1961.

Stevenson, Richard W. "G.E. Whistle Blower Could Face a Suit." *New York Times,* March 17, 1992.

Stevenson, Richard W. "Pentagon Lifts Ban of G.E. Unit." *New York Times,* June 6, 1992.

Stevenson, Richard W. "U.S. Accuses G.E. of Fraud in Israeli Deal." *New York Times,* August 15, 1991.

Stewart, Thomas A. "GE Keeps Those Ideas Coming." *Fortune,* August 12, 1991.

Taylor, John H. "General Electric: Whither NBC's Peacock." *Forbes,* March 4, 1991.

Tetzeli, Rick. "Business Students Cheat Most." *Fortune,* July 1, 1991.

Tully, Shawn. "GE in Hungary: Let There Be Light." *Fortune,* October 22, 1990.

Vise, David A. "GE to Buy RCA for $6.2 Billion." *Washington Post,* December 12, 1985.

Wald, Matthew L. "Four Decades of Bungling at Bomb Plan." *New York Times,* January 25, 1992.

Wall Street Transcript. "Corporate Critics Confidential: Electrical Equipment." July 24, 1989.

Welch, John F., Jr. "Quality Recovery for World Competitiveness." *Financier,* April 1983.

Welch, John F., Jr. "Shun the Incremental; Go for the Quantum Leap." *Financier,* July 1984.

Whitefield, Debra. "Welch: Going for the Leading Edge." *Los Angeles Times,* July 23, 1987.

Wickman, Roy. "Patients Killed by Radiation Blunder." *The European,* March 1–3, 1991.

Young, David. "GM's Rail Unit Chugs Ahead After Lean Spell." *Chicago Tribune,* March 17, 1991.

Books/Academic Articles/Teaching Cases

Auletta, Kenneth. *Three Blind Mice: How the TV Networks Lost Their Way* (New York: Random House, 1991).

Boulware, Lemuel R. *The Truth About Boulwarism* (Washington, D.C.: Bureau of National Affairs, 1969).

Burns, James MacGregor. *Leadership* (New York: Harper & Row, 1978).

Clinard, Marshall B., and Peter C. Yeager (with Ruth Blackburn Clinard). *Corporate Crime* (London: Free Press/Collier Macmillan Publishing, 1980).

Cox, James. A. *A Century of Light* (New York: Benjamin, 1979).

Etzioni, Amatai. *A Comparative Analysis of Complex Organizations* (New York: Free Press, 1961).

Fombrun, Charles, Noel M. Tichy, and Mary Anne Devanna, ed. *Strategic Human Resource Management* (New York: John Wiley & Sons, 1984).

Hall of History Foundation. *The General Electric Story 1876–1986: A Photo History* (Schenectady, NY: Hall of History Foundation, 1981).

INFACT. *Bringing GE to Light* (Philadelphia: New Society Publishers, 1990).

Jones, Robert, and Oliver Marriott. *Anatomy of a Merger: A History of G.E.C., A.E.I., and English Electric* (London: Cape, 1970).

Lydenberg, Steven D., Alice Tepper Martin, Sean O'Brien Strub, and the Council on Economic Priorities. *Rating America's Corporate Conscience* (Reading, MA: Addison-Wesley, 1986).

Magaziner, Ira C., and Mark Patinkin. "Cold Competition: GE Wages the Refrigerator War." *Harvard Business Review,* March/April 1989.

National Center on Education and the Economy, *America's Choice: High Skills or Low Wages* (Rochester, NY: National Center on Education and the Economy, 1990).

Neuman, Gerhard. *Herman and the German* (New York: William Morrow, 1984).

Noel, James L., and Ram Charan. "Leadership Development at GE's Crotonville." *Human Resource Management,* Winter 1988, vol. 27, no. 4.

Porter, Michael E. *The Competitive Advantage of Nations* (New York: Free Press, 1990).

Pucik, Vladimir, Noel M. Tichy, and Carole K. Barnett, ed. *Globalizing Management: Creating and Leading the Competitive Organization* (New York: John Wiley & Sons, 1992).

Stewart, James B. *Den of Thieves* (New York: Simon & Schuster, 1991).

Tichy, Noel M. "GE's Crotonville: A Staging Ground for Corporate Revolution." *Academy of Management Executive,* May 1989.

Tichy, Noel M. "The GE Transformation Story." For January 1989 Global Transformation Research Program.

Tichy, Noel M. "Setting the Global Human Resource Management Agenda for the 1990s." *Human Resource Management,* Spring 1988.

Tichy, Noel M. "Training as a Lever for Change." *New Management,* 1986.

Tichy, Noel M., and Mary Anne Devanna. *The Transformational Leader* (New York: John Wiley & Sons, 1986).

Tichy, Noel M., and Ram Charan. "Speed, Simplicity, Self-Confidence: An Interview with Jack Welch." *Harvard Business Review,* September/October 1989.

Young, Andrew, Daniel Levi, and Charles Slem. "Dispelling Some Myths About People and Technological Change." *IE,* November 1987.

Harvard Business School Cases

"General Electric Company." 9-113-121. 1964 (Revised 1970).

"General Electric Company: Aircraft Engine Business Group." Case B. 9-183-137. 1982.

"General Electric Company: Aircraft Engine Business Group." Case A. 9-183-136. 1982.

"General Electric Company: Appliance Division Advertising." 9-581-095. 1981.

"General Electric Company: Background Note on Management Systems: 1981." 181-111. 1981.

"General Electric Company: Business Development." 382-092. 1981.

"General Electric Company: Compliance Systems." 1-189-081. 1989.

"General Electric Company: Jack Welch's Second Wave." N9-391-248. 1991.

"General Electric Company: Middle Years." 9-370-160. 1969.

"General Electric Company: 1981 Audit of Management Systems." 181-112. 1981.

"General Electric Company: Origins of Early Development." 9-313-160.

"General Electric Company: Quality of Earnings Analysis." 9-182-243. 1982.

"General Electric Company: Reginald Jones and Jack Welch." N9-391-144. 1991.

"General Electric Company: Role of Staff 1982." 9-182-226. 1982.

"General Electric Company: The Executive Manpower Operation—David Orselet." 9-680-122. 1980.

"General Electric Company: Thermocouple Manufacturing." Case A, B, and C. 9-684-040. 1983.

"General Electric Company: Valley Forge." Case A through H. 1-189-009. 1989.

"General Electric Microwave Oven." 9-579-184. 1979.

Aguilar, Francis J., and Richard Hamermesh. "General Electric: Strategic Position 1981." 381-174. 1981.

Aguilar, Francis J., Richard G. Hamermesh, and Caroline Brainard. "General Electric: 1984." 9-385-315. 1985.

Collins, Neil, and John Quelch. "General Electric Company: Major Appliance Group: A through D." 9-585-053. 1985.

Hunker, Jeffrey, and John F. Cady, "General Electric: Clock and Timer Market Strategy." 9-582-031. 1984.

Porter, Michael, and Pankaj Ghemawat. "General Electric Versus Westinghouse in Large Turbine Generators." Case A, B, and C. 1980.

Other Sources

Anderson, Eric (MBA Student). "GE: Lighting's Marketing Strategy for Private Label, Consumer Incandescent Light Bulbs." Unpublished manuscript, Nov. 20, 1989.

Baughman, James. "Problems and Performance of the Role of Chief Executive in the General Electric Company 1892–1974." Unpublished manuscript, July 1974.

Charan, Ram, and Noel M. Tichy. "Cracking the Genetic Code for Global Competitiveness: Emotional Energy (E2)." Unpublished manuscript, 1988.

Coakley, Karen, and William Marsh. "General Electric: Strategy and Strategic Planning." Unpublished manuscript, 1980.

Dingell, John D., House of Representatives letter to Richard B. Cheney, Secretary of Defense, June 3, 1992.

Husen, Richard C. "Proceedings: Academy of Management 39th Annual Meeting." University of Georgia, August 8–11, 1979.

JD Power survey, "Customer Satisfaction of U.S. Versus Foreign Auto Companies," July 1992.

Kinnear, Connie. "GE Lighting Case." April 18, 1988.

Kinnear, Connie. "GE Plastics Story."

Kinnear, Connie. "GEMS Case." Unpublished manuscript, 1988.

Smidoly, Harold F. "Address and Papers by Harold F. Smidoly: Outside the Advanced Management Course." 1958.

Tichy, Noel M., Daniel Denison, Deborah Buhro, Jane Monto, and Patricia Woolcock. "National Broadcasting Company." The University of Michigan Graduate School of Business Administration, Teaching Case, October 1988.

University of Michigan. "General Electric Professional Relations Seminar: May 19–21, 1985."

U.S. Environmental Protection Agency. "Site Enforcement Tracking Report." January 13, 1992.

Wise, George. "General Electric's Century: A History of the General Electric Company from Its Origins to 1986." Unpublished manuscript, 1986.

HANDBOOK FOR
REVOLUTIONARIES

Noel M. Tichy

Introduction

Revolutionary Theater

The GE revolution shows that people can create radical organizational change from within, and they can do it while being financially successful. GE remade itself while earning record profits for over a decade.

Revolution is a call to leadership for all who have a desire to improve the world whether it be to revitalize a major corporation, a department within that corporation, or public sector institutions such as schools and hospitals. It requires taking on the dramatic challenge of creatively destroying and remaking organizations on a continuous basis. Revolution, driven by leaders with ideas and the heart and guts to bring them to life, will become a way of life. It's painful. In all facets of life, including business, one must master change. Faced with increasingly difficult discontinuities, we must redirect life's emotional energies. Leaders of any institution, private or public, are in the business of helping each and every employee generate high levels of positive emotional energy.

1. The Revolutionary Creed

Leaders Add Value to Their Organizations
The ultimate test of leadership is enhancing the long-term value of the organization. For leaders of a publicly held company, this means long-term share owner value. At every level of the organization, people must understand how their role contributes to value.

Leadership Creates Emotional Energy

One source of competitive advantage is the emotional energy level of the organization. In a fast-moving, complex, changing world, high levels of positive emotional energy lead to faster cycle times, higher quality, lower costs, and the ability to transform continuously.

Corollary: Emotional Energy Is about Ideas

Ideas empower people and provide the fuel for positive emotional energy.

The Goal Is Constant Revolution

The twenty-first-century winners will be those who are in constant revolution: One must embrace every change as an opportunity and not hesitate for fear of being wrong. Being wrong is okay. Change and then get on with it.

Revolutions Have Predictable Patterns

Revolutions follow a predictable set of dynamics. These can be understood and mastered by leaders.

2. The Three-Act Drama: Awakening, Envisioning, and Rearchitecting

Revolutions are predictable. The pain, the resistance, the breakthroughs and joys of successful passage from one phase to another can be understood and mastered.

A corporate revolution is a particular type of drama—a tragedy, perhaps, always with a catharsis and hopefully with a happy ending. For the people involved in the play, it's as gripping and deep as any classical plot. We think of corporations as machines but they are really more like theatrical troupes: Ideas, dialogue, and actions flow among the cast. Managers in the company are part of an ensemble cast demonstrating their skills and magnetism as they perform.

The protagonists of this drama are the people who seek change and set the revolutionary plot in motion. In General Electric's case, several dozen leaders sought to transform the culture radically. Jack Welch gathered them and came to symbolize their ideas, but they all acted as individuals. Inevitably, there are antagonists—people who hold tightly to the company's old ways. The struggle to change involves not just these two opposing groups but thousands of people. They all must deal with grief and deep feelings of loss as the old ways they know disappear. The end of a transformation is exhilarating and leads to a feeling of rebirth. Then the cycle must begin again.

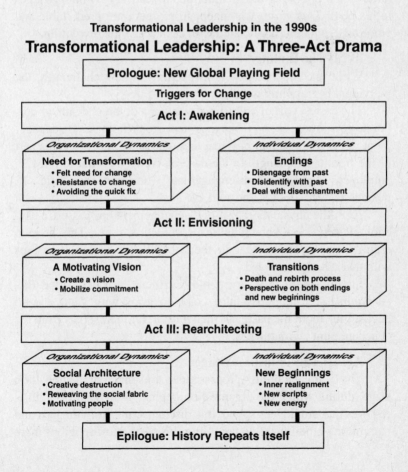

Transformational Leadership in the 1990s

Transformational Leadership: A Three-Act Drama

Prologue: New Global Playing Field

Triggers for Change

Act I: Awakening

Organizational Dynamics

Need for Transformation
- Felt need for change
- Resistance to change
- Avoiding the quick fix

Individual Dynamics

Endings
- Disengage from past
- Disidentify with past
- Deal with disenchantment

Act II: Envisioning

Organizational Dynamics

A Motivating Vision
- Create a vision
- Mobilize commitment

Individual Dynamics

Transitions
- Death and rebirth process
- Perspective on both endings and new beginnings

Act III: Rearchitecting

Organizational Dynamics

Social Architecture
- Creative destruction
- Reweaving the social fabric
- Motivating people

Individual Dynamics

New Beginnings
- Inner realignment
- New scripts
- New energy

Epilogue: History Repeats Itself

As the drama plays out in the organization, individual dramas take place within each person. These individual psychological dramas govern the flow of emotional energy in the organization. They are crucial to the success or lack of success of a transformational leader.

3. The Individual during a Revolution

Revolutions are fraught with emotions. Only those who have mastered the emotional issues are qualified to lead. As William Bridges in his book *Transitions* has mapped out, there are predictable and emotional dynamics associated with each act of the revolution.

Act I: The Ending

While the organization is awakening to new challenges, the individual is grappling with loss.

The easiest part of an ending, whether a divorce, death, or corporate revolution, is the *disengagement* from the past. Disengagement refers to the actual physical loss, and is the most obvious part of the trauma of change. In the case of Welch's revolution at GE, employees experienced disengagement when they were laid off, businesses were bought and sold, etc.

After the physical process of disengagement has passed, a psychological process known as *disidentification* starts. This process requires employees to untangle their old loyalties and relationships with that which has ended.

Finally, there is an even more difficult process called *disenchantment*. Employees must come to grips with what was so enchanting about the past, and then must sever themselves from the "enchantment" with the past.

Act II: The Transition Stage

The death and rebirth process that marks much of the transition stage, during which the organization begins to envision the future, requires that employees spend time disconnecting from the past and committing emotionally to the future. Just as in most religions there are processes (funerals, wakes, etc.) designed to aid family and friends of the deceased, employees *must* be given time to gain perspective on both the endings and the new beginnings. Employees of GE had to deal with this in the early and mid-1980s as Welch ended what most viewed as a tremendously successful century.

Act III: The New Beginning

Once employees have moved through the transition stage, they must be prepared for the frustration that accompanies failure as they replace old mastered routines with new ones. Many GE employees have only recently become comfortable with the new precepts at GE—ownership, boundarylessness, etc.

4. The Five Commandments of Revolution

GE's success has been driven by Jack Welch's obsessive desire to win, his ability to stay focused, and his distillation of five core principles that, when taken to heart, will guide any organization through revolutionary change:

1. **Know the Business Engine** Have a clear understanding of how an organization's capital and technical resources interact to create value.

2. **Understand the Human Connection** In order for the business engine to work, it must be linked with a clearly and carefully articulated vision of how the technical, political, and cultural systems of the organization support one another.

3. **Never Compromise on Performance** No excuses. You can make mistakes but you must own them. Take responsibility and move on. Never get stuck in the past.

4. **Be Candid and Forthcoming** Use face-to-face constructive conflict as a way to make key decisions.

5. **Never Be a Bully** But make the tough decisions that your situation requires. When you cause pain, show others compassion. Be hardheaded and softhearted.

5. How to Use This Handbook

This handbook provides guidelines for applying the powerful ideas from the GE revolution in a variety of situations.

The exhibits and activities are designed to help leaders work through a transformation. These are deep, thought-provoking exercises that provide help for people in various states of revolutionary development. Many of the activities are to be done individually and then discussed by the management team, preferably off-site.

This *Handbook* is designed to help leadership teams plan and guide their work over a several-year period. A corporate revolution is key to the long-term survival and health of the company. As such, it must be treated as the number-one leadership agenda and must draw proportionately on time, money, and leadership focus. Here are some questions and guidelines for leaders to resolve carefully before beginning the revolution:

1. **Time frame for activities**—Both the estimated period for the three acts of the revolution as well as the amount of effort of key leaders.

2. **Roles** of all key leaders—who has responsibility for what.

3. **Task forces**—many of the activities require multimonth task force activities.

4. **Internal staff and external consultant time**—resources, both expertise and facilitation skills needed.

6. Revolutions Take Time—Years

Plan on a multiyear effort. The three acts of the revolutionary drama described in the *Handbook* have already taken over a decade at GE. In preparing to undertake a revolution in your organization it is essential to be realistic about *time*. As you begin the journey, give this careful consideration and set expectations carefully.

The GE Revolution—The Time Dimension

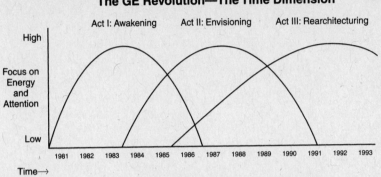

Act I: Awakening   Act II: Envisioning   Act III: Rearchitecturing

Your Revolution—The Time Dimension

Project what you anticipate to be the time for your revolution and how the three acts of the drama will occur.

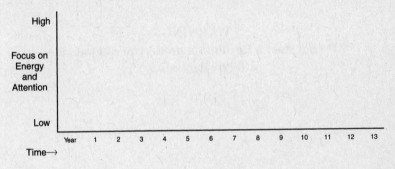

\<WARNING\>
\<Do not start a Revolution unless you can pass the following tests.\>

The Tests

One

The Organization Test:

How Much of a Revolution Do You Need?

Embracing the Top Line/Bottom Line Paradox

In any organization, there are two kinds of issues: hard and soft. Hard issues include finance, marketing, engineering, and manufacturing. Soft issues concern values, morale, communication, etc. The hard issues generally have the greatest effect on the bottom line (profits), whereas the soft issues have the greatest impact on the top line (total sales).

In the first phase of the GE revolution, Welch moved quickly and aggressively on the hard issues: taking the fat out of the bureaucracy, downsizing, divesting businesses in which GE couldn't win, and investing where he thought they could win. By 1985 the bottom-line profitability of GE was positively influenced by Welch's decisive action on the hard issues. Revenue growth and total sales, which are dependent on the trickier soft issues, were progressing at a slower rate.

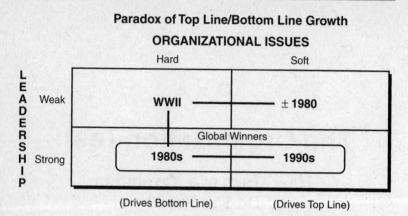

Paradox of Top Line/Bottom Line Growth

ORGANIZATIONAL ISSUES

STEP 1: Assess Your Organization: The Top Line/Bottom Line Paradox Test

In order to prepare for the revolution, take time to understand how well your organization is handling this paradox. The activities challenge you to assess:

1. Top-line/bottom-line trends and implications

2. The capacity for "hard issue" and "soft issue" leadership

This activity provides a catalyst for a lengthy discussion among the leadership team. Have individuals fill out the page individually, then discuss, debate, and draw conclusions.

Results and Projected Results for Your Company

[Fill in the historical numbers and project the future estimates.]

	2000	2001	2002	2003	2004	2005
Top Line [Sales]	____	____	____	____	____	____
Bottom Line [Net Income]	____	____	____	____	____	____

What Are the Implications for Your Company?

_____

_____

Assess Your Company's Leadership on Hard Issues:

Below Average for This Industry		Average		Best in Class for This Industry
1	2	3	4	5

Explain Your Rating:

_____

_____

Assess Your Company's Leadership on Soft Issues:

Below Average for This Industry		Average		Best in Class for This Industry
1	2	3	4	5

Explain Your Rating:

_____

_____

STEP 2: Crossing the Gap between "Old Way" and "New Way"
I like to describe the difference between "Old Way" and "New Way" companies in terms of sports. The old GE resembled a football team: Each player had carefully prescribed roles, yielding a carefully orchestrated pattern. The coach called all the plays. Even the strategic-planning guidebooks that governed GE policy were like the playbooks in football. The "New Way" GE is like hockey; roles are blurred, play flows uncontrollably from one side of the rink to the other, there are no time-outs, players adjust to new situations almost every moment and think for themselves while looking out for the team as a whole.

The "Old Way" paradigm of the twentieth-century corporate organization was anti-idea, built on a machine-age mentality. Business institutions created rational, nonemotional, "scientifically" sanitized bureaucracies. People in the organization were not expected to have ideas—the ideas were built into the bureaucracy through a variety of "scientific" practices ranging from time-motion concepts (prescribing how a worker was to do the job down to each physical move) to operations research (a set of quantitative planning tools). At AT&T there were volumes of policy and practice manuals specifying how almost everything was to be done. GE had its five-volume set of Blue Books on how to manage. The larger the bureaucracy, the more ideas were stifled. The focus rapidly became how to perpetuate the technical status quo in the organization, which, in turn, led people to dwell increasingly on the politics of turf protection and careerism.

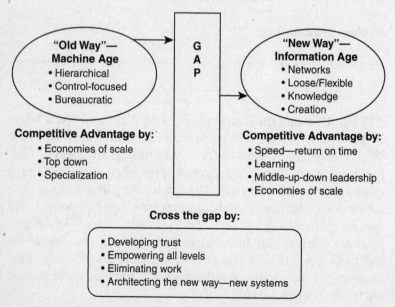

The Challenge—How Can Your Organization Cross the Gap?
THE TRANSFORMATION

"Old Way"—
Machine Age
• Hierarchical
• Control-focused
• Bureaucratic

G A P

"New Way"—
Information Age
• Networks
• Loose/Flexible
• Knowledge
• Creation

Competitive Advantage by:
• Economies of scale
• Top down
• Specialization

Competitive Advantage by:
• Speed—return on time
• Learning
• Middle-up-down leadership
• Economies of scale

Cross the gap by:
• Developing trust
• Empowering all levels
• Eliminating work
• Architecting the new way—new systems

The "New Way" organization is built on ideas that provide the energy for breaking frame with the past. Ideas change the direction and provide the emotional energy for moving the organization forward. Ideas are at the core of producing emotional energy for people—ideas about products and services, ideas about customers, ideas about organizations. The challenge for GE and other twenty-first-century winners is to create an environment where many people's ideas can be harnessed.

In order to cross the gap the following conditions are required:

Trust: Downsizing, delayering, and a lack of job security break the feeling of trust between the top and the middle management. It is necessary to rebuilt trust in order to take on the quantum leap from "Old Way" to "New Way."

Empowerment: Historically, power is held at the top of the control-oriented, machine-age bureaucracy. Top/down management is still dominant in the United States. As the transformation gap is crossed, this power must be shared with leadership at all levels, up, down, and sideways.

Eliminate Work: People get removed but not work. People are taken out of the organization but time is not taken to remove reports, approvals, meetings, and measurements. To cross the gap work must be taken out.

Vision: In order to have a true quantum change it is necessary to have a "New Way" vision. The social architecture needs to be articulated; those involved must have a clear idea about where they are going.

1. To what extent is there *trust* between the top and middle levels?

Very Low		Moderate			High Level	
1	2	3	4	5	6	7

Comments _____

_____

2. To what extent are middle managers *empowered*?

Very Low		Moderate			High Level	
1	2	3	4	5	6	7

Comments _____

_____

3. To what extent has unnecessary work been eliminated (reports, appraisals, meetings, measurements, etc.)?

Little/No Work Out		Moderate Work Out			Great Deal Work Out	
1	2	3	4	5	6	7

Comments _____

_____

4. To what extent is there a clear vision of the "New Way" organization of work?

No Clear Vision		Moderate Clarity			Very Clear Vision	
1	2	3	4	5	6	7

Comments _____

_____

5. Overall, where would you rate the organization on the transformation from "Old Way" to "New Way"?

Totally "Old Way"		Halfway There			Totally "New Way"	
1	2	3	4	5	6	7

Comments _____

_____

© 1988 Noel Tichy, Ram Charan.

STEP 3: Getting Down to Details—Why Do You Need a Revolution?

These questions help you systematically diagnose why your organization needs a revolution. It may take several months of task force, work, and off-site discussion to reach a final set of conclusions.

1) What is the hand you have been dealt?

<u>GE EXAMPLE</u>   <u>YOUR ORGANIZATION</u>

The Hand Welch Was Dealt— GE in 1980

- A strong balance sheet   _____

- Slow-moving bureaucracy   _____

- Productivity improvements of 1% to 2% per year   _____

- Nonglobal businesses   _____

- Modest technology   _____

2) What legacy is built into your organization's "genetic code"?

GE EXAMPLE   YOUR ORGANIZATION

GE's 100-Year-Old Heritage

GE was always a company of ideas about management and organization. It grew to be the most diverse company in the United States.

Its culture became very inward-focused and very bureaucratic under the fabric of "scientific management." It became the business school model for financial management, organizational design, strategic planning, development, and succession planning.

3) What is your bureaucracy like?

GE EXAMPLE   YOUR ORGANIZATION

The Old Bureaucracy

- Nine layers of management from CEO to shop floor

- Wedding cake shape of company—military-like nomenclature, all the same across the company

- Finance mafia—controlled by auditing, etc.

- Span-breaker—sector executives and staffs putting layers of reviews, procedures, etc., between CEO and actual people running the businesses

- Strategic planning process with over 100 planning staff at headquarters producing volumes of books and data for presentations

4) What are the core problems (hard and soft)?

GE EXAMPLE   YOUR ORGANIZATION

The Hard Issues

* Earnings growth average

* Cash flow a persistent problem
  because of high capital
  expenditures and working capital
  expansion

* Slow-growing electrical equipment
  core businesses still dominated GE

* Productivity growth 1% to 2%—
  and the operating margin stayed in
  the 7% to 9% range

* Large uncertainties in
  —Power systems where the
    energy crisis and Three Mile
    Island had devastated
    backlogs
  —Utah International because
    the Japanese were developing
    new coal supplies
  —International mini-GEs
    (Brazil, Canada, Spain, Mex-
    ico), which were high-cost
    entities not ready for the new
    emerging global competition

The Soft Issues

* Slow decision making

* Turf struggles

* Inward focus

* Lack of innovation

Two

The Mirror Test:

Do You Have the Head, Heart, and Guts to Lead a Revolution?

Revolution is a game for leaders. All of us have the capacity to be revolutionary leaders in our own sphere. The question is whether we want to apply our head, heart, and guts to the task. It is not possible to conduct the mirror test alone. Self-perception is always distorted. The steps outlined in this section include self-analyzing and feedback from others.

STEP 1: The Mirror Test—Take Time to Reflect on Your Personal Assessment

	WHAT IS REQUIRED	GE EXAMPLE	HOW DO YOU SEE YOURSELF?
H	Intellectual rigor,	• Ability to	
E	understanding of	Conceptualize	_____
A	business, and ideas	• Knowledge of	_____
D	that can win in the	Business	
	marketplace	• A Vision	_____

	WHAT IS REQUIRED	GE EXAMPLE	HOW DO YOU SEE YOURSELF?
H **E** **A** **R** **T**	Compassion, empathy, and fairness packaged in a tough love, absolute candor package	• Candor • Integrity • Compassion	_____ _____ _____
G **U** **T** **S**	Ability to make the tough calls, stand up to unpopular positions, take risks, and have the self-confidence to be simple	• Reality • Self-Knowledge • Simplicity • Speed	_____ _____ _____ _____

STEP 2: The Accomplishment Analysis

There is more to good leadership than making your numbers. GE uses a powerful analytic tool, the Accomplishment Analysis, to take an in-depth look at a leader's intellectual capability, ability to motivate staff, and capacity for risk-taking. At GE, specially trained members of the Executive Management Staff interview an individual, his subordinates, boss, and peers, focusing qualitatively on accomplishments, strengths, weaknesses, and potential. This activity is best organized by independent human resource staff or outside consultants. They need to interview the individual as well as key stakeholders, boss, subordinates, and customers.

Develop an Action Plan for Accomplishment Analysis

WHO NEEDS TO BE ANALYZED? (NAMES)	BY WHOM	BY WHEN
1. _____	_____	_____
2. _____	_____	_____
3. _____	_____	_____
4. _____	_____	_____
5. _____	_____	_____
6. _____	_____	_____

STEP 3: Survey of Top Leadership

In 1985, GE developed a Leadership Effectiveness Survey to see how well GE's leaders were adopting the new leadership values Welch advocated. The exhibit below lists the characteristics Jack Welch was seeking in the business and in leadership. The survey captures those dimensions.

Whenever individuals go to Crotonville, ten of their subordinates, peers, and bosses are asked to rate them. The individual also fills out the same survey, providing a self-portrait.

This process is worth developing in all organizations and can be started using a generic leadership survey that can then be customized as the organization clarifies its own set of values. The following page presents examples of ideas from a "Transformational Leader" assessment survey.

GE Value Statement

BUSINESS CHARACTERISTICS

LEAN

What—Reduce tasks and the people required to do them.

Why—Critical to developing world cost leadership.

AGILE

What—Delayering.

Why—Create fast decision-making in rapidly changing world through improved communication and increased individual response.

CREATIVE

What—Development of new ideas—innovation.

Why—Increase customer satisfaction and operating margins through higher value products and services.

OWNERSHIP

What—Self-confidence to trust others. Self-confidence to delegate to others the freedom to act while, at the same time, self-confidence to involve higher levels in issues critical to the business and the corporation.

Why—Supports concept of more individual responsibility, capability to act quickly and independently. Should increase job satisfaction and improve understanding of risks and rewards. While delegation is critical, there is a small percentage of high-impact issues that need or require involvement of higher levels within the business and within the corporation.

REWARD

What—Recognition and compensation commensurate with risk and performance—highly differentiated by individual, with recognition of total team achievement.

Why—Necessary to attract and motivate the type of individuals required to accomplish GE's objectives. A No. 1 business should provide No. 1 people with No. 1 opportunity.

INDIVIDUAL CHARACTERISTICS

REALITY

What—Describe the environment as it is—not as we hope it to be.

Why—Critical to developing a vision and a winning strategy, and to gaining universal acceptance for their implementation.

LEADERSHIP

What—Sustained passion for and commitment to a proactive, shared vision and its implementation.

Why—To rally teams toward achieving a common objective.

CANDOR/OPENNESS

What—Complete and frequent sharing of information with individuals (appraisals, etc.) and organization (everything).

Why—Critical to employees knowing where they, their efforts, and their business stand.

SIMPLICITY

What—Strive for brevity, clarity, the "elegant, simple solution"—less is better.

Why—Less complexity improves everything, from reduced bureaucracy to better product designs to lower costs.

INTEGRITY

What—Never bend or wink at the truth, and live within both the spirit and letter of the laws of every global business arena.

Why—Critical to gaining the global arena's acceptance of our right to grow and prosper. Every constituency: share owners who invest; customers who purchase; community that supports; and employees who depend, expect, and deserve our unequivocal commitment to integrity in every facet of our behavior.

INDIVIDUAL DIGNITY

What—Respect and leverage the talent and contribution of every individual in both good and bad times.

Why—Teamwork depends on trust, mutual understanding, and the shared belief that the individual will be treated fairly in any environment.

The Transformational Leader Survey
(SAMPLE ITEMS)

Act I: Awakening

Getting the organization prepared for the revolution and dealing with the forces of resistance and the psychodynamics of change.

> 0 Cannot Rate
> 1 Strongly Disagree
> 2 Disagree
> 3 Neutral
> 4 Agree
> 5 Strongly Agree

1. Is often first to identify changes in the · environment (societal, economic, political) which will impact business 5 4 3 2 1 0

2. In spite of resistance, consistently pursues the need for change 5 4 3 2 1 0

3. Is able to lead *others* to overcome fear and uncertainty in making change 5 4 3 2 1 0

4. Is able to help others overcome organization resistance to change 5 4 3 2 1 0

5. Avoids shortcuts and gimmicks for achieving organizational change 5 4 3 2 1 0

Act II: Envisioning

Generates ideas for the future success of the company and incorporates them into an exciting and motivating vision and mobilizes others around the vision.

1. Has described characteristics that his/her organization should have in the future 5 4 3 2 1 0

2. Can visualize the business through the eyes of the customer, i.e., is highly customer-conscious 5 4 3 2 1 0

3. Creates enthusiastic commitment for the vision of the business 5 4 3 2 1 0

4. Has a clear vision about the future of the business 5 4 3 2 1 0

5. Is able to help *others* disengage from the past and move into the future 5 4 3 2 1 0

Act III: Rearchitecting

Creatively destroying the old organization and architecting the new.

1. Can dismantle old bureaucracy and can create new organizational forms to fit the vision 5 4 3 2 1 0

Personal Characteristics:
Transformational leadership traits of the person.

1. Has high standards of personal conduct.........5 4 3 2 1 0

2. Learns from his/her mistakes 5 4 3 2 1 0

3. Insists on continuous improvement for self......5 4 3 2 1 0

4. Is able to engender a high level of motivation in others 5 4 3 2 1 0

5. Assumes responsibility for own mistakes.........5 4 3 2 1 0

6. Is trusted by others.........
...................5 4 3 2 1 0

7. Communicates openly and candidly with individuals at lower organizational levels..
...................5 4 3 2 1 0

8. Maintains sound business perspective in the face of dilemmas and paradoxes.............
..................5 4 3 2 1 0

9. Builds coalitions and networks across organizational lines to achieve important goals ....
...................5 4 3 2 1 0

STEP 4: Selecting the Varsity Team

The mirror test is not just for the top leader. It is a method of evaluating leadership capability at the top of the organization. A leadership team's success depends on the ability of all its members to communicate and cooperate.

Draw a diagram (see below) to assess the communication skills of the senior group: Circles indicate individuals, lines indicate

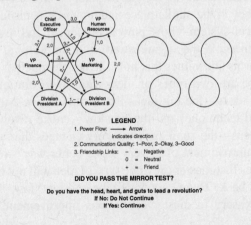

LEGEND

1. Power Flow: ⟶ Arrow
   indicates direction
2. Communication Quality: 1–Poor, 2–Okay, 3–Good
3. Friendship Links: – = Negative
   0 = Neutral
   + = Friend

DID YOU PASS THE MIRROR TEST?

Do you have the head, heart, and guts to lead a revolution?
If No: Do Not Continue
If Yes: Continue

linkages and authority relationships between individuals. Numbers indicate quality of communication: +, -, 0 indicate friendship links. After you identify who belongs in the network, identify each linkage between pairs of individuals. Show who influences whom, the quality of the communication between the individuals, and the effective links between the individuals—that is, the degree to which there are friendships. There is no room in "New Way" organizations for leaders who don't communicate.

STEP 5: The Idea Test

The fuel for the revolution is ideas because: (1) Ideas give meaning to life—throughout history spiritual ideas, ideas about justice and freedom, have been central to society. People's identities are tied to ideas they consider important. (2) There is nothing like the emotional kick that comes from putting your ideas into action. (3) Empowerment is at the core—the freedom to carry out one's ideas. Have an idea, try it out, and get feedback. It takes an enormous number and range of ideas to transform an organization: ideas about values and strategies, ideas for practical improvements, ideas about how to do small things a little more efficiently, and ideas for sweeping change. Ideas get people excited and get people moving. The tremendous energy of many motivated and focused people is what it takes to creatively destroy and rebuild the institution. There must be ideas about the technical system—how the company will make money in the marketplace and organize its resources to do so; the political system—how power, influence, and rewards will be used to energize the organization; and the cultural system—the shared norms and values that hold the people together.

There are two types of ideas vital to revolutionary success. Quantum ideas—the big ideas like No. 1 or No. 2 that throw old habits and techniques out the window—create revolutions. Incremental ideas—the small, evolutionary changes that yield the continuous improvement of "Every day a better way"—sustain them. Companies that master only one type of idea will not be winners. A few years back, Toyota generated the constant flow of incremental ideas necessary to master continuous improvement. Every company in the world wanted its just-in-time manufacturing system to be as lean and flexible as Toyota's. Toyota's bottom line was in great shape but the company wasn't generating the kind of quantum ideas that produce bold new products and top-line growth. Honda, with its innovative Accord and Acura lines, took the lead. A few years later, a wiser Toyota introduced the successful Lexus and Camry lines, proving itself to be a master of quantum as well as incremental ideas.

The table below shows the role of ideas in revolutionary organizations:

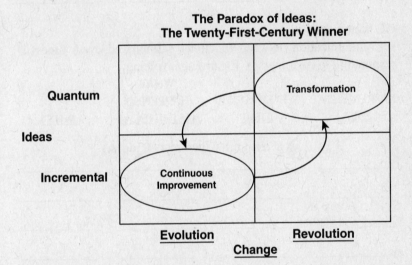

**The Paradox of Ideas:
The Twenty-First-Century Winner**

The exercise below is designed to help people understand what happens to ideas in your organization. After doing the individual work, discussion should focus on the analysis of what happens to ideas in your organization and why.

GE Quantum Ideas:
• Purchase of RCA • Swap of GE Consumer Electronics for Thomson's CGR medical-imaging business • Product breakthroughs, such as magnetic resonance.

QUANTUM IDEA	WHO HAD THE IDEA?	WHAT HAPPENED TO THE IDEA?	WHY?

(List one that you or someone in your organization had.)

_____	_____	_____	_____
_____	_____	_____	_____
_____	_____	_____	_____
_____	_____	_____	_____

GE Incremental Ideas:
• Communication between functions • Improved cycle times in responding to customers • Electronic invoicing.

INCREMENTAL IDEA	WHO HAD THE IDEA?	WHAT HAPPENED TO THE IDEA?	WHY?

(List at least three incremental ideas.)

_____	_____	_____	_____
_____	_____	_____	_____
_____	_____	_____	_____
_____	_____	_____	_____

STEP 6: Ideas for the Revolution

Welch led the revolution with three big ideas: The first strategy was to be No. 1 or No. 2 in any GE business and to get there by fixing, closing, or selling each of GE's businesses. This was the *technical* idea for GE's revolution. The *political* idea was a corporate structure that pushed most power out into the businesses, giving the businesses control of their destiny while at the same time integrating and holding certain powers at the center of GE. Finally, the *cul-*

tural idea for the GE revolution is captured in Welch's notion of "boundaryless" values and behavior—sharing to gain, partnering across all levels and boundaries within and outside GE. The GE ideas are portrayed in the diagram below:

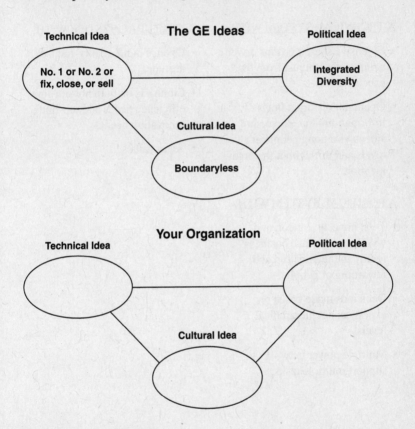

Have you developed core ideas for the (1) technical system, (2) political system, and (3) cultural system? Ideas about the three systems must be interwoven like the strands of a rope, mutually reinforcing each other.

The Technical, Political, and Cultural Building Blocks of an Organization

Ideas Create:

A TECHNICAL SYSTEM WITH:

- Extensive shared visions driven at all levels, not just from the executive suite.

- Open, nondistorted flows of information—up, down, and sideways among people at all levels and throughout the organization.

A POLITICAL SYSTEM WITH:

- Total honesty, candor, and willingness to face business reality in the selecting and rewarding of people.

- Decisions made based on expertise, not hierarchical levels.

- Multiple power networks to support multiple tasks.

A CULTURAL SYSTEM WITH:

- Open, candid, reality-focused attitudes

- Emphasis on both bottom-line efficiency needs and top-line innovation needs.

- Team values.

Three

The Readiness Test

Are You Ready for the Revolution?

Now that you have taken a look at reality, summarize your conclusions below. Note, this is a very serious and critical juncture. Leading a revolution means no turning back. Bridges do get burned and action must be taken.

Summarize your self-evaluation below.

Willingness: The Attitude toward Revolution

	LITTLE OR NO WILLINGNESS		MODERATE		GREAT AMOUNT OF WILLINGNESS
You as Leader:	1	2	3	4	5
Your "Varsity Team":	1	2	3	4	5
Your Organization:	1	2	3	4	5

Capability: The Talent, Skill, and Resources for Revolution

	LITTLE OR NO CAPABILITY		MODERATE		GREAT AMOUNT OF CAPABILITY
You as Leader:	1	2	3	4	5
Your "Varsity Team":	1	2	3	4	5
Your Organization:	1	2	3	4	5

Implications—Should You Start the Revolution?

_____

_____

_____

_____

Act I

Awakening

Kick-Starting the Revolution

Waking up the organization to the need for change is the most emotionally wrenching and terrifying aspect of a revolution. The protagonists have to shake up the status quo enough to release the emotional energy for the revolution. The first act of a revolution is creating a sense of urgency and dealing with the inevitable resistance to the new order. This was very tough in GE, as it is in all successful companies. The early Welch years, 1981–1983, were marked by tremendous resistance. Welch was viewed by many as "Neutron Jack" and was named toughest CEO by *Fortune* magazine in 1984. During this phase Welch analyzed the old GE—what was wrong with it, what needed changing, and what didn't. The early articulation of a change agenda, the dynamics of waking the organization, and the unfreezing of old mind-sets and cultures are the main scenes of the first act.

STEP 1: Create a Feeling of Urgency

Avoid the Boiled-Frog Phenomenon. The first major test of a revolutionary leader is the speed with which he wakes up the organization.

There is an old biological experiment that demonstrates a frog's lack of attention to a changing environment. The first step of the experiment is to place a frog in a pan of cold water. As the water temperature is raised from room temperature to boiling, the frog sits in the water, never jumping out, and is ultimately boiled to death, demonstrating the risk of new organizations that do not attend to their environmental changes. Welch avoided the boiled-frog phenomenon by taking quick, urgent action as the leader of the GE revolution.

Soon after becoming CEO in 1981, Welch gave a speech to his top 100 executives. He was visibly emotionally moved, trying to create a sense of urgency by saying:

> You own these damn businesses. The idea of coming into Fairfield, and Fairfield yells and exhorts and cheers, Big Daddy gets you, and then you come back with another plan a little bit better than the last time. It's an insane system we've built . . . Let's take it away. Number 1, it's ownership, leadership, responsibility—it's yours . . . Our strategic plan doesn't need a book this thick, it's for you to be the leaders in what you're in, to be No. 1 or No. 2 in the business you're in. That's the General Electric plan.

1) What is the rationale for change?

Start by carefully articulating why change is necessary; make certain the top leadership team is in total agreement.

GE EXAMPLE	YOUR ORGANIZATION
• Increasing global character of markets and competition	_____
• Slow top-line growth of business	_____
• New growth opportunities emerging	_____
• Need to be a nimble organization	_____
• Competitors were speeding up cycle times	_____

2) How vulnerable to the boiled-frog phenomenon are you?

GE EXAMPLE	YOUR ORGANIZATION
GE was a 100-year-old, successful, highly respected corporation in America, coming off a year of record net income with the previous chairman, Reginald Jones, who had been voted *Fortune*'s "Best CEO in the U.S." However, there was significant, underlying dry rot in businesses that would rapidly decline if not transformed in the 1980s. Inbred arrogance and complacency at GE made facing reality extremely difficult.	

STEP 2: Deal with Resistance

Welch's early exhortations did not result in resistance. In fact, most GE managers responded, more or less, with big yawns. They felt, "Hey, we're GE, we're the best, we've been around for 100 years, this guy Welch is just a lot of talk." But once Welch began to act, resistance started, albeit not for the reasons one might have expected. The nearly $3 billion divestiture of Utah International in 1983 elicited blasé "So what?" behavior on the part of some managers. It wasn't until the Housewares business was sold in 1984 (GE irons, toasters, and other small appliances) that GE managers woke up and figuratively started pointing at Welch and saying, "That son-of-a-bitch is starting to change us, now we have to resist him." And resistance comes in three forms: Technical, Political, and Cultural.

Types of Resistance

Technical resistance includes all of the rational reasons for resisting change: habit, prior investment, and inertia.

Political resistance is the response to the disruption to the existing power structure. Powerful coalitions are disrupted, resources are limited, and leaders often have to take blame for problems that were created in the organization.

Cultural resistance is due to mind-sets and blinders built up over the years, resulting in anchors that keep people in the past.

What Are the Major Forces Resisting Change in Your Business?

Diagnose the major forces of resistance: This is a critical step in the process as all of the leadership teams need to agree and work together. There is inevitably a great deal of conflict over resistance. This work often takes a day of intense debate and compromise to resolve.

1. Technical Resistance

CAUSE	GE EXAMPLES	YOUR ORGANIZATION
Habit and Inertia	GE managers had mastered a set of bureaucratic traditions. Welch's goals required doing things in a different way.	_____ _____ _____
Fear of the Unknown	GE managers were frightened by Welch's demand to go global. For many managers of traditionally domestic businesses, this caused anxiety and fear.	_____ _____ _____
Prior Investment	A tremendous amount was invested in training people to do things the "GE Way." This investment would allegedly be wasted if everyone changed.	_____ _____ _____

2. Political Resistance

CAUSE	GE EXAMPLES	YOUR ORGANIZATION
Resource Allocation	Resource allocation tends to be a zero sum game in the best of times. Welch told GEers to get higher productivity and more innovation with less overhead and less headcount. Doing more with less makes the normal politics of resource allocation even tougher.	_____ _____ _____ _____ _____
Indictment of Leaders	One exception to the "indictment of leaders" problem was Carl Schlemmer, the head of GE's Locomotive business, who invested $300 million in new plant capacity to overtake its competition, GM. When the bottom fell out of the market, Carl Schlemmer took full responsibility for having misjudged the market, and said, "I want to stay and clean up the mess." He went on to lead a very exciting turnaround—he faced his own personal indictment.	_____ _____ _____ _____ _____ _____ _____
Threats to Powerful Coalitions	The core businesses, such as Power Systems and Lighting, had dominated GE since they were founded: In 1980, 50% of earnings; by 1985 this number had shrunk to 25%. Their leaders resisted Welch as their power (investments, career opportunities, etc.) was threatened.	_____ _____ _____ _____ _____

3. Cultural Resistance

CAUSE	GE EXAMPLES	YOUR ORGANIZATION
Old Cultural Mind-sets	In Lighting, in 1984 and 1985, people reminisced about Thomas Edison, NELA Park, and the "good old days" of market dominance—while low-cost producers from Korea and elsewhere were eroding GE's market share. A history of dominance precluded Lighting's managers from perceiving a competitive threat. Their mind-sets were often "hard-wired" and immune to retraining.	_____
Sense of Security	Power Systems' several-year backlog of orders, its healthy earnings record, and its traditional technical superiority allowed the business's managers to feel secure even as their business was ending.	
Climate for Change	GE's stable 100-year-old bureaucracy was geared toward doing the same thing, the same way, for the millionth time; thus change was anathema to the organization.	

STEP 3: Fighting Resistance

Premise 1: Resistance Resides in the Chain of Command

The chain of command is where much of the resistance resides because people's vested interests are at stake.

a. You must stir up the total populace and begin developing new leaders for the new regime.

b. You must create a new set of values and templates.

c. You must invent mechanisms for socializing the work force.

Premise 2: Revolutionaries Replace the Current System with One of Their Own

Revolutionaries overturn the current system and replace it with one of their own devising. They do not rely on the chain of command to bring about quantum change—they grab the police, media, and education system. So did Jack Welch.

<u>GE EXAMPLE</u>   <u>YOUR ORGANIZATION</u>

The Police

GE's internal auditing staff, considered by many inside GE as the Gestapo and headed by the top finance executive, was the police. Welch eliminated many measures, created new measures, forced people to look at comparisons to competitors (not just to budgets), and redirected their focus to serving GE's businesses. Thus, rather than controlling it, corporate audit staff now does more and more consulting to help transform the organization rather than control it.

The Media

Welch took control of all his forms of communication, from board communication to security analyst presentations to using his own words and ideas when writing internal speeches.

The Schools

The GE Blue books, although not used for fifteen years, had still left their cultural imprint—they were symbolically burned. Welch said there are no more "textbook" answers. Leaders must write their own. He took direct control of Crotonville, and continues to appear every two weeks at Crotonville to interact in classes and redirect the overall Crotonville curriculum for everyone, from new hires to senior executives.

Act II

Envisioning

Mobilizing Commitment to a Vision

This is the act of the drama where emotion becomes more positive, where the frustrations and fears get channeled in new and exciting directions. The purpose of the revolution comes into focus.

Revolution requires emotionally exciting visions. The pain of change requires an image of the "New Way." The contemporary problem with vision is that for many leaders it has become a sloganeering "bumper sticker" campaign of platitudes such as "customer-oriented," "fast cycle-time," and "reengineered organization." Without intellectually substantial *ideas* to back these phrases, platitudes quickly become a source of ridicule for the "non-transformational leader." This ridicule leads to deep cynicism and alienation rather than the anticipated liberation of Act II.

In 1981 Welch clearly made this point when he spoke of the importance of having a central idea:

> You can express a vision to a broad number of people. People have to want to buy into your vision. You can implement it and together you can all win and reward yourselves and the company. That's what a good leader

does. He or she creates an open, caring relationship with every employee. If you can't articulate your business vision, if you can't get people to buy in, forget it. You won't be successful. It won't come from power and title.

The visioning process is a creative, often chaotic, multiple-iteration process. A vision is a group effort. It is what we believe to be important. It is a work in progress, an architectural rendering that constantly gets modified. We need to involve as many people as possible, think "out loud," and get feedback from many different stakeholders.

STEP 1: Preparation for the Vision— A GE Example

Before starting the creative visioning process, take time to carefully describe the current reality. Using the technical, political, and cultural framework, develop a set of summary descriptions for each box in the following chart. Each summary should be the result of intensive examination and discussion of the current organization and the manager who will be involved in the visioning process. The dialogue and discussion will help the teams work through their differences, sensitize each other to assumptions regarding what needs changing, and prepare them to think about the desired future. As soon as Welch took office, he spent six months visiting all corners of GE. These trips were his way of determining GE's reality—the TPC matrix on the following page summarizes this understanding. It represents GE's reality in 1980.

GE's Technical, Political, and Cultural Reality in 1980: The TPC Matrix

	STRATEGY	ORGANIZATIONAL STRUCTURE	HUMAN RESOURCE MANAGEMENT
T E C H N I C A L	• Diversify • Religious devotion to budgets • Grow high-tech businesses • Strategic planning	• Decentralize • Systematic structuring	• Engineer-dominated professional recruit • One pay system • Formal appraisals, work goals
P O L I T I C A L	• CEO as constitutionalist • Banker role	• Hierarchical • Functional boundaries • Political centralization	• Succession very formal/systematic • Rewards similar/lockstep • Approvals boss down
C U L T U R A L	• "Scientific management" • Decentralized philosophy—centralized behavior • Oligopolistic • Stewardship	• GE "way of doing things" • Core business culture dominance	• GE recruits screened for culture • Development used to shape culture • Appraisal and rewards "GE way" driven

What's the current state of reality at your organization? Fill in the TPC matrix for your organization today.

Your Organization's Technical, Political, and Cultural Reality Today: The TPC Matrix

	STRATEGY	ORGANIZATIONAL STRUCTURE	HUMAN RESOURCE MANAGEMENT
TECHNICAL			
POLITICAL			
CULTURAL			

STEP 2: The Nature of the Visioning Process

An example of this iterative nature of the visioning process at GE is the values statement. Welch was constantly reworking it, asking for feedback from all possible sources. The fundamental ideas remained the same throughout the drafts, but their articulation was reworked for a decade and revisions will continue forever.

1983: Main Points from Speech to Officers on Values

- Lean and agile
- Excellence
- Quality
- Entrepreneurship
- Reality and candor
- Communications
- Stewardship

1985: Main Points from Shared Values Statement

- Only satisfied customers can provide job security
- Change is continual; nothing is sacred
- Nothing is secret
- Constructive conflict flourishes
- Dealing with paradox is a way of life

1987: Main Points from Revised Shared Values Statement

- Respect for others
- Openness
- Change is continual
- Dealing with paradox is a way of life
- Constructive conflict
- Resource allocation is dynamic
- Everyone's contribution counts
- Doing the right thing is pervasive
- "Ownership"

1992: Main Points from Revised Shared Values Statement

- Create a clear, simple, reality-based, customer-focused vision and be able to communicate it straightforwardly to all constituencies.

- Understand accountability and commitment and be decisive. Set and meet aggressive targets with unyielding integrity.

- Have a passion for excellence. Hate bureaucracy and all the nonsense that comes with it.

- Have the self-confidence to empower others and behave in a boundaryless fashion. Believe in and be committed to Work-Out as a means of empowerment. Be open to ideas from anywhere.

- Have, or have the capacity to develop, global brands and global sensitivity and be comfortable building diverse global teams.

- Stimulate and relish change; do not be frightened or paralyzed by it. See changes as an opportunity, not just a threat.

- Have enormous energy and the ability to energize and invigorate others.

The visioning process is a creative, often chaotic, multiple-iteration process. Brainstorm and organize the ideas around central concepts and then get feedback and think out loud with many different stakeholders. This is akin to the architect doing many renderings, getting feedback, redrawing, rethinking, etc.

The vision must include quantum ideas in the technical, political, and cultural areas. These ideas provide the organizing logic for the transformation. These ideas must also reinforce each other. In order for GE to succeed, each of the three central ideas must contribute to each other. For example, being No. 1 or No. 2 with a very decentralized company could end up with GE as a mere holding company. Instead, Welch always believed there must be synergy between all the companies that make up GE. The political idea came about to provide the freedom for businesses to do their own thing as opposed to meeting the inward bureaucratic needs of the company. The glue that makes it all hold together is the shared values finally articulated under the concept of boundarylessness.

At GE it took Welch a very short period of time to articulate clearly the technical idea of being No. 1 or No. 2. Nonetheless this idea got discussed and revised many times in terms of meaning until it became deeply embedded in the collective mind-set of GEers.

The political idea, integrated diversity, with its paradox of decentralized businesses and collective GE action, took a lot longer to come into focus. Welch started with the idea of "ownership" of the businesses; the rendering was too fuzzy, managers misunderstood the concept, and until 1985, when the sector layer was removed from GE and the idea of businesses being directly connected to the office of the CEO occurred, the political idea for GE was not clear. Since that time the idea has been modified to its present articulation of integrated diversity, large freestanding businesses that can also cooperate with each other to accomplish overall GE wins in the marketplace.

. The glue to hold GE together is not bureaucracy, but a set of shared values and human networks across its businesses. The most intense of the visioning activities has been the process of articulating the value statement. Welch is constantly reworking it, asking for feedback from all possible sources.

The fundamental ideas remained the same, but their articulation was reworked for a decade and will continue to be revised forever. The technical, political, and cultural matrix provides a systematic framework for ensuring that the architectural rendering is complete, that all the major components of the organization are designed. It is never filled out at once, it is constantly revised, and it takes a period of years to get it approximately right.

STEP 3: Creating Your Vision

Remember, visioning is a process. It takes time and multiple iterations. Plan to give individuals time and opportunity to create their own visions of the future organization, then spend adequate time listening and sharing and working to create a common vision. The paradox is that visioning is not a democratic process. All revolutions are led by a minority of leaders, a committed core group. This does not mean they can't be highly participatory, but the top leadership must take a stand and must set stakes in the ground regarding core technical, political, and cultural ideas driving the revolution.

Your leadership responsibility is to create a vision of your organization that is:

- Challenging

- Easy to understand

- Not just one person's dream but indicative of a team's commitment

- Not fixed or static but capable of evolving over time

As you prepare for your vision, articulate a set of assumptions. Take time with the leadership group and develop your assumptions regarding the characteristics necessary for your company to win in the coming years. My personal list for this decade is:

- Marketplace challenges and strategy will be widely understood and provide the context for decision-making at all organizational levels.

- Efforts will be driven by shared visions and values rather than rules and policy pronouncements.

- Command from the top will be replaced by self-direction and teamwork.

- Human resources management will be directed toward building an ever-expanding pool of knowledgeable persons skilled in problem solving and developing others.

The matrix on the following page provides an analytic framework for capturing the creative work.

Do not start by trying to fill out the matrix. Use more creative processes such as having each member of the leadership team write his or her scenario of the future. I frequently have them write a *Fortune* article datelined three to four years in the future in which they journalistically describe where they would like to see the company at that point in time. Journalism requires them to paint a picture and describe in story form the people, corporate culture, and how the transition from today to that time took place.

The stories are then used to generate group discussion. Themes are identified and categorized into agreements and disagreements. This takes a number of days in off-site, open, constructive conflict-type discussions. The next step of working through the differences between group members can take months.

As the process goes along, try and capture the core elements of your vision in this TPC matrix.

Welch's 1990s Vision for GE

	STRATEGY	ORGANIZATIONAL STRUCTURE	HUMAN RESOURCE MANAGEMENT
TECHNICAL	• No. 1 or No. 2 • High-growth businesses	• Thirteen businesses • Share best practices • Boundarylessness	• Multiple pay systems • New staffing systems • Development as a continuous process
POLITICAL	• Integrated diversity	• No "wedding cake" hierarchy • Cross-functional teamwork • Empowerment, decision-making pushed to lower levels	• Rewards very flexible • Appraisals from below as well as above
CULTURAL	• Speed, simplicity, and self-confidence • Ownership • Share best practices • Work-Out	• Shared values • Many cultures • Common vision	• Human resource systems shape and mold boundarylessness • New staffing and support values

Your Vision

	STRATEGY	ORGANIZATIONAL STRUCTURE	HUMAN RESOURCE MANAGEMENT
TECHNICAL	_____ _____ _____ _____ _____	_____ _____ _____ _____ _____	_____ _____ _____ _____ _____
POLITICAL	_____ _____ _____ _____ _____	_____ _____ _____ _____ _____	_____ _____ _____ _____ _____
CULTURAL	_____ _____ _____ _____ _____	_____ _____ _____ _____ _____	_____ _____ _____ _____ _____

Act III

Rearchitecting

Introduction

Architecture: The art or practice of designing and building structures.
                                      —*Webster's Collegiate Dictionary*

Why "rearchitecting" when we know this is not a word? Because it captures the core challenge of Act III, the art and practice of redesigning and rebuilding the organization. Architecture is creative; it involves concepts and design as well as the practicality of the structure. Social architecture is the art of designing and building a complex organization. Revolutions require you to destroy, design, and then build the new organization creatively, thus, rearchitecting.

Act III was well underway at GE by the end of the eighties. Welch's vision began to emerge for the twenty-first-century organization, which he characterized with the word "boundarylessness." "Old Way" organizations were all about boundaries and compartmentalization and chains of command. The new organization would be free of these increasingly nonproductive strictures. Information would flow freely across functional and business boundaries from where it was developed to where it was needed. The boundaryless corporation would resolve the conflict between organizational size and speed. It would have the might of a large organization and the speed, flexibility, and self-confidence of a small one. Most important of all, it is the only way GE can accomplish the yearly productivity improvements required to span across all the businesses.

The only way to control your destiny is with ever-improving levels of productivity. This is the key portion of Welch's vision. Boundarylessness is the goal: Work-Out is the vehicle for getting there. Welch's statement in 1992, written in the 1991 annual report, defines this challenge well:

> 1991 did once again remind us how absolutely critical productivity growth is in the brutally Darwinian global market places in which virtually all of our businesses compete. We are aware, for instance, that if we had the same productivity growth in '90 and '91 that we had in '80 and '81, our '91 earnings would have been more like $3 billion rather than $4.435 billion. We also are acutely aware that without productivity growth it is possible to lose in twenty-four months businesses that took a half-century to build. Productivity growth is essential to industrial survival.
>
> But to increase productivity, you first have to clear away all the impediments that keep you from its achievement—primarily the management layers, functional boundaries, and all the other trappings of bureaucracy.
>
> We've been trumpeting the removal of bureaucracy and the layers at GE for several years now—and we did take out "sectors," "groups," and other superstructure—but much more remains. Unfortunately, it is still possible to find documents around GE businesses that look like something out of the National Archives, with five, ten, or even more signatures necessary before action can be taken. In some businesses you might still encounter many layers of management in small areas; boiler operators reporting to the supervisor of boilers, who reports to the utility manager, who reports to the manager of plant services, who reports to the plant manager, and so on.

Layers insulate. They slow things down. They garble. Leaders in highly layered organizations are like people who wear several sweaters outside on a freezing winter day. They remain warm and comfortable but are blissfully ignorant of the realities of their environment. They couldn't be further from what's going on.

GE Example:
Welch also used the analogy of a house with many floors and walls to represent the "Old Way" GE, pointing out the need to blow up all floors and walls—break down old bureaucratic boundaries—in order to create the new GE.

STEP 1: Assess Your Organization on Boundarylessness

Use the following chart to analyze where your organization currently is and what it should be doing in the future.

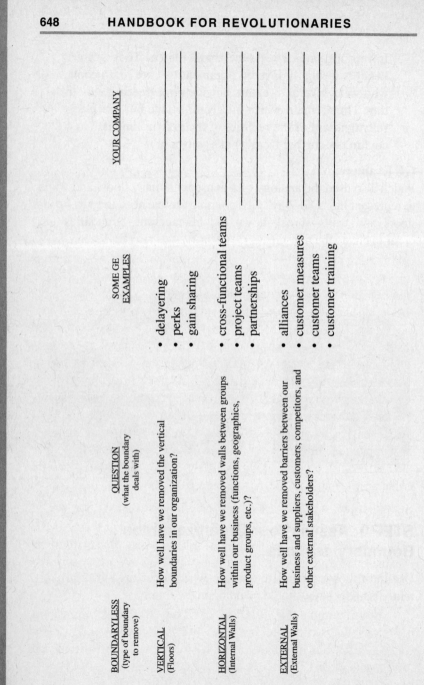

BOUNDARYLESS (type of boundary to remove)	QUESTION (what the boundary deals with)	SOME GE EXAMPLES	YOUR COMPANY
VERTICAL (Floors)	How well have we removed the vertical boundaries in our organization?	• delayering • perks • gain sharing	_____
HORIZONTAL (Internal Walls)	How well have we removed walls between groups within our business (functions, geographics, product groups, etc.)?	• cross-functional teams • project teams • partnerships	_____
EXTERNAL (External Walls)	How well have we removed barriers between our business and suppliers, customers, competitors, and other external stakeholders?	• alliances • customer measures • customer teams • customer training	_____

STEP 2: Social Architecture at the Top

Early in Act III, it is critical to start radically changing the way the top of the organization functions. Without this key building block none of the rest of the revolution will succeed. There are two fundamental reasons for this: (1) The top must "walk the talk" and role-model the new values and vision, and (2) the top is usually where a lot of the "Old Way" behavioral patterns are most deeply embedded and thus in great need of change.

Social architecture is a term that refers to the fundamental redesign of how people work together to get things done, who relates to whom for what, and how decisions are made. Examples at the top include all the resource allocation decisions made by top management, i.e., capital allocation, strategic direction, people allocation, as well as the coordination required to transfer technology, managerial learnings, and organizational best practices.

The challenge starts at the board level with a look at the key tasks, and who needs to do what with whom by when. The key conceptual building blocks of social architecture are: *People* (making sure that the right players are selected and put in the right roles); *time* (what goes on the corporate agenda and deciding on the appropriate cycle times. For example, should strategic reviews be held every year or on an as needed basis? Should succession planning take place annually or semiannually?); and *space* (where people and activities are physically located, how many hierarchical layers, what people and activities are networked, etc.).

GE Example:

The Corporate Executive Council is the centerpiece of the new GE. The old CEC was a formal monthly session where the heads of the businesses convened with the CEO to review businesses and discuss GE issues. The result was a very stilted, politically charged, "show and tell" session.

Starting in the mid-1980s the CEC began to meet quarterly in off-site settings with total informality. There is one agenda: "How do we, the heads of GE's thirteen major businesses—with Welch and Hood in the CEC, along with key corporate staff executives—

team together to be the world's most competitive enterprise." The meeting is designed to share best practices, looking for ways of getting synergy across GE's diverse set of businesses.

The meetings are run in a workshop-type setting. There are no formal presentations. Each of the key business leaders comes with material to share. There is open debate, ties or jackets are not allowed, long coffee breaks are scheduled, and informal time at night is planned so that people can network. There is total sharing of information with Welch acting as a facilitator. This bit of social architecture has now been replicated by GE's thirteen business heads in each of their businesses.

GE's Corporate Management System Study

In 1986 Welch commissioned a study of all the management processes at the top of the company. This study represents one way of doing your homework for social architecture at the top. As with the GE study, assign specific interviews to a key staff individual and/or consultant to collect data from the CEO, his/her direct reports, board members, and select executives one or two levels lower. Be systematic, objective, and dispassionate. This bit of social architecture has now been replicated by GE's thirteen business heads in each of their businesses.

On the following form, specify your diagnostic questions.

Questions Welch Used to Assess the Social Architecture at the Top

<u>GE EXAMPLE</u>   <u>YOUR ORGANIZATION</u>

Vision of what we want an operating business to be:

• How much scope? How much autonomy? How much delegation to head of business? Does delegation vary by the nature of the business, by our comfort with or the degree of tenure of its leader, or by the nature of the contemporary environment?

- How much differentiation are we comfortable in allowing in terms of such factors as organizational structure, nomenclature/officer titles, motivation and reward systems, operating style?

- How much communication laterally between businesses as opposed to vertically (CEO-Businesses)

Vision of what we want the Corporate Executive Office to be:

- What role and scope versus operating businesses?

- What added value should CEO provide over and above the bare minimum necessary to satisfy corporate requirements?

- If operating GE as a classic holding company represents one end of a spectrum and running GE as a highly integrated and centralized company represents the other end, where do we want to be on that spectrum?

- Will "where we want to be" vary with the economic cycle, our comfort level with and trust of our Business Executives or any other factor?

- What decisions do we *clearly* want to make at the CEO level, what decisions *clearly* at the business level, and what decisions require the application of judgment (on whose part) before deciding at which level?

Vision of what we want Corporate Staff to be (consistent with the agreed-upon visions for both the CEO and the operating businesses):

- What work *must* be done at corporate level to satisfy corporate entity requirements (e.g., financial reporting, tax accounting, share owner communications, etc.)?

- What work of a "staff" nature does the CEO want done at its behest to help CEO members carry out the vision of what the CEO should be and do?

- What work do we want done at corporate level (in which few areas) that ensures a homogeneous approach across the many and diverse businesses and cultures the company encompasses?

- What work do we want to carry out at corporate level for purposes of taking advantage of critical mass and cost-effectiveness parameters (e.g., Air Transport, Management Education, Pooled Services)?

Given these visions of what we desire in the future insofar as operating businesses, the Corporate Executive Office, and Corporate Staff are concerned, to what extent are the following consistent with those visions:

• Company *Policies* and the *Functional Procedures* which implement those Policies (including the delegations of authority contained therein)?

_____

_____

• Any management *practices* we have installed (whether documented or unwritten) which are *not* in sync with our stated Policies/Procedures?

_____

_____

• The recurrent annual *processes* which we utilize either at Corporate level, at Business level, or at both levels to manage the company?

_____

_____

How can we make the CEO more effective to manage a company one-third larger and significantly more complex than heretofore?

_____

_____

• Should the CEO meet more/less/ same as a collective body than at present?

_____

_____

• On what things is it critical that we all see the same things/hear the same words? On what things do we trust one another's judgment sufficiently to rely on one individual for sole source inputs on some subject upon which the CEO must make a collective decision?

_____

_____

_____

- What factors seem to be important in reaching timely decisions we feel comfortable with? What factors intervene when we must reach a decision *more quickly* than we're comfortable with? When a decision takes *longer* than we're comfortable with?

- When meeting collectively:
  —Are we too structured or rigid?
  —Too ad hoc and overly flexible?
  —Disciplined and linear or all over the ranch?

- Do we have enough "open" or "white space" days to allow us to carry out our individual responsibilities effectively? Comfortably?

- Are we oppressive, overly lax, or about right in our style of follow-up on operating matters over which we have approval authority?

- How effective are we in utilizing our CEO Staff? What do we need that we're not getting now? Ditto for those Corporate Staff Components whose role it is to service the staff needs of the CEO?

- What is the optimum balance between the CEO interacting with the company on a hierarchical basis (i.e., through those reporting directly to CEO members) versus "meeting the people directly" via appearance at Crotonville courses, Elfun presentations, plant visits, roundtables, etc.? Are we presently doing too much or not enough of the latter?

STEP 3: Companywide Involvement in the Revolution

Now that the top has been redesigned, it is time for a multiyear effort to involve every employee in the revolution. At GE, Work-Out is the name given to this process. As Welch stated in 1990:

> Work-Out is a fluid and adaptable concept, not a "program." It generally starts as a series of regularly scheduled "town meetings" that bring together large cross sections of a business—people from manufacturing, engineering, customer service, hourly, salaried, high- and lower-levels—people who in their normal routines work within the boxes on the organizational charts and have few dealings with one another.
>
> The initial purpose of these meetings is simple—to remove the more egregious manifestations of bureaucracy: multiple approvals, unnecessary paperwork, excessive reports, routines, rituals. Ideas and opinions are often, at first, voiced hesitantly by people who never before had a forum—other than the water cooler—to express them. We have found that after a short time, those ideas begin to come in a torrent—especially when people see action taken on the ones already advanced.
>
> With the desk largely cleared of bureaucratic impediments and distractions, the Work-Out sessions then begin to focus on the more challenging tasks: examining the myriad processes that made up every business, identifying the crucial ones, discarding the rest, and then finding a faster, simpler, better way of doing things. Next, the teams raise the bar of excellence by testing their improved processes against the very best from around the company and from the best companies around the world.

Work-Out sessions should include people from multiple levels and functions, and should be facilitated by trained internal staff and/or external consultants. In order to create trust and positive emotional energy, the process should initially be focused on bureaucracy busting. The following pages present examples from the launch of Work-Out in GE Medical Systems.

STEP 4: Launching a Work-Out Effort— A GE Example

In the fall of 1988 GE Medical Systems (GEMS) launched its Work-Out effort. Even though no two GE businesses approached the launch the same way, there are clearly some fundamental principles of building blocks. Use these case illustrations to think through your own launch process:

GEMS Prework Diagnosis

Work-Out began when some fifty GEMS employees attended a five-day off-site session. The participants included senior vice president and group executive John Trani, his staff, six employee relations managers, and informal leaders from technology, finance, sales, service, marketing, and manufacturing. Trani selected these informal leaders for their willingness to take business risks, challenge the status quo, and contribute in other key ways to GEMS. We participated as Work-Out faculty members.

The session took place after two important preliminary steps. First, we conducted in-depth interviews with managers at all levels of GEMS. Interviews uncovered many objections to and criticisms of existing procedures, including measurement systems (too many, not focused enough on customers' cross-functional conflicts); pay and reward systems (lack of work goals, inconsistent signals); career development systems (ambiguous career paths, inadequate performance feedback); and an atmosphere in which blame, fear, and lack of trust overshadowed team commitments to solving problems. Here are some sample quotes from our interviews:

> I'm frustrated. I simply can't do the quality of work that I want to do and know how to do. I feel my hands are tied. I have no time. I need help on how to delegate and operate in this new culture.

The goal of downsizing and delayering is correct. The execution stinks. The concept is to drop a lot of "less important" work. This just didn't happen. We still have to know all the details, still have to follow all the old policies and systems.

I'm overwhelmed. I can and want to do better work. The solution is not simply adding new people, I don't even want to. We need to team up on projects and work. Our leaders must stop piling on more and help us set priorities.

Second, just before the first Work-Out session, Jack Welch traveled to GEMS headquarters for a half-day round table with the Work-Out participants. Here are some sample quotes from middle managers.

To senior management:

Listen! Think carefully about what the middle managers say. Make them feel like they are the experts and that their opinions are respected. There appear to be too many preconceived beliefs on the part of Welch and Trani.

To senior management:

Listen to people, don't just pontificate. Trust people's judgment and don't continually second-guess. Treat other people like adults and not children.

About themselves:

I will recommend work to be discontinued. I will try to find "blind spots" where I withhold power. Any person I send to speak for me will "push" peers who resist change.

About themselves:

I will be more bold in making decisions. I will no longer accept the status quo. I will ask my boss for authority to make decisions. In fact, I will make more decisions on my own.

The Work-Out Session

The five-day Work-Out session was an intense effort to unravel, evaluate, and reconsider the complex web of personal relationships, cross-functional interactions, and formal work procedures through which the business of GEMS gets done. Cross-functional teams cooperated to address actual business problems. Each functional group developed a vision of where its operations are headed.

John Trani participated in a round table where he listened and responded to the concerns and criticisms of middle managers. Senior members of the GEMS staff worked to build trust and more effective communication with the functional managers. All the participants focused on ways to reorganize work and maximize return on organization time, on team time, and on individual time. An important part of the session was Bureaucracy Busting. There are several forms of Bureaucracy Busting. One that we developed is the CRAP detector (Critical Review Appraisal) of unnecessary work. Individuals are asked to look for CRAP, which can be unnecessary plans, approvals, policies, measurements, meetings, and reports. The CRAP detector is presented below and should be used to help identify ways you can begin rearchitecting your job.

Example: The Crap Detector

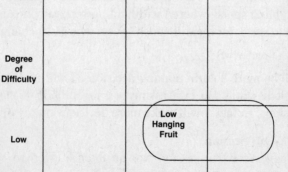

Critical Review Appraisal—Take Work-Out

IMPACT ON ORGANIZATION—
HOW MUCH IMPROVEMENT WILL RESULT?

DESCRIPTION: Use the CRAP detector to help individual and group start taking work out.

STEP 1: Review a typical work week—identify activities that do not add value to the customer—look for unnecessary:
>meetings
>reports
>measurements
>approvals
>procedures

STEP 2: Determine who needs to be involved to change it (assign a letter to each work elimination item):
>Me alone = M
>A partner = P
>My work group = G
>Intergroup (mine and another) = I
>Total organization = T

STEP 3: Indicate degree of impact and difficulty of change—place each item in the matrix.

STEP 4: Create an action plan for the "low hanging fruit" items that can be changed quickly and which have impact. Involve relevant parties.

The five-day session ended with individuals and functional teams signing close to 100 written contracts to implement the new procedures. There were contracts between functional teams, contracts between individuals, contracts between function heads and their staffs, and businesswide contracts with John Trani and his staff. This set the stage for phase one of Work-Out in GEMS, a series of similar workshops for hundreds of managers in 1989.

STEP 5: Human Resource Systems to Support Your Vision

Once you have used Work-Out to attain your vision, it is important to change the HR support function. Below are some suggestions:

HR Functions

Selection

Broaden criteria to include not only technical skill but . . .

- Facilitation, problem solving, and interpersonal skill
- Broad knowledge of the business
- Willingness to teach others

Appraisal Requirements

- Redefine success . . . elevate organizational management above career management
- Make mentoring paramount . . . the key to expanding the organization's expertise
- When weighing results, consider how obtained
- Take a longer-term view when judging an individual's contribution and career potential

Development

Since performance depends on each person knowing more than just his or her job, development is central.

Requirements:

- From executive development to organizational development
- From investments in high-potential human resources to investment in *high-leverage* human resources

Let those with innate desire and capacity help to develop others.

Rewards

If the many count, then reward structure must reflect this reality.

Not just issues of fair play but critical to:

- Attracting the right people
- Keeping them and their accumulated knowledge in the organization
- Providing high degree of stability for boundaryless organization to function effectively

Your Organization: What Changes Do You Need to Make to the HR Function?

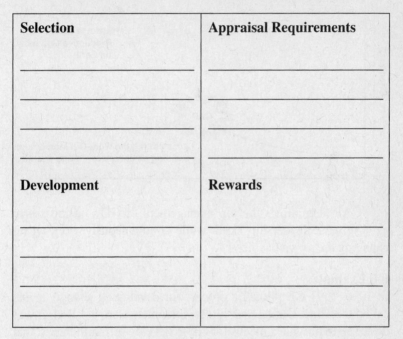

Selection	Appraisal Requirements
_____	_____
_____	_____
_____	_____
_____	
Development	**Rewards**
_____	_____
_____	_____
_____	_____
_____	

STEP 6: Continuous Revolution

In order to institutionalize your revolution's vision and ensure continuous change, it is necessary to make as many people as possible agents of change. At first, you will send people to Work-Out sessions and they will learn to redefine their jobs to meet the challenges of a changing business environment. But change is never finished. You must train leaders to lead their own Work-Out sessions.

After several years of Work-Out using teams of outside consultants as change agents, Welch felt GE was ready to develop its own army of change agents. In 1992 GE started at the top of the organization and started working down. The ultimate result was the Change Acceleration Program, or CAP. As the diagram below shows, CAP was designed to accelerate the rate of change within GE.

Change Acceleration Program

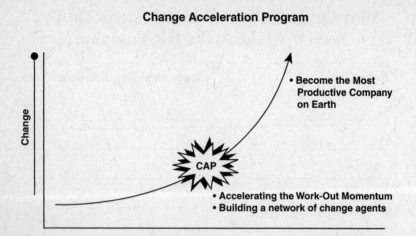

CAP also allows the top management of GE's businesses to gain valuable leadership skills while simultaneously working on changing their own businesses.

GE Example:
In 1990–1991 GE piloted a process for developing change agents called the Work-Out Leadership Development Series (LDS). It was designed to provide a means for GE to develop self-sufficiency, that is, have a critical mass of internal change agents cutting down on the reliance on external consultants.

LDS was designed to deliver development to individuals and teams from six GE businesses: NBC, Plastics, Motors, Medical Systems, EP&C, and the Audit Staff. Each team had a change project to complete during the LDS and each individual was to be developed as a change agent. The framework for development which guided the effort was based on the Transformational Leader Framework presented below.

Transformational Leader Framework

CHANGE MODEL

ACT I: Awakening

1. How to create a need for change
2. Dealing with resistance to change

ACT II: Envisioning

3. Developing a motivating vision
4. Gaining commitment of others to the vision

ACT III: Rearchitecting

5. Organization design skills
6. Human resource system design skills

Self As Instrument of Change

7. Developing the individual's change agent skill set

Your Organization—What Is Your Model for Leading Change?
Take time to discuss assumptions about how to lead change. Lay
out a conceptual framework and the rationale as the first step in
building a development process for change leadership.

KEY ELEMENTS OF MODEL   BRIEF DESCRIPTION

_____   _____

_____   _____

_____   _____

_____   _____

_____   _____

_____   _____

_____   _____

_____   _____

LDS consisted of three workshops spread over a six-month period. The six change agent teams had five to eight members. The change project constitutes the *action learning* component of the process. In addition, they learned new concepts and skills, and received considerable feedback from the faculty as well as peers and bosses.

The process is presented below:

WORKSHOP I

Facilitation Skills Workshop

- Group Dynamics/Group Development
- Role of the Process Facilitator
- Range of Facilitative Interventions
- Facilitating Work-Out Team Meetings
- Facilitation Lab

Aimed at helping participants learn skills and techniques to assist groups, manage group process, and become self-sufficient.

WORKSHOP II

Process Leadership Workshop

- Transformational Leadership
- Work-Out and Business Process Management
- Team Development
- Process Consultation
- Role of the Change Agent
- Application Planning

Aimed at helping participants learn concepts, skills, and techniques to take a more significant leadership role in the integration of Work-Out within their business; development of a focused, skilled, supportive team of internal change agents.

<u>WORKSHOP III</u>

Organizational Systems Workshop

- Systems View of Organizational Change
- Organizational Analysis & Diagnosis
- Intervention at an Organizational Level (Managing Conflict & Increasing Influence)
- Leading in a Boundaryless Organization

Aimed at helping participants gain the "big picture" view of organizational change and what it will take to reach Work-Out self-sufficiency and organizational "boundarylessness."

Your Organization

As a way of thinking through your own need for a Change Acceleration Program, do an analysis of your company's current effectiveness in each of the aspects of the change model. Use the framework on the next page:

Assess Your Organization's Effectiveness
(Plot your effectiveness for each dimension.)

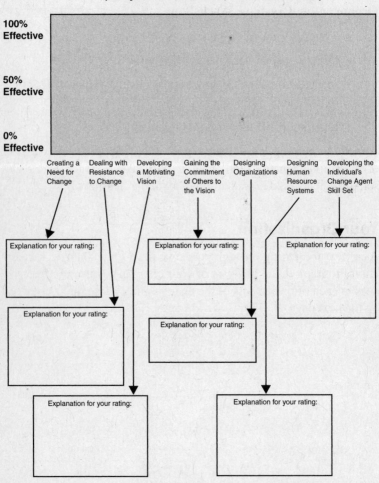

100% Effective

50% Effective

0% Effective

Creating a Need for Change

Dealing with Resistance to Change

Developing a Motivating Vision

Gaining the Commitment of Others to the Vision

Designing Organizations

Designing Human Resource Systems

Developing the Individual's Change Agent Skill Set

Explanation for your rating:

Explanation for your rating:

Explanation for your rating:

Explanation for your rating:

Explanation for your rating:

Explanation for your rating:

Explanation for your rating:

ACT I: Awakening　　　**ACT II: Envisioning**　　　**ACT III: Rearchitecting**

Your Challenge

Now specify your goals for designing continuous revolution processes in your organization.

<u>GE EXAMPLE</u>   <u>YOUR ORGANIZATION</u>

- Accelerate Work-Out self-sufficiency efforts

- Forge a true partnership for learning and development between Crotonville and businesses

- Create a critical mass of internal change agents

- Reinforce skill development with active experimentation and coaching on the job.

- Transfer GE Best Practices through site visits

- Position graduates as coaches

- Answer the call for "Act III"

How to Build a Change Agent Program

The top several hundred managers in most companies will require development as change agents. The final steps in the *Handbook* are presented to help guide you in this process.

Example of a Change Agent Program—Change Process (CP):
Over the last five years a set of social technologies has been developed to create a critical mass of change agents in a variety of companies around the world. The CP is designed to accelerate the transformation of companies by producing leadership teams with

the necessary skills to integrate various disciplines and programs useful today in successful companies—quality improvement, work reengineering, process mapping, visioning, cycle-time improvement, and other approaches—into a coherent, integrated agenda for change.

The program focuses on individual skill development *and* organizational change, using a variety of methods to solve important, immediate, critical business issues with leadership and change agent skills.

CP consists of a three-phase, action-learning process, delivered over six months with a combination of on-site and classroom activities to implement needed change in real time. Development of participants occurs both on line and through networking with other executives, interaction with facilitators, and structured learning experiences. The specific objectives are:

1. To build an effective leadership team which will drive the transformation agenda of each company.

2. To develop the individual skills of leaders to diagnose and facilitate individual, team, and organizational transformations.

3. To benchmark the best ideas and practices worldwide in order to accelerate the learning process and transformation of noncompeting consortium companies through creation of a rich learning system.

Fundamental Building Blocks of the Program

Change Process (CP) is both a lever for transforming your company and a powerful leadership experience. A unique set of building blocks, "social technologies," are used to achieve the five primary goals of CP: (1) Deliver on the change projects to make change in the company; (2) Develop change agent mind-sets; (3) Develop "change leadership" skills; (4) Develop change team skills; (5) Develop change networks. Each of the major building blocks is described below, along with the impact it has on each of the five goals.

The CP is delivered by creating a temporary system, that is, building a social organization with its own structure, leadership, and values. Compressed action learning puts individuals and teams under intense time and performance pressures. They must deliver strategic change to their organization while acquiring new skills and immediately using them to deliver on the projects.

IMPACT SCALE
○ = Little or no impact　◐ = Moderate impact　● = Strong impact

BUILDING BLOCKS	CHANGE PROJECTS	CHANGE MIND-SET	CHANGE LEADERSHIP	CHANGE TEAMS	CHANGE NETWORKS
Top Leadership Team: Ownership of the projects, selection and sponsorship of participants, and full involvement in the commitment process.	●	○	○	◐	○
Expert Faculty: Multidisciplinary faculty leading the process.	◐	●	◐	◐	◐
Coaching Role: Each team has a process consultant, someone selected and trained from the previous CLC who coaches the team.	●	◐	◐	●	◐
Process Learning: Team-building activities including "Outward Bound," learning about high-performing teams, systematic attention to feedback for each other.	●	◐	●	●	◐
Learning Feedback Loops: Collection of data and feedback to participants. (1) Survey pre-CP (self and others ratings of global leader behavior). (2) Team members provide feedback. (3) Coaches give feedback. (4) Another team analyzes and feeds back data. (5) Research team collects data and feeds back as part of program.	◐	◐	●	●	●
Commitment Processes: Throughout CP, individuals, teams, and the total group actively, publicly use processes for contracting and making "who, what, and when" commitments.	●	○	●	●	●
Concepts/Ideas: The CP faculty present participants with new conceptual tools dealing with global strategy, global operating mechanisms, time-based competitiveness, process loss, change processes, and leadership.	◐	●	●	◐	◐

Design Your Change Process

1. Specify Your Goals. Describe what outcomes you desire.

Mind-set _____

Leadership _____

Teamwork _____

Networking _____

Change Projects _____

2. Identify the Social Technology you will use in the Process.

WHICH BUILDING BLOCKS	DESCRIBE HOW IT WILL BE USED
1. Top Leadership Team	_____
2. Expert Faculty	_____
3. Coaching Role	_____
4. Process Learning	_____
5. Learning Feedback Loops	_____
6. Commitment Processes	_____
7. Concepts/Ideas	_____

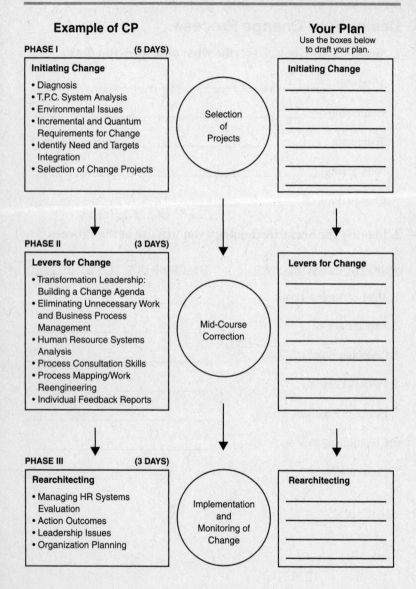

Example of CP

Your Plan

Use the boxes below to draft your plan.

PHASE I (5 DAYS)

Initiating Change

- Diagnosis
- T.P.C. System Analysis
- Environmental Issues
- Incremental and Quantum Requirements for Change
- Identify Need and Targets Integration
- Selection of Change Projects

Selection of Projects

Initiating Change

_____
_____
_____
_____
_____

PHASE II (3 DAYS)

Levers for Change

- Transformation Leadership: Building a Change Agenda
- Eliminating Unnecessary Work and Business Process Management
- Human Resource Systems Analysis
- Process Consultation Skills
- Process Mapping/Work Reengineering
- Individual Feedback Reports

Mid-Course Correction

Levers for Change

_____
_____
_____
_____
_____
_____

PHASE III (3 DAYS)

Rearchitecting

- Managing HR Systems Evaluation
- Action Outcomes
- Leadership Issues
- Organization Planning

Implementation and Monitoring of Change

Rearchitecting

_____
_____
_____
_____

EPILOGUE

Start the revolution all over again.

Index

A

accomplishment analyses, 63–64,
    281–283, 614–615
action learning, 161
    compressed, 163–164
    in Louisville, 249
actionable items, 246
advertising, 71
agility, 31, 32–33, 408
air cover, 71, 160
airplane interviews, 78
Alinsky, Saul, 164
alliances, best-of-class status in,
    227
AlliedSignal, 14, 76–77, 303
Allis-Chalmers, 57
American Express, 31
Anatomy of a Merger (Jones,
    Marriott), 207
Andrew, Nigel, 280, 321
Andrews, Eugene, 278
antitrust suits, 53, 54, 136–137,
    208
Apollo Computer, 77
application development, 70
ASEA Brown Boveri, 222
assembly lines, 32, 49
AT&T, 82
attitudinal positioning, 396
Austin, J. Paul, 45

Auto Auctions, 41
awakening, 596–598

B

backlogs, 95–96, 188–189
Ballmer, Steve, 321
Barriers, 279
Baughman, James, 93–94
    at Crotonville, 159–160, 161,
        329
    on GE bureaucracy, 50–51
    on Lighting's strategy, 207
    on reorganization, 184
    schools under, 101
    Tichy and, 165, 177–178
    values statement and, 174
    Work-Out and, 236–237, 242
Bayer, 73, 391
Bellaire, Florida, meeting, 93–94
benchmarking, 247
Benedetti, Carlo, 225
Bergen op Zoom plant, 73
"Best Practices," 195, 246–248,
    249, 299, 385
best-of-class status, 226–227
Black & Decker, 111–113, 220
Black Panthers, 164
Blue Books, 55–56, 70
Boca Raton, Florida, meetings,
    327–328, 339

Boesky, Ivan, 143
"boiled-frog syndrome," 96,
   627–628, 629
Bonsignore, Michael R., 14, 15
Borch, Fred, 52, 57–59, 78, 366
Borg-Warner, 41
Bossidy, Lawrence A., 99–100,
   185, 189
   Capital Services and, 75–77
   on CEC, 275
   CELC and, 166–168
   on GEMS, 259
   insider trading case and, 143
   proposed Honeywell
      acquisition and, 14
   Six Sigma and, 303, 334–335
   values statement and, 174
   on Welch's leadership, 253
boundaries, 476
Boundarylessness, 10, 83, 325
   assessing, 647–649
   co-location, 474–475
   community, 387
   control and, 196–197
   definition of, 33
   information sharing in, 198
   as value, 278–280
   Welch on, 294–295
   Work-Out and, 236, 241,
      244–245
boycotts, 135
Bradshaw, Thornton, 151
Bribery, 138
Brimm, Michael, 263
Buckley, Larry, 71, 74, 78
bureaucracy
   under Cordiner, 56–57
   corporate culture and, 49–51
   executive development and, 63

   at GE, 20–21, 44
   gotchas and, 60
   at RCA, 152–153
   turned against itself, 102–103
   Welch's skill in, 73–74
Bureaucracy Busting, 658–659
Burlingame, John, 77, 78, 100
   Utah International and, 89, 112
burnout, 5
Burns, James MacGregor, 162
Burton Group Financial Services,
   41
business engine, 103, 325, 378
   Opie and, 211
business portfolios, 39–41, 115,
   299–300, 347–348, 395
Business Week, 63
Bywater, Bill, 294

C

Calhoun, David, 144
Calloway, Wayne, 193
Calma, 41, 114, 116, 319
candor, 28, 161
   CEC and, 193–194
   employee relations and,
      127–128
   impact of, 198–199
   Welch's, 169–171
   Work-Out and, 301
capital allocation, 102–103
Carboloy, 41
Carpenter, Michael, 280
Carter, Jimmy, 45
Catch-22 (Heller), 268
Caterpillar, 489
Cave, the, 193–202. *See also*
   Crotonville

CBS, 150
CEC. *See* Corporate Executive
  Council (CEC)
central air conditioning, 41, 103
Chambers, John, 321
change
  Act I in, 33–34
  Act II in, 34–37
  Act III in, 37–38
  as continual, 175, 215–216
  coping with, 278
  Crotonville role in, 162, 164
  Immelt and, 348
  incremental, 91
  leadership qualities in, 64–65
  quantum, 33–38, 91, 374
  technology and, 222–223
  Welch on, 290–292
Change Acceleration Program
  (CAP), 251, 280, 334, 355
Change Agent Programs, 667–672
Change Process (CP), 667–672
changing before you have to, 28,
  48, 73
changing the game, 6–7
Chapperell Steel, 246
Charan, Ram, 263, 275–276
Chase Manhattan, 82
Chase Manhattan Leasing, 41
choir practices, 137
Churchill, Winston, 290
Citicorp, 31, 82
coaching, 320–321, 327–328
Coca-Cola, 45
coercive control, 196, 571
Coffin, Charles, 52–53, 358
  ethics under, 136
  strategic preferences of,
    558–559

Cohen, Eli, 323
collaboration, 278
collegial interaction, 185,
  192–193
co-location, 387, 474–475
combustion engineering, 222
commitment, 20, 196–197
communication, 25–26
  candid, 127–128
  constructive conflict in,
    169–171
  Crotonville and, 161
  in GEMS, 263–264
  and leading while being led,
    84–87
  Welch on, 291
  Welch's abilities in, 238
  of Welch's vision, 113–115,
    117
Compagnie des Lampes, 208
compensation
  GE system, 282–283
  incentive, 69, 214–215
  productivity and, 31–32
  shared values and, 274
  stock options, 277–278,
    282–283
  under Swope, 53–54
competition
  changes in, 30–32
  competitive advantage and, 28
  global, 5–6, 87–88
  Welch's redefinition of, 6–7
  Welch's views on, 98
competitive advantage, 28
  globalization, 87–88
  speed as, 85
competitive transparency, 6,
  87–88

complexity, 268
compressed action learning, 163–164
compressor failure, 199–201, 320, 439
compromise, 75
Con-Air, 112
conflict management, 344–345
conglomerates, 35, 113
Conseco, Inc., 346
consensus, 198
constructive conflict, 75, 571
    CEC and, 194
    criticism of, 188
    Crotonville and, 169–171
continuous improvement, 247, 253
control, 190–191
    types of organizational, 196, 571
Coolidge, William D., 361
Cordiner, Ralph, 52, 55–57, 137, 364
    task force of, 559
core circle, 113–115
Coronet Carpets, 41, 169–170
Corporate Entry Leadership Conference, 165–170, 330
Corporate Executive Council (CEC), 86–87, 90, 192–202, 381
    values and, 237–238
    Welch's satisfaction with, 274–275
Corporate Management System Study, 650–654
corporate planners, 102–103
Cosby Show, 150

cost cutting, 98–99, 214. *See also* layoffs
CRAP detector, 658–659
creative destruction, 91–92
credibility, 160
cross-licensing, 571–572
Croton-on-Hudson. *See* Crotonville
Crotonville, 87, 159–180
    action learning programs, 354
    CEC at, 193–202
    Corporate Entry Leadership Conference, 165–170, 330
    developmental processes at, 162–163
    discontent at, 147, 149
    global managers and, 230–231
    improvements at, 160–161
    as instrument of change, 162, 164
    Leadership Development Center, 329–332
    resistance at, 34–36
    in teaching infrastructure, 329–332
    Team Experienced Manager Course, 171–174
    values statement, 174–177
    Welch at, 319
    Welch on, 300
    Welch's investments in, 11
CT scanners, 75–76, 228–229, 304, 368
culture, organizational
    bureaucracy and, 49
    current GE, 7, 407–408, 414–415
    definition of, 48–49
    former GE, 20–21

globalization and, 259–260, 261–267
informality in, 327
at Lighting, 208–209
management of, 90–91
performance-driven, 160
power and, 245
TPC in, 88–91
values in, 83–84
Work-Out and, 38, 301
customer awareness trip, 128
customers
bureaucracy and, 21
satisfaction of, 247

D

Dammerman, Dennis, 59–60
Dance, Walter, 78
Darwinism, 71, 86, 320–321, 464
Dash 8 investment, 118–131
De Beers Consolidated Mines, 135
Deadly Deceptions, 135
decentralization, 55, 56
Decimus, 41
decision-making, 7, 37–38
compromise in, 75
Welch's method of, 69–70
defense contracts, 132–145, 149
Defense Industry Initiative on Business Ethics and Conduct, 140–141
delayering, 496–497. *See also* reorganization
Department of Commerce, U.S., 53
Department of Defense, U.S., 133–145

digitization, 13, 546–547
Dinks, 48
disenchantment, 92
disengagement, 598
disidentification, 92, 598
Disney, Walt, 193
diversity, 5, 273, 348–349
integrated, 83, 90, 195, 378, 449–450, 562–563
slides on, 562–563
Dotan, Rami, 135
Dotan case, 135
Doyle, Frank, 100
Drexel Burnham Lambert, 143
drives, 211. *See also* initiatives
Drucker, Peter, 29, 55, 88, 193
Du Pont, 136
Dunkirk, New York, meeting, 123
Dwyer, Jack, 120

E

e-business, 13, 304–306, 309, 325–326, 348, 541–544
Economic Advisory Board, 53
economies of scale, 265
Edison, Thomas, 4, 19, 52, 207, 358
Edison Electric, 208
egalitarianism, 87
Eickert, Stephen, 70, 73
e-learning, 336
Electrical Funds Group (ELFUN), 568
Electrolux, 77, 222
emotion
commitment and, 196–197
Housewares sale and, 111–113
Immelt and, 349–350

emotion (*cont.*)
  influence of, 85–86
  leadership and, 596
employees
  competing for talented, 310
  controlling, 191
  good of the company and, 119
  labor problems and, 126–129
  layoffs of, 99, 100–105, 110,
    128–129, 216
  morale among, 106–107, 147
  personal responsibility of, 33
  under Swope, 53–54
  upheaval of, 91–92
  winning over, 86–87
Employers Reinsurance Corp., 29,
    41, 109, 115
empowerment, 32, 204
  in "New Way" organizations,
    607–610
  Welch on, 296–297
  Work-Out and, 241
entrepreneurship, 408
environmental issues
  GE criticized on, 5
  nuclear plants and, 135–136
  Welch on, 288
envisioning, 596–598, 635–
    644
Ericsson, 258
ethics
  education programs, 144
  of facing reality, 131
  mirror test and, 133, 141–146,
    613–624
  prevalence of corrupt behavior
    and, 133, 134
  price fixing and, 57
  time-card scandal and, 131–145

Etzioni, Amitai, 571
European Commission, 347, 351
European Community, 225, 289
excellence, 397
excitement, 203–218, 293–294,
    309–310
executive management staff, 160,
    185, 281
Experienced Commercial
    Leadership Program, 355
external barriers, 279

F

facing reality, 8–9, 118–131
  attitudinal positioning, 396
  definition of, 28
  leadership and, 272–273
factory automation systems, 116,
    148, 434–435
Fanuc, 116, 434–435
fax networks, 195
Federated Department Stores,
    45
feedback, 170–171. *See also*
    communication
Financial Guaranty Insurance Co.,
    41
Financial News Network, 41
Fink, Daniel, 97
Flax, Steven, 110
flexibility, 263
Ford, Henry, 32
Ford Motor Company, 246
Fortune, 59–60, 137, 242–243
Frazier, Michael, 246
Frederick, Robert, 77
Fresco, Paulo, 217–220, 224–226,
    229

G

garbage events, 149
Gates, Bill, 321
Gault, Stanley, 63, 77
Gelco, 41
General Electric
  acquisitions of, 29, 41, 109,
    116, 148, 217–219, 425–
    426
  annual reports, 35–36
  antitrust suits against, 53, 54,
    136–137, 208
  audits, 144
  backlogs at, 95–96, 188–189
  Blue Books, 55–56, 70
  bureaucracy at, 20–21, 44
  business engine at, 35, 37, 39
  business units, 277
  CEOs of, 44, 52–60
  competitive technology position
    of, 46
  corruption at, 132–145
  criticisms of, 5
  cross-licensing agreements of,
    53, 207–208
  culture of, 7, 20–21, 49–51
  divestitures of, 29, 41, 89–90,
    103, 109, 111–113, 148
  dividend payments by, 47
  divisions at, 58–59
  e-business at, 13, 304–306,
    309, 325–326, 348
  environmental issues and, 5,
    135–136, 288
  financial performance of,
    28–29
  globalization, 87, 219–231
  history of, 19, 44–48, 52–60

holding company structure of,
    54–55
human resources system,
    280–283
initiatives of, 10–11, 12–15,
    337–342
insider trading case, 143–144
international business of, 87
issues facing Immelt, 347–348
job security at, 42
management development at,
    63–64
operating system of, 11–12,
    307–308, 340–341, 537–539
performance of, 43
portfolio of, 39–41, 115,
    299–300, 347–348
productivity rates of, 30, 46
progress stall at, 146–150
proposed Honeywell
    acquisition, 3–4, 14–15
RCA acquisition, 150–155,
    181, 418–419, 426
recognition of need for change
    at, 45–46, 64–65
reorganization of, 55, 90,
    124–128, 180–189,
    190–202, 203–218, 261, 262
resource massing at, 11
revenues of, non-U.S., 230
sectors, 180–183, 185–189
stock value of, 29, 47, 106, 149,
    296
strategy and performance
    reports, 393–555
teaching infrastructure at,
    329–337
Thomson S.A. acquisition,
    219–223

General Electric (*cont.*)
  three circles, 113–115
  time card scandal, 132–145
  timeline, 358–391
  value of, 3–4
  weak position of, 95–99
General Electric Aerospace, 134,
     249
General Electric Aircraft Engines,
     37, 40, 116, 288
  under Jones, 47
  market share of, 97
  Work-Out at, 249–251
General Electric Appliances, 40
  compressor disaster, 199–201,
     320, 439
  departments in, 58
  under Welch, 77
General Electric Audio, 258
General Electric Business
     Development, 246, 280
General Electric Capital Services,
     12, 30, 35, 40
  under Welch, 75–77
General Electric Consumer
     Electronics, 219–220, 228
General Electric Consumer
     Products and Services,
     75–77
General Electric Electro-Motive
     Division, 119, 120
General Electric Financial
     Services, 75, 97, 296
General Electric Gas Turbines,
     97
General Electric Housewares,
     111–113, 220
General Electric Industrial
     Systems, 40

General Electric Information
     Services, 192
General Electric Large
     Transformers, 115
General Electric Lighting, 40,
     203–218
  acquisitions of, 217–218
  antitrust suit against, 54
  as core operation, 115
  growth of, 37
  market share of, 97
  under Opie, 210–218
  Pro80 machines, 209, 212
  strength of, 207–210
General Electric Major
     Appliances, 106
General Electric Management
     Development Institute. *See*
     Crotonville
General Electric Medical
     Systems, 30, 40, 228–
     229
  cost structure of, 259
  Global Leadership Program,
     263–267
  globalization of, 219–223
  market share of, 97
  under Trani, 256–270
  Welch at, 74–75
General Electric Mobile
     Communication, 258
General Electric Motors, 97
General Electric Nuclear Power,
     104–105
General Electric Plastics, 40
  growth of, 73
  under Jones, 47
  LEXAN, 69, 70–71, 72–73
  market share of, 97

NORYL, 69–71, 72
Welch at, 48, 62, 68–74
General Electric Power Systems, 30, 37, 40, 222
goals of, 173
market share of, 97
General Electric Re-Entry Systems, 139–140, 143
General Electric Robotics, 170
General Electric Services and Materials, 185
General Electric Space Systems, 139, 141
General Electric Trading Company, 401
General Electric Transportation Systems, 40, 118–131
labor problems in, 126–129
restructuring of, 124–128
General Management and Technical Services Company, 134
General Motors, 31, 52–53, 82, 136
Genever-Watling, David, 189
Genstar, 41
Ginza event, 265
Giuliani, Rudolph, 143
global brains, 230–231
Global Leadership Program, 263–267
global learning, 554–555
globalization, 219–231
best-of-class status and, 226–227
competition in, 5–6, 31
competitive advantage and, 87–88
culture and, 259–260, 261–267

difficulty of, 224–225
free and fair trade and, 401–402
Jones's recognition of, 46
LEXAN and, 72–73
of Lighting, 217–218
of Medical Systems, 256–270
objective in, 302
overseas managers and, 230–231
resistance to, 226
results from, 546
GNA Annuities, 41
GNP companies, 28–29, 96–97
goals
shared, 273
stretch, 485–486, 490–491
Goldman Sachs Group, 178
Gomez, Alain, 219, 229
Goodyear, 63
gotchas, 60
Gotemba, Japan, course, 171–174
go-to-market, 269
governments, 288–290
Gross National Product, 96–97
GNP companies and, 28–29
Group Operating Council, 269
Grove City, Pennsylvania, plant, 120
growth
profitless, 57–59
revenue, 20–22, 204
GTE, 77
Gutoff, Reuben, 69, 70, 71, 74
guts, 279–280

H

Handbook for Revolutionaries, 593–673
hardware phase, 257, 463
Harrods/House of Fraser Credit Cards, 41
Harry, Mikel, 334–335
Harvard Business Review, 275–276
head, 279–280
heart, 279–280
Hergenhan, Joyce, 192
Hewlett Packard, 246
Hierarchy, 75
Hiner, Glen, 70, 95, 100, 184
  on CEC, 275
Hitachi Management Development Institute, 162
hockey, 67
Holy Grail, 58
Honeywell acquisition, proposed, 3–4, 14–15, 76–77, 313
  Immelt and, 352
  integration of, 347–348
  Welch and, 351
Hood, Edward, Jr., 77, 78, 100
  values statement and, 174
hope, 131
horizontal barriers, 279
hub-and-spoke structure, 184–185, 191–192, 381
Hughes, George, 361
human engine, 380
human resources
  best-of-class status in, 227
  GE system, 280–283
  vision support by, 660–661

I

IBM, 31, 82
  boiled-frog syndrome at, 96
  Sands Point School, 162
ideas. *See also* constructive conflict
  culture and, 562
  dialogue of, 91
  incremental, 620–621, 622
  power of, 80–92
  quantum, 620–622
  for revolutions, 620–623
Immelt, Jeffrey R., 3, 14, 344–345
  GE he will receive, 347–350
  in GEMS, 270
  leadership of, 351–352
  leadership pipeline and, 353–354
  as next CEO, 314
Impact program, 215
In Search of Excellence (Peters), 31
"Incredible Electrical Conspiracy, The," 137
indictment of leadership, 130
industrial parks, 572
INFACT, 135
inflation, 195
informality, 7, 327, 553–555
information
  boundarylessness and, 198
  in e-business, 306
  sharing, 309–310
  wallowing in, 75
  Welch's desire for, 72, 105–106
initiatives, 337–342
  innovation, 263
  Welch on, 298–299, 302–308

innovation, 21
insider trading, 143–144
integrity, 132–145, 547–
    548
International General
    Electric, 224
International Minerals &
    Chemicals, 69
International Union of
    Electronic Workers, 294
Internet Capital Group, 321
interpersonal skills, 197–198,
    278
Intersil, 41, 116
Itel Containers, 41

J

job security, 23–24
    CELC and, 167–169
    layoffs and, 100–101
    since the revolution, 30
    under Swope, 54
John F. Walsh Leadership Center.
    See Crotonville
Jones, Reginald H., 50, 368
    automation under, 116
    compared to Welch, 48
    financial controls of, 52
    management of, 45–48
    organizational structure under,
        58–60
    reorganization under, 75
    sectors under, 181
    succession process and, 61–65,
        77–79, 559
Jones, Robert, 207
J.P. Morgan & Co., 44–45
Just-in-Time programs, 249

K

Kaizen, 253, 335
Kane, Don, 50, 74, 78, 185, 278
    CEC and, 194
    Gotemba and, 172
    on reorganization, 190
    on risk, 186
    in succession process, 62–63,
        64–65
    values statement and, 174
Kanter, Rosabeth Moss, 88
keeping the car rolling, 256–
    257
Kerr, Steven, 178, 242
kicking the dog, 50, 186
Kidder Peabody, 29, 41
    insider trading case, 143–144
King, Martin Luther, 173
Klein, Joel, 355
knowledge sharing, 175
Knowling, Robert, 355–356
Kodak, 31
Kohl, Helmut, 87
Krach, Keith, 321

L

Late Night, 152, 153–155
layoffs, 99, 100–105, 110
    earnings goals and, 101, 564
    in Lighting, 216
    severance packages and, 103
    in Transportation, 128–129
Lazard Frères, 151
Lazarus, Ralph, 45
leadership, 28, 271–284
    CEC and, 197–199
    changes in Welch's, 251–254

leadership (*cont.*)
  framework for
    transformational, 663–665
  GE history of, 44, 353–354
  indictment of, 130
  knowledge sharing in, 175
  recruiting from outside, 280
  roles of, 327
  teachability of, 323–328
  transformational, 162–163,
    618–619
  types of, 273–275
  value added by, 595–596
  vision articulation and, 310
Leadership Academy (New York),
  356
Leadership Development Center,
  329–332
  Welch at, 319
Leadership Effectiveness Survey,
  615
Leadership Engine, The (Cohen,
  Tichy), 323
leading while being led, 84–87
lean and agile organizations,
  32–33, 408
  productivity in, 86
learning
  action, 161, 163–164, 249
  e-learning, 336
  results from, 547
Letterman, David, 152, 153–155,
  568
leveraged buyouts, 76
LeVino, Theodore, 77, 79, 100
  in succession process, 62–63,
    64
LEXAN, 69–73
Liemandt, Joe, 321

light bulb cross-licensing
  agreements, 53
Light Speed, 304
Loews Corp., 150
Los Angeles Times, 221

M

M/A Com, 77
management. *See also* Leadership
  Coffin and, 52
  competitive environment and,
    30–32
  imposition of control by, 82–83
  by objective, 55–56
  resistance of, 235–239
  shared practices, 450–451
  shared values and, 237–238
  speed and, 180–189
  Work-Out and, 235–255
Management Today, 44
managers, overseas, 230–231
Marconi, Guglielmo, 151
market share, 29
Marriott, Oliver, 207
matrix structure, 213–214,
  277–278
MATSCO case, 134
Matsushita, 77, 222, 228
McCabe, Donald, 133
McGowan, William, 111
McKinsey & Co., 58, 164
McNealy, Scott, 321
McNerney, W. James, Jr., 14,
  344–345, 353
"meatball, the," 111
media, 101, 238
mentors, 305
MGM-UA, 150

Michelson, Gertrude G., 45, 253
Milken, Michael, 143
Minderbinder, Milo, 268
mirror test, 133, 142–146
  revolution and, 613–624
mistakes, 130–131
Modan, Michael, 69–71, 73
Monsanto, 136
Montgomery Ward Credit, 41
morale, 106–107, 147
Morgan, J. P., 52, 53
motivation, 263
Motorola, 334–335
Murphy, Eugene, 153

N

Nacolah Life Insurance, 41
Nader, Ralph, 164
Nardelli, Robert L., 14, 344–345, 353
NASDAQ, 390
National Center on Education and the Economy, 31
NBC, 40, 112
  acquisition of, 150–155
  Welch on show at, 352
Nela Park, 572
"New Way" organizations, 607–610
New York Times, 111, 151, 221
Newsweek, 24
NIMBUS, 367
9/11 terrorist attack, 347, 352
No. 1 or No. 2, 83, 89–90, 94–95, 98, 300, 372, 417, 496
  creativity and, 115
  normative control, 196
NORYL, 69–71, 72

"not invented here" syndrome, 246, 301
no-wink paradox, 145
nuclear plants, 46, 104–105, 135

O

offerings development, 268
"Old Way" organizations, 558, 607–610
operating system, 11–12, 307–308, 340–341, 537–539
Opie, John, 189, 222
  Lighting under, 205–206, 210–218
  productivity and, 243
opportunism, planful, 72–73, 75, 81
  Thomson-CGR deal as, 227–230
order-to-remittance, 269
organizational structure
  bureaucratic, 49–50
  coercive, 196
  control in, 190–191
  holding company, 54–55
  matrix, 277–278
  normative, 196
  productivity and, 31–32
  sectors, 181–189
  spans of control in, 23
  TPC and, 88–91
  utilitarian, 196
orientation, 165–166
Orr, Verne, 139, 140
Orselet, Dave, 76, 78, 105
Osram, 208
Outward Bound, 163–164
Owens-Corning Fiberglas, 275

ownership, 26, 397
  globalization and, 224
  Welch on, 299
  Work-Out and, 243–244

P

paradox, 175
Parker, Jack, 78
paternalism, 54
Pathfinder Mines, 41
Paynter, Jim, 124, 126–127,
  128–129, 567
peer pressure, 199
Peiffer, Jack, 160, 174
Peiper, Chuck, 280
Pennzoil, 48
Penske Leasing, 41
people positioning, 396
performance goals, 103
performance reviews, 186
  interpersonal abilities in,
  197–198
perseverance, 20
Peters, Tom, 31, 88, 110–111, 115
Philips, 222, 358
  boiled-frog syndrome at, 96
  price-fixing with, 136–137
  Westinghouse acquisition, 205,
  209
Phoebus, 136–137, 571–572
pit. *See* Crotonville
planful opportunism, 72–73, 75,
  81
  Thomson-CGR deal as,
  227–230
planning
  corporate, 102–103
  real-time, 385

strategic, 57–59, 186, 403–404,
  409–410, 570–571
Polaris, 41
police, 101, 102–103
politics, 87, 90
  of speed, 180–189
Porter, Michael, 110
portfolios, 39–41, 115, 299–300,
  347–348, 395
  repositioning, 396
positioning, 395
PPO (polyphenylene oxide), 69,
  367
Pratt & Whitney, 116
Preston, Lewis T., 44–45
price fixing, 57, 135, 136–137
Pro80 machines, 209, 212
*Problems and Performance of the
  Role of Chief Executive in
  GE* (Baughman), 207
process mapping, 247, 248–251
product development, 46–47, 268
Product Services, 540–541
productivity, 20–22
  American, 31–32
  best practices, 247
  calculating, 558
  continual change, 215–216
  GE rates of, 30
  investments in, 401
  in lean organizations, 86
  in Lighting, 203–218
  stall in, 147
  Work-Out and, 235–255
products, best-of-class status in,
  227
profit-and-loss statements, 277
program investments, 395–396
promotions, 277–278

psychological contract, 275–276, 384

Q

Quality movement, 303–304
quantum change, 33–38, 91, 374
Quick market intelligence (QMI), 387, 389, 475, 489
Quick Response program, 249, 293, 389, 474

R

Rabinowitz, Stephen, 213, 214–215, 215–216
  at AlliedSignal, 572
  productivity and, 243
raising the bar, 226
RCA, 29, 41
  acquisition of, 112, 150–155, 181, 418–419, 426
Reagan, Ronald, 87
real-time planning, 385
rearchitecting, 596–598, 645–672
recruiting, 282
Reed, Charles, 69, 70, 71
Reed, Philip D., 362
reorganization, 190–202
  under Cordiner, 55
  Corporate Executive Council and, 90
  excitement and, 203–218
  of GEMS, 261–262
  hub-and-spoke structure, 184–185, 191–192
  in Lighting, 213–214
  matrix structure, 213–214, 277–278

speed and, 180–189
of Transportation Systems, 124–128
resistance, 22–23
  costs of, 187–188
  cultural, 630
  dealing with, 629–634
  end of, 108
  exhaustion *vs.*, 178
  to globalization, 226
  inevitability of, 290
  initial, 100
  from managers, 34–36, 235–239
  political, 630
  politics and, 90
  technical, 629–630
  toward Opie, 212–213
  toward Tichy, 177–178
  toward Welch, 24, 85, 86
  types of, 629–634
responsibility
  of employees, 33
  social, 397
return on equity, 29
revenue growth, 20–22, 204
revolution
  continuous, 661–663
  envisioning, 635–644
  Handbook for Revolutionaries, 593–673
  individuals in, 598–599
  mirror test and, 613–624
  organization test for, 605–612
  phases in, 596–598
  readiness test, 625–627
  rearchitecting in, 645–672
  vision articulation in, 113
reward and punishment, 283, 383

Richardson, Rick, 120, 127, 567
risk
  exposure to, 276
  performance reviews and, 186
Robb, Walter, 100
  Medical Systems under, 258
Rohatyn, Felix, 151
Roosevelt, Franklin, 53, 290
Roper, 41
Rowe, Brian, 100, 184, 201
Rubbermaid, 63
Runtagh, Hellene, 192
Ryland Corp., 201

S

S1/S2 strategy reviews, 342
Sands Point School, 162
Schenectady Works, 57
Schipke, Roger, 169, 184
  compressor disaster and, 200,
    201
Schlemmer, Carl, 118–131, 188,
    567
schools, 101. *See also* Crotonville
Schumpeter, Joseph, 91
scientific management, 18
  Cordiner and, 55
  under Jones, 45, 47
  obsolescence of, 60
self-confidence, 83, 280, 384, 453
service delivery, 269
services, best-of-class status in,
    227
services circle, 113–115
services initiative, 12–13, 546
Session C, 12, 281, 283, 339, 342
  Immelt and, 354
severance packages, 103

Sherman, Strat, 337
Sherman Antitrust Act, 53,
    136–137
Siegel, Martin, 143
Siemens, 205, 220, 222
simplicity, 83, 291–292, 453,
    491–492
Six Sigma, 13, 303–304, 306,
    334–336, 348, 389,
    515–521, 526–532
  results from, 546
  Welch and, 355
Sloan, Alfred, 19, 52–53, 353
social architecture, 4, 268–270,
    536–537
  assessing, 649–654
social responsibility, 397
Soderquist, Donald, 193
software phase, 257, 262–263,
    463
spans of control, 23, 303
speed, 83, 180–189, 384, 456,
    483–485
  as competitive advantage, 85
Stanley Works, 270
Stewart, Thomas A., 242–243,
    245
stock options, 277–278, 282–283,
    475–476
storyboards, 125
strategic planning
  under Borch, 57–59
  evolution of, 403–404,
    409–410
  staff eliminated, 186, 570–571
strategy and performance reports,
    393–555
Stretch, 485–486, 490–491
Stumberger, Ray, 63

succession process, 13–14,
308–310
Jones to Welch, 61–65, 77–79,
559
Welch to Immelt, 314,
322–323, 342–347
Superfund sites, 135–136
suppliers
as partners, 247
in Work-Out, 248–249
support
of executives, 34–36
process, 269
Swope, Gerard, 53–54, 136, 3
60
Swope Plan for American
Industry, 53
Sylvania, cross-licensing
agreements with, 53,
207–208

T

Takeuchi, Hiro, 172, 263
talent, competing for, 310
tax incentives, 413–414
Team Experienced Manager
Course, 171–174
teams
leadership and, 272
in Transportation, 125–126
teamwork, 32
in action learning, 164
CEC and, 199–201
incentives for, 200–201
at Plastics, 71–72
technology
GE competitive position in, 46
social architecture and, 268

structural change and, 222–223
value-driven, 288
technology circle, 113–115
tests
mirror, 133, 141–146, 613–624
organization, 605–612
readiness, 625–627
Texaco, 48
Thomson S.A., 152
Thomson-CGR, 41, 219–223,
257, 259–260, 441–442
planful opportunism and,
227–230
Thorn, 41, 217, 456
Three Mile Island, 46, 104, 369
Tichy, Noel, 83
as agent of change, 164–165
at Crotonville, 17–18, 159–160,
161
developmental processes of,
162–163
Handbook for Revolutionaries,
593–673
resistance toward, 177–178
values statement and, 174
Work-Out and, 242
Time, 151
time-card scandal, 132–145, 149
Tokyo Electric, 207–208
Tomasetti, Louis, 126, 187
Toshiba, 220, 222
TPC (technical, political,
cultural), 88–91
matrix, 637–638
training, 283
Trani, John, 220, 229
leadership of, 256–270
strategies of, 576
succession and, 345

transformational leadership,
162–163
framework for, 663–665
survey, 618–619
transparency, competitive, 6,
87–88
Travelers Mortgage, 41
trust, 294
loss of, 347
in "New Way" organizations,
607–610
Work-Out and, 241, 243–244
Tungsram, 41, 217–218, 456
Turner, Ted, 150
tyrannical behavior, 33–34

U

unions, 126–129, 294
United Electrical and Electronic
Workers, 126
United States
1980s economy of, 96–97
after 9/11 attacks, 347
competitive challenges facing,
31–32, 289–290
corrupt behavior in, 133–134
egalitarianism in, 87–88
global competition and, 87–
88
United Technologies, 14–15,
116
urgency, creating a sense of,
627–629
Urquhart, John, 187
U.S.S.R., 101
Utah International, 41, 89–90,
103, 112, 185, 230, 400
utilitarian control, 196

V

Value Decade, 285–288
values
boundarylessness as, 278–280
CEC and, 198–199, 237–238
commitment to, 196–197
Crotonville and, 161
as culture, 83–84
leadership and, 272
obstacles to transforming
shared, 564
orientation to, 165–166
rating on, 274, 283–284
shared, 18, 175, 271–284, 380,
564
soft, 471
statement of, 174–177,
326–327, 568–570,
616–617
Welch on, 291, 296–297
Van Orden, Paul, 51, 100,
105–106, 187
Vanderslice, Thomas, 77
varsity team, 619–620
vertical barriers, 279
vision
allegiance to, 183–184
articulating, 34–37, 113–115
envisioning, 635–644
human resources support for,
660–661
institutionalizing, 37–38
leadership and, 310
in Lighting, 206
in "New Way" organizations,
607–610
Von Clausewitz, Karl, 72
Von Moltke, Johannes, 72, 81, 227

W

Wall Street Journal, 188
war for talent, 310
Washington Post, 151
Way, Alva, 75
Weber, Max, 49
websites, 305. *See also* e-business
Weiss, Herm, 75
Weiss, Herman, 71, 75
Welch, Carolyn, 67
Welch, Grace, 66–67
Welch, Jane, 66
Welch, John, Sr., 66, 68
Welch, John F., Jr. (Jack), 372
  background of, 65–69
  on best practices, 299
  board support of, 25
  on boundarylessness, 286, 301
  bureacratic adeptness of, 73–74
  on business portfolios, 299–300
  on change, 290–292
  communication by, 117
  compared to Reg Jones, 48
  Crotonville and, 169–171, 300, 319
  definition of leadership by, 256
  description of, 5, 18–19, 24–25, 65–66
  on e-commerce, 304–306
  on empowerment, 296–297
  first job of, 4, 59–60, 68–69
  on globalization, 302
  on governments, 288–290
  on his mistakes, 116, 292–293
  on his retirement, 295
  Honeywell acquisition, 351
  information seeking by, 72, 105–106
  on initiatives, 298–299, 303–304
  as leader, 323–328
  leadership transformation of, 251–254
  legacy of, 313–314, 352–353
  listening by, 170–171
  management theory of, 75
  as Neutron Jack, 106–107, 558
  on number 1 and number 2, 300
  on ownership, 299
  philosophy of, 8–9
  power consolidation by, 101–103
  on productivity, 286, 287, 293–294
  religion of, 67–68, 138
  reputation attacks on, 110–111
  resistance against, 24, 85, 86
  in retirement, 355–356
  rules of, 27–28
  self-assessment memo of, 560–561
  on Six Sigma, 303–304
  on soft values, 286
  strategy of, 81–92
  succession process and, 61–65
  as teacher, 318–321
  time spent on personnel issues, 281–283
  track record of, 316–318
  on the Value Decade, 285–289, 296–297
  on values, 296–297
  vision communication by, 113–115
  on Work-Out, 300–301
Wendt, Gary, 345–346

Westinghouse, 57, 205, 222
   cross-licensing agreements
      with, 53, 207–208
   Philips acquisition of, 209
whips and chains, 205
White Consolidated, 222
White Inn meeting, 123
Wilson, Charles "Electric," 54,
   136–137, 362
Wilson, Charles "Engine," 54
Woodburn, Bill, 206
   on Lighting, 209, 216
   Tungsram and, 217–218
Work-Out, 10–11, 127, 178,
   235–255, 320–321,
   333–334, 451–452
   at Aircraft Engines, 249–251
   Best Practices and, 246–248
   Change-Acceleration Program,
      251, 280
   criticisms of, 254
   cultural change through, 38

exciting jobs and, 293–294
   goals of, 241
   launching, 655–659
   measuring success of, 254–255
   phases of, 572, 576
   process mapping by, 248–251
   Welch on, 300–301, 355
Works, the, 52
World Trade Center
   attack on, 352
Wright, Robert, 112–113, 189,
   201
Wriston, Walter, 57, 66

Y

Yokogawa Electric Works, 220,
   375
Yokogawa Medical Systems, 220,
   229, 257, 489
Yoshino, Mike, 172
Young, Owen D., 360